HANDBOOK TO LIFE IN PREHISTORIC EUROPE

HANDBOOK TO LIFE IN PREHISTORIC EUROPE

JANE McINTOSH

OXFORD
UNIVERSITY PRESS

OXFORD
UNIVERSITY PRESS

Oxford University Press, Inc., publishes works that further
Oxford University's objective of excellence
in research, scholarship, and education.

Oxford   New York
Auckland   Cape Town   Dar es Salaam   Hong Kong   Karachi
Kuala Lumpur   Madrid   Melbourne   Mexico City   Nairobi
New Delhi   Shanghai   Taipei   Toronto

With offices in
Argentina   Austria   Brazil   Chile   Czech Republic   France   Greece
Guatemala   Hungary   Italy   Japan   Poland   Portugal   Singapore
South Korea   Switzerland   Thailand   Turkey   Ukraine   Vietnam

First published by ABC-CLIO, Inc., 2006
130 Cremona Drive, Santa Barbara, CA 93116-1911

First issued as an Oxford University Press paperback, 2009
198 Madison Avenue, New York, NY 10016

www.oup.com

Oxford is a registered trademark of Oxford University Press

Library of Congress Cataloging-in-Publication Data
McIntosh, Jane.
Handbook to life in prehistoric Europe / Jane McIntosh.
p.   cm.
"First published by ABC-CLIO, 2006"—T.p. verso.
Includes bibliographical references and index.
ISBN 978-0-19-538476-5 (pbk.)
1. Prehistoric peoples—Europe.   2. Antiquities, Prehistoric—Europe.
3. Europe—Civilization.   4. Europe—Social life and customs.
5. Europe—Antiquities.   I. Title.
GN803.M46 2009
930.1—dc22   2008043485

1 3 5 7 9 8 6 4 2

Printed in the United States of America
on acid-free paper

CONTENTS

LIST OF ILLUSTRATIONS

LIST OF MAPS

LIST OF TABLES

ACKNOWLEDGMENTS _____

I am deeply indebted to the late David Clarke and Eric Higgs and their still flourishing colleagues whose inspired teaching first introduced me to European prehistory, and to my fellow students of those distant days and the other scholars I have since encountered with whom I have enjoyed many fruitful discussions. I owe special thanks to Dr. Alison Sheridan, who very kindly made it possible for my artist, Audrey McIntosh, to draw objects from the collections of the National Museums of Scotland.

INTRODUCTION _____

To produce a handbook to life in prehistoric Europe is a daunting task: The postglacial prehistory of Europe covers nearly 10,000 years, during which time there were enormous changes and momentous innovations, and the continent is an area of great environmental diversity, reflected in the contrasting lifestyles of the inhabitants of its individual regions. Antiquarians have been investigating Europe's remote past for hundreds of years, and it has remained the focus of attention of armies of archaeologists, equipped with a constantly growing arsenal of techniques for gathering data, both by excavation and by nondestructive means. The huge volume of material and information that has been recovered and the lively interpretive debates that it has sparked mean that a study of prehistoric European life in just one small region or short period can easily fill a whole book (and there are many such volumes). Nevertheless, there has been much that integrates Europe geographically and culturally, and some features of life that changed little through the ages. Europe has its own character and an overarching shared story that unites its disparate components.

For most of the long span of Europe's past it has been a land without writing, without named individuals, and without recorded deeds. This means that its history is almost entirely that of the ordinary individual, the hunter-gatherer, farmer, or metallurgist rather than the king. In this, prehistoric Europe is favored, for it focuses attention on the lives lived by the majority rather than on the exceptional lifestyles of the privileged elite (as is so often the case in recorded history). Evidence of the latter is not lacking, however, nor is material magnificence absent: The skills and expertise of prehistoric Europeans were often employed in the production of exquisite jewelry, elaborately woven cloth, beautifully made tools, and finely wrought weapons as well as in the production of more mundane objects. Though the palaces that have attracted excavators in other lands are absent, there are few monuments elsewhere in the world to rival Europe's massive megalithic tombs or great stone circles. And though individuals preserve their anonymity and many of their secrets, modern technology has made it possible to reveal parts of their life history in astonishing detail: the last meal they ate and their general diet, their genetic relationships, where they were born, what sort of work they had regularly performed, the exact year in which they felled individual trees to build houses or trackways, or the season in which they died.

Innovations in technology, such as remote sensing, examination with scanning electron microscopes, and DNA testing, constantly offer new scope for obtaining data, and archaeologists are constantly extending the boundaries of their investigations: Where once the focus was on uncovering individual burials and dwellings, now European archaeologists look at whole landscapes; at the opposite end of the scale they also examine the micromorphology of individual deposits of soil; they recover microscopic clues to tool use, and painstakingly collect tiny plant and animal remains to provide information on economy and environment. Chance discoveries, such as that of the Iceman in 1991, have also played a part in advancing knowledge of Europe's past. Hand in hand with the accumulation of data have been changing interpretations of those data, attempts to understand the course of development in prehistoric Europe and penetrate the human meaning behind the artifacts and monuments. This *Handbook to Life in Prehistoric Europe* is an attempt to give some account of what is known or surmised about these objects and structures and their authors.

1

GEOGRAPHY OF ANCIENT EUROPE

Europe is the meeting place of two contrasting environmental systems. On the one hand it is the western end of the vast continent of Asia, sharing extreme features characteristic of large landmasses. On the other it is a peninsula, girt on three sides by seas and enjoying aspects of the moderate maritime regime of islands. While largely part of the temperate zone, it runs from the fringes of the subtropical to the beginnings of the arctic regions. Substantial mountains and ranges of hills break it into many contrasting areas, but it also has extensive plains. While the topography favors the development of independent communities, the great rivers crossing the continent provide, with their tributaries, highways of interregional communication, as do the surrounding seas. Though Europe is rich in minerals, flora, and fauna, offering comfortable subsistence throughout its length and breadth, these resources are unevenly distributed, promoting the need for communications, movement, and exchanges to satisfy requirements that have developed since the earliest times, for shell and stone, metal ores and salt, furs and foodstuffs.

Topography, latitude, climate, and vegetation divide Europe into a number of major zones that have shaped the history of the continent, offering different economic opportunities to which its colonists and inhabitants have responded in a variety of ways at different times. Diversity has promoted independent development in the different regions while proving no barrier to the creation at times of much larger political entities.

THE MEDITERRANEAN

Sea

The southern part of Europe takes its form from the Mediterranean, of which it is the northern edge. The small relic of the once mighty Tethys Sea, the Mediterranean is saved from becoming a landlocked dead sea by the Strait of Gibraltar at its western end. Nine nautical miles wide, this narrow outlet links the Mediterranean to the Atlantic Ocean, allowing a limited tidal influx of ocean waters, which prevent the waters of the Mediterranean from stagnating but are insufficient to disrupt its calm surface and warm regime.

The warm waters of the Mediterranean support only limited amounts of plankton, and its coasts fall steeply below the water, so the sea is today relatively poor in marine resources, though a rich catch of migratory tuna is available annually. Lower sea levels and the absence of pollution made the Mediterranean seas less unproductive in the past. Seafaring developed early—obsidian at Franchthi cave in Greece obtained from the island of Melos shows that seagoing boats were in use before 9000 B.C. (while seafaring was already well established elsewhere on the globe tens of millennia earlier, as the colonization of Australia bears witness). At first the distances traveled were relatively small, but short voyages between adjacent regions allowed the eventual spread of ideas and commodities throughout the Mediterranean lands. By the second millennium B.C. navigation in the eastern basin regularly connected communities its length and breadth, from Egypt to Greece and beyond to southern Italy; in the west, the short distance across the Strait of Gibraltar proved no barrier to interaction between the peoples of Iberia and North Africa; while in the first millennium B.C. regular seaborne communications linked the entire Mediterranean basin.

Land

The relative ease of maritime communications contrasted with and compensated for the difficulties of those on land, for the Mediterranean regions of Europe are to a great extent made up of narrow coastal strips bordering mountains and high plateaus. In the west the arid inhospitable Meseta plateau covers most of the Iberian peninsula, a region scorchingly hot in the dry summer and cold and wet in the winter; the southern French coast is backed by the Massif Central and the Cevennes; the Apennines form a mountain spine throughout the length of Italy; across the Adriatic the Dinaric Alps stretch almost to the sea and run into the mountains of the Pindhus, Rhodope, and Balkan ranges, and in the south are the hills of the Peloponnese. The moun-

Map 1. *Political map of Europe*

tains, an ancient substrate covered by sedimentary deposits in the Tethys Sea, were uplifted and folded in the Tertiary period, and a number are still actively volcanic—Etna, Vesuvius, and Stromboli, for instance. A massive eruption that blew the center out of the Greek island of Thera around 1628 B.C.

adversely affected the climate of the whole of Europe. Though an ever-present threat, the volcanoes have some advantages, being the source of obsidian (volcanic glass), highly prized in antiquity for its sharpness and attractive appearance, and creating rich productive soils, those round Vesuvius being famous in Roman times for the quality of their vines.

Extensive areas of fertile level ground are rare in the Mediterranean, the largest being the Po plain and the Rhône delta, and their advantages for agriculture are offset by their tendency to flooding, making them not only marshy but also a breeding ground for malaria, a longtime scourge of Mediterranean lands. The region is relatively poorly furnished with rivers, and the majority of these carry water for only around three months of the year. Apart from the few plains and valleys, fertile ground for agriculture was available only in small patches on the lowlands and on the lower slopes of the mountains, while the uplands provided summer pastures for wild herbivores and domestic herds. The mountains also provided their share of mineral wealth: tin in parts of the Iberian peninsula, gold in the Balkan mountains, and copper in ranges spread across the basin, as well as stone.

Climate and Vegetation

Climatically, the Mediterranean basin enjoys mild winters, warmed by its sea, during which the bulk of the annual precipitation falls, starting in the west in October and driving toward the east. Most falls as rain, except on the mountains, swelling the streams and rivers into torrents that brought flooding and erosion during some periods, but which also carried sediments that were deposited, building up alluvial soils in their deltas in other periods. By April the rains are over and the temperature is rising, bringing six months of arid heat, exacerbated by hot winds blowing north from the Sahara. The mitigating effects of the seas decrease and the effect of the continental massif of Asia increases as one travels eastward, further raising summer temperatures.

The vegetation of Mediterranean Europe is determined by the climate, favoring species able to withstand the long summer drought but also allowing the growth of frost-tender plants. The potentially high productivity allowed by the high input of solar energy is not realized due to the restricted availability of water and good soils. Originally, woodlands including cork oak, chestnut, cypress, and other evergreens were widespread but human activity over millennia has seriously depleted them, trees being replaced by maquis and scrub. Among the native species, however, are vines and olive trees, which became pillars of Mediterranean agriculture. Cereal crops are sown in the autumn and harvested in the spring to take advantage of the winter rainfall and avoid the summer heat and drought. The climate also dictates the pattern of life for herd animals, with winters spent in the mild conditions of the lowlands and summers in grassy upland pastures: This and the vegetation have favored sheep, goats, and the omnivorous and fast-growing pig as domestic animals, while the natural fauna also includes boar along with smaller mammals and reptiles.

External Links

Sicily and the other smaller islands of the central Mediterranean divide the Mediterranean basin into two, while the eastern half is further subdivided by its topography. The Aegean, strewn with islands that are linked by short sea crossings, forms a natural unit that also includes the western portion of the Anatolia plateau. This in turn provides a bridge linking Europe to the vibrant world of the Near East, with which down the millennia Europe exchanged ideas, commodities, innovations, and peoples, and occasionally membership of shared political units—the Persian and Ottoman Empires, the ecumene of classical Greece, and the empire of Rome, for instance. These links go back far into prehistory; elsewhere in the Mediterranean cultural exchanges between its northern and southern shores were relatively limited until historical times, with the establishment of Phoenician trading outposts in Spain and North Africa.

The Aegean also leads into the Black Sea, whence the Mediterranean world gains access to the vast expanse of the Asian steppes and to the valleys of the Danube and other rivers leading into the heart of Europe. Farther west, the valley of the Rhône connects the French riviera with central Europe and gives easy access to other rivers flowing into the Atlantic and North Sea, while the Aude and Garonne link the western Mediterranean basin with the Atlantic coast of France. The Atlantic seaways are also accessible via the Strait of Gibraltar, but in general it was not until the first millennium B.C. that Mediterranean seafarers began to venture out of their *mare nostrum*—their own sea.

THE MOUNTAINS

Mediterranean Europe is sharply divided from the rest of the continent by an almost continuous belt of high mountains, starting in the west with the Cantabrian Mountains and the Pyrenees. From here the lower ranges of the Cevennes and the French Massif Central provide a slight reduction of the barrier, but they soon give way to the massive bloc of the Alps, rising as high as 4,500 feet (1,400 meters) and in places a formidable 150 miles (240 kilometers) wide from north to south. The Alps run without a break into the Dinaric Alps, which veer sharply south to join with the mountain ranges of the Balkans and Greece. At the same time the mountains continue farther north through the lower ranges of the Bohemian Foreland, the Moravian Heights, and the Sudetes into the high mountains of the Carpathian range, rising to more than 2,500 feet (800 meters). The Carpathians turn southward farther east running into the Transylvanian Alps, which are separated from the western edges of the Balkan mountains by the valley of the Danube. These eastern mountains encircle the fertile Carpathian basin, one of the few extensive plains of Europe. Lower mountains and hills fringe the northern edge of the mountain barrier, striking deep into Europe, from the Ardennes in the west through the Harz and Erzgebirge Mountains to the Sudetes in the east.

Despite their formidable height and extent the mountains do not present an impenetrable barrier since they are broken by many passes linking Mediterranean and temperate Europe. These were used by traders and other travelers from time immemorial and are still major access routes linking modern communities. The two major river valleys that cut through the mountains were corridors of immense importance for communications: in the west the Rhône valley and farther east the Danube valley, which rises on the north side of the Alps in central Europe, slicing between the Alps and the Carpathians to run through the Carpathian basin and the interior of the Balkans and thence to the Black Sea coast.

Topography and Vegetation

Within the mountains are upland valleys and wider basins and plateaus, their areas greater in the lower ranges and among the older mountains in the east. Forests cover all but the cold high reaches of the Alps and Pyrenees, where tundra vegetation is found; at higher elevations the trees are coniferous while the lower slopes share the deciduous woodland that is the predominant natural vegetation of temperate Europe. Valleys and plateaus offer generally limited opportunities for cultivation while the forests and pastures provide grazing for domestic and wild animals. Particularly favorable environments for human settlement, rich in wild plants, smaller land animals, and freshwater resources, were offered by lake margins during the drier periods of Europe's past, though the flooding brought by wetter conditions at times drove lake settlers away. The compression of environmental zones by elevation in the mountain regions made their lower slopes attractive for settlement since it offered a diversity of resources within a short distance as the crow flies. The mineral resources of the mountains were also attractive to early Europeans: Here stone and metal ores, often absent from lowland regions, were to be obtained, as well as salt, which was mined from the later second millennium B.C.

TEMPERATE EUROPE

North of the mountain barrier lie the European lowlands, a large part of them consisting of the vast

Map 2. *Topographical map of Europe*

North European Plain, stretching east from the Atlantic coast (and, before Britain became an island, from southern England) until it reaches the barrier of the Ural Mountains deep inside Russia. At their western end the lowlands extend round the Massif Central to continue south to the Pyrenees, while in the east beyond the Carpathians they run south to the northern shores of the Black Sea, meeting the delta of the Danube. From there, more restricted lowlands run northwest along the Danube: the Wallachian plain sandwiched between the Transylvanian Alps and the Balkan Mountains, and the mountain-encircled Carpathian basin. Smaller plains lie along the course of other rivers running through the lower mountains.

The steppe region on the eastern margin stretches to the borders of China in the east and connects with the Near East in the south. Home to nomadic pastoralists by the second millennium B.C., the immense steppe zone provided an influential corridor for communications between east, south, and west. Not only were ideas and innovations transferred via this corridor, but it also marked the route by which often aggressive groups pushed into Europe, on occasion driven by population movements that originated as far away as China.

In the north the Baltic Sea provided rich fishing for the inhabitants of the lands along its coasts. Southern Sweden and the southern tip of Finland form the northernmost extension of the temperate zone, sharing climate and vegetation with the northern coastal lands of continental Europe south of the Baltic. Numerous rivers rising in Europe's mountain spine link inland regions to the coastal areas to west, north, and south. The Danube and its tributaries, the Drava, Sava, Tisza, Morava, and others, flow into the Black Sea, which is also the destination of rivers farther east, the Dnestr, Bug, and Dnepr, which once shared a delta with the Danube, now drowned. The Danube rises in the Alpine Foreland not far from the source of the Rhine; together they provide a route right across the continent from north to south, the Rhine flowing north to debouch into the North Sea. To its east the North European Plain is traversed from the mountains to the North Sea by the Weser and Elbe, and to the Baltic by the Oder, Vistula, Nieman, and Dvina, linking Britain and Scandinavia with central and eastern Europe, while to the west the Meuse, Seine, Loire, and Garonne link the interior of western Europe with the Atlantic Ocean. A short overland journey links the Seine to the Saône, which flows into the Rhône, the main corridor between western Europe and the Mediterranean, while the

source of the Loire is also not far overland from the Rhône. Another route follows the Garonne, passes through the Carcassonne Gap, and reaches the Mediterranean via the Aude. These rivers are the highways by which people and goods have traveled across Europe down the millennia.

Climate, Flora, and Fauna

The climate of transalpine Europe is temperate, with mild summers and adequate to substantial rainfall year round, but major changes occur from west to east, and north to south. In the west and northwest the moderating influence of the surrounding ocean brings mild winters and relatively cool summers; moving eastward, the continental climate of the Asian landmass is progressively felt, bringing increasingly bitter and snowy winter conditions, lasting for many months. Winters are longer and colder as one moves north through the region, and summer temperatures rise as one goes south. In the southeast around the Black Sea and in the eastern Balkans as far north as the Carpathians, latitude combines with proximity to the warm seas of the Mediterranean and Black Sea to give hot summers, short relatively mild winters, and moderate rainfall, peaking in the spring and summer. The volume of rain across temperate Europe, brought in largely by northwesterly winds, decreases from northwest to south and east but rises with altitude, so the transalpine regions are well watered but not so the Carpathian basin. The Carpathians mark the boundary between the mild winters of the south and the long, cold snowy winters of central Europe.

The vegetation reflects the climatic and topographic variations. The coincidence of good rainfall and adequate sunlight makes temperate Europe an exceptionally rich natural environment, with a very high number of edible species. Rivers, lakes, and marshes were a source of many edible plants as well as providing fish and shellfish and attracting other wildlife such as wildfowl. Most of temperate Europe was originally densely forested, with mainly deciduous trees such as oak, hazel, beech, lime, and elder in the west; farther east, in central and eastern Europe, the forests were still predominantly deciduous but mixed with some coniferous species. As rainfall declined progressively eastward and southeastward, the natural forest became thinner, giving way to lighter woodland increasingly mixed with grassland, shading into the mixed desert and grassland of the steppe, a region with areas of good grazing originally supporting herds of antelope, aurochs, and wild equids, and with deep, highly fertile chernozem soils, but largely inaccessible for exploitation until the domestication of horses and the development of wheeled transport. The forests were home to a rich fauna, including several types of deer, aurochs, boar, bear, wolves, wildfowl, and rabbits and hare, and supported an abundance of other plant species. Millennia of intensive human exploitation of the forests has reduced their extent and diversity as trees were felled to provide fuel and timber, and cleared for agricultural land and settlement. In prehistory, however, transalpine Europe was a region of great natural abundance. Forest areas cleared for agriculture provided easily cultivable soils and pastureland, while fertile alluvial soils were available in the lower reaches of the rivers. A swathe of extremely fertile and easily worked loess soils (wind-deposited sediments) running across Europe from south of the Carpathian basin to the Atlantic coast of France attracted cultivation by the first farming communities in temperate Europe. Similarly attractive brown earth soils high in organic material and nutrients supported farming communities in other areas where drainage was good. Heavier soils, however, were not brought into cultivation until the introduction of the plow. Around the foothills of the Alps and in much of the North European Plain, moraine deposits of clay, sand, and gravel left by the melting of glaciers and ice sheets after the last glacial period created many areas of poor drainage: Here rivers, lake margins, and marshes provided a rich harvest of wild resources, but elsewhere in the region there were numerous areas of infertile heathland. Many areas of fragile poorer soils on the uplands were taken into cultivation during the Bronze Age and thereafter degenerated into heathland and moor, providing rough grazing but never subsequently usable for cultivation.

The mix of environments provided access to many valued resources: timber from the forests as well as honey, fruit and nuts, fodder, furs and hides; clay for making pottery and building materials; metal ores, particularly in the center and southeast; and outcrops of flint for making tools across the North European Plain from Britain to Poland and beyond. Iron, widely exploited from the first millennium B.C., was available in many areas of temperate Europe. From the north, around the Baltic and in Denmark, came amber, highly prized and widely traded.

THE ATLANTIC FACADE AND THE NORTH SEA

From Iceland to the Canaries and west coast of Africa, the Atlantic Ocean unites a range of environmental zones, linking them not only through seaborne communications but also through shared characteristics of great significance. The constant pounding of the seas has eroded the softer rocks, creating a coastline of many islets, rocks, shoals, and inlets, with promontories of harder Paleozoic rock left jutting into the sea, notably the southwest corner of Ireland, Cornwall, Brittany, Finisterre, and Cape St. Vincent. These provide both hazards to shipping and protection against the forces of sea and weather, combining with the drowned estuaries of numerous rivers to form many deep safe anchorages, such as Plymouth Sound, Rade du Brest, and the bay of Cádiz. In stretches where softer rocks predominated, notably the Gulf of Cádiz and the French coast south of the Loire, the sea has sculpted a smooth coastline upon which sand bars and beaches have developed. Often these form substantial dunes inland, impeding drainage and causing ponded-up lakes and great areas of marsh to form, such as the Marais Breton and Marais Poitevin in France and Las Marísmas in southern Spain. Unsuitable for farming and therefore unattractive to agricultural settlement, these waterlogged regions are a haven for wild plants and animals.

The interaction of tides, winds, and currents has dictated and controlled the patterns of movement around the Atlantic facade. Heavy gales bringing rough seas combine with cold and fog to make winter voyaging hazardous and best avoided, though not impossible. In the days of oar and sail most voyages were undertaken between April and October. Along most of the coast the prevailing winds are westerlies, but south of Cádiz these give way to the north-east trade winds that provide an easy passage southward down the African coast but make it difficult to return. This southern stretch of the European coast also has access via the Strait of Gibraltar to the Mediterranean. A strong west-to-east current aided mariners seeking to enter the inner sea, while outward-going vessels had to hug the shores on either side of the channel, but the main determinant of sailing direction was the wind, with mostly westerlies blowing January to February, April to June, and October to November, and mostly easterlies for the rest of the year. In general, Mediterranean sailors did not venture into the Atlantic until the first millennium B.C., but the Atlantic sea-lanes were plied by their own mariners from a far earlier date. In the north these passed through the Irish Sea to reach Scotland as far as Orkney and Shetland, perhaps even reaching Iceland, which seems to have been known to Atlantic communities by the time that Pytheas, a Greek explorer, circumnavigated Britain in the fourth century B.C. The Straits of Dover provided a passage by which seafarers could reach the North Sea and the coasts of northern continental Europe. The prevailing southwest winds favored voyages east through the Straits and the English Channel, while strong tides, which run for six and a quarter hours in one direction then reverse for the same length of time, could be used to sail west in a series of hops interspersed with anchoring to ride out the reverse eastward tide.

Many rivers give access from the Atlantic and the North Sea to the interior of Europe, some, like the majority of Iberian rivers, to the hinterland on the Atlantic side of the continent, others, particularly the Guadalquivir, Garonne, Loire, Seine, and Rhine, linking with rivers flowing into the Mediterranean and Black Sea, notably the Rhône and the Danube. Britain in the west is also well furnished with rivers, flowing down from the mountains that cover much of its western and northern parts.

The cold nutrient-rich polar waters that flow into the Atlantic and North Sea combine with the warm waters of the Gulf Stream arriving from the Caribbean; rich in plankton, they are home to numerous species of deepwater fish, such as cod and haddock, available in abundance until modern overfishing began to threaten their existence, and to sea mammals. In addition, the substantial continental shelf provides an ideal environment for shellfish and shallow-water fish species, similarly abundant in the past. Salmon and eels cross the Atlantic and enter British rivers during their breeding cycle, giving an important seasonally available resource. These resources place the North Atlantic and North Sea among the world's richest fisheries.

The Gulf Stream also significantly raises the temperature of the Atlantic coasts from Scotland to Galicia. This combines with the overall oceanic effect of the Atlantic on the west and northwest of Europe, including the islands of Britain and Ireland, to produce an equable climate, with mild winters and mildly warm summers.

Settlements along the Atlantic facade and the North Sea coasts were located to exploit both land and sea, taking advantage of good anchorages and safe places to beach ships, easy availability of fish and shellfish, access to rivers for water and transport and to their valleys, plains, and deltas for agricultural land. Estuaries and marshy stretches also offered abundant wild flora and fauna, including many edible species. In addition, many coastal locations were selected in order to exploit important mineral resources, such as the metal ores of the Río Tinto drainage, Galicia, Brittany, and western Britain, or the high-quality hard stones of the Irish and Welsh mountains. In the low-lying lands along the North Sea, settlement was at the mercy of the climate, attractive during dry periods, for example, during the second millennium, and flooded during periods of higher rainfall, as, for example, in the early centuries A.D., when many of those driven from their ancestral lands by flooding moved westward to invade the lands of their civilized neighbors.

THE FAR NORTH

From around latitude 65 degrees north, in an area encompassing most of Norway and Finland, and much of Sweden, leading into the great sweep of northern Russia to their east, one enters a different world. The west of the region is dominated by the Kjölen range of mountains, while the remainder is lowland dissected by numerous lakes and rivers. The climate here is subarctic, with extremely long, cold winters and short, cool summers. The predominant vegetation of the region is boreal coniferous forest, low in productivity of edible species attractive to humans, but supporting animals prized for their furs, such as fox, marmot, beaver, bear, and lynx, as well as elk and deer, and producing useful timber, including pine and spruce. Modest variations in the climate have a marked impact here, determining how far north it is possible to practice agriculture; in the warmer drier conditions of the second millennium B.C., for example, communities farmed in areas now too far north for crop cultivation. Nevertheless, the strongly leached podsol soils of the region offer only limited productivity. The prehistoric farmers of the region, therefore, made much use of the available wild resources as well.

The mountains in the west of the region and the narrow northern strip of land within the Arctic Circle, even colder and with little winter sunlight, cannot support trees but only low varieties such as dwarf birch and dwarf willows. Most of the vegetation of this arctic tundra is formed of mosses and lichens as well as sedges and other cold-tolerant species. It supports only a limited range of native fauna, such as Arctic fox and various migratory birds, but also large numbers of reindeer, which are herded by the hardy inhabitants of the region. Much of the ground is permanently frozen, and there is little development of soil, so cultivation is impossible. Similar conditions and vegetation are to be found in some of the high areas of the Alps.

ENVIRONMENTAL CHANGE

Although many of the conditions of modern Europe also operated in much of the past, there

have been many major natural and man-induced changes to the environment over the course of time. During the cold dry conditions at the height of the most recent glacial period, a massive ice cap covered Ireland, most of mainland Britain and Scandinavia, and part of the North European Plain, and lesser ice caps covered the Alps and Pyrenees and some adjacent areas. Most of the transalpine European environment was tundra, mixed in the south and east with parkland shading into steppe. Only in coastal and lowland areas of the Mediterranean were there forests. High winds caused massive erosion in the treeless European plains, creating large expanses of loess soil. Sea levels were much lower, adding substantially to coastal plains—for example, exposing half of what is now the Adriatic sea—and joining mainland Britain, Ireland, and continental Europe into a great plain extending far west of the present coast of France. The gradient of riverbeds running out into this plain was steeper, causing the rivers to flow faster in more deeply incised, narrower channels.

After the glacial maximum around 18,000–16,000 B.C. temperatures began to rise again, reaching levels similar to those of today by around 8500 B.C. Gradually the glaciers melted, releasing new lands for settlement in the north and Alpine regions. Relieved of their weight, parts of Scandinavia and northern Britain slowly rose (isostatic recovery), in places counteracting the loss to rising sea levels of coastal land. The progressive drowning of continental shelf around the Atlantic coast created a rich habitat for fish and shellfish, which was enthusiastically exploited by human groups; the lack of continental shelf in the Mediterranean made the development of marine food sources less marked here, and their advantages were outweighed by the progressive loss of the already restricted coastal lands. By 6000 B.C. the rising sea level had also drowned much of the plain in Europe's north and west, flooding the North Sea and creating the English Channel, separating Britain from continental Europe. The melting ice sheets had formed a huge body of freshwater north of Poland: by 5500 B.C. the North Sea broke through the narrow land barrier between Sweden and Denmark to turn this into the saline Baltic Sea. The Black Sea was also a freshwater lake until around 5500 B.C., when the Mediterranean broke through, drowning an enormous belt of coastal land around it. Other melting ice created many ponds and streams and a string of lakes across the north and east of Europe and others in the Alps: initially these lakes were relatively poor in nutrients, but within a thousand years they had become exceptionally fertile and productive locations, rich in plants, fish, and fauna. Only much later did silting significantly reduce their productivity and therefore their appeal for settlement.

The drowning of the continental shelf reduced the gradient of many rivers, while the hugely increased volumes of water flowing in them carried massive amounts of silt and other debris. These created new and extensive estuaries and areas of alluvium that were very attractive to plants, animals, and people.

As temperatures rose and rainfall increased, trees, grasses, and other vegetation spread from their refuges in southern Europe into most of the rest of the continent. For a period that lasted in different parts until 7000 to 5000 B.C., the Mediterranean zone became covered with deciduous forests, uniting their naturally high productivity with high levels of sunlight to achieve optimal conditions for sustaining

POSTGLACIAL CLIMATE AND VEGETATION

Date B.C.	Cultural Period	Climate Period NW Europe	Climate and Vegetation
11,500–10,800	Late Glacial	Alleröd	warmer and wetter coniferous forests in northwest
10,800–9600	Final Late Glacial	Younger Dryas	sudden dramatic drop in temperature very cold and dry subarctic conditions with open grassland and some trees in northwest

9600–8500	Mesolithic	Pre-Boreal	dramatic rise in temperature and humidity
			warm and wet
			coniferous forest (mainly birch and pine)
			  with some deciduous trees in northern
			  and central Europe, deciduous forest in
			  Mediterranean

8500–7200	Mesolithic/Neolithic	Boreal	warmer and dry deciduous forest colonizing central and northern Europe

7200–3800	Mesolithic/Neolithic/ Bronze Age	Atlantic	warmest and wet, mild winters,
			  long growing season
			deciduous mixed oak woodland with
			  elm and lime in northern and central
			  Europe—sudden very dramatic short
			  dip c. 6200 but afterward very stable
			  with very slight fluctuations

3800–1000	Chalcolithic/ Bronze Age	Sub-Boreal	slightly cooler but still warm warm summers, cold winters, dry
from 1000	Bronze Age/Iron Age	Sub-Atlantic	cooler and wetter growth of blanket bog

Sources: Barker 1985, Milisauskas (ed.) 2002, Mithen 2003, Price 2000, Renfrew and Bahn 2004, Arizona University 2005; Metindex 2005.

plant and animal life. Gradually, however, rising temperatures created hot dry summers in the Mediterranean that caused the northward retreat of deciduous forests and their replacement in the Mediterranean zone by the far less productive evergreen vegetation that today characterizes the region. This effect was felt earlier and more keenly in the eastern Mediterranean than farther west.

As deciduous forest pushed northward, cold-loving species like reindeer moved into the extreme northern regions of the continent where tundra developed and were replaced farther south by forest species such as red and roe deer. Between the deciduous forests and the tundra, boreal forests developed. Forests in turn created humic soils that encouraged the further development of vegetation. By around 4000 B.C. the pattern of European climate, environment, flora, and fauna approximated to the natural situation today. But humans had been making a significant impact on the landscape long before this time. The hunter-gatherer communities that became established throughout suitable locations in Europe developed ways of managing the environment for their own benefit, clearing areas of forest, using fire or bark-ringing, in order to encourage the development of open woodland with plant species attractive to themselves and their prey. The spread of farming as the preferred way of life, beginning around 7000 B.C. and penetrating most parts of Europe by 3000 B.C., exponentially increased the area of cleared forest and altered the vegetation of many regions, extending grassland, causing erosion, and in some areas producing degraded soils that have never recovered. The extension of human settlement into marginal areas in climatically favorable periods led in many cases to their permanent reduction to scrubland or bog. The effect of humanity has been to transform the landscape. Nor has this been only by direct and intentional actions, such as felling trees. The animals kept by farming communities have also been instrumental in destroying some aspects of the landscape and encouraging others: Pigs, for example, contributed to permanent forest clearance by destroying young regenerating growth. Wild animals became not only prey for food as before but also pests that threatened crops, encouraging their hunting, in some cases to extinction (as, for example, the aurochs, the massive wild cattle of Europe).

Superimposed on the human impact on the environment was that of natural climatic changes and occasional catastrophic events, with both local and more extensive effects. Fluctuations in temperature and rainfall have occurred throughout prehistory and history: Sustained temperature increases or decreases of only a few degrees have significant effects on the extent and range of different plants and animals, both in terms of latitude and of elevation, while higher rainfall can transform dry land into bogs and drown lake margins. Earthquakes and volcanoes have transformed the landscape in some areas, such as around Vesuvius: Devastating at first, volcanic eruptions have had longer-term benefits in the creation of highly fertile soils. In exceptional cases, such natural disasters have more widespread effects: In particular, the massive eruption on the Aegean island of Santorini (Thera) around 1628 B.C. threw enough debris into the atmosphere to block solar radiation for months, resulting in colder temperatures and causing a major setback to vegetation, particularly trees. Many significant cultural changes can be traced back to alterations in the climate and landscape, and vice versa.

READING

General

Milisauskas, ed. 2002, Clarke 1976, Butzer 1972, Hoffman 1983, Cunliffe 1994a, Kristiansen 1998, Champion et al. 1984: general survey; Scarre 1988, Black 1999, Philip 1991: maps.

The Mediterranean

Braudel 2001, Barker 1985: general; Perles 2001: Greece; Chapman 1990, Harrison 1996: Iberia.

The Mountains

Barker 1985, Sherratt 1997.

Temperate Europe

Barker 1985: general; Sherratt 1997: various regions; Bailey 2000: Balkans.

The Atlantic Facade and North Sea

Cunliffe 2001a, Sherratt 1997, Barker 1985: general; Reed 1990, Pryor 2003: Britain.

The Far North

Barker 1985, Price 2000.

Environmental Change

Scarre 1988, Jochim 2002c, Mithen 2003: late glacial and Mesolithic changes; Mellars 1994: glacial conditions; Harding 2000: Bronze Age.

2

THE DEVELOPMENT
OF EUROPE

Europe is both the westernmost extension of the continent of Asia and one, with West Asia and Africa, of the landmasses that ring the Mediterranean. At various times during its past it has received people, new materials, and ideas from its neighbors, while at others it has been those neighbors who have been recipients. Groups of humans penetrated Europe less than a million years ago and others arrived later, with fully modern humans the only survivors after around 26,000 B.C. Significant changes in their way of life took place in the wake of the climatic and environmental changes at the end of the last Ice Age around 9600 B.C. Initially, subsistence was based entirely on wild resources, but after 7000 B.C. farming communities using plants and animals domesticated in West Asia also began to appear in Southeast Europe, and by 3000 B.C. food production was the main way of life for most Europeans.

In the fifth millennium B.C. metalworking began in the southeast, using gold and copper, and by 2000 B.C. bronze was being manufactured across most of the continent, while iron came into use during the first millennium B.C. A diversity of burial practices was employed. Large mounds covered burials at various times, while Atlantic Europe had seen the creation of megalithic tombs from the fifth millennium onward. Monumental architecture was also employed for ritual structures, such as stone circles in the northwest and temples on Malta. Stone was used at times to construct dwellings, though houses were more commonly built of wood and clay. Domestic strongholds and fortified settlements sprang up in many areas at various times, and armed conflict can be traced back to the hunter-gatherer communities of the early postglacial period.

In the second millennium civilized societies emerged in Greece as well as along the southeastern shores of the Mediterranean, and during the first millennium appeared more widely in the Mediterranean. Their writings shed occasional specific light on their neighbors; most of Europe, however, remained prehistoric and therefore without a history of individuals and events. Archaeology, however, sheds considerable light on the way of life of ancient Europeans and the changes that took place.

One of the difficulties in writing a chronological account of prehistoric Europe is the uneven pace of development, both on a Europe-wide scale and more locally. Traditional labels such as *Neolithic* and *Bronze Age* refer to different time periods in different areas; and *Mesolithic* hunter-gatherers not only flourished in territories bordering those occupied by Neolithic farmers but for millennia were still the majority of Europe's population. The following account is therefore divided on the basis of absolute chronology into sections to which the traditional divisions of Palaeolithic through Iron Age have been broadly applied although they do not necessarily reflect the technology of all the areas under consideration at that time.

PALAEOLITHIC EUROPE (C. 1 MILLION TO 9600 B.C.)

Background

The record of human activity in the remote past is extremely patchy, and the remains of early people themselves are even more elusive. Problems with dating present a major handicap in chronicling Europe's earliest inhabitants and their activities as does the uncertain nature of some of the material. For example, crude chipped stone objects may be tools made by humans or the result of fracture by natural forces. While new and more sophisticated types of tool were created as time went on, simpler forms were not necessarily abandoned, and the apparent sophistication or crudity of tools made in a particular place also owes much to the quality of the stone available to the toolmakers, with the result that the typology of tools often cannot be used to give a broad relative date for the early sites where they have been found.

DATING THE EARLY PAST

While radiocarbon dating allows a chronological framework to be established for later European prehistory, and dates to be assigned to sites and other finds within this time frame, the greater part of the Palaeolithic occupation of Europe falls outside its range, which currently extends back only to around 50,000 years ago.

Other dating methods have therefore to be employed: many of these are applicable to natural processes, such as the accumulation of marine sediments or the eruption of volcanoes, which are not associated with human activities and can therefore only indirectly be used to date archaeological remains. Fluctuations in climate and vegetation reflected in cores taken from deep-sea and freshwater sediments and ice sheets are dated using various methods, including the countable annual layering of the sediments and ice sheets, correlation with paleomagnetic reversals, and uranium series dating. The latter is also applicable to stalagmites in limestone caves; and fission-track, potassium-argon, and thermoluminescence dating are also used on various types of rock that may under- or overlie archaeological remains.

Thermoluminescence can also be applied directly to some Palaeolithic artifacts: flint tools that had been subjected to heat, and accidentally or deliberately baked clay, such as hearths and, during the Upper Palaeolithic, some figurines. Animal teeth associated with human debris can be dated by electron spin resonance and by uranium series dating; and the remains of extinct fauna can also provide a relative date. The typology of stone tools gives some clues to relative date, too, although there are associated problems, as discussed above.

ICE AGES

Around 35 million years ago slight global cooling caused the development of the first ice sheets in Antarctica and from around 2.3 million (Pleistocene) ice sheets also developed in the Arctic, due to considerably increased cooling. Since then, the Earth has experienced numerous cycles of short glacial periods of extremely cold, usually dry conditions and short interglacial periods of considerable warmth and humidity, separated by much longer periods in which the climate was less extreme. The descent into glacial conditions was generally gradual, while warming after a glacial maximum proceeded much more rapidly. The course of these changes has been charted and dated using data from various sources that built up over very long periods: notably deep-sea cores that preserve a record of fluctuations in the oxygen-isotope composition of the oceans, reflecting the proportion of the Earth's moisture locked up in ice sheets; ice cores that record the annual extent of ice sheets; and pollen cores that show changes in vegetation, related largely to climate. In the last 750,000 years (Middle and Upper Pleistocene) there have been eight glacial-interglacial cycles, with the most recent interglacial period beginning around 130,000 years ago (Upper Pleistocene) and the last glacial maximum around 20,000 years ago. By c. 9600 B.C., temperatures had risen to a level comparable to today: This postglacial warm period, the latest in the continuing cycles, is known as the Holocene. Within this there have been further lesser fluctuations in temperature and precipitation, including conditions warmer and drier than today between c. 7000 and 1000 B.C.

Early Humans

INITIAL COLONIZATION

The evolutionary line that produced both chimpanzees and humans diverged by 7–6 million years ago, giving rise in Africa to a number of hominid species. By 2.5 million years ago, these included one or several small but relatively large-brained creatures that are assigned to our own genus *Homo* (*H. habilis, H. rudolfensis*). Around the same time, and probably made by *Homo*, the first (Olduwan) stone tools appeared, pebbles with a cutting edge made by striking off flakes.

A larger species of human (*H. ergaster/ H. erectus*) emerged around 1.9 million years ago and rapidly spread as far as China and Indonesia, a movement possibly spurred by climatic and environmental pressures or encouraged by the development of adaptations, such as successfully obtaining and eating meat, which allowed a population explosion and the colonization of new environments. At some time, possibly as early as 1.6 million and certainly by 500,000 years ago, humans began using fire: to cook, to keep themselves warm, and to defend themselves against predators. By 1.6 million, *H. ergaster* had developed more sophisticated (Acheulean) flake tools. These included the distinctive hand axe, carefully shaped by removing flakes from both faces of a large flake or small cobble to create a tool with a symmetrical shape and tapering point with sharp edges, probably used for many purposes, particularly butchering animals.

While remains of *H. ergaster* (alternatively classified as *H. georgicus*) have been found at Dmanisi in Georgia, on the edge of Europe, dated around 1.8 million years ago, evidence of an early human presence in Europe itself is confined to a few finds of possible but disputed stone tools. Cold winter temperatures (below 10 degrees Centigrade) may have inhibited advance into Europe until a later date when fire was under human control. The earliest indubitable evidence, dated c. 800,000 years ago, comes from Gran Dolina, Atapuerca, in Spain, where the bones of some six individuals belonging to an evolved form of *H. ergaster*, named *H. antecessor* or *H. mauritanicus*, were found in a cave. Cut marks and breaks suggest that these individuals may have been the victims of cannibalism. Another skull of similar age has been found at Ceprano in Italy: It may also belong to *H. antecessor* or to a separate species, *H. cepranensis*.

EARLY EUROPEANS

More detailed information on the lives of early Europeans comes from a number of later sites, dated after 500,000 years ago. Skeletal remains show a further evolution had occurred: These individuals belonged to a species with brains larger than earlier forms, known as *H. heidelbergensis*. Boxgrove in southern England has a number of working floors where flint tools, particularly hand axes, were made, using stone hammers for initial shaping and bone hammers for the finer work of finishing. Wooden spears, found, for example, at Clacton in England and Schöningen in Germany, were probably used for hunting: Faunal remains and other clues indicate that a considerable amount of meat, often from large animals, was consumed by these people, who also ate shellfish and perhaps some plant foods. Hunting was probably opportunistic rather than organized or regular, and meat was probably also scavenged. At Terra Amata in France arrangements of stakeholes and stones suggest the possibility of shelters built of brushwood stakes, perhaps covered by skins, containing a hearth and working floors. A few sites such as Wallendorf and Markleeberg in Germany seem likely to have been camps where people extracted good-quality flint for making tools.

MIDDLE PALAEOLITHIC

A massive deposit of human bones in a rock shaft, Sima de los Huesos, at Atapuerca in Spain, seemingly chosen as a convenient place to dispose of dead bodies, provides evidence that European hominids around 400,000 years ago were evolving toward the Neanderthals (*H. neanderthalensis*), a type of human that had emerged by 250,000 years ago. Short and strongly built, the Neanderthals had brains as large as those of modern humans; the later (after 70,000 years ago) "Classic" Neanderthals of Europe were even more stocky, adapted to cope with life in cold conditions. Their (Mousterian) stone tools included large flakes made by carefully preparing a "tortoise" core to enable a flake of predetermined shape finally to be struck from it. A range of other flake tools were also used, skillfully retouched to form artifacts for different purposes, including fine leaf points for use as projectiles. Stone for making these tools no longer came exclusively from the vicinity of the campsite: A small proportion (around 5 percent) might be obtained from more than 60 miles (100 kilometers) away and in a few cases as far as 200 miles (300 kilometers) away, though the rest came from no more than 12 miles (20 kilometers) away. On balance it seems that people obtained these materials themselves; there is little indication of interaction or exchange between groups.

Wood was also used for an increasing range of tools, including plates in one rock shelter (Romani, Spain). Microscopic examination of the wear on stone tools (microwear analysis) made by the Neanderthals shows that the majority had been used to work wood, making not only tools but also handles. Bone and antler were now also occasionally worked by flaking to make edge tools. Hides and furs from animals were prepared and may have been used for clothing as well as for constructing shelters.

Although some may have been roofed, the balance of opinion seems to be that most Neanderthal structures were windbreaks, usually associated with hearths. Much of the occupation evidence comes from caves and rock shelters. The harsh conditions of life are reflected in the Neanderthals' short life expectancy, few individuals surviving beyond age 40.

Neanderthal Life The powerfully built Neanderthals led a strenuous and often risky life, as many healed injuries show. Many of these injuries must have been inflicted during hunting, which probably involved close contact with the often large and dangerous prey such as aurochs (wild cattle). The Neanderthals' most common hunting weapon was a spear, of plain wood or wood with a stone tip, with which they stabbed their prey. Other hunting techniques probably included driving animals over cliffs, as at La Cotte on Jersey: This implies a degree of cooperation and coordination, perhaps involving some advance planning. Scavenging also provided some meat; small creatures such as shellfish, reptiles, and tortoises were caught; and some part of the diet probably derived from plant foods, although the evidence is rare and these would have been relatively scarce in the tundra and grassland that covered a considerable part of Europe during the colder periods. Resources available seasonally were exploited, and over the course of a year a group probably moved around within a territory of up to 40 miles' (65 kilometers') radius in order to obtain these. Campsites were selected to take advantage of differing environments where a diversity of resources could be obtained: Often these were located on the edge or slopes of river valleys. Desirable resources included not only foodstuffs but also good-quality stone for making tools.

Other aspects of Neanderthal culture are the subject of much debate. A few objects with simple engraved lines may be the beginnings of art, while it seems fossils and other curios were occasionally picked up and treasured, evidence of awakening aesthetic sensibilities. The survival of crippled individuals implies that they were cared for by other, able-bodied, members of their community or family. A number of skeletons have been found in situations that suggest deliberate burial, although not all scholars accept this. In a number of instances it is claimed that there were associated grave goods, such as pieces of meat, although in every case another explanation is possible for the claimed grave offerings, and bodies may have been disposed of for convenience rather than as a reflection of a notion of life beyond death. Some attested instances of cannibalism are similarly open to differing interpretations: there might have been symbolic reasons for cannibalism, as there have generally been in historical and recent times, or the practice might simply have been to provide food.

Another crucial question is whether the Neanderthals could speak. Cooperation in hunting and other shared activities, particularly those involving some forward planning, indicate that they were able to communicate in some way, perhaps using a range of manual signs and gestures, and some sounds, including, it has recently been suggested, singing and music, but the currently accepted majority view is that they did not have the cognitive abilities to create language and were probably physically incapable of articulating the full range of sounds that modern humans can make.

Modern Humans

Although the development of modern humans, *H. sapiens*, is still the subject of lively debate, the most widely held view is that they emerged around 200,000 to 150,000 years ago in Africa and from there eventually colonized the globe, replacing the populations of humans resident in other regions, probably without interbreeding with them, although some evidence suggests there may have been limited interbreeding between Neanderthals and modern humans in Europe. In West Asia, where Neanderthals coexisted with modern humans from around 100,000 years ago, there was no significant difference in the tools used by these two types of human, and it seems likely that they were culturally and intellectually similar for a long period.

CULTURAL TRANSFORMATION

Marked changes occurred around 60–40,000 years ago, which roughly coincides with the time when modern humans were moving into Europe (as indicated both by archaeology and by DNA studies). Large flake tools were replaced or complemented by slender blades modified to create a wide range of tools specifically designed for individual purposes. Many blades could be struck from a single core, representing a far more efficient and economical use of raw material. Stone blade tools were smaller and therefore more portable than before. As well as wood and stone, bone, ivory, and antler were now regularly used for making tools. From around 30,000 years ago these included needles, showing that for the first time garments were sewn. Other aspects of life, such as housing, art, indubitable burials, and sophisticated hunting practices, show that there had been a quantum change in human cognition and aesthetic sensibility. It has been suggested that this change was linked to the development of true spoken language. Language enables ideas to be exchanged and discussed and plans to be made; it also exponentially increases and enhances the quantity, quality, and nature of knowledge that can be handed down through the generations. Only modern humans are thought to have been capable of true speech. Recent DNA research appears to show that this was made possible by a genetic mutation in early modern humans, sometime between 200,00 and 100,000 years ago.

EARLY UPPER PALAEOLITHIC

The Aurignacian period began with the arrival in Europe of modern humans c. 50–45,000 years ago, first in the southeast but rapidly spreading west and north to occupy the whole of southern Europe from Spain and France to Bulgaria. The period was characterized from the start by the use of blade tools and the manufacture of jewelry and ivory figurines, as well as engravings and the recently discovered spectacular paintings at Chauvet cave in France.

At the same time a number of industries composed of tools displaying a mixture of Middle and Upper Palaeolithic technology appeared in parts of Europe from Russia to Spain, the best known being the Châtelperronian in northern Spain and France. These seem likely to have been made by Neanderthals who had come into contact with modern humans. The Neanderthals may have been incapable of inventing the new technology themselves,

but they were able to imitate it; and the quality of some of the tools made by earlier Neanderthals shows that they did not lack an aesthetic sense.

GLACIAL EUROPE

Modern humans and Neanderthals coexisted in Europe for at least 10,000 years. Although it is a debated issue, there is no evidence that modern humans deliberately wiped out the Neanderthals. Far more probably, their superior technology and cultural adaptability gave modern humans advantages over the Neanderthals in procuring the necessities of life and surviving cold conditions. Taller and less strongly built than Neanderthals, modern humans were physically adapted to a warmer environment but were able to devise cultural and technological means, such as efficient and sophisticated clothing, shelter, and hearths, to overcome their physical limitations so they were better able to exploit the full global range of environments available for settlement, and to cope with environmental and climatic change.

Between 30,000 and 25,000 years ago advancing ice sheets drove both Neanderthal and Aurignacian populations into a few favored areas of southern Europe, and by around 28,000, Neanderthals became extinct; Aurignacian industries continued in a few areas, including southwestern France, until 24,000 years ago. From around 30,000 years ago, however, new groups of modern humans (Gravettians) began to arrive in eastern Europe, perhaps from central Asia, bringing new technology, including basketry and cordage, fishing equipment, and eyed needles for sewing clothing. The new technology seems likely to have enabled modern humans to cope with the increasingly cold conditions, and Gravettian industries appeared over much of Europe between 30,000 and 27,000 years ago. The most distinctive Gravettian products were the models of women known as *Venus figurines*. At Dolní Věstonice in Moravia, and at other sites, there is evidence that clay models were fired with the intention of making them explode, perhaps for ritual reasons.

Housing was one of the principal ways in which people met the climatic challenge, constructing tents of hides stretched over a framework of timber or, in the east, of mammoth bones or tusks, sup-

2.1 A romantic view of Upper Palaeolithic Europeans. In reality, by this time prehistoric Europeans were wearing stitched clothing and hunting and defending themselves with spears and eventually bows and arrows; they also had control of fire, a powerful weapon against predators. (Figuier, Louis. *Primitive Man.* London: Chatto and Windus, 1876)

ported by stones. Often the floor was dug into the ground. Windbreaks and other structures were also erected in caves and rock shelters. Efficient hearths were constructed, ringed, and sometimes lined with stones. Many open-air sites belong to the Gravettian period, particularly in eastern Europe. Temperatures continued to fall, and during the period of extreme cold from c. 22,000 years ago leading into the last glacial maximum c. 20,000–18,000 years ago, the more northerly areas of Europe became sparsely populated or were abandoned and occupation was largely confined to caves and rock shelters. This period is known in western Europe (southern France and Spain) as the Solutrean (21,000–17,000 years ago), characterized particularly by very fine pressure-flaked "leaf" points made from carefully selected high-quality stone and too fragile for actual

use. Farther east, from Italy to Russia, less well studied industries continued from the Gravettian period and are known as Epigravettian.

Although no clothing itself has survived, the existence of needles shows that tailored garments were made. More detailed information comes from burials: In one at Sungir in Russia, the distribution of ivory beads that had decorated a man's clothes indicates that he wore trousers and a shirt or jacket with a hood or a separate cap. Tiny seashells, animal teeth, and fish vertebrae were also used as ornaments on clothing and as beads and pendants worn as jewelry, and many scholars argue that these were used to demonstrate identity, for instance as a member of a social group. Social interactions were probably of key importance in coping with the world in which the Upper Palaeolithic people lived. Connections between groups over a huge area spread the risks of life by providing a support network, for instance when resources became scarce in one region. The density of population, which rose enormously in this period, probably also made it vital to develop strategies for managing intergroup relations. Although people seemed to have been settled in small regional groups where conditions were favorable, communications between groups allowed the exchange of materials and ideas over long distances. The movement of commodities such as seashells, amber, fossil shells, and quality stone for tools over distances of up to 625 miles (1,000 kilometers) and the widespread occurrence of similar art objects underlines the extent of these connections.

ECONOMY

The economy of Upper Palaeolithic Europeans was more complex than that of their Neanderthal predecessors. While the latter seem generally to have obtained food opportunistically, Upper Palaeolithic people employed a range of organized strategies. It is likely some hunting involved the use of well-planned ambushes in which many people played individual but coordinated parts; remains of hides, drive lanes, and constructed cul-de-sacs (*kites*) have been found from the late Palaeolithic onward in the Near East, and similar devices may have been employed in Europe. The site of Solutré in France was selected to take advantage of a natural dead-end canyon that was used as a drive lane and trap in which to slaughter animals en masse; horses made up the majority of the prey at this site. People took advantage of the seasonal movements of big game animals to ambush large numbers in the autumn, cold-storing the meat in pits. People themselves also moved, often over long distances, to gain access to seasonally available resources in different areas. Settlements that have been found include short-term hunting camps and workshop camps for obtaining and processing stone for tools but also sites occupied for a season or year round. These settlements varied in size, suggesting the fissioning and fusion of groups at different times of year, depending on the distribution and density of available resources; some sites were of a considerable size, suggesting large groups at certain times of year, probably during the

winter when the community could live off frozen game and other stored food. The use of fire for thawing and cooking meat was critically important; cooking pits have been found in some of the Russian sites. While they made use of a wide variety of foodstuffs, such as plants, fish, birds, shellfish, small game, and wildfowl, the Upper Palaeolithic people also often concentrated upon particular species, for instance horses in the east and reindeer in southern France. Nets were made of knotted twine and were perhaps used for catching hares. The expanded and dedicated tool kit reflects improvements in the efficiency of hunting, and included spear-throwers, which extended the range at which projectiles could accurately be used.

AESTHETIC AND SYMBOLIC BEHAVIOR

The most dramatic demonstration of the intellectual and aesthetic sophistication of the Upper Palaeolithic people is their art. This ranges from engravings and paintings on the walls of caves and rock shelters, through engravings on stone plaques, to pieces of portable art, carved from bone, stone, antler, or ivory, or modeled in clay, of which the exaggeratedly female Venus figurines are the most famous exemplars. Early figurines, dated before 30,000 B.C., include several lion-headed men. The vast majority of surviving European Palaeolithic art dates from the Magdalenian period, after the last glacial maximum.

Many artworks were sensitive and beautifully observed portraits of animals, such as those used to decorate bone and antler tools such as spear-throwers. The purposes of this art are the subject of enormous debate, and no single explanation can account for all the diverse manifestations. Plausible explanations for particular objects or representations include records of the seasons and of common or unusual aspects of the environment, for the purpose of planning or education; representations of the experiences of shamans; totemic symbols; and simple decoration for pleasure and the enhancement of life. None can be proved though some can be ruled out; for example, the notion of hunting magic is undermined by the paucity of representations of the preferred prey species and the virtual absence of hunting scenes or depictions of wounded animals. The quality of the artists' aesthetic perceptions and their mastery of execution cannot be doubted, however. These are also apparent in the tools they created: Many new techniques, such as pressure flaking of stone and groove-and-splinter working of bone and antler, were developed to refine their production of artifacts, which were often things of great beauty as well as being efficient and practical.

The beginning of burials with grave goods, in graves dug both in caves and in open-air sites, also indicates intellectual development, since these were now clearly not simply a means of disposing of dead bodies, as might have been the case for Neanderthals, and imply some concept of an individual's existence beyond or outside death. Some of the graves contained multiple burials and might represent the interment of bodies that had been stored over the winter when the ground was too cold for graves to be dug. Grave goods such as jewelry, tools and weapons, and figurines were now commonly placed with the dead.

The Late Glacial Period

After the glacial maximum at around 18,000 B.C., conditions became slightly less cold, and a period of frequent fluctuations in the cold, dry conditions set in, bringing gradual changes in the vegetation and fauna of the continent. This late glacial period is known in western Europe as the Magdalenian, and was a time of considerable innovation and of the finest flowering of Palaeolithic art.

The environmental changes that took place in Europe during the later glacial period occurred gradually and therefore had a progressive impact on the way of life of the inhabitants of the region. Around 12,700 B.C. a dramatic rise in temperature and rainfall occurred (Bølling and Alleröd interstadial), reaching climatic conditions similar to today, followed by a dramatically contrasting period (Younger Dryas) around 10,800 B.C., when temperatures dropped steeply, causing some ice sheets to expand, before suddenly rising again around 9600. The climatic changes brought about gradual and fluctuating changes in the distribution of various animals and in the vegetation, with an increasing

number of trees and more grassland in the tundra and steppe and areas of forest expanding in more southerly parts of the continent. Areas abandoned during the glacial maximum were recolonized by animals and people, and Europe's population rose. Open-air sites greatly increased in number though caves and rock shelters were still the main places of settlement.

Many of the large herbivores hunted by Palaeolithic people, such as reindeer and horses, continued to thrive on the tundra and steppe and to provide a major part of the diet, though some species, such as musk ox and giant deer, gradually became extinct in Europe. Increased hunting efficiency was achieved through a number of innovations. Small blades manufactured during this period were probably set into shafts of bone or wood to make arrows: Definite evidence of bows and arrows, which allowed prey to be felled at less close range, is known by the end of the late glacial period. Dogs, useful during hunting expeditions and particularly for driving game, were probably domesticated—the first domestic animals. As temperatures rose, a diversity of foods became increasingly important, including birds, small mammals, fish, and various plants. Finds at La Riera, a cave in Spain, show that during the Magdalenian period shellfish gathered on the seashore became part of the diet of people who camped in the cave. Coastal sites, however, must generally lie in areas drowned by the later rise of sea levels so the importance of marine resources in the European late glacial period cannot be assessed.

The vast majority of surviving portable Palaeolithic art objects come from the Magdalenian period, including both figurines and engraved plaques, and decorated tools. Similarly, the greater part of the cave paintings that can be assigned a date come from this period, though cave painting was gradually abandoned as new areas were colonized in the later Magdalenian. Vividly portrayed animals provided the subject matter for most of the art.

As the ice sheets melted, new areas became available for settlement in the north, including southern Britain, the Low Countries, and Poland, and in the Alpine regions. By around 12,000 B.C., much of northern Europe was freed from the ice sheets and became tundra and steppe, with a progressively increasing amount of forest. Cold-adapted animals, including the large herds of reindeer, moved northward into the newly habitable regions, and some human groups moved with them. Deciduous forest developed in southern Spain, southern Italy, Greece, and the western Balkans. A large number of regional industries developed, characterized by different tool assemblages.

EARLY POSTGLACIAL EUROPE (C. 9600–5000 B.C.)

Early Holocene Climate and Environment

LAND AND SEA

After the briefly renewed glacial conditions of the Younger Dryas (c. 10,800–9600 B.C.), temperatures again rose very rapidly, marking the beginning of the Holocene period. Ice sheets and glaciers melted, increasing the volume of water in the seas and of moisture circulating in the air so that rainfall increased. Only northern Scotland, Norway and Sweden, and the Alps were still beneath ice sheets. Melting ice rapidly raised sea levels, drowning a large area of continental shelf west of the present Atlantic coast from Ireland to northern Spain and a narrower strip along the Portuguese coast, and the northern part of Doggerland (the land now beneath the North Sea between Scotland, northern England, and Denmark). In the Mediterranean, land exposed in the glacial period between Italy and the Balkans was drowned by the rising Adriatic Sea, and the narrow coastal strip around much of the Mediterranean coast began to be submerged. For example, Sicily lost about half its area and became separated from Italy while almost two-thirds of the coastal plain of the Argolid in Greece was lost by 8000 B.C. Glacial meltwaters also created many new lakes and ponds, particularly in northern and eastern Europe and

around the Alps. Initially poor in nutrients, these became rich environments within a millennium, though eventually they silted up.

By around 7000 B.C. Ireland had become an island, although southern England was still joined to continental Europe, and a substantial island existed where Dogger Bank is today. Ice sheets remained only over parts of Norway, Sweden, and northern Russia. In areas of the north previously under the ice sheets, rising sea levels were eventually offset by isostatic recovery: After being freed from the weight of the ice, the land rose gradually but very substantially with the result that some early Holocene beaches are now several hundred feet above sea level; the process continues today. Other areas, such as East Anglia, have sunk as the land has tilted. In the area that is now the Baltic Sea, a freshwater lake dammed by ice (Baltic Ice Lake) had existed during the glacial period: As sea levels rose, this became connected to the North Sea, growing greatly in size and becoming saline (Yoldia Sea). By 6500 B.C., however, land rising due to isostatic recovery dammed the inlet and cut off the Yoldia Sea, converting it into the freshwater Ancylus Lake, which lasted until the land was breached and the Baltic was again joined to the North Sea around 5500 B.C.

Between 6500 and 6000 B.C. the North Sea and English Channel reached approximately their modern form, severing the land bridge between Britain and the continent. Ireland continued to lose its coastal lands to the sea, especially in the north, until around 4400 B.C., when isostatic recovery began to tip the balance, raising the land, with the result that some beaches of that time are now several feet above present sea level. Most of the coastal lands around the Mediterranean were reduced to a narrow strip by the still-rising sea levels. The narrow straits between the Atlantic and the Mediterranean had remained open even when glacial sea levels were low but in the east the Mediterranean was separated by a land bridge from a substantial body of freshwater, the New Euxine Lake, which lay 500 feet (150 meters) below sea level. Around 5500 B.C. rising sea levels breached this land bridge, pouring huge quantities of saline water into the lake, which became the Black Sea, and inundating an enormous area of land around its coast, particularly on its northern side. American investigators working in this area suggest

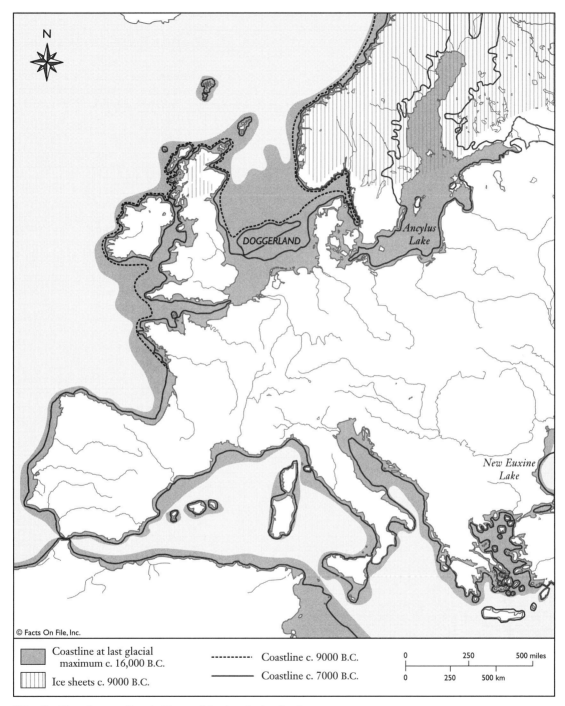

Map 3. *Changing coastlines in Europe following the last Ice Age*

N

DOGGERLAND

Ancylus Lake

New Euxine Lake

Coastline at last glacial
maximum c. 16,000 B.C.

Ice sheets c. 9000 B.C.

Coastline c. 9000 B.C.

Coastline c. 7000 B.C.

| 0 | | 250 | | 500 miles |
| 0 | 250 | | 500 km | |

© Facts On File, Inc.

that the memories of the survivors of this inundation gave rise to the Flood stories current in the Near East (though other scholars favor a Mesopotamian origin for the legend).

ENVIRONMENT

Freed of ice, new areas of tundra and steppe developed in the far north, attracting reindeer and other cold-loving animals, whose habitat was disappearing farther south. Some species, however, such as the giant Irish elk and the mammoth, were unable to adjust to the shrinking habitat and became extinct. Farther south the tundra and steppe became increasingly wooded as trees spread from their glacial refugia into regions now warmer and wetter than before: birch and pine initially, followed by hazel after 8000 B.C., then oak, lime, elm, and other deciduous species by 6000. Changing vegetation and the loss of coastal land to the sea brought about local extinctions, such as the wild ass and the aurochs in southern Greece.

In the Mediterranean rainfall rather than temperature had been the main factor limiting the spread of trees, which now flourished. By 8500 B.C. deciduous forest dominated by oak covered Iberia, Italy, and the Balkans, and had spread to most of Europe except Scandinavia by 6000 B.C. The early Holocene was a time of plenty in the Mediterranean, where a high level of annual sunshine hours, warm summer temperatures, and mild winters were coupled with the rich productivity and large number of edible species characteristic of deciduous forest; but by 7000 B.C. deciduous forest was gradually giving way to less productive evergreen woodland in the Mediterranean zone.

The deciduous forests produced nuts, fruits and berries, bulbs, roots, and tubers, while on more open ground grew legumes, pulses, and grasses including some wild cereals. A rich fauna inhabited these regions: herbivores such as red and roe deer, ibex and aurochs, other mammals such as boar and rabbits, as well as birds and snails. Marshlands, the margins of lakes and ponds, and the banks of rivers, particularly at their estuaries, were especially rich and diverse environments, offering not only land flora and fauna but also water resources such as fish, shellfish, turtles, and aquatic plants like water chestnuts, as well as wildfowl. The shallow waters of the drowned continental shelf around the tidal Atlantic coast and to a lesser extent the drowning coasts of the Mediterranean also furnished shellfish, such as mussels, limpets, and oysters, and in the seas there were fish, including sturgeon in the Black Sea, tuna in the Mediterranean, and cod, seabream, and saithe in the Atlantic, where there were also marine mammals such as seals and whales.

Early Mesolithic (9600–6000/5500)

ECONOMY

Human groups adapted their way of life to exploit these new circumstances. Success depended on flexibility in the strategies they adopted, enabling them to take advantage of opportunities and deal with shortfalls and fluctuations in their environment from season to season and year to year. It was important to make use of resources from a range of environments: People tended to settle for part or, later, sometimes all of the year in situations that allowed them to exploit a range of ecological settings, such as lake margins, rivers, estuaries, or coastal sites with access to woods, marshes, and upland. In northern Iberia, for example, some Mesolithic communities occupied coastal and estuarine locations (Asturian), exploiting aquatic resources, and game such as deer and boar, and their abundant settlements are marked by shell middens. Artifacts from these sites suggest line fishing and the use of drag nets. Other groups (Azilian) occupied both coastal and inland locations, including parts of the Pyrenees and Cantabrian Mountains, where game such as ibex were hunted. Caves and rock shelters as well as open sites were used for habitation. Mountain regions, such as the southern slopes of the Alps and the Cantabrian Cordillera, were exploited during summer months. Undifferentiated environments, such as the interior of thick forests, were generally avoided for settlement, though expeditions might be made into them.

Some groups continued traditional economies exploiting reindeer and other cold-loving fauna, but these were now confined to the north, which was progressively colonized as areas exposed by the melting ice sheets became available; eventually these animals and groups dependent on them lived only in the extreme north where tundra still existed. The gradual spread of forest favored herbivores, such as roe and red deer, whose pattern of life was less gregarious and involved far more restricted seasonal movement than that of the reindeer, horse, and other species hunted on the tundra. Hunting strategies had to be changed to deal with more solitary prey and terrain with reduced visibility. The bow and arrow, invented in the Magdalenian period, became more developed, using wooden arrows tipped with microliths to kill by slicing or penetrating the prey, or wooden arrows with blunt tips to stun or kill fur animals and birds without damaging their pelts. Burning sticks were also used to overcome fur animals for the same reason. Dogs became of great importance not only to aid in finding, flushing out, tracking, and driving game but also to pursue wounded animals and locate and retrieve prey fallen in the woods. Although in areas of open ground communal game drives might still be used as a hunting strategy, in the main hunters seem to have operated singly or with one or two companions. Pitfall traps and snares were also frequently used. Deer and boar were most widely hunted; elk and aurochs were also taken, as were rabbits in the Mediterranean, ibex and chamois in more mountainous regions, and birds everywhere, particularly around lakes, marshes, estuaries, and coasts. Hides from food animals were used for tents, clothing, and containers, but animals like beaver, wolf, otter, and pinemarten were also killed for their furs. Land snails and other small creatures were also exploited, and honey was obtained from the forests, as a Spanish rock painting attests. Meat could be dried or smoked for later use.

2.2 Hunting equipment: A Mesolithic barbed bone point from Denmark (left) and a Magdalenian (Late Glacial) biserially barbed bone harpoon head from France (right). Both would have been attached to long wooden shafts and were used for hunting large game. (Lubbock, John. *Prehistoric Times.* New York: D. Appleton and Company, 1890)

The great increase in plant foods, including roots, rhizomes, bulbs, tubers, leaves, fruits, seeds, nuts, fungi, and berries, available in the spreading forests and developing lake margins and marshes, must have led to an explosion in their importance in the diet. Many of them such as nuts and some tubers and fruits were suitable for storage for winter use. However, the evidence is limited, since most plants leave little trace in the way of imperishable waste material. Nevertheless, plant remains in water-logged sites, coprolites (preserved feces), tooth wear, and, most recently, isotope analysis of human bone attest the regular consumption of plants where they were available. Indirect evidence comes from microwear analysis, which provides information on the use to which tools were put, and from the introduction of new tools for obtaining and processing plant foods. Many of these used microliths, tiny blades and flakes of stone (usually flint) that made extremely efficient use of the raw material; these were mounted singly or together in wood or bone to make composite tools such as graters and knives. Grindstones and hammerstones were probably used for processing seeds, nuts, and other hard foods. Perforated round stones ("maceheads") may have been weights used on wooden digging sticks. Even in the early Mesolithic there is evidence of conscious management of plants and the environment. In particular, fire and bark-ringing were used to clear trees, reeds, and other dense vegetation, creating clearings and encouraging the growth of young shoots attractive to prey animals and of a variety of edible plants, such as nut-bearing hazel. In the north chipped flint axes were used probably to fell trees and certainly to work wood.

The coasts, lakes, estuaries, and rivers also furnished abundant fish and shellfish. New tools, including fishhooks, fish spears (leisters), and harpoons, were also devised to catch freshwater and marine fish, as were traps, weirs, and nets of wood and plant fibers, and special knives and "limpet picks" were used to prize shellfish from rocks and to open them. Like meat, fish could be preserved for use during lean times of the year. Huge shell middens, made up of a mixture of waste material of which seashells are the most bulky component, are the most visible remains of many coastal Mesolithic settlements. In the north marine mammals were also

exploited, the smaller ones like seals being hunted, though the whales eaten were probably usually stranded specimens. Coastal sites from the earlier part of the Mesolithic have been lost to rising sea levels, and it is therefore impossible to assess their relative importance, but certainly by the later part of the Mesolithic period marine and coastal resources were of great importance and coasts were the main focus of settlement in many parts of Europe such as the Atlantic regions. Numerous fish bones at Franchthi in Greece show that tuna fishing developed after 7000 B.C. to compensate for the reduction in land resources as the coastal plain shrank, and became increasingly important after 6000 B.C.

SETTLEMENT, MOVEMENT, AND SOCIETY

Seasonal movement to obtain resources available in different places at different times of year had been practiced in the glacial period. This continued, but new patterns were developed to exploit new resources or to accommodate the changing location of old. Deer, for example, were followed when they moved between lowland and upland grazing grounds, but the range of their seasonal migrations was far more restricted than that of Palaeolithic prey like reindeer; coastal locations were visited at seasons when spawning fish were present and lakes and marshes when migratory birds were expected. In the earlier part of the Mesolithic period, up to c. 6000/5500 B.C., communities seem to have been generally small and moved between seasonal camps to exploit these resources, traveling in the course of a year over a territory of around 50 to 100 miles' (80 to 150 kilometers') diameter or sometimes more. Seasonal movements brought groups into contact, allowing social relations to be maintained; communities could renew ties and exchange marriage partners but also make economic exchanges of goods. Raw materials and goods might travel substantial distances through a chain of such exchanges.

The development of boats for fishing permitted waterborne communications and exploration. In the earlier Mesolithic period evidence for these was indirect: a number of wooden paddles from various sites; tools and other human debris on islands, including Sicily, Corsica, and Sardinia by the eighth millennium B.C. From later Mesolithic times, however, dugout canoes survive from a few sites, including Tybrind Vig, which also yielded beautifully decorated paddles. One canoe from here was nearly 33 feet (10 meters) long and contained a clay hearth, presumed to be for night fishing, probably for eels. By 9000 B.C. people from southern Greece were visiting the island of Melos, from which they brought back obsidian. This was among a number of prized materials that were exchanged between communities, traveling long distances from their source; other included seashells and amber.

Evidence of Mesolithic housing is scanty, in most cases limited to sunken floors and traces of wooden stakes that may have supported walls of reeds or bark, or tents of hides, prepared using stone scrapers. In some cases, remains of a floor also survive, made of bark or clay, protected by a patch of sand where the hearth was built. Occasionally the hut foundations were built of stone. At Lepenski Vir in the Iron Gates gorge of the Danube the foundations of a number of trapezoidal huts built of stakes have been found. Within these there were remarkable limestone sculptures of fish-faced people with bulging eyes and open mouths. Art in general is far less well known than in the Upper Palaeolithic period. Pebbles painted with geometric designs of dots or lines are known in the early Mesolithic: These seem likely to have had some coded significance, now irretrievably lost. The rare finds of artwork such as the carved elks' heads among the grave goods at the later Mesolithic site of Oleneostrovski Mogilnik, however, show that there was no lack of skill or artistic creativity; but little has survived of the mostly perishable materials in which Mesolithic people worked. Late Mesolithic rock paintings in southern Spain and rock engravings in Scandinavia give rare, vivid glimpses of Mesolithic life, showing people at work, for example, hunting or collecting honey, and at leisure, for instance, engaging in communal dances. Masks made of deer skulls with antlers found at Star Carr in England may have been used in dances or other ritual activities although they may alternatively have been aids to hunting. Massive postholes near the site of the much later monument of Stonehenge once held posts made from huge pine tree trunks, erected in the eighth millennium B.C.—another elusive trace of Mesolithic symbolic activity.

Early Neolithic 7000–5500 B.C.

THE BEGINNINGS OF EUROPEAN AGRICULTURE

The postglacial period in the Near East had seen the rapid development and spread of farming as a way of life, including in Anatolia, Europe's nearest neighbor. Until c. 5500 B.C. northwest Anatolia was even linked to the far southeast of Europe by a small land bridge, destroyed when the Black Sea was flooded from the Mediterranean. In addition, Southeast Europe and Anatolia were linked by seas over which competent navigators in seaworthy boats had been active from at least 9000 B.C.

By around 7000 B.C., the first settlements of farmers were appearing in eastern Greece and on the island of Crete. Their domestic animals and crops included sheep and goats, wheat and barley, all introduced from the Near East, where these were staples. Also raised by Anatolian farmers were pigs, cattle, and various pulses. These may have been introduced, although wild boar, aurochs, and some cereals and pulses existed in the wild in Europe, and so they may have been domesticated locally. As farming spread across Europe, new domesticates were added to the range exploited, and there was probably some interbreeding between wild and domestic animals.

Although the original farming domesticates were introduced from the Near East, it is still debated to what extent these were moved by exchange between farmers and hunter-gatherers who were already changing their resource-management strategies or by immigrant farmers seeking new land as their populations expanded. Different scholars espouse different views, but it is widely accepted that the first farmers in Greece, the Balkans, southern Italy, and central Europe were mainly immigrants, while those elsewhere may have included immigrant farmers but were largely native hunter-gatherers who turned to agriculture as local economic or social conditions made it desirable to do so.

Mesolithic populations in many of the areas originally colonized by farmers, such as southern Greece and much of Southeast Europe, seem to have been low. Although in a few places Mesolithic

Map 4. *Postglacial hunter-gatherers and the spread of farming to 4500 B.C.*

and Neolithic communities came into contact, frequently the environments favored by each were not attractive to the other. Hunter-gatherers preferred coasts, lake shores, river estuaries, and other econiches with a wide range of easily accessible wild resources, while farmers often chose locations that combined access to water with well-watered stretches of open ground suitable for growing crops, such as river floodplains, where there was only limited diversity of wild resources. For instance, the loess soils favored by the first farmers in central Europe were avoided by hunter-gatherers.

In general, the first farming settlements in a region were small and few in number, and the associated culture often uniform over a wide area, such as the whole zone of the LBK (the first farmers in central Europe, from the western Carpathian basin to northern France and the Ukraine). Later settle-ments in a region were often larger and reflected some infilling of the landscape, giving greater density of occupation in the places first colonized and expansion into other ecological zones within the region. This internal expansion was often coupled with the development of regional variations in material culture, particularly apparent in styles of pottery. Some kind of defense or demarcation of the settlement, for example, by surrounding it with a ditch, developed in some regions, and in some cases was coupled with evidence for violence and conflict.

Sedentism, associated with farming but also with many later Mesolithic groups, allowed greater population increase than before; despite this, farming communities were for millennia the minority in most of Europe, and in some areas, especially Atlantic regions and the north, hunting and gathering remained the preferred way of life. By 3000 B.C.,

2.3 A fanciful reconstruction of early European horticulture. Such small-scale cultivation of fenced garden plots close to the settlement is likely to have characterized Neolithic farming in many parts of Europe. (Figuier, Louis. *Primitive Man.* London: Chatto and Windus, 1876)

however, farming was practiced throughout Europe and hunting was largely replaced by herding, but the exploitation of wild foods, particularly marine and riverine resources, was not universally abandoned.

GREECE AND THE BALKANS

Mesolithic occupation in Southeast Europe seems to have been sparse. Despite decades of investigation, very few Mesolithic sites are known in Greece, all but Theopetra in Thessaly being coastal; of these the best documented is Franchthi cave in the Argolid. Among the main resources exploited by the later Mesolithic occupants of Franchthi cave was tuna, caught by deep-sea fishing. Seaborne connections are therefore likely to have existed between coastal communities in the Aegean, providing links between Greece and the Near East, particularly Anatolia, a route by which domestic plants and animals and Neolithic objects may have been transmitted.

The long-lived Mesolithic occupation in Franchthi cave underwent a significant change around 7000 B.C., when new artifacts, including polished stone tools and pottery, and domestic animals and later plants appeared alongside the remains of wild foods and Mesolithic tools, and the size of the settlement increased. Although some scholars argue that this shows the indigenous development of farming, using domesticates obtained through contacts with farming communities in the Near East, more probably it reflects contacts and interactions with immigrant farmers who had settled in the region. A similar scenario can be argued at Lepenski Vir in the Iron Gates gorge of the Danube, where domestic animals appear alongside Mesolithic material around 6000 B.C.

Small numbers of farming settlements began to appear in eastern Greece and the island of Crete around 7000 B.C., and during the seventh millennium spread into Thessaly (Proto-Sesklo and Sesklo cultures). The farmers seem most likely to have come from parts of the Near East and Anatolia, probably by sea, bringing with them their full range of domestic animals and plants. Further expansion necessitated some adjustment to more temperate and continental conditions, with occasional summer rainfall and colder winters, but by 6000 B.C. farming communities had spread through the Balkans east of the central mountain ranges into

the southeastern part of the Carpathian basin, settling on fertile plains and avoiding other environmental settings. (Starčevo-Körös-Criş-Karanovo I complex). These settlements were generally small communities of 10 or 20 square or rectangular houses built of mud bricks or of clay on a wooden framework. Probably accommodating single nuclear families, they had a single room with a hearth or clay oven, a grindstone, and clay storage bins. Some of the later houses were more substantial, with a second story or a basement, or two interconnected rooms at ground level. Some settlements, such as the long-lived tell (settlement mound) of Karanovo in the Balkans, expanded as time went on and may eventually have contained as many as 60 houses. Although the first farming settlements may have been occupied only briefly, permanent settlements seem soon to have been established in many locations. Some of the settlements, particularly in the Balkans, were very long-lived, creating tells (mounds built up of debris from houses of clay repeatedly demolished and reconstructed). Where tells did not form, this was more probably due to the nature of the building material (wood that could be reused or burned) than to impermanent settlement.

The inhabitants of the earliest settlements in Greece may not have had pottery, which appears in Anatolian sites early in the seventh millennium; those of slightly later settlements made plain and later geometrically painted pottery and tools of polished stone as well as flint, obsidian, and probably wood, and may have decorated themselves with stamped designs using clay stamps (*pintaderas*). Sheep and goat, common in southern sites, were less common farther north, and their importance also decreased through time. Pigs and cattle were also kept. Wild creatures of many kinds, including deer, fish, boar, aurochs, fur animals, and wildfowl, were hunted, probably partly for meat and skins and partly to stop them eating the farmers' crops. These included wheat, barley, and pulses such as peas and vetch. Wild fruits and nuts, available in adjacent woodland, were collected and eaten, as other wild plants may also have been. Although the tools used by these farmers included a few polished stone axes, there is evidence of only limited forest clearance. Households probably cultivated their own plots and cared for their own animals, but cooking facilities placed outside the houses suggest that households ate together and shared food.

Spondylus shells from the Aegean and obsidian from the Aegean island of Melos found in Greek and Balkan sites, as much as 280 miles (450 kilometers) distant from their source, mark the existence of exchange networks throughout the region, probably though not certainly involving transactions over short distances in the context of kinship or other intercommunity ties. It is possible that some individuals specialized in obtaining such materials from their sources; there may also have been some exchange between farmers and hunter-gatherers in the areas in which they came into contact, with grain being exchanged not only for game but also perhaps for materials like obsidian obtained by hunter-gatherers on fishing expeditions. Obsidian and flint were used to make knives and other edge tools. In addition to pottery, which showed both overall stylistic similarities throughout the region and more localized variations, clay was used to make figurines depicting people and animals. These may have served some religious purpose. Although some are associated with possible shrines, such as a large centrally placed building in the Greek village of Nea Nikomedeia, most were found in ordinary houses, probably reflecting the domestic practice of ritual activities. Some burials were made within the settlement, but it is possible that most of the dead were cremated and interred outside the settlement.

THE EAST

To the east, the regions along the Bug and Dnestr Rivers were inhabited by communities living by hunting, gathering, and fishing. Some of their larger settlements in the river estuaries may have been inhabited year round and used as a base for seasonal expeditions, for example, into the Crimean mountains, where they occupied caves and rock shelters. Animals living in the grassland and forests, including antelope, bear, and deer, were among their prey. By about 6000 B.C., the inhabitants of some hunter-gatherer settlements on river terraces in this region, such as Soroki (Bug-Dnestr culture), began to include some domestic animals in their diet, keeping some cattle and pigs while still relying mainly on

wild resources. They also made distinctive comb-decorated or incised pots, often with pointed bases. These people probably acquired domestic animals and later cereals by trading with or raiding their farming neighbors on the northern shores of the Black Sea, where farming communities related to the Criş culture of the Balkans were established by the late seventh millennium. Other hunter-gatherer groups to their east also gradually acquired domestic animals and began to make pottery. Recently, a number of cemeteries have been found in the Dnepr rapids region of the Ukraine: Ranging in age across several millennia, some of these belonged to the late hunter-gatherer inhabitants of this region.

THE MEDITERRANEAN

Impressed Ware Cultures During the seventh millennium farming settlements also began to appear in southern Italy and eastern Sicily, areas with little Mesolithic population; these settlements became more numerous here during the sixth millennium and spread northward east of the Apennines, reaching northern Italy and thence spreading into the western Alps. The Po plain, occupied by hunter-gatherers, was not settled by Impressed Ware groups. After a short initial phase, settlements surrounded by one or several enclosure ditches were established in Italy; these are best known in the Tavoliere region of the south. Smaller circular ditched compounds within the settlement contained individual timber-framed houses. Settlements of various sizes are known, larger ones particularly in later phases. As in Southeast Europe, their inhabitants raised sheep, goats, cattle, and pigs and cultivated cereals. The trend of opinion is to regard these farmers as colonists from the eastern Mediterranean.

Native communities nevertheless played a major part in the gradual adoption of agriculture around the Mediterranean. Between 7000 and 6000 B.C. Mesolithic communities were coming under increasing pressure as their coastal land was progressively reduced by sea-level rises and as environmental changes deprived them of important resources. One response was an increased reliance on marine resources, including fish such as tuna whose exploitation required offshore navigation. Mediterranean islands were gradually colonized: Corsica and Sardinia during the ninth or eighth millennium, the Balearics during the later sixth millennium; Malta, which seems to have been devoid of native fauna, was probably not settled much before 5000 B.C. Seafaring encouraged interaction between communities the length and breadth of the Mediterranean and thus both ideas and goods from the farming communities of the Aegean made their appearance among coastal Mesolithic communities. These included pottery: From the seventh millennium B.C. a distinctive style of pottery decorated with impressions, particularly of seashells, (Cardial) Impressed Ware, began to be made by Mesolithic people from the Adriatic coasts of the Balkans through the islands and coastal regions of Italy and southern France to the southern shores of Iberia and north coast of Morocco and Algeria. Impressed wares were also used by the earliest farming communities in southern Italy, who were also making painted pottery by around 6000 B.C. Variations in the style and decoration of these impressed wares probably expressed the distinct identity of regional groups. Between 6000 and 4500 this pottery style also spread along the Atlantic coast from Portugal to France; networks of communication stretching from the Mediterranean coast of France to the Massif Central and to the Atlantic via the Garonne also spread knowledge of Neolithic technology and domestic animals to Mesolithic communities in the west.

Between 6000 and 5500 B.C. sheep and goats began to appear in Mesolithic caves and open settlements in the Mediterranean, their meat and hides supplementing those from hunted animals. They were known, for instance, in the long-established Mesolithic settlement of Grotta del'Uzzo in northwest Sicily, along with pigs, which may have been locally domesticated. The growing importance of domestic stock coincides in Sardinia and Corsica with a decline in the numbers of the native species *Prolagus sardus* (a kind of rabbit) and *Megacerus cazioti* (a deer), which eventually became extinct. Settlements with domestic sheep and goat and wild game and plant foods are known on the coast and in the interior of the Adriatic region of the Balkans (Danilo-Smilcic), where ditches enclosed settlements with houses and open areas for herding livestock; in southern France and southern Spain sheep, goats, and sometimes pigs appear alongside wild

resources. By the late sixth millennium domestic cereals, particularly barley, were also being adopted by hunter-gatherers from their farming neighbors. Pulses may also have been introduced, but it is at least as likely that local wild pulses, such as chickpeas, peas, and lentils, were taken into cultivation. Similarly, stocks of domestic animals were probably supplemented from local wild boar and aurochs.

Opinions are divided whether actual colonists were responsible for the spread of the Neolithic way of life into central and northern Italy and the western Mediterranean or whether all the farming communities that developed here grew out of local hunter-gatherer communities that had gradually adopted animal husbandry and cereal cultivation, reducing their reliance on wild resources through time; the latter seems more likely in many cases, but there is also some evidence of colonization. For example, in southern Portugal settlements with Impressed Ware, domestic animals, polished stone tools, and cereals appeared between 6000 and 5500 in areas (notably northern Estremadura) without previous Mesolithic settlement, while communities living by hunting, fishing, and collecting were concentrated in the valleys of the Tagus, Sado, and Mira: this could support the theory that farming communities in the region were incomers.

The distribution of sites where mixed agricultural and Mesolithic resources were exploited was largely confined to islands and coastal regions, reflecting the importance of seaborne communication; only later did domesticates begin to appear in inland sites in the central and western Mediterranean such as central Spain, southern France, and the Pyrenees.

Expansion and Development 5500–5000 B.C.

CENTRAL EUROPE

Linearbandkeramik (LBK also known as Danubian I). By 5500 B.C. farming settlements were beginning to appear in the western Carpathian basin and to spread into areas to the north and west of the Carpathian Mountains. Colonization of this region and beyond involved a number of adjustments since both climate and environment were significantly different from those of the southeast. Hot summers and mild winters were progressively replaced by mild summers and long, severe winters, low rainfall mainly in the winter by heavy precipitation over much of the year, including snow, and open woodland and scrub by dense forests. Once seen simply as an expansion by farming settlers from the Starčevo-Körös culture of Serbia and eastern Hungary, these colonists are now alternatively suggested to have been descendants of the Mesolithic natives of the Carpathian region who had adopted animals, crops, and agricultural practices from their Balkan neighbors. Whatever their origins, the rate of their spread was rapid, similar farming settlements appearing within 500 years in the Low Countries and northern France as far as the Paris basin and up to the southern edge of the North European Plain and the mouth of the Oder River. They also spread east into Moldavia and the western Ukraine during the fifth millennium. Rapid population growth seems likely to have fueled the progressive expansion into productive virgin territory where native hunter-gatherers were probably rarely encountered.

These settlements were confined to river valleys and particularly to loess soils, which occurred extensively across the region. Easily worked, well drained, and fertile, these windblown soils were also relatively free from forest, reducing the task involved in clearing the land before cultivation. Nevertheless, the artifacts used by the inhabitants of these settlements included many axes and woodworking tools, since these people relied heavily on timber from the adjacent forests for construction and tools, and for firewood.

Thousands of small settlements are known, generally with no more than six houses, and occurring about every one to two miles (one to three kilometers); in some regions settlement was composed of continuous ribbons of single houses, spaced at intervals of around 55–110 yards (50–100 meters). These dwellings were long, single-story houses with pitched roofs and overhanging eaves to deal with the rain and snow. The construction of these buildings must have been a matter for community cooperation; closeness to kin upon whom one could rely at need was one of the factors structuring the pattern

of dispersal in the new landscape, acting as a check on the otherwise relatively unlimited opportunities for expansion.

Distinctive unpainted pottery decorated with incised curvilinear lines and dots gives this culture its name: Linearbandkeramik (LBK). Polished stone axes and adzes were also characteristic LBK artifacts, designed for felling trees and woodworking, and perhaps as hoes for cultivation. Suitable fine-grained stone for making such tools, such as amphibolite, was exchanged over long distances, as were other goods and materials, including flint, pottery, and obsidian. Spondylus shells from the Aegean or the Black Sea show that exchanges took place not only between LBK communities but also with farming communities farther afield, with rivers providing transport routes.

Erosion of the surfaces of most LBK sites has severely limited the information available on houses and other aspects of life: Often all that remain are the stubs of the deep postholes of the houses' timber framework and of pits dug to provide clay for the walls. Some of the smaller structures may have been workshops or farm buildings. Many of the houses probably accommodated a single nuclear family while others may have been occupied by a larger family group. Alternatively, the larger structures, which might be as long as 145 feet (45 meters), may have served a different purpose, for example, as a shrine or community meeting house. Although most settlements were within easy reach of rivers or streams, some were not but had wood-lined wells to provide water.

The house walls were constructed of substantial wooden posts infilled with wattle and daub. Three rows of posts ran through the interior, supporting the gable roof. The central portion of the house was probably the area in which most daily activities took place, with hearths and working areas. One end of the house may have contained sleeping quarters and storage space, or may alternatively have been used to stall livestock. Above the other end of the house there was often a loft in which grain and other perishables could be stored. Cattle were now the main domestic animal, providing the bulk of the meat and possibly also being used to provide milk; pigs also increased in number, thriving on forage in the adjacent woodland. As well as the earlier staples, wheat,

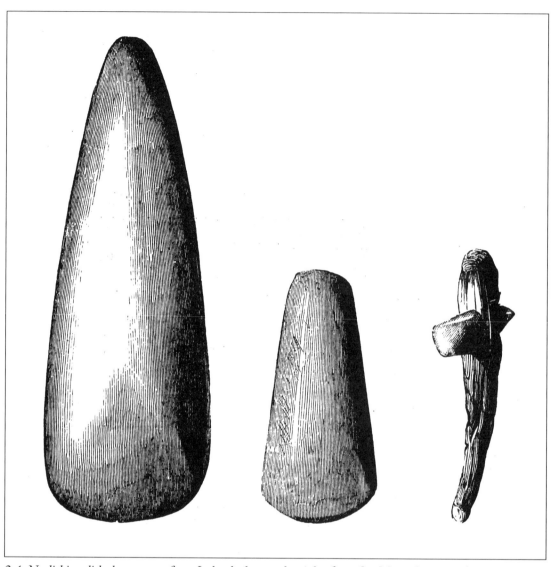

2.4 Neolithic polished stone axes from Ireland; that on the right, from Co. Monaghan, was found still in its haft, which was made of pine wood. These were not only woodworking tools but also served other purposes, including working the land for cultivation and killing opponents with blows to the head. (Lubbock, John. *Prehistoric Times.* New York: D. Appleton and Company, 1890)

barley, and pulses, LBK farmers may have grown goosefoot (chenopodium) and opium poppy, though these may just have been weeds of cultivation. Small plots were probably permanently cleared of their primary vegetation, in at least some cases by burning, and fertility maintained by crop rotation and manuring. At this stage the small numbers of farmers and the abundant land available meant that only a small amount was brought into cultivation, in general no more than that within a kilometer of the settlement. Domestic animals could have been pastured in fields or let to forage in adjacent woodland. Wild resources were also exploited: fish and wildfowl, deer, boar, and aurochs; fruit, nuts, and other plant foods, as well as leaves and other forage for the domestic animals. Some of these were probably stored for use over the winter.

In the west of the LBK zone, and to a lesser extent farther east, the dead were buried in small cemeteries of single graves; these were located beside larger settlements, or a central cemetery served a number of houses or hamlets in the areas of dispersed ribbon settlement. Both inhumation and cremation were practiced. The small number of graves and the distribution of different types of grave goods within them paints a picture of some differential access to resources, perhaps reflecting status differences, or different degrees of success among families or communities.

The loess of central Europe was an area largely shunned by hunter-gatherers, but when the LBK farmers reached the Atlantic and North Sea regions of the northwest they came into contact with Mesolithic communities, particularly on the coast and in river estuaries. Both conflicts and peaceful interactions must have taken place within this contact zone. Competition for land and resources may have encouraged the defense and demarcation of territory: Some LBK settlements in this region are surrounded by a defensive ditch, whereas elsewhere settlements were usually not enclosed. Food and other resources were probably exchanged between the communities, along with knowledge and expertise: Mesolithic groups acquired domestic plants and animals, pottery and ceramic technology, while some farmers adopted Mesolithic techniques of flint working or gained access to wild resources. The La Hoguette culture on the northwest edge of LBK may represent Mesolithic groups that had adopted pottery and domestic animals from LBK farmers.

GREECE AND THE BALKANS

Later Sesklo-Vadastra-Vinča-Karanovo III-Dudeşti By 5500 B.C. farming communities in Southeast Europe were very numerous and often large, reflecting a successful way of life and considerable population growth. Some were earlier settlements, such as the tell at Karanovo; others were new foundations in areas that had not previously been exploited. While the inhabitants of many communities were the descendants of the original farming colonists, others may have been people of hunter-gatherer stock who had adopted agriculture. The flooding of the Black Sea shores when the Mediterranean broke through around 5500 B.C. may also have driven many coastal farming communities to settle inland, for instance, in the previously sparsely settled lower Danube region. Although farming continued earlier practices, cattle were becoming more important, their numbers probably swelled by domesticating wild aurochs.

Desirable raw materials continued to circulate over considerable distances through exchange; in addition, some manufactured goods were also exchanged between groups, including local styles of pottery. Some pottery vessels were decorated with human features or even made in the form of people, and distinctive anthropomorphic figurines were also manufactured; these may have had some ritual purpose. Copper made its first appearance, initially being worked by cold hammering to produce small objects such as beads.

Settlements were for the most part undifferentiated, with no indication of any differences in status. A few, such as Sesklo in northern Greece, had a large structure in the center of the settlement. Some settlements were enclosed by ditches, perhaps for defense, although there is no evidence of conflict. In most areas the inhabitants continued to bury their dead within the settlement, generally in pits alongside or beneath their houses; however, in some regions, including the coastal region of Dobrogea on the Black Sea, an area where there is likely to have been acculturation of the local Mesolithic population, and on the Hungarian plain, some settlements began to have attached separate cemeteries in which some members of the community were buried.

THE ATLANTIC AND THE NORTH

The later Mesolithic period (from 6000/5500 B.C.) was a time of some stress for many hunter-gatherer communities, including those of western and northern Europe. By now the substantial plains of the north (Doggerland) had been drowned by the North Sea, the English Channel had separated Britain from the European mainland, and along the Atlantic coasts land continued to be lost. Around this time the Scandinavian land bridge that separated the North Sea from the Ancylus Lake was breached, converting the latter into the Litorina Sea, which eventually became the Baltic. In the interior rising rainfall and higher temperatures encouraged vegetation growth, resulting in forests that were larger, denser, and less penetrable, supporting fewer large animals as browsing became less easy: a less useful environment than the more open forests of earlier times. The development of lethal trapeze- or rhomboid-shaped arrowheads may reflect the need for greater hunting efficiency in the forest environment to counteract reduced visibility and penetrability; the growing importance of dogs may also have been related to this. In some sites dogs were accorded separate burial with associated grave goods. Forest also spread onto higher slopes of the mountains, reducing the area that provided upland summer grazing for herbivores.

The communities of the north and west responded to changing conditions by making more intensive use of established resources and incorporating new foods into their diet, in particular increasing their use of marine resources through coastal and deep-sea fishing and the hunting of sea mammals. The importance of fishing was reflected in the proliferation of devices for trapping or catching fish, such as weirs, nets, and leisters. Analysis of the human and dog bones at the inland hunting camp of Agernaes in Denmark shows that the inhabitants' diet was largely based on marine resources. Population increased overall, and in some areas settlements increased in size and permanence and decreased in number. For instance, in Portugal there was a shift from the earlier pattern of many small sites on the coast, in the estuaries of many rivers, and in inland limestone caves, to a concentration of settlement in the estuaries only of major rivers, especially the Tagus, Sado, and Mira, marked by massive shell middens. Most were probably occupied for most or all of the year, though some seem to have been short-occupation camps established to exploit particular resources. Chemical analyses of remains from the shell middens here show that half or more of the inhabitants' diet came from marine sources though land resources were also exploited. Farther north in Armorica there were also well-established coastal Mesolithic groups known archaeologically from their shell middens and burials at sites such as Hoëdic and Téviec. Remains from the middens show that fish and shellfish bulked large in the diet, but game, birds, and sea mammals were also eaten, as probably were plants though the evidence is very slim. Fur animals were also taken. In general, settlement in northern and western Europe was concentrated on the coasts although estuaries and lake margins where the produce of a range of environments was available were also favored for settlement.

Sites like these were probably occupied for all or most of the year. The well-studied later Mesolithic sites of Denmark (Ertebølle) show a pattern of sizable communities that spent much of the year in a large base camp usually located near the sea and generally marked by a large shell midden (e.g., Ertebølle itself). From here expeditions would be made by some members of the community to places where particular desirable resources were available at certain times of year, such as swans (e.g., Aggersund), piglets and pinemartens (e.g., Ringkloster), other fur animals (e.g., Agernaes), or eels (e.g., Dyrholm), but also to flint outcrops and other sites where material for tools could be obtained. Not all permanent settlements were coastal, however; for example, Auneau in the Paris Basin may have been occupied throughout the year.

As communities traveled smaller distances in their seasonal round, interaction between them grew in importance, and some commodities were moved far greater distances than before, up to 375 miles (600 kilometers). Substantial canoes were used for travel both by sea and by river. To this period also belong the first skis and sledges, found in the north. Stable isotope bone analysis from Téviec and Hoëdic also show the movement of women from inland communities to the coast as marriage partners. The widespread distribution of materials from distant areas shows that mechanisms existed to regulate intergroup relations peacefully; however, competition may well have spilled over into violence from time to time, and it has been suggested that the large formal cemeteries that appeared during this period, at coastal sites from Portugal and Brittany to Oleneostrovski Mogilnik in Russia, were created as an attempt to mark territorial ownership. Cemeteries of single burials are known at a number of large settlements along the Atlantic facade; those at Hoëdic and Téviec in Armorica differ in being communal graves in which individuals were buried over a period of time.

Neolithic Consolidation (Fifth Millennium B.C.)

Deciduous forests were continuing to spread northward, reaching Scandinavia and eastern Europe after 5000 B.C. Tundra became confined to the far north, now largely deglaciated, still home to reindeer, though many cold-loving animals had by now become locally or globally extinct. The productivity of lakes was beginning to decline as they became progressively infilled by organic material and soil, a process completed in many lakes by 4000 B.C. In the Mediterranean drier conditions brought the gradual replacement of deciduous forest by maquis and scrub vegetation, a process accelerated by the destructive effects of grazing animals.

Farming was established across much of Europe by 5000 B.C., but, except in the southeast and the Mediterranean, the numbers of farmers were still small. While some regions, such as dense forests, were virtually free of human occupation except at their margins, Mesolithic communities continued to thrive in many areas and still made up the bulk of the European population. In the west, along most of the Atlantic facade, in the north, and in the northeast, there was as yet no direct contact between hunter-gatherers and farmers, while in much of the rest of Europe, it was limited to the restricted areas selected for settlement by farmers. Where contact occurred, hunter-gatherers selectively adopted innovations as it suited them, acquiring polished stone axes by exchange, taking up pottery making, and obtaining domestic plants and animals. The well-established exchange networks operated by the Mesolithic people and the contacts facilitated by their partially mobile lifestyle meant that these innovations could spread widely, well beyond the zone of actual contact between farmers and hunter-gatherers. Environmental changes and the expansion of the farming communities put pressure on the Mesolithic lifestyle in some areas, and Mesolithic communities came to rely on domestic resources to supplement wild ones, the balance finally tipping over into a mainly agricultural economy in most areas by 4000 B.C.

The interaction and hybridization between Mesolithic and Neolithic traditions in many areas contributed to the growing trend of regionalization and the development of regional cultures. Another factor was adaptation to the specific conditions of different regions, contrasting with the relatively undifferentiated practices of the earliest farming colonists; in this, too, the contribution of the native hunter-gatherers, with millennia of knowledge of their local regions, was significant. Often farming communities that had previously ignored wild resources began to make some use of them, hunting and then eating animals that threatened their crops, augmenting their herds from wild stock, and using wild plants for fodder, food, and other uses such as dyes and medicines. The expansion of farming brought the colonization of land that was less easy to work than the soils such as loess that had first attracted farmers, and of less accessible areas such as uplands. Forests were progressively cleared, both to create new agricultural land and to provide wood for building and other purposes. The fifth millennium saw a considerable increase in farming population in temperate Europe as settlement expanded into new zones. The highest areas of population density, however, were most probably the coastal locations favored by Mesolithic communities, particularly in river estuaries. Here abundant and varied resources permitted sedentary settlement and allowed large and socially complex communities to develop. It is in this context that the acquisition of exotic goods such as polished stone axes may have gained importance. The growth of formal burials, often in cemeteries, may also be a reflection of developing complexity.

Population growth, the continuing erosion of the Mesolithic resource base, and interaction and competition between Mesolithic and Neolithic groups led in some areas to a more marked and self-conscious definition of group identity, shown for example in the development of megalithic tombs. Competition may also have developed into open conflict, both between hunter-gatherers and farmers and between communities of each. Mesolithic cemeteries include individuals who had suffered injuries inflicted by weapons. Some farming settlements may have been fortified, and there is evidence among these farming groups, too, of individuals or even whole groups that had met a violent end.

In the southeast, however, where agricultural communities had been established for well over a millennium, there is little trace of conflict. Settlements grew in size, and occupation expanded into new areas. Crafts flourished, and new technologies were developed. Native copper and gold had for many centuries been worked by cold-hammering in the areas where they were found, producing small objects such as beads. From around 4500 B.C., however, copper began to be smelted, at first in the Balkans and then in Spain, both areas rich in easily worked ores. The products of this early metallurgy continued to be objects of prestige value, such as ornaments, and took their place alongside other status symbols.

The Southeast

GREECE

Tsangli Then Dimini The fifth millennium saw an expansion of settlement in Greece, villages being founded both in Thessaly, where settlement was already well established, and in new areas such as parts of Thrace and Macedonia and a number of Aegean islands including the Cyclades. Some houses now had stone foundations. A few settlements had a large central building; at Dimini, a settlement founded in this period, this building was surrounded by a courtyard and a substantial stone wall.

Impressions of woven textiles at Sitagroi in Thrace around 5000 B.C. are the earliest direct evidence of cloth manufacture in Europe, although mats and baskets had been made from earlier times. Spindle whorls and loom weights appeared with increasing frequency in Greece and elsewhere.

THE BALKANS

Early Eneolithic (Karanovo IV-Vinča-Boian-Hamangia) In the earlier fifth millennium tell and flat settlements in the Balkans continued to grow and prosper, exploiting the easily worked and fertile soils of river valleys and dried-up lake basins. Copper and gold were still worked by cold-hammering and annealing, producing small objects such as fishhooks and beads. These were deposited among the grave goods in the separate cemeteries that were beginning to be created outside settlements in some areas such as Bulgaria.

Gumelnitsa-Karanovo V/VI-Vinča-Varna By 4500 B.C. tell settlements were often substantial and carefully planned, with houses laid out in rows, concentric circles, or blocks. Defensive ditches and palisades, with entrances placed at cardinal points, surrounded the settlements, which were often located in defensible situations on river terraces. Houses were often divided into several rooms, and in some cases they may have had a second story. Some structures were dwellings, while others were probably used for storage or other purposes. There was also some variation in the size of houses, suggesting differentials in status, though the larger structures might have been used for community purposes. The settlements were associated with a rich material culture, including fine painted pottery and many figurines.

It also included fine graphite-painted wares that were fired at a high temperature. Such command of pyrotechnology led to the smelting and casting of copper. Easily worked copper ores were widely available in the Carpathian and Balkan Mountains, often not far distant from farming settlements. The importance of copper is emphasized by the impressive mines at Rudna Glava and Aibunar. Copper and gold (obtained from rivers) were used to make ornaments and other objects such as axes and spearheads, reflecting growing metallurgical skills. The use of the new technology is most vividly displayed in the cemetery at Varna on the Black Sea, dated around 4500–4000 B.C. Here some 60 graves, around a fifth of the cemetery, contained ornaments and other objects of gold and copper, as well as others of spondylus shell and fine flint blades. The majority of these were buried in graves without bodies, where individuals were sometimes represented by clay masks, though a few of the richly furnished graves did contain skeletons. Most of the burials in the cemetery had some grave goods, their quantity and richness varying considerably.

Copper and gold objects probably enhanced and displayed the status of their owners. Metal ores were only one of the materials that were now sought by communities and widely traded; others included both prestige and everyday materials such as high-quality flint, pigments such as graphite for decorating pottery, stone for axes and grindstones, and probably many perishable materials such as furs. Manufactured goods also circulated, including pottery (perhaps traded for its contents) and stone tools. Analysis of the gold in the Varna cemetery shows that much of it came from distant sources in Armenia and the Caucasus, emphasizing the wide extent of contemporary trade networks.

THE EAST

North and east of the Balkans in the forest steppe villages of similar houses were built on promontories and other easily defensible locations, surrounded by ditches. From around 5000 B.C., Cucuteni-Tripolye farming communities were becoming established on the steppes of European Russia and the Ukraine, herding cattle, sheep, and goats and raising crops. LBK (Notenkopf) farmers also settled in this region during the fifth millennium, pressing gradually eastward. Their settlements appeared in the upper valleys of the Dnestr and Prut Rivers at the end of the fifth millennium; these had a fully Neolithic economy, with domestic animals, cereals, and other cultivated plants. Horses are among the animals represented in faunal remains in the forest steppe during the fifth millennium; these may have been wild or domestic or both and were killed or reared for meat. The culture of the region was predominantly pastoralist, and it is possible that horses began to be ridden for use in herding domestic stock and hunting or rounding up wild cattle and horses.

Away from the farming settlements the region was also inhabited by Mesolithic groups that combined hunting, fishing, and gathering with some stockraising, and probably followed a mobile lifestyle; similar communities stretched far to the east. In the region between the Dnepr and the Don settled communities with a mixture of hunting, fishing, and livestock rearing developed from the late sixth millennium, practicing a little cereal cultivation and using pointed-based pottery, microliths, and polished stone tools (Dnepr-Donets culture). Distinctive cemeteries (Mariupol complex) have been found in this region and areas to the east; these contain collective inhumation burials scattered with ochre and furnished with stone tools, boar's tusk blades, and a variety of ornaments; some cemeteries also contained piles of skulls.

THE CARPATHIAN BASIN

Tisza In the earlier fifth millennium settlements in the Carpathian basin grew in size and decreased in number. Cattle were now the main domestic animals raised, possibly for milk, and wild cattle and other animals were hunted. Some settlements included buildings that may have served as a shrine, furnished with unusual material such as figurines, clay animal heads, and anthropomorphic vessels.

Tiszapolgár By 4500, however, settlements were becoming smaller and more dispersed, often placed in elevated locations in the floodplains of the rivers. Emphasis turned to burial, with the appearance of large cemeteries as the probable focus of a number of settlements, replacing earlier practices of burial within the settlement or in small associated cemeteries. Within the cemeteries, the graves were carefully laid out, often in rows and never overlapping, showing that they were marked in some way. As in the Balkans, grave goods became more important, including prestige goods such as gold and copper ornaments, long flint blades, and stone or copper shafthole axes.

Mediterranean

WESTERN NEOLITHIC

During the sixth millennium in sites in southern France as far as the Loire valley and during the fifth millennium in other inland regions of the central and western Mediterranean, domestic animals and plants began to appear, often associated with Mesolithic-style flint tools and wild resources. The use of the latter declined, and by 4500 in most regions hunter-gatherer communities had been replaced by settlements dependent mainly on farming, such as the large villages in southern France and parts of Spain enclosed by ditches and palisades; ditched enclosures containing settlements continued in Italy. In southern Spain small hilltop settlements appeared, some surrounded by walls, with oval or rectangular huts. The Iberian interior was largely virgin territory when farming communities settled there, having apparently been unoccupied since the end of the Glacial period. In contrast, the Po plain was home to conservative hunter-gatherers (Castelnovian) who hunted deer and wild boar and exploited aquatic resources; this was one of the last regions to adopt agriculture. Here and in a number of other areas, some hunting and use of other wild resources continued alongside agriculture. Moving with domestic herds and flocks between seasonal pastures (transhumance) replaced seasonal movement to hunt wild herbivores.

In parts of northern Italy and in Alpine regions, lakeside villages of timber-framed houses developed, built on piles to counteract flooding; probably inhabited by descendants of Mesolithic people, these often showed continuing exploitation of many wild resources as well as farming. Villagers in the east were influenced by their LBK neighbors, while those in the west formed part of the Western Neolithic with its ancestry in the Impressed Ware cultures of the Mediterranean. Exceptional preservation of wooden objects and other perishable materials gives an unusually full picture of their lives; these objects included canoes and fishing equipment, bows and harpoons for hunting, and agricultural tools, as well as linen clothing, containers of birch bark and wood, food, fodder, and manure. Such settlements became more common in the fourth millennium.

Obsidian from four Italian island sources was extracted and exchanged on an increasing scale. High-quality flint and stone were also exchanged as was pottery, the latter probably as containers for some desirable commodity. Many regional styles of pottery developed, such as Chasseen in France and Cortaillod in Switzerland, but these styles shared a number of features, such as handles and round bases, and often they were undecorated. Copper began to be smelted in southeast Spain (Almerian).

Temperate Europe

ATLANTIC ZONE AND NORTHERN EUROPE

Mesolithic Society In various regions of the Atlantic facade and northern Europe, such as southern Portugal and Armorica, the marked shift to concentration on marine resources, initiated in the sixth millennium, became more intensive in the fifth. Favorable locations, particularly in river estuaries where coastal and riverine resources intersected and could often be combined with those of marsh and forest edge, were home to often large sedentary communities, their settlements marked by the vast shell middens that resulted from the exploitation of shellfish. In Denmark (Ertebølle culture), where Mesolithic settlement patterns have been intensively studied, the inhabitants lived for much of the year in these large camps, and from them were able to obtain a rich variety of foodstuffs and other resources within a few hours' walking distance. At some times of year, however, smaller groups from the community visited more distant locations, both elsewhere along the coast and inland, to obtain resources such as stone for tools and furs for clothing. These were not only used by the community that obtained them but also exchanged with neighboring groups; goods traveled long distances as a result of many such exchanges. Offshore islands also provided resources, and the sea yielded not only a great diversity of fish accessible from inshore fishing but also sea mammals and sea birds and deep-sea fish such as cod. On the Atlantic facade, deep-sea fishing promoted connections among communities right along the coastline. This was reflected in the appearance of shared practices, for example, the placement of deer antlers in some graves in Brittany and Scandinavia, and later probably in the rapid development of similar variations on the common theme of funerary monuments. Ritual practices may also have been developing in this period: a number of Ertebølle objects, including polished stone axes, have been found in bogs, and it is assumed that these were votive deposits.

Group identity was probably of considerable importance, and variations in the form of some everyday items may have been used to denote and emphasize membership of a particular community or regional group. In Denmark, for instance, such groupings have been detected at two levels: large-scale divisions on the basis of styles of combs, harpoons, and antler axes, possibly defining the territory of a related group of communities, and smaller scale variations in the shape of stone axes that may correspond to individual territories. As population rose, the necessity of demonstrating group identity and territorial affiliation increased. This may be reflected in the large cemeteries attached to a number of settlements. Distinct clusters of burials may represent separate clans or extended families. Practices varied: In Brittany one grave at Hoëdic was lined with stones as were a number at Téviec, where they were covered by small mounds; at Vedbaek in Denmark some of the bodies had been cremated, and there is evidence that may also represent exposure of the dead on a wooden structure before final disposal. Bones seem to have been rearranged in some graves, and in some cases bones were separated from the rest of the skeleton and treated differently, kept in the settlement or buried in ritual deposits, for instance. The nests of skulls at Ofnet in Germany may be an extreme example of this practice.

Grave goods, generally tools, weapons, and particularly ornaments, show some distinctions that may relate to status within the community; this seems to have been largely on the basis of gender and age. Young adult males were frequently the most richly furnished, with weapons and personal ornaments such as bear-tooth pendants. A few individuals who were accorded special treatment may have held a special position such as that of shaman. In some cases dogs were also buried, complete with grave goods, an indication of the degree to which they were integrated into community life.

Cemeteries also provide evidence of apparently widespread violence and conflict. A number of individuals buried in Mesolithic cemeteries had arrowheads embedded in their bones. Burials at Skateholm in Sweden and at other sites also included many individuals whose skulls had been fractured by heavy blows. Spanish rock engravings include some scenes that can be interpreted as battles between two groups armed with bows and arrows.

Hunter-Gatherers and Farmers   As farming became established as the main way of life in southern Europe, Mesolithic communities along the Atlantic coasts of Iberia and France gradually adopted domestic animals and Neolithic artifacts such as polished stone axes, grindstones, and pottery. Farther north the Mesolithic communities of the North Sea coastal regions and the North European Plain similarly acquired goods and technology from their farming neighbors (LBK and Danubian II). Interconnections between Mesolithic groups (Ellerbek, Swifterbant) in direct contact with farmers in the south of the North European Plain and those at a greater distance meant that, although geographically isolated from the farming settlements, by 4700 B.C. Ertebølle people were familiar with pottery and were making their own, in the form of coarse vessels with a pointed base.

Between 5000 and 4500 the prosperous Mesolithic communities that had occupied the Tagus, Sado, and Mira estuaries of southern Portugal abandoned their traditional way of life in favor of farming, a change reflected in their bones, analysis of which shows a steep decline in shellfish consumption. Mesolithic groups in the mountainous regions of northern Iberia, however, acquired animals, grain, and pottery from the farming communities with whom they came into contact but continued their traditional hunter-gatherer economy until the late fifth millennium. A similar picture holds good for other areas of dense Mesolithic settlement along the Atlantic facade and in northern Europe. Commodities and ideas, and probably also some individuals as marriage partners, were exchanged between Mesolithic and Neolithic communities, but food production was not adopted by the hunter-gatherers to any significant extent before 4000 B.C.

BRITAIN

Late Mesolithic settlements in Britain, best known from Scotland and Ireland, show a similar pattern to other areas of the Atlantic region, with a preference for coastal or estuarine locations and a mixed economy in which both aquatic and land resources were exploited, and there was movement to exploit resources in various locations at different times of the year. Woodlands were managed to create clearings attractive to hunted animals and to promote the growth of desirable vegetation such as hazel.

During the fifth millennium small numbers of farmers from the continent probably visited and settled in southern Britain, although traces of their presence are slight and their settlements elusive. Pottery, agricultural tools, domestic animals, and grain were present in Britain in the later fifth millennium, however, and by 3900 B.C. farming communities had spread widely in Britain, being established well inland and as far north as the Shetland Islands. Often they had a mixed economy, growing crops, raising animals, hunting, and fishing. While the crops and domestic animals were introduced from the European mainland and there seem likely to have been some immigrants, many of the farmers may have been Mesolithic people who had adopted the practices of agriculture.

CENTRAL EUROPE

Danubian II By 5000 or 4800 B.C. LBK settlements extended right across central Europe from the Carpathian basin in the south to the Paris Basin in the west and into the forest-steppe east of the Carpathians. During the fifth millennium LBK settlements in northern France increased in number and expanded over a wider area, including parts of Brittany and Normandy, where contacts and probably competition and conflict with the indigenous coastal hunter-gatherer communities must have occurred, as well as the development of hybrid groups. Farming communities also appeared in the Low Countries. Although some further outward expansion took place into parts of the North European Plain, high population densities of hunter-gatherers in Scandinavia and the east Baltic region probably discouraged or prevented any farther northward expansion by LBK farmers, and ecologi-

cal factors such as poor soils and the northern climatic conditions may have been equally important in deterring them from advancing farther. Productive contacts between farmers and hunter-gatherers can be seen in the appearance of Neolithic stone axes in the north and a unique find of a bow of Mesolithic type in a Danubian settlement. Furs and skins may also have been traded by the hunter-gatherers. In addition, hunting seems to have been of some importance to the Danubian farmers, with an increase in the bones of wild animals in many settlements.

After the rapid initial spread of LBK farmers across Europe, expansion in this region in the fifth millennium largely turned inward. While LBK farming had been largely confined to loess soil and along rivers, later farmers in the region also moved onto less easily worked soils and away from the river valleys, progressively filling in the huge region of central Europe from northern France to the Carpathians. Settlements were now often located on higher ground overlooking the valleys. The expansion of agriculture necessitated further forest clearance, although still only on a small scale.

While LBK had shown remarkable uniformity in its artifacts, the successor cultures, known collectively as Danubian II, developed different styles in their pottery (especially those known as Stichbandkeramik, Rössen, and Lengyel), and probably in other less durable artifacts, that must reflect the growth of regional traditions as communities became well established, adapted to the local conditions, and developed their own distinctive identity in ever more populous regions. Influences from neighboring cultures were also important in shaping these regional groups: in the south, the cultures of the Balkans, from whom they acquired some copper objects; elsewhere the local Mesolithic communities, including those of the Alpine regions. Skeletons showing signs of violent death present growing evidence of conflict toward the end of the LBK period when settlements were becoming more numerous and areas more densely occupied. Nevertheless, it seems unlikely that settlement density had reached the point of putting pressure on land and resources by this stage. Fighting may have occurred between LBK and Mesolithic groups, or between communities for reasons that remain a mystery.

Whereas the early settlers had built rectangular longhouses, Danubian II longhouses now tended to be trapezoidal in shape, with the entrance in the wider end. Often this opened into an outer room, behind which was the main part of the house, suggesting notions of privacy were developing. In some regions the previously open and often dispersed LBK settlements began to be nucleated and surrounded by palisades, possibly suggesting a need for defense, but also possibly to protect the crops grown in gardens attached to the houses from domestic and wild animals. Ditched enclosures, which now became widespread, may also relate to conflict, especially in the case of those, like Darion in southern Belgium, which contained longhouses. The majority, however, did not: it is thought that these may have been used to pen cattle or acted as meeting places for those living in the area, where activities such as dancing or ceremonies may have taken place. Communal gatherings in such enclosures may have had some ritual function, as is suggested by a range of deposits in their ditches, such as broken figurines and fragmentary human remains.

EARLY MEGALITHS AND FUNERARY MONUMENTS

During the fifth millennium substantial burial monuments appeared in several areas of western Europe.

The earliest examples seem to have been in Brittany, a region where both communal burial and the use of stone in grave construction had been known for some centuries. In the west of Brittany passage graves, consisting of a stone mound covering one or several burial chambers with an access passage, were being built by 4800–4500 B.C. Similarly early megaliths were constructed in Iberia, mostly passage graves in the southern regions of Alentejo and Estremadura, and simpler chambers in Galicia in the north. From the mid fifth millennium onward the practice of erecting stone funerary monuments gradually became widespread among communities along the Atlantic facade, from southeastern Spain and southern Portugal to Scandinavia, beginning, for example, in northern Iberia around 4000 B.C., at the time when farming communities developed here out of local Mesolithic roots.

A geographically overlapping tradition of building earthen funerary monuments (long barrows and long mounds) began around 4700–4000 B.C. in northern Europe. The mounds strongly resemble LBK longhouses in plan and details of construction and may have originated in Kujavia in Poland. On the other hand, they may have arisen first in the Carnac region of Brittany, a region impinged upon to the east by later LBK settlers, where sometime

2.5 *An early megalith from Plauharmel in Brittany, France, which consists of a long mound covering a series of passage graves* (Figuier, Louis. *Primitive Man.* London: Chatto and Windus, 1876)

between 4700 and 4400 B.C. long mounds of earth or stone began to be constructed, some covering small stone cists (stone boxes) with burials, and intimately associated with large menhirs (standing stones).

LATE NEOLITHIC (4200/4000–3000 B.C.)

During the fourth millennium important innovations brought major changes to the economy and way of life of prehistoric Europeans, promoting economic diversification, encouraging the exploitation of new terrain, intensifying international exchange networks, and in some areas supporting growing social inequalities.

The close of the fifth millennium saw further development of the process begun with the first farming settlements in the seventh millennium: the transformation of Europe from a continent of hunter-gatherers to one of farmers. From around 4000 B.C. there was a marked change in northern and eastern Europe. Mesolithic communities that had long been familiar with the products of farming while pursuing their traditional hunter-gatherer economy rapidly shifted to economies dominated by farming. Agriculture also became the dominant way of life of Britain from southern England to the Shetlands in the far north.

Farming now also dominated the economies of more southerly regions of the Atlantic facade and the interior of western and central Europe, where forest clearance was beginning to make a significant impact on the landscape, opening up land both for arable cultivation and for grazing domestic animals. From this period onward, farming became the mainstay of the European economy, though wild resources, such as marine fish and lake plants, continued to be important in some regions. In the northeast, covered by boreal forest, Mesolithic life continued little changed, although the people of the region gradually adopted the idea of making pottery, manufacturing a coarse ware decorated with comb and pitted designs; related groups occupied an area stretching east to the Urals. While there were now few purely hunter-gatherer communities, many farmers exploited some wild resources, and the picture of European economies was a patchwork of different adaptations.

Across much of Europe, cemeteries, funerary monuments, and nondomestic enclosures came to play a more prominent role in society, often acting as territorial markers or foci for communities that were often small and dispersed and whose settlements are elusive. In the north and west, megalithic tombs were becoming abundant, widespread, and extremely varied in their forms and associated rites, though collective burial was most common. In the southeast, a progressive trend toward social complexity was reflected in growing inequalities in the treatment of the dead, and some individuals were buried with prestige goods.

While the personality and distinctiveness of different regions and their cultures continued to develop, contacts between groups both within and between regions ensured that innovations spread widely, being adopted and adapted as appropriate. Major Near Eastern innovations, including the plow, wheeled transport, possibly woolly sheep, and the use of animals for traction and transport, reached Europe during the fourth millennium, some probably via the Balkans while others may have been introduced by people from the steppe, where nomadic pastoralism was now becoming an established way of life. Steppe incursions, marked by the appearance of characteristic burials as far west as the Hungarian Plain and by the introduction of the domestic horse to western regions, may have been partly responsible for the growth of defended settlements.

Population growth in areas that had been settled for millennia led to the colonization of new terrain, including considerable forest clearance, and intensified exploitation of lands already under cultivation. The plow (more accurately an ard, which broke the soil but did not turn the sod), allowed more difficult soils to be brought under cultivation, but more important, enabled forest soils that had been permanently cleared, and therefore colonized by grasses, to be broken for cultivation. Larger herds, their numbers made possible by their secondary uses, provided manure, which returned fertility to permanently cultivated ground. Oxen were used as draught

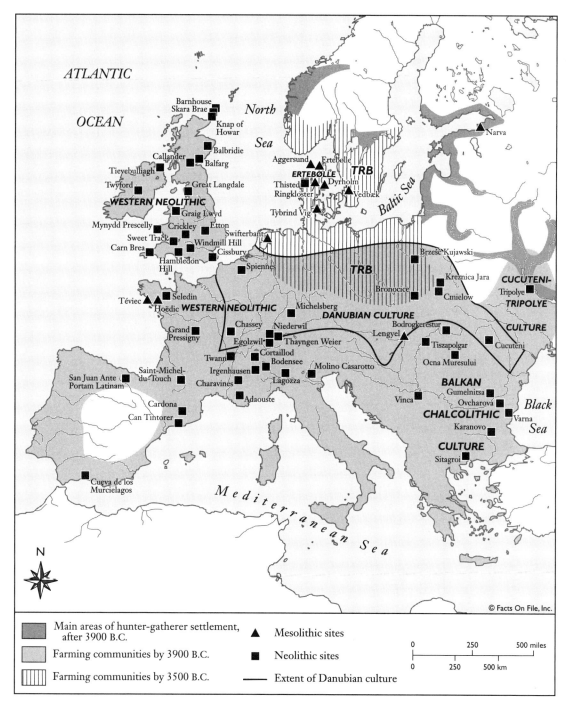

ATLANTIC

OCEAN

North
Sea

Barnhouse
Skara Brae
Knap of
Howar
Balbridie
Callander
Balfarg
Tieyebulliagh
Great Langdale
Twyford
WESTERN NEOLITHIC
Graig Lwyd
Mynydd Prescelly
Crickley
Etton
Sweet Track
Windmill Hill
Carn Brea
Cissbury
Hambledon
Hill
Spiennes

Aggersund Ertebølle **TRB**
ERTEBØLLE
Thisted Dyrholm
Ringkloster Vedbæk
Tybrind Vig
Swifterbant

Narva

Baltic Sea

TRB
Brześc Kujawski
Kreznica Jara
Bronocice
Cmielow
CUCUTENI-
Tripolye
TRIPOLYE

Michelsberg
DANUBIAN CULTURE
Téviec Seledin
Hoëdic **WESTERN NEOLITHIC**
Chassey
Niederwil
Bodrogkerestur
CULTURE
Grand
Pressigny
Egolzwil Thayngen Weier
Lengyel
Cucuteni
Twann Cortaillod
Tiszapolgar
Irgenhausen Bodensee
Ocna Muresului
Charavines Lagozza
Molino Casarotto
Saint-Michel-
du-Touch
Adaouste
BALKAN
San Juan Ante
Portam Latinam
Gumelnitsa
Vinca Ovcharová
Cardona
CHALCOLITHIC Varna
Can Tintorer
Karanovo

CULTURE
Sitagroi

Cueva de los
Murcielagos

Mediterranean Sea

Black
Sea

© Facts On File, Inc.

N

	Main areas of hunter-gatherer settlement, after 3900 B.C.	▲ Mesolithic sites
	Farming communities by 3900 B.C.	■ Neolithic sites
	Farming communities by 3500 B.C.	—— Extent of Danubian culture

0   250   500 miles
0   250   500 km

Map 5. *The further spread of farming to 3500 B.C.*

animals for pulling carts and plows. Cattle, sheep, and goats were now being kept partly for their milk, a practice that may have originated earlier.

Increased reliance on cereals at the expense of meat made it necessary to supplement the salt naturally occurring in the diet, and a number of sites started to produce salt by evaporating saline water; blocks of salt were among the goods that moved along the trade networks. Flint mining was also becoming a major industry to supply the growing demand for axes to clear woodland. Suitable stone was quarried or mined in many places such as England (e.g., Great Langdale stone ax factory) and their products widely traded. Highly prized attractive stone such as the banded flint from Krzemionki in Poland was exchanged over hundreds of miles. Such fine objects were often not used for functional purposes but as prestige goods, along with other prized goods and materials. Several major communications networks were in operation, such as the seaways of the Atlantic facade.

Metal objects were becoming more abundant and more widespread, although metalwork was still used generally for prestige items, including larger pieces such as shafthole axes. The growing importance of metallurgy, dependent on ores that were not uniformly distributed across the landscape, introduced a new element of inequality of opportunity between communities, allowing some to grow more powerful than others on the basis of mining, trading, or working copper. An independent center of metalworking developed in Spain, and copper also began to be worked in Italy. Metal objects were widely traded from the Balkan-Carpathian region into other parts of Europe, and the technology of extracting and working metal also gradually spread outward from the Balkans.

The Southeast

STEPPE PASTORALISTS

In the forest steppe groups of settled farmers raising stock, fishing, and hunting (Sredny Stog) were now well established, using cord-decorated pottery and burying their dead in flat graves with a few grave goods. Other groups in the same region constructed more substantial graves lined with stone slabs and furnished their dead with a richer array of grave goods. Farther east between the lower Dnepr and the Crimea similar mixed farmers and hunters (Lower Mikhailovka-Kemi Oba culture) built low mounds over their dead; small pottery censers associated with these people may have been used for heating cannabis, a custom known in the region in later times. All these groups shared the custom of scattering ochre over their burials. Imports from the metallurgical centers in the Caucasus and the Balkans early in the fourth millennium stimulated the development of a local metallurgical industry in the forest steppe during the later fourth millennium.

By around 3500 B.C. the inhabitants of the steppe region seem to have adopted a largely mobile lifestyle: Settlements were rare and burials are their best-known remains. The few known settlements, such as Mikhailovka, were fortified with ditches and stone walls. The potential for cereal agriculture in the steppe was limited, being restricted to river valleys, whereas its grasslands, stretching far to the east, offered abundant grazing for animals. While agriculture was practiced to some extent, stockbreeding, especially of caprines (including woolly sheep), seems to have been the mainstay of the economy. The horse, domesticated here during the fifth millennium, enabled pastoralists and hunters in this region to access the steppe pastures, at first only those on the fringes of the forest steppe, but with the advent of wheeled transport gradually beginning to make use of the pastures of central Asia, transporting their possessions in wagons drawn by oxen; late fourth-millennium burials sometimes contain the remains of such wagons.

These steppe nomads (Yamnaya) buried their dead in pits in the ground, often floored or lined with wood. Often these were covered by substantial barrows known as kurgans; ochre was often sprinkled on the bodies, and in the most impressive male burials the grave goods included weapons, animal bones, sometimes sacrificed women, and horse-headed scepters, taken to be a symbol of authority and status.

THE SOUTHEAST AND THE CARPATHIAN BASIN

Later Eneolithic Small groups of steppe pastoralists seem to have infiltrated the lands of their settled neighbors in the Balkans and the Carpathian basin. They are identified by their characteristic burials of bodies in a flexed position scattered with ochre, sometimes with horse-headed stone scepters; some graves were also marked by mounds. Steppe pastoralists may have been responsible for introducing to Southeast and central Europe a number of innovations, including wheeled transport and the practice of horse domestication; domestic horses had spread from the steppe as far as central Europe by 4000 B.C. Interactions between the nomads and settled farmers in the western Carpathian basin contributed to the rise of the Baden culture in southern central Europe from around 3500 B.C.

Relations between settled farmers and the intrusive steppe pastoralists may have been less than friendly; local population growth may also have been putting pressure on resources and creating the need for defense against neighbors, for fortified or defensible settlements developed in the southeast from around 4200–4000 B.C. Promontories and hills became favored places for settlement, and sites were generally smaller and more dispersed than before. Many tell settlements on the lower Danube were abandoned, and in the eastern part of the region, particularly along its border with the forest steppe region, the need for defense probably promoted the nucleation of regional settlement. Here some settlements, such as Dobrovody in Ukraine, were of massive proportions, perhaps housing several thousand people, though it is not certain whether all the houses within the settlement were simultaneously occupied. These settlements were not apparently fortified, but it is thought that the continuous ring of houses themselves acted as a barrier to aggressors. Abundant artifacts that could be used as weapons, such as arrowheads, axes, and spears, underline the suggestion of increased conflict.

The introduction of the ard allowed new land to be opened up on river terraces and in the foothills away from the river plains where earlier settlement had concentrated. Cultivation was extended onto previously uncultivated soils such as the plains and lower hillslopes of the Argolid. This process of expansion accelerated toward the end of the fourth millennium, with increased forest clearance.

Growing distinctions were apparent in the cemeteries. Grave goods differentiated men, with weapons, tools, and copper objects, from women, with pottery and ornaments, but also some individuals were singled out for more lavish provision of grave goods. Copper metallurgy was becoming more developed and more widespread, spreading into Greece, and products of the region were traded into areas far beyond, such as those occupied by the makers of TRB pottery to the north. Pottery jugs and cups with strap handles, known right across the region in the later fourth millennium, from the Carpathian basin to the Aegean, also reflect the breadth of communications at this time: They resemble silver and gold vessels in use at Troy in Anatolia.

The Mediterranean

By 4000 B.C. agricultural communities were well established throughout the central and western Mediterranean, although much of the interior plateau of Spain (*meseta*) was not settled until after 3000 B.C. Settlements were found in a variety of terrains, on fertile plains, beside lakes or in marshland, and in uplands. As in other parts of Europe, this millennium saw the adoption of the ard by many Mediterranean farming communities, allowing the spread of farming settlement, for example, in southern France. It also boosted occupation in the islands of the western Mediterranean. In Italy and southern France animal husbandry was becoming increasingly important, and the appearance of simple megaliths in the Pyrenees may reflect the development of pastoralist communities in the region practicing transhumance (the seasonal movement of livestock between different climatic regions).

In southern and central Italy and Malta plain pottery replaced the earlier painted wares (Diana culture), while across the region from northern Italy through France into Spain interrelated cultures made a variety of generally undecorated wares with lug-handles (Lagozza, Cortaillod, Chasseen, Sepulcros de Fosa). Trade increased in commodities such as obsidian, fine flint, and stone for axes. Burials in some Spanish and Breton sites included beads of an attractive greenish mineral, callais (variscite), which was intensively mined at Spanish sites such as Can Tintorer and perhaps in Brittany. The distribution of stone from various sources shows that routes through the Alps were in use, linking Italy with transalpine Europe. From one Alpine pass between modern Italy and Austria comes the frozen body of one of Europe's most famous inhabitants, the Iceman "Ötzi," who died here sometime around 3300–3200 B.C. Possibly a pastoralist tending his flocks in their summer pastures, he was wounded by an arrow and probably died while fleeing his attacker. He was fully clad when found, giving a rare picture of clothing, and was equipped with tools of wood, stone, and copper; his preserved body gives an insight into contemporary health and diet.

In Spain, as in the Balkans, copper metallurgy had begun before 4000 B.C. Italy and eastern Alpine regions now also saw the beginnings of copper metallurgy, perhaps based on technology acquired from the adjacent Balkan region though perhaps independently developed. Here and in other regions, arsenic was deliberately added to copper, or copper ore containing arsenic was selected, to produce an alloy harder than pure copper and therefore more useful for tools. The fact that the Iceman carried a metal ax may show that copper was not entirely reserved for prestige objects but was coming into use in daily life.

Burial practices became more diverse in the fourth millennium Mediterranean. In Italy some regions had simple graves containing single bodies; some preferred stone cists or graves surrounded by a stone circle, while others in southern Italy created rock-cut tombs (hypogea), a practice also followed in Sardinia, Malta, and parts of France and Iberia. The most elaborate were those of Malta, including the labyrinthine Hal Saflieni Hypogeum, which seems likely to have had a religious as well as a funerary function. Burial in cists or trenches and cave burials were popular in parts of Spain. Megalithic tombs, already widespread in the Atlantic regions of Europe, were also constructed in southern Spain, the Pyrenees, central France, and the western Mediterranean islands, as well as North Africa. These were often different in form from the (also very diverse) Atlantic megaliths: They included gallery graves in central France and cists surrounded by stone circles in Sardinia and Corsica. Others, particularly in southern Spain, were clearly related to Atlantic styles, comprising passage graves of various forms. In Malta aboveground temples constructed of huge stone blocks and with elaborate facades mirrored the structure of the subterranean hypogea. Many of these tombs or graves held collective burials.

Temperate Europe

NORTHERN AND CENTRAL EUROPE

TRB From around 4200–4100 B.C. a new style of well-made pottery appeared, probably first in Poland, and rapidly gained popularity across a wide area, from the earliest farming communities in Scandinavia and the North European Plain through the northern part of the region earlier occupied by Danubian farmers, from the Netherlands to the northern Ukraine. Known as TRB (Trichterrandbecherkultur—Funnel-Necked Beaker culture) from the shape of its most characteristic form, it included a range of vessels probably for drinking mead or beer: funnel-necked beakers, collared flasks, and funnel-necked amphorae. TRB assemblages also generally included flint and stone axes, including some whose fineness or functionally impractical shape suggests they were likely to have been prestige objects rather than merely tools. United by their characteristic artifacts, the people using TRB material, however, also had regional differences in many aspects of their culture, such as burial customs.

In the north they were acculturated Mesolithic people. Around 4200–4000 B.C. coastal communities in northern Europe shifted from a hunter-gatherer way of life to one in which farming was growing in importance, often using an ard in cultivation, though some groups inland seem likely to have continued for some time to rely mainly on wild resources. Domestic cattle were kept, probably mainly for milk, with oxen as draught animals. By late TRB times domestic horses from the steppe had made their appearance here. Polished stone axes for tree felling and woodworking were widely distributed in settlements and burial sites in Scandinavia and the North European Plain and seem to be associated with an increase in grass pollen and a decrease in tree pollen, suggesting extensive forest clearance. Nevertheless fishing and hunting or trapping game and fur animals were still practiced. Bog offerings, already known in Ertebølle times, continued: Polished flint axes, amber jewelry, and pottery, presumably containing food offerings, were deposited.

Elsewhere in the TRB zone coastal and riverine sites were also preferred by the users of TRB pottery, as were well-drained sandy soils. Settlements were now found not only in the main river valleys but also in those of smaller tributary rivers. They were quite often large and rather dispersed, containing a loose scatter of houses, pits, and working areas; there were also numerous small settlements. In some regions, such as Scandinavia, few settlements have been found. Round huts characterized some areas while others had long houses. The larger settlements were placed on higher ground, on the plateaus between rivers, and smaller settlements were found both in river valleys and in upland locations; the latter may have been camps occupied for hunting expeditions or during the summer months when herds were taken to upland pastures. The clearance of forest opened up grazing, allowing a greater emphasis on stock rearing.

Causewayed enclosures, large areas surrounded by interrupted ditches and probably palisades, which had appeared earlier in the Danubian area, now became widespread; some were settlement sites, probably the focus of local regional settlement, while others probably served some communal purpose. Similar enclosures were built by Neolithic groups in England, France, and the Rhineland. Communal feasting may well have been one of the functions of these enclosures, which seem to have served a ceremonial or ritual purpose as well as perhaps being the focus for social gatherings of the people of a region.

Some TRB groups, including those in the previous Ertebølle area, began to bury their dead in megalithic tombs from about 3700 B.C., while those in parts of Jutland and on the North European Plain from the Elbe to the Vistula practiced inhumation within a long earthen mound. Both frequently contained the collected bones of a number of individuals whose bodies had previously been exposed, though there were many different funerary practices. The megaliths here included dolmens (*dysser*) and passage graves.

Good-quality flint for making axes and other tools was quite abundant in the North European Plain and Scandinavia and was extensively mined. The highest quality flint, for example, from the Polish site of Krzemionki, was traded over several hundred miles. Similar distances were traveled by other prized materials, both within the TRB region and between it and adjacent cultural zones, such as Michelsberg to the west. Flint had been mined earlier, but production greatly increased to satisfy increased demand. Stone and other commodities circulated in the form of raw materials, roughed-out objects, and some finished goods. Perishable materials and goods must also have been exchanged. Copper from areas to the south beyond the Carpathians also entered the TRB exchange network; this included shafthole axes. Trade and other communications probably followed rivers, but over shorter distances wheeled carts drawn by oxen were now being used as is shown by the discovery of a cart track beneath a TRB long mound.

Globular Amphora While TRB continued in Scandinavia, around 3500 in much of central and eastern Europe TRB pottery was replaced by a type known as Globular Amphora after its characteristic baggy spherical jars with suspension loops; decoration on these and other vessels sometimes included cord impressions. Although like TRB Globular Amphora pottery was associated with mixed farming, pastoralism seems to have become increasingly important; a number of seasonal camps have been found. Settlements tended to be smaller and, though they were more numerous than before, overall population density seems to have decreased.

The importance of cattle was emphasized by a number of burials of cattle, a practice also found in a few late TRB contexts and in the Baden culture to the south. Globular Amphora funerary practices usually involved burials in twos, threes, or more, and often the bodies were incomplete. They were generally placed in cists or in flat graves, but in eastern Germany many were also inserted into the earlier TRB passage graves. Burials were accompanied by pottery, flint axes, and animal bones (especially pigs) which may represent a funeral feast.

Mining of flint at sites such as Krzemionki continued, and their products were distributed over a far wider area, Krzemionki flint now reaching around 370 miles (600 kilometers) from its source compared with around 110 miles (180 kilometers) in TRB times.

SOUTHERN CENTRAL EUROPE

In the region to the south of TRB, the introduction of the ard greatly facilitated the task of bringing forest soils under permanent cultivation. Forest clearance required an increasing number of stone and flint axes, procured mainly from TRB and Michelsberg mines and quarries to the north and west. Some of the stone axes may have been used in conflict; intercommunity violence became more common, with settlements more frequently located in defensible situations such as plateaus between river valleys and furnished with defensive ditches and palisades. The strength of the defenses also increased through time, with more ditches and palisades being added. Some of the fortified settlements probably served as places of refuge or ceremonial sites for the inhabitants of the surrounding area. Long mounds covered the remains of some individuals, but often little trace of burial practices survives.

By around 3500 B.C. this region saw the emergence of the Baden culture, which spread north into southerly TRB regions and south into the Carpathian basin. Houses become hard to detect, and it is thought that they were constructed with floor joists instead of posts, leaving little trace; such structures survive in the waterlogged lakeshore sites of the Alpine regions. Large-scale enclosures surrounded by substantial ditches and palisades sometimes with bastions may well have been settlements made up of such houses, now vanished; in parts of Bohemia this is confirmed since here the house floors were sunk into the ground, leaving evidence of densely packed villages. Influences from the contemporary cultures to the southeast promoted the continuing use of cemeteries in the Baden region. Cups in the form of four-wheeled carts are known from burials.

WESTERN EUROPE

In northern France and the Rhineland a culture related to TRB flourished, characterized by the style of pottery known as Michelsberg. This was also influenced by the cultures now established in western Europe, such as Cortaillod in Switzerland and Chasseen in France. In eastern Switzerland the Pfyn culture and other TRB-related groups developed. There was a considerable expansion of settlement in

Alpine regions, where lakeside settlements were common. Michelsberg sites are found on rivers and lakes. The occurrence of sites at different elevations indicates pastoral transhumance, with summer movements to higher pastures and winters in villages at lower levels; evidence from the Swiss lake villages indicates that the animals were stall-fed over the winter. Like TRB, Michelsberg people exploited both domestic and wild resources: The Swiss Lake villages give a particularly rich picture of the range of foods in use. Also like TRB, flint mines and stone quarries were becoming increasingly important.

The most complete information on domestic life in the Neolithic period comes from a number of lakeshore sites, particularly in Switzerland but also in France, where waterlogging has preserved organic material, including many linen textiles. Villages consisted of a number of small rectangular wooden houses, sometimes built on piles to raise them above flood level, which probably housed nuclear families. Food remains show that the inhabitants raised cereals, pulses, and some legumes, kept animals, fished and fowled on the lake, and gathered local wild plants foods such as apples and water chestnuts. They made clothing from woven cloth of reeds, linen, and, from around 3000 B.C., probably of wool, and tools of wood, bone, stone, and pottery.

ATLANTIC EUROPE

By the early fourth millennium farming became established as the main way of life in the region around the Atlantic coast, from Portugal and northwest Spain via France and western Britain to Scandinavia, but the people in this region frequently continued to exploit marine resources, thus also maintaining and intensifying seaborne links between communities. The diversity of their pottery and other artifacts and the variations within their economies were offset by shared practices of which the most obvious was the building of megalithic monuments. This had begun in the fifth millennium in Brittany and Iberia, and it became widespread along the Atlantic facade in the fourth and early third millennia, apparently acting as a very concrete and visible statement of a community's identity and ancestral rights to their territory, and probably reflecting reverence for the

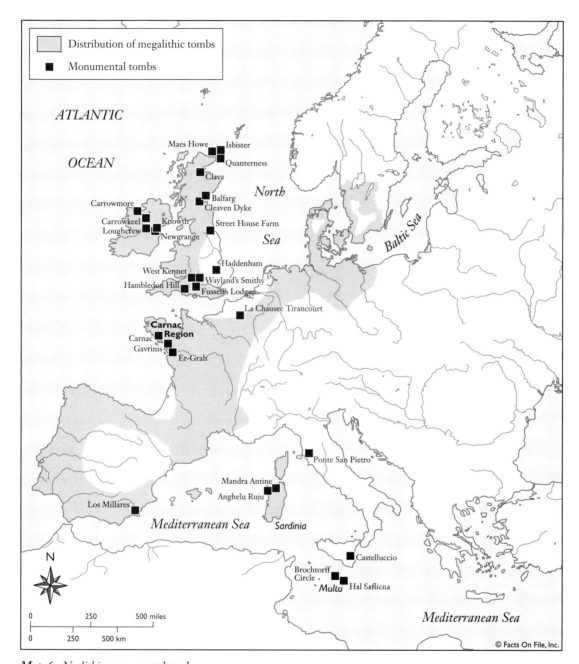

Map 6. *Neolithic monumental tombs*

ancestors. The majority of these were tombs, although there were some megalithic structures lacking a funerary purpose.

While a variety of funerary practices were associated with these monuments, they were generally communal graves in which funerary remains accumulated;

different local practices governed whether all members of the community were interred in these monuments, and if not, who were selected for burial; how their bodies or excarnated bones were arranged; and what, if any, grave goods were also placed there. Often the megaliths were enlarged or restructured at various times in the course of their period of use, and the practices associated with them changed.

Major concentrations of megalithic tombs were built in the earlier fourth millennium in southern Spain, southern Portugal around the Tagus estuary, Brittany, Ireland, Wales, western England, western and northern Scotland, and Denmark. Many of these were varieties of passage grave: a chambered tomb with an access passage, generally within a large stone or earthen mound. Many of the monuments had geometric or other designs carved on their stones or on associated objects, standing stones, or plaques. Stone plaques and small standing stones also sometimes bore anthropomorphic carvings. Axes were a common design in many areas, tying in with their symbolic or prestige use. The trade in stone axes reached considerable proportions: For example, the Sélèdin quarry in Brittany may have been producing around 5,000 axes per year, which were traded for several hundred miles along the coasts and inland along the Loire.

From around 3800 B.C. long mounds were superseded in Brittany by passage graves, and a number of the menhirs that had accompanied the long mounds were reused in the construction of these tombs, sometimes being broken into pieces before reuse. By around 3500 B.C. passage graves had ceased to be constructed in Brittany, although their use for burial often continued for centuries.

BRITAIN

Communal burial practices were followed in Britain, with considerable regional variation. In the east and in lowland Britain wooden mortuary chambers housed the remains of the dead, under earthen barrows that were generally rectangular or trapezoidal in form, though in some regions a round barrow was used. In contrast in western Britain, including Ireland, stone chamber tombs were constructed as part of the Atlantic tradition. The two modes of burial

were both found in the southwest. The different monuments, of which there were a variety of forms, generally contained the remains of many individuals, often deposited in the tomb after the bodies had been defleshed, probably by exposure. In some places this may have taken place on wooden structures within timber enclosures; in other cases the dead were probably exposed within earthworks such as the long ditched and fenced mortuary enclosures of Scotland.

Funerary monuments were often modified during the course of their use; other nonfunerary monuments were also constructed, such as cursuses (*see* page 262) and bank barrows. The construction of both funerary and nonfunerary monuments was a focus of communal effort, reflecting the status and power of a community; the ritual activity involved in constructing a monument or an addition to it may have had as much as or more significance than the finished monument.

Parts of Britain (England, Northern Ireland, probably Scotland) also saw the construction from around 4000 B.C. of causewayed enclosures, circular areas demarcated by rings of ditches interrupted by causeways, for various purposes, including the periodic congregation of communities who perhaps spent most of the year in small groups scattered across the landscape. At Hambledon in Dorset a series of causewayed enclosures included one that probably contained a permanent settlement. Of the other enclosures at Hambledon one was a necropolis in which the dead were exposed prior to burial within the associated chambered tomb. In the third, communal activities seem to have taken place and large numbers of cattle may have been periodically corralled or protected.

Early settlement sites are far less well known than the monuments, being constructed of perishable materials and difficult to discover; often traces of these buildings are likely to have been removed by intensive later agricultural activity. Most known houses were small; one exception was the substantial structure at Balbridie in Scotland, which resembled a Danubian longhouse in its layout. Later settlements, after c. 3500 B.C., became more substantial and show an expansion of farming onto soils such as gravel river terraces, a development facilitated by the introduction of the ard. Occasionally traces survive of land divisions: for instance, walls demarcating areas of land on Shetland, dated 3200–2800, and dry-stone walls enclosing fields in Ireland, dated around 3500 B.C. The use of stone instead of wood in Orkney has meant the preservation of several late Neolithic settlements such as Barnhouse and Skara Brae. Here dwelt a community of a few dozen people, living on agriculture and marine resources, and furnishing their intercommunicating houses with stone-built hearths, beds, and dressers.

From the Somerset Levels in western England comes uniquely preserved evidence of the Neolithic people's skillful management of woodland, including coppicing, a glimpse of practices that must have been far more widespread at the time. Among other things, the timber was used to build a sophisticated trackway across boggy ground around 3800 B.C.

A stone ax deposited as an offering beside the track was made of jadeite from Switzerland. Contacts between groups by sea and by river enabled such desirable materials to be exchanged over a wide area. Flint was mined, stone quarried, and potter's clay dug, poor material being used only locally while better-quality materials were exchanged. Prominent among the stone tools were those used for felling trees and working wood, including flint axes. Nevertheless, many of the tools were too fine or fragile for actual use and must have had a symbolic or prestige function.

CHALCOLITHIC (C. 3200/ 3000–2200 B.C.)

Permanent forest clearance in the fourth millennium led in many areas to soil degradation, particularly by erosion, and the replacement of regenerating secondary forest by permanent grassland. This was reflected in the third millennium in the decline, in many areas, of pigs, which required forest browse, and an increase in cattle, sheep, and goats, which could take advantage of the increased pasturage. While most earlier garments had been made from leather, the introduction of woolly sheep increased the production of textiles, previously made in small quantities from flax or other plant fibers. Spindle whorls and loom weights became common domestic artifacts. Pastoralism may have become of increased importance in mixed farming economies, and there may have been a shift to animal husbandry at the expense of arable agriculture. In many areas settlements are hardly known, suggesting impermanent occupation and possibly a mobile economy.

Population growth, coupled with land differentials and the limited distribution of key resources, promoted competition within and among communities and the need for resource management. More widespread signs began to appear of ranking within communities and within regions, and of intercommunity conflict and defense. These were reflected particularly in the different funerary treatment of individuals, with single burial progressively displacing the earlier rite of collective burial across western, central, and Mediterranean Europe, and the development of defended settlements, though competition was probably largely expressed by accumulating and displaying prestige objects and creating monuments rather than by armed conflict.

The practice of single burial reflects a considerable ideological shift, emphasizing the individual rather than the community as had been the case in earlier collective burials. This may well reflect a major socioeconomic change, with ties to land (place) becoming less important than ties to property (possessions), which were more susceptible to become vested in individuals. Property included both prestige goods, such as imported fine stonework and copper artifacts, and cattle, which could be built up into large herds but could also be rustled, giving plentiful scope for intercommunity conflict.

The need for prestige goods probably underlies the widespread adoption of new styles of pottery, particularly Corded Ware and Beakers, which were associated with other distinctive artifacts, such as battle-axes, archery equipment, and ornaments of metal and other exotic materials. Metal artifacts spread to most parts of the continent during the third millennium and copper and gold metallurgy were widely adopted; some Corded Ware groups may have practiced a limited amount of copper metallurgy, but in

Map 7a. *Later farming communities*

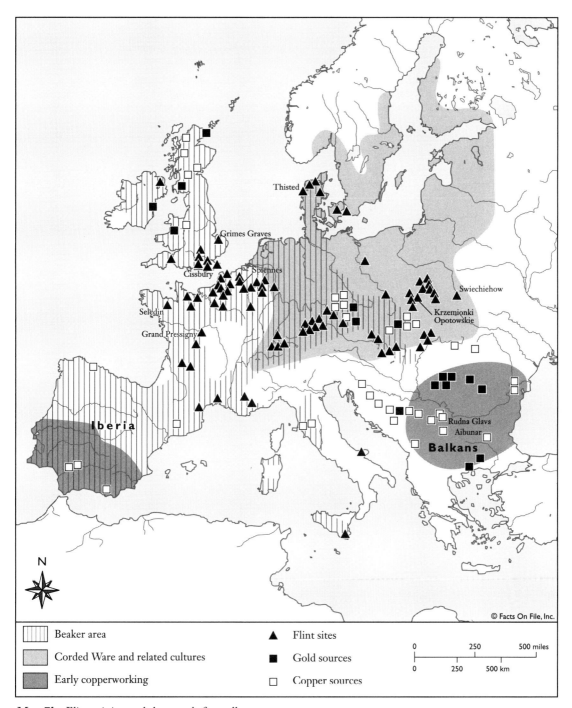

Map 7b. *Flint mining and the spread of metallurgy*

Legend:

Beaker area		▲	Flint sites
Corded Ware and related cultures		■	Gold sources
Early copperworking		□	Copper sources

Labeled sites: Thisted, Grimes Graves, Cissbury, Spiennes, Seledin, Grand Pressigny, Iberia, Swiechiehow, Krzemionki Opotowskie, Rudna Glava, Aibunar, Balkans

0   250   500 miles
0   250   500 km

© Facts On File, Inc.

western Europe the spread of metalworking was often associated with Beaker pottery. Horses, originally domesticated in the east and introduced into Southeast Europe by steppe people, were now being domesticated from local wild herds by the people in southern central Europe. From there they spread widely within the rest of Europe, being found, for instance, in Scandinavia in the late TRB or early Corded Ware period and in western Europe and the Mediterranean in Beaker contexts.

Before 3000 B.C. regional networks had operated, for example, by sea along the Atlantic facade, linking communities within a region, but with relatively few links to other regions; although a considerable volume of some goods, such as stone and flint axes, had circulated within these regions, the range of materials being traded had been relatively small. The third millennium saw a transformation in the scale and spread of trading networks across Europe and in the range of materials and goods that were exchanged.

Southeast

GREECE

The third millennium saw a great expansion of settlement in southern Greece. Here the introduction of woolly sheep brought significant changes to the pattern of agriculture, where the keeping of sheep had previously been limited and mainly for meat. Their use for wool and for milk, from which cheese could be made, increased their importance; land previously used for growing flax could now be used for other crops, while sheep made more extensive use of the rough grazing areas unsuitable for cultivation. Grapevines and olives may also now have been grown (although some scholars believe these were not cultivated until the second millennium); these crops used hillside land unsuitable for cereals or pulses, and their labor requirements did not conflict with those of arable agriculture. They provided oil, dried fruits, and wine, commodities that could be stored and traded, as could wool and woollen textiles.

Some larger settlements began to emerge, the focus of their immediate region. While the surrounding settlements were farms and agricultural villages, these centers also served other functions: They were the home of local leaders and places of storage for wool, grain, and other agricultural produce; they offered facilities for processing grain and provided an outlet for trade, reflected in the great increase in imported material. By the later third millennium these centers were becoming small towns of substantial well-built houses, sometimes fortified; often they included a large building or palace, such as the House of Tiles at Lerna in southern Greece. Industry, such as the production of obsidian blades, was focused in these settlements. The majority were near the coast, reflecting the increasing importance of sea contacts. At the same time many unoccupied or sparsely settled islands were colonized and others, such as Crete, saw a considerable population increase.

Metallurgy developed, flourishing particularly in the Cyclades, where copper and silver ores were available. The Cycladic Islands at this time also produced sculptured stone figures of sophisticated simplicity. Seaborne contacts were already well developed in earlier times, but the need for metal ores coupled with the topography of southern Greece, where land travel was far more difficult than communications by sea and where harbors and anchorages were plentiful, further promoted sea travel and the building of ships during the third millennium. Western Anatolia (including Troy), the islands of the Aegean, and southern Greece became a closely linked region in which innovations and materials circulated; through Anatolia this region was in contact with the civilized world of the Near East. The Cyclades, strategically located between Anatolia and the Greek mainland, benefited particularly from the international trade.

THE BALKANS AND CARPATHIANS

Toward the end of the fourth millennium there was a decline in metalworking in Southeast Europe that probably reflects pressure on the supplies of easily worked ores, which eventually became exhausted. Some late fourth-millennium artifacts from the Baden culture of the Carpathian region were made of the more difficult-to-work sulfide ores, which were relatively abundant in central Europe and which began to be worked in some quantity in the early Bronze Age.

In the early third millennium small numbers of steppe pastoralists (Pit Grave culture) settled in the Balkans and the Carpathian basin, creating hybrid cultures in some cases. Their presence was marked by the appearance of their characteristic burials in pits, often containing a wooden chamber, under kurgans (barrows); these often contained horses and warrior equipment. The use of round barrows and wooden mortuary chambers was adopted by local people and gradually spread from there into other parts of Europe. Incursions from the steppe occurred periodically and may have caused the abandonment of settlements in some parts of Southeast Europe, the strong fortification of others, and a move toward greater emphasis on pastoralism in the economy of the local communities (Ezero, Coţofeni, Vučedol, Schneckenberg, Karanovo VII).

Temperate Europe

CENTRAL AND NORTHERN EUROPE

Corded Ware and Battle-Axes In the last centuries of the fourth millennium a new complex emerged somewhere in the old TRB region from Jutland to eastern Poland and spread widely in the early third millennium, eventually extending from Finland in the north to Switzerland in the south and from the Netherlands in the west as far east as Moscow. This complex, known as the Corded Ware culture (Single Grave culture in Scandinavia; PFB or Protruding Foot Beaker culture in the Netherlands), is seen by some scholars as intrusive and is linked by them to movements of pastoralists ultimately from the steppe. Others point to local antecedents for many features of the culture and see the adoption of innovations as a reflection of new social demands. Few Corded Ware settlements have been found, and the culture is best known from burials, especially of males, under round barrows, furnished with beakers and amphorae decorated with cord impressions and sometimes small objects of copper, arrowheads, boar's tooth pendants, and stone "battle-axes." The bodies were placed in a flexed position, men generally on their right side, women on their left, also accompanied by cord-decorated pottery and some-

times ornaments. Not all burials were covered by mounds; in some cases the original mounds have been removed by later agriculture, but some may have been flat graves from the start.

The battle-axes are heavy stone shafthole axes with a flared blade, seemingly imitating the copper shafthole axes of the adjacent Carpathian and Southeast European zone; it is uncertain whether they were suitable for wielding in battle, but they were likely to have been prestige items. Cord-decorated pottery was a characteristic of the steppe region, as was single burial under a mound; such burials were known as far northwest as the Carpathian basin, where they probably represent the remains of small numbers of steppe invaders or settlers. Single burial was also the long-standing means of disposal among the farming communities of Southeast Europe and had for some centuries been associated there with status differentials expressed in associated grave goods. In northern and central Europe the rite of single burial is likely to have been adopted as a way of signifying the authority and status of the leaders who were emerging in increasingly hierarchical societies. The beakers, handleless vessels holding about a liter of liquid, may also have played a part in the distinction of the elite members of society; they may have held alcoholic drinks or possibly a brew containing cannabis, which was probably already being used by steppe communities.

The burials also contained the remains of animals. From these and the rare settlements it is clear that cattle and sheep and goats were increasingly important and pigs far less so; horses were also kept. The paucity of settlements has been interpreted by some as an indication that mobile pastoralism was the way of life of the Corded Ware communities, another possible link with the steppe communities. Although a shift toward pastoralism may have taken place in some areas, mixed farming was probably practiced in many areas, and there was considerable regional variation: For instance, Corded Ware is known from some of the Swiss lakeside villages, with their mixed farming economy in which wild resources still played an important part; was made by farmers in Lithuania; and was also used by other communities along the Baltic coasts for whom marine mammals were a major part of the economy. The few known settlements contained square or rectangular houses; in some areas settlements were smaller and more scattered than previously, while in other regions such as southeast Poland the population, which was declining overall, was concentrated in a smaller number of settlements that were larger than before. For example, Bronocice in southern Poland housed half the population of its region.

Corded Ware continued to be popular in Scandinavia when areas farther south adopted Beaker pottery. It also continued on the North European Plain and eastward into the edge of the steppe region.

WESTERN EUROPE

Iberia and Southern France The Tagus estuary in southern Portugal was able to support a dense population since it combined extensive fertile soils for agriculture with access to abundant marine resources. From around 3200 B.C. this region saw the building of a number of large fortified settlements such as Zambujal and Vila Nova de São Pedro (VNSP culture) with massive stone walls with bastions. Defense seems unlikely to have been the main reason for constructing these substantial fortifications, which were periodically enhanced by the addition of further layers of stone; status and intercommunity competition in ostentation seems a more likely explanation. Megalithic passage graves were constructed by these communities around the settlements. These housed collective burials and rich funerary offerings, including decorated plaques made of schist.

Similar fortified settlements were also built in Almeria, another region with substantial passage graves, notably at Los Millares, the most substantial settlement of the region (Millaran culture). A wide variety of native metals and metal ores, copper, silver, alluvial gold, and tin, were available in Iberia. During the later fourth and earlier third millennium, considerable amounts of copper were in use in southern Iberia, used for small objects like flat axes, chisels, daggers, and arrowheads. Trade throughout the third millennium along the Atlantic facade brought prestige materials such as metals, ivory, ostrich eggshells, and callais to centers of prosperity such as the Tagus estuary, Almeria, and Brittany.

At much the same time, what were perhaps fortified settlements began to be built in parts of south-ern France at sites such as Lébous and Boussargues. These consisted of drystone enclosures of walls incorporating circular or apsidal structures with corbelled roofs. These have been interpreted as bastions on a defensive wall, but are perhaps more convincingly seen as huts around the periphery of an enclosure in which animals were kept. These probably provided seasonal housing for shepherds grazing their flocks in upland summer pastures. Other, unenclosed, settlements were also known as well as cave dwellings. Caves might also house collections of burials, and many *dolmens simples* (stone cists covered by round cairns) were built on the limestone plateaus of southern France.

Beakers The fashion for cord-decorated pottery seen in the Corded Ware culture was matched slightly later and farther west by the spread of Beaker wares, possibly developed from or inspired by Corded Ware vessels and first appearing in the lower Rhine delta. Beakers had a rounded body and a long, slightly outward-sloping neck (inverted bell-shaped) and were decorated with horizontal zones of incised or impressed geometric designs, including cord impressions. Analyses of residues within the beakers suggest they were used for drinking alcohol, probably a form of mead with a flavoring of herbs or fruit, perhaps a socially significant ritual at the time. Beakers are known particularly from single burials, especially of males. As well as the beaker itself, these burials contained a package of other distinctive artifacts, including equipment related to archery, such as barbed and tanged flint arrowheads and stone wristguards; personal ornaments of exotic materials, such as sheet gold appliqués for clothing, belt buckles, and V-perforated buttons, often of jet; tanged daggers of flint or copper; and other small copper objects including awls.

The earliest Beakers, which had decoration over the whole vessel (AOO—All-Over Ornamented), began to be made in the lower Rhine region around 2800 B.C. These were often found with battle-axes, fine daggers of Grand Pressigny flint, and amber beads. AOO beakers became common in the northern part of western Europe, in the Rhine valley, the Netherlands, and parts of Britain and France. At around the same time a distinctively different type of Beaker vessel, known as the Maritime Bell Beaker,

2.6 The contents of a Beaker grave from Cul-duthel, Invernessshire, Scotland. The burial was accompanied by a beaker, an archer's wristguard, eight barbed and tanged flint arrowheads, a stone strike-a-light, an amber bead, and a belt ring. (Drawing by Audrey McIntosh, from material in the National Museums of Scotland, Edinburgh)

and Maritime Beakers were widely used in the period c. 2600–2300 B.C. Within a few centuries, various styles of Beaker vessels, along with the rest of the Beaker package of single burial and distinctive grave goods, were in use over a wide region including much of Britain, western and southern France, Iberia, and parts of North Africa, as well as Sicily, Sardinia, Switzerland, and parts of north and central Italy, where some burials contained horse remains, and eastern regions as far as the Carpathians. The Beaker assemblages were spread via both sea and land routes.

Some scholars believe that the Beaker package was spread by actual immigrants or by traders in search of desired materials, while others argue that they represent an ideology and set of status symbols that were readily taken up by the emerging leaders of increasingly hierarchical communities. Adoption of the package was eclectic: For instance, in Ireland a few Beaker pots were associated with the beginning of copper-working, but Beaker burial practices were not adopted; in Brittany, early Beaker vessels were succeeded by status symbols developed out of local traditions; while in Britain, the Beaker package was initially adopted in eastern England (an area with links to the Low Countries) and only later spread to other parts of the country where other traditions had been developing. In some regions Beaker practices were adopted wholesale and marked a sharp break with earlier traditions. In others there was some continuity: For example, final burials in some megalithic tombs contained Beaker material. Settlements belonging to the makers of Beaker pottery are elusive, and it has been suggested that they led a relatively mobile way of life, probably associated with pastoralism, though probably, like Corded Ware, Beaker material was used by communities practicing many economic strategies.

Metallurgy, Elites, and Trade   Although the earliest Beaker burials in the Rhineland lacked metalwork, in many areas, such as Britain, Beaker pots were associated with the introduction of copper metallurgy. In southern Iberia a well-established metal industry existed before the appearance of Beakers, and this region may have been the source of the metallurgical technology that spread through western Europe during the third millennium. The massive

decorated with thin horizontal bands often of herringbone combed designs, began to be made, possibly evolving in the Tagus region in southern Iberia. Maritime Beakers subsequently became popular along the Atlantic seaboard, especially in Iberia and France, but were known as far as the middle Rhine and reached the Netherlands by 2500. Both AOO

Iberian fortified sites such as Zambujal continued in use, perhaps as the home of the evolving local elite, whose rich burials were still to be found in the local megalithic tombs. The Millaran culture in southeastern Spain may have begun cultivating vines and olives at this time and may also have constructed simple dams for floodwater farming. The supply of imported luxury materials such as gold, copper, ivory, and callais increased in the Beaker period as demand by local elites grew to feed their need for prestige goods to display their status; power was demonstrated by the ability to control and manipulate the supply of such materials and competition between communities was expressed and achieved by such imports. Increased use of gold was reflected in the appearance of new Beaker jewelry such as basket-shaped earrings and sheet gold ornaments for clothing. Some regions such as the Tagus estuary and Brittany were centers supported by extensive fertile land; others such as Galicia benefited from their position on the communications routes to acquire prestige materials. The extent of international trade is shown by the fact that the products of a Breton ax factory around Quimper imitated the stone battle-axes made in northern Europe at this time. The attractive honey-colored flint from the Grand Pressigny mines was used to make long blades and daggers and was also traded in the form of cores, being distributed deep into northern and central Europe and being buried in single graves with AOO beakers or battle-axes. The sea and rivers such as the Loire provided the main arteries for trade. Brittany was a trade crossroads, where the Loire route from the Rhineland and the Low Countries intersected with the Atlantic sea routes. The first appearance of horses in Iberia and Britain was also associated with the Beaker complex.

Copper metallurgy was by now well established in Sicily and the Italian mainland. Tuscany, which had good local sources of copper ore, saw the development of a metal industry whose products appeared in the local Gaudo graves. Copper was used particularly for daggers and jewelry. Other material in circulation in Italy reflects contacts with the Aegean; in Sicily this included strap-handled pottery vessels imitating Aegean metal cups, and in the Gaudo region these contacts may have been behind the beginning of vine and olive cultivation.

Megalithic Developments In the later fourth millennium a new type of megalithic tomb, the gallery grave (*allée couvert*), began to be built in Brittany, and the practice spread along the Loire and Garonne into other parts of France, including the Paris Basin (SOM—Seine-Oise-Marne—culture). Gallery graves and their variants were megalithic chambers of rectangular form, where chamber and entrance passage were merged. Some were covered by a mound; others may not have been. They still contained collective burials, but in general the associated material was less impressive than that found in the passage graves. The inland areas of France, which had neither large areas of agricultural land nor mineral wealth, remained outside the area that adopted the Beaker package.

Rockcut tombs (hypogea), characteristic of some Mediterranean regions, were also constructed in the Champagne region of France, and these and other burial types known in the fourth millennium continued in use in many regions of the Mediterranean. Now, however, there were richly furnished individual burials, such as one of a man in the Italian (Rinaldone) hypogeum of Ponte San Pietro who was accompanied by the apparently sacrificed body of a woman and numerous grave goods, suggesting growing social inequalities. The striking Maltese temples and hypogea continued in use until around 2500 B.C.

By the late third millennium collective burial in megaliths was coming to an end over much of western Europe, ceasing in most French passage and gallery graves around 2200 B.C., when single burial came into vogue. Well before this, however, a number of megalithic tombs had been deliberately put out of commission, for instance, by blocking their entrances with rubble. In much of Britain and Ireland single graves became the norm from the later third millennium, associated with various styles of decorated pottery, including Beakers.

In Britain new monuments began to be constructed from the late fourth millennium, largely though not completely replacing megalithic tombs as the focus for community ritual. Henges, circular settings of wood or stone enclosed by a bank and internal ditch, began to be built, apparently first in northern Scotland, whence they spread through much of Britain, culminating in the elaborate stone version at Stonehenge, which went through a number of reconstructions along increasingly elaborate lines. Their purpose is still unknown, but it is likely that ceremonies of some nature, probably religious, were conducted there. Henges were associated with a new type of pottery, elaborately decorated, known as Grooved Ware, which was associated with ritual sites throughout the third millennium. A substance found in one vessel, black henbane, may have been used to induce trances. Grooved Ware is also associated with a few elaborate passage graves constructed from around 3300 B.C., after most passage graves had gone out of use. These had a substantial round mound covering a very long passage leading to a central chamber of sophisticated construction. They were confined to eastern Ireland, northern Wales, and Orkney. Late in the millennium western Ireland also saw the construction of wedge tombs, a simple type of gallery grave; these continued in use until at least 1200 B.C.

Circles of standing stones were erected in some parts of Britain. Recumbent stone circles, known in parts of Scotland, had a distribution that contrasted with that of henges. Alignments and avenues of stones were constructed in Britain and in Brittany, particularly at Carnac. Various studies suggest that the standing stones may have had an astronomical connection; the rare developed passage graves, such as Maes Howe and Newgrange, also have links with key astronomical events, such as the rising of the sun at the midwinter or midsummer solstice.

In some places a variety of monuments were constructed in association, forming a "ritual landscape," of which Stonehenge and Carnac are probably the best known. While megalithic tombs had belonged to individual communities, the ritual landscapes being created from the late fourth millennium were on a larger scale and less numerous, and must have united the efforts of a number of communities, reflecting a change in the organization of society. This can be seen clearly in Mainland, Orkney, where for the majority of the fourth millennium the island was divided into small territories, each with its own megalithic tomb; in the early third millennium these were replaced as the focus of communal building by a large and centrally located complex, including the impressive developed passage grave of Maes Howe, stone circles, henges, and standing stones. Other ritual landscapes included those of Stonehenge and Avebury. These remained the focus for ritual and communal activity for centuries despite changing practices: For instance, there are many Bronze Age mounds around Stonehenge.

THE BRONZE AGE (C. 2300/2200–1000/ 700 B.C.)

Early Bronze Age 2200–1800 B.C.

The technology of alloying copper with tin to make bronze was introduced to Greece, via Anatolia, from the Near Eastern world, where bronze had been in use since around 3000 B.C. Bronze manufacture, however, was probably developed independently in central Europe in the mid-third millennium, using Bohemian tin, and in Britain using tin from Cornwall. Use of the new alloy gradually spread across Europe, reflecting its strength and versatility compared to pure copper or copper-arsenic alloy. Many regions, however, continued to use copper alloyed with arsenic, a type of bronze that was stronger and more easily cast than pure copper.

By the end of the third millennium the growing demand for metal ores throughout Europe was having a marked effect on both the directions and intensity of trading networks. These were influenced by the rarity of tin and by changes in the types of copper ore exploited; easily smelted oxide and carbonate ores were in short supply by the Early Bronze Age, and attention was being turned to more difficult sulfide ores. The principal European sources of tin lay along the Atlantic facade, an area also rich in other metals; tin was also available from the Erzgebirge (Ore Mountains), and copper sources in the mountains of central Europe were exploited. The southeast probably had access to Near Eastern or steppe sources of tin. The bronze-using cultures of Europe

N

Atlantic

Ocean

North Sea

Eilean an Tighe

Ballinderry
WICKLOW MTS.
Great
Orme
Ross Island
Rathgall
Cwmystwyth
Mount Gabriel
Caldicot
Bigbury

Dalgety
Corbridge
Alderley Edge
Caergwrle Castle
Roos Carr
Dover Ferriby
Brigg
Shardlow
Swine Sty
Moor Sands
Dover
Langdon Bay

Baltic Sea

HARZ MTS.
ERZGEBIRGE MTS.

Hallstatt
Mitterberg
Hauterive-
Champreveyres
Frattesina

Galicia

Black Sea

Rio-Tinto
Chinflon
Huelva

M e d i t e r r a n e a n   S e a

Mycenae
Thera
Knossos

© Facts On File, Inc.

| | Sources of amber | | Sources of gold |
| | Sources of copper ore | | Sources of tin ore |

0   250   500 miles

0   250   500 km

Map 8a. *Bronze Age trade and industry*

Map 8b. *Bronze Age Europe*

Legend:
- Extent of Urnfield cultures by 9th century B.C.
- Principal areas of Bronze Age rock art

Atlantic Ocean

North Sea

Baltic Sea

Black Sea

Mediterranean Sea

Mediterranean Sea

Jarlshof
Linga Fold
Haga • Uppsala
North Mains
Corrymuckloch
Dalrigh • Balfarg
Behy-Glenulra
Cloonbrin
Dun Aonghasa
Dowris • Rathgall
Nors Thy
Borum Eshoj
Muldbjerg
Egtved • Trundholm
Guldhoj • Vikso
Voldtofte • Bredador (Kivik)
Hvidegard
Bush Barrow
Flag Fen
Elp
Seddin
Somerset Levels
Runnymede
Bargeroosterveld
Gwithian
Wassenaar
Dartmoor
Nebra
Zedau • Leki Male
Upton Lovell
Wilsford • Black Patch
Helmsdorf
Leubingen
Bad Frankenhausen
Kernonen
Velim
Schifferstadt
Etzeldorf
Unetice
Hagenau
Dampierre-sur-le-Doubs
Wasserburg
Straubing
Nitra
Spissky Stvrtok
Singen
Nitriansky Hradok
Jaszdozsa-Kapolnahalom
Camp Durand
Padnal
Hallstatt
Male Kosihy
Hatvan • Barca
Avanton
Wittnauer Horn
Toszeg
Füzesabony
Usatove
Hauterive-Champreveyres
Ledro • Val Camonica
Nagyrev
Hajdusamson
Castellaro di Uscio
Hagenau
Monkodonja
Otomani
Monte Bego
Arene Candide
Frattesina
Orastie
Pustopolje
Feudvar
Monteoru
Filitosa
Ezero
Donja Slatina
Huelva
Barumini
El Argar
Milazzese
Pantalica • Thapsos

© Facts On File, Inc.

N

0   250   500 miles
0   250   500 km

came to depend to a considerable extent on Atlantic metals, creating closer and more organized ties between the different regions of Europe.

A marked contrast had developed between the way of life in the southeast, where farming had been established for many millennia—large settlements were numerous, and land ownership was probably the main reflection of prosperity—and the areas to the north and west of the Carpathians, where, although arable agriculture was economically important, settlements were generally small, stock rearing was a major focus, and livestock may have been regarded as the main repository of wealth. Forest clearance continued, with many regions becoming permanently deforested. These included uplands that had begun to be settled during the third millennium. In some areas, such as Dartmoor in southwest England, traces of extensive field systems and land divisions marked by ditches, walls, fences, and hedges survive, with patterns of small cultivated fields set around small settlements and larger enclosures for pasturing animals.

Social and economic divisions in society were becoming more marked. New materials and increasing social complexity promoted the development of some economic specialization. Some individuals, particularly metallurgists, now engaged at least part-time in craft activities, and mining and trade may now also have been conducted by specialists. In addition, some specialist groups may have begun to emerge, notably pastoralists who adopted a more mobile lifestyle, whether exploiting seasonal pastures at different altitudes around and in mountains or the abundant grazing available in the steppe. Wealth and power were becoming concentrated in the hands of a few individuals in the community, and their status was expressed through visible and ostentatious use of valuable materials and conspicuous consumption, creating a substantial and continuing demand for the movement of exotic goods and materials. This is particularly reflected in funerary practices. Single burial was adopted over most of Europe, in some areas generally covered by a barrow while in others flat graves were usual and barrows reserved for a small number of elite individuals who were buried with personal finery and goods of fine craftsmanship and prized materials such as copper, gold, fine stone, jet, amber, and

faience, as well, originally, probably with perishable valuables such as furs.

International trade was stimulated by the increasing demands for prestige materials. Both the volume and the variety of goods and materials circulating increased, linking together many networks that had previously served the individual regions of the continent, allowing the circulation over vast distances not only of goods and materials but also of ideas, fashions, and belief systems. New communications routes were opened up and older ones more intensively used. As well as sea and river traffic, land routes through mountain passes were now more used, partly as a result of increased pastoral transhumance, making use of upland summer pastures.

Votive hoards became more common and sometimes very large. Originally thought to have been metallurgists' stock-in-trade, deposited for safekeeping in troubled times, hoards of metalwork seem more likely to have been votive offerings to the gods. Many such offerings were buried in the ground, while many others were deposited in particular places in rivers or lakes. The practice had begun in earlier times—as early as the Ertebølle period in Scandinavia—but now became more common and widespread; it continued not only throughout the Bronze and Iron Ages but into the post-Roman period in pagan regions. As well as serving religion, the ostentatious deposition of large amounts of valuable material must have demonstrated the power of individuals or communities to obtain supplies of such commodities, enhancing their prestige and status; this has been compared with the Northwest Pacific Coast Native American practice of potlatch, where a leader displayed his wealth and power by the deliberate destruction of foodstuffs and goods.

While flourishing trade shows that peaceful relations could exist among communities, the development of many defended settlements and the appearance of purposeful weapons indicates that conflicts now often led to real warfare. Bronze Age rock art from Scandinavia and the Italian Alps reinforces this impression by depicting scenes of armed confrontation. Bronze was made particularly into weapons. These included short ogival blades, either furnished with a hilt and used as a dagger, or mounted sideways on a pole for use as a halberd. Flat and shafthole axes were also made. All these indicate that Early Bronze Age people saw themselves as warriors. However, these weapons would not have been effective except at close quarters, suggesting that conflict may have taken place as single combat between champions. Other weapons were probably also used, particularly arrows.

THE AEGEAN

Small palace-centered economies had been developing in the later third millennium in the Aegean. Around 2200 B.C. the palaces on the mainland were destroyed by fire, the result of internal conflicts or invaders; those of the Cyclades declined; but on Crete development continued unchecked. The island's population lived mainly in villages and hamlets, but there were also a number of towns and a few substantial settlements. Mountain caves and high places were venerated, and a number of peak sanctuaries were constructed. Already Crete was in trading contact with Egypt.

Palaces developed on Crete within the substantial towns at Knossos, Mallia, and Phaestos and perhaps others from around 1950 B.C. (First Palace period) and came to dominate substantial territories. Here princes controlled the agricultural revenue of the surrounding countryside, which was stored in huge jars and storage pits, and supported artisans practicing a variety of crafts, including metallurgy and textile production. The palaces were administrative centers and home to the royal family. The demands of recording and organizing the revenues led to the development of Cretan Hieroglyphic writing. While the palaces themselves had a religious function, each palace was also associated with a sacred cave or a peak sanctuary located at the summit of an adjacent hill where votive offerings were made. The shrine at Anemospila on Mount Juktas was destroyed by an earthquake at the very moment when a human sacrifice was taking place there. This may have been the earthquake that destroyed many of the palaces around 1700 B.C.

THE STEPPE

In the steppe region the custom of pit burial continued to develop in the second millennium; bodies were now interred in chambers in the side of pits covered by tumuli (Catacomb Grave culture). This region was in close contact with the flourishing Caucasian metalworking culture of the eastern Black Sea and from there adopted many metallurgical innovations and styles of artifact, such as lugged chisels and axes of arsenical copper made in two-piece molds. From the steppe people these innovations also spread into Southeast Europe.

SOUTHEAST EUROPE

Settlements in this region of long-established agricultural communities were often long-lived and substantial, many forming tells where occupation continued unbroken from the fourth millennium while others were nucleated villages, surrounded by banks and ditches. In the south and east, however, many tells were abandoned in favor of hilltop locations. A few settlements, such as Vučedol, were heavily fortified. River floodplains, river terraces, and foothills were occupied, and communities lived by mixed arable farming and stockbreeding. Community members were buried in cemeteries associated with the settlements, usually in flat graves; in some areas these included richly furnished burials, and variations in the treatment of individuals seemed to reflect social differentiation.

Metallurgy included sophisticated casting techniques: Some developments took place locally; others were adopted from the Únětice industry in central Europe; and the region was also permeable to ideas and innovations from the Near East and from the adjacent steppe through which ideas were transmitted from the Caucasian metallurgical centers. Caucasian types included a distinctive battle-ax with a shafthole at one end and a deep fan-shaped blade, made by casting in a two-piece mold, with a clay core to produce the shafthole; this came into use in the Carpathian region in the later third millennium, along with other Caucasian metalwork. At the same time, however, there was a decline in the quantity of metalwork being produced, due to the exhaustion of the supply of easily worked local copper ores. Metal was now imported from central Europe, probably as *ösenringe*, and used sparingly for small pieces of jewelry. The Danube was probably the main route along which metal and other goods traveled, and other rivers

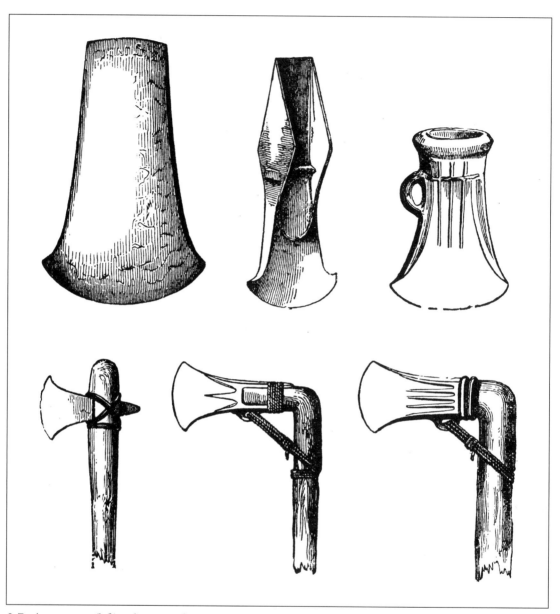

2.7 *A copper ax (left), a bronze palstave or winged celt (center), and a bronze socketed ax (right), all from Ireland, illustrating the development of different methods of hafting metal tools* (Lubbock, John. *Prehistoric Times.* New York: D. Appleton and Company, 1890)

were also important; settlements located at important nodes in the exchange network were able to acquire more substantial quantities of imported material, producing localized centers of wealth. These settlements also functioned as industrial and religious centers for their region.

CENTRAL AND NORTHERN EUROPE

Únětice The first alloying of copper and tin in central Europe probably took place around 2500, and by around 2200 B.C. bronze-working was established among groups north of the Danube, known collectively as Únětice; related cultures occupied the western Carpathian basin and the eastern Alpine region. Skilled metallurgists, the Únětice people developed the technique of casting-on to join pieces of metal, which they used to create daggers with solid hilts. They also became skillful at working sheet metal, producing fine beaten gold cups. Other Únětice products included massive bronze arm rings. One of the most characteristic products of the Únětice zone was the *ösenring*, made of copper from mines probably in the Austrian Alps, particularly Mitterberg. Ösenringe were cast copper rods hammered into rings and widely traded as ingots, to be alloyed with tin and made into other artifacts by those who acquired them.

Metalwork and technology from the Únětice area influenced regions farther to the west. For example, the technique of casting-on sparked imitations in the Atlantic zone, such as the Breton daggers with decorated hilts. The tin used by the Únětice groups to produce bronze probably came from alluvial sources in the Ore Mountains (Erzgebirge), but Atlantic metals, possibly including Cornish tin, were also in demand in central Europe and trade became more developed.

Many bronze objects were deposited in hoards, probably votive offerings but also reflecting conspicuous consumption to enhance prestige: Some hoards in Moravia contained 500 or more *ösenringe*. Most of the magnificent Únětice hoards were deposited around 2000 B.C., and the practice then ceased in central Europe until the Late Bronze Age.

The most magnificent arrays of metalwork come from barrow burials. Most people were buried in flat cemeteries, generally of inhumation burials (except in Hungary, where cremation was the norm), but as in western Europe barrows were erected over the remains of some elite individuals. A few exceptionally rich burials are known, notably Leubingen and Helmsdorf in Saxo-Thuringia and Łęki Małe in Poland; these were dated around 2000–1800 B.C. In each case an enormous barrow covered a wooden chamber in which the body of a man was laid surrounded by weapons and jewelry. The Leubingen man was accompanied by a young woman. The grave goods in his tomb included tools for carpentry and metalworking, and metalworking tools are known from other barrow burials, suggesting that craftsmen of the time could enjoy high status.

Scandinavian Late Neolithic/Dagger Period By c. 2200 the people of Scandinavia were burying their dead in stone cists, the men accompanied by flint daggers. Although not yet making their own metalwork, the influence of their bronze-using neighbors to the south and west, to whom they supplied amber, was seen in the skillful imitations of metal objects in finely worked flint and occasional imports of Únětice daggers and Irish axes.

WESTERN EUROPE

Atlantic The Atlantic region was rich in metals, with copper, silver, tin, and some gold in Iberia, tin and gold in Brittany, copper, tin, and gold in Ireland, copper in Wales, and tin in Cornwall. From the early second millennium these rich metal resources were increasingly exploited, both for local use and for export, often in the form of finished goods such as the gold lunulae (crescentic collars) made around 2000 B.C. in Ireland and traded along the Atlantic coast of France. Substantial copper mines developed; these included the Ross Island mines in Ireland, exploited 2400–2000 B.C. Amber, another highly valued material, was available in the Baltic region and on Jutland and was occasionally washed up on British coasts. Demand for these materials, rare or absent in much of continental Europe, drew the Atlantic into active trade relations with the European interior on a far larger scale than before.

Single burial was now the norm for the disposal of the dead, under round barrows in some areas such as southern Britain while in northern Britain, pits or cists were more usual, and there were some cremations. Often the barrow was defined or surrounded by a ditch or a circle of stones or posts. Success and prosperity was reflected in some areas, such as Brittany and the Wessex region of southern England, in the appearance of barrow burials furnished with a rich array of prestige goods. Cemeteries of these barrows developed over the centuries, probably representing chiefly lineages; those in Wessex fall into

two series, from 2000 to 1700 and 1700 to 1400 B.C. (Wessex Culture I and II). Wessex was an area also of great agricultural wealth, with good chalk soils providing not only arable land but also abundant pastures. The ritual landscape of Wessex had long been exceptional, and the continued elaboration of Stonehenge shows its enduring preeminence. Both Wessex and Brittany were situated at important nodes in trade routes, Wessex being linked by rivers to Ireland, the Atlantic seaboard, and the east coast of England and thence to the Low Countries and northern and central Europe. Brittany combined its strategic situation for trade with considerable mineral wealth. Here rich burials were placed in stone cists under small barrows.

Elsewhere the elite dead were also often placed under barrows with fine grave goods, though not in the same impressive concentration as those in Wessex and Brittany. Such prestige objects were made of Irish gold, bronze, amber from the Baltic, jet, shale, occasionally silver, and fine stone, and included a range of jewelry and ornaments for clothing, such as gold lunulae and jet necklaces, gold cups, and weapons such as metal daggers and flint arrowheads. Many items displayed exceptional craftsmanship, and it is likely that the craftsmen themselves enjoyed high status. A characteristic product of Brittany, traded into Wessex, was the copper or bronze dagger with a hilt decorated with gold pins, possibly inspired by Únětice daggers with organic hilts attached with metal nails. Handled cups in copper, gold, silver, shale, and amber made in various Atlantic regions may have been inspired by pottery vessels from Iberia or by beaten gold cups made in central Europe.

While in areas such as Wessex and Brittany the power of communities to obtain a supply of exotic goods was demonstrated by placing these in the burials of leaders, in other areas such as Ireland the

2.8 A flint dagger from Late Neolithic Denmark, made in imitation of the metal daggers that were in use at the time in areas farther to the south. The surface of this fine dagger was skillfully finished by pressure-flaking. (Worsaae, J. J. A. *The Industrial Arts of Denmark.* London: Chapman and Hall, 1882) conspicuous consumption of wealth was in the form of rich votive offerings, particularly of metalwork, deposited as hoards in the ground or in watery places. Among the pieces chosen for this were gold collars. The type known as lunulae were probably all produced in Ireland, of gold from the Wicklow Mountains; they reached parts of Britain and were buried as votive deposits in Brittany. They resemble the collars depicted around the necks of stone statue menhirs and may have been worn by images of gods. Southwest Iberia produced a different style of gold collars, which were mainly distributed in Iberia but reached as far north as northwest England.

In contrast to the abundant graves, settlements in Bronze Age western Europe are poorly known. Some of those identified in Britain, such as Black-patch, comprised a number of small round huts. Each family probably used a group of these huts for different purposes within normal domestic life. Groups of huts were often surrounded by a wall and had a large open space in the center where livestock might be penned.

Mediterranean In the Tagus region of Atlantic Iberia Beaker pottery was succeeded by decorated bowls associated with tanged bronze points, tanged daggers, and V-perforated buttons, as well as the rite of single burial (Palmela complex); similar material was associated with single burials in central Iberia (Ciempozuelas). From around 2200 B.C. settlement in southeast Spain, though still focused on Almeria, was concentrated in heavily defended hilltop locations (Argaric Bronze Age). With these were associated cemeteries of single burials in cists or large storage vessels furnished with fine dark undecorated pottery resembling metal forms, weapons including arsenical copper daggers and axes, silver rings and diadems, and sometimes small pieces of gold jewelry. Differences between graves in the wealth of associated material reflect developing social hierarchy in the region. Their metal objects, however, remained technologically simple, flat axes cast in one-piece molds being characteristic products.

Beaker material continued in use into the second millennium in parts of the western Mediterranean, including southern France and the Iberian interior, where megalithic tombs were also still used for burials. In southwest Iberia, however, single graves became the norm during the second millennium. These might be placed in stone cists or pits with a surrounding stone curb. In contrast to Almeria, few impressive grave goods were associated with these burials, the richest being furnished with little more than riveted daggers or small ornaments of gold. Settlement shifted away from the Tagus region, where it had been concentrated for millennia, focusing now on areas farther south where copper ores were available.

Individual burials were now general in the central Mediterranean as well; in Malta these were cremations. In northern Italy (Polada) many settlements were built in lakeside locations. Material from these sites show that the region was in contact with transalpine Europe and linked into the exchange networks across the continent, for example, receiving amber beads. In central Italy (Proto-Apennine) the central mountain spine of the Apennines, long a major barrier dividing east from west, was now becoming integrated into the mixed farming economy, providing summer pastures. The high elevations of the Alps, previously unsettled, also now began to provide summer pastures for the flocks of transhumant pastoralists who spent the winter at lower altitudes. These individuals may have combined their herding with mining, obtaining copper ores.

Middle Bronze Age 1800–1300 B.C.

Across much of Europe this period saw the replacement of burial in flat cemeteries by burial under round mounds (tumuli), a practice that already had a long history in parts of Atlantic Europe. Cremation began to be the preferred practice, however, in much of the latter region.

The Middle Bronze Age saw a marked increase in the scale and extent of bronze working. Prestige goods continued to dominate the use to which both bronze and other metals were put. For men these were weapons in particular, indicating the status of warrior was a key role in society. For women there was now an increased variety of ornaments, many elaborate and finely crafted, including pendants and bracelets. Pins with a head in the form of a

2.9 A bronze disc with fine spiral decoration worn by a woman found in a Danish tree-trunk coffin (Worsaae, J. J. A. *The Industrial Arts of Denmark*. London: Chapman and Hall, 1882)

four-spoked wheel reflect the high value attached to the chariot—the ultimate status symbol of the time, introduced to Southeast Europe from the steppe region and spreading thereafter into many parts of Europe. The ritual chariot of the sun, known from a bronze and gold example, complete with horse, from a votive deposit in a bog at Trundholm in Zealand, shows that this innovation had also found its way into religious symbolism.

International trade gained momentum, direct links developing across great distances, for example, between the elite of Scandinavian society and that of the Carpathian region. With the goods traveled ideas: knowledge of new techniques of working metals and other materials; new fashions in elite display, including weaponry, drinking vessels, and personal ornaments; and possibly new belief systems reflected in changing practices for the disposal of the dead and new religious symbolism like the spoked wheel.

The opening of the second millennium had seen the emergence of civilization in the Aegean. The demands of the Minoans and Mycenaeans for raw materials contributed to the volume of goods in cir-

culation, though the civilizations themselves probably only influenced their neighbors in the Balkans and the central Mediterranean; internal European trade had its own momentum, to which the Aegean world added little. Though the trade mechanisms in the rest of Europe are unknown, they are likely to have depended on agreements or alliances between the leaders of relatively small communities whose situation gave them control of the source or movements of desired commodities. These prestige goods enhanced the status of the leader within the community and the community within its local region, but were not the basis for the development of a significantly stratified society. The settlement evidence over much of Europe gives no hint of elite residences differentiated from those of the rest of society, display of status being reserved for burial.

A need for defense is shown by the growth of fortified settlements in Southeast Europe and elsewhere, including the tower houses of the Mediterranean islands. Their distribution across the landscape often suggests that they acted as a place of refuge for the inhabitants of small territorial units, probably during raids in which livestock were the main target. Conflict is also reflected in the development of new weapons, including spears with bronze heads. Daggers were now lengthened into swords, which made it possible to engage the enemy at arm's length rather than at the close quarters necessitated by daggers. Swords also became a vehicle for extensive innovation throughout the remaining centuries of the Bronze Age, reflecting both functional developments and fashion.

THE AEGEAN

Minoan Crete After the destructions around 1700 B.C., the major Minoan palaces were quickly reconstructed, generally on a larger scale (Second Palace period). Knossos became the dominant center, its king or priestly ruler exercising some authority over the whole island, and perhaps beyond. The island of Santorini (Thera), largely destroyed by a massive earthquake, probably around 1628 B.C., preserves in Akrotiri its ash-engulfed principal settlement, many two- or even three-storeyed houses with vivid wall paintings in the Minoan style. One depicts a scene of life on the island, with towns, substantial decorated ships, and soldiers bearing Cretan-style figure-of-eight shields.

While the Minoan royal family and their entourage resided in the palaces, the surrounding towns contained a number of large houses, probably home to the elite, and more modest structures including houses and workshops. Other smaller towns, like Gournia, also developed, as did villa estates in the countryside.

A full-fledged writing system, Linear A, was now in use for keeping records; from this it is clear that the Minoans were not Greek speakers. International sea trade flourished with Greece, Anatolia, and the southern Mediterranean as far west as Egypt, and Minoans are depicted in Egyptian paintings. This trade was highly organized and under the control of the palaces; the Minoans imported metal ores and other raw materials such as semi-precious stones, as well as foreign luxuries, and exported agricultural produce, particularly wine and olive oil, fine pottery, and other craft products. Minoan frescoes and other art include scenes of bull-dancing and the capture of bulls, as well as many creatures and scenes with animals, sea creatures being a particularly popular theme on painted pottery. Fine ivory carving and gold and silver working, especially manufacturing vessels and jewelry, were also among the crafts practiced in the Minoan palaces.

Around 1450 B.C. the Minoan palaces fell, possibly due to earthquakes or internal unrest, and at some stage Crete was taken over by the Mycenaeans from mainland southern Greece. The palace of Knossos was finally destroyed sometime in the early to mid-14th century B.C., and Chania in the west of Crete became the major center. With the 12th-century troubles associated with the Sea Peoples, the Cretans retreated to refuge settlements in the mountains.

Mycenaean Greece   Southern Greece saw the rise of a warrior aristocracy in the mid-16th century B.C., best known from the rich burials in the slab-lined Shaft Graves at Mycenae. Here a number of people were buried with gold masks and other finery, including a number of Minoan imports. Beads of Baltic amber as well as horse gear decorated with compass designs show that already links existed between this region and the societies of the Balkans, which had access to goods from the central European Tumulus culture and its trading partners in Scandinavia. The metalwork in the Shaft Graves, which included bronze daggers inlaid with designs in gold, silver, and niello, was the work of extremely gifted and skilled craftsmen, working under the control of local leaders.

Later rulers were buried in *tholoi* (corbel-vaulted chamber tombs) and lesser members of the elite in rock-cut chamber tombs, associated with the major centers such as Mycenae and Tiryns. These were fortified citadels with walls made of massive irregular dressed stones (Cyclopean architecture) enclosing a royal palace, storerooms, shrines, and housing. Outside the walls lay further houses and workshops. The conflicts suggested by the massive fortifications are borne out by the associated evidence of warfare, including weaponry, armor, chariots, and, from Pylos, records of the organization of coastal defense forces.

Minoan influences in 15th-century B.C. Greece were strongly felt and continued after Crete came under Mycenaean control. The Mycenaeans developed their own script, Linear B; being written in an early form of Greek, Linear B texts can be read but are mainly administrative documents, showing detailed control of agricultural production, industry, military equipment, and the distribution of rations. Crafts such as metalworking, ivory carving, textile production, and pottery making flourished.

While the Minoans had largely confined their trading activities to the eastern basin of the Mediterranean, the Mycenaeans ranged farther afield, seeking metal ores as far west as Sardinia and perhaps even Spain, where a few Mycenaean pots are known; Mycenaean pottery is more common in Cyprus, southern Italy, and Sicily, as well as the Levant, the entry point for participation in the extensive Near Eastern trade networks. Trade with their European neighbors gave the Mycenaeans indirect access to more distant materials, including amber from the Baltic. A wrecked ship, probably from Canaan in the Levant, which went down around 1300 B.C. at Ulu Burun off Anatolia, bore many goods probably destined for the Mycenaean world, such as tin, copper, and glass ingots, and plant materials for manufacturing perfumed oils, a Mycenaean export. Personal objects among the materials in the wreck suggest some of the crew were Mycenaeans. Copper was carried in the form of distinctive oxhide ingots; pottery was used to transport perfumes, oil, and spices, and large jars might also be used as containers for consignments of fine pottery vessels.

In the 13th and 12th centuries many cultures around the eastern Mediterranean, probably including the Mycenaeans, suffered attacks by seaborne raiders, known to their Egyptian victims as the Sea Peoples, who probably derived from a number of regions including Anatolia and Italy. Around 1200 many of the palaces fell, whether to these raiders or through internal conflicts is uncertain; others survived but with considerable loss of wealth and power as well as the cessation of written records. For several centuries, Greece underwent a dark age when overseas links were restricted and people lived in small communities with regional differences, for example, in pottery styles, that contrast with the cultural uniformity of the Mycenaean world.

THE STEPPE

Much information about the way of life of steppe pastoralists comes from their elite burials in catacomb graves. By the mid-second millennium these graves became more elaborate: They were now substantial barrows covering timber chambers that resembled houses (Timber grave culture). Some included chariots and horses among the grave offerings, a practice that was to become the hallmark of rich steppe burials.

Horses were essential to the maintenance of the steppe economy and by now were being used both for riding and for pulling light chariots with two spoked wheels, an innovation of the early second millennium that gave speed and mobility. Heavier four-wheeled wagons were still used to carry possessions and families as they moved across the steppe. By the mid-second millennium, the steppe region was being fully exploited, with nomadic pastoralists moving deep into central Asia to graze their animals in the scattered pastures of the steppe. This gave them access to new ore sources, copper from the Urals and copper and tin from the Altai, giving a new impetus to steppe metallurgy.

THE SOUTHEAST

By the early second millennium the substantial copper and gold resources of the Transylvanian Mountains were beginning to be exploited, leading to a major new Carpathian metal industry. Incised decoration was a characteristic feature of the metalwork, which included both local innovations and metallurgical and decorative techniques and designs borrowed from neighboring groups in central Europe and the steppe, such as casting-on, used for solid-hilted swords, and two-piece molds. Much of the Carpathian metalwork is known from votive hoards like that from Hajdúsámson in northeastern Hungary. This contained a sword with a solid hilt, across which had been laid 12 battle-axes. Decorative techniques such as compasswork, used to decorate metalwork, were also applied to pottery and horse gear in antler and bone. The people of the Carpathian basin traded widely, their metalwork reaching into Denmark (from which they received amber and probably furs), Italy and Greece, the Alpine foreland, and the Atlantic region.

As well as metallurgical innovations, the southeast continued to receive other ideas and goods from the east. These included horses, imported in considerable numbers, the harness elements for controlling them, including antler cheekpieces, and chariots with spoked wheels. Clay models of spoked wheels are known from the Carpathian region. The chariot rapidly became an important elite prestige possession, spreading across Europe.

Some substantial fortified settlements began to spring up, reflecting the prosperity of the Carpathian region, which now produced the finest metalwork in Europe. Many of those located in key places on the trade routes along the region's rivers were fortified with box ramparts. An outstanding example is Spišský Štvrtok in Slovakia, a site whose wealth is shown by a hoard of goldwork deposited in its interior. Most settlements had a surrounding bank and ditch and contained densely packed houses of wattle and daub.

The flourishing metalworking communities of the western Carpathian basin eventually became absorbed into the Tumulus culture, while those of the east turned their focus southward toward the developing Mycenaean warrior society in southern Greece and the cultures around the northern Black Sea.

Central Europe

Tumulus Culture After 1800 B.C. across much of central Europe the old tradition of burial in flat-grave cemeteries, which had operated for all but the most exalted members of society, was replaced by burial under round barrows (tumuli), often in a wooden coffin. The western Carpathian basin also became part of the Tumulus zone, which eventually stretched as far west as eastern France.

The Tumulus metal industry grew to rival that of the Carpathian basin in its trade network. Typical products of the industry included many types of jewelry and of weapons, including swords, socketed spearheads, palstaves, and armor to protect arms and legs. Some men were buried with a sword, while women were accompanied by jewelry.

Open-plan settlements of large post-built rectangular houses were usual across most of central Europe, from Holland to Hungary. Some settlements, however, were fortified, including a number of sites in Croatia with stone ramparts, such as Monkodonja, which had an elaborate gateway. The site of Velim in Bohemia, fortified with ramparts and ditches, contained a number of hoards of bronzes and goldwork, echoing the coincidence of hoards and fortifications seen at Spišský Stvrtok and perhaps suggesting that fortifications were to protect sites of ritual importance rather than people. Human bones, many with cut marks, were also interred in Velim's pits and ditches.

SCANDINAVIA

The Tumulus period saw the growth of direct links between central Europe and the north, Denmark trading via the Rhine and Oder with the Danube region and the Carpathian basin. The inhabitants of Scandinavia, a region without local sources of tin or accessible copper, now no longer merely imported metalwork and imitated it in other materials but actively sought to acquire metal from which to produce their own weapons and ornaments such as belt discs. Their metalwork shows strong central European influences, and they also imported fine metal objects such as swords, spears, and decorated axes. These weapons were among the prestige goods placed in hoards, along with local products, as offerings to the gods.

This period also saw the beginning of tumulus burial in this region for the elite of society, presumably the leaders who were able to organize the trade

in exotic goods and materials and their families. Bodies were wrapped in an ox hide or a blanket and placed in a well-made tree-trunk coffin, over which an earth-and-turf mound was erected. In a number of cases waterlogging has preserved these coffins and their contents, which included the woollen clothing and bronze jewelry worn by the deceased, personal possessions, and vessels and other objects of wood and birch bark. Some also contained goldwork. Long-distance trade links are emphasized by the discovery of Mycenaean folding stools in some of these coffins; while in Mycenaean graves as early as the mid-16th century Baltic amber beads were found. Dendrochronology (tree-ring dating) has shown that many of these coffins were buried between 1410 and 1360 B.C.

Later graves contained cremated remains instead of inhumations, often associated with miniature versions of appropriate grave goods such as swords and with small personal objects such as razors, but still placed within a tree-trunk coffin.

A further insight into life in Bronze Age Scandinavia comes from rock art, particularly common in Sweden. Although the context and content of this art is likely to have been religious, it provides some glimpses of life, such as men apparently engaged in single combat, armed with axes or swords; ships, often apparently manned by rowers; and men plowing with teams of oxen. The ships depicted were probably made of a wooden framework covered with skins.

WESTERN EUROPE

The Atlantic Zone   Barrow burials continued in many areas but none with the exceptional wealth of the earlier Wessex I and Armorican burials. Later burials were often inserted into earlier mounds or megalithic tombs or placed in cemeteries around them. In Britain, the Netherlands, and northwest France cremation became the norm, the ashes being interred in urns or large pottery vessels, generally with few grave goods. Much of northern and eastern France, however, became part of the central European Tumulus zone, with inhumation under barrows. Trade along the northern Atlantic coast continued to flourish, as did trade with the neighboring Tumulus region and Scandinavia, but Iberia was at this time relatively isolated: Tin bronze was not in use here, the local arsenic-rich copper producing a satisfactory form of bronze.

Metallurgy grew in importance, and new mines were opened in a number of areas such as the extensive Irish mines of Mount Gabriel, worked 1700–1500 B.C. Bronze was now being used for a great variety of tools and weapons, such as flanged axes, palstaves, sickles, chisels, socketed spears, and swords. Goldworking also flourished, particularly in Ireland, which produced a range of ornaments of sheet gold and of gold rods, some of them skillfully twisted into large torcs.

In northern France and Britain the organization of agriculture is apparent in some areas in the creation of land divisions, using lines of boulders or walls of stone or earth to demarcate field systems and grazing land. Dartmoor in England, for example, was divided up into a series of territorial units each containing arable, pastureland, and settlement areas. Here stone boundary walls (reaves) replaced earlier fences and hedgerows; the change from wood to stone reflects the completion during the second millennium of the process of deforestation across much of Europe.

Stone was also used for domestic construction in some areas such as upland Scotland, resulting in the survival there of many visible houses. These were substantial round houses with stone lower walls on which a superstructure of turf, timber, and thatch was constructed. In most areas houses were built of timber; in Britain these were large circular huts of posts with wattle and daub walls and thatched roofs; some were dwellings while others may have been used for weaving, cooking, and storage.

The Mediterranean and the Western European Interior Over much of the continent, houses were rectangular timber post-built structures, while lakeside settlements in Switzerland, France, and northern Italy often had log cabins, and in high Alpine valleys there were substantial plank-built houses with several rooms, including storage areas. Terramare settlements flourished in the Po valley; those beside lakes and rivers included houses supported on piles. In the high Apennines, which had previously been visited by people bringing their animals to summer pastures, permanent mixed-farming settle-

ments appeared by the mid-second millennium (Apennine Bronze Age), and there was also an increase in lowland settlements in central Italy. Southern Italy and the Aeolian Islands had small settlements of round huts, which were probably grouped to make up the living and working quarters of individual families. Built close together, sometimes in defensible locations such as the promontory settlement of Milazzese on Panarea, these small villages did not include space for animals, which must have been kept outside.

On Sardinia tower houses (nuraghi) began to be built. Initially these may have been the homes of single extended families of farmers, or places of refuge during armed raids. They consisted of a stone tower on two or three floors, with stairs and access corridors built into the thickness of the wall. Towerlike stone dwellings or places of refuge were also constructed in other Mediterranean islands: *torre* in Corsica and talayots on the Balearics. Megalithic tombs continued in use in the islands of the western Mediterranean, and highly distinctive forms were developed, including the *navetas* of the Balearics and the Sardinian "giants' tombs." Sardinia and the Balearics also had holy places with votive wells and offerings.

Trade through the Alpine passes into France and central Europe brought the central Mediterranean into the communications networks that crisscrossed transalpine Europe, their extent demonstrated by the presence of amber beads in the north Italian *terramare*.

Seaborne contacts between the islands and mainland promoted the circulation of goods, with Maltese pottery being traded to Sicily and Sicilian pottery to Lipari. Mycenaean trade brought Aegean luxuries, particularly perfumes, spices, and oil, carried in pottery, to southern Italy and the islands of Sicily and Sardinia, probably in exchange for copper and other raw materials. More than a hundred Mycenaean vessels were found in the Nuraghe Antigori on Sardinia. The technology of fine painted wheel-thrown pottery was introduced to the region by the Mycenaeans. At Thapsos on Sicily a large building with an extensive suite of rooms was built, perhaps reflecting the power developed by a local ruler as a result of contacts with the Mycenaeans. Impressive collective tombs of the Thapsos period were richly furnished with imported Mycenaean pottery as well as locally made bronzes. The traffic was not one-way: An Italian-style mold found at Mycenae suggests the presence there of a metal-worker from Italy.

Late Bronze Age 1300–1000/700

SETTLEMENT, ECONOMY, AND SOCIETY

After around 1300 B.C. farming practices gradually changed across Europe, becoming more intensive. In Britain, where there is good surviving evidence of land divisions, the pattern of small fields was in some areas replaced by much larger scale arrangements of banks and ditches (ranch boundaries) dividing the landscape into large blocks. Less is known about the partitioning of land in continental Europe. There is evidence for increasing rainfall after around 1100 B.C., causing many areas to become waterlogged. Trackways were constructed to enable people to travel over boggy areas, but the impact on farming was more drastic, leading to the abandonment of many fragile or marginal areas that had been brought under cultivation earlier in the Bronze Age. Overexploitation and deforestation also played a part in the transformation of these areas into blanket bog, acid soils, and barren heath.

Fortified settlements became widespread over most of Europe, though not in the north. Some took advantage of and enhanced the natural defenses of hilltops (hillforts). Others (stockades) were located on low-lying land, often on or by lakes, and were defended by substantial wooden palisades or elabo-rate ramparts of wood, stone, and earth. Late Bronze Age settlements were often larger than those of ear-lier times and contained a larger number of houses, often densely packed within the settlement defenses. Some settlements seem to have had their layout planned, while others show a haphazard internal arrangement. These forts were presumably the place of residence of the local leader and his immediate cir-cle. The majority of the population, however, still lived in small farming settlements scattered across the countryside where one or a few families lived sur-rounded by their fields and pastures. Farming was the main occupation of most people, only a few being engaged in other activities such as metallurgy. Very probably the fortified settlements would act as a place of refuge for the rural population during raids; they could accommodate larger numbers than in earlier times, suggesting that leaders now dominated more extensive territories. Even so, the scale of conflict was still small, raiding parties being unlikely to number more than 100 and probably far fewer. Armed expedi-tions were often successful, since few fortified settle-ments managed to last more than a century before being destroyed and usually abandoned.

The emphasis on weaponry among bronze work in hoards and graves right across Europe supports the importance that seems to have been placed on warriors and warfare, as do Mediterranean bronze sculptures and carved standing stones depicting weapons or individuals as warriors. Much of the expertise of metallurgists was invested in producing parade armor, including shields, cuirasses of beaten metal, and elaborately decorated horned helmets, whose function was to impress rather than protect. Swords combined function with ostentation, new designs constantly being developed, offering greater efficiency or a more impressive appearance or both, and these were rapidly adopted across Europe. Chariots pulled by horses were still the ultimate sta-tus symbol, and horse gear was increasingly made in bronze.

METALLURGY

Despite the scarcity and uneven distribution of tin, by the Late Bronze Age almost every region made substantial use of bronze. New technology devel-oped, including the working of sheet bronze from which were produced a wide range of objects such as armor, buckets, and cauldrons, frequently deco-rated by methods such as repoussé work. The armor, while it must have served to finely display status, did not offer much real protection, and in battle, leather armor and shields of wood or boiled leather must more commonly have been used to give protection. The exploitation of European metal sources had now become so well developed that bronze was common enough to be used for everyday tools. Most of this was tin bronze, but copper was also alloyed with lead, for reasons unknown. One possible explanation is that lead made it possible to increase the quantity of bronze available, given the rarity of tin; another is that the soft lead alloy facilitated the casting of complex shapes. The occurrence in hoards of some objects made largely or entirely of lead also suggests the possibility that lead was used for items made for deposition as offerings, a context in which strength and functionality would be irrelevant. Techniques in use now included cire perdue (lost-wax) casting, which could produce elaborate objects, such as figurines and objects with complex surface decoration. Single-use clay molds and elaborate multiple-piece molds were now in common use, producing sophisticated shapes such as the lur of Scandinavia; molds impressed in firm sand were probably also used for casting. Ireland and Scandinavia were centers of particularly fine gold working, where complex and elaborate cast objects included vessels and ornaments such as bracelets and gorgets. Improved pyrotechnology also made it possible to begin producing true glass, which was made in small quantities across Europe from northern Italy and Switzerland to Ireland and was used for beads.

Copper circulated in the form of the plano-convex ingots that formed at the bottom of the bowl-shaped furnaces after smelting. Occasional shipwrecks show that there was extensive movement not only of raw materials but also of scrap metal around the Atlantic facade. Similarly extensive trade in metal and other goods flourished on the continent, carrying considerable quantities of materials over long distances. For example, whereas in earlier times, British bronzes had been made mainly with local ores, such as those from Great Orme, the majority in the Late Bronze Age used metal from continental sources, especially from the Alps. Particular weapon types, such as flange-hilted swords, are known right across Europe. Weapons were among the most common artifacts exchanged; others included amber, glass, and salt. This began to be mined at Hallstatt in the Austrian Alps, which continued as a major center of salt production in the Iron Age. The rich grave goods in the cemetery here reflect the wealth that exploitation of the salt mines brought to its community. At a number of other places in Europe where salt springs occurred, salt was produced by evaporation, either by heating brine in coarse clay vessels or by allowing natural evaporation in clay-lined pools.

Metal smiths enjoyed considerable status and were probably few in number. Larger communities may have had resident smiths, but smaller ones may have had to rely on itinerant metalworkers. That even small communities had access to metalworking skills and bronze tools and weapons is shown by the discovery of crucibles and broken clay molds in small settlements such as Dún Aonghasa in Ireland and Jarlshof on Shetland.

From around 1000 B.C. iron also began to be worked, though its impact was not at first widely felt. Iron ores occur far more widely than those of copper and particularly tin, making iron a metal within the reach of ordinary people for everyday tools once it came into widespread use. At first it was only worked in the south, where it was made into weapons that are known from tombs in parts of the Balkans and Italy.

DEATH AND RELIGION

The Late Bronze Age saw a major transformation in funerary practices with the spread across much of Europe of the practice of cremation. The ashes were placed in urns of various distinctive types, which were buried in vast urnfields. Whether this represents a significant change in belief or merely a change in fashions is uncertain.

While burials were generally poorly furnished with grave goods, much metalwork survives in hoards, which became common and widespread. Unlike earlier hoards, which mainly contained fine objects, these Late Bronze Age hoards were often collections of broken or recycled tools or sometimes weapons. Their meaning is disputed, some scholars seeing them as the stock-in-trade of metalsmiths, while others consider that they continued earlier votive practices. Votive offerings of more impressive objects accumulated in lakes and rivers such as the Rhine and Thames. A particularly lavish hoard, of some 400 objects including many swords and spears, comes from the estuary of the River Odiel at Huelva in Spain (although some scholars interpret this as a shipwreck). Certain caves and rock fissures also attracted offerings and were perhaps imitated in the shafts and wells in which an accumulation of small offerings have been found. Other probable ritual sites included unusual and as yet unexplained wooden structures such as that at Bargeroosterveld in Holland. Rock art, also likely to have a ritual context, continued in Scandinavia and was also found in other areas, including Val Camonica and Monte Bego in the Alps where representations include scenes of plowing and housebuilding, textile manufacture, and metalworking, as well as warfare.

A number of Late Bronze Age artifacts seem likely to have had a religious function or meaning. These included the magnificent Scandinavian lur, a type of horn or trumpet that may have been sounded during rituals, and bronze model carts bearing symbols such as birds, discs, and spoked wheels. Birds and particularly ducks were a widespread and common symbol, occurring as figurines in pottery and metal, as attachments on cauldrons, and as motifs on ceramic and metal objects.

URNFIELDS

Considerable population growth had taken place along the middle and lower Danube, an area characterized by flat cemeteries and fortified settlements. By the 14th century this area saw the beginnings of a practice that was to become widespread. Cremation had been the usual method of disposing of the dead in Hungary in the Early Bronze Age and had been adopted by some areas to its north and west in the Middle Bronze Age. Now cremation became the norm throughout the central Danube region. The ashes of the dead were collected and placed in urns, which were buried in large cemeteries (Urnfields). The practice spread from there into mainland Italy, and eastern and central Europe in subsequent centuries. By the ninth century B.C. cremation had spread farther, being adopted in much of western Europe as far as northern Iberia, where close cultural ties with southern France may reflect limited population movement across the Pyrenees. Britain and the Atlantic regions, the Low Countries and northern Europe, however, remained outside the Urnfield zone, although cremation was a common practice in these regions. Despite the widespread popularity of cremation, inhumation was not entirely abandoned; some cemeteries contained a few inhumations, while a few had more inhumations

than cremations. In some areas cremations might be covered by a small barrow, while in western regions burials were often placed within ditched enclosures. The cremation burials were generally poorly furnished with grave goods, which usually comprised only pottery and sometimes small metal objects such as razors or pins, fibulae (safety-pin brooches), and other jewelry. In the area north of the Alps, however, a few rich burials were furnished with fine tableware for feasting, a sword, and a wagon that was burned on the funeral pyre.

NORDIC ZONE

Although the Bronze Age inhabitants of Scandinavia relied entirely on imported copper and tin ore, nevertheless by the Late Bronze Age bronze artifacts were in common use here. Some have been recovered from votive deposits in bogs, including objects whose use seems most likely to have been religious, such as lurs.

As cremation became the standard rite over most of Europe, it also became much more common in Scandinavia. Here, however, the ashes were buried as bodies had been previously, in full-sized graves. Many were now surrounded by a setting of low stones in the shape of a boat; similar boat burials come from northern Germany. A few massive barrow burials also date from this period in Scandinavia and northern Germany, for example at Lusehøj on the island of Funen in Denmark and Uppsala in Sweden. At Seddin in northeast Germany the mound was 420 feet (130 meters) in diameter and covered a vaulted stone chamber in which rich grave goods had been placed. Here and in other large barrow burials the grave goods reflect the deceased's elite status as a warrior, including in some cases a wagon.

Although there are a number of rich burials, probably of individuals able to engage profitably in international trade, society in the north remained small scale. The basic unit of settlement was the small farm or hamlet, housing one or a few families; this region did not see the development of fortified settlements. The exceptional barrow burials lie at important nodes in the routes linking the north with the Urnfield region; trade seems to have been managed by a few chiefs able to enhance their position through the acquisition of prestige goods and to manipulate other leaders by controlling the supply of such goods to them.

MEDITERRANEAN

By the 12th century the nuraghi (tower houses) in Sardinia were becoming more substantial, with extra lobes or bastions added to the original tower; some may now have housed entire villages, while others had associated villages of round houses, also constructed of stone. Among the products of the local bronze industry were distinctive human and animal figurines, made by cire perdue casting. Warriors were a common subject, as they were on Iberian grave stelae and Corsican statue menhirs.

On Sicily a substantial stone building, the *anaktoron* (palace), was constructed at Pantalica, a settlement of several hundred people. Although Mycenaean imports were far less common than in the earlier Thapsos culture, much of the material, such as the wheel-made pottery, showed Aegean inspiration.

After the collapse of the Mycenaean civilization, trade contracted and Greece no longer exploited the metal sources of the central Mediterranean. Italy's long-standing trade links across the Alps now became more important. Much of mainland Italy saw the adoption of Urnfield practices and artifacts during the 12th century (Protovillanovan culture), as did southern France. Nevertheless, trade within the Mediterranean did not cease. According to tradition, Phoenician traders from the Levant were beginning to explore the central and western Mediterranean in search of metal ores. For some centuries there were close interconnections between the east and west Mediterranean, between the Mediterranean and the Atlantic, and across the Alps and along the Danube into temperate Europe, shown by the distribution of distinctive objects: for example, carp's-tongue swords, of Breton origin or inspiration, in Sardinia and northern Italy; Cypriot fibulae in France and Iberia.

THE ATLANTIC ZONE

Atlantic Europe also lay outside the Urnfield cultural area, though closely linked to it by trade. While cremation was still practiced here, other rites,

which left no archaeological trace, were also widespread. Hoards were abundant and so were fortified sites. Many earlier open settlements were now enclosed within a wall, suggesting an increased need for defense.

Technological advances in metallurgy, such as the working of sheet bronze, and fashions in sword styles and other artifact types spread from the Urnfield region to the west, where local styles of metalwork, producing such objects as bronze cauldrons and socketed axes, also developed and spread. The substantial movement of goods is highlighted by finds of ships wrecked on the Atlantic coast, such as that at Langdon Bay off the south coast of England, which carried a cargo of continental, mainly French, swords, axes and palstaves, mostly broken and so apparently scrap metal. Britain lay at the interface between the three major provinces of Late Bronze Age Europe: the Urnfield zone, whose axis was the Rhine-Danube corridor, the Nordic zone, and the Atlantic region; it was also a conduit for material and ideas to and from Ireland.

THE IRON AGE (C. 1000/700–100 B.C.)

By the end of the second millennium B.C., iron working was becoming established over much of the Near East, and it spread rapidly through Europe in subsequent centuries: Beginning in Greece and the Black Sea region in the 11th century, between 1000 and 800 B.C. it spread into the Balkans and eastern central Europe and was introduced into Italy and coastal Iberia by the Greeks and Phoenicians; iron working spread through central and western Europe as far as Britain by 700 B.C. By the late second millennium B.C. Scandinavia had a flourishing bronze-working industry based entirely on imported metals. When iron-working technology spread through Europe, the curious situation arose that iron-rich Scandinavia for some time resisted its adoption, preferring to retain the older bronze-working traditions: Iron working did not begin here until 600–500 B.C.

Map 9. *Early Iron Age Europe*

Iron working required different techniques to bronze working, objects being forged by hammering rather than being cast (casting required pyrotechnology beyond the skills of Europe until much later times, although the Chinese had mastered this technology by the seventh century B.C.). Some objects were made from steel, produced by heating iron in the presence of carbon. When properly quenched and tempered, iron has greater hardness and a keener edge than bronze, making it preferable for tools and weapons, and by 400 B.C. iron was in common use for everyday objects across Europe.

As iron became more common for mundane objects, bronze was channeled into the production of lavish prestige objects, such as luxury tableware, parade armor, horse gear, and jewelry, all made by skilled craftsmen. These were vehicles for the distinctive and vigorous Celtic art style that developed in the later first millennium, also seen in stone sculptures and objects of other materials such as gold, silver, and jet. Among the techniques employed were glass inlay work, enameling, and the use of compasses to produce geometric designs.

Deteriorating conditions, with lower temperatures and a marked increase in rainfall, around the end of the second millennium, brought an end to cultivation in many areas, fragile lands becoming heath or bog, suitable only for grazing or abandoned altogether. However, the development in the later Iron Age of the true plow, furnished with an iron plowshare and coulter, allowed heavier but highly productive soils to be taken into cultivation. Iron tools also improved productivity: These included spades and hoes as well as scythes for mowing the hay used for overwintering domestic stock.

Iron ores were widely available and abundant, making iron more accessible than copper and tin. The change from bronze to iron had a significant effect on trade and international relations, since the local availability of iron allowed communities and regional groups to be more independent than before. Nevertheless, trade networks were maintained and continued to develop, carrying both luxury goods and materials and necessities such as salt. Patterns of trade reflected the distribution of resources: As iron working became more important, for example, areas with rich iron deposits flourished. Salt was mined in the Alps and produced from seawater in some regions. Trade followed the rivers and sea lanes; land transport was harder but still important, including traffic through the Alpine passes.

Mediterranean Europe saw the rise of the city-states of the Greeks, Etruscans, and Phoenicians, and the empires of Carthage and Rome, and the inevitable development of competition among them. These states gradually spread their influences over much of Europe through trade, peaceful contact, conflict, and conquest. The Mediterranean powers sought land for settlement and raw materials such as metal ores and furs, as well as slaves, offering in exchange luxury goods, particularly wine, which were used by native chieftains to enhance and emphasize their status. The traffic was not one-way: Celtic warriors invaded both Greece and Italy and sought their fortunes as mercenaries.

Conflict was an important feature of life within temperate Europe, too. Population growth and environmental problems put pressure on resources, which brought conflict: warfare was common and hillforts continued to develop in many areas. These were home to the tribal chief and often a considerable community, a place of storage for tribal wealth in grain, a center of industry, and a refuge for the local farmers and their livestock when they were threatened by enemies. Numerous weapons reflect the warlike nature of the society, and in the later Iron Age the burials of chiefs often included a chariot, used in war either as a transport or as a mobile fighting platform. Classical references to the inhabitants of transalpine Europe emphasize the importance of warfare in their societies, and the bravery and ferocity of their warriors. Warfare was an honored way of life; warriors enjoyed high status and successful war leaders could attract an ever-growing band of followers. Feasting and drinking played a major part in the lives of the warriors, and fights often broke out between individuals. War bands raided their neighbors not only for booty but also for glory, and battles probably often took the form of single combat between champions. The majority of members of society, however, were farmers, although there were also craftsmen and priests.

Funerary practices were very varied: They included burial in flat-grave cemeteries, under massive tumuli or under smaller barrows, cremation and subsequent burial in urns or chambers, and practices that have left no trace. Some individuals were sacrificed, their bodies deposited in lakes and rivers; votive offerings of metalwork and other valued items were also placed in such watery locations. Offerings were also deposited in deep shafts and severed heads were displayed in occasional shrines. Religion played a major role in society. Although some worship took place in built shrines, particularly in late centuries, much of it was conducted in holy sites such as groves or by water such as lakes, springs, and rivers. According to classical writers Celtic (Gallic and British) religion was conducted by Druids, whose most sacred base was the island of Anglesey (Mona to the Romans); these were not only priests but also teachers, the repository of tribal knowledge, and lawgivers.

Classical authors in their writings for the first time provide literary evidence of the societies of temperate Europe, inhabited in the west by groups they knew as Celts and in the north and east by Germanic peoples, while in the southeast dwelt the Thracians and farther east in the steppe, Scythians and other nomad groups. Often the names of tribes (or confederacies, often known by the name of the leaders' tribe) are given; the presence of groups of the same name in different areas or different groups in an area at different times reflects the fluidity of political organization and the loose ties between groups and territory. As well as shedding additional light on the way of life of these peoples, classical sources provide some historical information, notably about the migrations of the Celts. A few individuals emerge from the generally anonymous canvas, such as Brennus, who led the Celts into Greece, Burebista king of the Dacians, and Vercingetorix, whom Caesar defeated.

Mediterranean States

PHOENICIANS AND CARTHAGINIANS

The Phoenicians inhabited a number of coastal city states in the Levant such as Tyre and Sidon and were fine seafarers and traders. By ancient tradition they began to prospect for metals and establish colonies in the west by around 1100 B.C., although the earliest secure archaeological evidence of their presence dates from the ninth century, at Nora on Sardinia. Thereafter they settled on the Mediterranean and Atlantic coasts of Iberia and North Africa, coming to dominate the southern half of the western Mediterranean. Major colonies included Gadir (Cádiz) on the Atlantic coast of Spain and Carthage in Tunisia; established in 814 B.C., the latter gained control of the Phoenician colonies after the mother cities in the Levant were conquered by the Babylonians in 573 B.C. The Carthaginians held land in Sicily, North Africa, and Spain and had colonies down the west African coast at least as far as Mogador. Their expansion brought them into conflict first with the Greeks and then with the Romans, by whom they were narrowly defeated in the First Punic War (264–241 B.C.). This led them to strengthen their hold on southern Iberia, but renewed hostilities

with Rome (218–202 B.C.) resulted in the loss of their Iberian territories, despite the brilliant generalship of Hannibal. After its conclusive defeat in the Third Punic War Carthage was sacked in 146 B.C.

GREECE

Greece In the ninth century Greek city-states began to emerge in Greece and Asia Minor: small cities controlling an agricultural hinterland and governed by aristocracies, and later oligarchies or democracies. Over the centuries competition between states made warfare a regular part of life, and most states raised citizen armies at need; in Sparta, where the citizens controlled and oppressed a subject people (Helots), whom they had to keep from rebellion, militarism was a central feature of life and was carried to extremes. Trade, shared religion, and shared culture acted as counterweights to conflict, and the pan-Hellenic games held at regular intervals (of which the Olympic games were the most important) served to sublimate interstate aggression.

Trade with the Levant introduced alphabetic writing, which the Greeks modified to create an alphabet that fully recorded all the sounds of their speech. Literacy rapidly developed, writing being used to record not only economic and political affairs but also history and literature and the ethnography of neighboring societies. Arts and crafts flourished, reaching their peak in fifth-century Athens. After the Greeks' success in repulsing two invasions by the mighty Persian Empire in 490 and 480 B.C., Athens became the foremost power in Greece, combining democracy at home with high-handed imperialism in the states with which it was in principle allied. By the 430s its actions and attitudes had provoked war with Sparta, into which much of Greece was drawn, to the detriment of all. In the tragic aftermath, when Sparta, Thebes, and Athens vied for power, the barbaric northern state of Macedonia was able to seize control progressively of all of Greece and under Alexander conquered most of the known world, spreading Greek culture from Egypt to the borders of India, in Hellenistic kingdoms consolidated by Alexander's successors.

Greek Colonies In the eighth century growing populations and limited agricultural land in Greece encouraged expanding city-states to look overseas for land to settle; the earliest known colony was established by Euboea at Pithecussae in central Italy around 775 B.C., and others were founded in eastern Spain, southern France, central and southern Italy and Sicily, and around the shores of the Black Sea during the eighth to sixth centuries. These colonies took the overflow of population from their home states and sent home grain and other produce, but they also acted as trading stations that could tap the resources of the European interior and the Atlantic coast. The Greeks also established a warm trading relationship with the Tartessians on the southern Atlantic coast of Iberia, but after a major confrontation in 537 (battle of Alalia), in which Greeks fought Etruscans and their Carthaginian allies, the southern Iberian route to the Atlantic metal sources was closed to the Greeks, who turned instead to routes through France. A key settlement here was Massalia (modern Marseilles), founded by Phocaea around 600 B.C., which gave access via the Rhône to central France and Germany and to the trading networks leading on from there.

Greek colonies in Italy and particularly Sicily became involved in power struggles against the Etruscans and Carthaginians, as well as sometimes taking sides in the internal conflicts of Greece. Allied for a time with the rising Roman state against the Carthaginians, they were eventually swallowed up by its expansion. By 146 B.C. even the Greek mainland had fallen to the Romans.

ETRUSCANS

In the ninth century a number of substantial settlements developed in central Italy (Villanovan culture), surrounded by sizable cemeteries of cremation burials, sometimes placed in urns shaped like huts, with grave goods including *fibulae* (brooches). The Villanovans controlled substantial supplies of copper, tin, and lead from the Colline Metallifere, and the abundant iron deposits of Elba. Iron began to be worked here occasionally in the 10th century and became more common from the eighth century. The region's mineral wealth attracted trade from the Greeks and Phoenicians through the eighth century; this introduced luxury goods, such as Greek pottery, sparking the rapid development of local imitations.

At this time richer burials suggest the emergence of a ranked society.

The Etruscans, who developed a civilized society in this region from around 700 B.C., were descendants of the Villanovans. Twelve city-states emerged by the seventh century B.C., allied in a religious league and sharing a vivid and distinctive culture into which they wove ideas and innovations adopted from their Greek neighbors and from farther afield in West Asia. They enhanced the high agricultural potential of the region by innovations in farming management, increasing productivity. They built roads and bridges, elaborate water systems, and massive city walls and gates, as well as a variety of chamber tombs, sometimes painted with scenes of life, including feasting and dancing.

Trade and industry were key elements in the Etruscan city-states. Exploitation of the local metal ores enabled the Etruscans not only to satisfy local demand but also to supply considerable amounts of metal ore and finished goods to their Greek neighbors in central and southern Italy and Sicily. In the sixth century the Greeks came to dominate the northern part of the western Mediterranean basin. Squeezed out of trading in the western Mediterranean seas, the Etruscans expanded to the north and sought new markets across the Alps and through their eastern ports of Spina and Adria, which gave them direct access down the Adriatic to Greece.

Expansion beyond their heartland by 500 B.C. brought the Etruscans control of much of northern Italy, and of areas of Italy to their south, including Rome, then a small town. Within a century of the Romans' expulsion of their Etruscan kings, however, the Roman state had grown strong enough to challenge and then defeat the individual city-states of the Etruscan league, climaxing in the capture of Veii in 396; the process was complete by the second century. While Etruscan culture underlay much of that of the Romans, the Etruscan states and Etruscan identity were obliterated.

ROME

Traditionally founded in 753 B.C., Rome was a series of linked villages that gradually coalesced into a town when it was part of the Etruscan ecumene in the sixth century. In 509 B.C. the Romans expelled their Etruscan king and founded the Republic. The sack of Rome by a band of Celtic freebooters around 387 B.C. dealt a serious blow to Roman pride and self-confidence, making them for centuries oversensitive to renewed Celtic threats and exaggerated in their responses. Expansion in the late fourth and third centuries brought the Romans up against Etruscans and central and southern Italians, whose territories they were able to absorb. For a while the Greek states in Italy were their allies against the Carthaginians, but eventually they too were taken over. Their crushing defeat of the Carthaginians by the mid-second century brought the Romans control of the former Carthaginian empire in North Africa, Iberia, and Sicily, and left them without an opponent in the western Mediterranean. At the same time they conquered Greece. Over the following century the Romans continued to expand, gaining control of the rest of Iberia, whose metal ores in particular were a major attraction, southern France, parts of North Africa, western Anatolia and the Levant, and the Adriatic coast of the Balkans. By the second century A.D. they had also conquered the rest of Europe west of the Rhine-Danube line and ruled a significant part of West Asia.

Southeastern Europe

THRACE

Macedonia straddled the region between civilized Greece and the societies that the Greeks knew as barbarians. The inhabitants of the Balkans from the western Black Sea up into the Carpathian basin were referred to by Herodotus and other Greek authors as Thracians and were said to be related to the Trojans. Although they farmed the region, their main settlements were strongly fortified sites in upland regions, where they practiced pastoralism and exploited iron sources. Like the steppe nomads with whom they had close ties, they were warriors and horse riders, as well as cattle rustlers. Hoards buried when trouble loomed, for example, when huge bands of Celts invaded the region in the third century, contained numerous vessels of gold and silver, elaborately decorated with designs that reflect both local traditions and styles and ideas adopted not only from their neighbors, the Greeks and Persians, but also from distant India, central Asia, and even China. Similarly, what is known of their religion from classical sources and archaeology indicates that the Thracians shared some beliefs and practices with Zoroastrianism and Tantrism.

While the majority of the population were probably cremated and their ashes buried in flat-grave cemeteries, the Thracian elite were buried in rock-cut tombs or under barrows, sometimes accompanied by a sacrificed wife, and furnished with impressive gold and silver vessels and jewelry; the monumental royal tombs were modeled on Macedonian *tholoi*. The establishment of Greek colonies on the Thracian coast allowed local elites to enhance their prestige by acquiring luxury goods such as wine and wine-drinking vessels. Thracians were also employed by the Persians as mercenaries. By the fourth century B.C. the Thracians were using silver coinage. Numerous Thracian tribes are referred to by classical authors; while many remained politically fluid, some strong leaders were able to carve out tribal states, such as that of the Odysai between Macedonia and the Black Sea, with its capital at Seuthopolis. This state expanded and contracted, depending on the strength of its kings, eventually becoming a client kingdom of the Romans, who annexed it in A.D. 46.

STEPPE CULTURES

Beyond the Thracian lands lay the steppe, stretching across Asia to the borders of China and inhabited by pastoral nomads and horse-riding elite warriors armed with swords, spears, and efficient composite bows and armor-piercing arrows, whose movements and conflicts sometimes impinged upon Europe. In the early centuries of the first millennium the Cimmerians were active both as raiders and as mercenaries in the northern regions of the Near East and in Asia Minor, and they or related groups may have made incursions into eastern Europe. Close relations between steppe nomads and the more settled inhabitants of the Balkans provided one of the routes by which Europe acquired steppe-bred horses, used for riding in Europe from around 800 B.C.

By the seventh century, when the Greeks began establishing colonies on the coasts of the Black Sea, the Cimmerians had been displaced and the Caucasus and adjacent steppe region were home to the Scythians, a name that covers both elite warrior horsemen and steppe pastoralists, and farmers settled in the river valleys, whom they dominated. The Scythians buried their dead kings in wooden chambers under substantial barrows, accompanied by sacrificed horses and retainers, often in large numbers, and with lavish grave goods. Frozen tombs of similar steppe groups found at Pazyryk in the Altai region of central Asia have preserved wonderful clothing, cushions, saddles, horse gear, wall hangings and other textiles of woven or felted wool, leather, and fur, as well as imported Near Eastern carpets and Chinese silk; extraordinary carved wooden objects; and tattooed bodies. Scythian burials lack the preserved organic materials but have yielded a treasury of gold work that shares their decorative themes and exuberant style, in which animals are prominent. Gold objects, including vessels, combs, and other personal ornaments, also depict scenes of life, including milking, hunting, and preparing sheepskins; some of these pieces show artistic influences from their Greek neighbors with whom the Scythians had a lively trade, exchanging grain and slaves for luxury goods, including wine and drinking sets. By the mid-sixth century strongholds were developing in the forest steppe, of which the largest was Belsk (probably ancient Gelonus), a vast site enclosed by a rampart 20 miles (33 kilometers) long; it contained villages, industrial areas, and granaries, but was probably mainly a seasonal meeting place for nomadic groups with their animals. By the third century the Scythians had settled in the Crimea and had been replaced on the steppe by another nomad group, the Sarmatians.

Temperate Europe

When classical writers began to refer to the inhabitants of western and central Europe, they called them Celts (Keltoi, Celti), Gauls (Galli), or Galatians (Galatae). These people spoke a number of related languages, from which modern languages such as Welsh descend, and were organized in tribes that often acknowledged interrelationships. By the second century Celtic-speaking tribes occupied most of the area from Iberia to the Carpathian basin, mixed in some areas with other tribal groups, such as the Iberians. How far back in time one can use the label "Celt," however, is debated, and it is customary to apply the term only in the later Iron Age (La Tène period, from c. 500 B.C.). Celtic speakers were also present in Britain by the time of Roman contact; whether they settled there during the later first millennium or were descended from the earlier indigenous inhabitants is hotly debated. The Atlantic coastal region, including Britain, was culturally distinct from the La Tène zone for most of the pre-Roman Iron Age, as it had been for millennia, although trading relations made it open to influences and ideas from the continental interior. La Tène metalwork, for example, was imported into Britain, and its decoration inspired new native art styles.

The demands of the Mediterranean powers for raw materials, such as metals, and slaves had a major impact on the scale of trade and production in temperate Europe, bringing the two systems into a close relationship, which culminated by the first century A.D. in the Roman conquest of Europe up to the Rhine. By this time many Celtic tribes had become partially urbanized, with substantial fortified settlements that were the political, religious, economic, and industrial foci of their area.

In the north and in the east societies remained smaller in scale. The tribes of this area, like the Celts, were warriors as well as farmers; they had many religious practices and other aspects of culture in common with the Celts, and enjoyed both trading and warring relations with them. The Romans knew these tribes as Germani and considered them distinct from the Celts, a distinction reinforced by the later frontier of the Roman Empire at the Rhine, with the Celts inside and the Germans outside, but in reality the boundary and tribal identities were probably rather fluid until crystallized by Roman realpolitik.

IBERIA

The long-established metalworking traditions of Iberia were given a new stimulus by the arrival of foreign traders in search of metal. Traditionally, the

Phoenicians founded a port-of-trade at Gadir (Cádiz), an island near the estuary of the Guadalquivir, around 1100 B.C., and certainly by the eighth century Phoenician trading settlements were established along the Atlantic coast of southern Iberia, situated at the mouths of rivers to gain access to the region's metal ores, particularly silver, gold, and tin, while other colonies were founded on the Mediterranean coast. The major native settlement of Tartessos, which is probably to be identified with modern Huelva at the mouth of the Río Tinto, channeled some of the material from the interior to the Phoenicians, and in exchange the Tartessians acquired jewelry, ivories, bronze vessels, and other items of superb Phoenician craftsmanship, as well as goods from elsewhere in the Mediterranean carried by Phoenician traders, such as amphorae of Greek oil and fine Greek pottery. Many of these items, acquired by the local elite, were deposited in rich burials, such as those at Carmona, or found their way far inland through trade or social networks.

Additional colonies were established farther north on the Atlantic coast of Iberia in the eighth century, again giving the Phoenicians access to metal ores. Mediterranean demand for these stimulated native mining and production and trade along the Atlantic facade. By 550 southern coastal Iberia was part of the Carthaginian sphere, while farther north the Greeks had established a colony at Emporion (Ampurias). The Greeks also traded directly with the Tartessians in the sixth century despite the presence of the long-established Phoenician port-of-trade at Gadir; hostile relations with Carthage would have barred them from the region from the fifth century. Around the trading settlements and in the Tartessian hinterland the native Iberians developed an increasingly civilized way of life, with emerging towns and an art style that blended native traditions with ideas borrowed from their Mediterranean trading partners. Farther north in the interior were tribes known collectively as the Celtiberians, who from the sixth century were burying their warrior elite with weapons and sometimes horse trappings. They maintained close links with communities across the Pyrenees in southern France. By the fourth century they too were becoming urbanized, living in heavily defended hilltop strongholds and developing their own written language.

THE ATLANTIC

The inhabitants of Atlantic Iberia were distinct from those farther east, forming part of the still active Atlantic trading network. By the fourth or third century Carthaginian traders probably reached the coast of Galicia, from which they could access additional metal sources. It is possible this region was the area known as the Cassiterides or Oestrymnis, from which the Carthaginians and later the Romans obtained tin; the Greeks also derived tin from here, either via the Phoenicians or by direct involvement in Atlantic trade via the rivers of France. Alternatively, these names may refer to Cornwall, which was also trading tin to foreigners and which was known to the literate Mediterranean world. Cornish tin was traded across the Channel to Gaul and thence by river to the Mediterranean.

The mineral resources of the Atlantic continued to be in demand in the European interior, and the growing requirements of the distant Mediterranean states increased the quantities of raw materials that entered the trading networks, although Mediterranean luxuries only rarely reached the northern areas of the Atlantic system, western France, Britain, and Ireland. Southern England was a crossroads where the Atlantic network intersected with that of the continental interior. At times it was more closely linked to the one than the other. In the eighth and seventh centuries Britain and Ireland were closely integrated into the continental trade network at the expense of their involvement with Atlantic trade, but from the sixth century onward the European interior accessed Atlantic resources, including those of Britain and Ireland, along the Loire from Brittany, which now became the main middleman between the two networks, also trading its own metals and other resources. By the fourth century Britain was also enjoying access to continental trade across the North Sea again. The routes by which goods moved also spread the designs and techniques of Celtic art, which were enthusiastically adopted and built on by communities in Brittany, Britain, and Ireland.

During the first millennium a variety of defended settlements characterized western regions within the Atlantic zone. The *castros* of Galicia varied in size; these were nucleated settlements of stone houses inside stone defenses on hilltops. Their inhabitants used decorated pottery, and their leaders wore distinctive gold torcs. They created stone sculptures of warriors and bulls, and their rituals involved the use of stone sauna baths. In Brittany most people lived in farmsteads defended by a bank and sometimes a ditch. Souterrains, underground chambers accessed by tunnels, were associated with the settlements and may have been used for storage. Banks and ditches were also used to cut off headlands, forming cliff castles in which people could take refuge but which may also have had a ritual function. The people of coastal Brittany also erected dressed stone stelae, sometimes decorated, which may have been territorial markers. In southwest England and Wales the situation was similar: the landscape was densely settled with defended farmsteads ("rounds" and "raths"), and in Cornwall these had *fogous*, stone-built subterranean chambers probably used for storage; there were many cliff castles, too. Cliff castles were also built in western Ireland, where stone forts surrounded farmsteads and larger settlements. In western and northern Scotland various forms of impressive circular stone cellular houses and towers, the brochs, wheelhouses, and duns, were constructed, home to individual families or larger communities; these may have been built more to impress the neighbors than to ward off their aggression. Other settlements were defended by being located on artificial or natural islands within lakes (crannogs).

CENTRAL AND WESTERN EUROPE

Hallstatt C: Eighth and Seventh Centuries
Influences and possibly incursions from the steppe around 800 B.C. introduced the practice of horse riding. Horses themselves may have been imported from the steppe region, where nomadic pastoralists buried important individuals in wooden chambers under mounds, accompanied by weapons, horses, and sometimes vehicles. This practice may have inspired the appearance in central Europe, in the prosperous region between southern Germany and Bohemia, of a number of wealthy burials in which the body was laid on a wagon for a bier and was accompanied by a set of weapons, bronze horse trappings, and other fine goods. Other well-endowed burials had similar grave goods but lacked the high-

est status symbol of the wagon. These burials reflect growing differentiation in society and the status accorded to warriors.

The salt mines at Hallstatt entered their period of greatest prosperity in the seventh and sixth centuries, reflected in the rich array of artifacts placed in burials here, including bronze buckets and jewelry, swords and daggers of bronze and iron, some with gilded hilts, and fine pottery. The salt in the mines has preserved many of the organic objects used by the miners, including leather backpacks in which they carried out the lumps of salt. By the fifth century, however, Hallstatt had been eclipsed by new mines at Dürrnberg bei Hallein farther north.

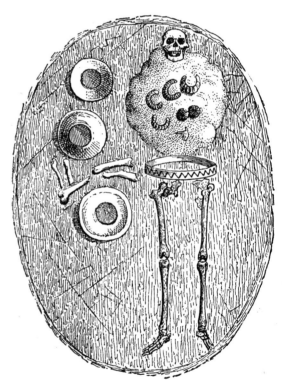

2.10 A burial from the Iron Age cemetery at Hallstatt. This individual was partially cremated, his torso being reduced to ashes that were deposited in the pots placed within the grave. (Figuier, Louis. Primitive Man. London: Chatto and Windus, 1876)

Hallstatt D: 600–450 B.C. The establishment of a Greek colony at Massalia around 600 B.C. had a significant impact on the patterns of trade and power within transalpine Europe. Expeditions by Greek traders in search of raw materials brought them up the Rhône and Saône to the Burgundy region of France. From here it was a short distance to the Seine, which linked central France to the North Sea coast and by a short sea crossing to Britain. Burgundy also gave access to routes into southern Germany, significantly west of the area where the richest Hallstatt C burials had taken place. In both Burgundy and southern Germany the preexisting native chiefdoms, focused on a few substantial hillforts, gained symbols of power and prestige through trading as middlemen with the Greeks, receiving wine and luxury goods, some, like the enormous Vix krater (wine-mixing bowl), made to cater to barbarian tastes for ostentation. Wine amphorae, Etruscan bronze flagons, and fine Greek Attic pottery were prominent among the imports in exchange for which the Greeks received gold and other metals, furs, amber, and slaves. Many imports ended up as grave goods in the burials of chiefs who, as in the preceding Hallstatt C period, were often placed on wagons in wooden chambers under large earthen mounds: Prominent examples include the Hohmichele barrow at Heuneberg and the Hochdorf barrow; in the latter the wagon was loaded with grave goods while the chief was laid out on a bronze couch. Now, however, among the grave goods weaponry came second to equipment for drinking, not only imported vessels but also local items such as drinking horns; feasting had become the means by which a chief demonstrated his status. Smaller barrows set around the chief's tomb housed the remains of the local elite.

The chiefs and their entourage dwelt in fortified hillforts, but the majority of the tribe farmed within the surrounding countryside, a pattern repeated across Europe at this time. The German hillfort of Heuneberg gives a striking illustration of the value placed on exotica: While for the most part the hillfort's ramparts were, like others of the time, timber-framed constructions of wood, stone, and earth, at one stage these were replaced by Mediterranean-style walls with bastions, built of clay-brick on a stone footing.

Over much of the rest of western Europe a similar but less prosperous society flourished, consisting of small tribes mainly of farmers living in villages or farmsteads, giving allegiance to a chief based in a hillfort. The latter maintained an entourage of elite warriors who spent much of their time in hunting or in raiding their neighbors.

La Tène A: 500–400 In the sixth century the Etruscans expanded into northern Italy, where they encountered Celts, who were beginning to settle there. This and the loss to the Greeks of their western Mediterranean trade encouraged the Etruscans to develop trade across the Alps. The importance of routes through the Alpine passes is underlined by occasional finds of hoards, such as a collection of gold torcs and armlets deposited at Erstfeld along the route through the St. Gotthard pass. Trade to the Burgundy–south Germany region that had been the main sixth-century beneficiary of Mediterranean trade declined in the fifth century when Greek interest in the Rhône corridor decreased in favor of other routes between the Mediterranean and the Atlantic.

Mediterranean goods such as Etruscan beaked flagons now began to appear in the regions farther to the north, east, and west, with particular concentrations of wealth appearing in Bohemia and the Marne/Champagne and Moselle/middle Rhine regions. The growing importance of iron contributed to the rise in importance of the Hunsrück-Eifel area (middle Rhine) since the region had abundant iron deposits. Some of the Mediterranean goods were moved through trade, while others were probably booty from raiding expeditions into Italy or accumulated by Celtic mercenaries who had fought for the Etruscans. This is reflected in the distribution of imported luxuries, which occurred more widely but in smaller concentrations than before. The growing prosperity of these regions was marked by a series of wealthy burials placed on two-wheeled chariots, for example, at Somme-Bionne in Champagne.

The trade in Mediterranean luxuries contributed to the emergence of La Tène ("Celtic") art, which drew on Greek, Etruscan, and Phoenician designs, motifs, and shapes and reworked them with native traditions to produce a vibrant style of decorated metalwork, particularly concentrated on weapons, vessels, and ornaments. Some of the designs were repeated on pottery and presumably on perishable materials such as wood and textiles. Geometric and

Map 10. *Europe in the Early La Tène period*

abstract designs were combined with symbols such as the duck that harked back to the artwork of the Bronze Age. Celtic craftsmen exercised a range of metalworking skills, casting elaborate shapes, decorating bronze and gold objects with engraved, cut-out, and repoussé designs, inlaying objects with glass or coral, and adding small animal figures or grotesque human heads. Beginning on the middle Rhine, Celtic art styles were adopted widely across transalpine Europe, although they made little impression on Iberia, which had its own styles of artwork.

Substantial settlements with many urban features, such as Vače, were developing at the head of the Adriatic, but, in contrast to western and central Europe, Mediterranean luxury goods played little part here. Instead, the elite used local products such as glass beads, sheet bronze goods, and decorated bronze buckets (*situlae*). The latter were also popular in northern Italy, an area where native cultures received influences from the Mediterranean world at second hand via the Etruscans.

Outside the regions that developed direct trading relations with the Mediterranean, many communities continued to live in hillforts or lowland stockades, which increased in number in the sixth and fifth centuries. These fortified settlements acted as local chiefly centers and refuges in times of attack, and often contained storage facilities for large stocks of grain. Some of these fortified settlements housed sizable communities—Biskupin in Poland, for example, contained more than 100 houses—and were centers of considerable craft activity, such as Závist in the Czech Republic. Few Mediterranean luxury goods entered the systems by which goods circulated in these areas, but trade in

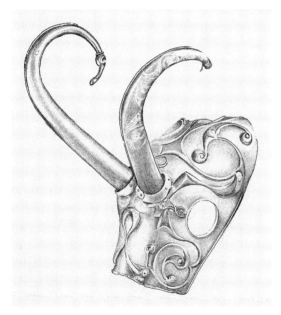

2.11 The chamfrein or pony-cap found in a peat bog at Torrs, Kirkcudbrightshire, Scotland, a fine example of the decorative bronzework owned by the elite of the later Iron Age. The two bronze drinking horns found with the pony-cap were added to it in recent times. (Drawing by Audrey McIntosh, from material in the National Museums of Scotland, Edinburgh)

the regional products of transalpine Europe continued, carrying raw materials, such as coral and metal ores, and manufactured goods such as swords. In Britain many hillforts were abandoned after around 400 B.C., but those that survived in many cases endured for centuries.

La Tène B: 400–275 Migrations After about 400 B.C. Mediterranean trade into transalpine Europe seems to have ceased. Trade across the Alps may have been disrupted by the Celtic migrations that began in earnest around 400, while in southern France the Greek colony at Massalia had ceased to trade up the Rhône, instead becoming involved in local power struggles.

As populations rose in western and central Europe, some groups, attracted by the wealth of the Mediterranean world or because resources in their homeland were under pressure, left to seek their fortune, either as individual tribal bands or as larger confederations of groups from a number of tribes. In some cases these were bands of young warriors looking for booty and adventure; in others cases they also included women and children and were seeking new lands to settle. Some Celts had settled in northern Italy in the sixth century B.C. Around 400 B.C. their numbers were swelled by a substantial influx of Celts, known to the Romans as Gauls; these included Insubres and Boii, who settled around Milan and in the Po plain, respectively. An army of freebooters descended on the Etruscan cities, defeated a Roman army at Allia, and swept south, sacking Rome around 387; the Romans paid a large bribe to induce them to return to the Celtic settlements of Gallia Cisalpina. Regarding them thereafter as a significant threat, the Romans eventually conquered the Cisalpine Celts between 232 and 190 B.C.; the Boii resettled in Bohemia.

During the late fifth and early fourth centuries, Celtic groups also moved eastward, settling along the Danube and in the Carpathian basin, and raiding into Illyria. Alexander the Great, on a punitive raid in Thrace, encountered a group of these Celts, known to the Greeks as Galatians. In 281–279 a huge Galatian confederation swept south into Macedonian Greece. Here the army quarreled and split, one group continuing southeast into Asia Minor, where they established a Galatian warrior aristocracy; this lasted until the Romans conquered the region in the first century B.C. The other group under Brennus continued south into Greece, intending to loot the treasuries of the shrine at Delphi. A Greek army stoutly defended the shrine and eventually the Celts were driven off, with the loss of Brennus and 26,000 men, according to Greek sources, though they may have succeeded first in plundering the shrine.

Partly as a result of the migrations, by the third century Celtic tribes and La Tène culture were spread over a huge area from France to the Balkans, with the related Celtiberians over much of Iberia. There was a substantial area settled by Galatians in Anatolia, and the inhabitants of much of Britain and Ireland may also have been Celts.

In northern Europe and Scandinavia, small settlements accommodating only a few families continued to be the norm. These contained houses, in some cases including stalled shelter for the family's livestock, and other buildings for agricultural or domestic use.

The abundance of bogs in Denmark, the Low Countries, and Britain have made them particularly fertile regions for recovering evidence of the widespread European practice of offering sacrifices in watery places. These included not only valued possessions but also people who were ritually killed, often using several methods in conjunction. Offerings frequently accumulated over long periods in the same, hallowed, place; they included fine jewelry, weapons and parade armor, metal vessels, and other objects including slave chains. Among the objects thus deposited at Gundestrup in Denmark was a fine silver-gilt cauldron decorated with a number of scenes featuring ritual practices and gods. Although it ended its life in Scandinavia, it was probably manufactured in Thrace and incorporated ideas from much farther afield, including India, as well as Celtic Europe.

An exceptional votive deposit at Hjortspring off Jutland contained a boat and a considerable quantity of weapons. It is thought that this was a thanksoffering for victory, comprising the arms of a defeated army of at least 80 men.

LA TÈNE C-D 275 B.C. TO THE ROMAN CONQUEST

Iberia and Southern France Around the Mediterranean coast of France some native tribes responded to the presence of Greek colonies by developing defended settlements with Greek features, such as street planning and construction in dressed stone, but retaining markedly nonclassical aspects, such as the religious preoccupation with severed heads. Other settlements, particularly Montlaures, Carcaso (Carcassonne), and Tolosa (Toulouse) on the Aude-Garonne route, developed at strategic points on the routes that linked the Greek colonies with Atlantic France. Silver coins copied from Greek prototypes began to circulate among the tribes of southern France. By the third century B.C. Roman traders were also active in the coastal region, trading with Greek settlements. When in 154 B.C. the Greek towns were threatened by hostile hill tribes, Massalia sought military help from the Romans.

Victory in the Second Punic War in 206 B.C. won the Romans the Carthaginian territories in southern and eastern Iberia, giving them control of the gold, silver, and copper mines as well as extremely productive agricultural land. While some Iberians welcomed the Romans as liberators from Carthaginian rule, others rose against them. Native resistance escalated in 154, when the Lusitanians in the southwest rose in revolt and the Celtiberians in the center of the peninsula were drawn in as their allies. It was not until 133 B.C. that the Romans succeeded in subduing these regions, treating conquered towns with extreme brutality. When the Celtiberian stronghold of Numantia fell after a long siege, most of its inhabitants were sold into slavery.

The Romans accessed their Iberian possessions overland along the coast, a route that was threatened by hostile tribes, including the Saluvii, who also posed a threat to the Greek and friendly native towns of southern Gaul. The Romans mounted a campaign against the Saluvii, Allobroges, and Arverni in 125–121 B.C., savagely sacking the Saluvii's oppidum (tribal center) at Entremont; they thereafter decided to annex the region to safeguard their interests, creating the province of Gallia Transalpina, stretching inland up the Aude and Garonne. In succeeding years they founded a port at Narbo (Narbonne) and seized Tolosa, gaining control of the Garonne route to the Atlantic and thus direct access to the Atlantic trade network and its mineral resources; their participation increased the volume of goods in circulation.

Map 11. *Europe in the Late Iron Age*

Legend:
- Expansion of Roman state by 201 B.C.
- Expansion of Roman state by 100 B.C.
- Expansion of Roman state by 44 B.C.
- Celtic languages in 1st century B.C.
- ·········· Dacians under Burebista

0   250   500 miles
0   250   500 km

Eastern Europe   The eastern Alps, source of copper, iron, and salt, saw the emergence of a small state, the kingdom of Noricum, with its capital at Noreia (Magdalensberg). This became a center of iron working, producing, among other goods, welded swords that were in considerable demand among neighboring communities. After an initial confrontation over settlement in the Aquileia region (at the head of the Adriatic) around 180 B.C., the Romans and the people of Noricum established friendly relations.

Around 120 B.C. a confederation of tribes from Jutland and the North European Plain, under the leadership of the Cimbri and Teutones, started to migrate south, moving first into the middle Danube, whence they expelled the Celtic Scordisci tribe. They then attacked Noricum and defeated a Roman army that was sent against them. Moving on to raid southern Gaul, they reignited opposition to the Romans among the tribes the latter had subdued a decade before. After further defeats, in 109, 107, and 105, the Romans at last won decisive victories against the Cimbri in 102 and the Teutones in 101. The barbarian threat was averted, but the Romans remained sensitive to potential trouble from Celtic Europe.

Noricum continued to flourish as a state in the first century, trading with both Celtic Europe and the Romans; in 70 B.C. the Noricans started to issue their own coinage. The importance of Roman trade is emphasized by the establishment around 100 B.C. of a Roman trading colony outside the oppidum of Noreia. By the end of the first century B.C. Roman advances into the Balkans, bringing the lands up to the Danube under Roman control, made it expedient for the Romans to annex Noricum, too.

To the southeast of the Roman provinces along the Danube lay Thrace. This was left as a client kingdom by Augustus but was annexed by the Romans in A.D. 46, giving them control of all the lands on the west side of the Danube, which with the Rhine formed a natural frontier.

North of the Danube the Dacians, a group related to the people of Thrace, inhabited the uplands of Transylvania. Around 60 B.C. they expanded, forming a large state known as Dacia in the Carpathian basin and the areas beyond to the south, under the rule of King Burebista and his priest Deceneus, although it contracted again after Burebista's murder in 40 B.C. The Dacians attacked the Black Sea towns but imported grain and sold slaves for silver coin to settlements on the Adriatic, becoming increasingly influenced by Mediterranean culture. The state was strengthened by King Decebalus from the 80s A.D.; raids on the adjacent Roman provinces provoked confrontation, and between A.D. 105 and 107 the Romans defeated the Dacians and annexed their ter-

ritory, sacking the complex of fortified settlements and sanctuaries at Sarmizegethusa, where they found huge quantities of gold and silver. Many of the inhabitants of Dacia fled, leaving the Romans in control of the mineral wealth of a depopulated area. This extension of Roman territory beyond the natural frontier of the Danube proved too costly to maintain, and around A.D. 250 it was abandoned.

Oppida   Control of southern France and its routes into central Europe and the Atlantic network gave the Romans access to European markets for their wine and the tableware for drinking it in style. In exchange they obtained metals and other raw materials, furs, hides and hunting dogs, grain, and especially slaves, needed in increasing numbers to work on Italian farming estates.

The territories adjacent to areas now under Roman control began to reflect Roman influences. Roman styles of architecture appeared in the developing tribal centers (oppida), and it is possible that Mediterranean influences played some part in the emergence of these Celtic towns. Mediterranean luxuries were in demand, and a softer lifestyle began to develop among the tribes of central Gaul, a factor in the ease with which these were bought under Roman control in the mid-first century. Roman institutions were also adopted by some of the tribes in the Roman sphere of influence: The Helvetii in Switzerland, for example, replaced kingship with rule by elected magistrates.

From the later second century onward, fortified tribal centers began to emerge in France and elsewhere. Known as oppida, they had many features of towns, acting as the administrative, political, and industrial center for tribal groups farming the surrounding countryside. They replaced the earlier hillforts, sometimes being located in the same place, but generally not, though they were usually strategically placed for defense. Strongly fortified with ramparts of stone, timber, and earth, they might have additional defenses such as a glacis, dikes, and thorn hedges, and the gateways were often complex defensive structures with outworks.

Within the fortifications of an oppidum were residential areas, often laid out as a planned settlement with streets. The houses could be small or more substantial rectangular wooden structures, sometimes with stone foundations. In many cases the influence of Roman architecture could be seen in the design of the houses, especially those of the elite and the tribal chief or king. Many craftsmen lived and worked within the oppidum, bringing industry under the control of the tribal leader. Industrial activities included working in bronze, glass, gold, and other fine materials, as well as creating more everyday objects such as iron tools and weapons and pottery. The introduction of the potter's wheel now made it possible for Celtic craftsmen to mass-produce fine vessels such as pedestalled jars and other luxury tableware associated with wine drinking.

Many oppida also contained a mint as tribal kings adopted the idea of coinage. High denomination coins may have been used to reward royal followers or as a medium of exchange with other tribal leaders, while lower ones facilitated ordinary transactions, indicating the beginnings of a market economy. Coinage also served as a vehicle for royal propaganda. One part of the oppidum was set aside for religious installations; these could include built shrines but also ritual pits and other Celtic sanctuaries.

While many continental oppida were relatively compact settlements, often strategically located on elevated ground, those in southeast England often enclosed huge areas: Camulodunon, for instance, was more than 10 square miles (16 square kilometers) in extent, enclosing a royal residence, separate settled areas, burials, a sanctuary, and a great deal of open ground.

Outside the southeast, and in other backward areas of the Celtic world, as in much of the Germanic lands, territories were smaller and centered on hillforts or other defended sites, which provided a focus for the tribe and a defense in time of need but housed only the chief and his entourage.

Gaul In the first century B.C. the personal ambitions of individual Roman leaders began to affect their policies toward the barbarians. In 58 B.C. the Helvetii, a tribe in Switzerland, decided to move west to settle in central Gaul. Seeing this as both an indirect threat to the Roman province of Gallia Transalpina and an opportunity for glory, Julius Caesar turned them back by force, causing the deaths of several hundred thousand of them. In the same year intertribal conflict in Gaul and the activities of a band of Germanic mercenaries under Ario-

vistus gave Caesar further opportunities for involvement in Gaulish affairs and justification at home for a policy of annexation. Over the period 58 to 53 B.C. he successfully attacked a number of Gallic tribes, bringing the whole of France and Belgium up to the Rhine under Roman rule and mounting two expeditions against British tribes that had given support to their colleagues, the Veneti of Brittany, a major player in the Atlantic trade network whose fleet Caesar destroyed. The Romans dealt brutally with their opponents, virtually wiping out the Belgae and Eburones, who had resisted strongly. Opposition to the Romans became united in the winter of 53–52 B.C., and almost all Gaul rose against them, sucking in Caesar's Gallic allies. The Gallic forces were led by the chief of the Arverni tribe, Vercingetorix, who enjoyed considerable success until his army was besieged at Alesia in 52 B.C. The Romans' superior discipline and siegecraft brought them victory and Vercingetorix surrendered. The fall of another stronghold, Uxellodunum, the following year ended Gallic resistance. Gaul lay devastated, with more than a million of its inhabitants slain or enslaved, the countryside ravaged by the military campaigns and Vercingetorix's scorched earth policy, and its wealth seized by the conqueror. It was not until after the Roman civil war ended in the victory of Octavian (Augustus) in 31 B.C. that steps began to be taken to organize Gaul within the empire. At this time, too, the Romans conquered the remaining, northwest, corner of Iberia.

Britain Though unconquered, the southeast of Britain now became more strongly focused on the Roman world, importing wine, Roman and Gallic luxury tableware, and exotic foods such as olive oil and fish sauce for feasting; these also appeared in their burials. The Atlantic sea trade now became less important than cross Channel trade, moving the center of prosperity from the south coast to the southeast and the Thames estuary.

Tribes in the adjacent regions who were in trading relations with the southeast received limited quantities of such imports, but people continued to live in farmsteads and small villages, with hillforts as their tribal centers. Craftsmanship displayed in goods such as jewelry and weaponry was of a high standard but reflected native Celtic traditions rather

2.12 Pacifying the natives: A detail from the Roman distance slab found at Bridgeness on the Antonine Wall in Scotland, briefly held as the Roman frontier in Britain (Drawing by Audrey McIntosh, from material in the National Museums of Scotland, Edinburgh)

than Mediterranean stylistic influences. The regions to the north and west, the Atlantic zone, were unaffected, continuing their traditional way of life.

The Catuvellauni, previously based at Verlamion (St. Albans), became the most powerful tribe, conquering the Trinovantes of the east and seizing control of their center at Camulodunon (Colchester), which became the major focus for trade with the continent. Their rivals in the south, the Atrebates, allied themselves with the Romans and were rewarded when the Romans under the emperor Claudius invaded and conquered Britain in A.D. 43. The Romans rapidly gained control of the already partially civilized south and east half of England and went on to pacify the north and west, including a

massive attack on Mona (Anglesey) to destroy the power of the Druids. Despite the setback of the rising under Boudicca in A.D. 60, by the early second century the Romans were firmly in control of England and part of southern Scotland. The empire in Europe had now reached its maximum extent, with Ireland and most of Scotland outside it; these areas retained their traditional way of life.

AFTER THE ROMAN CONQUEST

Barbarians

Germanic tribesmen had often become involved in Celtic tribal conflict, and on several occasions during his campaigns Caesar had crossed the Rhine on punitive expeditions against them. The Rhine provided a natural frontier, beyond which dwelt Germanic tribes with whom the Romans engaged in a long-running and ultimately unsuccessful conflict. Unlike the Celts, who by the second-first century B.C. were developing a form of urban society, in which they had acquired a taste for the trappings of civilization, the Germani were still organized in small tribes with fluid boundaries and no higher authority. This meant that, whereas the Celts could be subdued by the capture of their oppida and leaders, the Germani engaged in endless guerrilla warfare against which the Romans could make no enduring headway. The lowest moment for the Romans came when Germani led by Arminius, who had served in the Roman army, destroyed three Roman legions.

Conflict did not, however, prevent the exchange of materials, objects, and ideas between the Roman and the barbarian worlds, and Roman glassware, for example, has been found in pagan burials well to the north in Scandinavia. Huge quantities of silver as well as Mediterranean luxury goods and wine were exchanged for materials such as furs and for slaves for which the Romans had an inexhaustible need—calculated at 140,000 per year. Within a radius of around 120 miles (200 kilometers) of the frontier, gold and particularly silver coins were valued, suggesting that a market economy was developing in areas adjacent to the empire. Beyond this, wine and the tableware to drink it from were popular and reached far north into Scandinavia. Rivalry and conflict among Germanic tribes allowed the Romans to forge alliances with some against others, as had earlier been the case with Celtic tribes, and Germanic mercenaries were often recruited into the Roman army as auxiliaries; this offered them both the opportunity to engage in warfare, their preferred way of life, and far greater material rewards than were available through local warfare. By the late fourth century A.D. barbarian recruits formed the bulk of the Roman army due to a shortage of manpower in the empire.

Population growth, pressure from neighbors, and other factors meant that migrations frequently took place within the barbarian territories, and on occasion these spilled over into Roman territory and were repulsed with varying degrees of difficulty. The problem was particularly acute in the mid-third century. By the fourth century A.D. political and economic troubles were plaguing much of the Roman Empire, and agreements were made with friendly Germanic tribes that allowed them to settle in depopulated areas, in some cases acting as a military buffer against hostile tribes. In A.D. 406 the Rhine froze, allowing hordes of Germanic tribesmen to cross into Gaul. Pressure from the Huns, steppe nomads who had swept west from their original home on the borders of China, pushed some tribes into the Balkans in the late fourth century, threatening Byzantium, now the principal capital of the Roman Empire. During the following century, the Western Roman Empire, including Rome itself, gradually fell to these tribal groups, while the Eastern Empire retained control only of the southeastern remnant of its European territory, along with parts of West Asia. The extent to which Roman institutions and culture were preserved in these overrun territories depended on a number of factors, such as the attitude of local dignitaries, the degree to which the barbarian group had already absorbed Roman ways from prolonged contact and interaction, and the speed at which resistance collapsed. In Britain, which put up a strong fight against the Angles, Saxons, and other invaders, Roman culture was all but lost, while in Gaul, which was quickly overrun, it remained strong.

Within the Empire

Roman policy toward conquered areas favored Romanization. Towns were founded to replace tribal centers, often at or near existing oppida, such as Verulamium (St. Albans), or developed out of Roman forts placed at militarily strategic places, such as Eboracum (York). Deliberate Roman foundations were intended to set a civic example to the natives and were structured around a forum, with its administrative and public buildings, including a temple to the imperial cult; other important buildings intended to inculcate the Roman way of life might include a bathhouse, a theater, or an amphitheater. Local chiefs or princes and their elite followers were encouraged to reside within the town, though they might also have country estates, and to take up civic duties, which included funding the provision of some amenities and offices.

Town houses and country villas often followed Roman models in their layout, décor, and facilities, and their owners adopted aspects of Roman dress and culture. Roman luxury goods, such as Samian pottery and classical jewelry, were used to display wealth and importance. Many Roman industries were established in conquered territories, and native industries adopted Roman methods of production and distribution. A market economy became established, and many businesses and estates became the property of absentee owners who lived in Italy or other central parts of the empire. Recruitment to the army and the granting of land to veterans in the area in which they spent their final service created conditions for considerable mixing of ethnic groups throughout the empire.

Nevertheless, being part of the Roman Empire did not entirely change the way of life of its new subjects, particularly those of lowly status and those dwelling on its periphery, in areas such as Wales. Small farmers continued as they had done for millennia, and there were few innovations in agriculture outside the large industrialized villa estates. Native crafts, such as making domestic pottery and textiles, continued as before, while Celtic art styles and traditions still flourished, exemplified by the fine metalwork that was produced. New media were embraced and blended with traditional styles, such as the decidedly unclassical designs of some mosaics.

Despite the Romans' suppression of the Druids, they preferred to tolerate or assimilate rather than destroy the religions of their subject peoples, at times embracing them themselves, as long as these did not conflict with the imperial cult, which was also an avowal of allegiance to the emperor. Many Celtic sacred places continued to be venerated; in some cases in their original form, in others replaced by Roman temples dedicated to the Celtic deity or to the latter alongside a Roman equivalent. When in the fourth century Christianity was adopted as the empire's official religion, many earlier pagan shrines were converted to churches, but earlier traditions lingered, becoming in some cases woven into local Christian belief and practice.

Earlier traditions in many other aspects of life also endured or resurfaced after the fall of the Roman Empire and made a significant contribution to later life in Europe. Subsistence farming in many areas such as highland Scotland changed little between prehistoric and recent times. The social structure of chief, warriors, and peasants familiar from the Iron Age was echoed in later times, for example, in Ireland, and the mythology of gods and heroes survived in later folk tales and oral literature and has inspired literature, music, and even political doctrines down the ages. The exuberant art of Celtic Europe continued to develop not only in the metalwork of later times but also in illuminated manuscripts, textiles, and other craft products. Europe's languages have hardly been added to since prehistoric times, and have spread across the globe, while DNA studies now reveal that the majority of Europeans today are descended from people who inhabited the continent more than 20,000 years ago.

READING

Palaeolithic

Renfrew and Bahn 2004: dating; Barton 1997, Jochim 2002a, 2002b, Stringer and Andrews 2005: general survey; Scarre 1998: Terra Amata; Gamble 1994: ice ages, colonization of Europe, Nean-

derthals; Barton 1997: Boxgrove; Barton 1997, Jochim 2002b, Mellars 1994, Van Andel and Davies, eds. 2004: modern humans; Mithen 1996, 2005: prehistoric cognition.

Early Postglacial

Milisauskas, ed. 2002, Whittle 1994, 1996, Mithen 1994, 2003, Champion et al. 1984, Barker 1985, Thorpe 1996, Price, ed. 2000: general survey; Jochim 2002c, Dennell 1983: Mesolithic; Uscinowicz 2000, Mitchell 2004, Dolukhanov 2003: postglacial climate and environment changes; Clarke 1976: environment and Mesolithic economy; Noe-Nygaard and Richter 2003: Mesolithic hunting techniques; Zohary and Hopf 2000: cultivated plants; Shwarz 2001: tuna; Van Andel and Runnels 1987, Halstead 1996, Perles 2001, Doumas 1994: Greece; Bailey 2000, Garašanin 1994: Balkans; Merpert 1994: east/steppe region; Luning 1994, Bogucki 2000: LBK; Fontana and Guerreschi 2003: Mesolithic in Alpine regions; Guilaine 1994, Barnett 2000, Binder 2000, Zilhao 2000: western Mediterranean; Straus and Morales 2003: Mesolithic Iberia; Cunliffe 2001a, Araujo et al. 2003, Bradley 1998: Atlantic facade; Verjux 2003, Scarre, ed. 1987: France; Barclay 1998, Finlayson 1998, Darvill 1987, 1996: Britain; Thomas 1996, Verhart 2003, Louwe Kooijmans 2003: northern Europe.

Neolithic Consolidation

Milisauskas and Kruk 2002a, Whittle 1994, 1996, Sherratt 1994a, 1997, Champion et al. 1984, Barker 1985, Thorpe 1996, Price, ed. 2000: general survey; Jochim 2002c, Dennell 1983: Mesolithic; Clarke 1976: environment and Mesolithic economy; Van Andel and Runnels 1987, Halstead 1996, Perles 2001: Greece; Bailey 2000, Garasanin 1994: Balkans; Merpert 1994, Lillie 2003, Dolukhanov 2004: east/steppe region; Guilaine 1994, Binder 2000, Zilhao 2000: western Mediterranean; Straus and Morales 2003: Mesolithic Iberia; Cunliffe 2001a, Schulting 2003, Araujo et al. 2003, Bradley 1998: Atlantic facade; Verjux 2003, Scarre, ed. 1987:

France; Barclay 1998, Darvill 1987, 1996: Britain; Thomas 1996, Kaelas 1994a, Zvelebil 1996, Petersen 2003, Noe-Nygaard and Richter 2003, Louwe Kooijmans 2003, Fischer and Kristiansen, ed. 2002, Fischer 2003, Price 2000: northern Europe.

Later Neolithic and Chalcolithic

Champion et al. 1984, Whittle 1996, Cunliffe 2001a, Sherratt 1994a, 1997, Milisauskas and Kruk 2002b: general survey; Halstead 1996, Van Andel and Runnels 1987: Greece; Harmatta 1992, Garasanin 1994, Merpert 1994, Mallory 1989: steppe cultures; Luning 1994: central Europe; Barclay 1998, Bewley 2003, Pryor 2003, Ashmore 1996, Darvill 1987, 1996, Budd 2000: Britain; Cunliffe 2001a: Atlantic.

Bronze Age

Champion et al. 1984, Sherratt 1994b, Harding 1994, 2000, 2002, Kristiansen 1998, Cunliffe 2001a, Mohen 1996, Demakopoulou et al. 1999: general survey; Sherratt 1997, Budd 2000: metallurgy; Halstead 1996, Van Andel and Runnels 1987: Greece; Fitton 2002: Minoans; Taylour 1983, Chadwick 1976: Mycenaeans; Peroni 1996, Jorge 1999a: Mediterranean; Dolukhanov 1999a: steppe; Kovacs 1999: Southeast Europe; Jockenhovel 1999, Vandkilde 1999, Pare 1999: central Europe; Jensen 1999, Christensen 1999: Scandinavia; Hingley 1998, Barclay 1998, Bewley 2003, Ashmore 1996, Darvill 1987, 1996: Britain.

Iron Age

Cunliffe 1994b, 1994c, 1997, 2001a, Kristiansen 1998, Collis 1984a, Wells 2002, James 1993, Twist 2001, Berresford Ellis 1988, Green, ed. 1995: general survey; Taylor 1994, Kristiansen 1998: steppe cultures; Taylor 1994, Marazov 1998: Thracians and Dacians; Spivey and Stoddart 1990, Barker and Rasmussen 1998: Etruscans; Cornell and Matthews 1982: Romans; Sacks 1995: Greeks; Cunliffe 2001a, Harrison 1988: Iberia, Cunliffe 2001a: Atlantic; Wells 1980, Collis 1984a: Hallstatt D/La Tène A trade; James 1993: Celtic migrations; James 1993, Caesar 1951: conquest of Gaul; Armit 1997, Hingley 1998, Bewley 2003, Darvill 1987, 1996, Cunliffe 1995: Britain.

3

ECONOMY

AGRICULTURE

Early European agriculture was conducted on a small scale, often using the land immediately adjacent to houses. Only with the introduction of the ard (simple plow) were larger fields opened up; forest clearance now began to increase, and more areas were brought under cultivation, gradually transforming the landscape. New crops, notably grapes and olives, and the beginnings of irrigation and water control brought greater productivity to the Mediterranean from the third millennium, alongside greater economic and sociopolitical complexity. Much of the marginal or fragile land taken into cultivation during the second millennium turned to bog or moorland in the less favorable conditions of the Iron Age and has not been cultivated since then; but the first millennium also saw the beginning of cultivation on heavier soils using iron-shod ards with coulters. Many aspects of agriculture, however, did not change, some practices and tools continuing in use even to the present day.

Crops

Prehistoric European agriculture was based on cereals and pulses, supplemented by a number of other domestic and wild plant foods. Fields of cereals were usually invaded by weeds, which were often harvested along with the cultivated grain; sometimes these were separated from the grain and discarded, but frequently they were eaten with it. The mixture of plants identified as forming the last meal of several Iron Age bog bodies probably owed much to the presence of such weeds of cultivation among the wheat or barley crop. Some of these weeds, such as oats and gold-of-pleasure, were deliberately grown as crops in their own right in later prehistory. The range of plants under cultivation increased through time, with species domesticated in Europe being added to those initially introduced from the Near East; there was, in particular, a substantial increase in the Late Bronze Age (Urnfield period) in the range of crops regularly grown; and the introduction of olive and vine cultivation in the Bronze Age Mediterranean eventually significantly changed the pattern of cultivation across much of the region.

CEREALS

Cereals were brought into cultivation in the Near East early in the Holocene period and from there were introduced into Europe, where they provided the main carbohydrate component of the diet as well as some protein; cereals were served as cooked grain or ground into flour from which bread and gruel or porridge could be made. Some cereals were also grown for fodder, and their straw could be used for many purposes, such as feeding animals, thatching, and weaving containers.

Wheat Wheat has been the main staple of most European farming communities since the beginnings of European agriculture. The earliest cultivated wheats in the Near East were emmer and einkorn, hulled varieties that have to be pounded to release the grain. These were the wheats introduced into Europe by the first farmers in the southeast, and they spread throughout Europe. Ovens identified in some settlements may have been used to parch the grain to loosen the husk before pounding.

Most other cultivated wheats are free-threshing, shedding their naked grains when threshed, and so are easier to process. Emmer and its descendant durum (or macaroni) wheat are hard wheats with low gluten content, unsuitable for making leavened bread but with great elasticity so better for making gruel, sauces, and pasta; they can also be cooked as whole grains. Free-threshing wheats spread across the Mediterranean alongside emmer in the Early Neolithic (Impressed Ware culture) and into Alpine regions by the Middle Neolithic. Durum wheat became the main variety cultivated in southern Europe by the Late Bronze Age.

A cross between emmer and a wild cereal, goat-faced grass, gave rise to spelt, a hulled wheat high in gluten, which probably arose in Transcaucasia, from where it reached eastern Europe by the fifth millennium B.C., being cultivated in the northeastern half of Europe throughout later prehistory. Spelt was particularly useful in the north as it was tolerant of cold and wet conditions and had a short growing season.

Free-threshing varieties of high-gluten wheat, breadwheat and club wheat, also spread widely from the Early Neolithic period onward. These wheats, particularly breadwheat, are suitable for making leavened bread. Except in the Mediterranean region, however, emmer and spelt remained the principal wheats under cultivation into the Roman period. The importance of breadwheat and clubwheat increased in the Bronze Age as they could be grown on the heavier soils that were being taken into cultivation.

Wheat straw could be used for making mats, baskets, and thatch and was probably also strewn as animal bedding; however, it did not make good fodder.

Barley Barley, two-row and six-row hulled and naked varieties, was brought to Europe by the first farming settlers and was grown along with wheat. A less popular crop than the latter, it nevertheless had the advantage of tolerating poorer or more saline soils and drier or colder growing conditions, making it particularly suitable for cultivation in the Mediterranean and allowing it to be grown in northern areas beyond the range of wheat. Barley became a major crop in the Mediterranean and in parts of the rest of Europe, its importance increasing in the later Neolithic and Bronze Ages. This may reflect its use for making beer, one of the alcoholic beverages thought to have been a socially significant drink among cultures such as TRB.

Barley was also grown as animal feed; both the husks and the straw could be used as fodder as well as the grains.

Oats Native to the Mediterranean basin, oats initially occurred as a weed growing among wheat and barley; it began to be deliberately cultivated in parts of northern and western Europe only toward the end of the second millennium B.C., when it offered the advantage of being suitable for growing on the acid soils that were developing in some areas and in

3.1 A 19th-century view of Iron Age agriculture. Though, as shown here, cereals were indeed the main crop, Iron Age landscapes were divided into much smaller fields. (Figuier, Louis. *Primitive Man.* London: Chatto and Windus, 1876)

the wetter conditions of the period. Oats was grown both as a food for humans, made into porridge or griddle cakes, and as fodder, its straw also being used to feed animals.

Rye Rye was introduced as a weed of cultivation, probably from the east since it was not present among the cereals on Early Neolithic sites in Greece and the Balkans. Its deliberate cultivation began by the later fifth millennium in the Balkans (Gumelnitsa culture). Its earliest occurrence elsewhere in Europe is in a number of TRB settlements where small quantities of rye were found mixed in with wheat and barley. Being very tolerant of prolonged cold, rye was grown particularly in Britain and in northern and eastern Europe, and was cultivated in the Iron Age to make use of acid soils. Deep plowing from the Iron Age onward also assisted the growth of rye.

Millet Probably domesticated in central Asia, broomcorn millet (*Panicum*) was present in a number of LBK and other Neolithic settlements in eastern Europe. By the Early Bronze Age millet, which could be grown quickly and withstood drought and high temperatures, began to be cultivated in northern Italy and in the Late Bronze Age in northern Greece, and spread to northern and central Europe early in the Iron Age, in later times becoming a major subsistence crop for poor farmers. During the Bronze Age foxtail millet (*Setaria*) also came under cultivation in parts of Europe, becoming more widespread in the Iron Age.

PULSES

A number of pulses (legumes) were introduced to Europe at the same time as wheat and barley, to which they were an important complement, providing protein and renewing soil fertility by fixing nitrogen: They were therefore often grown in rotation with cereals, a practice that may date back to the Early Neolithic. Although highly nutritious, pulses often contain toxins that need to be removed by soaking or rendered harmless by cooking. They were mostly served boiled whole or in pottage, but could also be ground into flour.

The early introductions included pea, bitter vetch, and lentil, which were grown by the first farmers in the southeast, the Mediterranean, and central Europe. Chickpeas may also have been introduced but were rare. Pulses continued to be staple crops alongside wheat and barley throughout European prehistory. Peas were particularly popular in LBK and other Neolithic cultures but declined in favor of lentils and beans in the Bronze Age. Although unpopular in post-Roman times, when it became regarded as a famine food and was generally grown only as a fodder crop, bitter vetch was cultivated in large quantities in Neolithic Southeast Europe; elsewhere in Europe, however, it was rare or absent. Neolithic and Bronze Age communities in Greece and the Balkans also grew considerable amounts of grass pea (chickling vetch); elsewhere this pulse, which is dangerous if consumed in large quantities, was not popular, though it is known from some Neolithic French sites. Spanish vetchling, a related species, was cultivated by the Minoans and their contemporaries in the Aegean Islands, and lupins may also have been brought into cultivation in the Bronze Age Aegean.

Chickpeas, native to parts of the Mediterranean, may have been brought into cultivation by the early farming communities of the region (Impressed Ware culture); vetch and peas also grew wild in the Mediterranean and were gathered by the Mesolithic population before being cultivated by Impressed Ware groups.

Broad beans were added to the range of cultivated pulses during the late Neolithic in the western and central Mediterranean and in central Europe. Their cultivation spread to other parts of Europe during the Bronze Age, occurring, for example, at Blackpatch in southern England and Biskupin in Poland. Being salt-tolerant, beans were grown in preference to other pulses by farmers exploiting the salt marshes that developed on the North Sea coast during the first millennium B.C.

VEGETABLES

Familiar Varieties Since most vegetables leave little archaeological trace, it is difficult to construct a complete picture of what was grown in prehistoric Europe. Many of those recorded in classical literature are likely to have been grown in earlier times, and green and root vegetables native to Europe were gathered long before they were brought into cultivation.

Occasional discoveries of seeds show that cabbages were grown in southern England in the Bronze Age and oil-seed rape, turnips, and carrots in the Iron Age; celery, carrots, cabbages, and turnips were also among the plants used by the Neolithic and Bronze Age inhabitants of the Swiss lake villages; as celery does not grow wild in this region it may already have been cultivated. Although wild European radishes were probably eaten, the cultivated variety was probably domesticated from a different species in the eastern Mediterranean. Members of the cabbage family are native to both Mediterranean and Atlantic Europe; they were probably brought under cultivation in the latter region since cultivated varieties are descended from Atlantic wild cabbages. Several varieties are referred to in Roman literature, possibly including broccoli, but the great diversity of brassicas, including cauliflower and Brussels sprouts, was a much later development.

Lettuces were popular with the ancient Egyptians and were cultivated by the Greeks and Romans but did not spread beyond the Mediterranean until medieval times. The Greeks knew cucumbers, a crop that ultimately derived from India. Musk melons, domesticated in the Near East or Egypt, were grown in the Aegean in the Late Bronze Age and classical times.

Chenopodium Chenopodium, known also as Good King Henry, fat-hen, or goosefoot, occurred as a weed of cultivation and was also deliberately grown, for example at the LBK site of Lamersdorf and by Neolithic and Bronze Age Swiss lake villagers. It was used both as a leafy vegetable and as a source of seeds that could be cooked in gruel or ground into flour for making bread. Dried plants also made good winter fodder for animals. In addition, it was sown late in the spring and could therefore be planted as a catch crop if a field of cereal failed.

Oil-Bearing Plants One of the crops introduced by the first farmers in Southeast Europe, linseed (flax) was probably grown both for its fibers and for its oil-rich seeds. Gold-of-pleasure (*Camelina*, false flax) was grown initially as a weed of cultivation, but by the third millennium it was being deliberately cultivated for its oil-bearing seeds in eastern, southeastern, and central Europe. It became more common in the second millennium, being found in large quantities, for example, in Middle Bronze Age central European sites. By the Iron Age it was cultivated particularly in coastal northern Europe, being well suited to poor sandy soils. Members of the mustard family native to Europe, such as turnip, mustard, rape, and radish, probably also provided oil though the evidence is scanty.

FRUITS

A variety of fruits were brought under cultivation in the Near East and China in antiquity, but across much of Europe, fruits were generally gathered wild by farmers as well as hunter-gatherers for much of the prehistoric period. Since the fruit of trees grown from seed can differ greatly in taste, size, and other important characteristics from those of the parent tree, cultivated trees are generally clones, grown from cuttings, suckers, or grafts. Many types of nut, however, such as hazel and walnut, can successfully be produced from trees grown from seed.

Mediterranean Crops Of the fruits native to the Mediterranean, grapes, olives, pomegranates, and figs, which can easily be propagated from cuttings, began to be cultivated during the Bronze Age, while carobs, which require grafting, were certainly grown by Roman times. Nonnative fruits were a late introduction: Peaches and apricots, which are native to central and East Asia, quinces, which derive from Iran and the Caucasus, and citrons, which are native to India, were all introduced to classical Europe via the Near East during the first millennium B.C., and other citrus fruits did not arrive until Islamic times or later.

Cultivation of the grape, olive, and fig began at some point in the Bronze Age in the Aegean; all had previously been domesticated in the Levant and had long been gathered as wild fruits in the Mediterranean. They are well adapted to the arid summers of the region and grow well on poor soils on hillslopes. Vines tolerate a wider range of conditions, and grapes probably grew wild well into central Europe. Grapes could be used as fresh fruit, dried for storage as raisins and sultanas, or made into wine, which could not only be stored but also traded; Mediterranean wine became a lucrative export of the Greeks and later the Romans to the elites of Iron Age temperate Europe. Olives were also useful for both storage and trade; they were picked unripe and preserved to be eaten as fruit, or left till ripe and pressed for oil. Figs, like grapes, could be eaten fresh or dried and stored.

Olives require little attention once the trees are established, but the tender young plants need protection against the summer drought and careful tending, including regular pruning. Grape vines also need considerable attention when young and repeated annual pruning. Cultivated figs benefit from being grown alongside wild figs to allow cross-pollination; wild fruits attached to cultivated trees (a process called caprification, known to have been practiced by the Romans) encourage pollination by the fig wasp. The cultivation of these crops therefore required an intensification of the agricultural regime to integrate field crops with vine and olive cultivation (Mediterranean polyculture), and some scholars link this to the emergence of greater social complexity in the regions where it was adopted.

Wild grapes can be used for wine making and despite their acidity were widely gathered in prehistoric Europe, so the appearance of large quantities of grape seeds in Late Neolithic northern Greece need not indicate cultivation; by the late third millennium, however, grapes were almost certainly being grown in southern Greece. At a similar time they may also have been brought under cultivation in southeast Spain by the Millaran culture. Although they were also grown by the Argaric culture of this region, it was apparently not until the first millennium B.C. when the Phoenicians and later the Greeks began to colonize the western Mediterranean that grapes and olives began to be cultivated in other parts of Iberia and in southern France. Expansion of settlement in Dalmatia onto the stony karst area and the construction there of terraces probably related to the introduction of polyculture here in the second millennium. Southern Italy may have seen some cultivation of grapes and olives in areas influenced by the Mycenaeans; Apennine Bronze Age sites may have produced wine, since they have yielded abundant grape pips and fine drinking vessels; and grapes, figs, or olives may have

been cultivated at some Bronze Age sites (such as Monte Leoni in northern Italy). The Etruscans, however, were the first Italian culture to establish an integrated regime of Mediterranean polyculture, in the eighth century B.C., followed by the Romans, who introduced olives into the remaining parts of the Mediterranean and grapes both there and into suitable regions of temperate Europe.

Fruit Trees Other varieties of fruit trees, notably apple, pear, plum, and cherry, which grew wild across most of Europe and were extensively exploited in prehistory, require grafting for satisfactory propagation, a technique practiced by the Chinese and probably not known in Europe until classical times; the Romans were probably responsible for the spread of the practice into other parts of Europe. However, some apples recovered from Late Neolithic lake villages had some characteristics found only in cultivated varieties. These settlements also yielded pears and plums that may have been cultivated. This evidence suggests arboriculture had been developed by this time in Europe, but what form this might have taken is unclear, since trees grown from seed are extremely variable in the qualities of their fruit, and apples, pears, and plums cannot usually successfully be propagated from cuttings or suckers.

Berries Raspberries, strawberries, elderberries, and other berries were gathered wild, as blackberries are still today; they were probably not brought into cultivation in prehistoric times in Europe, although strawberries may have been grown by the Mycenaeans.

Nuts Like fruit, nuts were gathered by both farmers and hunter-gatherers. Hazelnuts were particularly popular; its growth was encouraged by hunter-gatherers and early farmers, and it was later planted. Both walnuts and sweet chestnuts may have grown wild in parts of postglacial Europe though the evidence is thin; chestnuts were cultivated in later Bronze Age Spain and walnuts by the later Iron Age and classical times; the Romans were probably responsible for the spread of their cultivation outside the Mediterranean. Almonds, native to the Mediterranean, can be grown from seed or grafted. Cultivation was mainly designed to select against the bitter variety of almond containing deadly prussic acid, which can, however, be removed by leaching. It is likely that almonds came under cultivation around the same time as vines and olives.

OTHER CROPS

Fibers   Flax was grown both for its oil-producing seeds and for its fibers, which were made into linen. It was among the crops first introduced into Europe from the Near East, was cultivated by LBK farmers, and spread widely both in temperate Europe and in the Mediterranean. Nettles were also used for making cloth; a fine white textile recovered from a Late Bronze Age site at Voldtofte in Denmark proved to have been made from nettle fibers. The development of wool for textiles from the Late Neolithic period onward reduced the reliance on plant fibers, though these still continued in use.

Hemp (cannabis) was also used for making cloth in temperate Europe, although its fibers and the resulting textiles are coarser than linen. Since it was resistant to seawater, it was particularly useful for making sails. Hemp seeds occur in a few European sites from LBK onward, and possible hemp cloth was found in a Late Neolithic French site; hemp textiles were certainly in production by the Iron Age in Thrace and Greece. Hemp fibers were also used to make rope.

Bark fibers were used for making nets and cordage from Mesolithic times onward; examples have been identified as coming from willow and linden trees. Reeds, grasses, and other wild plant fibers were also used in various ways, particularly for making baskets, bags, and rope. Esparto grass baskets and bags, sandals, and even clothing were found with Late Neolithic burials in Cueva de los Murciélagos in Spain, a cave whose aridity has allowed the preservation of many organic remains. The use of esparto grass was probably confined to Iberia, but other grasses may have been more widely used. Ötzi the Iceman (late fourth millennium) wore a cloak that had been made from grass, and his shoes were stuffed with grass to keep his feet warm.

Drugs   Various narcotic substances were probably in use in prehistoric Europe. Poppy, a native Mediterranean species, was already present in central Europe in LBK settlements and in western Europe, Swiss lake villages, and northern Italy by the fourth millennium. A basket of poppy heads was found with the burials in Cueva de los Murciélagos. Poppy was a source of oil, and its seeds were eaten, but their most probable use was for producing opium. Cannabis, grown for its hemp fibers, was also employed as a narcotic by people of the steppe, perhaps by the earlier fourth millennium, and this use may also have been adopted in Europe, for instance, by the Corded Ware culture. Other drugs included black henbane, found in Grooved Ware pottery in Chalcolithic Scotland and probably used to induce trances.

Herbs and Spices   The evidence of these is patchy, and it is often difficult to determine whether they were collected or cultivated. Coriander was used in Bronze Age Greece; dill and cumin are known from the Late Neolithic in the Swiss lake villages. Saffron, made from crocus flowers, was probably used widely in prehistoric Europe as both a food flavoring and a dye, but the first evidence of this comes from Bronze Age Aegean art, such as the famous fresco from Thera (Santorini) in which ladies are shown gathering saffron.

Dyes   A number of plants were used for dyes, including saffron. Safflower was under cultivation by the early second millennium at the Balkan site of Feudvar. Literary sources show that madder and dyer's rocket were cultivated by classical times, but they were probably used much earlier. Woad was used in Europe by the first millennium B.C. as a dye for cloth, but recent work on preserved bodies suggests that apparent classical references to woad as a body paint have been misinterpreted; azurite (copper sulfate) was more probably used.

Domestic Animals

Domestic sheep, goat, and probably cattle and pig were introduced into Europe from the Near East at the same time as the first cultivated plants, and animal husbandry remained an integral part of European agriculture as it was gradually adopted across the continent. As forests were progressively cleared, many communities increased the size of their domestic herds, particularly of cattle, for example, the TRB inhabitants of central Europe. Some groups also developed specialist pastoral economies. Hunter-gatherer groups in contact with early farmers often acquired domestic animals from their farming neighbors or domesticated animals themselves from local stock: For example, groups in Belgium contemporary with LBK farmers kept domestic pigs and cattle, the latter domesticated from local wild cattle and larger than LBK cattle.

Kept at first for meat, animals later became important also for their secondary products: milk, wool, and traction, as well as leather and manure. Horses were domesticated later but rapidly became important, particularly in warfare. The range of domestic animals increased through time, though many animals that contributed significantly to the European diet were never domesticated.

The relative importance of crops and domestic animals varied both regionally and more locally, as did the relative proportions of the different domestic animals. Wild stock were often important in boosting the supply of domesticates or introducing new blood by interbreeding with them.

PIGS

Although pigs were domesticated in the Near East and were probably introduced into Southeast Europe, wild boar were widespread across prehistoric Europe, and wild stocks must have provided a significant proportion of European domestic pigs. In medieval Europe domestic sows were tied up in the woods to encourage them to interbreed with wild boars, and deliberate or serendipitous interbreeding between wild and domestic stock must have taken place in antiquity. This might account for the large and savage breed of pigs said by the Roman author Strabo to be kept by the Celts, although excavated pig bones indicate that Celtic farmers usually had quite small pigs.

The preferred environment of pigs was shady woodland, where they could forage for a range of plants such as nuts. As Europe's forests were progressively reduced by clearance and the extension of agriculture, in some areas the importance of pigs declined in favor of cattle and caprines, though this was not universally so. Pigs are omnivorous so they can be fed on domestic waste and can find food in a wide range of environments. They also breed prolifically and grow fast so they are a good source of meat; they were therefore always an important component of the mixed farming economy of prehistoric Europe, kept by permanently settled groups and probably generally left to forage around the margins of the settlement and farmed area rather than penned, although some Iron Age settlements have small structures that might have been pig sties.

While pigs were kept mainly for meat, lard, and leather, they could also be used for preparing ground for cultivation by trampling it and thoroughly grubbing up the surface, destroying weeds and turning the soil, and at the same time manuring it.

CATTLE

Cattle were domesticated in ancient Anatolia and may have been introduced to Europe, but it is likely that many European cattle were domesticated in Europe itself, from the massive and ferocious aurochs (*Bos primigenius*) that remained part of the native fauna until its extinction in recent times.

Initially cattle were kept for their meat and their skins used for leather. Later they were also kept for milk, which became a major resource, probably generally in the form of cheese. Although it is not clear at what time milk began to be exploited for food, the presence of some older animals among the LBK cattle and of pottery sieves that may have been used in making cheese, suggest the possibility that some LBK cattle were kept for milking. By the later Neolithic such evidence was widespread, and milk and milk products had became an important part of the economy for many communities. Prehistoric European cows could probably each produce around 800–2,400 pints (500–1,500 liters) of milk per year. On many Celtic settlements about a third of the cattle bones come from juveniles killed for meat while the rest were mostly cows kept for milk and for producing calves; these went together as prehistoric breeds of cow would only let down their milk in the presence of their calf.

By the later fourth millennium cattle, usually oxen (castrated bulls) but sometimes cows on small farms, were also being used as beasts of burden and for traction, pulling carts and ards, although skeletal evidence from fifth-millennium Greece suggests they were being used to pull heavy loads even earlier. They attained adequate strength for these tasks at around three to four years old. Castrated beasts were more docile and so easier to handle; they also put on more weight and so many communities also castrated the male cattle intended for meat production. A number of fourth-millennium cattle figurines from northern Greece depict them with baskets or panniers on their backs.

Many representations of carts and plows, for example, on TRB and Baden culture pottery, in Bronze Age rock art, and as figurines of pottery and bronze, show they were drawn by pairs of oxen, although some seem to have required teams of four. These representations, along with wooden yokes recovered from waterlogged sites, such as Fiave in Italy and Loch Nell in Scotland, show that two methods of harnessing were used. In one the yoke was attached to the animals' horns, while in the other the yoke was molded to fit across their withers. One horncore from TRB period Bronocice in Poland bore the marks of the cord with which the horn had been attached to the yoke.

Cattle required regular access to water, which placed some constraints on where they could be kept. They could generally find adequate grazing on the forest edge and, as woodland was cleared, in the grass that grew up to replace it, as well as on the river floodplains, marshy ground, and other areas unsuitable for cultivation. Causewayed enclosures, known from Neolithic Britain, France, and parts of the Danubian cultural region, may have been used for corralling large numbers of cattle, among other functions.

In the dry summers of the Mediterranean cattle needed to be fed stored food such as grain and pulses, except in the few areas, such as the floodplains of large rivers, where pastures were available, so in southern Europe their numbers were relatively low. In contrast they were generally the most important domestic animal in much of temperate Europe, from LBK times onward. In cold regions they had to be kept inside during the winter, where they were stall fed. Longhouses in LBK and later settlements might have a part set aside for stalling animals, often with stall partitions, or cattle might be kept in separate byres, as they were elsewhere,

for example, in Switzerland. Much of the fodder needed to keep them during the winter months could be obtained from the wild, forests and wetlands providing leaves, ivy, twigs, shoots, and other plant material. Fodder could also be grown: Many of the legumes used to restore soil fertility could be fed to animals, as could rape and other leafy crops. In later periods meadows to provide hay could be part of the field system, and the straw from cereal crops also provided some cattle feed. The introduction of the iron scythe in the Iron Age made the mowing of hay easier than it had been with the sickles previously in use.

One building in the Cortaillod settlement of Egolzwil had been used to stall cattle that had been fed on leaves, mistletoe, and hay. The pupae of houseflies were among the debris on the floor of the building, evidence that dung had accumulated there. In central and western Holland, Neolithic cattle were not stalled, but the practice developed in the Bronze Age and was common thereafter. It is suggested that this reflected a need to collect dung for manuring fields to increase productivity; and this seems to have been true in other regions, too. Stalls and byres might also reflect the increased importance of milking, since it was more comfortable for the milker to operate indoors in winter.

Where grazing and fodder were limited, milch cows and oxen would be kept year round, other animals being slaughtered in the autumn and their meat preserved by smoking, drying, or salting. Oxen, which provided neither meat nor milk but only traction, were an expensive commodity. A team might be kept as the communal property of a community or owned by the elite; smaller communities probably continued to rely on human labor for preparing the ground for cultivation, or used cows to draw their ards. Special treatment was accorded to the plow team to ensure that they were fit for their heavy task; this might include extra feeding or special fodder (such as grain). They were also likely to be kept in the settlement and treated as individuals like pets, since docility was essential in ensuring their cooperation in plowing.

As well as meat and milk, cattle yielded hides for leather, fat for tallow, and bones and horns for making tools. They were also popular as sacrificial victims among the Celts.

CAPRINES

Caprines, domesticated in the Near East, were introduced into Europe in the seventh millennium B.C. Both sheep and goats can find food in a wide range of environments, including rough or mountainous terrain; goats are both more agile and able to eat a wider range of plants, but they are more difficult to manage, and their hair is less useful than the sheep's wool, so there has generally been a strong preference for keeping sheep.

Wild caprines move seasonally between lowland winter and upland summer pastures and this transhumant seasonal movement has been a regular feature of domestic caprine herding, too, although small numbers could be maintained year round on vegetation available near the settlement. In much of temperate Europe the numbers of caprines that were kept increased as forests were cleared, opening up areas for grazing.

Both sheep and goats were milked; although evidence of this is elusive, milking of caprines probably began around the same time as that of cattle. In the Mediterranean, where caprines were the main domestic animals, they were also the main providers of milk, probably usually used to make cheese; in temperate Europe cattle were probably the main milk providers, but sheep and goat milk was also used.

Sheep Sheep were originally hairy like goats, their wool being a short winter undercoat shed in the spring. Woolly sheep, which were originally bred in the Near East, were introduced into Europe during the fourth or third millennium, and by the Bronze Age wool was in widespread use for manufacturing clothing and other textiles. From the primitive breeds of sheep kept in prehistoric Europe the yield of wool may have been around 2 pounds (a kilogram) per animal.

There is evidence from many sites of a change in the age and sex structure of flocks with the development of wool production, with an increase in the numbers of adult sheep and particularly wethers (castrated rams), which provide the best and most abundant wool. Sheep could continue to produce wool until they were seven or eight years old. Meat, milk, and wool production could be combined, as at the third millennium Swiss site of Ledro, where many of the sheep were killed young for meat; half the adults were ewes kept for their milk and to produce lambs, and most of the rest were wethers that were kept until they had produced two or three fleeces and were then slaughtered.

Specialist sheep herding became increasingly important with the advent of wool production. For example, in southern Greece the Minoan and Mycenaean palace economies depended significantly on the production of large quantities of wool for domestic use and export. From the later Neolithic period onward some alpine communities developed a strong pastoral bias, making use of high pastures for summer grazing. The people of the Michelsberg culture of Switzerland, for example, kept their animals around their villages in winter, while in the summer the flocks were driven to upland pastures where the herdsmen lived in temporary camps.

Bronze Age sheep were similar to the modern primitive Soay sheep, which are small, agile, and intelligent, bearing wool that is plucked rather than shorn. Bone combs, known from many Iron Age sites, may have been used to collect their wool during the spring molt. Other larger varieties were also kept by the Celts; these were shorn using iron shears. Some ewes had small horns, others were hornless, as were some of the rams, while some had four horns.

As sheep are hardy, they were generally kept outside throughout the year, although in harsh winter conditions they might require fodder, such as hay. They were susceptible to foot-rot and liver fluke, both prevalent in damp pastures; evidence of the mollusk host of liver fluke has been found in some sites such as the Late Bronze Age Dutch settlement of Hoogkarspel.

Goats Although sheep were generally preferred to goats, it was usual to keep a small number of goats in every flock, as they are said to calm sheep and are frequently used to lead the flock to and from pastures. Some Celtic farmers kept larger numbers of goats for meat, though still in considerably smaller numbers than sheep. Goatskin makes good leather, and the hair can be used for rope and textiles.

DOMESTIC FOWL

Ducks and Geese Geese were kept by the Celts and exported to the Roman world by the Gauls, though no archaeological evidence of them survives on Celtic sites. Both ducks and geese are likely to have been kept in earlier times, too, but the evidence is lacking, although ducks featured prominently in religious symbolism.

Chickens The domestic chicken was bred from the Indian jungle fowl and eventually reached the West; it was known from Bronze Age contexts onward in Europe. The Greeks and Romans kept a larger breed of chicken, some of which were imported into Celtic Europe. Chickens were generally kept only in small numbers, providing mainly meat but also eggs in the spring.

HORSES

Horses were domesticated in the European steppe before 4000 B.C. and rapidly spread from the east into the Balkans and central Europe, and thence to western Europe, reaching Spain and Italy by the later third millennium as one element of the Beaker "package." From the second millennium B.C. horses were used to draw war chariots, a perquisite of the elite. Horses were particularly important in the steppe, where they were used by pastoralists herding their flocks. Steppe peoples also milked their horses; the milk could be fermented into an alcoholic drink (kumiss). Horses were widely valued by European societies, particularly for their role in warfare, and horses or horsetrappings were deposited in elite graves in many areas and periods. Although originally used by people on the steppe margins to provide meat, horses were generally kept for riding or traction, though they might also be used as beasts of burden. A line of hoofprints found beneath a Bronze Age house at Ullunda in Sweden shows that the horse that made them had been carrying a load, perhaps in panniers.

Celtic horses were a small breed, around 1.2 to 1.4 meters high at the withers. It is therefore not surprising that Celtic tribes like the Veneti of northern Italy set store by the taller horses of the Scythians, which they obtained by trade and on occasion

buried with their chieftains. The Celts probably did not generally eat horse meat, although at Danebury hillfort in England there is evidence that old horses were killed and butchered. From Celtic religious art and the presence of horses in elite graves and in shrines as sacrificial victims it is clear that horses enjoyed a special status in Celtic society, associated with elite cavalry and chariot-riding warriors and with the important fertility goddess Epona.

Studies from Iron Age settlements show horses were often kept in loosely controlled breeding herds that were periodically rounded up to take out two- and three-year-old male colts, which were then broken in for riding or traction. Alternatively, they might be more closely managed.

Riding It is a subject of much debate when horses began to be ridden; some scholars argue this happened at the time of their first domestication in the fifth millennium B.C., while others consider this was not much before the later third millennium, when horse riding was firmly attested in Mesopotamia.

The control of ridden horses was at first entirely dependent upon the rider's use of knees and hands, perhaps with the addition of a rope noseband. Nose rings to which reins were attached were used for control in the third and second millennia in the Near East; finely decorated antler cheek pieces are known from the Balkans and the Carpathian basin by around 1800 B.C., but it is unknown whether the harness from which these came was for riding or for pulling a vehicle. Bronze bits were developed in the Near East before the mid-second millennium but were not employed in Europe until around 1300 B.C.; these were generally in the form of a bar. A cloth might be spread on the horse's back; saddles, invented in the steppe, were used in Europe during the later first millennium and had pommels at the four corners to keep the rider secure. Stirrups, however, were not invented until the sixth century A.D.

Other Equids Donkeys were domesticated in the Near East and appeared in the Aegean in the Early Bronze Age and somewhat later in other parts of the Mediterranean. Thereafter donkeys and mules (a donkey-horse cross) became the main pack animals of southern Europe, though they could also be used for pulling small carts or plowing light soils. They

3.2 *A detail from a reconstruction of prehistoric life. Dogs were the first domestic animals in many parts of the globe and were regular residents of human settlements, where bones have been found bearing their teeth marks.* (Figuier, Louis. *Primitive Man.* London: Chatto and Windus, 1876)

were probably introduced into Celtic Europe by Roman troops.

DOGS

Dogs were the first animals to be domesticated, from wolves, which are animals whose social organization and nature made it easy for them to integrate into human communities. Dogs were kept by hunter-gatherers in many parts of the world by the early postglacial period. They were used particularly in hunting, for tracking, running down, and retrieving game. They were also useful for guarding people and livestock. Rock art scenes indicate that dogs were also used for herding, though, as today, this may not have been a widespread practice.

By the Iron Age there were a number of different breeds of dog in Europe. The most common Celtic dog resembled a greyhound. Large dogs were bred for hunting, a sport of the elite, and were highly prized by the Romans, who listed them among the desirable commodities that they imported from Britain.

On the evidence of bones showing signs of butchery, it would seem that some Celts also ate dogs, but this is unlikely to have been a common practice. Dog skins were also used.

CATS

Although domestic cats had been present in Egypt for millennia, they are thought not to have been introduced into Mediterranean Europe until the first century B.C. However, cats were found throughout the occupation of the Iron Age hillfort of Danebury in England; these may have been wild cats scavenging in the settlement where stored grain would have attracted rats and mice, but they may equally have been domestic.

WILD RESOURCES

Until the seventh millennium B.C. exploitation of wild resources was the only way of life in Europe, and it continued to be that of the majority of the European population long after the introduction of agriculture. In the far north game, sea mammals, and fish remained the main sources of food, supplemented by limited animal husbandry. Many farming communities made extensive use of wild resources, and most took some things from the wild, such as fodder, wild fruits, fish or herbal remedies, as people do even today. Fishing has continued to supply the main livelihood of many coastal communities, while by the Iron Age hunting had for some been transformed into a pastime, though for others trapping game remained a necessity. Farmers continued to manage woodland for many purposes, as their Mesolithic predecessors had done. Few wild resources useful to humans were neglected: Honey, for example, was gathered, as rock paintings from Late Glacial Spain attest. Beeswax was collected for use in the cire perdue casting of bronze, and by the Iron Age domestic bees were kept for honey and wax.

While many later Mesolithic sites show year-round occupation, many resources were available only at certain times of year in certain environments:

Some large mammals such as red deer moved between summer upland and winter lowland pastures; certain fish species migrated to annual spawning grounds; different plants ripened at different seasons in different areas; seabirds' eggs were available in the spring on seaside islands and cliffs. Many Mesolithic groups, therefore, moved seasonally to exploit the full diversity of their landscape, while other occupied a base camp from which seasonal expeditions were made by part of the community. Sedentary Ertebølle hunter-gatherers on the Danish coasts, for example, sent parties out at different times of year, inland to hunt piglets, migratory wildfowl, and fur animals, and to other coastal locations and offshore islands to take eels, swans, and seals. Pastoralists also moved between pastures and were therefore in a position to hunt and collect seasonally available resources.

Plants

Many of the plants that were undoubtedly exploited in prehistory have left little trace in the archaeological record. Only exceptional environments such as waterlogged settlements (particularly Swiss and other lake villages), arid caves, and the guts of bog bodies have yielded direct evidence, while other clues have been extracted from such indirect sources as pollen profiles. Of plants known to have been eaten or used in other ways, some are cultivated today but we do not know when they were domesticated, while some are not grown today but were cultivated in the past.

A huge range of wild plants from many different environments were exploited by prehistoric Europeans. Deciduous woodland was particularly rich in species edible to humans. It seems probable that the Mesolithic inhabitants of Europe took full advantage of the diversity of plant resources offered by the wild, even where evidence is lacking. Many of these plants were also used by farmers, and in much of western and northern Europe the situation was for a long time reversed, cultivated plants being used by people largely dependent on wild resources, such as the Neolithic Fiorano and Cortaillod communities settled around lakes in northern Italy and Switzerland.

TREES

Wild fruit and nuts were harvested for food, and many could be stored for the winter. Those known to have been exploited included apples, crab apples, pears, cherries, cornelian cherries, olives, plums, figs, and sloes; acorns, chestnuts, walnuts, almonds, beechnuts, hazelnuts, stone-pine kernels, and pistachio. As well as being stored whole, apples were dried, as were other fruits such as figs, and nuts were roasted to aid their preservation. Hazelnuts were particularly popular, turning up in considerable quantities all over Europe—in a pot beside the Neolithic Sweet Track in the Somerset Levels, as part of the last meal of one of the Iron Age men sacrificed in Lindow Moss, in Mesolithic caves in the Jura and Bronze Age settlements in Italy and Britain, for example. Mesolithic people probably deliberately encouraged the growth of hazel trees by clearing patches of forest, since hazel was one of the first and most vigorous trees to colonize such clearings. Acorns and chestnuts could be ground into flour; they were also very palatable to animals and so were used as fodder or forage, for example, in the managed *dehesas* of later prehistoric southern Europe. Leaves also provided fodder, preferred by animals to hay.

Bark was collected from many trees. Birch bark had many uses, including decorative strips on some Cortaillod pottery vessels; it was frequently made into containers. Bark fibers (bast) were used to make cords and textiles: Cloth woven from lime, oak, and willow bast was found in the Swiss lake villages. Birch wood or birch bark when carbonized produced pitch, which was used as an adhesive: This was identified as the means used to attach flint points to arrows carried by the Iceman, for instance.

OTHER PLANTS

Berries are one of the few wild plant foods that have left traces of their consumption, mainly from the Swiss and north Italian lake settlements: These included bilberries, strawberries, raspberries, rosehips, dewberries, haws, and elderberries. A number of settlements have also yielded evidence of wild grapes, which could have been fermented into wine. Juniper berries are known from the Cardial Impressed Ware site of Le Baratin in France, while seeds from settlements such as Iron Age Glastonbury in England, TRB Swifterbant in Holland, and Early Neolithic Chevdar in the Balkans show that blackberries were widely enjoyed. As well as being eaten as they were, berries could be made into drinks; native American Indians used to pound berries and meat together to make the long-lasting food staple, pemmican, and something of this sort might have been produced in Europe also.

Among the possessions found with the Iceman (c. 3300/3200 B.C.) were two pieces of birch fungus threaded onto strips of fur: these may have been a folk remedy. Mushrooms were recovered from Cortaillod sites in Switzerland as were water chestnuts; at the contemporary Italian site of Molino Casarotto the latter were of far more importance in the diet than cereals. Other water plants likely to have been eaten included watercress, wild rice, and club rush. Various wild seeds were gathered while buds, flowers, shoots, and leaves, such as nettles, plantain, knotweed, and sorrel, must also have been eaten and used in other ways. Plants could supply flavorings, medicines, dyes, and even poisons for use in hunting. Those that grew in the fields alongside crops (weeds of cultivation), such as common cleavers and chess, were often gathered and eaten, either along with the crop or harvested separately. Others such as oats, chenopodium and gold-of-pleasure were eventually cultivated as crops in their own right. Plants more familiar as domesticates, such as lentils, were also gathered from the wild.

Considerable use was made of wild plants for forage, animals being turned loose to graze at the forest edge or in the rough ground bordering fields and beyond. Grass was one of the main such plants, but many shrubs and bushes and other plants were also eaten, particularly by goats. Managed resources, such as coppiced woodland and water meadows, had to be fenced or bounded with ditches, banks, hedges, or walls to protect them from grazing animals.

Reeds, rushes, sedges, and osiers were gathered for making cords, mats, baskets, and thatch, as well as floor coverings and bedding for people and animals. Reeds grew best if managed by being harvested annually. Cords could also be made of vines such as wild clematis (old man's beard), an example of which is known from Bronze Age Bad Frankenhausen. Nettles were also a source of fibers.

Roots, tubers, rhizomes, and bulbs, such as bracken rhizomes, wild garlic, and lily bulbs, must also have been enjoyed, despite the lack of evidence.

GATHERING

Tools such as sickles and knives of flint, bronze, or iron were used to harvest wild plants, while nets, baskets, and bags would be used for carrying what had been gathered. Querns could be used to grind wild seeds and other plants as well as cultivated grain. Some of the flint microliths characteristic of Mesolithic technology may have been set in wooden boards to form graters for preparing roots and other such foods.

Animals

The use of wild fauna is better attested than wild flora since bones preserve well in many soil types (though not in acid bogs), but the bones of smaller creatures may often have been missed in excavations. Animals were hunted not only for food but also for their hides and fur, their bones, horns, and antlers from which tools were made, and their sinews, which were used for fastenings. Shed antlers were also collected, to make tools like mattocks and hammers. Farmers also killed animals to protect their crops. In later prehistory hunting became a sport, though pursuing dangerous game like aurochs and boar had presumably always been viewed as a male demonstration of courage and skill.

LARGE MAMMALS

The deciduous forests of Europe were home to a number of large mammals that played an important part in the diet of Mesolithic people: These included roe deer, red deer, wild boar, aurochs, elk, and horse. In the more open terrain of the steppe horses were particularly important as a source of food, while in the far north the large prey were mainly reindeer and elk. These all continued to be exploited by the farming inhabitants of their regions, horses being domesticated in the fifth millennium and subsequently used for herding in the steppe. In the Balearic Islands of the western Mediterranean the myotragus, a creature resembling a chamois, and on Corsica the deerlike megacerus were important to their Mesolithic inhabitants. Chamois and ibex were hunted in the mountains from Mesolithic times onward.

SMALL MAMMALS

Rabbits, hares, and squirrels were among the creatures caught for food both by the Mesolithic people and by farmers. Foxes, wolves, beavers, wild cats, badgers, bears, otters, lynx, and martens may also have been eaten but were mainly taken for their furs or hides. Blunt-headed wooden arrows were used by hunters to stun these animals in order not to damage their pelts, and smoke and traps were also used.

OTHER CREATURES

Wildfowl and other birds such as swans, cranes, and mallards taken in marshes and on rivers and lakes were an important source of food for both Mesolithic and farming communities, while seabirds such as cormorants, gulls, and puffins were also eaten. Songbirds and game birds such as grouse were snared or stunned with blunt arrows. One Late Neolithic megalithic tomb in Orkney at Isbister contained the remains of eight sea eagles, which may have had some symbolic significance for the community. A similar interpretation seems likely for the Mesolithic burial at Vedbaek in Denmark, where a stillborn baby was laid on a swan's wing beside his mother.

Other small creatures that were eaten included snails and tortoises, and lizards, frogs, snakes, and perhaps beetles must also have been caught.

HUNTING

Early hunters had used spears, either attacking animals directly or using spearthrowers to propel the spear from a distance. They also used throwing

3.3 A fanciful picture of hunting in the Iron Age, a period when hunting was an elite sport as well as a way of supplementing domestic food supplies. Wild boar were among the most dangerous prey in postglacial Europe. (Figuier, Louis. *Primitive Man.* London: Chatto and Windus, 1876)

sticks or boomerangs. Bows and arrows came into use late in the last glacial period and were particularly effective in the Holocene woodlands, where it was difficult to get close to game; several fine Mesolithic and later bows have been recovered from waterlogged sites. Slings, nets, snares, and traps were also used, including an ingenious spring-loaded wooden trap used to catch deer.

Late Glacial or Mesolithic Spanish rock art suggests the possibility of communal game drives, though there is no direct evidence of this practice as there had been in earlier times. In general it seems likely that hunters operated alone or in small numbers, aided by dogs. Horses also helped in hunting, giving the hunter speed to match that of his prey.

While big game were hunted by men, many of the smaller creatures were pursued or trapped by women and children, who were also largely responsible for the collection of plant foods.

Aquatic Resources

Rivers, lakes, and marshes provided a rich harvest for hunter-gatherer groups, and many chose to settle in the vicinity of water. Here they had access to many water plants, small mammals like water rats, turtles, and wildfowl, as well as larger game coming to drink or graze on wetland vegetation. Equally attractive was the seashore, where plants such as samphire and sea kale could be gathered and there were seabirds and their eggs to be had. Some seaweeds were edible, and coastal farming communities such as those of Orkney also used seaweed as manure, while in northern Scandinavia it was used as fodder. Freshwater and marine fish and shellfish were a major resource, while the seas also offered marine mammals.

When farming was adopted by Atlantic and Mediterranean communities, the central importance of marine resources declined, but these were not abandoned, and many coastal communities continued to fish; similarities between the artifacts of different regions and the movement of raw materials imply interregional connections in the Atlantic that may have been maintained by groups pursuing schools of seasonally migrating fish, and deep-sea

fishing similarly encouraged interregional contacts in the Mediterranean.

Like the meat of land animals, that of marine mammals could be dried, smoked or salted, as could fish. Fish could also be used as a fertilizer for cultivated ground.

FISHING

The rich cold waters of the Atlantic and North Sea teemed with fish, including cod, saithe, herring, haddock, sardine, mackerel, conger eel, whiting, flounder, and turbot. Many of these came inshore at certain seasons to breed, when they could be caught with lines or spears, but they were also caught offshore from seagoing boats.

The Mediterranean offered smaller and less varied stocks, but the annual arrival of spawning tuna offered an abundant spring harvest to fishers able to pursue them offshore with boats and nets; this had begun by 9000 B.C. if not earlier.

Salmon, sturgeon, and eels were most easily caught when they came into rivers to breed, offering seasonal plenty (for comparison, native Americans of the northwest dependent on seasonal salmon runs were able to evolve a prosperous sedentary way of life). Other palatable fish in the rivers included trout, pike, perch, carp, bream, roach, catfish, barbel, and grayling.

Rods and lines were used to catch inshore and freshwater fish; fish hooks were found on many prehistoric sites. Limpets in Neolithic settlements in Orkney were probably collected for bait, and the stone watertight boxes in the houses at Skara Brae may have used for soaking limpets to soften them for this purpose. Spears and harpoons were also used, including leisters (fish spears). Fishing nets are known from a few waterlogged sites, including part of a large seine net of willow bast with pine floats from Antrea in Finland; the widespread use of nets is implied by the discovery of many of the weights that were used to hold them down. Net sinkers of small stones wrapped in bark and bark net floats were recovered from the Swiss Neolithic settlement of Twann, while fish traps of basketry and fish weirs have been found in some rivers, such as a Mesolithic example from Tybrind Vig in Denmark. In some cases prey were captured and kept alive until

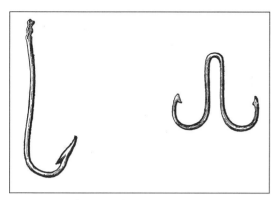

3.4 *Bronze fishhooks found in Swiss lakeside settlements. Fishing remained an important source of food for many communities throughout prehistory.* (Figuier, Louis. *Primitive Man.* London: Chatto and Windus, 1876)

required: For example, bell-shaped pits in the LBK settlement of Brześć Kujawski were used for keeping fish and turtles.

SHELLFISH

Huge mounds of discarded shells show the widespread importance of shellfish such as limpets, mussels, oysters, whelks, razorfish, clams, and cockles to the Mesolithic inhabitants of Europe, particularly of the Atlantic. Though the calorific contribution of shellfish was small, they could provide a critical resource at times of the year when other sources of food were limited. Freshwater mollusks were also eaten, for example, in the Italian Neolithic site of Molino Casarotto. Crustacea such as crabs, shrimps, lobsters, and crayfish were caught and in the Mediterranean octopuses and squid.

MARINE MAMMALS

Grey, Greenland, ringed, and common seals, caught when they came inshore to breed or pursued at sea, became important as a food source in northern Atlantic regions by the early postglacial; dolphins and porpoises were also taken. Sperm, blue, and killer whales were also eaten: these were probably beached animals in most cases, but by the later

Mesolithic it seems they may also have been hunted in the open seas of the North Atlantic, a dangerous and difficult undertaking. Harpoons were used for hunting marine mammals.

In addition to their meat, marine mammals were rich in blubber, providing not only a vital source of dietary fat but also oil for cooking and lighting. Seals were also hunted for their skins.

ECONOMIC STRATEGIES

Early European arable agriculture was largely confined to light, easily worked, and well-drained soils such as the loess of central Europe, the patches of crosta soil around Tavoliere settlements in Italy, the light loams favored by the Egolzwil culture of the central Swiss plateau, or the chalk and gravels of southern England. Preferred locations often lay in the zone between the edges of alluvial plains and the surrounding hillslopes, areas that offered grazing for domestic animals.

As the number of farming settlements increased, settlement and cultivation spread onto other light soils that were poorer or harder to cultivate, such as sandy interfluves, dry plateaus, alluvium, forest soils requiring clearance, and upland regions. The cultivation of these areas was often facilitated by the use of the ard, introduced in the fourth millennium.

Progressive forest clearance greatly increased the area under cultivation through time. Flooding could pose a problem on alluvial plains, which were gradually settled by farmers: those of northern Greece during the late fourth and early third millennia, for example, the difficult Po plain only during the second millennium. Hillslopes, widely used for pasture, came under cultivation in parts of the Mediterranean from the third millennium onward with the domestication of the vine, olive, and fig. Warmer and drier conditions in the earlier second millennium allowed the extension of cultivation onto marginal soils, many of which subsequently became permanently degraded, suffering erosion or podsolisation or becoming heathland or blanket bog. The introduction of the iron plowshare and coulter brought a further extension of arable agriculture onto deep heavy soils such as clays and heavy valley bottom soils.

Many environments initially avoided by farmers were attractive to hunter-gatherers for the abundant and varied wild resources that they offered: These included coastal land, marshes, river estuaries, lake shores, and mountains. As farming became more widespread, these saw the development of communities in whose economic life wild resources played a major part: coastal farmers and fishers; lake dwellers relying both on wild and domestic animals and plants; farmers keeping livestock in wetlands; pastoral communities moving seasonally with their herds into alpine pastures; and many other strategies that mixed arable agriculture, pastoralism, and the exploitation of wild resources in different ways to make use of all Europe's diversity of environments.

While early farming communities were largely self-sufficient in food, in later times farmers or communities often specialized in some aspects of farming, producing surpluses of grain, livestock, and secondary products to trade with their neighbors or more distant communities. For example, the Iron Age tribes of Illyria traded cattle and horses with the Greeks in return for wine, and Strabo lists grain, cattle, hides, and hunting dogs among the commodities exported by Britain to the Roman world in the first century B.C. As society became more complex, farmers might also be required to produce food and other commodities such as wool to support the leaders on whom they depended for physical and spiritual protection. Some communities or groups emphasized particular animals or crops, producing large numbers as part of an integrated system or in order to trade. For example, the people of the hillfort of Eldon's Seat in southern England seem to have concentrated on raising sheep on downland, while horses predominated at another hillfort, Bury Hill; in Late Bronze Age Tuscany, certain sites specialized in raising sheep, while others concentrated on cattle or pigs. Nevertheless, in many parts of Europe, small communities practicing subsistence farming continued to exist into Roman times and after.

Mixed Farming

FIELDS

Temporary or Permanent Fields? It used to be thought that farming in much of temperate Europe, particularly in the region of the Danubian cultures, involved swidden agriculture: clearance of virgin forest, a few years of cultivation, then abandonment for a decade or two to allow forest to regenerate and fertility to be restored. It is now thought more likely that plots were permanently cleared and cultivated continuously. Fixed fields also seem likely in the Early Neolithic of other areas such as Greece and the Balkans, and were probably the norm throughout prehistory. Experiments show that the fertility of permanently cultivated fields would decline gradually over a long period, but it could be maintained by crop rotation, fallowing, and manuring. Rotating legumes with other crops would have been particularly effective. Manure was applied to the land directly, by pasturing animals in fallow or harvested stubble fields. Dung was also collected from stalled animals and spread on fields; in Late Bronze Age and Iron Age Holland and Germany this was collected in muck heaps and periodically mixed with soil from pits before being applied (*plaggen* cultivation). As well as using animal manure, fields close to the settlement could be fertilized with night soil and domestic waste, evidenced by scatters in fields of small pieces of domestic debris such as potsherds. Seaweed was used for manure in the Orkneys and probably in other areas with access to the sea.

Field Systems In LBK there was limited clearance of ground around the settlement, extending less that a mile from it, and in many cases the fields were more like gardens, covering part of the ground immediately adjacent to the houses. In the Italian Tavoliere, early cultivation was similarly confined to small patches of suitable soil adjacent to the settlements, a pattern repeated in other regions of Europe. Later settlements made use of wider areas of cultivated land.

Good evidence of the layout of fields comes from occasional finds of field boundaries made of stones or banks and ditches, or traces of fences. An early example is the 2,500-acre (1,000-hectare) fourth-millennium B.C. field system traced at Ceide in Ireland, which had stone walls and cross walls enclosing rectangular fields of various sizes. Extensive land divisions of a similar age are known from Orkney, Arran, and other British islands. Surviving field systems are known mainly from Britain, but examples also come from Scandinavia and the Low Countries. Boundaries may have originated in the practice of leaving a thin strip of uncleared ground around the edge of cultivated plots on which hedges, including such vegetation as brambles, thorn bushes, and roses, would have acted as a natural barrier to wild animals. Others may have begun as accumulations of stones removed from farmland during ground preparation and dumped along the field edges.

Square and rectangular fields such as those known from Bronze Age Wessex seem likely to have been used for cultivation, while systems of long, narrow strips like those from Bronze Age Dartmoor (marked by low walls known locally as *reaves*) may have been used to graze animals, their shape perhaps allowing the animals to be confined to selected areas using temporary, movable, barriers. Fields generally remained small throughout prehistory. Bronze and Iron Age Celtic field systems were made up of a series of small fields, each one probably the size that could be dealt with in one day, for plowing, sowing, weeding, or harvesting. For example, settlements in Holland on sandy soils were associated with fields around 165 by 165 feet (50 by 50 meters) in size, separated by low ditches, which also provided limited drainage, while those in Denmark were delimited by banks. Lynchets that show the outline of fields cultivated on sloping ground, for example, at Blackpatch in southern England, again emphasize their small size.

Blocks of such fields clustered around settlements; land farther from the habitation was not delimited. Farming settlements in later first-millennium Scandinavia were often associated with an infield-outfield system, with fenced hay meadows and arable fields fertilized with manure adjacent to the settlement and more distant pastures linked to the settlement by a droveway. Similar arrangements are known in Iron Age Britain. A number of larger-scale boundaries formed of banks and ditches (ranch boundaries) occur in later Bronze Age and Iron Age Britain, frequently crosscutting earlier field systems, indicating a change in the arrangement of local land

use or land tenure. Larger hillforts and oppida often included fields within their defenses, for example, at Manching.

While land boundaries may have been designed to indicate land ownership, particularly in later periods, a principal function must always have been to keep animals, wild and domestic, away from growing crops and managed woodland.

GROUND PREPARATION

Various tools were used to break new ground or prepare previously cultivated ground for sowing. In addition, animals could be used to prepare ground: The use of pigs to trample the surface and grub it up is attested ethnographically in both recent times and antiquity.

Hand Tools   The small fields of early farmers were cultivated using hand tools; these included digging sticks. The ground could be broken up with a hoe or mattock or dug with a spade, all of which are still used in horticulture. The marks of a heart-shaped spade have been found in the second-millennium settlement of Gwithian in southern England, and a spade made of maplewood was found in a well in the LBK settlement of Erkelenz-Kückhoven. The abundant shoelast celts, a particular form of polished stone ax or adz associated with LBK settlements, have also been interpreted as hoe or mattock blades; these would have been bound to the short arm of an L-shaped haft of wood or antler. Even after the introduction of ards, peasant farmers are likely to have continued to use hand tools to prepare the ground in their small fields, given the high cost of maintaining a plow team; and they had other uses, hoes, for example, being used to break up clods of earth after plowing. Double-ended spades that resemble paddles have been found in Danish bogs, as have spades designed for cutting peat. The use of iron in the first millennium greatly increased the efficiency of such hand tools, producing spades, for example, that cut more cleanly and easily and deeper into the ground.

Ard and Plow   The earliest plows, introduced into Europe in the fourth millennium B.C., were actually ards. These consisted of a pointed wooden share to gouge through the ground surface, attached to a long shaft by which it was drawn along, generally by a pair of oxen harnessed to an attached yoke. The plowman followed behind holding an upright stilt attached to the share to guide the direction in which the ard traveled through the ground. Marks made by ards have been uncovered under a number of later Neolithic and Bronze Age barrows, from Britain and Denmark to Switzerland; they often run crisscross, probably in order to break the ground more thoroughly. Examples of the ards themselves have been recovered from bogs in northern Europe and Alpine lake villages, while representations of plowing, with teams of two or sometimes four oxen, are found among the Bronze Age rock engravings in Scandinavia and northern Italy.

Several varieties of ard seem to have been in use for different purposes. The rip ard (or sod-buster), which penetrated deeply and probably needed a team of four oxen, was the only type suited to breaking ground that had lain fallow or had not previously been cultivated: no examples have been found, but experiments suggest that the plow marks discovered under barrows must have been made with such a tool. Two other types, the bow ard and the crook ard, are exemplified by the actual examples recovered from the bogs at Donnerupland and Hvorslev, respectively; the former, which has a wider undershare behind its tip, was used to stir up ground that had been cultivated in the previous year, uprooting any remaining weeds and aerating the soil; the latter was drawn through prepared ground to make drills for sowing. A related tool found in a Danish bog at Satrup Moor is known as a rope traction ard: this was like a heart-shaped spade with a very long handle. Two perforations near the back of the blade allowed a rope to be passed through by which the ard could be drawn through the ground by one man, while another used the handle to force the ard blade into the ground.

Ards allowed the ground to be tilled to a greater depth than was possible with hand tools and greatly increased the area that could efficiently be cultivated. Regular use of the ard would have been effective in keeping down weeds. It facilitated the expansion of settlement, allowing new soils to be brought under cultivation, such as the sandy soils of central Europe, of which use began to be made in the third millennium B.C. Sowing seed in furrows or drills greatly increased the seed-to-harvest ratio: The wastage rate with broadcast seed could be as much as three-quarters, whereas drilled seed almost all germinated.

Whereas hand tools could be used by either sex, and ethnographic evidence shows that hoe cultivation is frequently the task of women worldwide, plowing required male strength, and so the beginning of plow agriculture may have seen a revolution in gender relations.

Equipping ards with shoes or tips of stone, bone, antler, or bronze improved their efficiency and ability to penetrate the ground and protected them from rapid wear. By the Late Iron Age, ards were equipped with iron plowshares and coulters, making it possible to break much heavier ground than had previously been possible, such as clays. These ards also penetrated more deeply into the soil, encouraging the growth of deep-rooted crops such as rye. Some may have been true plows with a moldboard, able to turn the sod; Pliny recorded that these were used by the peasants of the kingdom of Noricum.

OTHER AGRICULTURAL TOOLS

Grain may have been harvested with sickles, those of the Neolithic period being made of flint blades, held in the hand or set into wooden or bone handles. Later sickles were also made of bronze and, from the first millennium B.C., of iron. Evidence shows that LBK farmers harvested only the ears of grain, possibly picking them by hand, leaving most of the stalk in the fields, whereas Bronze Age farmers in the same region, using metal sickles, cut the crop closer to the ground. Sickles could also be used for other tasks, such as harvesting straw, cutting reeds for various purposes, or gathering grass or bushy plants like gorse for fodder. Iron scythes, which also appeared in the Iron Age, used to mow hay for fodder, were a great improvement on the sickles that had previously been used for this purpose.

Other iron tools included pruning knives, billhooks, and reaping hooks, probably used to cut a variety of plants. Stone tools used in earlier times included unretouched flint flakes for cutting reeds and axes for felling timber.

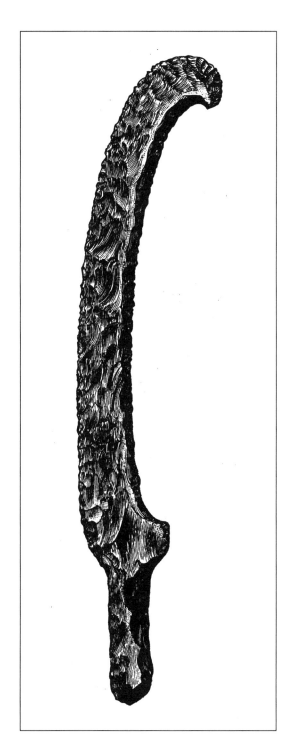

CULTIVATION

Mediterranean farmers planted their cereal crops in the autumn to take advantage of winter rains, then harvested them in the spring or early summer. In contrast, in much of temperate Europe wheat and barley were sown in the spring and harvested in the late summer, avoiding the winter cold, taking advantage of year-round rainfall, and waiting for summer sun to complete ripening. The increased range of cereals grown in the first millennium allowed the development of a rotation system, for which there is evidence in central Europe, with winter-sown crops such as rye, oats, and winter wheat alternating with winter fallow and spring-sown millets. In regions where the risk of severe frosts was lower, such as Britain, wheat and barley could also be autumn sown, extending the growing season and increasing the yield (although also risking crop failure if the winter was very severe). Cereal straw was important in its own right and might be harvested with or after the grain. Legumes and many others of the fruit and vegetables would not be harvested at one time but gathered as they ripened.

Growing crops had to be protected against animals, probably a major reason for surrounding fields with ditches, fences, hedges or walls; wild animals were also killed to discourage their predation, incidentally providing extra meat. Weeding would have increased crop yield, so the presence of many weeds of cultivation among harvested grain suggests that certain plants were considered a desirable addition to the sown crop, increasing its palatability and reducing the risk of total crop failure. Such plants could be gathered with or before the grain harvest.

AFTER THE HARVEST

Except for that portion set aside for planting the following year, grain, nuts, and pulses were often parched in ovens to remove moisture, inhibiting

3.5 An unusual flint sickle or curved knife from Late Neolithic Denmark, perhaps imitating examples in bronze (Worsaae, J. J. A. *The Industrial Arts of Denmark.* London: Chapman and Hall, 1882)

germination in storage; carbonized remains show that sometimes the parching was overenthusiastic. Fruit was also dried as well as stored fresh. Parching grain made it easier to remove the husks from hulled cereals; the grain was then pounded to break the husks before winnowing. In the wetter conditions of the Iron Age corn dryers were also developed in temperate Europe. Simpler methods were used in the small Iron Age settlement of Poswietne in Poland, where hay was dried on wooden frames and a shed with a central hearth was used to dry sheaves of grain. Drying beans and peas, grain and leaves, other crops and particularly hay all required considerable labor.

Harvested grain was probably threshed on a threshing floor in a windy spot in or adjacent to the settlement, either by driving cattle over it or by beating it with flails. A possible threshing floor is known from the Neolithic Swiss settlement of Thayngen Weier. The threshed grain was then winnowed with baskets or sieves to remove the husks. Some farmers were careful to separate weeds of cultivation from the crop before threshing, but often these were allowed to remain and were eaten with the grain. Some of the rock engravings in Val Camonica and Monte Bego in northern Italy have been interpreted as representations (as seen from the hillside above) of fields, corn stacks, and threshing floors. A ring of postholes at Twisk and circular drainage ditches at Bovenkarspel in Holland, associated with carbonized grain, have been interpreted as the remains of such corn stacks. Hay was also built into stacks for storage, protected from the rain with thatching; single posts within a circular depression may be the remains of these. A pitchfork recovered from the Somerset Levels may have been used for handling stalks of grain, hay, or other plant material such as reeds.

STORAGE

Various methods of storing of grain and other foodstuffs were employed in different areas and at different times. Pits were often used initially for storage and turned over to rubbish disposal at a later stage. Surprisingly, experiments have demonstrated that pits store grain well, even in wet countries like Britain, as long as they were covered with an airtight seal, using clay, for example, covered by soil: A crust of germinated grain quickly forms around the edges in contact with the ground, using up the oxygen and releasing carbon dioxide, creating an environment that preserves the rest. However, once the pit was opened, it could not be resealed, so it was not suitable for storing grain for daily use.

Wooden granaries consisting of a roofed platform raised on posts were widely used, particularly in the Iron Age, for storing grain, pulses, and other plant material, out of reach of domestic pigs and rodents; examples included the four-post structures associated with each house on the Urnfield settlement of Zedau and a six-poster from Late Bronze Age Elp in Holland. Such granaries were particularly used on wet sites such as the Swiss lake villages, where they were combined with storage vessels; in drier environments sacks or baskets may have been used instead of pots. The ground plan of LBK longhouses suggest the use of loft space for storage. Such raised storage buildings gave protection against animals such as domestic pigs and rodents. Pottery vessels and bins were also used. Liquids such as wine and oil could be stored and transported in vessels of stone, leather, or pottery. A well-preserved Early Neolithic house at Slatina in Bulgaria had 14 clay-lined pins arranged beside a domed oven; six of them still contained a considerable quantity of carbonized grain and pulses.

ANIMAL HUSBANDRY

Livestock were generally reared as part of a mixed economy. The relative proportions of the different animals kept depended to a considerable degree on the nature of the environment, with sheep and goats predominating in most of the Mediterranean, while cattle were the principal domestic animals in most of temperate Europe. Local conditions were also important, different crops and animals being suited to various types of terrain. For example, cattle were the main domestic animals in Bronze Age settlements on the Po plain, while caprines predominated in villages in the surrounding mountainous regions. Pigs were kept only by sedentary communities as they cannot be herded over any great distance.

The purposes for which animals were raised also determined their relative importance. The beginning of milking saw an increase in many regions in the numbers of cattle or caprines or both that were kept, while a number of cultures, such as those of Bronze Age Greece, greatly increased the size of their flocks after woolly sheep were introduced.

Other, more localized, considerations might determine which animals were kept. For example, on the Bronze Age site at Runnymede in England it is thought that pigs were in the majority because of the local presence of liver fluke to which cattle and caprines were more vulnerable than were swine.

Providing food for livestock was a major concern. In the early Neolithic when settlements were small and most land was uncleared, pigs could forage in the neighboring woods or scrub, while cattle and caprines grazed on the forest edge or on nearby hillslopes. Later, when much of Europe's forest cover had been cleared, pigs could forage around the settlement and in remaining patches of woodland, but could also find food in most types of terrain. Areas of uncleared scrub vegetation were suitable for caprines, and grassland and wetland for cattle, horses, and sheep. Trackways, such as those in the Somerset Levels, were constructed from the Neolithic period onward, to give access to islands of solid ground within wetlands that could be used for grazing.

Animals could be turned into the fields to graze the stubble and remaining weeds of cultivation after the harvest, at the same time enriching the soil with their dung. Fodder crops were also grown, including oats, some pulses, and leafy vegetables; straw from cereals provided animal feed and surplus grain and other crops could be used. In some areas barley was grown specially for animal feed. In the field systems of Celtic Europe meadows were often included to provide hay for winter fodder. Wild plants, such as leaves, reeds, sedges, and ivy, were also gathered for fodder. The need to provide adequate supplies of food set some limits on the numbers of animals that could be supported by a farming family or community, and involved making decisions: in particular, balancing the increased area that could be cultivated using an ard against the amount of land that had to be cultivated just to raise and maintain plow oxen.

The meat of animals killed in the autumn to spare the need for overwintering them was preserved, by smoking, drying, or salting. Livestock as well as providing meat and secondary products were also a means of managing fluctuations in conditions. Surplus agricultural produce in good years could be used to build up and maintain larger herds or flocks, which could then be used for trade or as reserve food supplies for leaner years. In temperate Europe, by the Bronze Age and probably earlier, stock, particularly cattle, were probably the main form of wealth, herd size reflecting the prestige and status of individuals or communities. They were also vulnerable, however, and cattle rustling was probably a major form of Bronze Age and Iron Age conflict, as it was in post-Roman Europe. Enclosures within hillforts and oppida may have been used for penning cattle when danger threatened.

Woodland Management

Areas of woodland were carefully managed from Mesolithic times onward. Dense impenetrable forests were attractive neither to people nor to game; traces of carbon and pollen profiles show that Mesolithic groups created clearings by controlled burning of trees or by ringing the bark to cause the trees to die. Such clearings were quickly colonized by hazel and other plants, attracting game such as red deer as well as providing nuts, fruits, and other human food. Fruit and nut trees were also pruned to improve their productivity. Later, domestic animals, particularly pigs and goats, contributed to the clearance of forest by eating young shoots and saplings and thus preventing the regeneration of woodland in cleared plots.

Farming communities that required large quantities of wood for building houses, fences, and trackways and making tools, carts, and many other wooden objects, also managed adjacent woods to control the types, sizes, and shapes of timber available. This might involve planting, pruning, and thinning trees, tasks whose benefits might be reaped only decades or even centuries later. In the shorter term oak, ash, and elm were coppiced, their trunks cut down to leave a low stool from which shoots grew up to form straight poles up to 8 inches (20 centimeters) in diameter. These were harvested when they reached the desired size and were used as stakes for fencing and posts for construction. Hazel and alder were also coppiced to produce thin rods cut after about seven to 11 years and used for making baskets, wattle, hurdles, and fish traps. As the tender young shoots of coppiced trees grew low, areas of managed woodland had to be fenced to exclude browsing animals, both wild and domestic. Trees such as willow could also be pollarded, the top of the tree trunk being cut off, encouraging the growth of a mass of small straight branches. Coppicing and pollarding seem likely to have been practiced from Mesolithic times onward. Coppiced wood was used in the Sweet Track in the Somerset Levels in England, dated to the winter of 3807–6 B.C.

The properties of different timbers were well appreciated, and woodland was managed to ensure that a regular supply of appropriate timber was available for every purpose. For example, trackways in the Somerset Levels were built of oak or ash planks, alder corduroy or brushwood paths, or hurdles of hazel or alder rods. At Mesolithic Tybrind Vig a dugout canoe was made of lime, with paddles of ash; at a number of sites pine was used for arrows.

Tools that required curved or angled components, such as ards, could be created by soaking and bending or joining pieces of wood, but timbers grown to the desired shape were stronger. These might be selected from naturally distorted branches, but growing branches were also trained into shape.

In addition to timber, woodlands were managed to provide fodder and fuel. Acorns and other nuts could be collected for feed or the animals driven into woodland to forage for them. Leaves for fodder were gathered in the summer and dried on racks. Since stripping leaves in quantity would be injurious to the tree, it is likely that they were preferentially gathered from trees already earmarked to be felled for timber. Fallen twigs and bark were gathered for kindling; bracket fungi were also useful for this, and tree and vine prunings and fruit kernels could also be burned. Felled timber and fallen branches were sawed into logs and stored for winter use. The production of charcoal was also important since it provided the huge quantities of fuel needed for metalworking, an important industry for much of prehistory: It is estimated that it took around 300 pounds (140 kilograms) of timber to produce 2 pounds (1 kilogram) of copper.

Intensification and Specialization

IRRIGATION AND WETLANDS

From the late fourth millennium B.C. Millaran farmers and their Argaric successors in the arid region of southeast Spain may have constructed simple dams and ditches for floodwater farming, channeling winter or spring floodwaters from adjacent streams onto arable land. This is disputed, however, and there is no supporting evidence from the plant remains that irrigation was practiced until the Argaric Bronze Age, when flax and other crops began to be grown here.

While floodwater farming was a strategy that allowed cultivation in arid regions, in temperate lands seasonally flooded land could be used at other times of year as water meadows for pasturing animals; these were made use of particularly in the Iron Age. Marshes also provided grazing and fodder as well as a rich variety of wild resources.

MEDITERRANEAN POLYCULTURE

The intensive system of agriculture that developed in parts of the Mediterranean during the third and second millennia B.C. integrated the cultivation of cereals and pulses on plain and valley soils with the raising of grapes, olives, and figs on the poorer soils of the hillslopes. Crops could also be interplanted, vegetables, and other crops benefiting from the shade and increased soil warmth of land beneath the trees. Since these crops needed attention at different times of the year, this system made it possible to raise overall productivity, but at the expense of increasing the amount of labor required by agriculture.

TREES AND ANIMALS

From the mid-third to mid-second millennia parts of southwest Spain were exploited as *dehesas:* managed oak woodlands. Parkland with holm and cork oaks and other trees were used to provide pasturage for pigs, which grew fat on acorns and chestnuts; cattle, horses, sheep, and geese could also find food there, including acorns, leaves, and tree prunings. The trees were planted, pruned, and protected while young, and were also used to make charcoal and provide fuel. Similar pastoral regimes may have been practiced in other regions of the Mediterranean.

PASTORALISM

Settled communities could increase the numbers of livestock they owned by sending them with part of the community, generally young men, to seasonal pastures outside the farmland; for example, taking sheep and goats into the uplands where summer grazing was available. It has been suggested that stock from Neolithic tell settlements in Thessaly and the Balkans were taken in the summer to graze on nearby river floodplains. Floodplains might also provide winter grazing, as has been suggested for the Neolithic farmers of the Tavoliere in Italy, while fens and marshes might be used for summer grazing, for example, by Chassey farmers in Provence or prehistoric villagers in East Anglia. In third-millennium southern France farming settlements on the Garrigues Plateau were linked to small enclosed structures away from the farms, interpreted as shepherds' huts, as well as transhumant use of higher pastures in the Grand Causses. Upland caves in southern France and elsewhere seem to have been seasonally occupied by shepherds and their flocks. Summer transhumance into the high pastures of the Apennines also developed as part of the Bronze Age expansion of land use in Italy.

Pastoralism was one way of increasing productivity when the land suitable for arable agriculture was fully settled or when overexploitation or climatic change had reduced its fertility: This, for example, may account for the shift to pastoralism in the third-millennium Balkans. It also allowed the exploitation of regions where arable land was rare or absent. In regions such as the steppe and the Alps, communities developed that devoted themselves largely or entirely to pastoralism, raising large herds of cattle or flocks of sheep and moving either seasonally or when local grazing became depleted. Steppe pastoralists also kept horses on which they could move rapidly and easily when herding their flocks. In alpine regions pockets of hillside land could be cultivated by largely pastoral communities to raise a few crops, their fertility enhanced by applying liberal quantities of manure.

Pastoral groups in modern times are often also involved in trade, carrying materials between settled communities, and other activities, and it is likely that in prehistoric Europe the same was true: For example, it is thought that pastoralists exploiting the high pastures of the Alps were involved in the beginning of metal-ore extraction in this zone.

Pastoral groups often have and had a range of symbiotic arrangements with settled communities, contracting to take villagers' animals along with their own to summer pastures or trading animal products such as wool, leather, cheese, and manure for grain. This seems likely to have been the relationship between the inhabitants of the Bronze Age *terramare* settlements on the Po plain, who practiced mixed farming, raising wheat, cattle, and pigs, and settlements in the adjacent mountains, such as Arene Candide and Castellaro di Uscio, who were herding sheep and goats, and using imported grain and pottery that they had exchanged for wool.

READING

Agriculture

Barker 1985, 1999, Whittle 1996, Harding 2000, 2002, James 1993, Milisauskas and Kruk 2002a, Reynolds 1987, 1995, Thorpe 1996: general; Milisauskas 2002b, Wells 2002, Noble 2003: arable agriculture; Zohary and Hopf 2000, Kiple and Ornelas 2000, Zeuner 1954: crops; Barber 1991: fibers; Forbes 1954a, Pyatt et al. 1995: dyes; Midgeley 1992: TRB; Sherratt 1997, Cunliffe 1993, Mercer, ed. 1984: animal husbandry; Bökönyi 1991: Iron Age; Cunliffe 1993: cats; Mercer 1990: causewayed enclosures; Bailey 2000: Balkans.

Wild Resources

Clarke 1976, Barker 1985, Mithen 1994: general; Midgeley 1992: TRB; Cunliffe 2001a: Atlantic; Finlayson 1998: Scotland; Spindler 1995: Iceman; Hodges 1971: traps; Wickham-Jones 2003, Rowley-Conwy 2002a: shellfish.

Economic Strategies

Coles, B. 1987, Coles and Coles 1986, Reynolds 1995: woodland management; Harrison 1996, Barker 1999: *dehesas*; Gilman and Thornes 1985, Barker 1999: irrigation; Reynolds 1995, Bailey 2000: storage; Kuster 1991: Manching; Arca 1999: fields in rock art; Bowen 1961: fields.

4

SETTLEMENT

The picture of European communities recovered by archaeologists is quite patchy. In the southeast where mudbrick was used in construction and tells often formed, housing is well known; in lakeside settlements where organic materials are preserved, including parts of timber houses, the picture is very full; in some areas stone was used for building impressive structures that still stand, such as the brochs of Scotland and the nuraghi of Sardinia; but in much of Europe where houses were of wood and settlements often small and difficult to locate, much of the evidence for the presence of farmers comes from funerary contexts rather than settlements, and the picture is worse for hunter-gatherer and pastoral communities, whose settlements were often occupied only for short periods and whose housing was often made largely of perishable materials. Aerial reconnaissance and landscape surveys, coupled with artifact and burial distribution studies, have achieved some success in reconstructing the pattern of settlement in some areas, but the picture of settlement in many eras and regions, particularly rural and small-scale occupation, is still significantly dependent on chance discoveries, and there are many gaps in our knowledge.

CONSTRUCTION

Domestic structures in prehistoric Europe were generally constructed of local building materials, and where necessary the style of traditional architecture was modified in line with what could be achieved with the materials available—in prehistoric Orkney, for instance, where timber, the traditional building material, was scarce, houses were built of local stone and an appropriate style of construction was developed.

Architecture also related to the local environmental and climatic conditions, taking into account such factors as shelter from summer heat or winter cold, and the volume and severity of precipitation. The needs of animals might also be taken into account in house designs, providing stalls for them either within the house or in separate outbuildings.

Social and cultural factors also influenced architectural design and the choice of materials: These included the size of the domestic unit, ranging from nuclear families through extended families to communities, the relative importance given to individual or household privacy and interaction, gender and age-related organization, and the arrangement of domestic and industrial activities. Status was also important in determining the form of structures and their material: An extreme example is the wall surrounding the hillfort at Heuneberg, part of which in one period was reconstructed in mud brick, a Mediterranean building material unsuited to the central European climate but adopted here for ostentation during the period of trade between the local chief and the Greeks.

Building Materials

MUD AND CLAY

Mud, particularly clay, was important as a building material in the Aegean and Balkans and later in the Mediterranean. It was generally mixed with straw, dung, animal hair, grass, or another temper to reinforce it and prevent cracking. The mixture was used as pisé (packed mud) or shaped into mud bricks. Clay was also used to mold internal features of houses such as hearths, storage bins, shelves, and benches, as well as ovens inside or outside the house. The use of mud, mud brick, and daub in settlements that were occupied continuously for many centuries or even millennia, such as Karanovo, resulted in the formation of tells, mounds that gradually developed as new houses were constructed over the leveled debris of their predecessors.

Mud was also used as the mortar between courses of mud brick. House floors throughout Europe were often made of beaten earth or covered with clay. Mud was widely employed as the main constituent of daub, in some areas a mixture of 60 percent soil, 30 percent clay, and 10 percent temper, in others just clay and temper. This was used to create a strong, hard, weatherproof surface covering walls made of wattle or timber, and could be further protected by applying a lime wash, which gave an attractive and durable finish.

WOOD

Roundwood The ubiquity of postholes as the remaining trace of buildings attests the importance of timber posts in construction throughout Europe. These might form the framework of a timber building with the spaces between them filled with other walling material such as wattle or planks. Poles or split posts could also be used themselves to form the walls of houses, set vertically side by side or arranged horizontally in log cabins. Posts formed the framework of subsidiary structures such as small storage buildings, and were used for some of the internal fittings of a house, such as loom uprights. Corduroy floors and paths of poles or logs were built in some settlements. Pairs of uprights with a lintel were also needed to frame and reinforce doorways; some houses had an additional pair of posts forming a porch in front of the door.

A few prehistoric European houses had a second story, its floor constructed of planks or poles covered with wattle and plaster, supported by internal posts. More commonly, these were used to create a loft over part of the house, used for storing grain and other produce and perhaps as sleeping quarters.

Substantial posts were chiefly used as roof supports, arranged in various ways. In some houses they were part of the wall framework, while in others they formed internal rows or rings, often with a timber rail fastened to their tops using a carpentry joint such as mortise and tenon.

Posts were usually set in postholes and packed with stones. Less commonly, the posts could be set into sole plates or sleeper beams laid on the ground surface or slightly sunk into it; this method was used particularly in damp settings where the ground was not firm. Experiments have shown, however, that the strength of the overall design of post-built structures kept the posts vertical and that they could therefore be erected directly on the ground surface, without postholes (making them archaeologically invisible). In settings such as lake margins and land liable to occasional flooding, posts were also used as piles to support a solid platform upon which houses were constructed. These are better known than most constructional elements, being preserved in a number of waterlogged sites.

Planks Planks, split or sawed, were used for building the walls of some houses and smaller buildings, for internal fittings, and for other domestic structures, such as the lining of wells. Floors could also be made of planks, though beaten earth was more common, and planks were also used to construct platforms as the base for houses in wet conditions.

Wattle Wattle was one of the main construction materials of prehistoric European houses and other structures. It consisted of two components: a series of upright stakes driven into the ground and a number of rods, often of coppiced hazel, alder, or willow, interwoven between the stakes. Wattle was used for the walls of small roundhouses and to fill in the spaces between the posts of timber-framed houses. In some Greek Neolithic houses bundles of reeds stood on end between the posts were used instead of interwoven rods.

This arrangement of wattle and posts on their own was adequate for fencing and the internal partitions of houses, but the exterior walls of houses for people and animals and of buildings for storing perishable materials required the protection of daub, probably generally applied inside and out in a thick layer.

Brushwood Brushwood was employed to cover damp ground, for example, forming a platform on marshy ground in the early Mesolithic camp site at Star Carr in England. Brushwood tied in bundles or pulled together could also have been used to make the frame of temporary structures, over which a covering of hides or cloth could be stretched. Some trackways were constructed of brushwood, and it was combined with piles to make artificial platforms for settlement, such as the crannogs of Iron Age Britain.

Roof Timbers Poles or beams provided the main framework for house roofs. In the Aegean some houses had flat roofs of poles laid as horizontal rafters across the tops of the walls and covered with brushwood or wattle and packed earth or mud plaster. Flat roofs were also common in the Mediterranean in later periods. Many early Aegean houses, however, like those of the rest of Europe, had pitched roofs. The lower ends of the roof beams were supported on the tops of wall posts or by transverse or ring beams running between them; in some cases the ends of the roof beams rested on the ground itself. At the apex of roofs in rectangular houses the rafters could be supported on a ridge pole running between the main upright posts of the house. The framework could be strengthened with transverse rods or beams.

In roundhouses the roof poles had to be relatively few in number, to avoid congestion at the apex. Shorter rafters, supported at the bottom but not reaching to the top, were added and the whole structure fastened together with rings of rods tied to the rafters or woven in to form a basketry framework.

STONE

Stone was used for construction in areas where timber was scarce and stone abundant, such as upland

4.1 The interior of one house in the Neolithic settlement of Skara Brae in Orkney. The shortage of wood on the island meant that stone was used to build both the houses and their fittings, such as beds and shelves. (TopFoto.co.uk, photo Richard Harding / Uppa.co.uk)

areas of Britain and France. In the Orkneys the local stone was gray flagstone, which naturally breaks into flat straight-edged slabs that were easily built up in drystone layers to form walls. Drystone masonry could also be built of other types of stone, skillfully slotted together by experienced builders to create a great variety of houses as well as walls along field boundaries and around settlements, and other structures. The roof on stone houses could be supported on wooden timbers (or in Orkney whalebone) or constructed as a corbelled dome of stone.

More elaborate constructions were frequently built of stone: These included defensive structures, such as settlement walls in some areas, and religious and funerary monuments such as megaliths and stone circles, as well as fortified domestic buildings such as brochs and nuraghi.

Stone was also sometimes used for the foundation courses of houses built mainly of wood or mud brick. In addition, there were elements of domestic structures that were often of stone, such as hearths and door pivots. Cobbled or stone-flagged floors inside houses and covering courtyards are also known in some places.

ROOFING MATERIALS

Roofs do not generally survive, and their form and building materials are generally reconstructed on the basis of structural clues from the remains of walls and foundations, debris from fallen or burnt roofs, experimental data, and ethnographic information on more recent European houses. In some cases stone-built houses were roofed in stone by corbelling, but most roofs were constructed upon a timber framework, using a variety of roofing materials. Often the roof timbers were interwoven with rods to form a wattle base, but an alternative was a mesh of strong cord strung between the beams in both directions. A layer of brushwood was another alternative. In southern Europe the wattle or brushwood could be covered with earth or plaster; elsewhere turf, peat, and thatch were generally used.

Thatch Straw, reed, seaweed, or heather thatching is suitable for use on both round and rectangular houses. The timber framework for thatched roofs needed to be pitched at an angle between 45 and 55 degrees. The thatching material was probably tied in bundles, laid across the timber framework, and fastened together. Tough cords with stones tied at each end could be placed over the thatch to weight it down and help keep it in place.

Turf and Peat   Turfs were a common roofing material and were also built up around the outside of houses in cold areas such as Scotland to strengthen and insulate them. The turfs were cut and laid grass side down over the roof framework. Another layer, grass side up, was laid on top. This created a solid covering that was both warm and weatherproof but which also allowed smoke to seep out. Peat blocks were used in the same way. Alternatively, a single layer of turfs laid facedown could be covered with a layer of straw or other thatching material.

Other   Branches covered with leaves were also suitable for roofing. Temporary structures, such as tents and huts in short-lived camps, were probably covered with hides, though textiles such as felt and woollen or linen cloth might also be used, as might bark, stripped from the tree in sheets. Stones and branches were often used to anchor the lower edge of these nonrigid materials; in eastern Europe some Palaeolithic communities used mammoth bones and tusks for this purpose and for the framework of their houses.

HOLES

Many structures in the settlements of prehistoric Europe were cut into the ground. The most ubiquitous were pits, used for storage and the disposal of rubbish. Other holes were dug to deposit votive offerings, to increase space beneath the loom for long pieces of weaving, to make wells, as graves, and for many other purposes. Some pits were lined with clay, wood, or stone, but most were simply holes.

Pit houses have been reported from sites across Europe; in many cases these are likely to have been holes dug for other purposes, particularly as quarries for the large quantities of clay needed for daub. Some circular or irregularly shaped pits formed the lower part of small huts.

On a larger scale ditches and their complementary banks also played an important part in construc-

tion. Many British roundhouses were surrounded by a bank-and-ditch enclosure, demarcating the domestic space attached to the house; similar house plots were found in other settlements such as the Impressed Ware settlements on the Tavoliere in Italy. Ditches and banks were also used as field boundaries and to enclose settlements, probably with a hedge or palisade on the top of the bank, and were used to mark the perimeters of a number of monuments, such as the British henges and cursuses, but also the many types of barrow constructed by various European societies.

In Iron Age Atlantic Europe more elaborate subterranean structures were created for storage, perhaps with a religious dimension. These souterrains were essentially underground tunnels and chambers, though each region had its own form.

Life Expectancy of Houses

The wood from buildings preserved in waterlogged sites can often be dated precisely, using dendrochronology. This has provided unexpected information on the lifespan of wooden buildings, at least on wetland sites. A number of Neolithic settlements, including Hauterive-Champréveyres in Switzerland and Charavines-les-Baigneurs in France, are made up of buildings that were abandoned after 10 to 25 years, and that had often undergone repairs during their lifetime. An even clearer picture comes from around the shores of Lake Constance (Bodensee), where between c. 3940 and 3825 B.C. a number of villages were constructed within an area around five miles (8 kilometers) across. The dendrochronological dates of these villages show that they were built consecutively, each being occupied for 10 to 15 years before a new village was built a short distance away and the old one abandoned.

The short life expectancy of these buildings may have resulted from their damp location; studies on dry-land settlements suggest that timber buildings could last for 50 to 100 years before they needed to be renewed. Here the rebuilding also often involved a change of location, although this might be over a distance of feet rather than miles. The formation of tells in Southeast Europe demonstrates that in some areas the same settlement site might be occupied for hundreds and even thousands of years; but here also experiments and ethnographic observation have shown that the individual mud-walled buildings probably had a life expectancy of only around 15 to 20 years.

DOMESTIC ARCHITECTURE

Although a few complete or largely intact houses have survived, in most cases the houses of prehistoric Europe are known only from the few traces they have left at ground level: the lowest courses of stone walls, floors with scattered domestic debris surrounded by the postholes and stakeholes of the house walls, and at worst, as in some LBK houses, little apart from the bottom portion of the postholes. From these traces many different conjectural forms of houses have been reconstructed. Sometimes these have been tested in experiments that have provided many insights into structural requirements and possibilities. Other information can be gleaned from contemporary house models and from burial structures thought to imitate houses, though these cannot be uncritically accepted as replicas of real houses.

Houses built of wood and other perishable materials are difficult to find; although some may be revealed by aerial reconnaissance and others by chance discoveries, for example, during modern ground clearance for construction, such houses are usually found when sites are examined that have been identified on the basis of other material, such as scatters of pottery or associated earthworks. This means that the more numerous and substantial the artifacts and other remains left by a settlement's inhabitants, the better the chance of their buildings being identified. Thus the homes of settled farmers, with their stone querns and pottery vessels, are far more frequently found than those of mobile hunter-gatherers and pastoralists whose seasonal or periodic movements made it imperative that they were not burdened with many material possessions.

The majority of European houses were either round or rectilinear, ranging from square to extremely elongated, though a few were trapezoidal or other shapes. Many of the few Mesolithic structures that have been traced were round, as were those of many later communities in the Mediterranean and Atlantic Europe. Square and rectangular houses were the norm in Southeast Europe, while through central Europe and into the north, west, and northeast longhouses were built. The pattern was by no means so clear-cut, however: early houses in Britain were square or rectangular, later ones round; roundhouses occurred in the Balkans and rectangular ones in the Mediterranean; Scandinavia had both round and rectangular houses; and in later times rectangular houses were sometimes the choice of the elite in areas like southern England, where roundhouses were the norm. Some houses fell into neither category: the wedge-shaped houses of Mesolithic Lepenski Vir, for example.

Ephemeral Housing

Many of the homes of prehistoric Europeans, particularly mobile hunter-gatherers and pastoralists, have left little or no trace since they were made of perishable materials and lacked substantial foundations. Often the only clues are the remains of hearths and the patterns made by the material that people discarded inside and outside their dwellings. Even permanent settlements, however, such as those of the early farmers of western Europe, have often left little structural evidence.

A number of temporary or even permanent camps are known largely from platforms constructed to protect the inhabitants from the damp in river- or lakeside locations. For example, at ninth-millennium Star Carr in England a simple platform beside a lakeshore was made by laying branches, brushwood, stones, and moss on the boggy ground beside the lake. The inhabitants of Molino Casarotto, a Neolithic settlement in northern Italy, built small wooden platforms along the lake margin, one with a substantial hearth. In neither case do traces survive of the shelters constructed on the platforms: At Star Carr these may have been tents or other flimsy temporary shelters, but at Molino they were probably huts.

MIDDENS

Shell middens, great mounds of discarded shells of marine and sometimes freshwater mollusks, are the most visible remains of sites occupied by coastal Mesolithic communities, but excavations of such mounds have yielded little trace of structures apart from hearths. Recent excavations of a midden at West Voe in Shetland, however, identified the remains of a possible structure beside the shell midden, and it is likely that more extensive exploration of the area around shell middens would lead to the discovery of camp sites and shelters.

TENTS AND TEMPORARY HUTS

Despite the difficulties of identifying temporary structures, a number have been found. Often these had a sunken floor, sometimes covered with clay or bark. The hearth was often surrounded by stones and sometimes set over a patch of sand, to reduce the risk of the fire damaging the hut. Sometimes stones were used as the foundation for these shelters, but usually they were made of wood, generally in the form of stakes that supported a covering of hides, bark, or reeds.

Terra Amata Supposedly the earliest houses in Europe, dated around 380,000 B.C., were excavated at Terra Amata in France, shelters constructed by early humans for a short stay. Sharpened stakes were pushed into the ground in a rough oval and fastened at the top. Two larger branches were erected inside as tent poles to support the roof. The shelter may have been covered with skins, held down by a ring of stones around the outside. Inside, a hollow held the fire, protected from the wind with a screen of stones, and scatters of discarded material marked where the occupants had undertaken various activities such as making stone tools.

Staosnaig (Scotland) A circular pit 13 feet (4 meters) wide was packed with charred hazelnut shells and domestic debris. This is believed to have been the lower part of a house before it was turned over to rubbish by its Mesolithic owners. A number of smaller pits surrounding it had been used for roasting the hazelnuts.

Timmeras (Bohuslan, Sweden) A pit was dug into sloping ground in a Mesolithic winter camp here, and four posts were erected in a square to support some kind of roof. Inside was a hearth containing charred food debris.

Le Baratin (southern France) This was an Impressed Ware open-air camp site where people lived in huts or tents. These had a central post and a series of posts around the outside, with river pebbles laid to form circular floors.

Divostin IA (Serbia) Around 6000 B.C. three temporary shelters were erected near the Divostinski stream, each consisting of an irregular hollow with a superstructure of branches and twigs covered with mud and clay. In the center of the floor was a hearth built of clay over a foundation of stones.

CAVES

From Palaeolithic times up to the present day, caves and rock shelters have been used to provide a ready-made place to camp or live permanently, sheltered from the weather and from predators. Often these offered adequate accommodation as they were, but in many cases some modifications and improvements were made to increase their comfort. These included hearths, windbreaks constructed of stakes or wattle and hides, and partitions of similar construction, used, for example, by pastoralists to pen their flocks at night. These simple structures could be built inside the cave or on the surrounding ground, extending the area of shelter provided by the cave. A number of caves in Bulgaria occupied during the Bronze Age contained wattle-and-daub structures.

Mesolithic Houses

Although details of most Mesolithic houses are elusive, in the Iron Gates gorge of the Danube in

Southeast Europe where a number of fishing communities existed in the eighth to sixth millennia B.C., well-defined house plans have been recovered. Lepenski Vir is the best known site, but others such as Vlasac had similar structures.

Wetland sites in Scandinavia, Latvia, and Estonia have also yielded the remains of substantial houses; these may have been exceptional in their solid construction and the carpentry skills they display, but more probably they represent the rare preservation, due to waterlogging, of building practices that were more widespread among later Mesolithic communities. These were rectangular huts, 7 to 20 feet (2 to 6 meters) long, built of posts and bark, with a central hearth placed on a layer of sand.

Lepenski Vir (Serbia) The settlement here consisted of about 25 huts set in natural and excavated hollows in the ground. These huts were trapezoidal in plan with their entrance in the wider, rounded end. Their walls were built of posts set diagonally into the ground, sloping to form the roof, and perhaps covered with hides. The floors were plastered with a crushed limestone and gravel mixture and painted red or white. Within each was a central pit lined with limestone blocks that held the hearth. Limestone slabs placed on end surrounded the hearth. Others laid flat may have been used as tables or work surfaces. Near the hearth in many of the houses was a carved limestone block depicting a fish-faced individual. Carved stones laid flat near the hearth are thought to have been offering tables or altars. A number of individuals were buried beneath the house floor at the back of the hearth.

Eyni (Estonia) Wooden beams were sunk into boggy ground as the foundations for rectangular houses of wooden uprights with two or four internal posts supporting the roof. The floor in one house was of wooden boards laid on a grid of beams; others had a covering of pine or birch bark.

Square and Rectangular Houses

Rectangular houses of various shapes and sizes, including square, were built in most parts of prehistoric Europe. Ancillary buildings such as granaries were also generally square. The majority were built of timber, with a post frame, walls of wattle and daub, and a pitched roof. In some regions, such as the Alpine lake villages, the walls might alternatively be built of planks. Some rectangular houses had stone foundations. Mud brick and pisé were also used, particularly in Southeast Europe. Floors were generally of beaten earth, but in some houses, particularly in lakeside settlements, the floors were built of planks, laid directly on the ground or raised above it.

The posts and stakes forming the framework of the house were generally driven into the ground, but in some Alpine villages and in the Baden culture sleeper beams with a hole at each end were laid on the ground surface and the corner posts were driven through the holes. Above this a wooden floor was laid and the house constructed above it, using sole plates (perforated planks) or joists to hold the uprights of the walls. Houses of this type in Bohemia had sunken floors.

SOUTHEAST EUROPE

Early houses in Greece were square or rectangular, constructed of mud brick or with a timber post and wattle framework plastered with clay. They ranged in size from 20 feet by 26 feet (6–8 meters) to almost twice these dimensions. Houses were similar in the Balkans, their walls built of timber posts and wattle covered with daub made of chaff and clay obtained from quarry pits along the sides of the house; these pits were subsequently filled with domestic rubbish or used as graves. Sometimes the inside walls of the houses were painted. The house floor might be of beaten earth or covered with clay or wooden planks.

Most early houses had a single room with a hearth with a clay surround, though some were divided into two. Some houses had a clay oven inside the house, while in other cases the ovens were built outside the houses. Clay was also used to construct storage bins and benches, while stone grindstones and clay-lined basins were also regular features. Some houses in the Balkans contained clay "altars."

Later, by the mid fifth millennium, houses in the region were similar but often larger, and in some cases their walls were built of substantial wooden planks, while others were still of posts with wattle and daub; some now also had stone foundations. Some houses were subdivided into two or sometimes three rooms, while others had a basement. In some cases there may have been an upper story or loft over some of the rooms, accessed by ladder.

Nea Nikomedeia (Greece) A two-roomed post-built house was among those in the Early Neolithic settlement of Nea Nikomedeia. The smaller room may have been the kitchen; it had a plaster bench along one side with a hearth and a storage bin set into it. The house also had a porch.

Slatina (Bulgaria) The well-preserved plan of a sixth-millennium house was excavated at Slatina. It was 42 feet by 33 feet (13 x 10 meters), constructed of posts, wattle, and daub, with three large posts in the center supporting the apex of the roof. The floor was of wooden planks covered with clay, probably renewed annually. There was one large room with a small room partitioned off at the back for storage; here were found tools and a clay box on feet (possibly a house model, interpreted as a shrine). The hearth was just inside the house's doorway, and in each of the front corners was a large wooden structure, probably a bed. One of the back corners was the kitchen area, with 14 clay-lined storage bins containing wheat, barley, and beans, a quern, and a large domed oven. Two more containers stood near the other corner. Between the kitchen and the bed was a loom, while against the opposite wall was a wooden platform. A four-post screen stood in the center of the floor between the beds; this shielded the interior of the house from view through the doorway.

OTHER AREAS

The houses of the first farmers in southern Italy are best known from the Tavoliere region. They were small rectangular timber-framed buildings, the more substantial examples with stone footings, and each was set within a small horseshoe-shaped ditched compound.

Some houses in hamlets and villages in the Alps and other upland areas were small rectangular or square huts, while others were longhouses. Lakeshore houses were originally thought to have been built over open water, an idea largely disproved by later investigations. These have shown that the houses were generally erected on the margins of

lakes where the ground was often boggy and where there might be occasional flooding. To raise them above the damp, the houses were therefore constructed on plank platforms supported by timber piles, or the ground level was artificially raised. A few north Italian settlements of the Bronze Age, however, were indeed constructed over open water; surviving piles from these settlements are as much as 30 feet (9 meters) long. In high Alpine valleys there were substantial plank-built houses with several rooms, including storage areas. Some had stone foundations and occasionally stone-paved floors. One at Padnal contained a rectangular cistern of larch posts and planks sunk into the ground.

The earliest houses in Britain were square or rectangular, though few are known. Most were small, although a growing number of larger halls have recently been found. The majority of later houses in Britain were circular, but some Iron Age houses were also rectangular, for example, those from sixth-century Crickley Hill.

In many other regions the earliest houses were small rectangular structures. Those in Scandinavia had round corners and their roofs were supported on a central row of posts. Later houses were often more substantial.

Knap of Howar (Orkney, Scotland) At Knap of Howar two rectangular houses with rounded corners, 25 feet (7.5 meters) and 31 feet (9.5 meters) long, respectively, were constructed in the fourth millennium. They had thick walls of drystone masonry, surmounted by a timber-framed turf roof. Several internal posts helped support the roof. Upright slabs divided the interior into two rooms in one case, three in the other. The furnishings included wooden and stone benches, hearths, stone-lined storage pits set into the floor, which in some rooms were paved with stone, and shelves and cupboards built into the thickness of the walls. Similar houses in timber or stone are known from other parts of Neolithic Britain.

LOG CABINS

In the Alpine regions, both in lakeside villages and on upland plateaus, houses were often built of logs. For their foundations poles were laid horizontally on the ground and held in place by vertical posts at the corners, sometimes set in sole plates. The walls above were made from further poles arranged horizontally. Log cabins were also built in other parts of Europe, for example, in the large EBA stockaded village of Biskupin.

Biskupin (Poland) The tightly packed houses in the four-acre (1.5-hectare) fortified settlement of Biskupin were built to a standardized design, in rows that shared a common roof. The walls and floor were constructed of split timbers set horizontally into grooves cut in the posts framing the house. The roof was thatched with reeds, and gaps in the wall timbers plugged with clay and moss. The house was divided into a small room for sleeping, with a communal bed, and a larger room for domestic activities, with a central hearth constructed of stone to protect the timber from fire. A loft, accessed by ladder, was used for storage. A porch or entrance hall ran the length of the outside at the front; here the domestic pigs were kept.

Longhouses

Longhouses were a particular design of timber-framed rectangular house in which the width was generally far less than the length. First appearing in Europe in LBK settlements, various types of longhouse became common from the Neolithic period onward in areas as far apart as Switzerland, the Carpathian basin, the Low Countries, northern France, Poland, and parts of Scandinavia; they were still in use in Germanic regions in post-Roman times. Some longhouses, such as those in Scandinavia, had stone footings.

RECTANGULAR LONGHOUSES

LBK longhouses were long single-story rectangular structures with a substantial timber-post framework infilled with wattle or in some cases wholly or partly with planks. The walls were covered with clay dug from large pits alongside the houses. The roofs were steeply pitched to shed rain and snow; they had gable ends and overhanging eaves to protect the walls from the wet.

The houses varied in length, some being a suitable size for a single family, others probably accommodating the separate households of an extended family, probably each with their own hearth. The longhouses were generally 33 to 100 feet (10 to 30 meters) long by 16 to 23 feet (5 to 7 meters) wide. Three internal rows of substantial posts ran longitudinally through the house, supporting the roof and dividing the house into aisles. Internal partitions were often used to divide the aisles into separate rooms. Some would have been sleeping places, others places for storing tools and equipment or food or undertaking various activities. In some houses one end was reserved for stalling livestock. At the opposite end there may have been a loft where grain and other perishables could be stored in the dry. The hearth or hearths were centrally placed and surrounded by working areas where food preparation and other domestic activities took place. Apart from the hearths, however, few of the fittings and furnishings of the houses survive.

TRAPEZOIDAL LONGHOUSES

Danubian II longhouses, particularly those of the Rössen and Lengyel groups, were similar to those of LBK, but were now trapezoidal in shape, with their entrance in the wider end wall. In some this opened into an outer room, suggested to have been a reception area in which residents could interact with visitors while domestic activities took place in the main part of the house, behind a partition wall. In Poland in settlements such as Brześć Kujawski, these houses had walls of close-set posts or planks. Many trapezoidal longhouses had no internal posts, others had fewer than before, and the roof was carried by additional posts in the walls. Often there were internal partitions, separating the house into two or three rooms.

TERPEN

Longhouses built on the *terpen* of the North Sea coast in the late centuries B.C. and early centuries A.D. were constructed of wattle and daub, buttressed externally with sloping timbers. An internal timber frame of posts and beams supported the roof poles, which were covered with thatch or turf. The floors were of beaten earth. Internal partitions of wattle separated the domestic quarters from the byre and divided the latter into stalls.

HALLS

A large fourth-millennium building similar to a longhouse but wider in proportion to its length was found at Balbridie in Scotland. This was a building of exceptional size, 43 by 85 feet (13 by 26 meters), rectangular with rounded corners, walls built of substantial posts, and internal partitions. The purpose of this structure was uncertain, its size suggesting that it was a communal hall rather than a domestic house. A number of similar buildings, however, have been found in various parts of Britain in recent years; one was excavated at Callander in Scotland in 2001 and this had internal partitions and seems, like many longhouses, to have been designed to house domestic stock at one end and the household at the other. Houses of similar form are known from northwest France and the Netherlands.

Circular Houses

The rare Mesolithic houses that have been identified were frequently round or elliptical and in Atlantic Europe and parts of the Mediterranean circular houses were also the more common form. Circular houses varied in size from small huts used for single purposes such as cooking or storage to houses as much as 70 feet (22 meters) in diameter that could accommodate a large extended family. Most roundhouses were of timber, though some had stone walls. It would also have been possible to build houses of turf, as occurred in historical times, but this would have left no trace.

PIT HOUSES

A few Mesolithic and early Neolithic pits have been identified as pit dwellings. In general these took the form of a shallow wide pit of approximately circular shape, often quite irregular, surrounded by walls of posts or stakes with wattle and daub. In some cases a central post held up the pitched roof.

Divostin Ib (Serbia) A number of early Starčevo huts here were formed of deep elliptical hollows 12 to 16 feet (4 to 5 meters) in diameter, surrounded by wattle-and-daub walls. A central post supported by

stones held up the roof. The huts contained hearths, and in one a niche had been cut into the hut wall.

Howick (Northumberland, England) A large Mesolithic coastal house, apparently occupied for at least a century around 7800 B.C., was around 20 feet (6 meters) across with a sunken floor. A ring of posts inside the house and a ring of stakes stuck at an angle around the edge of the pit supported some form of roof covering, probably of turf or thatch. A number of hearths and debris from stone tool working were found inside the house.

TIMBER ROUNDHOUSES

Most roundhouses were built of wood. In some cases roundhouses had walls of timbers placed in a circular slot. More commonly they were built of wattle. Small houses had walls of stake-framed wattle and daub, forming an upright circular basketlike structure broken by an opening for the doorway, which was reinforced by strong timber doorposts and a lintel. Larger roundhouses required an additional framework of an internal ring of posts with a ring beam to prevent the roof poles sagging. The roofs were of timber and wattle covered with thatch or turf. In some cases, for example, in many Iron Age British houses, two posts outside the door formed a porch, with a separate pitched roof. Many roundhouses had a pair of large postholes opposite the doorway; these held the uprights of a warp-weighted loom placed to give good light for weaving.

Roundhouses in Britain were often surrounded by a small bank and ditch, forming a courtyard around the house.

STONE ROUNDHOUSES

In some regions, such as upland Britain, roundhouses were constructed of stone, usually built up as drystone walls with an inner and outer face. Many of these houses were quite small. Their roofs, like those of timber roundhouses, were of timber covered with turfs or thatch.

In Bronze Age Scotland houses known as hut circles were constructed with low stone walls built up with turfs or soil. The roof was the usual timber framework supporting heather or straw thatch; in some cases the roof poles rested on the ground. These houses were often a substantial size, some as much as 50 feet (15 meters) in diameter. Timber partitions often divided the outer part of the house into bays with timber-planked floors; these might be used for sleeping or working. In some a ring of internal posts probably supported an upper floor. In the Iron Age some hut circles became more elaborate, with features typical of broch architecture such as an entrance passage and double walls with cells or passages between them.

ELABORATE TIMBER ROUNDHOUSES

Various types of large timber roundhouses constructed in Iron Age Scotland also had internal divisions. In ring-ditch houses the outer part of the interior was often dug out slightly and paved with stone; it is thought that this part of the house was a byre for sheltering livestock. The central part of the house was raised and may have been used for storage. A ring of posts supported an upper floor accessed by ladder, which provided living quarters for the family.

Domestic Strongholds

In Britain during the first millennium defensive structures were built to house families or small communities and protect them against raids by their neighbors; they were probably also designed to impress. These were stone-built houses of various forms, sometimes with a surrounding stone wall, of which the towering brochs were the most elaborate. The majority housed single or extended families; only in Orkney at a late date did they include more sizable communities.

BROCHS

Numerous brochs were constructed in Skye, northeast Scotland, Orkney, and Shetland, and a few elsewhere in Scotland, mainly in the first century B.C. and the first century A.D. They were round towers, constructed of drystone masonry forming an outer walled ring, 15 feet (4.5 meters) or more thick, surrounding an open interior 30 to 40 feet (9 to 12 meters) in diameter. The outer ring consisted of two walls, one inside the other, the outer wall tapering markedly inward so that the gap between the two walls narrowed with height. Cross slabs joined the two walls at regular intervals upward, giving structural reinforcement and forming the floor of passages. The double-wall construction also provided valuable insulation. Frequently the lowest part of the walls was built as a single solid wall, while in other cases (known as ground-galleried brochs) the hollow-wall construction started at the base. A massive entrance passage with an enormous lintel led from the outside into the broch's interior. A short way down the passage was a heavy wooden door that could be closed and fastened with substantial wooden drawbars; behind this was a guard chamber built into the wall. A staircase in the wall often led up to the galleries, which were probably used for storage.

Timber housing was built in the open interior, sometimes with posts set into the ground. A ledge (*scarcement*) of stones projecting from or set back into the inside wall at various levels provided support for the cross timbers, roof beams, and a turf or thatch roof. Brochs on Orkney generally had internal structures built of stone slabs or masonry, and sometimes they formed part of a larger complex, with an adjoining or surrounding walled courtyard. A developed form of roundhouse, found at Bu on Mainland, Orkney, and dated around 600 B.C., may have been ancestral to the broch; it consisted of a substantial wall, later thickened by adding an outer skin, pierced by an entrance passage, which surrounded an internal space of about 30 feet (9 meters) in diameter divided into chambers by stone partitions, which may also have helped support a roof.

It has been suggested that the brochs, which are strongly similar, were constructed by specialist broch builders who traveled around accepting commissions from any household or community that could afford to employ them.

Mousa (Shetland) The best-preserved broch, still standing to a height of 43 feet, six inches (13.3 meters), with an 18-foot (5.5 meter)-thick wall around an 18-foot (5.5 meter)-wide interior space. Three large cells were built into the solid base of the wall, with cupboards in their sides and windows through into the broch's interior. A stair ran contin-

4.2 The broch at Mousa on one of the Shetland Islands, Scotland (Lubbock, John. *Prehistoric Times.* New York: A. Appleton and Company, 1890)

uously from the first gallery through four higher galleries to what is today the top of the walls. This broch was probably exceptional in its height, a feature made possible by its relatively narrow diameter.

AISLED ROUNDHOUSES AND WHEELHOUSES

Two types of fortified farmhouse were constructed in the Western Isles of Scotland and on Shetland, Scotland. The wheelhouse was a round drystone structure with a series of roof-height radiating piers built out from the wall, resembling the spokes of a wheel in plan. These supported the roof and divided the house interior into chambers. The center, free of piers, contained the hearth, often built of stone and with a stone cooking tank beside it. A stone-lined passage gave access to the interior. The aisled roundhouse was similar, but the interior was divided by free-standing rather than integral piers; these gave support to the radiating beams on which the thatched or turf-built roof was constructed. Both were developments from the earlier roundhouses, and most date from the last centuries B.C. and first two centuries A.D.

Cnip (Isle of Lewis, Scotland) A wheelhouse was built at Cnip within a coastal sand dune. A passage and a large pit excavated in the dune were lined with drystone walling. The cells formed by constructing the pillars of the wheel were roofed with stone corbelling and covered with turf, and a timber-and-turf roof was erected over the center of the house, while stone slabs were used to roof the passage, also covered over with turf.

DUNS

In southwestern Scotland, particularly in coastal areas but also in the interior of central Scotland, numerous duns were constructed in the late first millennium B.C. These were drystone fortified roundhouses of somewhat irregular shape with a defended entrance and guard cell behind. They had roofs of timber and thatch and were similar to brochs but on one story only. Frequently they were located on hilltops.

COURTYARD HOUSES

In the late second century B.C. courtyard houses were constructed in Cornwall. In these a strong stone wall enclosed a paved courtyard with stone-built rooms around it, some residential, others for keeping animals or for storage. Fogous (underground chambers) were often associated with these houses.

Mansions

A number of prehistoric settlements contained a house distinguished in some way from the rest, for instance, by its size, its location in a separate enclosure, or the number and variety of ancillary buildings associated with it; these are interpreted as the residence of the local leader. Qualitatively different houses, however, are rare. Two are known from Bronze Age Sicily, the *anaktora* at Thapsos and Pantalica, which had stone foundations, an entrance vestibule, and an extensive suite of rooms; these were probably inspired by contact with the Mycenaeans. Similarly, the Greeks and Romans had some influence on the architectural form of the elite residences that appeared in some of the French and Iberian towns in the last centuries B.C. In others, however, elite houses followed native traditions, with large houses set in a palisaded enclosure, often with a number of ancillary buildings. For example, several Early La Tène sites in Bohemia have court residences, such as the one at Droužkovice. Here a large square area enclosed by a double palisade contained a smithy and a large timber house 21 by 23 feet (6.5 by 7 meters) with a stone wall on one side, while a small adjoining enclosure contained a large sunken-floor ancillary building. Recent discoveries suggest that the chiefs associated with some hillforts, such as Závist and Heuneberg, may have resided not in the hillfort itself but in a mansion in a settlement outside.

Storage Facilities

CLAY RECEPTACLES

Many houses in Southeast Europe had large built-in clay-lined storage bins. Pottery was also widely used for storage, particularly in settlements in damp locations such as lake margins. In the Iron Age amphorae were used for transporting and storing wine and other liquids such as olive oil and fish sauce.

TIMBER STRUCTURES

Small structures represented by four, six, or nine postholes are often associated with individual houses or placed elsewhere within settlements in many parts of Europe. These posts probably supported timber platforms with wattle superstructures and roofs, which were used as granaries and storage facilities for hay and other produce. Many timber houses also had lofts for storage.

PITS

Perhaps the most common and widespread form of storage facility was the round pit dug in the ground and capped with clay. Even in cold, wet Britain pits were used to store grain and other commodities, and experiments have shown that they work efficiently with little wastage from mold or other damp-induced conditions.

SOUTERRAINS

Underground passages and chambers were created in the farmsteads and villages of Scotland, Ireland, Cornwall, and Brittany from the Late Bronze Age to the early centuries A.D. They were perhaps designed to store foodstuffs that required a low temperature, such as meat, milk, and cheese. Charred grain found in one at Red Castle in Scotland shows that grain was also stored there. It is thought that they may also have had a religious significance.

The souterrains took various forms. Those of Brittany were fully subterranean. A shaft was sunk into the local rock, and a series of side chambers were excavated from it. Those of Orkney and Shetland, known also as earth houses, were also entirely underground. They consisted of a low underground passage opening into an oval chamber at its far end, accessed via an opening from the floor inside a roundhouse. Sometimes they were cut through bedrock, but often they were reinforced by walls built along the sides, while the passage and chamber were generally roofed with slabs. Sometimes stone pillars reinforced the roof of the chamber.

In Cornwall, where the structures are called fogous, a trench was dug in the ground and lined with stone walls over which capstones were fitted. The souterrains on the Scottish mainland, sometimes referred to as weems, were similarly constructed. Like the earth houses of Orkney and Shetland, they were accessed from inside the houses.

Wells

Most settlements were located near water sources, but some had wells instead. These were deep pits lined with wicker, planks, or hollow tree trunks. The earliest known example, from the LBK settlement of Erkelenz-Kückhoven, was around 45 feet (14 meters) deep and was lined with massive oak planks, notched to slot together. Dendrochronology shows that it was dug in 5089 B.C., and another in the same settlement was constructed in 5057 B.C.

SETTLEMENTS

For much of European prehistory and in many areas the majority of the farming population lived in individual farmsteads or small hamlets of a few nuclear or extended families. In the southeast, settlements were more nucleated from the start, and villages soon became the norm, many of them growing to a substantial size. Substantial villages were less common in other parts of Europe, although by the Late Neolithic there were some concentrations of people within defended settlements. In later times larger settlements appeared in many regions, but small communities still generally housed the bulk of the population. Apart from the Aegean and Italy, true towns did not emerge in Europe until the Late Iron Age.

As well as houses for people, farmsteads, hamlets, and villages generally contained accommodation for livestock, simple enclosures in many cases, though in the more inclement areas such as central Europe and the Alps, byres or stalls were often provided to shelter them in winter; stalling animals also made it easy to collect their dung for manuring the fields. Settlements also generally included provision for storing grain and other produce, often in separate buildings, pits, or lofts, and some had sheds or barns to store equipment. Farming settlements included hay and corn stacks and areas for processing crops; these are archaeologically elusive, but a possible threshing floor was identified in the Neolithic Swiss settlement of Thayngen and possible corn stacks at Twisk in Switzerland and Bovenkarspel in Holland.

Domestic industries, such as pottery making, weaving, cooking, and making and repairing tools generally took place within the home or in the open air, but in some settlements there were separate buildings for these activities. Some villages and farmsteads also saw the practice of specialist industries (for example, Gussage All Saints, where bronze harness and vehicle fittings were made), although more commonly such production tended to be concentrated in the major settlements. There was also specialist settlements housing the people working in extractive industries such as mining and salt making.

Towns and often hillforts reflected a society in which there was a social hierarchy and some division of labor. These settlements, therefore, had houses of different sizes, and sometimes of different designs, belonging to the elite, artisans, and farmers, as well as workshops. These settlements might also have a shrine. Facilities for storing large quantities of produce and sheltering large numbers of livestock were also present in many major settlements, which were often the place of refuge for the local rural population.

Farmsteads and hamlets often had gardens for growing food within the settlement and intensively cultivated fields immediately outside, with grazing and sometimes further fields beyond. Some of the hillforts and oppida also included fields. In nucleated settlements, however, the houses were closely packed, and all the cultivated land lay outside the settlement.

Since water was a necessity, most settlements were located within easy reach of a spring, stream, or accessible river, although in some cases other considerations, such as defense, made this impossible, and their inhabitants relied on wells where these were possible or rainwater, caught in cisterns, barrels, or large jars.

Defense was often important in the siting and layout of settlements. Most commonly the defenses took the form of ditches and banks, probably topped with fences or hedges, but some settlements had more substantial defenses, such as wooden palisades or walls of wood and stone. The lie of the land might also be harnessed to protect the settlement. Perhaps the most extreme example is the promontory fort or cliff castle, a feature of parts of Iron Age Atlantic Europe, where the settlement was on a spit of land defended at its neck by banks and ditches and surrounded on all other sides by steep unclimbable cliffs.

Temporary Settlements

Many inhabitants of prehistoric Europe, such as hunter-gatherers and pastoralists, miners and traders, led lives that involved seasonal or periodic movement. Few of their campsites have been located, however, and most are known only from hearths and scatters of discarded material, with occasionally traces of a hut or two.

In several periods of European prehistory few settlements are known in some areas, and it is thought that the people pursued a mobile way of life in which they occupied temporary settlements with insubstantial buildings. This has been suggested, for instance, for the Beaker and Corded Ware periods and for many areas during the Bronze Age, when burials are far better known than settlements. While in some cases this must reflect the reality of the situation, in others it is due to chance in discovery. For example, the paucity of settlement evidence led archaeologists to believe that mobile pastoralism played the major role in the Neolithic British way of life, but the discovery in recent years of many farmsteads has completely altered the picture.

Mesolithic Villages

Well-preserved remains of hunter-gatherer houses are rare, and rarer still are settlements whose layout has been preserved and excavated. One exception is the group of Mesolithic settlements found in the Iron Gates Gorge of the Danube, dated to the eighth to sixth millennia B.C., some probably occupied for short periods, others permanently inhabited by communities that relied heavily on fish and river resources. Of these the best known is Lepenski Vir. Here some 25 trapezoidal houses were arranged with their wide ends facing the river. The houses were frequently reconstructed, but in most phases of the occupation they seem to have been divided into two groups and there was one larger house. A similar division into two clusters of houses was found at other settlements such as Vlasac. In Lepenski Vir people were buried within the houses, whereas at Vlasac the graves were arranged around the outside of the houses.

Small Farming Settlements

OPEN SETTLEMENTS

In many parts of Europe farmsteads, hamlets, and villages were generally unenclosed settlements of timber buildings; this has made them harder to discover than settlements defined by banks and ditches or constructed in stone or those that created tells, all of which have left traces visible without excavation. Those that have been found take many different forms, depending on environmental, economic, and social conditions as well as cultural traditions.

Padnal (Grisons, Switzerland) Located in a mountain valley, this settlement was founded around 1700 B.C. in a natural hollow that was made more suitable by leveling and terracing the ground. Five or six houses with walls of posts and planks and sometimes stone foundations were constructed in a row with a gap in the middle. They were all small square or rectangular structures, 13 to 16 feet (4 to 5 meters) long, with a hearth. By the 14th century the settlement had grown to eight or nine houses arranged in three rows, still with a central gap between. They now all had stone foundations, some had stone-paved floors, and those on the southern side were now larger, up to 30 feet (9 meters) long, and divided into two or three rooms. The settlement was still occupied in the eighth century, when there were at least three houses.

Dampierre-sur-le-Doubs (France) A Late Bronze Age valley-bottom village of small rectangular post-built houses, abandoned due to flooding, it was later reoccupied and new houses constructed. The later settlement had 28 houses, three of them with wooden floors, and one larger one with an apsidal end, perhaps the residence of the village leader. The houses were laid out in groups of two to four, possibly representing the homes of families within an extended family group. Outside the village was a cremation cemetery.

LONGHOUSE SETTLEMENTS

The settlements of LBK, the first farmers in temperate Europe, took two forms. In some cases the houses were grouped in hamlets of six or fewer longhouses; in other cases the longhouses were strung out in a continuous ribbon, each house separately sited around 150 to 350 feet (50 to 100 meters) from its nearest neighbor. In some the houses themselves included stalls for the animals, while in others there were smaller buildings of the same design, which probably served as barns or byres, and some settlements had a single, much longer roundhouse, up to 145 feet (45 meters) long, which was perhaps a community hall or shrine. People were often buried within the settlement, but there were also some separate cemeteries shared by a number of hamlets. Most LBK settlements were unenclosed, but a few were surrounded by one or more ditches. Around the houses and within a half-mile (1-kilometer) radius were areas of cultivated ground, probably protected from animals by fences, in which the crops required by the household were raised.

In the following period, Danubian II, these longhouse settlements became more nucleated and were more commonly surrounded by a bank and ditch or fence; some were also larger. In addition, in some areas there were sometimes associated ditched enclosures. Similar settlements continued throughout prehistory and into Roman times and beyond in many areas of temperate Europe, from Switzerland to Scandinavia.

Elp (Drenthe, Netherlands) The settlement excavated on a sand ridge at Elp was a farmstead occupied in the later Bronze Age, with one large longhouse 80 to 100 feet (25 to 30 meters) long, a smaller house or barn, and two sheds, one large and one small. A number of times during the life of the settlement a new longhouse and subsidiary buildings were constructed on an adjacent part of the ridge and the old ones abandoned or demolished. The longhouse was divided into two parts, with human habitation in one and stalls for around 30 head of cattle in the other. The smaller house accommodated another 15 or 20 cattle or was also divided into separate sections for people and a smaller number of cattle. The larger shed had sturdy posts supporting a platform and was probably a granary; the smaller shed may also have been for storage. A U-shaped enclosure at the end of the house perhaps surrounded haystacks to protect them from the pigs kept in the farmstead. Small fields must have surrounded the farmstead, fertilized with the manure collected from the stalled cattle. Those associated with similar settlements were demarcated by ditches.

Hodde (Jutland, Denmark) A late prehistoric village was built at Hodde in the first century B.C. within a fence with gateways that gave access to the surrounding fields. Around 20 small longhouses made up the settlement, each including stalls for the animals and with its own barns and other subsidiary buildings, surrounded by its own fence; at its greatest extent there were 27 houses. In the center of the settlement was a village green, and in one corner was a separate enclosure within which were a much larger house, belonging to the village chief, and storage buildings.

CAUSEWAYED ENCLOSURES

Circular or subcircular enclosures were constructed in the sixth to fourth or third millennia in much of Europe, particularly southern Britain and central Europe, where they were associated with some groups of longhouse settlements. These enclosures were demarcated by one or more banks and ditches interrupted by causeways, from which they take their name *causewayed enclosures*. Although some of the causeways served as entrances to the enclosure, others resulted from the method of construction, in which ditch segments were separately excavated, perhaps by different groups of people. The enclosures seem to have had many different functions. Some may have been the venue for communal ceremonial or social activities. Others, it has been suggested, may have served as corrals periodically used to keep together a large number of animals. A number of causewayed enclosures were defended settlements: Several British examples of this sort suffered attacks.

In eastern central Europe more regular ditched enclosures known as roundels are also associated with longhouse settlements; these were circular, with one or several ditches and several palisade rings, but apparently no banks, interrupted by four entrances. None of these seem to have been occupied by houses, and a community function seems most probable.

In southern France fifth- and fourth-millennium enclosures of various sizes, defined by interrupted ditches and stretches of palisade, including large ones such as that at Saint Michel du Touch, contained pits and hollows filled with burnt stones; these may also have been used for communal activities rather than for settlement.

Stepleton Enclosure (Dorset, England) One of three causewayed enclosures on Hambledon Hill, the Stepleton enclosure was about 2.5 acres (1 hectare) in extent. In its first phase of use it had one ditch and a bank enclosed within a timber rampart.

Pits, domestic debris, and some fragmentary traces of structures inside it suggest that people lived here; their wasteful use of food might imply that they were an elite group. A stillborn baby was buried in the side of the ditch. Later, a more massive ditch was dug, backed by a box rampart built of oak timbers, and the enclosure was incorporated within a ditch and rampart system enclosing the whole hill; these defenses were later strengthened. Despite this, the settlement was attacked and burnt to the ground; one man fleeing with a child was shot in the back with an arrow, and others also died.

ENCLOSED VILLAGES

Settlements of various sizes were constructed in Italy from the seventh millennium onward, and these are particularly well known in the Tavoliere in the south, where the villages were made up of rectangular houses within small round ditched enclosures. Cobbled areas within these villages were probably used for various activities such as food preparation. The settlement was defended by one or several ditches, sometimes as many as eight; sometimes bodies were buried in these ditches.

Ditched settlements have also been found in parts of the Mediterranean and western Europe, some containing square or rectangular houses, others houses that were round or oval. Only in waterlogged settings have these yielded good structural information. Elsewhere the evidence is often difficult to interpret; for example, the Neolithic causewayed enclosure of Saint-Michel-du-Touch in southern France contained hundreds of large hollows filled with burnt stones. Some scholars see these as the foundations of huts in a populous village, while for others, more convincingly, these were cooking places, the result of feasting when the scattered inhabitants of a large area came together to celebrate.

Passo di Corvo A large Early Neolithic settlement on the Tavoliere, Passo de Corvo was an irregular 70-acre (28-hectare) enclosure bounded by a continuous ditch; on one side there was a parallel ditch and in the adjacent stretch a third. Within this were around 90 horseshoe-shaped ditched hut compounds. Attached to the enclosure was another ditch enclosing a further 100 acres (40 hectares).

ROUNDHOUSE FARMS AND HAMLETS

Small enclosed settlements of roundhouses—farmsteads, hamlets, and villages—were built in various parts of Atlantic Europe and the Mediterranean. In some, small roundhouses were grouped together to make up the living and working quarters of individual families. In others the household was accommodated in a single large roundhouse where they performed their daily activities together.

In second millennium southern Italy and the Aeolian Islands some settlements of small roundhouses were located in defensible situations such as promontories. The houses were grouped close together, making it necessary to pen the domestic animals outside the settlement.

In many settlements in Bronze and Iron Age Britain, a bank and ditch, fence, or wall enclosed groups of small roundhouses and an area of open ground in which the animals might be penned at night. Each house cluster contained a large residential roundhouse and a group of others, of the same size or smaller, which were used for other activities such as cooking, storage, and weaving. In addition to the huts there were small four-post structures, probably granaries, drying racks, and other agricultural structures. Farmsteads like this could exist singly or be grouped into hamlets of three or four households or larger villages. Often Iron Age farmsteads were surrounded by banjo-shaped banked and ditched enclosures. These probably had a fence or hedge on the top of the bank, serving to keep livestock in or out as required but not providing serious defense. A few similar farmsteads have been found that were unenclosed; given the difficulty of discovering them, these may well have been common. In Atlantic Britain a variety of forms of enclosed farmstead and village were constructed: For instance, in Cornwall these were small villages of courtyard houses with fogous, garden plots attached to the houses, and small fields around them.

Black Patch (Sussex, England) A Late Bronze Age settlement with; four house platforms of which one was excavated, this comprised a large domestic roundhouse thought to have been used by the males of the household for craft activities and also used for storing the farmstead's grain in pits, flanked by sev-

4.3 A reconstruction of a small Iron Age roundhouse settlement, c. 400–c. 150 B.C., based on the settlement excavated at Dawley in London, England (TopFoto.co.uk., (c) Museum of London/HIP, Photographer: Derek Lucas)

eral smaller roundhouses where the women lived and performed their daily tasks such as cooking and weaving. Other small houses may have been used for stalling animals. Two ponds provided the water needed by the people and animals of the farm. The settlement was surrounded by wattle fencing, and beyond this were fields and pastures.

Industrial Settlements

Raw materials such as stone, flint, and metal ores were often mined by groups of people who visited the source area periodically, camping there for some time before returning to their homes elsewhere. For example, in the TRB period the people who mined flint at Krzemionki Opotowskie in Poland came from the settlement at Cmielów in the nearby Kami-

enna valley while those who mined copper at Cwmystwyth in Wales probably lived near the coast at the mouth of the Ystwyth, some 20 miles (30 kilometers) away. In some cases, however, and increasingly from the Bronze Age, permanent settlements developed in these areas, inhabited by people who specialized in mineral extraction. These took various forms, depending on local conditions, but some became extremely wealthy, with populations in the hundreds.

Dürrnberg bei Hallein (Salzburg, Austria) Salt extraction at Dürrnberg began around 600 B.C., and by around 400 the Dürrnberg mines had eclipsed the earlier mining complex at nearby Hallstatt, less accessibly located. In the sixth century the miners lived on hillslopes near to the mines. Settlement expanded over a wider area in the fifth century, with a concentration on the slopes of Mosterstein of houses, metal foundries, and workshops where pottery was made and glass worked. Another village was situated in the Ramsautal valley, with pottery, leather, bronze, and iron workshops. Above this on a high spur of the Ramsaukopf surrounded by precipices a hillfort was built, thought to have been the residence of the local chief. The neck of the spur, the only access route, was defended by massive walls of drystone construction. Each community working the Dürrnberg mines had its own cemetery, located near their houses but on high ground unsuitable for settlement. The grave goods from these cemeteries, both imports and local craft products, reflect the wealth that trade in salt brought to Dürrnberg.

Wetland Settlements

Preservation by waterlogging means that lakeside and other wetland settlements have yielded far more detailed evidence of house construction, settlement organization, and domestic life than most other kinds of settlement.

LAKE VILLAGES

In lakeside locations in northern Italy, France, and the Alps, settlements were built on damp lake margins on platforms supported by piles, which lifted the settlement above the level at which there was danger from flooding. A few Bronze Age lake settlements were built over open water. Many villages were small, with around eight or 10 houses; some early lakeside settlements were hamlets of three or four houses or farmsteads, while others, particularly in later periods, had considerably more houses. Larger settlements were arranged as parallel rows of houses separated by paths, to make best use of the restricted space. Various types of houses were built, including square or rectangular huts and log cabins. Others were timber-framed longhouses with clay floors and wattle partitions, some containing stalls for animals, while in other cases there were separate byres in which the animals spent the winter, being stall-fed on leaves and other plant material. Raised granaries constructed as platforms supported by

posts were commonly used for storage, to keep foodstuffs well above any dampness, but houses might also have storage jars. In later settlements there were also craft workshops. Corduroy pathways of timber connected the houses within the settlement, which was enclosed within a wooden palisade. Some villages had more substantial defenses, particularly at their entrances. In many cases in which dendrochronology has been used to study the history of individual houses, it seems that the lake dwellers occupied a settlement for only a short period, often no more than 20 years and rarely more than 70, but that they then constructed a new settlement nearby, occupying the general area often for thousands of years.

Niederwil (Lake Bodensee, Switzerland) A Pfyn village in which the original houses were small huts; later in its 50-year existence, longhouses with internal partitions were also built here. The houses were arranged in terraced rows. The village probably housed around 100 to 150 people, or fewer if the houses were not all occupied at the same time. A strong palisade surrounded the settlement, and there was also an area where sheep and goats were stalled.

Twann (Lake Bienne, Switzerland) This lake village was occupied periodically throughout the Neolithic period, from Cortaillod to Horgen; on 21 occasions rising lake levels forced the villagers to move elsewhere, but the site was reoccupied when lake levels fell again. The settlement has yielded many artifacts made of organic materials, including dugout canoes and even a preserved loaf of bread.

Thayngen Weier (Lake Bodensee, Switzerland) This Pfyn hamlet of eight or 10 single-roomed houses was occupied sporadically for around two centuries, growing eventually to around 30 houses. Part of the settlement was given over to crop processing, with a threshing floor. There were also barns for storing fodder and cowsheds.

Hauterive-Champréveyres (Lake Neuchâtel, Switzerland) Five settlements were found in this locality, the oldest a Palaeolithic campsite of the Magdalenian period. The site was reoccupied in the Neolithic period and again in Hallstatt times. Dendrochronology has provided details of the life of one Neolithic settlement here: The first house was built with timbers felled in spring 3810 B.C., and in the same year five others were constructed. Nine years later, another house was added, and an oak fence was built around the settlement, which also included other small buildings. Repairs were periodically carried out on the houses, but around 3793 B.C. the hamlet was abandoned.

Charavines-les-Baigneurs (Lake Paladru, France) Around 2750–2730 B.C. people constructed two rectangular houses and subsidiary buildings of pine wood at Charavines and added five more over the next four years. One house was rebuilt five years later, and all saw repairs and maintenance over the next few years, but around 22 years after the hamlet was founded, its inhabitants abandoned it. Thirty-six years later, people returned here and built another farming settlement, using a variety of different types of timber, but after 21 years this was flooded by rising lake levels and the people moved away. The inhabitants of this hamlet grew wheat, barley, and flax, but also collected wild fruit, nuts and berries, and they made textiles and rope from wool and flax.

TERRAMARE

During the second millennium B.C. farmers spread into the Po plain, where flooding was common. In many cases, therefore, their settlements, known as *terramare*, were built on artificial mounds, raised 10 to 13 feet (3 to 4 meters) above the surface of the plain. The mounds were constructed of clay, domestic rubbish, branches, and other organic material, sometimes packed into wicker baskets. Piles driven into the marshy ground held these in place, and some *terramare* had substantial timber revetments. Settlements varied considerably in size and were

4.4 A 19th-century reconstruction of one of the Bronze Age Swiss lake villages (Figuier, Louis. *Primitive Man.* London: Chatto and Windus, 1876)

generally of rectangular post-built houses, though log cabins, houses built on sleeper beams, and roundhouses are also known. Some *terramare* were surrounded by a moat or ditches, for drainage and perhaps defense.

TERPEN AND WIERDEN

In the easily flooded salt marshes that developed during the Iron Age along the North Sea coast, artificial mounds of clay, animal dung, and domestic refuse up to 20 feet (6 meters) high were raised. On these mounds, known as *terpen* in the Netherlands and *Wierden* or *Wurten* in Germany, settlements ranging from farmsteads and hamlets of two or three longhouses to sizable villages were constructed. The longhouses included stall provision for the cattle, whose dung was collected for use as manure. A supply of freshwater for drinking was assured by using wells and cisterns to catch and store rain. The limited arable land in the vicinity of these settlements was cultivated to grow cereals and legumes, but cattle were the main focus of the economy, pastured on the marshes in summer and stall-fed on hay from these meadows in the winter; other domestic animals and fish also contributed to the food supply.

Ezinge (Friesland, Netherlands) A timber-fenced farmstead was established on a *terp* at Ezinge around 500 B.C., consisting of two longhouses divided into domestic accommodation at one end and a byre at the other, along with a solidly built large rectangular building with nine rows of five posts supporting a platform, probably a granary. The settlement grew larger in later centuries, with five to 10 longhouses arranged radially, with the domestic accommodation facing the center of the settlement, where there was a pond, and the byre ends opening onto a track running around the outside of the houses. Around 400 A.D. the settlement was destroyed by fire.

Feddersen Wierde (Germany) This began as a farmstead in the first century B.C.; several others were added, each on their own mound, but in the first century A.D. these were combined into a single large *terp* on which a village of around 30 longhouses was built. Around A.D. 450 flooding brought about its abandonment. The village had a larger aisled house set apart within a palisade and ditch, which may have been the residence of the village chief. Within this compound were workshops where craftsmen made objects of leather, wood, bone and antler, iron, and bronze. Material from the great house included Roman imports. Cattle were stalled in the compound, and there were also granaries, suggesting that the chief who lived here controlled local production. Many of the individual longhouses had nine-post granaries or sheds, and the village also had a large hall for community use.

CRANNOGS

Numerous Scottish and Irish lakes, and a few elsewhere in Britain, contain crannogs, natural islands built up with additional material or wholly artificial islands. These were created from the Neolithic period onward, though most were constructed in the Iron Age. Crannogs were largely built as defended settlements, but other methods of protecting settlements, such as timber palisades, would have been less labor intensive, suggesting that the construction of a crannog also conferred prestige. Many crannogs were the base for a single farmhouse, though some held villages, while others were merely places for fishing or catching waterfowl, or corrals to protect domestic stock from wild animals. Some were located near the shore, others well out into the lake. Access to some was via a wooden causeway, sometimes with a section that could be withdrawn like a drawbridge; others could be reached only by boat.

Crannogs were built up of every kind of wood, from piles driven into the lake bed as the foundation and edging for artificial islands, to waste timber, brushwood, and discarded wooden artifacts used as the base for a wooden platform. Stones and boulders and layers of peat and clay or marl might also be dumped into the lake as the base on which the timber island was constructed.

Milton Loch (Dumfries and Galloway, Scotland) A crannog on Milton Loch, occupied around 700–300 B.C., had a single large roundhouse 42 feet (12.8 meters) in diameter, divided into rooms with internal partitions. A wooden walkway ran around the outside of the house. Linked to the mainland by a wooden causeway, the crannog also had a small

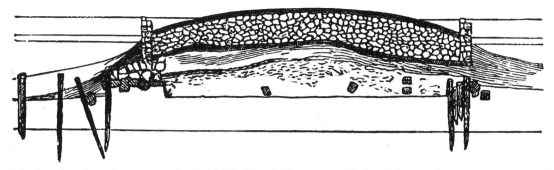

4.5 A section through a crannog in Ardakillin Lough, Roscommon, Ireland, showing how it was constructed of wooden posts driven into the lake bed, holding in place layers of stone and earth (Lubbock, John. *Prehistoric Times*. New York: D. Appleton and Company, 1890)

harbor inside two extended arms of the crannog platform that formed jetties. At least two other crannogs were also constructed near the edge of this loch (lake).

Glastonbury (Somerset, England) This Iron Age village was constructed on an artificial island of clay mounds and timber in what was then a lake but is now land. The settlement began around 150 B.C. with a few roundhouses and sheds set in circular enclosures. Over time new houses were built, and a palisade was constructed around the crannog, with a landing stage. At its height the settlement housed around 200 people but later declined in size. The village was composed of large roundhouses with smaller ancillary buildings in which domestic and industrial activities took place, including cooking, spinning and weaving, metalworking, pottery making, woodworking, and basket making. One larger house may have housed the village chief. Large numbers of sheep were grazed in the nearby sedge wasteland in summer and were driven onto the surrounding hills in winter when the land around the village was waterlogged; the making of woollen textiles was probably an important local industry. The villagers cultivated fields on the adjacent dry land, caught fish from the lake, and killed wildfowl with clay slingstones. Several log boats and a number of lathe-turned vessels and wheel naves were among the wooden objects recovered from the village.

Forts, Towers, and Fortified Farms

In the Atlantic region, Iberia, and some islands of the western Mediterranean, stone-walled structures were built at various times during the fourth to first millennia. Some were intended to house communities and protect them against raids by their neighbors, others appear not to have been defensive, but in many cases the stone structures were also designed to impress. In some regions settlements were defended by stone ramparts or multiple banks and ditches. In others the defenses included towers, which may have been used as a place of refuge for the inhabitants of farms scattered over the surrounding countryside, or as a place of residence or of defended storage.

CHALCOLITHIC IBERIA

A few sites surrounded by massive walls appeared in the late fourth millennium in the Tagus estuary in southern Portugal and Almeria in southeast Spain. The walls, which often had bastions, were remarkably thick. Little evidence suggests warlike activity at the time, and it is likely that the walls were built more for show, to gain local prestige, than for defense. Beside the settlements were megalithic tombs. These sites continued in use into the late third millennium, perhaps as the home of the evolving local elite whose rich burials were still to be found in the local megalithic tombs. Housing within these fortifications is poorly known.

Zambujal (Portugal) Located on a peninsula, Zambujal was surrounded by a circular wall up to 13 feet (4 meters) thick, with a single entrance, and outside this two further arcs of walling, all with bastions. A rock-cut ditch 13 feet (4 meters) wide lay between the inner and middle walls. The walls were frequently modified and added to. A cemetery of megalithic tombs lay outside its walls.

Los Millares (Almeria, Spain) Los Millares was constructed on a rocky promontory that was encircled by three massive walls. Inside was a smaller walled area. In its first stage the entrance to the settlement was through a gap in the outer wall, but this was embellished through time, and in its final stage was an elaborate gateway with barbicans projecting more that 38 feet (12 meters). A number of circular bastions lay along the outer face of the wall. Smaller walled enclosures lay outside, along with a cemetery of 80 passage graves.

NURAGHI, *TORRE*, AND *TALAYOTS*

Stone tower houses were built in the Mediterranean islands during the second millennium; these are known as nuraghi in Sardinia, *torre* in Corsica, and *talayots* in the Balearics. They were built with a double wall enclosing stairs and passages that gave access to chambers on two or three floors in the tower's interior. The top of the tower was closed with a corbelled vault. Early towers stood alone and were probably the home of small groups such as single extended families, but they might also act as places of refuge for a wider community during armed raids. However, in the 12th century B.C. stone bastions or lobe-shaped extensions were added to the exterior at ground level. These formed a fortified village housing the entire local population, giving them protection against intercommunity raids. Alternatively, a village of stone houses might be constructed around the base of the tower. Increasingly, the tower itself came to be the residence of the community's chief.

MOTILLAS AND *MORRAS*

In the Early Bronze Age, around 2200–1500 B.C., monumental stone towers known as *motillas* or *morras* were constructed in southeast Spain, surrounded by several circular masonry defensive walls. These were locally spaced at regular intervals of around 10 miles (15 kilometers) or less and provided the focus for settlement in the *meseta* plains, an area where the limited availability of drinking water was a crucial determinant of settlement location. These towers resembled the nuraghi and other towers of the western Mediterranean islands in form and in the associated way of life. The settlement around the tower might reach up to 7.5 acres (3 hectares) in extent.

These towers had a square or rectangular base with walls three feet to four feet, six inches (1 to 1.4 meters) thick and of varying heights, sometimes more than 20 feet (6 meters). External walls were added through time. The area inside these walls was divided by partitions of wood, stone, and mud into separate areas used for industrial activities and for large-scale storage, for instance, of grain, while the inhabitants of the complex lived in the houses outside the walls. In contrast, the contemporary cultures of the uplands had large complex stone-built settlements, but no evidence of central storage.

BROCHS

In the later first millennium the tower houses known as brochs were erected in parts of Scotland. While in most of the region these were elaborate farmsteads, in Orkney they became the focus of larger settlements. It is thought that these Orcadian brochs were the residence of the local leader, while the surrounding houses were the homes of his followers.

Gurness (Mainland, Orkney) A ground-galleried broch here was surrounded by a courtyard and a massive enclosure wall. Between the wall and the broch a complex of closely packed semi-detached stone houses grew up, eventually accommodating 30 or 40 families. The settlement was in use for around three centuries. In the broch interior stone had been used to construct partitions, tanks, and a hearth.

Jarlshof (Shetland) A long-lived prehistoric farmstead was founded here in the Neolithic period, favorably located by a natural harbor, freshwater, arable land, and pasture. In the later Iron Age a broch was constructed here, half of it now removed by coastal erosion. The entrance lay in the now vanished part, while on either side of the interior space there was a cell built into the wall at ground level. In the center of the broch interior a well 13 feet (4 meters) deep had been cut into the bedrock. A courtyard surrounded by a wall still standing to 10 feet (3 meters) high had been constructed outside adjoining the broch; in this an aisled roundhouse was later built. At a later date this was abandoned and a wheelhouse was partially built over it, along with at least one other wheelhouse in the courtyard and another inside the broch. Settlement in this favored spot continued into Viking and later times.

FORTS AND BLOCKHOUSES

A number of fortified farmsteads were built on promontories on Shetland in the later first millennium B.C. These consisted of a walled enclosure with farm buildings probably built as lean-to wooden structures around the inside of the wall. Some had a blockhouse just inside the entrance in the wall; these were substantially built stone structures, containing small chambers, and sometimes with an attached wooden structure at the rear. They created a monumental gateway to the enclosure and might have been the residence of the owner of the complex who, by analogy with similar structures in Ireland in historical times, may have been the local chief, a view reinforced by a number of cases, such as at Clickhimin, where the blockhouse was later replaced or superseded by a broch.

D-SHAPED FORTIFICATIONS

In the second and first centuries B.C. a number of D-shaped fortifications (semibrochs) were built in Skye and the adjacent Scottish mainland, formed of a semicircular wall or hollow double wall with the straight side of the D along a cliff or precipice edge. Like brochs, these fortifications were entered through a strongly built passage containing a stout door fastened when closed with substantial wooden bars.

STONE FORTS

In western Ireland small communities occupied homesteads with multiple stone defensive walls known as stone forts; some date to the first millennium A.D., others go back to the Late Bronze Age. Some were built on cliff edges, others inland. The massive inner wall, in some cases as much as 18 feet (5.5 meters) high, surrounded the settlement of huts in an unbroken ring with staircases enabling people to climb over.

Dun Aonghasa (Aran Island, Ireland) Occupied from the late second millennium B.C. into the first millennium A.D., this was a small settlement on the edge of a sheer cliff, enclosed by a semicircular stone wall and later expanded with the addition of a larger subrectangular outer wall beyond which an area of *chevaux-de-frise* had been constructed. Another wall enclosed an area of land beyond.

CLIFF CASTLES AND PROMONTORY FORTS

Cliff castles and promontory forts were a feature of first-millennium Brittany, Ireland, and western Britain, and are mentioned as places of refuge by Caesar when he was campaigning in Gaul. Headlands with steep cliffs projecting into the sea were fortified by digging one or several sets of banks and ditches across their landward end. Some were permanently occupied, others probably used only in times of need. They may also have served a religious purpose; classical authors mentioned that such places were sacred to the gods. On Shetland some cliff castles had a broch built inside.

ROUNDS, RATHS, AND DUN ENCLOSURES

From the late second millennium into the Roman period, the inhabitants of parts of western Britain were densely settled in defended farmsteads, known as rounds in southwest England and as raths in Wales. These were settlements of a few roundhouses and storage structures built within a substantial drystone or bank-and-ditch enclosure with a stone revetment. In western Scotland similar drystone masonry enclosures were constructed, known as dun enclosures. Contemporary settlements in western Brittany were similar: farmsteads defended by a bank and sometimes a ditch.

PASTORAL ENCLOSURES

In southern upland sites in France the late fourth and third millennia saw the construction at sites such as Boussargues and Lébous of polygonal walled enclosures of drystone masonry. Their corners were formed by a series of round or apsidal buildings with corbelled roofs, opening into the interior. Inside these were hearths and pottery vessels; they were probably houses, occupied by pastoralists who penned their animals in the center of the enclosed space. Unenclosed settlements and cave sites in the same area were probably also occupied during the summer months by pastoralists.

Tells

The early settlements in the Balkans and Greece were small villages of around 10 to 20 houses, though they grew in size as time went on, frequently forming tells, though these were absent in some areas. In the Balkans some villages contained as many as 60 houses. In Greece, although the houses contained hearths, outside ovens in the settlement seem to imply that the inhabitants of the village cooked and ate together; in Balkan villages the ovens were generally inside the houses. Some villages also included a larger house, whose purpose is uncertain; it might have been a communal hall or perhaps a religious structure. Burials were interred in various places: under the houses, around their outside, or at the edge of the settlement.

In tell villages, known as far north as Hungary, the houses were placed close together, and in some they were arranged in rows. As the tell rose, the houses often became more tightly packed. By the mid-fifth millennium, some of the Balkan villages had achieved a considerable size and were often planned, with the houses arranged in rows or concentric circles or laid out in blocks. The buildings included both residential houses and ones used for storage and other purposes, including as workshops for people who by this time may have been specialist artisans. Some houses were larger than the rest; these were either for community use or were the residences of an emerging elite. Villages often also had a house that is thought, on the basis of its con-

tents, to have been a shrine; many figurines were found in them. The village was generally well defended, both in its location and by building a ditch and palisade or a stone wall around it, broken by gates at the cardinal points.

By the late fourth and third millennia the need or desire for protection grew, with settlements being sited in defensible locations such as promontories and hills, the defenses becoming more substantial, and many of the earlier tell settlements being abandoned, probably at least in part due to steppe incursions. While some settlements were smaller and more dispersed, others were very large and were the home of the regional population, perhaps numbering several thousand. Tell settlements continued in lowland and upland sites well into the Bronze Age.

Nea Nikomedeia (Greece) Nea Nikomedeia was a village of rectangular houses with floors of mud over reeds, timber walls plastered with reeds and mud, and reed roofs. Clay ovens were placed outside the houses as were rubbish pits, while the houses contained clay-lined basins. One larger house with six others around it may have been a shrine: It contained figurines instead of domestic debris. The settlement was occupied for around 2,000 years, being abandoned around 5000 B.C.

Karanovo (Bulgaria) This village was occupied almost continuously for more than 2,500 years, from the sixth millennium onward, creating a lofty tell 39 feet (12 meters) high and around 10 acres (4 hectares) in extent. In the Early Neolithic it was a village of around 15 to 60 houses, most with one or two rooms, laid out in rows. Several houses with three rooms were separated from the rest of the settlement by a fence. In the fifth millennium Karanovo had about 50 houses, extending right to the edge of the tell; some were now larger than before, in some cases with ditches around them.

Dimini (Thessaly, Greece) This settlement was founded in the fifth millennium. A large three-roomed building (*megaron*) was constructed in an elevated position in the center of the village, surrounded by a large courtyard and a stone wall. Other concentric walls and cross walls created several other courtyard areas, each containing a large house, areas for preparing food and craft activity, storage facilities, and other buildings. The remains from some of the houses suggests that several households made spondylus objects on a scale beyond their immediate needs.

Jaszdozsa-Kapolnahalom (Hungary) This 20-feet (6-meter)-high tell was defensively located in a river meander. A rampart and ditch surrounded a large area, with ground between it and the base of the tell; in one part of this area were storage pits and in the other houses. An internal rampart and ditch encircled the tell, on which houses were laid out in parallel rows with alleys between. These houses were rectangular, of log-cabin construction, with hearths and ovens inside. During the period of its occupation in the earlier second millennium, the settlement rose 8 feet (2.4 meters) in height.

Hillforts and Fortified Villages

Fortified settlements situated in defensible locations such as promontories and plateaus were appearing in Southeast Europe by the fourth millennium, and these became more widespread in later times. While some were small, others were large nucleated settlements, which seem to have housed the majority of the population of an area. In the late second millennium hillforts also began to appear over a wide area: strongly fortified hilltop or hillside fortified sites that often served mainly as places of refuge rather than permanent settlements, though the latter are also known, particularly in the Iron Age. Some lowland fortified sites also served as temporary refuges rather than being permanently occupied. Many sites took advantage of naturally defended locations, such as promontories, steep hills, or islands; these were enhanced by defensive walls, palisades, banks, and ditches, and their entrances were often strongly protected by gateways and defensive works. Many types of fortification developed, using timber, soil, and stone in a variety of ways.

FORTIFIED VILLAGES

By the Late Bronze Age fortified villages were widespread across Europe. Those that were not situated to take advantage of defensible locations were heavily fortified with strong palisades or ramparts of wood, stone, and earth. These settlements contained evidence of industrial activity, particularly metalworking, and often they seem to have been producing quantities of goods in excess of the settlement's requirements. A number, including Barca and Spišský Štvrtok, contained hoards of gold work, but their layout and domestic architecture give little indication of social hierarchy; such distinctions tended to be reserved for expression mainly in funerary practices and grave goods.

Barca (Slovakia) A small Otomani settlement of closely packed rectangular houses was located on a high promontory overlooking the confluence of two rivers, which bounded it on two sides. The other two sides of the settlement were protected by a wide ditch and a substantial bank topped by a palisade.

Wittnauer Horn (Argau, Germany) This Late Bronze Age settlement of 26 houses was situated on a long, narrow spur. Most of the houses were built along the three sides of the spur, while two were in the center. A massive rampart 33 feet (10 meters) high defended the narrow neck of land giving access to the settlement.

Biskupin (Poland) This large village was occupied for about 300 years from around 730 B.C. Entirely occupying a peninsula in a lake, it was surrounded on three sides by water and on the fourth by boggy ground, which also underlay the settlement. Birch and alder branches and other wood, sand, clay, and stones were used to form a platform upon which the settlement was constructed. A timber bridge linked it to the firmer ground beyond. It was further defended by a massive timber rampart with a tower guarding its gateway, and a substantial breakwater of oak and pine stakes set at 45 degrees around the outside protected the settlement from erosion by the lake waters. Inside, the village was laid out as terraced rows of log cabins with shared roofs. Some houses contained industrial waste and were apparently the homes and workshops of specialist artisans making objects of bronze, leather, and bone. The settlement contained more than 100 houses and would have housed a population of around 700 to 1,000 people. Between the rows of houses and around the entire settlement between the houses and the stockade ran corduroy causeways built of logs. The settlement was clearly designed and built as a single operation; calculations show that it required the timber of around 100,000 trees and around 900,000 man-hours' work to complete; depending on the size of the workforce it could have been built in one or two years.

Spišský Štvrtok (Slovakia) This was a second-millennium fortified village of 26 two-roomed houses, the larger, more substantial ones being arranged on a separately fortified central acropolis around an area paved with stones. Hoards of gold work were deposited beneath the floors of some of these houses. A stone-faced rampart and ditch lined with stone defended the settlement, with towers guarding the gateway.

Camp Durand (Vendée, France) This was a Bronze Age village of several hundred inhabitants, with craft areas and stock enclosures as well as houses, within substantial drystone ramparts with gate towers.

CASTROS

Throughout the first millennium B.C. and into the early centuries A.D., defended settlements known as *castros* were constructed in large numbers in northwestern Iberia, particularly in Galicia. These were strategically located on high ground and had massive stone walls up to 20 feet (6 meters) thick surrounding the settlement. Some were further fortified with *chevaux-de-frise*. These *castros* varied in size, from small settlements to large villages, generally of roundhouses built of stone with straw roofs. The villages also included stone subterranean saunas, perhaps intended for religious or medicinal purposes. *Castros* were also located in hilly areas farther inland, where they were associated with cremation cemeteries. In the valleys of the middle Douro there were villages of roundhouses that sometimes formed tells. Under Roman influence from the late second century B.C. some *castros* became more urban in character, with regular planned streets.

Citania de Sanfins (Pacos de Ferreira, Portugal) A developed *castro* of the early Roman period in Iberia, more than 37 acres (15 hectares) in extent and housing perhaps as many as 3,000 people, the settlement was divided into regular blocks, like Roman *insulae*, each subdivided into plots containing a group of four or five roundhouses, probably the home of an extended family.

HILLFORTS

Fortified sites were built in hilltop locations from the late second millennium and became a common feature of most of Europe during the first millennium, although their use was not continuous or contemporary in all areas. Some were defended villages, but in many cases they were fortified areas within which only a part was given over to workshops and houses, probably those of the local chief and his entourage. Hillforts offered a place of refuge to the dispersed rural population and a place of safety in which the grain produced by the surrounding farms could be stored; pits and granaries were often present in large numbers. Some hillforts also had provision for corralling many livestock. The defenses were generally formed of banks and ditches and timber-framed ramparts.

The Breiddin (Powys, Wales) A 75-acre (30-hectare) hilltop site occupied from the Early Bronze Age was fortified in the early first millennium. A substantial rampart of earth and stone reinforced with timber was constructed, within which there were houses, a furnace, and four-post granaries. A square pond in the center of the hillfort provided a water supply for those living or taking refuge in the hillfort.

The Heuneberg (Baden-Württemberg, Germany) A hillfort enclosing around 7.4 acres (3 hectares) on the summit of a hill overlooking the Danube, the Heuneberg was occupied on and off from the Middle Bronze Age to around 500 B.C., including the period in the sixth century B.C. when

Greek traders were active in the area. The local chief benefited from the trade, and this is reflected in the imported pottery found in the hillfort. A timber-framed box-rampart surrounded the hilltop, except in one phase during the period of Greek trading contact when part of the rampart was replaced by a mud brick wall with bastions, an impractical Mediterranean novelty. Some buildings had floors paved with clay bricks and were possibly the houses of the elite. A house built in the large settlement of Talhau below the hillfort, which has a number of rooms, may also have belonged to the local chief. In the hillfort some of the houses were timber framed, while others were constructed on sleeper beams. There were also granaries, workshops for making glass, bone, bronze, and iron objects, textiles, and pottery, and furnaces for smelting iron. Larger barrows in the land around the hillfort, including the huge Hohmichele barrow, housed a number of richly furnished burials.

4.6 Aerial view of the Trundle, an Iron Age hillfort, Sussex, England (TopFoto.co.uk, English Heritage/Heritage-I/HIP Photographer: EH/RCHME staff photographer)

Danebury (Dorset, England) This 13-acre (1.5-hectare) hillfort was located on the summit of a low hill, and was occupied from around 1000 B.C. to A.D. 100. Within the hillfort there were areas of housing, accommodating around 300 to 350 people at its maximum extent, and workshops where weaving and ironworking took place. The greater part of the interior, however, was given over to storage pits and four-post granaries, thought to have provided defended storage for the crops of the inhabitants of the 20 or more farming settlements in the river valley below. The hillfort was surrounded by a massive earthen rampart and ditch and had two gateways; the southeastern one was greatly elaborated in the later phase of occupation here, after 500 B.C. In the same period an outer rampart was added, enclosing an additional area that probably provided a corral for the livestock of the local farms in time of trouble.

VITRIFIED FORTS

Some Scottish hillforts of the last centuries B.C. were defended by stone ramparts reinforced with timber. Many of these were subjected to fire, which reached such a temperature that the stone became fused into a solid, glassy form, giving rise to the name "vitrified fort" for these hillforts. It used to be thought that the firing happened during enemy action or was undertaken by the inhabitants to strengthen the wall, but current thinking is that it was a deliberate and symbolic act of destruction, the razing of the fortification.

Towns

Towns began to appear in the late first millennium over much of Europe, with considerable populations and large-scale industrial activity. Some, like those of southern France and southern and eastern Iberia, became urbanized under the influence of neighboring communities of settlers from the civilized societies of Carthage, Greece, and Rome. In other areas, however, such as Thrace, the head of the Adriatic, or central Europe, urban societies owed their prosperity and emerging social complexity to other factors such as international trade and the rise of industrial production, particularly of iron. Some towns developed from preexisting settlements, but most were new foundations; in temperate Europe these are known as oppida, a term borrowed from the Romans. In western and southern Europe these continued to develop up to the time of the Roman conquest, whereas north of the Danube most were abandoned by the late first century B.C.

CLASSICALLY INFLUENCED TOWNS

In the coastal regions of southern France and Mediterranean Iberia, and into the interior along the Garonne and other rivers, the presence of Greek, Carthaginian, and later Roman settlements, traders, and prospectors exercised considerable influence over the native population. Here by the third century towns were developing with a number of features inspired by their classical neighbors. Buildings often used dressed stone and mud brick and were arranged in a planned layout. In other respects, however, they were firmly rooted in local tradition, as, for example, in the severed heads associated with the public building in Entremont.

Entremont (France) Entremont was founded as the capital of the Saluvii in the second century B.C. (or perhaps earlier). The region had been exposed to classical influences since the Greeks established a colony at nearby Massalia around 600 B.C., and this is reflected in the layout of the upper town at Entremont in a grid pattern of streets lined with two-story houses of mud brick on stone foundations. Large pottery jars (*dolia*) were placed beside the houses to catch rainwater. A stone wall with towers surrounded the upper town, situated in the southwestern corner of the site, and another encircled the whole area of the settlement. A public building was situated between two towers of the inner wall. Above its open pillared portico this building had a hall whose floor was decorated with geometric patterns in black and white stone. In contrast to these classically inspired features, however, the facade of the building was adorned, in very Celtic style, with severed heads attached to it with nails. The northern and eastern portions of the oppidum may represent areas into which the settlement expanded as the population grew. Workshops and industrial facilities such as furnaces were also located in the lower town, whose layout was less formal. Olive presses reflect the local production of oil. The town fell to a Roman assault in either 123 or 90 B.C.

Numantia (Spain) A fortified settlement was founded in the seventh century on a flat-topped hill at the confluence of three rivers. According to Strabo, the settlement was taken over, probably in the third century B.C., by a Celtiberian tribe, the Arevaci, who drove out the native inhabitants and constructed a town of around 60 acres (23 hectares). This town reflected classical influences in its layout, having two wide main streets paved with round stones intersected by others to form a grid around which the rectangular houses were built. These were constructed of wooden uprights, walls of mud brick or compressed earth and straw, and roofs of branches on timber beams. They were divided into three rooms: The central one contained the hearth, while a stair from the outer room led down to a cellar. An inner patrol wall ran along the west side of the town's defensive wall. The latter was at its strongest in the stretches where the natural defenses were limited; it was built of stones and had bastions at intervals. The town was besieged and captured in 133 B.C. by the Romans, who razed it to the ground.

OPPIDA

Native towns, known as oppida, began to appear across temperate Europe from France to Slovakia during the second and first centuries B.C., possibly inspired to some extent by growing familiarity with the towns of the Mediterranean world. Generally, oppida were founded on a new site, in a prominent location on high ground, a prime situation for commanding communication routes, and for physically and psychologically dominating the surrounding region. Occasionally, they were built over an earlier settlement, and some were situated on a river plain: both are true of Manching. They were generally surrounded by impressive ramparts with elaborate gateways, but these were probably as much for show and for controlling the movement of people and goods as for defense. Oppida were the tribal administrative and political centers, places of refuge for the rural population, and they also played a key economic and religious role. They were very much larger than earlier settlements.

Houses were often laid out along streets, and their size and style often reflected the social status of their owners, with stone being used by the more wealthy. Within some oppida there was a fortified citadel on the highest ground, and it was generally here that elite housing was located. Part of the settlement was taken up by the workshops in which a number of industrial activities took place such as bronze and iron working, pottery production, jewelry manufacture, and the creation of objects in wood, bone, glass, and stone; often goods such as iron tools and pottery were mass-produced. Oppida generally also had a mint; the presence of weighing equipment and low-denomination coins implies the existence of a market economy. Amphorae and other Mediterranean imports show that the inhabitants of these towns participated in international trade.

The larger oppida also included farms with arable and pasture land, granaries and other storage facilities, and, when required, could accommodate the rural population of the region: For example, when Caesar besieged the oppidum of Avaricum (modern Bourges), the capital of the Biturges, its inhabitants, including those who had taken refuge there, numbered 40,000—of whom Caesar slaughtered all but 800. Some oppida, such as Bibracte, continued in use as towns after the Roman conquest, but in most cases the Romans founded a new town on the adjacent lower ground. Farther east oppida fell to local aggressors such as the Marcommani and the Dacians.

Noreia   (Austria) The kingdom of Noricum, which owed its prosperity to control of salt and metal ores in the eastern Alps, had its capital at Noreia, now identified with the oppidum of Magdalensberg. The town, founded in the second century B.C., occupied an area of around 865 acres (350 hectares). It was a center of iron production; numerous furnaces and quantities of iron slag were found here. The Romans had close trading links with Noreia from the mid-second century, and around 100 B.C. they established a trading colony on the low ground below the mountain eminence on which the oppidum stood. Commercial accounts scratched on the cellar walls of some houses give details of the trade conducted through this outlet, with Norican iron objects such as anvils, hooks, and cauldrons being exported.

Závist   (Bohemia, Czech Republic) Founded in the early second century B.C. over an earlier settlement, the oppidum of Závist was reputedly a town of the Boii, a Celtic tribe whose arrival in the fourth century may have brought about the abandonment of an earlier hillfort in the area. The six-mile (9-kilometer)-long fortified perimeter of the oppidum, made up of several concentric ramparts, encircled an area of more than 375 acres (150 hectares), including both hilltops and the valleys between them. A massive gateway controlled access to the interior; this was restructured a number of times. Immediately inside the gate was an area of workshops, particularly focusing on working iron. Elsewhere within the oppidum were areas of housing, religious precincts, and farms, and gold and silver coinage was also minted in the town. Three other gates were later added to the circuit of the wall. An area to the north of the oppidum was also fortified in the latest phase of the town's history; this may have been a place of refuge. Závist was destroyed by fire around 25–20 B.C.

Manching   (Bavaria, Danube valley) An undefended village specializing in craft activity was replaced by or evolved into an oppidum in the late second century. The town was strategically placed for agriculture and riverborne communications, on the alluvial plain of the River Paar south of the Danube; its situation on low ground necessitated the building of massive defensive ramparts. Its five-mile (7-kilometer)-long *murus gallicus* wall enclosed a huge area, some 940 acres (380 hectares) in extent, and protected a number of areas of settlement and industry, crop-processing areas and numerous fields, growing barley, some spelt and emmer, legumes, and flax. In some parts of the town, houses were arranged along streets, with numerous pits at their rear. The houses of the elite had cellars, prestige goods such as horse trappings, and keys to lock their doors, something unknown before the advent of towns. Several areas were devoted to workshops for different crafts, producing a range of goods in bronze, iron, glass, bone and antler, leather, and wood, and minting coins. Pottery made here included the graphite ware that was traded to the Rhine valley and central Germany, and the oppidum imported many Mediterranean goods, particularly wine and the fine bronze and pottery tableware to drink it in style. Storage facilities for grain, probably received as tribute, included barrel-shaped pits and four-post structures. Settlement here ended in the mid-first century B.C.

Bibracte (Burgundy, France) Bibracte (modern Mount Beuvray) was an oppidum of around 320 acres (135 hectares) covering several hilltops and the valleys between, enclosed in a *murus gallicus* wall three miles (5 kilometers) long, which had a single defended gateway. Inside the gate was a street lined with buildings with stone foundations; houses and workshops where iron, bronze, and glass were made into tools, weapons, and jewelry; glass beads were a specialty. Farther into the oppidum there were a number of springs and streams for water and other areas of housing, including elite residences on the saddle that dominated the settlement. In the farthest corner from the entrance gateway there was a large square sacred enclosure containing votive deposits. Bibracte was the capital of the Aedui, allies of the Romans; Caesar wintered here in 52 B.C. during his campaigns in Gaul.

TERRITORIAL OPPIDA

In Britain nascent urbanism took a different form: the creation of vast, loosely enclosed sites known as territorial oppida, strategically placed for trade and the control of communications. They are exemplified by Verlamion and Camulodunon, successive capitals of the Catuvellauni, but less impressive examples were widespread in the southern and eastern half of England. Massive earthwork defenses (dikes) surrounded a very extensive area within which were concentrations of activity, including settlements, cemeteries, shrines, industrial areas, and cultivated land. The royal oppida in the southeast contained mints. Both the earthwork defenses and some of the major buildings within them were sited to impress; this was probably the main function of the dikes as they did not provide effective defense.

Camulodunon (Essex, England) Camulodunon (modern Colchester) covered an area of 10 square miles (16 square kilometers), lying between two rivers and defended by a series of dikeworks on the western side. Within this there were concentrations of settlement separated by open ground, which was probably cultivated or used for pasture. The main area of settlement, at Sheepen, contained houses and workshops where pottery making, metalworking, enameling, salt making, and other crafts and industries were practiced and coins minted. A cult enclosure, probably of the god Camulos, was located at Gosbecks Green near the elite residential area, which was located in an enclosure on a hill: probably the "Fort of Camulos" from which the settlement took its name and which was probably the earliest settlement within the oppidum. At Lexden there was a cemetery containing a number of graves and two large barrows, one covering a cremation burial in a large pit, accompanied by a rich selection of grave goods, including a medallion of the emperor Augustus and a Roman ceremonial stool, both probably diplomatic gifts from the emperor to the local king. This probably predates the foundation of the oppidum around the beginning of the first century A.D. Camulodunon began as the tribal center of the Trinovantes, but after their fall to the Catuvellauni, the latter made it their capital in preference to Verlamion; a small settlement within the oppidum subsequently became the capital of the Roman province of Britannia until sacked by Boudicca in A.D. 60.

LANDSCAPES

Marking Territory

The division of the landscape into territories exploited by different groups must date back far into the prehistoric period. Ethnographic evidence indicates that mobile hunter-gatherers such as the Palaeolithic and earlier Mesolithic inhabitants of Europe would have had well-recognized exploitation rights in a range of locations spread across the landscape (their annual territory), giving them access to the resources they required at different times of year. Often kinship ties would give each individual the right to join any one of several groups and participate in the exploitation of that group's annual territory.

Sedentary communities, on the other hand, generally had smaller territories, more distinctly marked, and more rigidly enforced. Investment in the alteration and maintenance of a piece of land for agriculture changed the nature of the relationship between people and landscape. Instead of a system of structured but flexible rights to the natural produce of the landscape, sedentism in general and farming in particular brought a close and possessive relationship between people and the land they permanently occupied and farmed: ownership of the land itself rather than rights to its produce.

An inevitable consequence of the growth of land ownership was the desire and need to demarcate and mark territory. This was done in many ways. Fields or garden plots were surrounded by wooden fences; by walls, particularly in areas where the ground was stony and rocks or stones had regularly to be cleared from the fields before cultivation; or by banks or ditches and usually both together, often combined with a thorn hedge. These would have served not only to identify the land of a family or community but also to keep out wild and domestic animals. Similar means could be used to demarcate settlements, keeping wild animals out and domestic animals in and making a statement of possession to outsiders; although they could be defensive, palisades, banks and ditches, and walls, even substantial ones, probably served primarily as a community or household statement, demonstrating ownership and the ability to raise and maintain such boundaries. In second-millennium Dartmoor and other areas of late Neolithic and early Bronze Age western Europe, territorial demarcations of stone were constructed across large tracts of landscape, used for settlement, arable agriculture, and pasture.

On this larger scale the community's right to a section of the landscape, including not only fields but also pastures and woodland, water supplies, and other essentials, as well as areas of sacred or cultural significance, were often emphasized by the erection of monuments in prominent locations where they could be seen and understood by those entering the territory. In Atlantic Europe during the Neolithic period tombs were used as territorial markers in this way and were therefore placed in prominent, visible locations. In some areas these took the form of long barrows, in others megalithic tombs. These monuments not only visibly demonstrated the manpower that could be mobilized to build them, and acted as impressive markers, but by holding the bones of some or all of the community's dead they also emphasized the ancestral links between the local community and the territory, a visible sign that ownership had been vested in the community since time immemorial.

From the later fourth millennium in Britain and Brittany, the role of visible symbols of power and local ownership of territory shifted to stone circles, henges, and other impressive religious monuments, and across Europe round barrows covering the burials of leaders gradually took on this role.

Settlement themselves might also serve the purpose of marking territory. The settlement mounds (tells) that developed in Southeast Europe were prominent features of the landscape. Other settlements might be made more obvious and impressive by constructing substantial fortifications that served more for show than for defense: For example, the Chalcolithic villages of Iberia, such as Los Millares and Vila Nova de São Pedro, had massive walls, frequently made more massive by adding extra skins of stones, although the local need for defense seems to have been negligible. The same was probably true, for example, of the defended homesteads and settlements of the Atlantic region in the Iron Age; structures like the brochs of Scotland were probably designed as much to impress outsiders as to defend against them. Hillforts and oppida were also located to be visible and impressive.

In contemporary Galicia stone animal heads were placed to delimit the pastureland belonging to a community and life-size statues of warriors by the settlement entrance, and in other parts of western Iberia granite models of bulls and boars (*verracos*) were similarly used as territorial markers. These probably had a religious significance as did the stone stelae raised in Brittany. In every area and period ways were found to mark territorial ownership.

People in the Landscape

The distribution and density of modern settlement in Europe is a poor guide to the situation in the past. For much of the postglacial prehistoric period, a large part of the land was covered with dense uninhabited forest; although this was gradually reduced by clearance, the forest cover was still extensive in many areas well into post-Roman times. Other areas were also uninhabited because the land could not be exploited with the technology available at the time. In addition, the small population of Europe—perhaps 1 to 5 million in the Neolithic period and around 30 million by the end of the Iron Age—meant that during earlier prehistory settlement could be confined to the areas easiest to exploit, and only later did pressure from expanding population cause people to move into more challenging areas or adopt more labor-intensive ways of life.

MESOLITHIC

Before about 7000 B.C. Europe was inhabited exclusively by hunter-gatherers, whose preferred habitats included coasts, the shores of lakes, rivers, and estuaries, the vicinity of marshes, and sites with access to a range of environments. These people also often moved with the seasons, following herds to upland pastures, visiting offshore islands, and making expeditions into woods and other terrain where particular foodstuffs and other necessary or desirable resources were available. Although the favored areas became densely settled and exploited, there were huge tracts of Europe that were uninhabited and unexploited at this time.

The success of the Mesolithic lifestyle led to a substantial growth in hunter-gatherer populations through time, with many large permanent settlements, particularly in coastal regions, and by the later sixth millennium there is considerable evidence of violence, presumably between communities competing for the same favored areas. Forest management offered one way to increase resources, with some forest edges being cleared by fire or by bark ringing to encourage the growth of hazel and other species that thrive in open woodland, and to attract prey animals; this made only minor inroads into the forest cover, however. Another means adopted by later Mesolithic people was to expand exploitation of the sea; while fishing had earlier been confined to inshore waters, deep-sea fishing now took place.

Finally, there was the option of increasing economic productivity by taking up aspects of agriculture: keeping domestic animals and planting a few crops. To some extent this was possible within the preexisting settlement pattern; many communities in Mediterranean and Atlantic Europe continued to occupy coastal, lakeshore, and other favored locations but practiced a mixed economy. Some communities, for instance, around lakes in Switzerland and northern Italy, relied heavily on wild resources, supplemented by some farming, for millennia; and many Atlantic communities continued to place considerable emphasis on fishing. By around 3000 B.C., however, most Europeans were dependent to a greater or lesser degree on farming, and their choices of settlement location reflected this.

EARLY FARMING

Farming communities began to appear in Europe in the seventh millennium, and at first settled on land with light, easily cultivated soils and access to water and land suitable for grazing; in some regions this required a limited amount of forest clearance. In Greece and the Balkans settlement was mainly in river valleys, in dried-up lake basins, and at the edges of alluvial plains. In Italy settlements were adjacent to patches of easily cultivated soils within the Tavoliere plain and other lowland areas. From the later sixth millennium farmers settled on loess soils on river terraces in central Europe and as far west as the Paris Basin, and east of the Carpathians similar locations were taken up in the fifth millennium. The land needed for farming was still very restricted in extent, often little more than gardens around the houses, and usually extending less than a mile from the settlement. Grazing for the small numbers of domestic stock was also available within the vicinity of these settlements, though seasonal pastures in adjacent areas might also be used: For example, inhabitants of some Greek and Balkan villages probably grazed their animals on the river floodplains in summer, while Italian communities sought pastures in the hills around the plains.

The initial spread of farming in the seventh to mid-fifth millennia did not affect western or northern Europe, but these areas saw the advent of agriculture during the following 1,500 years, as did areas farther east. While some farming settlements were located to continue some exploitation of wild resources, particularly those of the coast, many appeared in new areas: areas where, as before, soils were well drained and easy to cultivate, such as the chalk land of southern England. At the same time, in the regions where farming communities had previously been established, settlements begun to appear in new locations as well as continuing in the old: in smaller river valleys and on the higher ground between rivers in temperate central Europe; on the open plains of Thessaly and the Balkans, where previously settlement had concentrated on the margins; in the interior of southern and central France; around lakes in northern Italy and Switzerland; and in previously unoccupied Mediterranean islands, including Malta and a number in the Aegean.

MOVING OUT AND FILLING IN

As populations continued to grow, the increasing need for food and other resources was met by agricultural intensification, expansion into new areas, and economic diversification.

The introduction of the ard (simple plow) in the fourth millennium made it possible to take larger areas of land into cultivation and saw a shift from gardens within or small fields close to the settlement to more extensive fields in the landscape around it. In some areas networks of small fields enclosed by walls, hedges, or banks and ditches were laid out; these are known particularly from Britain. New areas not previously cultivable, such as British gravel river terraces and Jutland sands, could now also be farmed. The use of animals to pull carts and carry loads also made it feasible to cultivate land at a greater distance from the settlement than when farmers had had to walk to their fields and carry tools and produce themselves. The expansion of cultivated land necessitated an increase in forest clearance, but it was not until the third or second millennium that this began to make a significant impact on the extent of Europe's forest. The cultivation of new plants also allowed higher productivity

from the land surrounding the settlement: For example, in third-millennium Greece and later other areas of the Mediterranean these included grapes and olives. A greater emphasis on stock raising in many areas also increased productivity and proceeded in tandem with forest clearance.

New areas continued to be colonized as the centuries passed and populations grew. The *meseta*, the dry interior plateau of Iberia, saw settlement begin during the third millennium; settlers practicing mixed farming also spread into upland plateaus in southern France, Britain, and many parts of Europe. The swampy lands of the Po plain, previously thinly occupied by hunter-gatherers, saw the emergence of agricultural communities (the *terramare*) in the second millennium. Nomadic pastoralists, equipped with wagons for transporting their belongings and horses for herding their animals, were responsible for the colonization of the steppe. In the first millennium the low-lying lands of the North Sea's southern coast saw the construction of artificially raised ground to allow farming settlements to be established there, while artificial islands were built in some lakes in Britain and continental Europe for settlement and defense.

Some of the expansion into other regions had been made possible by the development of specialist pastoral groups who traveled seasonally between settlements at lower elevations and camps in the upland or mountain pastures of the Alps, the French Grand Causses, and other highland regions. Some communities established permanent settlements in valleys and other areas within the mountain ranges where pockets of arable land were available; the fertility of their fields was maintained by large quantities of manure from domestic flocks that were protected from the severity of the winter climate by being housed in byres where they were stall-fed. These communities integrated arable and pastoral agriculture, most of the inhabitants living year round in the settlement while some individuals took the flocks and herds to summer pastures higher in the mountains. Pastoralists might also obtain grain from lowland groups with whom they traded wool and dairy produce.

EMERGING COMPLEXITY

Symbiotic relationships between pastoral and agricultural groups were only one aspect of growing specialization and interdependence. Communities were also emerging, by the second millennium if not before, that specialized in other activities such as mining, satisfying the growing demand for stone, metal ores, salt, and other commodities. While some resource procurement was by seasonal visits, in other cases a community was permanently resident near the source of tradable materials, depending to a varying degree on imported grain and other foodstuffs obtained in exchange for the commodities that they extracted. By the first millennium many such communities existed; some, like the salt-mining settlement at Hallstatt, became extremely wealthy on the proceeds of their activities, as the rich burials in their cemetery attest. In tandem it became necessary for farming settlements to increase agricultural production in order to have a surplus with which to trade.

Growing populations were matched by growing social complexity. In some areas during the fourth and third millennia, and in many during the second and first, elites emerged who exercised some control over local production and trade. This was reflected in the second millennium in the emergence of settlements at nodes in the trade networks from which local leaders could control the movements of goods, and from around 1100 B.C. in the development of hillforts as centers providing leadership, defense, and perhaps some manufactured goods and a religious focus for the surrounding farming population, as well as being involved in long-distance trade. Hillforts became widespread in the first millennium. Some grew in size through time and came to control larger areas; in some cases a single large hillfort replaced a number of smaller ones in an area.

Far larger and more complex were the oppida and other towns that emerged in the last three centuries B.C. An oppidum might replace a number of hillforts or large villages, or these might survive as a lower tier in the settlement hierarchy, still central to their own area but subordinate to the tribal capital. During his campaigns in Gaul Caesar noted that the population dwelt in farmsteads (*aedificia privata*), villages (*vici*), and towns (*oppida*), and he also mentions *castelli* (hillforts?). Oppida, many of which had a population of several thousand, served

a wide area as centers of trade and industry, offering services and a market, and a wider political focus: The principal oppida were the seat of government for a wide region.

EBB AND FLOW

Expansion into new areas continued throughout prehistory. In parts of the Mediterranean such as Almeria in southeastern Iberia, communities developed irrigation techniques that allowed them to cultivate land that was too dry for rain-fed agriculture. During the second millennium higher temperatures and lower rainfall allowed the spread of farming into areas that had previously been unsuitable for cultivation, such as many upland areas in western and central Europe, and regions that had previously been too wet, such as the Po plain. In the late first millennium the development of the coulter and iron plowshare, and in some areas the moldboard plow, opened up the cultivation of clays and other soils, for instance, in valley bottoms, that had previously been too heavy for agriculture. By the time of the Roman conquest Europe was densely settled, with a diverse pattern of settlements ranging from farmsteads to towns.

But the pattern of development was by no means uniform progress. Colder, wetter conditions from the late second millennium turned many upland and marginal areas into blanket bog and moorland, never again to be cultivable, and suitable only for rough grazing. Flooding and swamp growth in parts of the North European Plain caused many major settlements to be abandoned, leaving only farmsteads and hamlets; many lakeside settlements, in Switzerland and elsewhere, were also abandoned. Similar patterns of advance and decline were experienced by other areas at different periods for various reasons such as overexploitation; for example, overgrazing and consequent erosion may have been, at least in part, responsible for the abandonment of many settlements in the Balkans in the early third millennium.

Changes in the exploitation of other resources also affected the patterns of regional settlement. For instance, the exhaustion of the easily worked carbonate and oxide ores of the Balkans and the shift to mining sulfide copper ores changed the focus of metallurgical exploitation in southeast and central Europe from the Balkans in the fourth millennium to the Alps and Carpathians in the later third, while the spread of iron working in the first millennium completely altered the pattern of mining, metallurgy, and trade. Regions rose and fell in importance, and this had consequences in the pattern of trade networks and the settlements dependent on them. For example, major alterations to trade networks and settlement hierarchies came with the penetration of the European interior by Mediterranean traders from the sixth century B.C.

Political factors also played a major role in determining settlement patterns. Competition between communities often erupted into armed conflict, sometimes resulting in the destruction of settlements. Sites therefore not only began to be fortified but also were often shifted to more defensible locations, sometimes accompanied by a decline in population. Hillforts, domestic strongholds, and other defended sites are well known in the Bronze and Iron Ages in western and central Europe, and strongly fortified sites appeared in the Balkans at an earlier date. In addition to local conflict communities might suffer from the attacks by external raiders such as periodic incursions by nomads from the steppe and the movements of large confederacies of Celts. In some regions such as Dacia and Gaul, the Roman conquest brought massive depopulation and economic collapse.

READING

Construction

Perles 2001, Taylour 1983: Greece; Armit 1997, Turner 1998, Reynolds 1995: Britain; Whittle 1996: Neolithic; Harding 2000: Bronze Age; Coles 1973: experimental construction; Coles, J. 1973, Coles, B. 1999, Audouze and Buchsenschutz 1992: life expectancy of houses.

Domestic Architecture

Barker 1985, Milisauskas, ed. 2002, Champion et al. 1984: general; Mithen 2003: Mesolithic; Whittle 1996, Thorpe 1996: Neolithic; Harding 2000, Kristiansen 1998: Bronze Age; Reynolds 1995: Iron Age; Bailey 2000: Balkans; Cunliffe 2001a: Atlantic region; Darvill 1996: Britain; Ashmore 1996, Barclay 1998, Hingley 1998, Armit 1997, Ritchie 1988: Scotland; Ritchie 1995: Orkney; Turner 1998: Shetland; Lumley 1969, Scarre 1998: Terra Amata; Hernek 2003: Timmeras; Leighton 1999: Thapsos, Pantalica; Waddington et al. 2003, Denison 2003c: Howick; Mellars and Dark 1998: Star Carr; Zvelebil 1987: Eyni; Melton and Nicholson 2004: West Voe; Shepherd 2000, Scarre 1998: Skara Brae; Denison 2001: Callander; Rowley-Conwy 2002b: Balbridie; Smrz 1991: Drouzkovice.

Settlements

Milisauskas, ed. 2002; Barker 1985: general; Whittle 1996: Neolithic; Harding 2000, Kristiansen 1998, Audouze and Buchsenschutz 1992: Bronze Age; Cunliffe 1997, Twist 2001, Audouze and Buchsenschutz 1992, James 1993, Collis 1984a, Berresford Ellis 1998: Iron Age; Bailey 2000: Balkans; Midgeley 1992: Poland; Cunliffe 2001a: Atlantic region; Trump 1980: Mediterranean; Skeates 2002: Tavoliere; Caesar 1951: Gaul; Darvill 1996, 1987, Parker Pearson 1993: Britain; O'Brien and Harbison 1996, O'Kelly 1989: Ireland; Lenerz-de Wilde 1995, Chapman 1990: Iberia; Ritchie 1988, Hingley 1998, Armit 1997: Scotland; Ritchie 1995: Orkney; Turner 1998: Shetland; Thrane 1999a: Scandinavia; Mercer 1990, Cizmarova et al. 1996, Darvill and Thomas, eds. 2001, Oswald et al. 2001, Varndell and Topping, eds. 2002: causewayed enclosures; Fokkens 1998, Todd 1972, 1994, Dixon 1976, Graham-Campbell, ed. 1994, Barker 1985: terpen, Feddersen Wierde, Ezinge; Armit 1997, O'Kelly 1989, Morrison 1997, Piggott 1995, Reed 1990: crannogs; Coles and Coles 1986, Rahtz 1993, Clarke 1982, Bewley 2003: Glastonbury; Grimal 1964, Barker 1999: terramare; Coles 1984, Garrison 1997, Egloff 1987: lake villages; Coles 1999: Hauterive-Champréveyres; Bocquet et al. 1987: Charavines;

Giardino 1992, Bonzani 1992, Becker 1992: nuraghi; Pericot Garcia 1972: *talayots;* Moosleitner 1991: Dürrnberg; Zvelebil 1987, Champion and Champion 1982, Scarre 1998: Biskupin; Cunliffe 1993, 2003: Danebury; Martinez 1991: Numantia; Maier 1991a, Haselgrove and Millet 1997, Collis 1984b, 1995: oppida; Motyakova et al. 1991: Závist; Maier 1991b: Manching; Maier 1991a: Bibracte; Kurz 2005, Maier 1991a: Heuneberg; Scarre 1998: Entremont; Millett 1990, 1995, Darvill 1996: Camulodunon.

Landscapes

Barker 1985, Milisauskas, ed. 2002, Sherratt 1997, Cunliffe ed. 1994: general; Whittle 1996: Neolithic; Harding 2000, Kristiansen 1998, Audouze and Buchsenschutz 1992, Thrane 1999a: Bronze Age; Audouze and Buchsenschutz 1992, Collis 1995, Bevan 1997: Iron Age; Renfrew 1973, Renfrew and Bahn 2004: megaliths as markers.

5

TRADE AND TRANSPORT

TRADE

Changing Patterns

Ethnographic evidence gives some insight into the range of ways in which exchange may have operated in antiquity. The distribution of materials and the patterns of their movement provide some indication of the mechanisms that operated at different periods, and for the later first millennium literary evidence is also available.

DIRECT PROCUREMENT

Some materials were obtained by directly visiting their source. In Palaeolithic and early Mesolithic times, seasonal movements to obtain different food resources were organized also to include visits to areas providing raw materials, such as stone for tools. For instance, Mesolithic people in the eastern Mediterranean fishing offshore for tuna obtained obsidian from the island of Melos during their voyages.

In later Mesolithic times, when many communities were settled year round in base camps, expeditions were regularly made at certain times of year to obtain raw materials; many of the Ertebølle people of Denmark, for example, lived on the coast but visited inland sites and offshore islands to obtain furs, various seasonally available foodstuffs, and stone for tools. Farming communities also obtained some of their resources in this way: for example, the lack of permanent settlements near flint mines such as Grimes Graves in England suggests that the miners were people from communities elsewhere who visited occasionally to extract the flint they required. In later times the movements of pastoralists enabled them easily to continue direct resource procurement. For example, pastoralists taking their flocks to high Alpine pastures for summer grazing were probably the first to extract copper ores from sources at these elevations.

RECIPROCITY

In addition, even in Palaeolithic times, some goods and materials circulated beyond the range of possi-ble direct procurement. Ethnographic analogy and the pattern of distribution indicate that in early times the prime mechanism was through gift-giving, often highly structured, between kin or between exchange partners with whom formal relationships were maintained. Some of these transactions took place within the context of ceremonies such as marriages and funerals, which involved feasting (the provision of food by the host family or community) and gift-giving. On many occasions gifts would pass in one direction rather than be exchanged, but through time these gifts would balance out. Typically, the movement of commodities by such gift exchanges created a pattern of slow falloff in quantity with distance from source (down-the-line exchange) as each family or community made use of some of the materials they obtained and passed the rest on to their kin. Since the act of giving was often of more significance than the gift itself, this could result in the movement between communities of the locally available commodities as well as exotic ones.

UNEQUAL TRANSACTIONS

The movement of goods through gift-giving continued throughout prehistory (and still continues), but by the Late Neolithic period this was overlaid by other mechanisms that circulated goods or materials more widely and in greater quantities, and which allowed communities greater control over what they received.

Gift exchanges served to cement family and intercommunity bonds and were not designed to profit the participants directly. In contrast exchanges between individuals outside kinship relationships were made with the intention of profiting on the transaction. Since the value attached to a commodity would increase with the distance from its source, however, this could be achieved without disadvantage to either party.

Farmers required large quantities of stone for making axes and other tools for forest clearance, cultivation, working timber for constructing houses, trackways and fences, and other purposes. Social relations among farmers and among the increasing complex hunter-gatherer communities demanded a supply of materials, such as shells, attractive stone, amber, gold, and copper, that could be made into personal ornaments and display goods, as well as exotic artifacts such as nonlocal pottery. During the fifth to third millennia these needs promoted the development of trading networks to ensure the regular supply of these goods. Commodities still changed hands many times and moved over short distances with each exchange, but ultimately traveled hundreds of miles from their source. Communities near the source areas of particular desirable materials now invested time and effort in procuring them in order to be able to participate in the trade networks that would in turn bring them other materials that they required, and some goods were produced in quantities beyond those needed by the individual household or community, for the purpose of trading.

While metal initially served an exclusively social function, for making display and prestige goods, with the development of copper alloys during the third and second millennia, the shift to the more widely available sulfide copper ores, and the spread of metallurgical technology over the European continent, arsenical and tin bronze began to be used also to make tools and particularly weapons, increasing demand for metal in the trading networks. In the second millennium tin became the principal metal for alloying with copper; its main sources were Cornwall, the Bohemian Ore Mountains, and probably Galicia, although smaller amounts could be obtained from other sources such as Brittany and parts of Italy. The universal need to obtain tin for bronze, which was used to make an ever-increasing number of practical and prestige artifacts during the second millennium, stimulated the development of more highly organized trading networks, which united the earlier regional circuits that had operated along the Atlantic coast and through different parts of continental Europe. The developing social hierarchy of the period was due at least in part to the benefits to be gained from active and organized participation in the trade network: leaders emerged and settlements in key locations on the trade routes grew prosperous. It is likely that trade links now covered much longer distances, with direct transactions between leaders or communities in widely separated regions to some degree replacing the earlier chains of short-distance exchanges. Large votive hoards of metalwork, deposited in the ground or in watery

places, reflect the huge numbers of metal artifacts in circulation, while the presence of Baltic amber in the Aegean and Mycenaean folding stools in Denmark both emphasizes the enormous geographical spread of the trading networks and illustrates the circulation of a wide range of commodities: these included goods and materials for everyday practical use and ones of social importance or ritual significance.

ASYMMETRIC TRADE

The Mycenaeans trading with the European interior seem to have participated in the established trade networks. In contrast, in the Mediterranean they made direct contact with their source areas, sailing to southern Italy and Sardinia to obtain copper ore. They may even have reached Spain, although the Mycenaean pots found there more probably reached the region through the existing trade networks among the people of the western Mediterranean basin. Some centuries later, the Phoenicians reached the Atlantic coast of Iberia, where they established a trading colony at Gadir (Cádiz), and other Phoenician colonies were founded in Spain, Sicily, Sardinia, and North Africa, where the key settlement of Carthage soon grew large enough to establish its own colonies in the western Mediterranean. In the eighth and seventh centuries Greeks also settled on the Mediterranean shores of Spain and in Sicily, as well as in southern Italy and on the southern French coast. From here they traded up the Rhône into eastern France and southern Germany.

The arrival of these eastern Mediterranean traders, prospectors, and settlers created new patterns of trade, cross-cutting the networks already in existence and diverting raw materials from their established consumers. Ethnographic analogies and the archaeological finds from the regions in which these civilized traders did business suggest that they first made appropriate gifts (such as the massive Vix krater) to the local rulers to secure trading agreements and then supplied them with prestige goods and luxuries, such as Phoenician gold jewelry and ivory work, as well as Greek wine and the vessels to serve it, in exchange for raw materials obtained from the local area or further afield: Tartessian silver, central European copper and gold, Cornish tin, Baltic amber, and other commodities. Ominously, they

5.1 The Vix krater, an enormous vessel for mixing wine, probably given as a diplomatic gift by Greek traders to a barbarian chief at the French hillfort of Mont Lassois, with whom they were attempting to establish trading relations. The bronze krater was eventually placed in the grave of the "Vix princess." (Drawing by Audrey McIntosh, from material in the National Museums of Scotland, Edinburgh)

also sought slaves, unlikely previously to have been a traded item. New prestige goods enabled local leaders to outcompete local rivals and provided them with new gifts to reward their followers. The elite also acquired a taste for wine.

When the Greeks abandoned their Rhône trade in favor of trade through their Black Sea colonies, other contacts developed between the Mediterranean world and barbarian Europe that ensured that Mediterranean wine and luxury goods continued to flow into the European interior. These were no longer so asymmetric: Many Mediterranean goods reached transalpine Europe as pay or booty acquired by Celtic mercenaries and raiders in Italy

and the eastern Mediterranean; Celtic settlers in the Po plain mediated exchanges between the Etruscans and other Italian communities and the Celts of western and central Europe; and new trade networks developed that included the Mediterranean civilizations.

MARKET ECONOMIES

In the later Iron Age urban centers developed in many parts of Europe and gradually a market economy began to emerge, that is, trade that involved no relationship between the parties to a transaction, and that operated through the medium of coinage or other objects (such as currency bars), which provided standardized and locally guaranteed units of value to which different commodities could be related (i.e., given a price). Production became centered on the towns, which had workshops making a wide range of goods. The urban centers offered goods and services to the farmers and other rural population of their area in return for agricultural and other rural produce, some on the basis of long-established relationships of kinship, clientage, and tribal social hierarchy, but others on a pure monetary basis, and money also mediated transactions between locals and outsiders. Weights, scales, and balances also appeared at this time. There were also professional merchants and traders, operating privately rather than at the behest of their leader; it is uncertain whether such freelance traders operated in earlier times, but probably unlikely before the later Bronze Age.

Coinage Although the civilizations of the Near East had long used silver and other valuable materials as media of exchange, and the cultures of prehistoric Europe may similarly have used objects like *ösenringe*, the first coins (units of metal stamped with the mark of an issuing authority that guaranteed their weight and quality) were issued in Ionia around 700 B.C. Their manufacture implies both the ability to control closely the purity of metal and the technology for weighing accurately. Coinage became widespread in the Greek world by the sixth century and in much of the Mediterranean basin thereafter. Standardized stone weights and iron ingots were used in Celtic Europe in the late first millennium B.C.

The first Celtic coins, which appeared in the early third century, were modeled on the gold and silver coins brought home as pay by Celts who had worked as mercenaries in the eastern and central Mediterranean. These early coins were generally of gold in the more northerly regions of western and central Europe and silver in the south and east; they were probably used by chiefs and leaders as a convenient standard unit of wealth for rewarding their followers or making gifts to other leaders. By the early second century native higher denomination coins were being minted across Europe from France to Transylvania and the Balkans. Many copied the gold staters of Philip II of Macedon and his son, Alexander the Great. At first the copies were quite faithful to the originals, but the designs progressively disintegrated.

As parts of Celtic Europe began to develop towns and a more complex economy, the need for media of exchange grew, resulting in the development of lower denomination coins, especially in eastern France and central Europe, by the early first century B.C. In the later second century coins of the Belgae, settled in the Seine basin of Gaul, began to be used in Kent, and native coins based upon them soon followed. The first British coins were struck in potin, (high-tin bronze) but by around 80–60 B.C. gold coins were also being minted here. In the later first century B.C. and the early first century A.D. the tribes of south and east England each developed their own coinage.

Commodities

No settlement can be located to give access to everything a community requires for daily or occasional use; even in the Palaeolithic period people required stone for making tools as well as food, water, shelter, and security from predators, and through time the list of commodities regarded as essential or worth making an effort to acquire grew longer and the distances over which they were obtained often grew greater.

Tracking the movement of such commodities is far from straightforward. Many of the materials known from literary sources to have been impor-

tant in trade, such as foodstuffs and furs, have long since vanished. Others lack the characteristics that would allow them to be matched to particular sources. Manufactured goods may be the product of a particular community, but they may also be local copies, implying the movement of ideas rather than goods, and it is not always possible to distinguish these. Technological innovations, however sophisticated they may seem, are not necessarily the brainchild of a single community, so their appearance in separate areas need not imply that they are derived from a single source. (The long-running debate about the Aegean or local origin of the faience beads in Early Bronze Age Britain, now resolved, is a classic example of such difficulties.) Heavy reliance is therefore placed on commodities that can be characterized (examined physically or chemically to identify a characteristic pattern of trace elements or mineral inclusions) and therefore matched to precise sources, such as obsidian, or that come from a single or restricted source, such as amber; these act as markers for the circulation of other goods. Commodities in circulation at any period can also conjecturally be matched to sources shown by archaeological evidence to have been exploited at that time, though such evidence is often absent, and other evidence may be needed to establish which of several potential sources actually supplied a particular region.

STONE

Flint Silicate stone, particularly flint, that could easily be knapped was used from the Palaeolithic period for making cutting, boring, and scraping tools and was still in use into recent times for making gunflints. Flint occurs widely in Europe and was at first derived from surface outcrops, though by Mesolithic times it was also beginning to be mined. The homogeneous nature of flint makes it difficult to characterize, and most flint objects can therefore not be matched to a source. Some attractive types of flint, however, can be identified on the basis of their distinctive color and patterning. These were mined and widely traded in the third millennium, and were often made into objects intended for display rather than for use as tools. The principal sources of these flints were in parts of northern and western Europe, including eastern and southern England, Belgium, western France, Jutland, Zealand, and Scania, Rügen in Germany, Poland (particularly in the Holy Cross mountains), and the Ukraine. Farther south the Apennines yielded a pink flint used in lowland sites, and Bulgarian flint was widely used in eastern Europe. Objects made from these fine flints were traded over great distances, that from Grand Pressigny in France being found as much as 500 miles (800 kilometers) away.

Obsidian The attractive volcanic glass, obsidian, from which exceptionally sharp-edged tools can be made, can be characterized on the basis of the presence and relative proportions of different trace elements, patterns that are unique to each volcanic formation. Obsidian on the island of Melos was being actively sought by the inhabitants of the Aegean by around 9000 B.C.; it is known from the Mesolithic settlement at Franchthi cave and was important in the early and later Neolithic settlements of Greece, in some cases being the main type of stone used for making blades. Sources on Sardinia, Pantelleria, Lipari, and Palmarola were exploited by the Neolithic inhabitants of Italy and southern France. Obsidian from the Slovakian and Hungarian mountains was already being used in the early postglacial period by people living in the Danube valley and was widely circulated among the Neolithic inhabitants of the Balkans. It was also acquired by the inhabitants of Olszanica in southern Poland and of other LBK settlements, generally in the form of cores.

Hard Stone Fine igneous and metamorphic rock was used for making axes, chisels, and other cutting tools from the Neolithic period onward; the stone was ground into shape and then polished, making tools that were more durable than those of flint. The pattern of mineral inclusions allows the stone to be matched to a source area and often a precise source. Although suitable stone was quite widely available, particularly fine outcrops were intensively exploited and their products exchanged or traded over considerable distances, particularly during the third millennium B.C.; individual settlements often contained the products of several different sources.

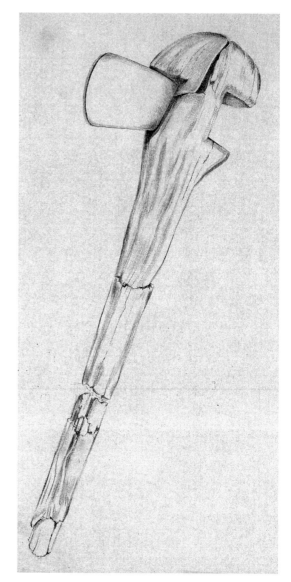

5.2 *A Neolithic stone ax still in its wooden handle, found in a bog at Shulishader on the island of Lewis, Scotland. The ax was made of porcellanite, a type of stone probably traded from Antrium in Ireland.* (Drawing by Audrey McIntosh, from material in the National Museums of Scotland, Edinburgh)

Other Stone Many types of stone were exploited for making tools, figurines, and other objects, generally within an area relatively close to their source. One exception was abrasive stone, which was used for making grindstones, important in everyday life for grinding grain. Such stone was relatively limited in its occurrence, and good-quality stone, such as the basalt from Mayen in Germany and Niedermendig lava from the Rhineland, was widely traded, particularly during the Iron Age.

Building Stone Stone for domestic construction was generally obtained from the local area, but for building monuments suitable stone might be brought by their builders from some distance, at considerable effort. The Grand Menhir Brisé at Carnac, a vast 355 short tons (348 tonnes) in weight, was dragged over 2.5 miles (4 kilometers) from its source, while the 82 bluestones used at Stonehenge (averaging 1.5 short tons each) were transported over 150 miles (240 kilometers) from the Prescelly Mountains of Wales.

METALS

Metallurgy began in the Balkans and Spain in the fifth millennium, and the technology was adopted and developed across Europe in the following millennia, Scandinavia being the last major region to begin working metal, its industry based entirely on imported ores. The patchy distribution of metal ores was a major stimulus to the development of trading networks and mechanisms that ensured the regular supply of metal ores and metal objects, resulting by the second millennium in many shared cultural features across Europe. Metal artifacts were initially rare prestige goods of social significance, but gradually also included many tools necessary for everyday life.

Various methods of characterization have been used in the attempt to match metal artifacts with the sources of the ores from which they were made, and recently lead isotope analysis has yielded useful results for lead, silver, and copper. But there are major difficulties: Many of the ore sources exploited in antiquity were small and have been worked out or are now unknown, and the mixing of ores, particularly by reusing scrap metal, makes characterization difficult or meaningless. The picture of prehistoric

European metal extraction and trade is therefore incompletely known.

Some metal ores such as malachite, azurite, and haematite (red ochre) were also used as pigments, the use of red ochre going back deep into Palaeolithic times.

Gold Alluvial gold was available in the rivers of the Balkans and was worked by the fifth millennium. Not all gold used in the Balkans was obtained locally, however: a significant proportion of the gold objects found in the Bulgarian cemetery of Varna came from more distant sources in Armenia and the Caucasus.

By the late third millennium local gold sources were being exploited in Iberia, Brittany, and Ireland, and both unworked gold and artifacts such as personal ornaments were being traded in the Atlantic region. Around the same time the Otomani and Únětice cultures of the Carpathian basin and central Europe were making cups of sheet gold from sources in Transylvania and Bohemia. Gold was used and traded in increasing quantities from the later second millennium onward. In the late centuries B.C. much of the gold in use in Celtic Europe came from the Mediterranean as coins paid to Celtic mercenaries and melted down as bullion.

Copper Copper working began in the Balkans and Iberia during the fifth millennium, based on native copper and easily worked local oxide and carbonate ores. During the fourth millennium copper objects from the Balkans were being traded as far as Scandinavia, but by the late fourth millennium these ores were running out. The Fahlerz sulfide ores of the Harz and Slovakian Mountains and the Austrian Alps, which contained arsenic and antimony, now began to be mined and traded. By the later third millennium copper metallurgy was also being practiced in western Europe and Italy, using sulfide copper ores from many sources.

At the same time copper began to be alloyed with tin to produce bronze. Ore, smelted metal, and bronze artifacts were being widely traded by the second millennium, both Atlantic and central European sources being exploited, while metal from sources outside Europe was also traded into the southeast. By the Late Bronze Age bronze was common enough to be widely used for manufacturing tools as well as weapons and ornaments, even in Scandinavia, which imported all its copper and tin. Artifacts such as axes and swords were widely traded, and two wrecks off the English coast show that scrap metal was also moved between regions as a raw material.

Tin The sources of tin in Europe were extremely restricted, and its trade was therefore of key impor-

tance in determining the patterns of communications across Europe. Cornwall was perhaps the principal source, though Galicia and the Bohemian Ore Mountains were also important. Small quantities were also obtained from Brittany, parts of Italy, and Iberia, and perhaps Ireland and Serbia, and probably from the steppe and the Near East.

Lead and Silver The main sources of silver in prehistoric Europe were the silver-lead ores of Iberia, the relatively pure silver of the Bohemian Ore

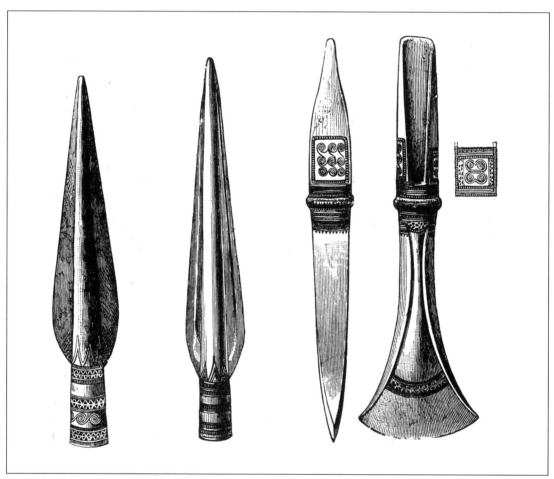

5.3 Two fine Bronze Age spearheads and a palstave from Denmark, skillfully decorated. All bronzework in prehistoric Scandinavia was made from imported metal ores. (Worsaae. J. J. A. *The Industrial Arts of Denmark.* London: Chapman and Hall, 1882)

Mountains, and the electrum (gold and silver alloy) of Transylvania. Outside these regions silver was little used, but lead was traded and in the Atlantic region was alloyed with copper in the Late Bronze Age. In the Late Iron Age, however, a considerable quantity of silver began to circulate in transalpine Europe as a result of trade with the Romans.

Iron and Iron-Age Metalwork   During the early first millennium iron came to replace bronze as the main metal for making tools and weapons, allowing bronze to be devoted to the production of personal ornaments and prestige objects such as parade armor, mirrors, horse trappings, and fine tableware. Iron ores were widespread and most regions were able to use local sources, although the iron from major sources such as the eastern Alps, the Holy Cross Mountains of Poland, the Hunsrück-Eifel area, and Etruria was also exported. Iron artifacts, particularly weapons, also circulated widely in the first millennium, as did objects of bronze, including decorated vessels, jewelry such as bracelets, and bronze cauldrons.

DECORATIVE MATERIALS

Glass and Faience   The technology used for producing faience was developed in the Near East in the fifth millennium but may also have been independently invented in central Europe in the early second millennium, from whence it reached Britain and France. Analyses of the composition and manufacturing details of faience beads show that they were locally made in a number of different regions, such as Wessex and southern Scotland.

Glass began to be produced around the same time, probably in the Bohemian Ore Mountains, and circulated in central Europe. During the Late Bronze Age glass beads made in the Aegean and Italy were traded widely, and during the first millennium glass production became increasingly common across Europe and the range of forms, colors, and decoration diversified. Raw glass was widely traded and worked into beads, bracelets, and other small objects in oppida and other major settlements, for local use and for export.

Amber   Neolithic coastal communities such as those that made Pitted Ware are known to have col-

lected, worked, and traded amber to their Globular Amphora neighbors in the fourth millennium, a pattern that probably characterized most of prehistory. The volume of amber in circulation can be gauged from the discovery at Rospond, a TRB site in Poland, of a cache of some 1,100 pounds (500 kilograms). Most amber came from the coasts of the Baltic or the North Sea coast of Jutland, but some was carried by the sea to the eastern shores of Britain and to other North Sea coasts. It was traded as far as Iberia, Italy, and Greece, and was particularly popular in the Iron Age.

African Materials   The prehistoric inhabitants of Iberia obtained ivory from northwest Africa. During the first millennium the Phoenicians and Carthaginians injected supplies of both African and Indian elephant ivory into the Mediterranean trading networks, and possibly hippopotamus ivory. Some of this was traded into the European interior, where it was used mainly for small objects. Ivory sphinxes and ornaments of Mediterranean manufacture are known from a wealthy Hallstatt D burial at Grafenbühl, and ivory chains were among the goods said by Strabo to have been imported by the British in the late first century A.D.

Trade in ostrich eggshells followed a similar pattern, being imported from North Africa by the people of southern Iberia from the late third millennium and circulating more widely in Europe, though not in any quantity, from the later second millennium through the activities of Phoenician and Aegean traders.

Other Materials   Many attractive materials were used in the areas in which they occurred, at various times in prehistory, but generally did not circulate outside these regions. Jet, lignite, and cannel-coal (all forms of coal), and shale found in various parts of Britain were used occasionally for making jewelry in the Mesolithic and Neolithic periods. From the Early Bronze Age jewelry and clothing accessories of these materials became more common and circulated widely in Britain. Vessels were also made from lignite and shale. A related stone, sapropelite, found in Bohemia, was worked in the Iron Age to make bangles, which were traded in central Europe as far as Switzerland.

Schist was used in the fourth millennium in southwest Iberia to make decorated plaques and "crosiers," objects with a probable religious significance. In the same period callais was used to make beads in northern Iberia; this material was used more widely in Iberia and in Brittany during the late fourth and earlier third millennium, but its use ceased thereafter.

Shells were used for making ornaments by the people of coastal communities who ate their contents, but some also circulated widely from Palaeolithic times onward. During the Mesolithic period spondylus shells from the Aegean were traded throughout the Mediterranean and in the Neolithic period reached LBK settlements of central Europe. Dentalium shells circulated among the communities of the Aegean and the Balkans during the same periods.

Decorative stones, such as jasper, chalcedony, and jadeite, were used to make ornaments and other valued objects, particularly in the Neolithic period. Some were traded over considerable distances, such as the jadeite polished stone ax from the Alps that was deposited in the Somerset Levels in England.

Mediterranean coral gained widespread popularity in Iron Age Europe, where it was used for inlays, jewelry, and amulets.

PERISHABLE GOODS

Timber Much of Europe was forested in antiquity, and in temperate Europe the wood required for building houses, vehicles, and boats and for manufacturing a range of goods was usually locally available to communities. Where it was not, other materials were substituted: For example, houses on Orkney, as at Skara Brae, were constructed of stone instead of timber.

In the Mediterranean, forests and woodland were more restricted and timber had to be obtained from areas often far from the communities that required it. Timber was among the goods sought by the Greeks in the first millennium B.C. as they established trading colonies around the Mediterranean and Black Seas.

Furs and Hides Roman authors record furs and hides among the goods they obtained from Britain, Gaul, and northern Europe. Although there is no archaeological evidence of trade in these perishable materials, it is likely that in prehistoric times, as in recorded history, furs were an important export from Scandinavia, and they were probably among the goods exchanged by north European hunter-gatherers in return for the agricultural produce of farmers such as LBK.

Slaves The classical world, particularly the Romans, had a great need for slave labor. They obtained many slaves directly through warfare and raiding, but others they purchased from Celtic or Germanic tribes who had themselves acquired the captives in wars or raids. Dramatic evidence for the British slave trade comes from slave chains discovered in the hillfort of Bigbury in Kent and among the votive offerings deposited in the Welsh lake of Llyn Cellig Bach: circles of iron that were fixed around the necks of captives, fastened together in a line with chains. Transalpine Europe was probably supplying classical cultures with slaves by the sixth century B.C., when the Greeks began to trade up the Rhône. The Celts themselves made relatively little use of slaves, so the acquisition of war captives seems to have been largely for export, and the existence of an export market for slaves may indeed have stimulated raiding.

Animals The appearance of domestic caprines among the fauna in hunter-gatherer settlements such as those of the Ertebølle in the north, the Bug-Dnestr culture in the east, and Impressed Ware groups in the Mediterranean implies their original acquisition from farming groups. These animals were probably acquired by raiding or mutually profitable exchanges in areas where intrusive farming communities came into contact with native hunter-gatherers and by gift exchange among those hunter-gatherer communities that had no direct contact with agricultural settlers. Trade in and exchanges of animals, for instance, between pastoral groups and settled communities, must have continued throughout prehistory, but it is hard to demonstrate after the initial appearance of nonlocal species in a region. The Roman author Strabo recorded that the Celts exported large quantities of salted meat, particularly pork, to Italy and Rome.

Strabo also listed hunting dogs among the Roman world's valued imports from Late Iron Age

Britain. In the other direction the Celtic world acquired donkeys from the Romans, probably as a result of Rome's conquest of Gaul. Domesticated horses had been introduced into Europe during the fourth millennium, initially probably by incursive steppe nomads. Although horses were bred thereafter by European communities from local stock, the larger steppe horses continued to be prized and were among the goods acquired by European communities from the Scythians.

Wine   In the sixth century B.C., when the Greeks began trading up the Rhône with the chiefdoms of France and southern Germany, among the main inducements they offered were wine and the luxury tableware with which to serve it: Etruscan bronze flagons and fine Attic pottery. As a diplomatic gift to the leader at Mont Lassois they presented the Vix krater, theoretically a vessel for mixing wine with water, but extravagantly large and ostentatious. This unique object, made to order in Sparta or Magna Graecia, was transported in pieces and reassembled by the Greeks in situ, as Greek letters labeling its sections demonstrate.

Some centuries later, the same inducements, wine and a wine service of fine pottery, were offered, with equal success, by the Romans to the leaders of Celtic tribes in Gaul and Britain. The Romans exchanged the wine at what was for them a very favorable exchange rate, a slave for one amphora of wine, as against five to six amphorae in Rome, for by the late centuries B.C. large Roman estates were producing a surplus of wine that they were very happy to unload on the barbarians who could offer valued raw materials in exchange. The volume of trade can be deduced from the quantities of amphorae found on settlements in southern Gaul in the second century and those of northern Gaul and southern England in the late second and first. These were used to transport wine by sea, while for land transport it was more practical to move wine in wooden barrels and skin bags, both referred to in classical texts; these have left no trace.

Salt   Salt was a vital dietary supplement for prehistoric farmers whose daily fare was cereal based, and was also important as a preservative. It was obtained by evaporating brine from seawater, salt springs or salt marshes, or mined from deposits of salt crystals

or brine within rocks; sources in the Halle region of Germany and the Salzkammergut area of Austria were particularly important. Surface deposits of salt were being exploited at Cardona in Catalonia during the fourth millennium. By the later Neolithic salt was being produced from brine in a number of sites in eastern and central Europe and the Alps, such as Barycz in southern Poland and Ocna Mureşului in Romania. Salt production greatly increased in the Late Bronze Age, salt being mined and evaporated from seawater as well as from brine springs and pools. Salt production was a major Iron Age industry, for instance, at Droitwich in England, Seille in France, and Bad Nauheim in Germany, but especially from Hallstatt and Dürrnberg bei Hallein in Austria. A number of Iron Age settlements, such as Camp de Château in eastern France and Hallstatt itself, became wealthy on the proceeds of salt extraction, and salt was a major item of trade.

MANUFACTURED GOODS

Pottery   Despite being both heavy and breakable, pottery was often traded in prehistoric Europe, presumably mainly by water. In many cases pots served as containers for perishable goods; these can sometimes by identified by residues that have survived inside the vessels, but are usually unknown. Some types of pottery, however, were used exclusively for transporting specific known commodities and are therefore very informative. In particular, Roman amphorae were used to ship wine and other foodstuffs to various regions, including Celtic Europe; variations in the form of these amphorae provide very specific information about this trade. For example, from the late second century B.C. Roman wine was transported in a type of amphora known as Dressel type 1A. Considerable quantities were shipped to Brittany and thence into southern England via the port of Hengistbury Head on the Solent. After the Roman conquest of Gaul, however, around which time the style of amphora became taller and thinner (Dressel type 1B), the focus of Roman trade here shifted to southeast England, operating between the Seine-Rhine region and the Thames. Fish sauce and olive oil were also shipped to this region, in different styles of amphora (Dressel types 6–11 and 20).

Pottery was also traded for itself, usually as a luxury or prestige commodity. In the Iron Age fine Greek drinking vessels accompanied the wine traded into sixth-century barbarian Europe, and fine Gallic and Roman pottery was traded alongside the wine that reached southern England in the first century. Although the quality and appearance of pottery vessels must themselves have been attractions, the circulation of different styles and forms of pottery often related principally to their meaning: Particular pottery vessels might display wealth, demonstrate social status, or indicate participation in a religious or social activity. In some cases it was the pottery that circulated, in others just the style, with the pottery itself being locally made. For example, in third- and early second-millennium Britain a succession of wares appeared first as prestige goods and gradually became more common and less valuable, until they became the common domestic ware, and a new prestige ware appeared: these included Grooved Ware, Beakers, and Food Vessels. Each probably represented more than a fashion in pottery shape and decoration when it first appeared, being used in socially and ritually significant activities involving alcohol, drugs, and the disposal of the dead.

In other cases pottery was traded for utilitarian reasons. The graphite coating on Late Iron Age pottery made in Brittany, for example, was an effective heat diffuser, and thus this ware was traded for culinary use. Graphite-bearing clays were extracted in central Europe during the Bronze and Iron Ages, and graphite-tempered wares made from this clay were particularly popular east of the Rhine from the second century B.C.; they were attractive as well as practical.

Textiles The vast majority of textiles in prehistoric Europe were manufactured in the home, of locally grown flax and other plant fibers and of wool from domestic flocks. In the Late Iron Age some more intensive production may have taken place; woollen garments were among the commodities that the Romans imported from transalpine Europe, including the *sagum*, a heavy cloak that could also be used as a blanket, and the *byrrus*, a thick hooded cloak resembling a duffle coat, both made from the coarse wool of Gallic sheep, which repelled rain and

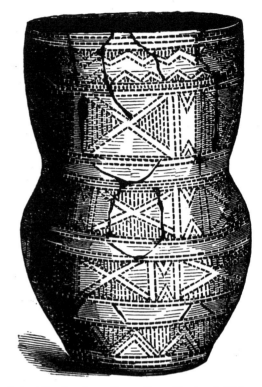

5.4 A Beaker from Green Low, England. This distinctive ware was popular over much of western Europe; although sometimes connected with the supposed movements of a "Beaker Folk," the spread of Beaker pottery probably illustrates the spread of fashions and ideas. (Lubbock, John. *Prehistoric Times.* New York: D. Appleton and Company, 1890)

insulated even when wet. Those made by the Nervii of Belgium were most highly valued, but British products also commanded a good price.

Silk, made in distant China, occasionally reached the elite of Iron Age Europe, probably via the nomadic cultures of central Asia.

Routes

Topographical features, vegetation, natural hazards, and other environmental constraints and opportunities must always have been of major importance in determining which routes were used, and so these often stayed the same down the ages. Other, human, considerations, however, dictated the choice of routes in use at any one time: the pattern of settlements across the landscape; the nature and technology of the transport available at the time; the creation or existence of constructed roads and trackways, ferries, and bridges; the extent to which forests had been cleared; the purpose of the journey being undertaken; the relationships between the traveler and his or her community and the communities through whose territory the traveler might pass (ranging from actively welcoming through neutral and placable to violently hostile or dangerous); and so on.

LAND

Routes in the interior often followed rivers. These could be traveled by boat, often the most practical means of transport, particularly when transporting bulky goods. Travelers on foot or with vehicles and animals needed supplies of water, which were readily provided by rivers. The banks of rivers often formed easily used pathways, relatively free of vegetation, and river valleys created routes through hills and mountains that would otherwise present an obstacle. River valleys were also frequently the best route to the sea, especially where there were coastal cliffs. Conversely, rivers often presented a barrier separating the lands on either side, and routes followed riverbanks to the places where crossings could most easily be made, whether by fords, ferries, causeways, stepping-stones or, in some cases, bridges (such as La Tène).

Away from the rivers, hills and mountains played a major role in determining the routes that were followed. Passes through major mountain barriers channeled communications as did saddles between hills, and routes across and around hills and mountains remained unchanged for millennia unless the topography itself changed, as a result of events such as rockfalls or earthquakes.

In areas without significant relief such as the steppe and the North European Plain, other constraints operated to dictate routes, such as the availability of water and the distribution of marshy ground.

SEA

In coastal regions and lands with dissected or mountainous topography, communications were often easier by sea than by land; this was true, for example, both of Greece and of Scandinavia. Most sea voyages were likely to have been over short distances, such as between the coastal sites or islands exploited at various times of year by Mesolithic hunter-gatherers like those who visited Oronsay in the Hebrides, Vaengo So and Dyrholm in Denmark, or the Greek island of Melos. Fishing expeditions also took people out to sea; although many fish were caught in coastal waters, some such as ling were fished in deeper water; similarly, sea mammals could be taken on shores where they came to breed or were beached, but they were also pursued and caught out at sea.

Longer voyages may nevertheless have been undertaken from early times. Some were by pioneers colonizing coasts and islands, either deliberately setting out to reach visible or suspected land (such as Shetland, visible from Orkney) or returning to places where they had made unintentional landfall after being driven off course by storms. Some fishing expeditions may also have involved longer journeys, following the annual migration routes of fish such as cod. Familiarity with distant seas and the lands they edged led to voyages undertaken to obtain, directly or by trade, the materials and products of other regions. By 4000 B.C., therefore, if not earlier, the sea-lanes from Anatolia to the Shetlands and Scandinavia were known and being traveled, probably generally as a series of overlapping shorter routes known to the inhabitants of each region.

Classical sources show that seafarers, whenever possible, followed the coasts and preferred to voyage by day, putting in to camp on shore each night; it is unlikely that prehistoric Europeans differed in this respect. The ability to do this, however, depended on local conditions such as the availability of beaches or inlets where landings could be made, the currents and depth of water along the shore, and the absence of dangerous rocks, and some journeys inevitably involved crossing open water for several days on end, without possibility of landfall. The most dramatic example of this is the journey to Iceland, apparently familiar to Scottish seafarers by the later first millennium: a voyage of six days, possibly broken by landing in the Faroes.

ATLANTIC SEABOARD AND THE WEST

Archaeological evidence such as the distribution of materials away from their source areas, similarities in megalithic architecture between different regions, and the colonization of islands (including Shetland by 3900 and possibly 5500 B.C.) shows that the sea-lanes of the Atlantic were well known to the people of the Atlantic facade by the fourth millennium and probably considerably earlier. By the time that the Mediterranean voyager Pytheas recorded his observations of Britain and the north, Iceland was known as a land of volcanoes and frozen seas six days' journey from Scotland; it is uncertain whether Pytheas himself visited Iceland, but it had probably been known to north European seafarers long before this period.

Seafaring along the Atlantic coast generally operated in several overlapping and interlinked sections, which also linked with overland routes into the European interior along the major rivers.

The Gulf of Cádiz, centered on Huelva and Cádiz, was the southernmost section of the European Atlantic sea-lanes, from the northwest corner of North Africa to Cape St. Vincent. Travelers between the Atlantic and the Mediterranean unable to pass through the Strait of Gibraltar could travel overland, following the Guadalquivir inland from the Gulf of Cádiz to the pass of Despeñaperros and thence along the valley of the Segura River to the Costa Blanca. The Guadalquivir, the most important river in southern Iberia, also gave access to a region rich in metal ores.

From Cape St. Vincent to Cabo da Roca the Atlantic seaboard was dominated by the estuary of the Tagus, a major focus of prehistoric settlement. The river, navigable for 120 miles (190 kilometers) gave access to the Spanish *meseta*. From Cabo da Roca to Finisterre was the final west Iberian section of the Atlantic coast, and from this region the Douro provided access into the interior of Galicia, another major area of settlement. These three maritime regions were probably linked by regular contacts, and in the first millennium Finisterre in Galicia (Oestrymnis), a major source of tin, was probably the northern limit of most Phoenician and Roman sailing expeditions.

The northern (Cantabrian) coast of Iberia, the southern margin of the Bay of Biscay, presented a narrow coastal strip backed by mountains, with no easy access to the interior. While some local shipping connected the inhabitants of this coast with one another and with the southern French Atlantic coast, the main sea-lane from northwest Iberia crossed the Bay of Biscay directly to Brittany, a major node in international trade routes. From here sea routes led to Cornwall, which maintained important links with Brittany throughout most of prehistory, into the English Channel and into the Irish Sea. The latter formed a further section of the Atlantic seaways, as well as providing east-west links between Ireland and the British mainland, and led to routes along the west coast of Scotland to Orkney and Shetland and thence to Iceland or Scandinavia.

FRANCE

While Atlantic communities traveled the Atlantic sea-lanes linking Iberia to Brittany, the main routes for Mediterranean access to the Atlantic lay along the rivers of France. North of the Pyrenees, a route ran along the valley of the Aude and through the Carcassonne Gap, to link up with the Garonne, which flowed out into the Atlantic through the Gironde estuary. Major settlements, including Narbo (Narbonne), Tolosa (Toulouse), and Burdigala (Bordeaux), emphasize the importance of this route in the later first millennium, but it was a major line of communications far earlier, for example, providing the route by which the Beaker "package" spread to the Golfe du Lions and eastern Spain. Inhospitable sandbars and marshy shores stretched north and south from the mouth of the Gironde, but a sea crossing linked it to the Bay of Quiberon and thence to the coasts of Brittany. Farther north the mouth of the Loire, another major trade artery, also opened into the Atlantic just south of Quiberon.

The Loire and its tributaries led into the Massif Central and the area to its north, from which a short overland journey brought the traveler to the Rhône-Saône corridor. This led south into the Mediterranean, a route exploited by the Greeks, who established a major trading settlement at Massalia (modern Marseilles, a major port to this day). For much of prehistory this was the main route linking southern Brittany and the Atlantic to the Mediterranean. The Loire-Rhône axis also led north to the Rhineland and routes into the heart of Europe. Farther north the Seine was also a short journey from the Rhône-Saône corridor; this gave access to the English Channel.

THE NORTH

Short sea crossings linked Britain and northwest France across the English Channel: from the western part of the Breton peninsula to Cornwall, and from the Rance estuary and the mouth of the Seine to the Solent shore of southern England, a coastline rich in natural harbors from which five major rivers, the Frome, Stour, Avon, Test, and Itchen, led into the English interior. This was one of the main axes of communication between Britain and continental Europe at many times in prehistory; in the first century B.C., for example, the substantial volume of traffic along this route is shown by the concentration of wine amphorae from Gaul at the port of Hengistbury Head.

East of the Solent the English Channel narrows in the Straits of Dover, the gateway between the Atlantic and the North Sea, where the complex pattern of winds and tides made local knowledge essential for passage. Another major route between the interior of Britain and the continent was the crossing between the Thames and the Seine and the Rhine; with the Roman conquest of Gaul this superseded the Solent shore as the main trade route, leading to the development first of Colchester and then of London as major centers of international trade.

Britain's eastern seaboard, with major rivers such as the Humber giving access to the interior, provided many further links across the North Sea with the rivers of the Low Countries and the North European Plain and with the coasts of Scandinavia. In the northern lands communications were mainly by sea since the mountains and dissected terrain of Scandinavia made overland travel slow and difficult. The narrow neck of land at the base of the Danish peninsula, however, offered an overland shortcut between the North Sea and the Baltic, which must have been used in prehistory as it was in historical

times. The Baltic and the Gulf of Bothnia in turn linked Scandinavia and Finland with northern Russia and the lands of the eastern North European Plain.

CENTRAL AND EASTERN EUROPE

The major rivers crossing the North European Plain were the main arteries of communications between the north and central Europe. The Oder and the Vistula connected the Baltic with the area to the north and east of the Carpathians, and the Oder valley cut a passage through the mountain barrier, between the western end of the Carpathians and the Sudetes, into the Carpathian basin and Hungarian Plain. The Vistula linked to the Dnestr, providing an eastern route to the Black Sea.

Farther west, routes followed the Elbe and Weser south from the North Sea, but the Rhine was the major highway, linking British and North Sea traffic with the rivers of France in the west and the Danube to the south.

The Danube formed the principal route south from the Alpine foreland, carving a passage into the Carpathian basin. Joined by the Drava, Sava, Morava, and other rivers that gave access to the mountains of the western Balkans, and by the Tisza and other rivers descending from the Carpathians, the Danube formed the Iron Gates Gorge, which created an exit from the Carpathian basin between the Carpathians and the Balkan Mountains, flowing from there into the Black Sea. The Rhine-Danube corridor, therefore, was the major north-south route through the center of Europe, but it could also be a barrier to communications between east and west.

SOUTHEAST EUROPE AND THE MEDITERRANEAN

While the lands bordering the north of the Black Sea were relatively open, the mountainous terrain of Greece and the western Balkans made land communications difficult and favored travel by sea, through the Aegean and Adriatic Seas, the former connecting Greece with Anatolia and the seaborne trade routes of the eastern Mediterranean, the latter linking the Balkans with eastern Italy. At the head of the Adriatic the valleys of the Drava and Sava provided a route around the Julian Alps into the Carpathian basin and transalpine Europe, much used through the ages.

Sea routes in the Mediterranean generally stayed close to land. European connections between the east and west basins of the Mediterranean, therefore, passed through the hazards of the treacherous Straits of Messina between Italy and Sicily: the location of "Scylla" and "Charybdis" of classical ill repute. The coastal lands of western Italy, France, and Spain permitted some travel, but communications in the western Mediterranean basin, as in the east, were largely by sea. For example, the distribution of obsidian from the island of Lipari shows that it was brought by sea to various locations on the Calabrian coast, from which it was traded into the interior, rather than taken to the closest land, Sicily, and traded overland from there. From the western basin of the Mediterranean the Rhône gave access to the interior of Europe. Other well-traveled routes led from northern Italy through the Alpine passes into France and Germany; a cache of gold torcs and armlets hidden beneath a rock at Erstfeld provides striking evidence of the passage of a Celtic trader along the route leading through the St. Gotthard Pass. In contrast, passes through the Apennines were few and difficult to negotiate, channeling southward travel by land or sea along the east and west coasts of Italy.

As in the Atlantic, early travel in the Mediterranean involved numerous short and overlapping routes. Most followed the coasts, but there were also routes between islands and between the islands and the mainland. These were generally used only at certain times of year, depending particularly on seasonal patterns of currents, winds, and weather. Evidence shows that while Sicily, Corsica, Sardinia, and Crete were settled and incorporated into communications networks early in the postglacial period, it was not until the late sixth millennium that the Balearics and Malta were settled. During the second millennium international trade linked the civilizations of the eastern Mediterranean basin, including the Egyptians, the states of the Levant and Anatolia, and the Minoans and Mycenaeans. The Mycenaeans also established long-distance trade routes as far west as Sardinia by the 14th century B.C., and a few centuries later the Phoenicians were establishing trading colonies in the central and western Mediterranean, followed in the eighth century by the Greeks; the entire length and breadth of the Mediterranean was now being traversed by seaborne traders. In the absence of literary evidence it cannot be conclusively determined whether long-distance expeditions were made earlier, but archaeological evidence indicates close links among the inhabitants of the Tyrrhenian Sea and many contacts among the cultures of the western Mediterranean basin, illustrated, for example, by the rapid spread of the Beaker package.

The Strait of Gibraltar formed a bottleneck that restricted communications between the Mediterranean and the Atlantic seas. Only at certain times of year when the wind direction was favorable was it possible to sail from the Mediterranean into the Atlantic; a strong current made it easier to sail from west to east, but this was still dependent upon favorable winds. As the winds were not always reliable, passage of the Straits could sometimes be delayed for several months. Nevertheless, during the sixth millennium communications or the movement of colonists through the Straits brought Neolithic plants and animals to Estremadura in southern Portugal, the first demonstrable connection between the seas. Unknown numbers of prehistoric seafarers made the journey in either direction before the Phoenicians in the 11th century established the first historically recorded Mediterranean colonies on the Atlantic seaboard.

LAND TRANSPORT

Foot

Most travel by land was on foot: Over short distances people walked between their settlement and their fields or pastures or visited relatives in neighboring settlements; traders and itinerant craftsmen walked over longer distances, as did transhumant pastoralists, accompanied by pack animals. The Iceman, who died in the Alps some 5,000 years ago, was journeying on foot, carrying his equipment in a backpack and on his person. Mercenaries, attested in the Iron Age, also traveled considerable distances from their native villages in western or central Europe as far as Egypt, North Africa, and Greece, while bands of Celtic raiders penetrated Asia Minor.

From the later Mesolithic period onward, transport over snow was facilitated by the use of skis, sledges, and snowshoes, though the evidence is very slim. Examples of Mesolithic sledges and skis were found in north European bogs; a pine-wood runner found at Mesolithic Heinola in Finland came from a large sledge, probably drawn by dogs; part of a Bronze Age burial chamber at Pustopolje in Bosnia was made from a reused sledge runner; and a Catacomb Grave kurgan at Novaya Kvasnikova in Volgograd contained a burial furnished with a sledge with wooden runners. Sledges were also probably widely used for carrying goods even without snow, although there is no clear evidence of this; they were used in this way into recent times in Britain.

Vis I (Russia) At this eighth-millennium Mesolithic site fragments of skis were found, made from substantial hardwood logs. One ski had an elk's head carved on it; this acted as a brake.

Animals

By the fourth millennium, if not before, animals were being used for transport: Farmers used cattle for localized transport; dogs probably drew sledges in the north; pastoralists may have loaded some goods onto their sheep and goats, as in more recent times (a sheep could carry loads around 22 pounds (10 kilograms) in weight); and by the second millennium horses were probably employed as pack animals. Donkeys were used to carry goods and people in the Near East and the Mediterranean in the Bronze Age, but they were not introduced into temperate Europe until Roman times. The date when horses began to be ridden is uncertain; people in the Near East began to ride horses by the late third millennium, but this only became significant there in the first millennium, when cavalry became important in warfare. In the steppe, however, horse riding may have begun earlier. It is not possible to establish

whether the antler cheek pieces that have been found in the steppe and the Carpathian basin in the early second millennium formed part of a harness for riding or for traction. Art, literary accounts, and trappings in graves demonstrate that horse riding was practiced by the Iron Age in transalpine Europe. Horses were valuable possessions and were probably owned only by elite individuals.

Vehicles

Wheeled vehicles appeared in eastern and central Europe during the fourth millennium and were drawn initially by oxen. Analysis of ox bones from the TRB settlement of Schalkenburg shows pathological changes to the hip bones, which indicates that the animals had been used to draw heavy loads, and a pot handle from TRB Krężnica Jara depicts a pair of yoked oxen. These animals continued to pull wagons and plows in later times, though horses might also be used. Horses served mainly to draw chariots, used by the warrior elite in warfare. Elite burials with wheeled vehicles as biers or grave goods demonstrate the importance attached to them; these appeared in the steppe from the late fourth millennium and occasionally in Bronze Age northern Europe, and in a number of Iron Age chieftains' graves.

Models and artistic representations on pottery depict the early vehicles as four-wheeled wagons

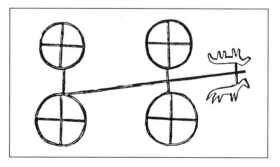

5.5 A Bronze Age rock carving of a wagon drawn by two horses, from Scandinavia (Worsaae, J. J. A. The Industrial Arts of Denmark. London: Chapman and Hall, 1882)

with solid wheels and frames. Wagons in the steppe sometimes had an arched superstructure, making the wagons into shelters while the nomads were on the move; these are not known in Europe, where carts and wagons were probably used mainly for transporting goods over short distances. The introduction of lighter spoked wheels in the second millennium provided the impetus for the development of two-wheeled vehicles whose main use was for transport into battle; by the first millennium the war chariot had further developed into a fighting platform with a light wicker superstructure. Four-wheeled wagons continued in use for transport.

In the absence of made roads, the utility of wheeled vehicles for transport was relatively restricted. Cart ruts on tracks preserved on old land surfaces, for example, beneath barrows, show that vehicles were used, but except in areas of flat unbroken terrain with little vegetation, such as the steppe, their use was probably generally over short distances, such as on the well-beaten tracks between fields and settlements and on paths giving access to water transport; sometimes trackways were built to facilitate the use of such paths.

Roads and Tracks

Travel overland generally followed paths along river valleys when the ground was dry. Alternative routes ran along higher ground, for use when conditions were too wet in the valley bottoms. These higher paths also gave a good view of the landscape, allowing travelers to see their route clearly. The Ridgeway, running along the northern edge of the Berkshire Downs, is a well-known example of such routes, used continuously from remote antiquity up to the present day; it forms part of the Icknield Way, which runs from East Anglia to the south coast of England. Both in valleys and on higher ground paths were formed and fixed by constant use. Where they ran between fixed features, such as embanked field boundaries, continuous use might create a hollow way, the ground along the path being eroded by the passage of people and domestic animals, especially cattle; these are a common feature of Iron Age farming landscapes in Britain. Small portions of paths

have occasionally been located, such as the 65-foot (20-meter) stretch preserved beneath the mid-fourth-millennium TRB mound at Flintbek in Germany, which bears the wheel ruts of carts.

TRACKWAYS

Where routes had to traverse difficult terrain such as boggy ground or shallow water, trackways might be constructed. These are known from various areas in Europe, notably England, Ireland, the Netherlands, southern Scandinavia, and Lower Saxony, and have been intensively investigated in the Somerset Levels in western England. They ranged in complexity and substance from handfuls of brushwood strewn over boggy patches on footpaths to carefully constructed roads of large timbers. Some substantial wide roads in northern Germany, such as Ipfweger Moor, were as much as 6 miles (10 kilometers) long and were constructed of massive split logs laid side by side over supporting timbers, along which wheeled vehicles could have been driven. Tracks might also be built over stretches of ground that saw intensive use by wheeled transport, such as that at Wittemoor. Some, such as Corlea in Ireland, may also have built, at least in part, as a demonstration of the power and prestige of local leaders.

Star Carr (Yorkshire, England) The oldest built track in Europe, a series of split trunks of poplar or aspen laid in parallel across a short stretch of boggy ground, was discovered between the camp area and the lake at the well-known ninth-millennium Mesolithic settlement at Star Carr.

Wittemoor Trackway XLII (Lower Saxony, Germany) A two-mile (3-kilometer)-long corduroy road was constructed here around 135 B.C. and kept in careful repair. It is thought to have been built to take carts loaded with iron ore to the River Hunte, where the ore was loaded onto boats for further transport to the main highway of the Weser.

Corlea 1 (Co. Longford, Ireland) This massive timber road, 13 feet (4 meters) wide and 1.24 miles (2 kilometers) long, is of Iron Age date, and runs across two stretches of boggy ground. It was constructed from at least 375 mature oak trees: Roundwood sleepers were laid longitudinally on the ground and covered by a series of planks, each of which had a hole at either end through which pegs were driven into the bog to hold them in place.

SOMERSET LEVELS

The Somerset Levels in western England is a wetland region that in periods of heavy rainfall, as in the Iron Age, has had large stretches of shallow water, reed marsh, or swamp, while at other times, when the climate has been drier, it has been peatbog. Access to the resources of dry islands within the Levels was by boat when the area was flooded, but in order to cross boggy areas the people of the region, living on the surrounding higher ground, built trackways across the Levels. The earliest, known as the Sweet Track, was constructed of timber felled in the winter of 3807–6 B.C.; it was used and repaired for around 10 years and then abandoned. This substantial track was built by laying a rail, made of poles of ash, alder, hazel, and elm, across the wet marshy ground. Pairs of large roundwood pegs were driven into the marsh diagonally across the rail, forming a V-shape above it into which a surface of oak and ash planks was laid and anchored at intervals with smaller pegs of coppiced hazel driven into the peat through holes in the planks.

Some later trackways in the Levels were simple paths made of bundles of brushwood laid over the damp surface. Others were made of hurdles of coppiced hazel, pegged down on the bog surface. Individual panels were laid side by side and fastened together with withies or the ends of the hurdle rods. The Eclipse Track, created in the second millennium, was made of a continuous length of hurdling, composed of individual panels that had been joined by weaving in extra rods that ran over the breaks between them.

WATER TRANSPORT

Except in mountain regions, water provided the easiest form of transport, especially of goods in bulk.

Both inland and seagoing boats were in use by the Mesolithic period. As well as fishing and carrying cargo, boats were used as ferries to take people and animals across rivers and lakes and between islands, and to carry war bands on raiding expeditions.

Boats

Boats suitable for use on rivers and other inland water must have been used in the earlier Mesolithic period; although none have yet been recovered a number of paddles have been found. From the later Mesolithic onward various river craft have been found, but the record is very patchy; a number of sturdy dugout canoes have been discovered, but less substantial boats such as coracles and rafts have rarely survived and often only fragments of plank-built vessels have been recovered. Boats built of planks are known from the late third millennium onward, but may have been in use earlier. Boats are depicted in the rock art of Scandinavia, but it is not possible to gain much insight into their construction and appearance from these schematic representations. Rather more informative are occasional models, such as the Caergwrle Castle shale bowl inlaid with gold from Bronze Age Wales, showing oars and ribs, the Iron Age sheet gold vessel from Broighter in Ireland, the fifth-century B.C. gold model from Dürrnberg in Germany, fitted with pivoted oars, and the Roos Carr wooden boat model fitted with an animal figurehead from Late Bronze Age Humberside, England, in which stand five warriors. No prehistoric European seagoing vessels are known; several wrecks have been found, but in every case they have been identified only from the distribution of their surviving cargo since no structural remains of them have survived. Evidence of seafaring, therefore, comes indirectly from evidence of the colonization of islands such as the Hebrides during the Mesolithic period, the distribution of traded goods and materials, the presence of deep-sea fish and sea mammals among food remains, and literary sources of the classical period.

RAFTS

Rafts may have been used in the Mediterranean and on lakes and rivers in the European interior, but

5.6 A reconstruction of log boats under construction and in use. In many cases the work of hollowing out the tree trunk was made easier by heart rot, which destroyed the tree's center. (Figuier, Louis. *Primitive Man.* London: Chatto and Windus, 1876)

would not have been suitable for use on the cold seas of the Atlantic and the north. None survive before Roman times, but two rafts from second-century A.D. Strasbourg made of logs fastened together with wooden pegs and probably cord lashings recall classical descriptions of vessels used by the Celts. Caesar, for instance, refers to the Celts' use of log rafts to cross rivers.

DUGOUTS

Dugout canoes are the first known water craft, the earliest surviving examples, from Pesse in the Netherlands and Noyen-sur-Seine in France, dating to the eighth millennium B.C., and they continued in use throughout prehistory; they include a mid-fourth-millennium example from the Charente in France, a late third-millennium example from Locharbiggs in Scotland, and a number of later boats from English and Danish rivers and estuaries, Swiss lakes, and elsewhere. Their use in eastern Spain is mentioned by the Roman author Strabo. Dugout canoes were heavy, not very stable, and not easily maneuverable, so they must generally have been used in relatively calm waters such as rivers and lakes. Those known at present were not seaworthy; paired (joined) boats, described by Caesar in use by Celts on rivers, would have been stable enough for use on the sea, but there is no indication that any of the known specimens were joined in any way.

Canoes were fashioned from long straight tree trunks, the majority of oak, though lime, pine, and sometimes aspen or ash were also used. The outside was shaped using adzes and axes of stone or metal, while the inside was hollowed out with tools (including wedges) or fire, or both. Heart rot was common in mature oak trunks, making it necessary to fill in the stern end of the canoe with a transom board, fitted into a groove.

Tybrind Vig (Fyn, Denmark) Two dugout canoes dated around 4400 B.C. were found in this later Mesolithic settlement. The larger one was 31 feet (9.5 meters) long, carved from a lime tree trunk, with a square-cut stern, and could have taken a crew of six to eight people. A hearth of clay and sand had been constructed in the center of both canoes; it is suggested that this reflects their use for night fishing for eels. Also found were 10 heart-shaped paddles of ash, two of them beautifully decorated with geometric patterns.

Hasholme (North Humberside, England) A large logboat from Hasholme was dated by dendrochronology to 322–277 B.C. Nearly 42 feet (13 meters) long and 3 feet 6 inches (1.4 meters) broad, it was fashioned out of an oak trunk that was around 800 years old at the time of felling. Heart rot throughout the trunk made it easy to hollow out but also made it necessary to close both ends, by inserting a transom at the stern and a sophisticated arrangement of timbers at the bows, fastened with cleats and treenails. A steering platform was added at the stern. A series of holes along the sides may have taken lashings that secured covers to keep the cargo dry. The vessel's final cargo when it sank was joints of beef.

Brigg (Lincs, England) This early first-millennium B.C. logboat was made from a whole oak tree trunk, with oak bottom planking and a fitted oak transom at the stern. Repairs had been made to it by sewing or lashing on wooden patches, caulked with moss. The vessel was 48 feet (14.78 meters) long and its girth near its butt was 19 feet (5.9 meters). Raised ridges inside may have marked the stations of three pairs of paddlers. A platform at the stern allowed steersmen to operate steering paddles. It could carry a crew of up to 26 paddlers or a crew of five with a cargo of around 5.6 short tons (5.5 tonnes).

Björke (Sweden) This first-century A.D. logboat, 23 feet, three inches (7.16 meters) long, was modified by the addition of a plank to each side to make a higher-sided vessel; these were fastened with iron rivets and lashed to cleats in the dugout's base.

HIDE AND BARK BOATS

Hide boats such as coracles and currachs were probably used from the Mesolithic period, when deep-sea fish such as ling and sea mammals such as seals and even perhaps whales were caught at sea, and have continued in use into modern times; they were frequently mentioned by classical authors, showing their regular use from Iberia to Britain. Tantalizingly little evidence of these, however, survives: soil traces of a wicker framework, possibly such a boat, from an Early Bronze Age burial at Dalgety in Scotland, a possible coracle used for a burial in the Early Bronze Age cemetery at Barns Farm, also in Scotland, another from Corbridge in northern England, and one timber possibly from a currach at Ballinderry in Ireland. These vessels were constructed of a wicker framework covered with hides; sometimes they might have ribs and a keel of light timbers. Some rock engravings from Scandinavia and Russia may depict such boats, and they are known to have been used in the Mediterranean by the mid-first millennium B.C. They were very versatile, being easily constructed, very buoyant, stable enough for sea transport, and light enough to be carried, for example, between rivers or along stretches of river too dangerous for navigation. They ranged in size from one-man circular vessels propelled with a paddle to boats with sails and oars that could accommodate up to a dozen people.

Similar light seaworthy vessels may have been made from bark, carefully cut from the tree trunk as a cylinder or half-cylinder and shaped by soaking and heating. If one piece of bark was too small, the boat could be extended by sewing on extra pieces, caulking the joints with resin. The ends were also sewn together and a wooden framework inserted. The earliest example of a bark boat from Europe dates to the first millennium A.D., but such boats could have been made from Mesolithic times when suitable trees became available.

Broighter (Co. Derry, Ireland) A model boat of sheet gold, dated to the first century B.C., may depict a currach. It was equipped with nine pairs of oars and rowing thwarts but also had a stepped mast and a steering oar. The boat was also furnished with a four-hook anchor, boat hooks, and poles, probably for punting.

PLANK-BUILT BOATS

Vessels built of planks are known by the Bronze Age and are probably depicted in rock art. The earliest surviving evidence is one of the three boats from Ferriby, dated around 2000 B.C.; a single plank from another such boat, found at Caldicot in Wales, also dated to the earlier second millennium B.C.

These boats were built of planks split from tree trunks, generally of oak, and green timber was probably preferred for ease of shaping. Timbers for boat building were often stored underwater to give them the pliancy necessary for shaping the boat; heat, tension, and pressure were applied to warp the timbers into the desired shape. Prehistoric European boats were probably all built as a shell of planks to which the internal framework was added; the alternative method, constructing a framework over which the shell was built, appears in boats built in Britain and on the Rhine during the Roman period, and may have been a local development inspired by the earlier technology of hide boats (essentially a skeleton covered by skins, translated here into planks).

Boats built with a keel were stronger and more stable than those without, which were not suitable for use on the open sea. The keel also provided a step for a mast, which could also be stepped in shears; although none of the surviving prehistoric European vessels had provision for a mast, Iron Age European sailing ships were recorded by classical authors, such as those of the Veneti, a sea-trading Gallic tribe in Brittany.

Prehistoric examples have been found only of the less stable vessels suitable for river and estuarine use; they were often flat-bottomed, long, and narrow. Three British seaworthy vessels are known from the Roman period, however, from Blackfriars in London, Barland's Farm on the Severn, and St. Peter Port in Guernsey, and it is possible that the partially preserved Dover boat was also a seagoing craft. Caesar's description of the ships of the Veneti (which numbered around 220, a sizable navy) indicate that seagoing vessels had a shallow draught to allow them to operate in shoals and shallows and a high prow

and stern to allow them to ride heavy seas. He thought that their use of leather or hide rather than cloth for sails was also designed to stand up to rough weather. The sole remnant of such a vessel so far discovered is an iron anchor with 22 feet (6.5 meters) of iron chain, from a hillfort near Poole Harbour in southern England. Deep-hulled ships with a mast and yardarm supported by stays and a side rudder for steering are depicted on the coins of the British king Cunobelin. Sails were used on Mediterranean shipping by the beginning of the second millennium and may well have been adopted by Atlantic seafarers from the Phoenicians around the end of the millennium.

The earliest plank-built vessels were constructed of planks sewn together with strong thread, bast cord, or withies of yew or willow. They were either fastened by tying short threads through paired holes in adjacent planks or by running a continuous thread through the timbers. Often the boats were designed so that the fastenings were countersunk, to prevent them being snagged or abraded. Treenails were also used to fasten together plank boats, and iron nails were beginning to be used by the fifth century B.C. Cleats and transverse timbers were also used to hold the planks together. The gaps between the planks were caulked using a variety of materials: These included moss and well-greased wool, while seaweed (possibly reeds in actuality) was reportedly used by the Veneti. Oil and fat were used to make the boat timbers waterproof and to discourage the growth of plants.

Dover Boat (Dover, England) Part of an oak plank boat stitched with yew withies, originally probably around 42–49 feet (13–15 meters) long and up to 7 feet (2.2 meters) wide, dating from the 14th century B.C. was found at Dover. It had been partially dismantled, but enough remained to show that it was of sophisticated and complex construction, and it was probably a valuable seagoing vessel used in trade across the English Channel.

(North) Ferriby (North Humberside, England) Three plank-built boats were found here, dated to the earlier second millennium B.C. The bottom portion was of four planks cut with an adze from half-logs of oak, two fastened end to end forming a keel that rose in a curve at the stern, flanked by a bottom strake on either side from which rose sides of a further three strakes. Adjacent planks were fastened with a tongue-and-groove joint and stitched with single strands of yew tied through paired holes. Transverse timbers that passed through cleats sticking up from the bottom planking also fastened the planks together. All three boats were flat-bottomed and may have been propelled with paddles or poles since there was no provision for stepping a mast or shipping oars; they would have been used in rivers or estuaries but were not suitable for seagoing.

Brigg "Raft" (Lincs, England) This was the lower part of an early first-millennium shallow flat-bottomed boat built of oak planks sewn with a continuous thread of willow and caulked with moss. Timbers fastened at right angles to the bottom planks through cleats reinforced them. The vessel was probably used as a ferry to carry people and livestock across the Ancholme River and would have been propelled with punt poles or paddles.

Rhine (Belgium, Netherlands, France, and Switzerland) The Rhine has yielded a number of boats of the first to third centuries A.D., probably of the type that had been used on inland waterways in the pre-Roman period. These were flat-bottomed vessels with low vertical sides, their planks held together by ribs fastened to them with clenched iron nails.

CLINKER-BUILT

By the fourth century B.C. the forerunners of the clinker-built boats and ships that were to become typical of northern Europe began to be made. In these vessels the planks overlapped. Like flush-built plank boats these were often sewn, but they might also be fastened using scarf joints and treenails or clenched strake fastenings.

Hjortspring (Island of Als, Denmark) Dated around 350–300 B.C., this is the earliest known example of a clinker-built boat. Around 46 feet (14 meters) long, it consisted of seven limewood planks sewn together, with a keel and side strakes, thin hazel ribs lashed to cleats, and seats for 20 rowers

who propelled the boat with paddles. It had been deposited as a votive offering, along with the arms of around 80 men, and was probably a vessel used by a marauding war band, perhaps offered in thanksgiving by the locals who had managed to defeat them.

ROCK ART

Bronze Age rock engravings, known particularly from Sweden and Norway, frequently depict boats, but so schematically that it is impossible to say what the vessels they represent really looked like and how they were constructed. Features frequently shown include massively upturned ends, both at prow and stern, a beak or projection at water level, possibly to protect the boat against damage when beaching it, and a series of vertical dashes along the gunwales, variously interpreted as crew members, oars, or unknown structural elements. Similar depictions are found on some of the contemporary artifacts, particularly razors, and on the Nebra sky-disc.

SHIPWRECKS

Most evidence for the movement of goods comes from knowledge of the sources of raw materials and manufactured goods and finds of these goods and materials along their distribution routes and in the settlements or burials of their final owners. Very rarely, more direct evidence has been found where boats carrying traded goods foundered and have been rediscovered, though no structural evidence of the boats themselves has survived. Even these finds are not always clear-cut evidence of sea trade; many scholars, for example, regard the Huelva material as a massive votive offering rather than a wreck.

Huelva (Huelva, Portugal) Dated to the mid-10th century B.C., a collection of around 400 objects was found in the mouth of the Odiel River opposite the important Tartessian town of Huelva. The objects included swords, daggers, spearheads, some of them made in Ireland, a helmet, and a number of *fibulae* (safety-pin brooches) from the eastern Mediterranean.

Moor Sands (Devon, England) Eight 12th-century B.C. bronzes, including two Breton palstaves and an

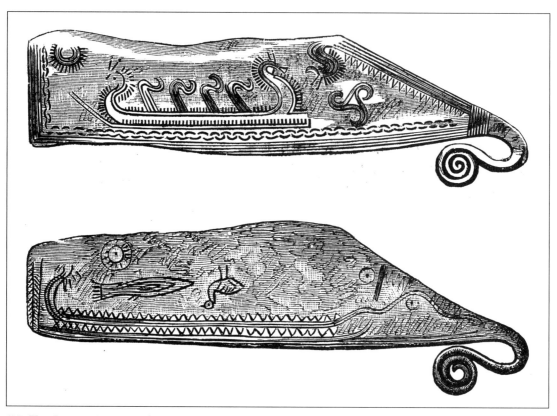

5.7 Two Bronze Age razors from Denmark bearing designs in the form of boats (Worsaae, J. J. A. *The Industrial Arts of Denmark.* London: Chapman and Hall, 1882)

Urnfield-style sword, were found in the sea off Moor Sands at Prawle Point. Although no timbers were found, it is thought that these bronzes came from a vessel carrying scrap metal, wrecked on a voyage from Brittany to a destination in southwest England.

Langdon Bay (Kent, England) More than 350 fragmentary bronzes of continental manufacture, including median-winged axes, palstaves, rapiers, spearheads, pins, and bracelets, were found just outside Dover harbor, a third of a mile (500 meters) from the shore. They are believed to have been the cargo of a now-vanished ship that sank around 1150 B.C. while bringing scrap metal to Britain for reuse. The sole British-style artifact among the collection was a socketed ax, probably the property of a crew member.

Bigbury Bay (Devon, England) Forty-four tin ingots, varying widely in shape and size, were found near a reef in the Erme estuary. They cannot be dated, but their lack of uniformity suggests that they were made by small-scale independent prospectors, possibly in the Late Iron Age, when Roman sources refer to "knuckle-shaped" tin ingots from Cornwall, a description that matches two of the smallest ingots that were found here; these were said to have been transported by the locals in skin boats, a likely vessel to have been carrying this small cargo.

Water Travel

Surviving boats and those described by classical authors had a shallow draught, which would have allowed them to be run aground on beaches or sloping riverbanks or to be moored in shallow water without damage. This made it unnecessary to provide quays for loading and unloading boats, although harbors and sheltered anchorages were still important for sheltering vessels from stormy weather. Jetties, landing stages, and causeways over boggy ground were built in a number of rivers and estuaries; sometimes making use of a superannuated boat as part of the framework. A Bronze Age barge was found at Shardlow on the River Trent in England beside a causeway under construction; it had been carrying stones for building the causeway, and it seems that it and the causeway were destroyed at the same time, perhaps by a flash flood.

The shallow draught of these vessels also reduced the problems of navigation in shallow waters, though knowledge of local hazards such as rocks and treacherous tides or currents would have been essential for safe seafaring and navigation in estuaries and inland waterways. Sounding leads to gauge the depth of shallow water and identify the seafloor sediments were in use by the late centuries B.C. in the Mediterranean and probably the Atlantic; surviving examples were suitable for use in waters up to 50 fathoms (100 meters) deep. Landmarks would have been used to determine location on coastal and inland voyages, but out of sight of land the sun by day and stars by night were undoubtedly used; knowledge of the heavens by prehistoric Europeans is implied by features of some megalithic monuments (See "Megalithic Astronomy," chapter 8). Other useful indications included the patterns of tides, winds, sea swell, and cloud formations, the movements of birds and fish, and clues coming from the land such as smells and the recognizable sediments discharged by particular rivers. The fourth-century A.D. Roman poem *Ora Maritima*, which reused material from the sixth-century B.C. *Massaliote Periplus*, included details of landmarks and other features used to recognize places along the Atlantic coast during a voyage, and undoubtedly such information was handed down orally by prehistoric sailors long before it was recorded in writing.

READING

General

Cunliffe, ed. 1994, Mithen 2003, Milisauskas ed. 2002, Whittle 1996, Harding 2000, Champion et al. 1984.

Trade

Renfrew and Bahn 2004: theoretical trade patterns, characterization; Cunliffe, ed. 1994, Sherratt 1997, Milisauskas ed. 2002, Champion et al. 1984: European trade; Nash 1987, Briggs 1995, Kellner 1991, Wells 1995b, Cunliffe 1997, Champion et al. 1984: coinage; O'Brien, ed. 1999, Sherratt 1997, Scarre, ed. 1988, Darvill 1996: traded goods and materials; Klassen 2002: Ertebølle; Collis 1984a, James 1993, Wells 1995b, Cunliffe 1995, Bökönyi 1991, Sacks 1995: Iron Age trade; Liversidge 1976: Roman trade; Winghart 2000, Sherratt 1997: bronze; Ammerman 1985: obsidian; Cunliffe 1994c, 1995, Darvill 1987: wine; Whittle 1996, Kaelas 1994a: amber; Harrison 1988, Cunliffe 2001a: Phoenician trade; Boardman 1999, Cunliffe 1994c, Collis 1984a, Wells 1980: Greek trade, Biel 1986: Vix.

Routes

Cunliffe 2001a, Milisauskas, ed. 2002, Scarre 1988, Black, ed.1999, McGrail 1995, Darvill 1996, Philip 1991, Kristiansen 1998: general; Turner 1998: Shetland; Cunliffe 2001b: Iceland; Giardino 1992: Sardinia; Pearce and De Guio 1999: North Italy.

Land Transport

Milisauskas and Kruk 2002a, 2002b, Sherratt 1997: general; Mithen 1994, Jochim 2002c, Barker 1985, Harding 2000: skis, sledges, snowshoes; Pearce and De Guio 1999: sheep; Midgeley 1992: oxen; Coles

1984, 1987, Coles and Coles 1986, Raftery 1999, Mellars 1999: trackways.

Water Transport

McGrail 1998, 1983, 1995, Delgado, ed. 1997, Cunliffe 2001a, 2002, Denison 2002, Harding 2000, Fenwick and Gale 1998: boats; Denison 2003a: Shardlow; Denison 2003b: Hasholme; Coles 1984, Mithen 1994: Tybrind Vig; Whittle 1996: Noyen; Sheridan 1999: Barns Farm; McGrail 1983, 1998, Cunliffe 2001a, Finlayson 1998: sea travel; Fenwick and Gale 1998, Harding 2000, Cunliffe 2001a: wrecks.

6

INDUSTRY AND CRAFTS

WOOD

Throughout prehistoric Europe wood was used to make a wide range of tools, while in temperate regions timber was also the main building material. Wood was also universally important for fuel, both for domestic use and for industrial processes, such as firing pottery and smelting metal. Although the primary forest was extensively cleared to obtain land for farming and provide timber, from early times woods were also managed by coppicing and pollarding to control the production of timbers suitable for many purposes. The properties of different types of wood were well understood, and they were carefully selected to fulfill different functions: oak, ash, and elm for planks, hazel and alder rods for wattling and hurdles, yew for bows, and pine for arrows, for example.

Like other organic materials, wood is rarely preserved, most examples of surviving wooden structures and artifacts coming from waterlogged sites such as the Alpine lake villages and the bogs and fens of northern and western Europe. Other sources, however, point to the ubiquitous use of wood and yield some information on woodworking and exploitation. Pollen spectral analyses provide some clues to the growth, decline, and management of forests and the species within them. Postholes, stakeholes, and other archaeological features, such as the discolorations sometimes left in the soil by decayed wooden objects, provide a substantial amount of structural information, and occasional skeuomorphs, such as the joints used at Stonehenge, reveal details of carpentry techniques and other ways in which wood was used and worked. The remaining inorganic portions of composite artifacts can also be revealing: For instance, the layout of metal fittings in a grave may show the form of the wooden vehicle of which they were once part.

Felling and Preparation

The abundance of flint and stone axes in Neolithic Europe shows that trees were generally felled by chopping with an ax. Axes for this purpose were later made of bronze and then iron. Trees might also be killed by cutting a complete ring of bark from them; the wood could then be left to season before the tree was deliberately felled or was knocked down by the elements. Pollen diagrams and studies of preserved wood, particularly in the Somerset Levels, indicate that woods were managed over the long term, trees being encouraged to grow by judicious thinning of saplings, with a view to use several hundred years later.

The major tasks of felling trees and trimming timber were undertaken with axes, while in the Somerset Levels flint flakes were used to perform detailed trimming. These flakes were backed by the natural cortex and were not retouched. Wooden wedges and wooden mallets, along with stone and metal hammers, were used for splitting felled wood into planks.

Oak planks used to build the Sweet Track in the Somerset Levels were of two types, illustrating the technology in use by the early fourth millennium. Some planks were from massive trees over four centuries old. These had been split radially, producing wedge-shaped planks around 16–20 inches (40–50 centimeters) wide. Younger, more slender trees were also used, and in order to obtain planks of the same width, these were split tangentially, a far more difficult and skilled operation.

Woodworking and Wooden Artifacts

Wood was probably used for, or formed part of, the majority of tools and weapons, from spades to plows, from arrows and spears to chariots, from the handles of axes and hafts of daggers to pit props and boats. Occasional translations of these objects into more durable materials and rare finds of actual wooden objects give some clues to the range and ubiquity of wooden artifacts in prehistoric Europe. Only certain tasks were beyond the capabilities of wood: Points and edges for cutting harder materials had to be made of stone or metal, though wooden spears and digging sticks were perfectly adequate for penetrating flesh and soft soil; equipment destined for direct contact with fire, such as cooking vessels, crucibles, or tongs, had also to be of materials other than wood, such as pottery or metal. Probably the most striking objects of wood are the statues, probably of deities, that have been recovered from a few waterlogged sites, such as the Iron Age figures from Ballachulish in Scotland and Ipfweger Moor in Germany, where they were placed beside a trackway, and the large number of votive figurines from Sources-de-la-Seine in France; a small Mesolithic figurine of a person was also found in Holland. Many of the finest wooden objects were made by Mesolithic groups, including elaborate fish traps, skis from the Russian site of Vis, one of which was decorated with a carved elk's head, and two paddles from the Danish site of Tybrind Vig, which bore geometric designs. Different woods were used for different purposes, in some cases within the same object: For example, a solid wooden Bronze Age wheel from Flag Fen was made of alder planks held together with oak braces and ash dowels, while an Iron Age spoked wheel from Holme Pierrepont, also in England, had a birch hub, oak spokes and dowels, and an ash felloe.

TOOLS

Stone tools used to trim and shape wood included axes, adzes, gouges, chisels, awls, small saws, spokeshaves, burins, and knives. Small grooved sandstone blocks through which wooden rods were drawn were used in the Neolithic to make straight arrowshafts. Metal allowed the development of a wider range of woodworking tools and improvements in the efficiency of some existing tools; metal axes, for instance, were sharper and more durable than those of stone. By the sixth century B.C. the sawn planks used to construct the wooden burial chamber in the Hohmichele barrow attest to the use of a large timber-yard saw. From a similar date a pole-lathe began to be used in temperate Europe to turn wooden vessels, wheel naves, and other suitable objects as well as artifacts of other materials such as shale. Iron drill-bits were among the carpentry tools that were found in the Spanish Iron Age village of La Bastida.

JOINTS AND FASTENINGS

Various ways of joining timbers were employed. The trilithons and circles at Stonehenge made use of mortise-and-tenon and tongue-and-groove joints that must have been copied from woodworking. Structures from lake villages in the Alps, the Somerset Levels, and other waterlogged sites show these joints were widely used, along with scarf joints, sockets, dovetail joints, braces, notches, grooves, dowels, and wedges. Other means of fastening used on preserved boats also included sewing, cleats combined with transverse timbers, treenails, and iron nails.

CONSTRUCTION

In temperate Europe wood, and particularly oak, was the usual material for construction. Occasionally tree trunks were used with little or no modification, most famously for the extraordinary monument at Seahenge, a tree set upside down in the ground, exposing its roots. Trimmed tree trunks, roundwood posts and logs, and split tree trunks were also employed in constructing monuments such as the British henges, palisades and gateways, houses, roads and trackways, rafts, mortuary chambers, and the piles on which lakeside settlements were raised, as well as the strange Bronze Age shrine at Bargeroosterveld. Some of the timbers used were massive: Oak posts up to 3 feet (1 meter) in diameter and 4,400 pounds (2,000 kilograms) in weight were already in use by the Neolithic period, and even earlier the pine posts erected at Stonehenge in the eighth millennium B.C. measured up to 32 inches (80 centimeters) in diameter. Split tree trunks were hollowed out with fire and adzes to make dugout canoes and coffins. Tree trunks might also be trimmed to make beams or split into planks for making boats, buildings, vehicles, roads, coffins, sledges, and other large constructions, while branches were used to make smaller objects such as tools, vessels, and handles. Wells were often lined with wood, ranging from wickerwork or planks to hollow tree trunks. Coppiced and pollarded trees such as hazel and alder produced straight poles, rods, and withies, which were often woven into hurdles or used as wattle for trackways, fences, houses, the framework of chariots and hide boats, and other larger-scale construction, as well as baskets, mats, and other smaller-scale objects, including pegs and treenails. Withies were widely used for bindings. Bark was also used for making objects and as twine or cordage. Brush-wood was both used for constructing trackways and combined with piles to form artificial islands such as the crannogs of Iron Age Britain. Waste timber was used as fuel, probably along with timber felled for the purpose; this was either burned as wood in domestic fires or made into charcoal for industry.

TRACKWAYS

Hurdles were probably used for many purposes such as fencing. Preserved hurdles used to construct trackways on the Somerset Levels were made from slender pliable rods of coppiced hazel, alder, or birch, with thicker rods for the sails. Sails laid out singly or in pairs or threes formed the skeleton of the hurdle panel, usually as a number of short rods laid widthwise, although occasionally, as in the third-millennium Honeybee Track, the sails were laid longitudinally. The smaller rods were then woven in and out of the sails to form the hurdle. Longer pieces of hurdling could be made by fastening panels together with withies, or creating a continuous strip by weaving in extra rods to cover the joins between panels, as in the Eclipse trackway.

Other trackways in the Somerset Levels, Saxony, and elsewhere were constructed of split timbers or planks, including the sophisticated fourth-millennium structure known as the Sweet Track, which had a plank walkway suspended above the boggy surface on a rail crossed by pairs of large pegs. In contrast, some trackways were no more than bundles of brushwood laid on the ground.

DOMESTIC EQUIPMENT

One of the most basic uses of wood was to provide handles for edge and pointed tools such as axes, picks, and chisels. Flat axes of metal and polished stone or flint axes were often mounted in an antler sleeve, which was slotted into a wooden haft or were mounted directly in the haft, using cords or sinews for binding. Some axes had the wooden shaft passing directly through a shafthole; this could be fixed more firmly by driving in wooden wedges. Flanged axes were mounted into the split end of a knee-shaped handle; as use would tend to wedge the ax more firmly into the handle end, risking splitting,

such axes often had a stop ridge at the base of the flange. A similarly shaped handle with a solid end was used in socketed tools. Some metal objects were cast with side loops through which a binding could be passed to attach the handle more firmly or prevent its loss if the handle worked loose from the socket.

Apart from cooking vessels, a large proportion of domestic equipment was of wood. This included spindle whorls and loom frames, spoons, bowls, and plates for storing and serving food, and containers like the decorated jewelry box from Late Bronze Age Gross Hafnung in Switzerland. Fine Iron Age woodwork included a flat-bottomed bowl from the Lake Village at Glastonbury. Carved from a single piece of ash, with a small hole at either side which may have held a handle, this vessel was decorated with elegant crosshatched swirls. The most impressive vessels carved from a single wood block were tubs or cauldrons such as the poplar example, one foot (30 centimeters) in diameter, from Iron Age Altarte Glebe in Ireland, which had lugs on its shoulder holding movable yew handles. Wooden vessels found in the Ertebølle site of Christiansholm bear a strong resemblance to the pottery made by the Ertebølle people and may have provided the inspiration for its form.

Furniture was probably limited but might include wooden storage chests, beds, or shelves. Miniature tables and chairs are known from some Balkan Neolithic settlements, as well as wooden beds from an Early Neolithic house at Slatina in Bulgaria, while Skara Brae in Orkney had dressers, seats, and box beds of stone, in the absence locally of wood. A folding stool with an otter-skin seat made in the Mycenaean world was buried in a Danish tree trunk coffin at Guldhøj. Classical sources state that the Celts sat on the ground or on cushions, though the sources do refer to low wooden tables. On the other hand, the carbonized remains of a piece or pieces of fourth-century furniture inlaid with engraved bone, carved with high relief decoration, and ornamented with cast-bronze figurines was found at Cancho Roano in Spain; perhaps a chest of drawers, it shows that furniture was not only used in some places but also could be elaborate.

Many wooden artifacts, such as ards, were made in several pieces. Iron Age buckets, barrels, and

6.1 A wooden bowl decorated with tin pins from a Bronze Age tree-trunk coffin in Denmark (Worsaae, J. J. A. *The Industrial Arts of Denmark*. London: Chapman and Hall, 1882)

even tankards were often stave-built, and some were ringed with bronze bands; they might also have decorative bronze handles and other fittings, and a few examples were sheathed in metal. Buckets from the Wilsford Shaft in England were made of staves with a disc base slotted together and bound with withies.

ATTACK AND DEFENSE

Wood was an adequate material for arrows, spears, pronged fish spears, and other hunting equipment and weapons used on unprotected enemies, though frequently objects intended to penetrate were tipped with stone, bone, or metal, and these would have been a requisite against armored foes. Weapon hilts were often of wood and so were scab-

bards. Wood was probably the usual material for shields, though boiled leather shields were also effective; sometimes these materials were combined; wooden molds were used to form leather shields.

Wood played a major part in the construction of defenses, such as palisades, gateways, and the famous *murus gallicus*, and was the main component of war chariots.

WHEELS

Introduced into Europe in the fourth millennium B.C., wheels were initially constructed of solid wood, either a single piece or made up of three planks fastened with dowels. In the second millennium the spoked wheel was invented in the Near East, and its use spread rapidly, allowing the construction of much lighter, faster, and more maneuverable vehicles, including war chariots. These wheels were constructed of wooden spokes fastened at the center into a hub and at the edge into a wooden rim (felloe or felly) made of pieces of wood joined together, a construction method that continued into Roman times in the Mediterranean. In temperate Europe, however, by around 600 B.C. skilled artisans had devised a more advanced wheel whose felloe was constructed of a single coppiced pole, formed into a circle by heating and bending, its ends fastened with a scarf joint secured with an iron clamp, and the whole protected by an iron tire, held in place with iron nails. By the second century B.C., however, Celtic craftsmen had perfected a technique that required no nails. The tire was heated to make it expand, allowing it to be slipped over the felloe, which it held tightly when it cooled and contracted.

TEXTILES, BASKETRY, NETS, AND MATS

Only rarely has direct evidence of prehistoric European cloth, basketry, and related materials been preserved, being found in waterlogged sites, more rarely in arid locations, and in a few other exceptional settings, including salt mines. Indirect evidence comes from impressions left by textiles on metal, pottery, and other materials, from equipment used in textile manufacture, from artistic representations of clothing and textile manufacture, and from literary references by classical authors. Finds from northern Europe and elsewhere show that mats and baskets, nets and cords were being made in Europe from Palaeolithic or Mesolithic times onward, and cloth was being woven from early in the Neolithic period in parts of Europe, eventually becoming ubiquitous. Impressions on clay from Dolni Věstonice and other Czech sites suggest plain weaving may have begun as early as 27,000 years ago. The discovery, complete with his clothing and equipment, of the Iceman ("Ötzi"), who died around 3300 B.C., has added considerably to our knowledge; interestingly, none of his clothing was made of woven cloth.

Fibers and Other Materials

The majority of surviving textiles from prehistoric Europe were made of wool or flax. Most linen textiles were found in Neolithic lake villages, where the alkali conditions do not preserve wool; most Bronze Age textiles are of wool and come from Scandinavian burials in acid environments that destroy vegetable fibers; it is hard, therefore, to establish the relative importance of the two fibers, though it is thought that wool became the main fiber for making European textiles after the advent of woolly sheep.

Some textiles were made of other plant fibers (bast), including nettles, hemp, tree bast, and grass. Animal hair was also used; for example, a Bronze Age woolen textile from Sheshader in Scotland also incorporated horse and cattle hair, and a fine sash of black horsehair was part of an Iron Age votive offering recovered from a peat bog at Armoy in Ireland. Cotton cloth was probably not known in the Near East until the first millennium B.C., and in Europe it appears first in fifth-century Athens; a rare luxury, it did not penetrate prehistoric Europe. Silk, however, though similarly exotic, was known to the elite of Iron Age Europe.

The fibers used for making cloth could also be used for manufacturing cord and rope, nets and bags, as could many other materials, for example, a cord from Bronze Age Bad Frankenhausen was made of wild clematis. Mats, sandals, and baskets were also made from plant fibers such as esparto grass, reeds, and rushes.

FLAX

Linum usitatissimum was one of the early crops extensively cultivated by European farmers, but, as it was grown also for its oil seeds, its presence does not necessarily imply the use of its fibers. Rare remains of textiles, however, show that linen cloth was made in the Neolithic period. From the Bronze Age its importance probably declined in favor of wool, but it continued in use.

Flax produces a smooth, strong fabric of a golden color that is easily bleached by being laid out wet on grass, but it is difficult to dye.

Preparation   Flax for making fibers was best harvested before the seeds ripened; the later before ripening the harvest took place, the stronger and coarser the fibers produced. These were extracted by retting: the stalks were first dried then soaked in water or urine to cause all but the fibers to decompose. They were then dried again, and the fibers were separated from the decayed material by pounding (braking and scutching) and combing (heckling). Bronze Age pits used for retting flax have been found at West Row Fen and Reading Business Park in England, and a heavy wooden bat for braking and two types of tool for heckling, a wooden board set with thorns and a split rib bone, are known from the Swiss lake villages; these resembled tools used in Europe in more recent times.

OTHER PLANT FIBERS (BAST)

Hemp was used to make coarse cloth and rope, and was particularly useful as sailcloth. The plant was probably cultivated as a narcotic (cannabis), at least by the first millennium, but blue-dyed cloth possibly of hemp is known from the Neolithic site of Adaouste in France; hemp cloth was found in a Late Bronze Age hoard from Scotland; and it was made by steppe nomads and in Southeast Europe in the Iron Age.

The inner bark of certain trees, including lime, oak, and willow, contained fibers (tree bast) that were used to make cord, netting, and cloth, including an Early Mesolithic net of willow bast from Korpilahti in Finland.

Nettle fibers make a fine soft cloth and, given their natural abundance on disturbed ground (particularly that fertilized by urine), must have been widely used for cloth, although the evidence is rare: a single fragment of white cloth made of nettle fiber from a Late Bronze Age tomb at Voldtofte.

Preparation   Hemp fiber was extracted from the plant in much the same way as flax. Nettle fiber could also be separated by retting or by boiling together with ashes.

WOOL

Primitive sheep such as the modern Soay shed their wool, which was collected by plucking or combing it from the animal; suitable combs were common on Iron Age sites. Other larger breeds, known from the Iron Age, had to be sheared, using iron shears. The fleeces of these primitive breeds varied in color, from white through fawn and reddish brown to dark brown and black; like modern Icelandic yarn the natural colors of these wools would have allowed considerable patterning in the textiles produced from them. White wool also absorbs dyes well, making it the most suitable fiber for manufacturing colored cloth.

Preparation   The dirty greasy wool was washed in cold water, either before or after shearing or plucking, then combed to remove pieces of plant and other debris and to align the fibers. These were then ready to be spun into worsted thread, a strong though coarse yarn.

Alternatively, after washing, the wool could be carded to produce woolen yarn, which is soft and elastic but weaker; the textiles known from prehistoric Europe, however, were all of worsted rather than woolen thread.

SILK

Silk was produced in China and probably reached the west via central Asian nomads whom the Chinese used to bribe with silks and other luxuries to buy off their raids. A locally made woolen chemise in the great Hohmichele barrow in Germany, dated to the sixth century B.C., was embroidered with silk and also used silk threads for part of the weft; these threads probably came from a piece of silk fabric that had been unraveled and respun. Silk is also known from the roughly contemporary Hochdorf barrow.

ESPARTO GRASS

Native to southern Spain and North Africa, two different genera of esparto grass were used in prehistoric Spain to make a variety of textiles. A great range of esparto-grass artifacts were found with late third-millennium burials in the cave of Cueva de los Murciélagos. These included baskets, bags, sandals, tunics, belts, and caps, and even a necklace, made by plaiting, coiling, twining, or weaving the grass fibers. Esparto grass could also be made into cords and ropes, particularly used for ships' rigging, but was not used outside its local area in prehistory.

Preparation   Esparto grass leaves were harvested by pulling them off the living plant. These were then dried and retted in seawater.

OTHER MATERIALS

A range of stiffer plant materials was employed to make baskets and mats, including rushes, reeds, sedges, bark, and straw (particularly from wheat), as well as thin pliable woody materials such as osiers. Long, unretouched flint flakes were used in the Somerset Levels to cut reeds; other cutting instruments such as flint and metal sickles and knives were also used over much of Europe.

6.2 The contents of a Danish Bronze Age tree-trunk coffin from Treenhoj in Jutland, including two woolen caps, two nested wooden boxes, a coarse woven woolen cloak, a fringed woolen shawl, and a woolen shirt with a belt (Worsaae, J. J. A. *The Industrial Arts of Denmark*. London: Chapman and Hall, 1882)

Spinning

Yarn was spun from prepared fibers, using a drop spindle (often of wood and thus rarely preserved) weighted by a spindle whorl of wood, pottery, cut-down potsherds, metal, or stone. It has been suggested that the Swiss lake villagers used different spindles for spinning flax and wool, the former with a conical whorl, the latter with a small disc. Rare examples of wooden spindles complete with thread were found in a Horgen site at Sipplingen-Osthafen.

The spinner also needed a distaff to hold the raw wool while she spun, but as this need only have been an ordinary stick, none have been identified. The spinner shown on the Iron Age pot from Sopron in Hungary may be holding a distaff.

Weaving

THREAD

When spinning, the spindle is twirled in a clockwise or anticlockwise direction, producing thread with a Z-twist or S-twist, respectively; most European thread was Z-spun. Two-ply yarn was obtained by twisting two threads together in the opposite direction from that in which they were spun, producing Zs and Sz plies. By combining the different threads, interesting textural differences and patterns could be introduced into woven cloth.

LOOMS

Narrow pieces of cloth, bands, and belts were woven on a simple band loom, probably the backstrap loom in which the warp threads were held in tension between a band around the weaver's waist and a rod attached to something else, such as the weaver's feet or a tree. Though none have been found, the narrow strips of cloth they produced are known from European sites of the Neolithic period onward.

Warp-weighted (upright) looms may have been developed from the band loom in Southeast Europe or Anatolia in order to weave wider and longer pieces of cloth. They consisted of a frame made of strong wooden uprights with a crossbar at the top to which the warp threads were attached. Weights tied to the bottom of the warp threads held them under tension. Warp-weighted looms were in use by the Early Neolithic in the Körös culture of Hungary and gradually spread north, east, and west, being known in later Neolithic Switzerland and Italy and becoming widespread in the Bronze Age. Archaeological evidence for upright looms is often found: sometimes in the form of a pair of postholes inside a house and more commonly as triangular, annular, or conical weights of baked clay or stone with a hole in the narrower end, sometimes found lying in a line between or near the postholes. Occasionally a pit was dug between the posts, probably to allow a longer piece of cloth to be woven. The stylized picture of a woman weaving on the Iron Age pot from Sopron may depict this: The weaving descends far below her feet into a space delimited by parallel lines.

Representations of looms on rock engravings from Val Camonica also show the weights as well as the shed bar and one or several heddle bars, used to raise part of the warp. Plain weave required one heddle bar, twill needed three. No examples of these or of other weaving equipment such as the bars used for beating up the cloth and bobbins for passing the thread through have been certainly identified, although tubular clay objects with a slight waist from Early Neolithic Elateia in Greece are claimed to have been bobbins. In western Europe a bone or antler comb with short teeth was used for beating down the weft to ensure a tight weave.

Normally, cloth was woven by a single individual (a woman on the basis of known depictions), but looms with posts set several meters apart suggest that women on occasion collaborated to weave cloth up to 10 feet (3 meters) wide, and this is borne out by some finds of textiles from Danish Bronze Age coffins.

The use in Early Iron Age Denmark of a different kind of upright loom for weaving tubular cloth has been deduced from a few examples of such cloth found at Egtved and Trindhøj.

OTHER EQUIPMENT

Some bands of surviving Iron Age cloth show the characteristic twists produced by tablet weaving, in which the warps are threaded through holes in the corners of a series of square flat tablets that act as heddles. Some of these tablets were found at Deibjerg in

Denmark and some, made of boxwood, in a grave at Cigarralejo in Spain, both of the La Tène period.

TYPES OF WEAVE

Although loom weights and spindle whorls show that weaving dates back to the sixth millennium B.C. in Europe, surviving examples of the textiles themselves are not known before around 3000 B.C. These show that the cloth was generally tabby weave, a plain fabric in which the weft threads went alternatively over and under each warp thread in one row and the reverse in the next; some were basket weave, similar to tabby but weaving pairs of warp and weft threads. Variations in the appearance of the cloth were achieved by making the warp threads thicker than the weft or vice versa (faced weave), or by making patterns using different combinations of S-spun, Z-spun, Sz-ply, and Zs-ply threads, which caught the light differently (shadow stripe). For example, a belt from the oak coffin at Borum Eshøj had a band of Z-spun warp threads between two bands of S-spun warp threads. Other patterns were achieved using extra weft threads that were floated over the main weaving; a particularly elaborate fabric from the Neolithic Swiss site of Irgenhausen was decorated with solid triangles made in this way. Another Swiss textile was ornamented with tiny beads made from perforated seeds, sewn on, and other examples of such work are known. Often the borders of the cloth were made separately or woven with a different set of sheds to allow the patterns to be more elaborate than the main cloth. A separately woven band was often used as a starting border, its weft threads being made very long to form the warps of the main cloth. A linen cloth from the lake village of Ledro apparently had designs stamped on it. Little terra-cotta stamps (known as *pintaderas*) were found from the Early Neolithic period in various parts of Europe, assumed to have been used for stamping people or cloth, but this is the only example known of the actual use of such things. Some Bronze Age textiles were embellished with embroidery, and in Scandinavia, where netting had a long history back to Mesolithic times, netting techniques were also used to add edges to garments.

From the Late Bronze Age twill also began to be made. The weft threads were passed over and under two or more warp threads, in each row moving one warp thread along from the previous row to produce a diagonal or step pattern. Other twill patterns included lozenges, herringbone, and zigzags. Examples of twill are known from a number of Bronze and Iron Age sites, including the Austrian salt mines of Hallstatt and Hallein; unlike other environments in which textiles have survived, the salt mines preserved the colors of textiles, too, making it possible to appreciate the colored plaids that were now also being made. Some first-millennium textiles had a border made by tablet weaving; the earliest example known in Europe comes from Hohmichele, and there were many from later sites, including the grave at Cigarralejo in which the tablets for weaving such borders were found.

Additional variety was introduced by the choice of thread. Although most cloth was made from a single type of fiber, some pieces from both Switzerland and Denmark were made using flax for the warp and wool for the weft, and silk was used in one predominantly woolen textile from Hohmichele. The wool-and-linen textiles date from the third millennium and may reflect the period when wool was coming into use but was not yet preferred to linen.

Other Cloth-making Techniques

FELTING

Wool, which has a scaly surface unlike the smooth surface of plant fibers, can be made into a strong fabric by felting. The woolen cloth is soaked and warmed and then beaten or kneaded, causing the scales to interlock. Early European textiles seem often to have been felted to make them warmer and more weatherproof. From the Late Bronze Age this practice declined since the new twill weave in common use also had these properties and because felting would blur the fine colored designs now being made.

PLAITING

The ends of woven bands and belts were often finished off by plaiting, in some cases ending in tassels.

Plaiting might also be used for the closing border of larger pieces of woven cloth.

SPRANG

A technique called sprang, rather similar to cat's cradle and producing an open elastic material like a net, was practiced across prehistoric Europe and survived into recent times in some regions, though it was widely superseded by knitting (which was not known until the third century A.D.). It was used particularly to make hairnets and caps, such as a fine example from Borum Eshøj.

TWINING

Various techniques similar to basket making were sometimes used; two have been identified from European textiles. In one, weft-wrapping, a thread was passed around each warp thread in turn; in weft-twining a pair of threads were passed round either side of a warp then across each other before passing on to the next warp thread. Both produce a textile resembling netting. Neolithic examples of this technique are known from Cueva de los Murciélagos in Spain, using esparto grass.

Dyeing

Although a range of muted colors, from white to dark brown, was available naturally, wool (especially white wool) was also dyed. Bast fibers like linen did not take up dyes nearly so readily and required pretreatment with tannic acid, but some basts were also dyed. Most vegetable dyes are fugitive, requiring the textile to be fixed by boiling or steeping in a mordant (often alum for acid dyes or tannin for basic dyes) and sometimes also in a developer, such as ammonia (urine), which enhanced or altered the color.

Dyes known to have been used include red ochre, producing a range of colors from yellow through red to brown; the fermented leaves of woad for blue and for red the blood of the cochineal beetle, which lives in the kermes oak of the Mediterranean. Both of these colors were known from bast fibers in a Neolithic burial at Adaouste in France, associated with the remains of a paste made from kermes

insects. Madder and safflower may have been used for red, and saffron and the roots of dyer's rocket for yellow. The pale green color known from a Hallstatt textile may have been achieved by using a yellow dye along with iron as a mordant.

Baskets, Mats, Nets, and Cords

CORDS AND ROPES

Twisted cord was being made in Europe during the Palaeolithic period; the cast of a three-ply cord of plant fiber was found in the famous decorated cave of Lascaux. Later cords and ropes were made of twisted or spun fibers, such as a flaxen rope from the Neolithic settlement of Charavines in France, or twisted or plaited from grass and rushes. Baskets were made using a twisted or plaited cord or bundles of grass, reeds or other materials gradually coiled from the center outward and secured by stitching; these are known from the Swiss lake villages and from Cueva de los Murciélagos in Spain, where they were made of esparto grass; impressions of others are known from many sites. The Iceman wore a cloak made of long grasses plaited together at the top and fastened at intervals by twining. He also had a backpack made out of a bent hazel frame, two boards of larch, and a quantity of two-ply grass cord.

NETTING

Mesolithic and later nets were made from fibers or cords using a variety of knotted and knotless techniques. The Iceman had a loose-mesh net made of two-ply grass strings, perhaps for catching birds. Netting inside his shoes held in place grass stuffing to keep his feet warm.

MATTING AND TWINING

Stiff grasses, reeds, rushes, and similar materials were interwoven in a manner similar to weaving but without need of a loom. Impressions of such mats are known from many prehistoric sites, including Early Neolithic Nea Nikomedeia in

Greece, showing basket weave, faced weave, and various twill patterns.

To produce a thicker and less rigid mat or a container, bundles of rushes laid side by side were bound together by threads interlaced between them in a variety of ways, producing a range of patterns. A Neolithic bag of coiled wood slivers bound with grass twine was found in a peat bog at Twyford in Ireland. It was made in two pieces fastened together and had handles of plaited straw. Many different types of twining were used in the Swiss lake villages and on baskets, bags, and sandals from Cueva de los Murciélagos. A flint dagger worn by the Iceman was kept in a scabbard of lime-tree bast fibers fastened at intervals with twined grass cords.

WICKERWORK

Rods such as birch twigs and small branches were used to create a framework for wickerwork constructions, which ranged from small baskets to substantial fish traps. Bindings of other materials, such as split roots, osiers, bark fibers, and rushes, were used to secure the framework by twining. Many of the surviving examples come from Mesolithic sites; later examples include many from Swiss and other lake villages.

BARK

Containers made of folded birch bark are known on Mesolithic sites, and other bark containers were found in LBK wells at Erkelenz-Kückhoven. Ötzi the Iceman also had two containers made of folded birch bark, stitched with strips of bast. Net sinkers of pebbles wrapped in bark and tied with thin bark strips were recovered from the Swiss village of Twann. An early second-millennium sewn bark coffin cover was found at Dalrigh in Scotland. The man buried in the richly furnished Hochdorf barrow wore a conical hat of bark.

LEATHER AND FURS

The use of leather for artifacts and clothing can generally only be guessed since in the majority of situations leather decays. The rare examples that survive, however, from the Danish tree-trunk coffins, bogs, and a few other unusual contexts, provide clues to the widespread importance of leather for containers, garments, and other artifacts. Much of the clothing of the recently discovered Iceman, who died around 3300/3200 B.C., was made of leather and none of it of woven textiles. The salt mines of the Early Iron Age have preserved leather backpacks, bags, and shoes. Shields were made of wood or leather, and boiled leather would have made effective body armor. Hides and furs were also probably used as rugs and covers.

Furs were known as exports from Celtic Europe and the north during the Iron Age and must have been traded in earlier times. They were probably among the goods exchanged by the Mesolithic Ertebølle groups among themselves and with their LBK neighbors; the Ertebølle site of Ringkloster was an inland camp for hunting wild piglets and pinemartens, while people camped at Agernaes to hunt other fur animals.

Sources

Domestic and wild animals whose hides were frequently used included cattle, goat, sheep, and deer. Fur-bearing animals hunted by Mesolithic people and probably exploited in later prehistoric Europe included polecat, badgers, pinemartens, wild cats, lynx, beavers, otters, wolves, and foxes. The pelts of domestic dogs were probably also used. The Iceman's clothing was made from the leather and fur of cattle and goat, red deer, mountain goat, and bear.

Treatment

In warm regions raw hides could be shaped and then dried, for use as bags, coverings, and bindings, but in the damp conditions of most of Europe they had to be converted into leather. Hides were soaked or allowed to putrefy slightly to loosen the epidermis and hair, which were removed by scraping while fat and other tissue were scraped away from the inside. Tools of stone and bone used for scraping hides are known from the Palaeolithic period onward, and metal ones in later times. The simplest way of curing hides was by smoking; this seems to have been the method used to prepare the leather from which the Iceman's clothing was made. A more effective method was to work a tanning agent into the skin to prevent putrefaction and to make it water-resistant. The skin was stretched and rubbed with fat, or it could be treated with alum (tawed) or salt or a mixture of both, or soaked in tannin, derived from oak-galls or oak, chestnut or pine bark, then stretched and worked with a blunt instrument to soften it. Several of these methods might be used in conjunction. Leather could be made hard by boiling it. Lumps of haematite were used in Neolithic Orkney for buffing the surface of leather to give it a glossy finish.

Leather Objects

Depending on the degree of working and the choice of tanning agents, leather could be made extremely soft and pliable or hard and tough enough to be cut with a saw, making it suitable for a wide range of artifacts, including armor, containers, shoes, and clothing, as well as coverings for wooden shields and boats.

Leather bags were probably made from Palaeolithic times onward, and early Neolithic pottery often seems to imitate the form and details of leather vessels or bags, some, for instance, indicating a wooden hoop at the neck and shoulder of a bag to keep it rigidly open, and stitching to hold the hoops in place, imitated as decorative lines. Leather vessels filled with water were used for cooking by dropping in heated stones; this is attested to in Mesolithic Scandinavia and was probably still taking place in Bronze Age Britain. A few molded leather bowls and beakers are known from Neolithic Europe. Leather backpacks with a wooden framework were preserved in the salt mines at Hallstatt. A bag from the Dürrnberg salt mine had a leather drawstring.

Pieces of leather were often fastened together to make garments and other objects, either by lacing with sinews or thin leather thongs or by sewing. Bone awls were used to make holes; these are known from Neolithic Orkney, and in the Bronze Age cemetery of Singen in Germany awls were placed in

female graves, suggesting that some leatherworking, at least, was undertaken by women. A Neolithic dagger sheath from Stade in Germany was made of a single piece of cowhide fastened up the back with very fine leather thongs and lined with a piece of tawed sheepskin to cushion the edges of the dagger. Other leather sheaths and scabbards are also known,

6.3 The Iceman, showing his grass cloak; leather coat, shoes, quiver, and belt; fur cap and leggings; and wooden backpack. In his hand he is carrying a yew bow stave and a copper ax. (Drawing by Audrey McIntosh, after drawings and information in Spindler, Konrad. The Man in the Ice. London: Orion, 1995)

and the Iceman carried a quiver of deerskin. Tawed leather was said by Caesar to have been used for sails by the Veneti, a seafaring Breton tribe.

Although most surviving prehistoric shields are of metal, these were probably in the minority in their time, being intended for display more than for defense, while those used in battle were probably generally of wood or boiled leather. A surviving example from Cloonbrin in Ireland was in the form, well known from bronze examples, of a circle with a V-shaped notch, strengthened with a pattern of ribs and bosses. A leather cap was stitched over the central boss, and a handle was laced onto the back behind it. Also from Ireland come examples of wooden shield molds into which leather, softened with water, was beaten with round-headed punches. Armor such as breastplates and greaves may also have been made of boiled leather; Sardinian Bronze Age art shows figures wearing leather tunics and kilts, perhaps reinforced with small bronze bosses.

Various items of leather and fur clothing have survived. The Iceman wore a deerskin coat, calfskin shoes, a fur cap with a chin strap, fur leggings, a calfskin belt with a pouch, and a loincloth of leather. Fur and leather were used for sewn caps and hoods, including some of leather with a fur lining or trim. Calfskin shoes from the Dürrnberg salt mines were made of a single piece of leather bent into shape and stitched at the heel, while a shoe from the tree-trunk coffin at Guldhøj had a leather sole and a cloth upper. Dressed skins varied in color depending on the tanning agent used, going from white (alum) and buff (fat) to reddish brown (tannin), but they could be dyed to give a greater range of colors, either all over or selectively to produce patterns. Designs might also be added by embossing the surface; tools for doing this have been found in Neolithic Orkney.

Harness and other horse equipment were often of leather with some metal components. A leather bag found in the Iron Age settlement of La Tène contained the tools used by a leatherworker; these included half-moon knives and awls for cutting and piercing the leather as well as chisels, punches, and gouges for shaping and decorating saddles and other harness.

Bone, Horn, Antler, and Ivory

Bone, horn, and antler were widely used to made tools and ornaments, both in their natural state or slightly modified, and as the raw material from which a variety of objects were fashioned. The use of these materials began in the Palaeolithic period, as did that of ivory, and they were still important in the Iron Age.

Bone, Horn, and Antler

SOURCES

Shed antler was collected and antler taken from hunted deer. Red deer antler was the most generally used, though elk antler was made into mattocks in the early postglacial period. Domestic animals provided a supply of horn and bones, of which longbones, metapodia, and shoulder blades were particularly used; the bones of hunted animals were also employed, including teeth. Coastal communities also used the bones of marine mammals such as whales, while fish vertebrae and bird bones were also used.

WORKING

Flint and later metal knives and saws were used to work the material. Pieces of antler for making points and other small tools were removed by cutting two parallel grooves along the length of the antler and undercutting the piece between them, which was then levered out (groove-and-splinter technique). Antler could be made easier to work by soaking to soften it temporarily. Horn is relatively soft and could be easily cut; if soaked and boiled, it can be split into layers that are translucent. It is also a flexible material; this property was exploited in the manufacture of composite bows where horn was laminated with wood and sinew to produce a bow with a greatly increased range. Fish hooks were shaped by drilling a hole in a disc of bone, then cutting away one segment to form a curved and pointed hook. Pumice washed up on the beaches of Orkney was used to work bone by rubbing, shaping the bone tools and creating sharpened points.

ARTIFACTS

Heavy Work Antler tools were widely used in mining flint and metal ores, particularly as picks and wedges; the strength and springiness of antler make it an ideal material for the job. Picks were made by removing all the tines except the lowest; the removed tines were then used as wedges, as were animal metapodia. Antler tools left with two tines probably served as rakes. On occasion, antler was also used for pit props. Cattle shoulder blades found in mines were probably used as shovels or rakes; they were not strong enough to have been used to shovel up flint nodules or smashed ore, but may have been used to clear the remaining small debris. Small unmodified bones in the Great Orme copper mine may have been used as scoops to extract the copper ore from its soft limestone matrix.

Antler hammers and mattocks, perforated to take a wooden haft, were in use by Mesolithic times; longbones and whalebone were also used as hammers. In Neolithic Britain antler was also carved into mace heads, which may have been prestige or ceremonial objects.

Whale ribs and jawbones were employed as sledge runners and as building material by coastal communities where wood was scarce, as at Skara Brae, where they formed roof beams.

Lighter Work A large range of small tools was made of these materials by Mesolithic hunter-gatherers, and many of these continued in use into the Iron Age, along with new types. Stone chisels and axes were often set into an antler sleeve, which was then mounted in a wooden haft. Handles, hafts, and weapon pommels might also be made of bone or antler, while antler awls and chisels were also used from the Mesolithic period onward; seal bones were also made into awls. Other artifacts included fishing equipment such as fishhooks, fish gorges, harpoons, and leisters; points and arrowheads; antler cheek pieces for horse harness, often decorated; spoons for eating; polishing tools made

of animal metapodia for working leather; spatulas for modeling clay; and small combs and bird bones for decorating pottery. Spindle whorls were often cut from discs of bone or antler. Threaders for weaving were made from small bones and needles from bone slivers, while weaving combs were carved from animal bone, whalebone, or antler. In the Iron Age dice were also among the wide range of bone and antler objects. Boars' tusks were sometimes modified for use as blades or fishhooks. A grave of the Wessex culture at Wilsford contained a bone whistle. A few surviving horn objects include a ladle from a Beaker burial at Broomend in Scotland and some dagger pommels. In the Iron Age, if not before, horns were used as drinking vessels; in the Hochdorf chieftain's burial chamber, dated around 550 B.C., nine drinking horns bound with bands of gold and bronze were hung on the wall.

Among his equipment Ötzi the Iceman carried a fine bone awl for punching holes in fur or leather or perhaps for use as a tattooing needle; some pieces of antler from which to make arrowheads; an antler spike in a lime-branch sleeve, which was probably used for sharpening flint tools by fine retouching; and an antler point among whose many uses were skinning animals and splicing cord.

Ornaments and Clothing Accessories Bone and antler were used for pendants, pins, and beads in Mesolithic sites, as were fox canines and fish teeth and vertebrae. Beads and pendants continued to be made throughout prehistory, including perforated beaver incisors, boars' tusks, and deer teeth, and the later repertoire also included pins with elaborate heads, rings, toggles, spacer beads, belt hooks, and belt fastening rings. The grave goods in the Bush Barrow from Early Bronze Age Wessex included a wooden staff decorated with a series of bone rings with zigzag edges. Figurines and decorated objects were also on occasion carved of bone or antler: For example, the fifth-millennium Romanian site of Cǎscioarele yielded a female figurine decorated with carved dots and holes; an antler beam from the Mesolithic site of Sjöholmen in southern Sweden was intricately decorated with geometric patterns; and bone idols carved or painted with eyes and geometric patterns were made in Chalcolithic Spain.

Ivory

Mammoth ivory was used for making tools, ornaments, and figurines in the Palaeolithic period, but with the extinction of the mammoth Europe ceased to have a native source of ivory. The Neolithic inhabitants of Iberia imported elephant ivory from the Maghreb and made it into small objects such as wands, combs, and figurines, while in the Beaker and succeeding periods it was made into V-perforated buttons. In the Iron Age ivory was imported from Africa or South Asia via the Near East and the Mediterranean world. Phoenician traders brought ivory to their trading posts in Iberia, where they, or local people to whom they had taught their skills in ivory working, made the ivory into fine elaborate objects such as the decorated combs found in the elite tombs at Carmona. An ivory-carving workshop has been identified in the native Iberian settlement of El Castillo de Dona Blanca, opposite the Phoenician settlement of Gadir. Being an extremely hard material, ivory was more difficult to work than antler, and drills were generally used. This and its rarity meant that it was used mainly as a decorative inlay on metalwork or for small ornaments.

STONE

Stone was used for making tools from the earliest times and continued in use even after the introduction of metal tools, both as a cheaper alternative and to perform tasks for which metal was less suitable, such as grinding. Stone was also used in construction. Attractive kinds of stone such as agate and jadeite were made into jewelry and other display objects; stone imitations of metal axes and daggers were also made by groups with limited or no access to metal ores or artifacts.

Flint

From early in the Palaeolithic period onward, people used flint and other easily fractured silicate stone (such as chert, jasper, and chalcedony) to make stone tools for a wide range of purposes. In the postglacial period these included axes, scrapers, knives, daggers, and arrowheads, as well as microliths used to create the cutting edge for many different tools. Tools made of exceptional types of material, such as obsidian (volcanic glass) or the honey-colored flint from Grand Pressigny, were highly prized for use or display; and a high value was also placed on objects whose manufacture required great skill, such as exceedingly long blades. Where flint was limited or unavailable, other types of stone such as quartz or limestone might be flaked into tools, although these materials were less easily worked and often produced inferior results.

FLINT MINING

Flint occurs as seams of nodules in chalk, sometimes exposed at the surface by weathering or other natural action. Flint for making everyday tools could be widely obtained, but the finer material needed for exceptional objects was mined in a few locations and widely traded in the third millennium. Fine chocolate-colored flint was quarried in the Holy Cross Mountains as early as Mesolithic times, although most Mesolithic flint came from surface outcrops.

Early flint mines were shallow pits cut into the chalk to follow flint located at the surface. These were succeeded by more substantial trenches that could be as much as 13 feet (4 meters) deep and 33 feet (10 meters) long. Underground seams were later mined by excavating a shaft. Some were wide at the top, tapering to a narrow waist and continuing down, sometimes as much as 33 feet (10 meters), till the flint seam was struck. The lower shaft was then widened as the flint and chalk were quarried away as far as was safe, forming a bell-shaped pit. More complex mines were created by sinking a shaft to the level of the seam of flint and following the seam with narrow galleries, leaving pillars of chalk between them to support the roof. The galleries were pursued until they became too poorly ventilated for work to continue. Shafts as deep as 52 feet (16 meters) are known and galleries as much as 100 feet (30 meters) long. Poor-quality seams might be ignored, and the shaft continued downward until a good seam was located. Once a shaft was abandoned, it became a dump for the waste material; abandoned galleries were also back-filled with the quarried chalk.

In wider shafts access from the surface was probably via a wooden ladder, while in narrower shafts a series of wooden struts was probably set across the shaft for the miners to climb. Wood may have been used to reinforce shafts and galleries, and occasional notches found in the sides of galleries may have held roof beams; however, the evidence is limited and in general flint mines relied on chalk pillars for support. Sometimes extra supports were built of chalk or antlers were rammed into place as props.

The flint was mined using antler picks, which were effective in prising the nodules out from the soft chalk; picks were also made of animal long bones or flint. Stone axes and hammers were also used, as were wedges of antler tine or pieces of bone. Occasionally in hard rock fire-setting was also used. Shovels made of wood or animal scapulae were used to gather up the excavated material, using antler rakes. The work was probably conducted mainly by natural light, but in some cases chalk lamps burning animal fat were used to give extra light. The flint was placed in baskets or leather bags, which were taken to the surface, probably usually by hauling them up with a rope run over a beam at the top.

Cissbury (Sussex, England) Mining began before 3000 B.C. at Cissbury, where some 200 circular and rectangular shafts were dug with galleries, some interconnecting. Sump holes to collect rainwater and prevent it running into the galleries have been found at the base of some of the shafts. Small windows were cut in some of the supporting chalk pillars between galleries to allow daylight through.

Grand Pressigny (Indre-et-Loire, France) Grand Pressigny was the source of an attractive honey-colored iron-rich flint resembling copper, which was used to make long blades from cores known locally as *livres de beurre* ("pounds of butter"). The Grand Pressigny mines were worked over a long period, from the Palaeolithic to the Bronze Age, but their peak of production was from around 3000 to 2400 B.C. Their

products reached as far as Jersey, the Netherlands, and western Switzerland, more than 200 miles (350 kilometers) from their source, and occasionally pieces traveled as far as 500 miles (800 kilometers). The flint was extracted from shallow pits dug into the hillsides and valley floor of an area several miles in extent.

Grimes Graves (Norfolk, England) The mines extend over an area of around 22 acres (9 hectares). At least 366 shafts are known, ranging from open pits three to seven feet (1 or 2 meters) in diameter and 10–13 feet (3–4 meters) deep, to bell-shaped pits and deep shafts with galleries, up to 40 feet (12 meters) deep. Three seams of flint were mined, of which the lowest ("floorstone") was the best. Bone, mainly of sheep and goat, may be the remains of miners' feasts. An arrangement of a polished ax of Cornish greenstone, two antler picks, and the skull of a rare bird, the phalarope, in one gallery may have been a votive offering. While mining here began around 3000 B.C., the majority of the mines date from the Late Neolithic and Early Bronze Ages, around 2000 B.C.

Krzemionki Opatowskie (Poland) Attractive banded flint was mined here. More than 1,000 shafts were dug over a narrow area around 2.5 miles (4 kilometers) long. Shallow pits were excavated here in early TRB times, while in the later TRB and Globular Amphora periods shafts up to 50 feet (15 meters) deep were dug with galleries up to 100 feet (30 meters) long. Although a number of other mines offered attractive flint, which was used by the TRB and Globular Amphora cultures (for example, white-speckled flint from Świechiehów, chocolate-colored flint from the Radom area, banded Jurassic flint from the Craców area, all in Poland, and flint from Volhynia in Ukraine), their preferred material for making axes was the striking banded flint from Krzemionki Opatowskie, which was traded as far as 370 miles (600 kilometers) from the mines.

Obourg (Belgium) This was a mine worked by open trenches, occasionally linked by galleries. In one the skeleton of a miner was found, holding an antler pick; he had been killed by a roof fall.

6.4 *Section through a flint mine at Grimes Graves, Norfolk, England, showing the main shaft and galleries* (TopFoto.co.uk, ©2004 English Heritage, Photographer: Terry Ball. Reproduced by permission of English Heritage/HIP/TopFoto)

Spiennes (Belgium) A mining site worked particularly by the Michelsberg culture, it extends over an area of about 150 acres (60 hectares) and included both early open pits and a systematic network of narrow shafts and interconnecting galleries, which exploited an inclined seam of flint. Most of the shafts were vertical, but some were inclined. Several inferior seams were rejected, and the shafts sunk to a better seam, between 16 and 50 feet (5–16 meters) below the ground surface. In one inclined shaft the mined material was hauled to the surface up a wooden chute.

Thisted (Jutland, Denmark) Source of high-quality Senon flint, mining began here in the fifth millennium. Conical pits 13–16 feet (4–5 meters) wide were dug to the flint seams, which lay around 13–16 feet (4–5 meters) deep, and from here galleries up to 16 feet (5 meters) long were cut. Working floors where the material was roughly shaped lay on the surface between the pits.

TOOL MAKING

Various types of flint were suited to manufacturing different tools. For example, the banded flint from Krzemionki Opatowskie was excellent for making axes but not suitable for blades; the reverse was true of the flint from Obourg, which was used to make long knives and scrapers; Świechiehów spotted flint could be used for axes but was particularly good for making blades, as was the honey-colored flint from Grand Pressigny.

Blades and flakes, used as knives and as blanks for daggers, arrowheads, scrapers, and other tools, were struck from a prepared core and were finely retouched or pressure-flaked. Cores were also knapped to make axes.

The flint nodules were frequently roughed out into axes at or near the mining site, a task that could have taken as little as 10 minutes to perform. Large objects, such as thin-butted axes up to 20 inches (0.5 meters) long, could be shaped only from freshly exposed flint and therefore had to be roughed out at the mine. Working floors were located at many mining sites, but in the TRB period the flint mined at Krzemionki Opatowskie was taken to Cmielów in the adjacent Kamienna valley, where both roughouts and finished axes were made.

Obsidian

Obsidian is a natural volcanic glass, which has an attractive translucent appearance and ranges in color from black to green; it also flakes to produce the sharpest edges on any man-made object. It has therefore, not surprisingly, been highly prized wherever it has been found. The European sources of obsidian were on the Aegean island of Melos, the central Mediterranean islands of Lipari, Pantelleria, Palmarola, and Sardinia, and the Slovakian and Hungarian mountains.

WORKING

Obsidian was knapped using the same methods as for flint. It was probably worked into blade cores at or near its source. These were then used in settlements to produce long, slender blades that might then travel to more distant settlements.

Polished Stone Tools

Fine igneous and metamorphic rock such as dolerite, greenstone, and tuff were used for making polished stone tools such as axes and chisels. These tools were less fragile than those made of flint, and the polished edge retained its sharpness for a longer time.

SOURCES AND QUARRYING

Local outcrops of suitable stone were exploited where available, but fine outcrops were actively sought and their rock quarried and carried over long distances; thin section analysis of the composition of different rocks allows them to be matched to their source, enabling a picture of the movement of hard stone to be built up. In Britain, for example, more than 30 sources were exploited, including Great Langdale, Tievebulliagh (porcellanite), Mynydd Prescelly, and Graig Lwyd (greenstone), and material from farther afield such as jadeite from France and the Alps was also occasionally obtained.

Often suitable stone had been subjected to weathering and pieces of various sizes spread over the area around the outcrop, from which they could easily be picked up. Where this was not the case the rock face was quarried, on occasion being followed into the hillside in a small tunnel (adit). Horizontal or inclined rockfaces were also quarried, forming small open pits.

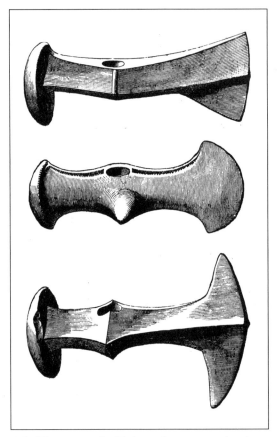

6.5 Three stone shafthole ax-hammers or battle-axes from Denmark (Worsaae, J. J. A. *The Industrial Arts of Denmark.* London: Chapman and Hall, 1882)

Sélèdin (Brittany, France) A mining complex extending over a third of a square mile (1 square kilometer), which was in operation for more than a millennium, it probably produced around 6 million dolerite axes. These supplied around half the axes used in Brittany, and were traded along the Loire and the coasts throughout northwest France and occasionally beyond.

Great Langdale (Cumbria, England) The mountains above Great Langdale contain a gray green volcanic tuff highly suitable for making tools, and this was mined by Neolithic groups who probably visited

on many occasions. Some of the stone was hewn from vertical faces, some quarried in open pits or small adits. In addition, some stone was available on the screes below, due to weathering. The stone was roughed out into ax blanks on working floors on the screes or the valley floor below. Stone was obtained from Great Langdale by visiting groups throughout the earlier Neolithic, but after around 3300 B.C. the quarrying became more organized and on a larger scale. In this later period axes from Great Langdale were traded to almost every part of Britain.

Mynydd Prescelly (Wales, Great Britain) The igneous rocks of the Mynydd Prescelly mountain ridge included rhyolites and dolerites attractive for making axes and other tools, among which was the bluestone (spotted dolerite) from which some of the standing stones at Stonehenge were also made. The rock is strongly weathered, so stone for toolmaking could readily be obtained without quarrying, while the larger blocks could be levered out.

WORKING

Generally, the raw material for axes and other polished stone tools was roughly shaped at source by flaking or pecking with a hammerstone. These rough-outs were then often traded or exchanged over long distances before reaching a settlement where they were ground and polished into their final shape using grinding stones or polishers of abrasive materials such as sandstone. Felsite was used in Shetland to produce beautiful thin "Shetland knives," flat oval discs with highly polished faces and sharp edges, which were probably for show rather than use.

Axes and other tools were hafted in handles or sleeves generally of wood or antler and were bound in place with rawhide, sinew, or bast. Some tools, however, such as the battle-axes of Neolithic northern Europe as well as hammers and mace heads, had a shafthole through which the haft was passed. This was made by drilling, probably using a bow drill, or by abrasion with a stone, sand, and water. Other stone objects in which holes were made included loomweights and spindle whorls.

Beorgs of Uyea (Shetland, Britain) A stone tool working site where felsite was roughed out into ax and knife blanks before being taken elsewhere for finishing. A hollow from which felsite had been quarried was roofed with stone slabs to form a shelter in which some of the working was done. Broken rough-outs and working debris were scattered around. The felsite was used to produce maces and axes, which were distributed as far as northern England, and Shetland knives, which circulated only locally.

Other Stone

Abrasive stone and stone with a pitted surface were sought for grindstones and querns; these included good sandstone, conglomerates, and volcanic stone such as basalt. Such stone was not generally available locally so suitable stone was mined and widely exchanged, particularly in the Iron Age. Basalt for making querns was mined at Mayen in the Eifel region of Germany by the fifth millennium, and this source continued to be worked into Roman times. Niedermendig Lava quernstones imported from the Rhineland occur in several Early Bronze Age sites in southern England. Other such quarries also existed in the Neolithic and increased in number and output in the Late Iron Age when the rotary quern came into use and a substantial trade in millstones developed, using rivers for transport.

Tools of sandstone, pumice, and other abrasive stones were used to produce the polished surface on axes and other stone tools. Pebbles of local stone for use as hammers or anvils and for other purposes were collected from beaches and screes and often required no modification before use. In Orkney and Shetland sandstone cobbles from the beach were flaked to make cutting tools known as "Skaill knives." In Shetland slate was used for knives, choppers, and lids; it occurs in layers that were easy to quarry and split. Slate was also used for Mesolithic tools in the Baltic region.

Various types of stone were used to make figurines, stelae, vessels, and other carved stone objects. These included the curious decorated balls of igneous camptonite found in Orkney and northeast Scotland. In the Chalcolithic whetstones made of hard, fine-grained stone began to appear alongside the metal tools that they were used to sharpen.

Building Stone

Building stone was obtained locally and used for domestic construction in some parts of Europe such as Orkney, where, in the absence of timber, it was the main building material. Monuments, however, in some cases were constructed from materials brought in from a considerable distance. Stonehenge, an outstanding example, was constructed of massive sarsens from the Marlborough Downs, some 18 miles (30 kilometers) away, and of bluestones from the Prescelly Mountains in Wales. In some cases stone for building was available as glacial erratics or fallen rocks and boulders. In other cases it had to be quarried. The gray flagstone used in Orkney occurred in horizontal beds and split naturally into flat straight-edged slabs, which were easy to lever off if not already detached.

SALT

Meat consumption provided enough salt to keep hunter-gatherers healthy, but as people came to rely increasingly on cereal-based agriculture, salt to supplement that available in their diet became necessary as well as being desirable to impart flavor to food. Salt was also used for preserving meat and fish, and in making cheese and tanning hides. Two main sources of salt were available: deposits of salt crystals and brine within rocks, particularly in parts of central Europe, which could be mined; and the sea, salt springs, and salt marshes, where salt was extracted by evaporation.

Salt Mining

The earliest evidence of salt mining comes from Catalonia in Spain, where the Muntanya de Sal salt dome at Cardona seems to have been exploited by the Sepulcros de Fosa culture during the fourth millennium B.C. They extracted the salt from open pits using stone picks and hammers, many broken examples of which have been found around the mountain. Such surface deposits are rare, the only other being in Romania, and most salt deposits are within mountains, from which they were mined by excavating adits (tunnels sunk into the side of a hill) and shafts with galleries, some as much as 1,000 feet (300 meters) deep.

Salt mining probably began in the Late Bronze Age and is best known from the Early Iron Age when the mines at Hallstatt and Dürrnberg bei Hallein were most active. Salt being a preservative, not only the stone, metal, and antler tools of the miners but even their perishable clothing and equipment have been recovered. These included baskets and wood-framed leather backpacks for carrying blocks of salt. The salt was mined with picks, those at Hallstatt being elegant long bronze blades with a sleeve fitting an L-shaped wooden handle. The pick was placed against the salt deposit, and the base of the handle was tapped with a wooden mallet, cutting a groove that allowed blocks of salt to be levered out. These were gathered up with wooden shovels. Bundles of sticks bound together as torches were used to provide light in the Hallstatt mines. Wooden supports were used to brace the walls and roofs of the tunnels, but accidents did happen and several bodies of miners killed by rock falls were found at Hallstatt.

Hallstatt   A mining complex in the Salzkammergut, where rock salt was extracted from the mid-second millennium onward; previously the inhabitants of the area had used brine from natural springs. Its time of greatest production was around 1000–600 B.C. The mines are concentrated in three areas, the eastern group, worked from the eighth century, being the most productive. Here deep shafts gave access to the salt deposits, which were followed in a series of side tunnels running up to the surface. The wealth generated by the mining operations is reflected in the cemetery attached to the settlement of Hallstatt, which contains many burials, particularly of the seventh and sixth centuries, with fine pottery, bronze vessels and jewelry, and weaponry, including many bronze swords. After a decline in the fifth century, a devastating landslide in the fourth brought an end to operations in the eastern mines.

Dürrnberg bei Hallein   This mining complex, which was close to Hallstatt but better situated for communications, rose to prominence in the fifth century and was probably responsible for Hallstatt's decline; mining probably began here in the late second millennium B.C. Two of the graves in the cemetery here contained chariot burials, and many had rich grave goods, including local Celtic and imported Mediterranean pottery and bronze vessels.

Salt Production

Salt extraction from seawater became an important industry in the Iron Age. Shallow tanks or ditches were dug along the seashore where high tide would fill them, with barriers to stop the water draining back into the sea. Impurities and debris in the water settled to the bottom of these tanks as the seawater gradually evaporated, leaving a concentrated brine. This was drawn off and heated in thick-walled coarse pottery vessels so that the remaining water evaporated, leaving salt crystals, which were often pressed in molds to form briquettes of salt. Often these vessels were deep rounded or conical bowls that were supported over the fire on pedestals or firebars. The debris from this process, known collectively as *briquetage*, has been found in many coastal sites where people probably camped for limited periods to make the salt; there are no associated settlements. Saltmaking sites in eastern England have mounds known as "red hills," made up of briquetage and burnt earth.

Briquetage has also been found on inland sites exploiting salt springs in some regions, dating from the Neolithic onward. In other areas the brine from salt springs was left in large shallow clay-lined holes to evaporate naturally.

METALLURGY

Nuggets of naturally occurring (native) copper and gold must have been regarded as stones with unusual properties from remote antiquity; by the sixth millennium they were being cold-hammered into simple objects such as beads. Annealing (heating) metal to make it more malleable allowed a greater range of simple shapes to be made, such as fishhooks and pins; it also countered the brittleness produced by repeated hammering. By the mid-fifth millennium in the Balkans and a little later in Spain, copper ores were also being mined and smelted and more substantial objects such as axes, spearheads, and chisels were being made by casting in open molds. This technology gradually became widespread across Europe over the following millennia, and more complex molds came into use, producing tools and weapons with shaftholes and other more elaborate objects. Techniques for working gold also became more varied and sophisticated. Copper began to be alloyed with various metals, of which tin was the most important, producing bronze, which was stronger than copper; during the second millennium bronze came into use in most of Europe. Silver-lead ore was also used in the few areas where it was available, notably Spain. Silver objects began to appear in the Beaker period, and by the later second millennium lead was used for many purposes, including alloying with copper. From the early first millennium iron began to take the place of bronze as the metal from which tools were made, while bronze and other metals were used for a wide range of ornamental and prestige goods. A number of Iron Age decorative objects involved the combined use of several metals to give contrasting color and surface appearance or to eke out precious metals with base ones; iron and bronze, copper and brass, gold and silver, or a lead core covered by sheet bronze or gold, for instance.

The distribution of different ores and metals to some extent dictated the pattern of development, but contacts between regions enabled technological innovations in metallurgy to spread across the continent and gave rise to major metalworking industries even in areas that had to import all their metal.

Mining and Prospecting

Metal ore that had eroded from metalliferous lodes occurred in some areas in river alluvium (placer deposits) and could be recovered by panning. This was done by mixing alluvial gravel with water in a dish and swirling the contents to separate the lighter soil from the heavier grains of metal ore; the former was allowed to wash over the edge of the dish while the metal ore settled in the bottom. The rare metals gold and tin were often obtained by panning. In some cases the eroded ore was deposited as eluvial deposits on the hillside below the parent lode; eluvial gold, tin, and galena could be recovered by ground sluicing.

By tracing the source of alluvial metal, people could locate rocks containing metal ore. Weathered ores on the surface could often be recognized by their bright colors: reddish iron deposits, bluish or greenish copper, for example. The location of ores might also be marked by the presence of particular plants that tolerated metal-rich soils toxic to most vegetation.

As the most common metal among the Earth's minerals, iron was present in many ore deposits bearing other metals, and in some cases both iron and other metals were mined at the same site at different times, as at Rudna Glava in the Balkans, where copper was mined in the fifth millennium and iron in Roman times. The shape and extent of metalliferous veins depended on their conditions of formation and the subsequent history of the rock: For example, some formed narrow but deep veins following rock fissures, while others were broken into discontinuous and well-separated sections by extensive faulting; some had been subjected to erosion and redeposition.

THE PRINCIPAL ORES AND METALS EXPLOITED

Native metals Naturally occurring pure metals: gold, copper, silver

Azurite Blue copper carbonate

Malachite Green copper hydroxy-carbonate

Fahlerz Chalcocite and other sulfide copper ore containing trace elements of many other minerals including arsenic, antimony, silver, lead, cobalt, and nickel

Chalcopyrite Double sulfide of copper and iron

Cassiterite Stannic dioxide, a black-colored tin ore

Galena Lead sulfide, generally containing a small proportion of silver sulfide

Magnetite Magnetic oxide of iron

Haematite Red to reddish black iron oxide

Pyrite Iron sulfide

MINING METALS

The character of the ore deposit to some extent dictated the form of mining that took place. Where lodes were identified at the ground surface, they were mined by digging open pits and by cutting adits and trenches following the lode. Deposits occurring at some depth were mined by sinking a shaft and excavating radiating galleries. Evidence of timber supports has been found in copper mines. Ventilation must have been a concern in ancient mines, since it is calculated that stale air would make it impossible to work more than 13 feet (4 meters) along an unventilated gallery. Interconnecting galleries and paired shafts may have been a deliberate attempt to deal with this problem; fires may also have been used to draw air through the network of shafts and galleries.

The principal method used for mining metal ore from the hard rock in which it was found was by fire setting, which could be used very precisely. A pile of brushwood and sticks or logs was built against the rock face and was lit and left to burn, probably for several hours. The poisonous fumes meant that the area had to be evacuated while the fire burned. Water (or vinegar, according to Roman sources) was often poured over the hot rock to aid cracking, though this was unnecessary as the fire alone was effective in causing the rock to fracture. However, the water cooled the rock, making it easier to begin work.

Stone hammers, antler picks and levers, and wood and antler wedges and spikes were then used to break off the fractured rock. Bronze or bronze-shod tools such as chisels and wedges may also have been used sometimes, though the evidence is thin; when iron became common, however, chisels, hammers, adzes, and spikes of iron were regularly employed as were iron or iron-shod shovels. The antler and bone tools have decayed away in the usually acid environment of metal mines, though a few mines have conditions that have allowed their

preservation in large numbers, and marks on the walls of mines show they were widely used. The hammerstones were rounded cobbles, often with a central groove for hafting. Most, weighing a few pounds, were swung by hand against the loosened rock face, but much larger ones were probably suspended in a cradle, while very small ones were probably held in the hand for use in small or awkward spaces. In soft rock fire setting was unnecessary, and mining was undertaken with just stone and antler tools, as in the Bronze Age copper mines at Alderley Edge in England.

The quarried rock was crushed using stone anvils and hammers. Even after bronze and iron tools came into use, stone was still often used for crushing. This took place either outside the mine shafts or pits or, particularly in the case of deep mines, adjacent to the working face so as to minimize the weight of material that had to be carried out. The ore fragments were picked out of the crushed rock by hand. Short-handled wooden shovels or animal scapulae were used to shovel the ore into baskets, wooden troughs, or leather bags that were hauled with leather ropes along the floor to the entrance of the adit or the base of the shaft, from which they were carried to the surface. Outside the mine the rock could be crushed more finely and the ore rinsed out by panning; this seems to have happened at Mount Gabriel, where stone-crushing tools and stone slabs for finely grinding the rock have been found.

Both mining and metalworking required considerable quantities of timber, and it has even been suggested that the increased deforestation to supply the needs of the mines in regions such as Wales and southwest Ireland contributed significantly to the environmental degradation from forest to blanket bog in the earlier second millennium B.C.

Río Tinto (Spain) The rich metal deposits of Río Tinto and Chinflon in Huelva (ancient Tartessos) were worked in the Bronze and Iron Ages and intensively by the Romans, who constructed a remarkable ladder of waterwheels for mine drainage. Continuous veins of malachite at Chinflon were mined in the Chalcolithic period by digging trenches along them, and the surface deposits of copper oxide ores at Río Tinto were probably also mined but rapidly worked out. Wooden beams and rock shelves across the Chinflon trenches were used as the base for equipment to lift out the ore. Later prehistoric mining at Río Tinto concentrated on the minerally enriched deposits below the substantial iron gossan layers, in which gold, arsenic- and antimony-rich sulfidic copper, and argentiferrous jarosite ores were found. The latter were lead sulfide ores with an exceptionally high silver content, now completely worked out. As the gossan was impenetrable, access to these ores depended on locating surface exposures of the enriched layer, which could be followed under the gossan. Cueva del Lago may have been one such way in, now destroyed by modern mining; Late Bronze Age silver-smelting slag was found here. Shafts dug at Chinflon in the Late Bronze Age with steps cut into their sides would have given access to a major chalcopyrite ore lode, but may have been purely exploratory. Traces of the miners' camp were found nearby.

Copper and Copper Alloys

Native copper was made into beads and other small objects by cold-hammering, grinding, or annealing and hammering, but around 5000 B.C. copper was being smelted at Anza in Macedonia, and by the mid-fifth millennium in many Balkan sites, from easily worked oxide or carbonate ores. Around the same time casting was made possible by the development in the Balkans of high-temperature kilns for firing fine graphite-coated pottery.

The Fahlerz ores that began to be used from the late fourth millennium often contained a significant amount of arsenic or antimony, and the smelted ore produced a type of bronze that was harder and therefore more useful than pure copper and that had a lower melting point. Arsenic- or antimony-rich ores were deliberately selected. In the mid-third millennium tin came into use and began to be alloyed with copper, at first in Bohemia and separately in Britain; an early second-millennium burial at Buxheim in Bavaria contained a necklace of segmented tin beads. Despite its rarity tin became the main alloying metal. Bronzes usually contained around 5–10 percent tin and were generally made using chalcopyrite copper ores. In the Late Bronze

Age lead was also alloyed with copper, though it produced a softer metal.

SOURCES

Copper Ores   The weathered upper levels of the copper ore body contain oxide and carbonate copper ores such as malachite and azurite, with native (pure) copper on the surface. At the base of the weathered levels is found the pale clayey sulfide copper ore known as Fahlerz, which often contains high concentrations of impurities such as arsenic and antimony. Below these are unaltered copper sulfides such as chalcopyrites. In areas that have been subject to glaciation, such as the Alps, the weathered upper layers may be absent.

6.6 *Two elaborately decorated bronze axes found in a Danish bog, where they were probably placed as votive offerings* (Worsaae, J. J. A. *The Industrial Arts of Denmark.* London: Chapman and Hall, 1882)

Native copper occurs as small particles or sometimes nuggets. It was known and exploited from early times in areas where it occurred, including parts of the Balkans, such as the Tisza valley. The earliest European metallurgy developed in settlements adjacent to sources of easily worked oxide and carbonate ores in the mountains of the Balkans and southern Spain. Copper mines began to be worked at Rudna Glava, Aibunar, and other Balkan sites. When the Balkan sources began to fail in the late fourth millennium, attention shifted to the Fahlerz ores of the Harz and Slovakian mountains of central Europe and particularly the Austrian Alps; these were harder to work and often occurred at higher altitudes and were therefore less accessible. Fahlerz ores often contained arsenic or antimony; the resulting alloy was significantly stronger than pure copper, and it is clear that these ores were deliberately selected. The proportion of arsenic or antimony in the finished objects was carefully controlled; in some cases the ore contained around 30 percent arsenic, but the copper objects never contained more than 7 percent. It seems therefore that arsenic was added to copper ore or pure copper to the arsenic-rich copper ore, as required. Sulfide ores were far more abundant than carbonate and oxide ores, being found in many parts of western and central Europe, including major sources in the mountains of Bohemia and Transylvania and along the Atlantic facade; many of these began to be worked in the later third millennium B.C. Ring ingots (ösenringe) of very pure copper probably from Alpine sources circulated widely across Europe around 2000 B.C.

Tin Tin was extremely rare, and when tin bronze began to be widely used in Europe, the adjustment of networks to obtain tin made a very significant difference to the pattern of trade in Europe. The main sources exploited in prehistoric times were Cornwall, Galicia, and the Bohemian Ore Mountains (Erzgebirge), where copper was also available; other sources occurred in Brittany, other parts of Iberia, Tuscany, Sardinia, and possibly Serbia and Ireland. Tin from steppe sources may have been available to people in Southeast Europe, while those of the Aegean may also have had access to tin from Anatolia.

Tin was generally obtained from alluvial (placer) deposits in rivers, in the form of black pebbles of cassiterite (tin oxide), though in some cases it was recovered from eluvial deposits by ground sluicing. Tin mines in Spain were worked before Roman times, and tin may also have been mined in Cornwall, though no ancient mines have been located there.

Rudna Glava (Serbia) Malachite ore was mined here from the later fifth millennium, using funnel-shaped pits 50–65 feet (15–20 meters) deep, of which around 40 are known, though more recent iron working has destroyed much of the early evidence. Sometimes the top of the pit, which cut through loose material, was reinforced with stone walls. The shafts were stepped above the ore vein to protect the miners from debris falling from the mouth of the shaft. The ore was mined with stone hammers and antler picks, probably without using fire setting. Finds of fine Vinča pottery in the mines may have been votive offerings.

Aibunar (Bulgaria) From this source of malachite, mined in the fifth millennium and exchanged throughout the Balkans and beyond, the ore was obtained by cutting narrow trenches up to 260 feet (80 meters) long and 33–65 feet (10–20 meters) deep. Antler picks, two heavily used copper tools, an ax-adz and a hammer-ax, large hammerstones, and the bones of three miners were found here.

Ross Island (Ireland) The arsenic-rich sulfidic copper ores at Ross Island were exploited around 2400–2000 B.C. by people using Beaker pottery. Tools recovered from the mines include ox-scapula shovels. The ore was broken up at the mine site and taken to the nearby hut encampment, where it was roasted and smelted in bowl furnaces. Flat axes made from Ross Island ore were widely distributed in the British mainland.

Mitterberg (Austria) Chalcopyrite ore was mined at Mitterberg during the Bronze Age from wide pits that were often extended into adits and shafts with galleries up to 330 feet (100 meters) long, forming an extensive network. Mining was discontinued in the main shaft around 1020 B.C. due to the depletion of the ore. Ladders made of notched tree trunks were used to give access to the galleries, some of which were exploratory, searching for veins that had run out. Fire setting was used as the main method of mining, and water to cool the rock was brought in in bronze buckets or wooden troughs made of hollowed split tree trunks. The rock was crushed in the mine, using bronze hammers, and was graded using wooden sieves with a hazel twig mesh. A windlass was used to draw bags of ore to the surface. Outside the mines the crushed ore was separated by hand or in wooden water-separating devices built alongside a stream. Roasting beds and smelting furnaces have also been found. Many of the miners may have lived in the small nearby settlement of St. Veit-Klinglberg.

Cwmystwyth (Wales, Britain) Here a substantial open mining pit was extensively worked from around 2000 to 1400 B.C. and continued in use into the Iron Age. It was dug to exploit the visible top part of an extensive deposit of chalcopyrite, Comet Lode, 3–20 feet (1–6 meters) wide, which ran down the side of the valley. The pit is around 80 feet (25 meters) long and at least 23 feet (7 meters) deep, with some small galleries cut in its sides to follow ore-filled fissures (*vugs*). Iron carbonate and galena also occurred there, and the latter was exploited by the prehistoric miners. Beach cobbles used as hammerstones here had been brought from the mouth of the Ystwyth River, some 20 miles (30 kilometers) away; many were found in the waste material tipped down the hillside, along with oak charcoal from the fire setting. As the mines increased in depth, flooding began to be a problem; this was dealt with by installing guttering made of alder logs, which drained the water into a sump from which it could be bailed out. Waterlogged remains found here included baskets of hazel withies and ropes.

Mount Gabriel (Ireland) Malachite ore, along with some copper sulfide ore, occurred here as many small discontinuous veins, which were mined in the period 1700–1500 B.C. by digging numerous small pits, of which around 30 are known. As the rock was hard, all the mining was by fire setting. Tools found here include a shovel made of alder wood, a number of sharpened oak sticks used to prize off flakes of rock, and a handle for a hammerstone made of twisted hazel withies, as well as pine splints that had been burnt as torches. It is estimated that around 20–28 short tons (20–27 tonnes) of ore were taken from the mine over the two centuries of its use.

Great Orme's Head (Wales, Britain) A very extensive underground network of mines, one of the largest in prehistoric Europe, with shafts up to 230 feet (70 meters) deep and galleries as much as 1,000 feet (300 meters) long, was worked at Great Orme from around 1700 to 700 B.C. Early work here exploited surface deposits, but the mines soon expanded underground, following the ore deposits. The ores mined here were chalcopyrites; arsenic was added when the ore was worked, to produce arsenical bronze. The parent rock was limestone, giving an alkaline environment that allowed the preservation of numerous bone and antler tools, including unmodified bones used as scoops to gouge out copper ore. Very large stones weighing up to 65 pounds (30 kilograms) that had clearly been used for pounding the rock were probably operated using a cradle suspended from timber uprights. Fire setting was probably unnecessary, given the softness of the rock. Work began here with large open pits to mine the surface outcrops of ore. Veins of ore were then followed underground. Many of the animal bones found in the mines seem likely to have come from the meals eaten there by the miners. The ore was crushed at the site, using mortar stones, and washed in a spring before being taken to Pen Trwyn, about a mile (1.5 kilometers) from the mine, where it was smelted.

Galicia (Spain) Cassiterite ore was available in the rivers of Galicia and was probably exploited from the Bronze Age onward. The classical world knew the region as the Cassiterides or Tin Islands, from which the Phoenicians and their successors obtained considerable quantities of tin.

Cornwall (Britain) This was possibly the chief source of tin in antiquity. Analyses of the first bronze artifacts in Britain, made around 2000 B.C., have shown that they include tin that chemically matches that from Cornwall. No ancient mines have been located here, since extensive later mining and erosion have probably obliterated all trace of ancient working, but these analyses have demonstrated that Cornish tin was being worked by 2000 B.C. Classical references show that Cornwall was one of Europe's main sources of tin in the later Iron Age. Diodorus Siculus refers to the mining of surface deposits of tin and the manufacture of astragalus-shaped ingots in Belerion (Cornwall); ingots in this shape have been recovered from an undated ancient wreck off the Devon coast at Bigbury Bay. Tin-smelting slag was found in barrows at Caerloggas in Cornwall.

SMELTING

Copper Oxide and carbonate ores could be smelted simply by heating them with charcoal in a reducing environment, but sulfide ore had first to be roasted in an open bonfire to drive off the sulfur and some of the trace elements and to oxidize the ore. The copper ore was mixed with charcoal for fuel, and iron oxide or sand could be added as a flux. The ore was smelted in a bowl furnace covered by clay walls with a hole at its base to tap the slag and to force in a draught using bellows; a temperature of 1,470 degrees Fahrenheit (800 degrees Centigrade) was required. A base possibly of such a furnace was found at Muhlbach in the eastern Alps. Iron, a common element of sulfide copper ores, and other impurities were removed as gas, or settled in the slag, while the copper produced by the smelting process settled in the furnace base, forming a bun-shaped (plano-convex) ingot. In the eastern Mediterranean "oxhide" copper ingots were made, some of which were traded into Europe, where they are known from Sardinia and Sicily and fragments from a hoard in Germany.

Tin The ore was roasted and ground to a powder. At first this was probably mixed with copper ore and the two smelted together to produce bronze in one operation. Later, it was smelted separately to produce pure tin and then mixed with copper, giving greater control over the relative proportions of the two metals.

WORKING

Native or smelted copper could be worked into simple shapes by cold-hammering, or by hammering and annealing; working by hammering and annealing was also necessary to remove the blistering and unevenness of the smelted copper. Cold-hammering was also used to sharpen the edge of cast copper tools.

Copper required a temperature of 1,981 degrees Fahrenheit (1,083 degrees Centigrade) to melt; the technology for achieving this was available in the Balkans by the fifth millennium. The smelted copper was placed in a clay crucible and heated with charcoal inside a clay-lined furnace with a chimney. A forced draught was necessary to achieve the required temperature, so a tuyere to take a blow pipe or bellows was inserted at the base of the furnace. Hot crucibles were probably handled using tongs or paired poles of green wood.

Once copper could be melted, it was used for casting. At first open molds were employed; the shape of the desired object was carved into a stone block, but simpler molds were also made by pressing a shape into firm sand and pouring metal into the resulting impression. Common objects in the fifth-millennium Balkans included flat axes and awls, but also heavier objects such as shafthole axes and hammers. Open molds produced objects shaped on the lower side and flat on top, probably generally treated as blanks that were then worked into their finished form by grinding, hammering, and annealing.

Two-piece molds are known in Europe in the later third millennium, though they may also have been used earlier in the Balkans to cast shafthole axes. These molds were often made of clay, which could be formed around a reusable wooden pattern, or of stone or metal; in the case of metal molds, the inside was coated with graphite to prevent the molten metal sticking to it. Metal was poured into the mold, and when the object cooled the mold was removed. The remnants of the casting process, notably the slight seam formed at the junction of the mold pieces and the flashes from the mold's vents and filling hole, were then removed by hammering and the blade might be sharpened or the object heated to allow it to be bent. The metal was also often polished to give the object a smooth surface. Two-piece molds enabled more complex shapes to be made, such as flanged axes, daggers and halberds with a midrib, and ax heads with a side loop by which they could be bound more securely to their handle.

A clay core might be inserted to create a shaft-hole in the finished object. The most characteristic

6.7 Reconstruction of a bronze founder's workshop (Figuier, Louis. *Primitive Man.* London: Chatto and Windus, 1876)

early product of this technique was the battle-axe, made in the Carpathian region and widely imitated in stone. Bronze was easier to cast than copper, encouraging the development of more complex shapes. Únětice metallurgists developed a technique of surface enrichment of tin in bronze objects to give a silvery finish. Other Únětice innovations included casting-on, in which a cast object was partially inserted into the mold for an additional part before the molten metal was poured into the mold; solid metal hilts were added to daggers using this technique, which also enabled larger objects to be created and broken objects to be repaired.

The Únětice metallurgists also made small vessels and ornaments from beaten metal sheets. By the later second millennium bronze bars hammered out into sheets were being used to create much larger objects such as buckets, cauldrons, shields, and body armor.

These were hammered into shape over a wooden form and decorated with repoussé bosses and ribs, which also gave extra strength. Sections were held together with rivets, often arranged in patterns, and handles were added by casting-on. Objects made in two-piece molds now included swords, socketed spearheads, pins with decorated heads, and socketed axes. They were often decorated, using a variety of techniques, including engraving, chasing, and repoussé, with chisels, punches, and gravers. Elaborate designs were drawn with compasses. Some Iron Age bone plaques from Loughcrew in Ireland may have been used as test pieces on which to design these compass patterns before executing them on the metal itself. Several pairs of Iron Age compasses were found in the Spanish settlement of La Bastida. Red-hot bronze was drawn through holes in a drawbar or hammered into a swage (groove) on the stone anvil to create wire; this was used to make applied decoration or twisted singly or in strands to form pins, bracelets, and neck rings.

More complex objects were made in reusable stone or bronze multiple-piece molds or by lost-wax (cire perdue) casting. For the latter a model of the desired object was created in wax, with or without a clay core, and sometimes with elaborate surface decoration. This was encased in clay and fired. The wax ran out, leaving a hollow interior or a thin space between the outer mold and inner core (held in place by pins) into which the metal was poured. When the metal had cooled, the clay mold was smashed. The alloying of lead with copper in the Late Bronze Age would have facilitated casting in these elaborate molds as the lead-copper alloy runs more easily than tin-bronze when molten. Cire perdue was used to create elaborate shapes such as Irish horns or the figurines from the Nuraghic culture of

Sardinia. Some complex objects such as the Scandinavian lurer were cast in separate pieces with locking joints that were fixed together. Tin was sometimes made into small objects like beads; it was also used as a solder for joining pieces of bronze.

In the first millennium, when tools were more usually made of iron, bronze was mainly used to manufacture ornaments and other prestigious objects. These included horse harness, parade armor, vessels, and jewelry such as pins, torcs, and fibulae. Bronze even more than before became a vehicle for displaying artistic and technological versatility, skill, and inventiveness. Objects of sheet bronze became both more common and more elaborate; these included exceptional creations such as the bronze wheeled couch in the Hochdorf barrow. Sheet bronze was also used for cladding on objects such as wooden buckets and for decoration. Some bronze cauldrons had a base of iron, producing an attractive bichrome heat-resistant vessel. Copper, tin, and bronze were also combined with other metals for decorative effect. Bronze was sometimes used to plate iron, while bronze or copper were occasionally plated with tin or silver or gilded.

Other decoration was achieved by inlaying bronze with coral and glass, held in cells of metal (cloisonné). By the late centuries B.C. the art of enameling had been mastered. Finished bronze objects were often polished, using sand or a stone to grind the surface smooth and oil and wax to create a sheen, using a piece of wool.

Brass was probably not manufactured in prehistoric Europe, although some bronzes contained zinc from impurities in the copper ore. Some Late Iron Age objects also contained zinc derived from Roman brass used as scrap metal and a few late objects were made of brass, for example, a number of sheet brass objects in a hoard found at Tal-y-llyn in Wales.

Gussage All Saints This second-century B.C. British Iron Age farmstead was also a specialist bronze industrial site where horse harness and vehicle fittings were produced by cire perdue casting. Debris left here included small bone tools used to model the objects in wax, iron punches and chisels, triangular crucibles, a small billet of bronze, and broken clay molds for various harness elements such as bits, terret rings, strap ends, and linchpins. Iron was also separately worked here.

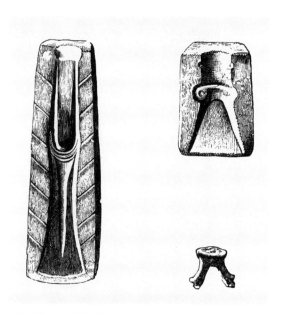

6.8 *Two mold halves, for casting a bronze palstave (left) and a bronze ax (right), as well as the plug of metal that formed at the top of the mold when the molten metal was poured* (Worsaae, J. J. A. *The Industrial Arts of Denmark*. London: Chapman and Hall, 1882)

Gold

The appearance, rarity, and incorruptibility of gold have caused it to be regarded as a precious material almost everywhere it is known. A great proportion of gold work from ancient Europe comes from burials where it was used as the material for many prestige grave goods.

SOURCES

Gold occurs generally in its native (pure metal) form, which often includes some other metals such as silver, copper, platinum, iron, or tin as impurities; electrum, a natural alloy of gold with larger amounts of silver, was also known. Gold is often found in eluvial and alluvial (placer) deposits. In rocks gold is found in the upper, oxidized levels. Important sources of gold in prehistoric Europe were known in Ireland, Iberia, and Transylvania, and smaller sources in Bohemia, parts of the Balkans, Wales, and France. Gold used at Varna in the fifth millennium also came from more distant sources in Armenia and the Caucasus.

Though some was mined, much of the gold obtained in antiquity was recovered by panning alluvial deposits. A third-century B.C. panning operation was found at Modlesovice in Bohemia, where the wooden troughs used were preserved. Gold was often present in minute amounts in the placer deposits from which tin ore was panned; in historical times this was carefully collected by tin miners and stored in a quill. Mined gold-bearing rock was crushed to a fine powder and the gold separated from the rock dust by panning or washing over a collecting medium such as heather or a sheepskin to which the gold adhered while the lighter rock particles were washed away.

Wicklow Mountains (Ireland) Alluvial gold and possibly alluvial tin were panned in the Wicklow Mountains, where gold was probably also mined from the late third millennium, providing the basis for a magnificent gold-working industry.

WORKING

As gold is soft and easily worked, gold objects were generally produced by cold-hammering or heating and hammering; at first simple shapes such as beads, pendants, and rings were made. By the fifth millennium B.C. at Varna, however, gold was being made into more ambitious shapes that probably involved casting as well as hammering. An exceptional piece from Moigrad in Romania was a sheet-gold disc weighing 26 ounces (750 grams) and measuring 10 by 12 inches (24 by 31 centimeters).

In the Bronze Age gold may have circulated in the form of small "bullet" ingots from which it could be cold-hammered into sheet gold. Small pieces of gold could be welded together by burnishing, enabling larger objects to be made. Many of the great variety of techniques used for working copper and bronze were also applied to gold, such as shaping thin sheet gold over a form, casting in simple or multiple-piece molds, making wire, and decorating with repoussé, chased, engraved, stamped, and compass-drawn designs. Ornate gold cups and elaborate ornaments were made by many Bronze Age groups. In the Iron Age gold work was sometimes inlaid with coral or glass.

Gold was also worked by its own particular techniques, including granulation and filigree, and objects of other metals were sometimes gilded. Many gold artifacts were extremely fine and elaborate, and some involved substantial quantities of gold. Artifacts made in several pieces were joined by sewing with gold wire or by soldering using an alloy of copper and gold. This alloy was also commonly used in the later Bronze Age and in the La Tène period to make artifacts, saving on gold and giving a richer color; in the Iron Age silver was often also added, making a ternary alloy. The appearance of objects made of the latter was sometimes enhanced by depletion gilding. Gold was also used to decorate objects made of other materials, such as Chalcolithic buttons covered with gold foil, Early Bronze Age daggers decorated with tiny gold nails, and Iron Age bowls, helmets, and other objects with solid or openwork sheet-gold cladding or appliqués. At Varna and a few other early Balkan sites some pottery vessels were decorated with gold paint.

Varna (Bulgaria) At this cemetery dated around 4500–4000 B.C. 61 out of some 300 graves contained gold objects, totaling around 13 pounds (6 kilograms) of gold. These included discs and sheet-gold appliqués to decorate clothing, amulets, decorations on clay masks, a tube that may have been a penis sheath, and even a solid gold model astragalus, as well as beads, bracelets, and rings. Hollow tubes to cover the wooden shafts of stone hammer-axes may have been cast. The abundance and variety of gold objects here contrasts with the small numbers of beads and rings found elsewhere at this time.

Wessex (Britain) A series of rich barrow burials in the region around Stonehenge, dated around 2000 to 1700 B.C., included some with objects of fine sheet gold that were apparently the work of a single craftsman. His products included a lozenge-shaped chest ornament and a smaller lozenge, a belt hook and gold-wire inlay for the handle of a copper dagger, associated with the man buried in the Bush Barrow; a lozenge plate and button- and pendant-covers buried with a cremation in the same barrow cemetery at Wilsford; and a rectangular plate, button-covers, cones, and cylindrical beads with a secondary cremation at Upton Lovell.

Ireland (Britain) Irish gold working, using gold from the Wicklow Mountains, began around 2200 B.C., producing sheet-gold discs, basket-shaped earrings, and lunulae (crescentic collars), elaborately decorated with incised or punched geometric patterns. A greater range of objects was made in the second millennium, including torcs, tress rings, and other objects made using twisted strips or rods of gold, and sheet-gold armlets with chased or repoussé ribbed decoration. Even greater versatility was displayed in the first millennium; products included small objects such as earrings and amulets covered with intricately decorated gold foil, massive solid gold dress-fasteners, and gorgets. The latter were great collars of fine sheet gold decorated with ribs and ropes of fine twisted wire to which gold disc terminals had been stitched with gold wire. The decoration of the discs and body of the gorgets used many techniques, including repoussé, raising, chasing, and stamping.

Thrace (Bulgaria) Grave goods buried in Thracian royal tombs in the later first millennium B.C. demonstrate remarkable mastery of metalworking, using gold

6.9 A gold torc from Clonmacnoise in Ireland, made from a loosely twisted flat strip of gold with expanded terminals that loop together (Lubbock, John. *Prehistoric Times.* New York: D. Appleton and Company, 1890)

and silver from the Apuseni Mountains in Transylvania. The ornaments include necklaces of gold beads and pendants decorated by granulation, repoussé, filigree, and soldering on patterns in fine gold wire; gold brooches with cloisonné enamel; necklaces made of chains of silver wire; and silver, gilded silver, and gold appliqués for sewing onto clothing. Silver dishes, bowls, and jugs had gilded and finely decorated bands and bosses, while other silver vessels, pieces of harness, and armor bore gilded relief figures and scenes such as horsemen hunting. A hoard known as the Panagyurishte treasure comprised nine gold vessels decorated with solid and hollow figures and relief scenes.

Torcs Bronze Age gold torcs (neck rings) were made from skillfully twisted flanged metal bars or wire, with knob or rod terminals. Similar torcs were produced in the Iron Age along with torcs and bracelets of tubular gold sheet or cast solid gold, sometimes with elaborate relief decoration. The sixth-century B.C. "princess's" grave at Vix included a torc of thick sheet gold with elaborate terminals whose decoration included tiny cast figures of a winged horse, chased and punched designs, and delicate filigree work. The terminals of torcs often bore elaborate decoration, including figures and geometric designs. Among the most impressive examples were the torcs found at Snettisham in England, which included some made of gold wires twisted in strands that were then twisted together and attached by casting-on to massive cire perdue cast terminals.

Silver and Lead

Silver was not widely available in Europe, but occasional silver pins and other ornaments and a few weapons are known from eastern and central Europe and Italy from the third millennium onward, some of them Aegean or Anatolian imports. Chalcolithic and Bronze Age Spain was an exception, producing a number of diadems, beads, and rings, while a few silver cups are known from France in the same period. Its use became more widespread in the Iron Age.

Lead had many uses, from the humble functions of mending metal objects, filling holes in them or adding weight to improve their balance, through providing small parts and attachments on bronzes, to occasionally being made into small objects entirely of lead, such as weights or beads. Gold was sometimes eked out by making objects with a lead core. Lead was used in the Late Bronze Age in western Europe to alloy with copper, producing a metal that was easier to cast.

SOURCES

In the Erzgebirge (Bohemian Ore Mountains) native silver and veins of a very pure silver ore containing cobalt, nickel, and arsenic occurred. Silver-lead sulfide (galena) deposits known as jarosites, which formed at the base of the weathered horizon in some metalliferous rock, were favored as the source of silver and lead in antiquity. These were composed mostly of lead with a variable amount of silver, usually small. The most important source of silver was the silver-rich jarosite of the Huelva area of Spain, worked by the Late Bronze Age if not earlier.

Silver also occurred in a natural alloy with gold, known as electrum. The proportions of the two metals varied, giving in different regions a metal that more closely resembled either gold or silver. The electrum of the Apuseni Mountains in Transylvania was extensively used in the Iron Age.

SMELTING AND WORKING

Silver-lead sulfide ore was first roasted to drive off some of the sulfur it contained, producing litharge (lead oxide). This could be used as it was or could be reduced to lead by heating in a furnace with charcoal, a process that drove off the remaining sulfur as sulfur dioxide. At every stage the lead still contained the silver and trace elements that had been present in the ore. The smelted metal could be used as lead or the silver could be extracted by cupellation.

Impurities in silver could also be removed by cupellation; in this case the silver was mixed with lead before the process began. The metal was heated to red heat in an open crucible and air was blown across the surface, driving the lead off as lead oxide gas. This was the method used to extract silver at the Río Tinto mines in Spain, where an extensive deposit of silver-smelting slag has been found. In the first millennium much of the silver from here, which was mined and smelted by local people, was traded with the Phoenicians established on the coast. It was also extensively used locally for small vessels and ornaments, such as fibulae, bracelets, and torcs, which were often made of twisted wires or bars, sometimes with knots, loops, and other decorative features worked in. Another major center of Iron Age silver working was in Thrace, where silver was used alongside gold. A silver-plated iron torc with cow's-head terminals from Trichtingen in Germany may also have been of Thracian workmanship.

Gundestrup Cauldron (Denmark) This famous Iron Age gilded silver cauldron was constructed of 13 panels of silver sheet decorated with repoussé high-relief designs with engraved and chased detail. These were soldered together with tin to form an interior and an exterior frieze, and were attached to a sheet-silver bowl with a gilded central disc and a circular iron rim. Many of the scenes shown and artifacts depicted, such as torcs and carnyxes, seem purely Celtic, but others show features from regions as distant as India, such as elephants, and the workmanship suggests it was of Thracian manufacture.

Iron

Red ochre, hydrated iron oxide, was known and used as a pigment from the Palaeolithic period onward, iron pyrites were often employed as strike-a-lights, and meteoritic iron was occasionally gathered and used. Iron ore was not worked, however, until relatively late. Iron was known in the Near East by the late third millennium, and in Greece in the late second millennium, becoming widespread by 700 B.C. However, some later Bronze Age bronzes in temperate Europe have decorations that seem to have been made with iron punches, and one such punch was found in Holland; iron drill bits are also implied by holes drilled in some Late Bronze Age metalwork, so it seems likely that a limited amount of iron was in circulation at this time. It probably was first pro-

duced as a by-product of smelting sulfide copper ores, which often contain iron.

The technology of iron working differed markedly from that of other metals. In the ancient world only the Chinese achieved the technology necessary for the manufacture of cast iron, Europeans being confined to making wrought iron. Since iron was inferior to bronze in strength, until the practice of carburization was mastered in the early centuries of the first millennium B.C. its earlier adoption may have been linked to the difficulties of obtaining a sufficient supply of tin or good-quality copper to satisfy contemporary demand for metal tools and weapons. By the later first millennium iron was being used to make a great range of everyday tools accessible to most people, and iron-smithing was practiced in most settlements of any size.

SOURCES AND EXTRACTION

Iron occurred as meteoritic iron, but most iron came from ore in rocks. The weathered upper layers of iron-bearing rock oxidized to form a range of iron oxides, including haematite and magnetite in rock forming a reddish crust known as iron-hat or gossan; these were the ores most commonly exploited, by digging open pits or by collecting nodules from the surface, though some deeper mines were also worked. At the base of the weathered horizon, iron potassium sulfates formed, and below this were unaltered sulfides such as iron pyrites. In some regions eroded magnetite formed placer deposits of black sand, which was recovered by ground sluicing and exploited as iron ore, for example, by the Etruscans in Elba and Populonia. Bog iron (limonite, a type of brown haematite found in bogs) was used in some parts of Europe.

Unlike other metals, particularly tin, iron ore was widely available and plentiful, local supplies serving the needs of most areas. Sources of iron of wider importance included the eastern Alps, the Holy Cross Mountains of Poland, the Hunsrück-Eifel area, and Etruria. Most iron could be obtained from the surface by open pit mining.

SMELTING AND WORKING

Iron ore was usually smelted close to its source as its bulk made it difficult to transport. The ore was lay-

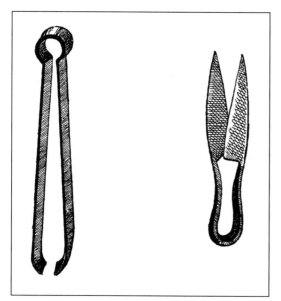

6.10 Iron pincers and shears found at La Tène in Lake Neuchâtel, Switzerland (Figuier, Louis. *Primitive Man.* London: Chatto and Windus, 1876)

ered with charcoal and heated in an enclosed shaft furnace with a steady forced draught created with bellows to a temperature that had to be maintained between 2,000 and 2,200 degrees Fahrenheit (1,100 and 1,200 degrees Centigrade). The furnace was then often smashed to remove the resultant spongy mass of impure iron, known as the bloom. This had to be repeatedly worked by heating to red-hot in a forging fire and hammering, to separate the iron from the slag. Iron production was often on a large scale and was an expensive process, 2 pounds (1 kilogram) of useable iron being the end product of a smelt whose firing used 20 pounds (10 kilograms) of charcoal and involved around 25 man-hours' work, in addition to that required for mining, charcoal-burning, and other associated tasks. The wrought iron was often forged into ingots of various shapes that were probably designed to demonstrate the quality and consistency of the iron; common forms were a square-sectioned bar with tapering ends and a flat bar with a flanged end. These are also known as currency bars since they were probably used as a medium of exchange.

The iron ingots were traded widely, to be worked into artifacts on settlements; scrap iron recycled from broken artifacts was also used. The smiths produced the required shape by repeated heating in a hearth and hammering on an anvil. Use of charcoal in the smithing process caused carbon to combine with the iron to produce steel, a harder metal than wrought iron; repeated working increased the proportion of steel present. Carburization could also be achieved by spreading a layer of fine charcoal particles across the anvil before forging the iron object on it, producing a case-hardened artifact that had a steel shell and an iron interior. By the later Iron Age the technique of quenching the steel had also been mastered; this involved plunging the white-hot object into water to cool it rapidly, increasing its hardness but also making it brittle. Objects were then often tempered by being heated and slowly cooled. This reduced their brittleness at the expense of reducing their hardness; skill was required to achieve the right balance between quenching and tempering. Case-hardened objects, however, required no tempering since the brittleness of the quenched steel was offset by the softness of the iron. Pieces of iron could be welded together by heating them to red heat and hammering them together. Wrought iron was used for many different artifacts, steel generally only for edged tools, including swords. The earliest iron objects imitated those in bronze, but gradually shapes more suited to the methods of iron working were produced. Some of the finest swords were made from strips of wrought iron and steel welded together, combining the flexibility of the iron with the hard edge of steel, or were case-hardened to produce a thick steel shell. Another exceptional product was iron mail, a Celtic invention around 300 B.C. This was made by forging iron rings and individually interlocking them.

Noricum   The iron ore of the kingdom of Noricum in the eastern Alps was particularly good since it contained a considerable amount of manganese, an element that increased the malleability of iron. Noreia (Magdalensberg), its principal oppidum, therefore became a major center of iron working, where numerous furnaces and quantities of slag have been found. Its iron was famed in the Roman world, where it was known as *ferrum noricum*.

Coin Production

Coinage of gold and silver began to be used in much of Europe during the third century B.C. Lower-value denominations began to appear in the first century: small silver coins and coins of bronze and potin.

Coin blanks (flans) were produced in molds, the metal for each having been exactly weighed out or the molds carefully made to produce flans of exactly the same size. Large molds with 50 or more holes were used for mass-production. The flans were placed between two engraved bronze or iron dies, and the upper one was struck a single hard blow, impressing the design from both dies onto the faces of the flan. As the designs were cut into the dies, they appeared in relief on the coins.

Occasionally, coins were cast in clay molds. This method was used for making potin coins in Kent in Britain: a two-piece mold was made using a strip of papyrus to form the coin blanks. The design was scratched into the fired clay with a stylus before the

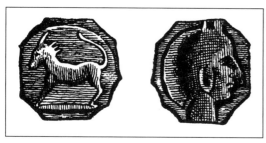

6.11 A Celtic bronze coin found at La Tène in Lake Neuchâtel, Switzerland (Figuier, Louis. *Primitive Man.* London: Chatto and Windus, 1876)

coins were cast. As the holes in the mold ran into each other, this produced a strip of coins that were then cut apart.

CERAMICS

The world's first pottery was made in Japan before 10,000 B.C., and deliberately fired clay objects were being produced even earlier in various parts of the Palaeolithic world. The Near East saw the development of pottery before 7000 B.C., and sometime during the seventh millennium pottery began to appear on Greek farming settlements. The idea or technology of pottery production spread across Europe with the spread of farming, being taken up by sedentary hunter-gatherer communities in areas such as the forest steppe of eastern Europe and Scandinavia.

Pottery served two main purposes: storage and cooking. Other containers, such as skins and baskets, could also perform these functions, but pottery was more efficient and more versatile. On the other hand it was both more fragile and heavier than the alternatives and was therefore not suited to a mobile lifestyle, being used almost exclusively by sedentary communities, although it was also traded or used as containers for traded goods, mainly moved by water transport.

In addition, pottery was attractive and capable of being made into many shapes and decorated in an almost infinite variety of ways, so it rapidly became a vehicle for making cultural statements, for instance, as status symbols or demonstrations of participation in a religious or social practice, such as that associated with the widespread Beaker pottery.

Pottery Production

Different clay and filler mixes, surface treatments, and firing conditions were used to make pottery for different purposes, such as watertight wares for heating liquids and porous fabrics to keep liquids cool.

CLAYS

Clay suitable for making pottery was widely available, particularly red clays that contain iron oxides, and most communities were able to dig potter's clay from sources nearby. Nevertheless, fine or unusual clays were prized and vessels manufactured from them were widely traded; these included pottery made from the gabbroitic clay of the Lizard in Cornwall, which was transported throughout southwest England.

CLAY PREPARATION

Raw clay was often spread out to weather and periodically turned and knocked about, breaking down any lumps. The clay was worked to make it smooth and even so that it would not distort during drying and firing. Large impurities were removed by hand, and the clay might be washed and settled or strained to obtain fine particles. If necessary a filler (temper) was added to reduce the clay's stickiness; this was particularly necessary for the very plastic red clays. Some clay already contained mineral particles that could act as a filler, but others that might be added included ground shell, calcined flint, chopped straw, fine sand, or grog (ground-up pottery). The clay and filler were thoroughly mixed with water and kneaded to obtain a plastic, well-blended material free of air bubbles.

POTTERY MAKING

The simplest method of forming pottery is by pressing a hollow into a ball of clay and thinning the sides between finger and thumb; this may have been the method by which some of the earliest pottery was made. Most European pottery, however, was built up of coils or rings of rolled strips of clay; the surface was then smoothed with a rib bone, a wooden beater and anvil, or a damp cloth. The base of the vessel might be made by pressing clay into a mold, and then the body of the vessel would be built up in coils; large storage vessels often were made this way. Pots might be made in several separate pieces, such as body and neck, often with a carination at the point of attachment. They might also be built up of slabs of clay, as was some of the Greek Early Neolithic pottery. Lugs were pinched out from the side of the vessel or attached and smoothed on, as were footrings, feet, and handles, though these might also be attached through holes poked into the vessel's side. Lips and spouts were usually pinched out. Curved incised decoration had to be executed at this stage as only straight lines were practicable when the pottery had dried to leather hard; impressed or rusticated decoration was also applied at this stage.

Pots were often formed on a flat stone, mat, or sherd that could be turned during their manufacture. It is possible that the turntable (tournette), a flat disc seated on a pivot, was used in prehistoric Europe. In the second millennium B.C. the potter's wheel was adopted by the Minoans from the Near East and gradually spread through the Mediterranean. It was introduced into temperate Europe during the second half of the first millennium B.C., reaching Britain by the first century B.C. Wheel-thrown vessels usually had flat bases, while those formed in other ways might have round, flat, or pointed bases.

After shaping, the vessels were left to dry slowly and evenly, in the air in warm regions or near the hearth or in a drying oven in cooler lands. When the vessel was leather hard, portions of its walls might be shaved with a knife to reduce their thickness. Incised, excised, or impressed decoration could be added at this stage, and the surface was frequently slipped and burnished with a stone, bone, or piece of shell to reduce its porosity. Greek Early Neolithic pottery, for example, was very highly burnished and glossy. Lugs and other additions could be luted on to the leather-hard vessel, using slip as an adhesive; applied decoration such as knobs, bosses, or bands of clay or clay pellets could also be added. The vessels

were then allowed to dry further; when they were white-hard, with almost no remaining water, they were ready for firing. At this stage they could be decorated by painting.

FIRING

The temperature to which pottery was fired determined its final state. Firing to a temperature above about 840 degrees Fahrenheit (450 degrees Centigrade) would drive off the water from the clay, producing terra-cotta, a usable but porous and friable pottery. At a certain temperature (the sinter point) the surfaces of the clay particles fused, producing a hard impermeable fabric known as earthenware. However, at a certain higher temperature, the clay particles would melt, causing the pottery to collapse. These temperatures varied, depending on the mineral composition of the clay, but the sinter point generally lay between 1,800 and 2,200 degrees Fahrenheit (1,000 and 1,200 degrees Centigrade). In some clays the sinter point and melting temperatures were very close, while in other, more suitable, clays they were widely separated.

Bonfires The simplest method of firing was in the domestic hearth, the vessel being turned periodically to ensure even, overall firing. A related method, widely employed even in the Iron Age, was bonfire (clamp) firing. The pottery was stacked on the ground or in a pit, with fast-burning fuel such as brushwood arranged below and above it and mixed in, and the whole heap was often covered with earth, turf, or dung to damp the fire and conserve the heat, allowing it to burn under control for around three days, a technique similar to charcoal burning. The fired pots were allowed to cool naturally, probably for as long as a week. Temperatures in a bonfire firing could rise as high as 1,740 degrees Fahrenheit (950 degrees Centigrade), but the firing was often uneven and the level of wastage could be high. The use of poorer fuels such as peat, for example, in prehistoric Orkney, resulted in the production of softer, less durable pottery.

Kilns Simple updraught (vertical) kilns consisted of a hearth enclosed in a stone, clay, or brick chamber, with a perforated clay floor above the hearth on which the pots were stacked. The kiln was sealed by a dome of clay, stone, or even dung with a hole left for a chimney; this was removed or smashed after each firing in order to take out the fired pots. These kilns allowed higher temperatures to be achieved and gave better control of the conditions of firing, allowing unblemished polychrome pottery to be produced. However, the number of vessels that could be fired at one time was smaller, and kilns required pieces of wood or charcoal for fuel rather than the more readily available brushwood, dung, straw, or peat that could be used in a bonfire firing. Horizontal kilns in which the pottery was stacked beside the hearth and the air drawn through the chamber by a flue provided better firing conditions, with higher temperatures being possible.

Firing in an oxidizing environment resulted in the production of pottery with a red surface, while firing in a reducing atmosphere (with little or no oxygen coming into contact with the pottery) would produce a gray or black surface. Pottery might also be blackened by smoking over a fire, allowing soot particles to fill the pores in the pottery, or by applying a magnetite slip to the vessel before firing.

The graphite-painted wares of the Balkans imply that the ability to produce controlled high-firing temperatures had been achieved by the fifth millennium. Updraught and horizontal kilns are known from prehistoric sites in various parts of Europe, but bonfire firing also continued into the Late Iron Age.

Eilean an Tighe   A potter's workshop was found in this second-millennium Hebridean site. Clay was available locally and was tempered with grit from the shores of the adjacent loch, ground on site with heavy stone pestles. Pieces of pumice were used for smoothing the surface of vessels and a burnisher was also found. The pottery was fired in horizontal kilns built of stone blocks packed with turf and roofed with stone slabs. The kilns had a paved hearth, and stone slabs acted as baffles protecting the pots in the firing chamber from direct contact with the fire. A narrow flue led away from the firing chamber. Birch and willow wood were used as fuel.

Pottery Vessels

SHAPES

The earliest pottery was made in simple shapes, often imitating the containers of such materials as leather and basketry that were already in use. Although forms suited to the ceramic medium were quick to develop, imitations of vessels in other media also continued to be produced on occasion. Fine metal vessels, for example, were reproduced in pottery, presumably for those without access to the metal prototypes. Pottery vessels were developed for particular purposes: For example, a range of vessels including strainers and large open bowls appeared in the fourth millennium across much of Europe, probably connected with milking and processing milk for making cheese. Jars for storage, bowls for cooking and serving food, cups and beakers for

6.12 A collared flask, one of the distinctive range of vessels made by the TRB culture in Neolithic northern Europe (Worsaae, J. J. A. *The Industrial Arts of Denmark.* London: Chapman and Hall, 1882)

drinking, and urns for burying the dead were among the shapes regularly used. The introduction of the potter's wheel greatly facilitated the shaping of vessels, giving rise to forms with many changes of direction in their profile.

From the beginning, European pottery had a variety of different base forms: round, pointed, and flat, with ring bases or feet; some later vessels also had pedestals. Vessels might have spouts or lips for pouring; handles or lugs for lifting or suspension, such as the unusual *Flute-de-Pan* handles of French Neolithic Chassey Ware; necks or collars, such as the range of urns from Late Neolithic and Early Bronze Age Britain; rounded, straight-sided or carinated profiles; and many other variations in shape.

Many cultures also experimented with more unusual or fantastic designs: TRB flasks with a thin clay disc collar around their long necks; Danish Late Neolithic bowls with eye motifs; Otomani jars with large spiky bosses; Eastern European jars with painted or modeled human faces on their necks; or the tiny Early Bronze Age British "grape cups" whose surface was covered with small balls of clay resembling a bunch of grapes. Some cultures produced pottery in the form of people, animals, or objects, such as the cups made by the Baden culture in the shape of wheeled vehicles.

DECORATION

Many methods were available to give an attractive appearance to pottery. Clay and slip selection provided a range of possibilities for the color and appearance of the finished vessels. Decoration could be applied over the whole surface or part of it, in various patterns. Zones of decoration were common and were perhaps related to the introduction of the tournette (turntable).

Surface Deformation The surface of the newly formed or leather-hard vessel could be decorated with incised lines (e.g., LBK) or impressions using a fingernail, a bird bone, a stick, a shell (e.g., Cardial Impressed Ware), or a twisted cord (e.g., Corded Ware, Beakers), or the surface could be stamped (e.g., some Iron Age wares), combed (e.g., some Mesolithic wares) or rusticated. Surface roughening in these ways improved the user's grip on the vessel.

Appliqués Clay pellets, bands or rolls of clay, and even figures were added to some vessels at the leather-hard stage and might themselves be decorated by impressing or incising. For example, the Encrusted Urns of Early Bronze Age Britain were decorated with applied rosettes, swags, and zigzag bands of clay, often bearing slashed incisions. Some Hungarian Iron Age pottery had human or animal heads molded on the handles.

Slips and Glazes Further color and textural differences could be achieved with a surface coating. The simplest form was a slip, made from a wash of fine clay, either that used in making the pottery (self-slip) or a contrasting clay. The slip might be applied to the whole of one or both surfaces or painted on as designs. Patterns might also be produced on vessels dipped into or washed with slip, by previously covering parts of the vessel's surface with a material such as wax or grease that would repel the slip but which would burn off during firing to reveal the unslipped surface (reserved slip decoration).

Other minerals such as haematite, graphite, and mica could also be applied by burnishing, slipping, or painting. Some of these permitted the surface to be burnished to a lustrous finish or metallic sheen, such as the Iron Age Black-Burnished wares.

Painting Designs could be applied to part or all of the white-hard vessel's surface by painting, using a variety of mineral pigments such as ochre and other natural earths. These could be mixed to produce a range of colors. Although the first pottery in Greece was undecorated, it was not long before the farming communities in Southeast Europe began to make pottery painted with red or white geometric designs. A great range of such designs was popular in many areas and at many times, but occasionally representational art was also applied to vessels, such as those of the Hallstatt period from Sopron in Hungary, which show scenes from everyday life.

Other Ceramics

Clay was also used to produce a range of other objects. These included many domestic tools, such as spindle whorls and loomweights, fishing-net weights, beads and pendants, molds for casting metal objects, coin molds, *pintaderas* for stamping designs on cloth or people, and Vinča culture inscribed tablets. In construction clay was used as daub for wooden structures in temperate Europe and made into mud bricks or used as pisé in the southeast. Clay was also used to build kilns and furnaces for firing pottery or smelting metals. Traces on some Mesolithic baskets show that they were lined with unfired clay to render them watertight.

FIGURINES

Many cultures also used clay to manufacture figurines and other models, for a variety of purposes of which ritual is likely to have been the most common. Some figurines were in the shape of animals. The majority, however, were human, ranging from clay rods with a few facial and sexual features to carefully modeled naturalistic figures. These figurines might also bear geometric designs. In some cases whole scenes were modeled in clay: For example, an arrangement of miniature people seated on chairs and tables with pots from Ovcharovo in Bulgaria. Miniature models of houses were common in the tell settlements of the fifth-millennium Balkans. Many of the cenotaphs in the Varna cemetery contained clay masks.

VITREOUS MATERIALS

Glassy materials were produced from a mixture of grains of silica such as sand, or ground quartz, flint or rock crystal, with lime (calcium oxide) and an alkali such as soda or potash; these acted as fluxes. Small amounts of metallic oxides were also often added to give color. Heating the mixture caused the grains to adhere (sinter), producing frit. If the surface melted to produce a glaze, the material is known as faience; this could have a core of frit or of powdered quartz containing little or no flux. It is often difficult to distinguish archaeological finds of frit and faience, since the thin glazed surface of faience objects can easily be weathered away. Frit and faience were being produced in the Near East by the mid-fifth millennium B.C., along with glazed stone beads, and the technology had reached Crete by the third millennium. True glass requires a considerably higher temperature in order to melt the silica-alkali-lime mixture completely. While glass beads were occasionally produced in the third millennium, it was not until around 1600 B.C. that glass was being made regularly in the Near East; both glass vessels and glazed pottery appeared around this time. A vitreous glaze could also be applied to metal, forming enamel; this was developed in the later first millennium.

Faience and glass were made into vessels in the Near East and the Mediterranean, but generally only ornaments, inlays, and small figurines were produced in the rest of Europe, though some small glass vessels were made in the earlier Iron Age. Roman blown and sophisticated molded glass objects were imported as valued luxuries by Iron Age communities, but the technology to produce them was not adopted.

Faience

Blue or turquoise faience beads found in early second-millennium central Europe, Britain, and France, and occasionally elsewhere, were originally thought to have been imported from the eastern Mediterranean. While those found with Mycenaean beads on the Aeolian island of Salina are likely to have been Aegean imports, analyses of other European examples have shown that they were made of local materials, though it is still a matter of dispute whether the technology was derived from the Near East or independently invented in Europe. Britain probably acquired the knowledge of faience manufacture from central Europe through the trading contacts that took Cornish tin into continental Europe.

Faience beads were produced in a number of places, probably in small quantities as required, a necklace at a time, from a paste made with water and ground quartz or a sand-alkali-lime mixture. The alkali used in some Scottish faience beads was found to be derived from seaweed ash, while the composition of some of the English beads resembled that of early glass beads in central Europe, with a high potash content.

Various methods were used to shape the beads, which included spherical and ring beads, stars, quoits and segmented beads, barrel and biconical beads. Often the paste was wrapped round a straw and then cut into beads. Segmented beads in Wessex were often made by rolling a cylinder of paste against a ridged surface, whereas in Scottish examples a sharp tool was used to indent segments on the paste cylinder. The glazed surface was in some cases produced by dipping the paste bead into a semi-liquid glazing mixture (sand-alkali-lime and copper oxide), while in others it was made by mixing the powdered glazing material into the paste, whence it migrated to the surface as the body paste dried.

Glass

Glass was produced by slowly heating a sand-soda-lime mixture until it melted; the temperatures achieved in prehistoric Europe did not eliminate all the gas present, so the glass that formed was opaque. Clear glass requires a higher temperature and slow cooling in an annealing oven.

True glass may have been produced in Bronze Age Europe in the Ore Mountains (Erzgebirge), where the silver ore contained cobalt among its impurities. Experiments have shown that cobalt-blue glass was probably produced as a natural by-product of the smelting of this silver; the glass was unlikely to have been discarded but was probably used like gemstone. Cobalt-blue glass beads have been recovered from the nearby early Únětice cemetery at Nitra in Slovakia, dated around 1800 B.C. Many glass beads are known from Urnfield burials in central Europe, and a few glass beads from other second-millennium European sites, probably of central European manufacture; these were various shades of blue and green, colors derived mainly from cupric oxide combined with firing in oxidizing conditions.

In the Late Bronze Age glass with a high magnesium content was imported from the Mediterranean and used in various parts of Europe to manufacture glass beads. In contrast, glass made in temperate Europe was low in magnesium but high in potassium (from potash). Evidence of its production is known from Frattesina in the Po plain in Italy, while finds of this glass come from a number of sites, including

6.13 Four of the glass gaming counters that were among the grave goods in the late first-century B.C. grave at Welwyn Garden City, Hertfordshire, England (TopFoto.co.uk, © The British Museum/ HIP, Photographer: Unknown)

Hauterive-Champréveyres in Switzerland and Rathgall in Ireland. Most regions, however, did not make glass until the Early Iron Age; the presence of 20,500 glass beads in six graves at Stična in Slovenia gives some idea of the quantities being made by this time.

The Urnfield beads were ring- or torus-shaped, and some were decorated with trails of molten glass in a contrasting color, such as yellow (from antimony) or white (from tin oxide), wound round the bead in a spiral or arranged as "eyes" made of concentric circles of different colored glass, sometimes around a boss. These designs continued into the Iron Age when eye-beads became increasingly popular; many such beads and brooch decorations were made in Aquileia, around the head of the Adriatic. In Hallstatt, Istria, and some other settlements in the sixth or fifth century small bowl-shaped glass vessels with vertical ribs and handles were found; these were probably locally made. Glass was also treated like gemstone and cut or ground to produce cloisonné inlays for many metal objects such as bronze jugs, bracelets, and fibulae. The glass used for this was usually colored sealing-wax red with cuprous oxide and lead fired under reducing conditions; this is thought to have been a Celtic invention around the fifth century B.C. Glass inlays also provided the eyes of statues like the bronze seated figure from Bouray, France, which has one surviving blue and white glass eye. No furnaces for manufacturing raw glass have been discovered, but many oppida and other large settlements contained workshops where raw glass was remelted and made into a range of ornaments, including beads, rings, pendants, the heads of pins, and parts of fibulae; these were generally shades of blue or blue green. Bracelets, which were made from the mid-third century B.C., were a product particular to Celtic Europe. From the second century B.C. massive ring beads and occasionally small figurines were made, and glass was manufactured in a range of colors, including blue, green, turquoise, yellow, white, amber color (from iron oxide), violet or purple (from manganese), and colorless, the latter being technically the hardest to produce since it required the selection of iron-free sand or the addition of manganese dioxide to neutralize the yellowish color imparted by the iron oxide often present in sand.

Enamel Enameling, in which glass was fused to the surface of metal objects, replaced glass inlay in the Late Iron Age. Glass was ground with water to a very fine paste, which was packed tightly into raised (cloisonné) or cut-away (champlevé) cells in the metal object. After drying, the object was heated in a furnace until the glass fused. Finally, the enamel surface was ground and polished. Many Late Iron Age metal objects such as pieces of jewelry, horse harness, and parade armor were decorated with enamel work; although a variety of colors were sometimes used, red was the favorite.

Frattesina (Po valley, Italy) This settlement had an extensive range of industries producing objects of metal, bone, horn, ivory, amber, ostrich eggshell, and glass. While Mycenaean sherds show that the inhabitants of Frattesina were in trading communications with the eastern Mediterranean, the composition of the glass shows that it was locally manufactured. Among the finds here were crucibles containing traces of glass, partly fused glass, lumps of blue and red glass, the raw material from which beads would have been made, along with finished and partially formed beads.

Meare (Somerset, Britain) A workshop for making glass beads was among the industrial remains in the Iron Age wetland village of Meare, probably the site of a seasonal trading fair. Finds here included a mold for making beads (this was originally identified as a broken bead). Among the workshop's products were white beads with yellow spiral decoration, known as "Meare spirals," which were traded into Ireland.

OTHER MATERIALS

Many other materials were exploited particularly for making jewelry or decorating weapons and fine metalwork. These included shell, jet, and amber. Some materials might be made into larger objects, such as lathe-turned shale bowls.

Coal and Shale

Various kinds of coal were prized for making ornaments and other small objects; of these the finest is jet, which takes a high polish and has electrostatic properties that were probably considered magical in antiquity. Lignite (brown coal) and cannel-coal were also used. Shale, an argillaceous rock often found associated with coal, and sapropelite, a related stone, were often used in the same ways as jet and other coals.

SOURCES AND EXTRACTION

Jet was mined from the cliffs of Whitby in England and used from Neolithic times onward for making jewelry. This was widely circulated, but local substitutes were also used; these included lignite, Kimmeridge shale in southern England, and cannel-coal in Scotland and Derbyshire. Shale, which occurs in large blocks, was also made into handled cups in the Early Bronze Age, and in the Iron Age lignite and shale were made into vessels. Kimmeridge shale from the Isle of Purbeck region of the Dorset coast was dug from the cliffs where it outcropped and exported over much of southern England as roughouts or finished bangles. Sapropelite was found in Bohemia, where it was worked in major settlements such as Mšecké Žehrovice and exported as far as Switzerland.

WORKING AND ARTIFACTS

Lignite was made into beads by Mesolithic people at Star Carr in the earlier Mesolithic. In the Chalcolithic and Bronze Age Whitby produced finished objects of jet that were widely circulated, especially spacer-bead necklaces and bracelets, V-perforated buttons, sometimes carved with geometric designs, and other clothing accessories such as belt fasteners, large rings that were perhaps cloak fasteners, and necklaces of beads and spacer beads; some of the beads were covered with sheet gold. Other types of jewelry were made in various places of the local materials, such as necklaces of cannel-coal disc beads in Scotland. Local materials were probably used particularly to replace broken elements in necklaces and bracelets of jet beads, but also for whole imitation necklaces: these might have more strands than the Whitby examples. More unusual objects included a polished mace head inlaid with gold studs, a shale cup, and a later bowl in the shape of a boat found at Caergwrle Castle in Wales, of shale inlaid with gold showing the ribs of the boat, the oars and shields of the rowers, and the waves of the sea. Later Bronze Age jewelry included rings and bracelets of Kimmeridge shale, worked at Eldon's seat and other Dorset coastal sites. Cannel-coal was worked in Derbyshire at Swine Sty.

Jet, shale, and lignite continued in use for ornaments such as rings, bracelets, pendants, and beads in the Iron Age, along with sapropelite, which was widely used in Europe for making bangles. Shale objects also included spindle whorls and decorated discs. In the Late Iron Age shale was worked by turning on a lathe to fashion vessels and bracelets. Sapropelite, in contrast, was carved into bracelets from slabs of the material, cutting out a disc from the center, which was then discarded.

Hengistbury Head (Dorset, England) An extensive settlement occupied from around 800 B.C., its

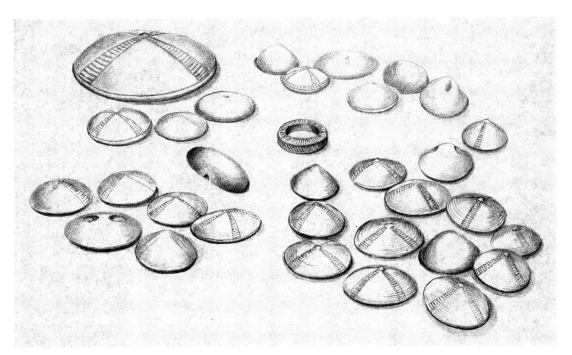

6.14 A collection of conical shale buttons decorated with ladder patterns and a shale belt ring (center) from a later-third-millennium cairn burial from Harehope in southern Scotland (Drawing by Audrey McIntosh, from material in the National Museums of Scotland, Edinburgh)

industrial activity included the working of Kimmeridge shale and possibly salt production. At its peak in the first century B.C.–early first century A.D., it was an important industrial and trading center extracting silver, and producing and exporting lathe-turned shale amulets and bracelets, bronze work, salt, and glass.

Schist

Schist was used in southwest Iberia for making plaques and crosiers during the fourth millennium; they are known particularly from megaliths. The plaques, flat subrectangular sheets of schist, were highly decorated with geometric patterns and were often anthropomorphic in a stylized way, the designs arranged to suggest clothing while two holes at the top formed eyes; it has been suggested they were intended as idols. The crosiers were curved objects decorated with similar geometric designs.

Graphite

Blocks of graphite on early postglacial sites in the Balkans attest to its early use as a decorative material. In the fifth millennium graphite from the Rhodope and Stara Planina Mountains began to be used in this region to decorate the interior and exterior surfaces of pottery, either by painting or by drawing with a lump of graphite. A high temperature, in excess of 1,800 degrees Fahrenheit (1,000 degrees Centigrade), was required to fire graphite-decorated pottery. Graphite was also later used in the manufacture of metal objects as a coating on the inside of molds to prevent the molten metal sticking to them.

Graphite-bearing clays, found, for example, near Třísov in Bohemia, were extracted in several parts of Europe in the Bronze and Iron Ages to make pottery with a fine black appearance. Graphite-tempered wares were manufactured on a large scale in the later centuries B.C. in the eastern part of Celtic Europe and graphite-coated wares in Brittany, where graphitic schists occurred in a number of places; this pottery was effective at spreading heat and was therefore favored for the manufacture of cooking vessels.

Coral

Coral was imported from the Mediterranean in the Iron Age and used particularly for inlayed decoration in metal vessels and jewelry, such as the Basse-Yutz flagon, particularly in the period 600–300 B.C. It was also made into beads and rings, including spacer beads. Unworked pieces of coral were also carried as amulets: Classical sources indicate that coral was supposed to ward off the evil eye.

Amber

Amber is fossilized resin and particularly that of the now-extinct pine, *Pinus succinifera*. It was highly prized for its appearance and for its electrostatic properties, which were probably regarded as magical. Its regular association with other exotic and prestigious materials, such as gold or jet, underlines its value in antiquity.

SOURCES

The shores of the Baltic in Latvia, Lithuania, and Poland, and the North Sea coast of Jutland were the main source of amber in prehistoric Europe, but some amber from this region also washed up on the North Sea coasts of Britain and the continent. Along with furs it was one of the main products of the north, exchanged throughout prehistory and later for goods and materials from farther south.

WORKING AND ARTIFACTS

Amber was widely circulated in the north from the Palaeolithic period onward, when it was used for making beads. Mesolithic amber artifacts included beads and pendants from Denmark and England, a carved elk's head from Denmark, and other figurines. Workshops and hoards of unused amber and amber ornaments are known from Neolithic times onward in Poland. In addition to beads, the TRB inhabitants of Poland made pendants in the form of miniature axes.

By the third millennium amber was being traded over a much wider area, reaching as far afield as Los Millares in Spain, where it was placed in a few elite

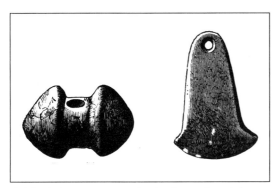

6.15 Amber ornaments in the form of a miniature hammer and a miniature ax, from Late Neolithic Denmark (Worsaae, J. J. A. *The Industrial Arts of Denmark.* London: Chapman and Hall, 1882)

burials in passage graves. Amber was among the materials used for beads by the makers of Beaker pottery. Amber V-perforated buttons and necklaces of amber beads and spacer-plates replaced those of jet as key prestige apparel around 1800 B.C. in Britain with the rise of the Wessex culture; these are known also in Scotland, Brittany, central Europe, southern France, southern Italy, and Greece. In the Mycenaean Shaft Graves in the latter region spacer beads identical to those of southern England were found. Spacer beads were a very distinctive product, used to separate and hold together strings of beads in a necklace. A spacer bead was made by carving a rectangular plaque of amber and cutting perforations through its width; these were often extended at the ends into V-shaped holes joining adjacent perforations. Amber discs and pendants mounted in gold are also known from Wessex burials; a contemporary Breton grave at Saint-Fiacre contained an archer's wrist guard of amber, while an amber cup was found in a grave at Hove in Sussex, England.

Amber beads continued to be made in the later Bronze Age, and in Jutland and England amber was also used for sword-hilt decorations. From the late second millennium until the sixth century B.C. the Italians and especially the Etruscans were major consumers of the supply of amber, and amber was among the materials worked in the settlement of Frattesina in northern Italy. Italy was a major producer of amber

artifacts during the Hallstatt period; these were traded even into the Baltic region. Amber was a frequent material for Iron Age pendants, rings, and beads, but also for inlays on bronze ornaments. A number of Iron Age settlements have evidence of amber working, including large quantities of unworked amber, for example 3,100 pounds (1,400 kilograms) stored in pits in the Polish settlement of Wroclaw-Partynice. Large amber beads were lathe-turned in the later Iron Age.

Upton Lovell   In this richly furnished burial of a Wessex-culture woman, the accompanying grave goods included a gold plaque with geometric decorations, a gold-plated shale cone, gold beads and studs, a grape cup, and a pottery jar. The woman also wore a five-string amber necklace held together by an arrangement of two-, three-, and five-hole spacer beads.

Callaïs

Also known as variscite, callaïs is an attractive green or turquoise-colored stone (hydrated phosphate of aluminum) that takes a high polish; it resembles turquoise but is considerably softer. It was used particularly to make beads and was popular with the people of the Neolithic and Beaker periods in Iberia and Brittany. By the later third millennium, however, it was no longer in use, perhaps suggesting that supplies had run out. A related material, kaolinite (hydrated aluminum silicate), was used in the Balkans to make beads during the Neolithic period.

No source of callaïs has been identified in Brittany, but the nature of the local rock suggests that it may have been located in the Morbihan region, in a part of the coast that is now submerged. In Iberia it was mined at a number of sites, particularly Can Tintorer in northeast Spain, where mineshafts up to 165 feet (50 meters) long have been found.

Many graves of the fourth-millennium Sepulcros de Fosa culture in northern Iberia contain beads made from callaïs. In the late fourth and earlier third millennium callaïs was popular in the Tagus and Alentejo regions of Iberia, and callaïs beads were also found in a tomb at Monte da Mora in northwestern Iberia on the Mino River. Contemporary French chamber tombs also contain necklaces made of callaïs beads and pendants, and large pendant rings.

Decorative Minerals

Many attractive materials, including such gemstones as carnelian, jasper, and chalcedony, metal ores such as malachite, azurite, and haematite, and other minerals such as marble, quartz, and steatite, were used for making beads and other ornaments, particularly in the Mesolithic and Neolithic periods. Nodules or lumps of these materials were treasured as precious objects or ground for use as pigments; red ochre was particularly widely used, and had been included in graves from the later Palaeolithic, presumably with a ritual or apotropaic purpose. These materials might also be used to make other objects, such as marble figurines and bowls in the Balkans and Aegean, the widely exchanged Late Neolithic stone axes made of Alpine jadeite, and the steatite urns at Linga Fold in second-millennium Orkney, made from material imported from Shetland.

Shell

Shells were among the exotic materials that circulated in Europe from Late Glacial times onward, valued for their appearance and ease of use as ornaments. Coastal communities that gathered and ate shellfish also used the shells for ornaments: For example, Mesolithic necklaces including perforated cowrie-shell beads were found on Oronsay in Scotland, while the Early Neolithic inhabitants of Franchthi cave in Greece made substantial numbers of cockleshell beads, chipping out discs from the shells, which they then perforated with drills and ground down into rings. They also used dentalium, a shell popular and abundant in the Aegean and Balkans throughout the Mesolithic and Neolithic periods; one Varna cenotaph contained 2,200 dentalium beads. On inland sites snail shells were used, for instance, in a Mesolithic bead bracelet at Vlasac in the Danube Gorges.

Spondylus shells from the Aegean were among the imported materials used in Mesolithic and Neolithic sites in the Mediterranean basin and the Balkans and as far north as the LBK settlements of central Europe. As well as beads, spondylus was made into buttons, pendants, appliqués, rings, and bracelets. The Neolithic settlement at Dimini in northern Greece may have had several households specializing in the manufacture of spondylus objects.

Ostrich Eggshell

The Millaran inhabitants of southern Spain obtained ostrich eggshells from North Africa for use as prestige goods. Ostrich eggshells continued to circulate as an exotic and valuable material in later times, traded into Europe by the Phoenicians, who obtained them directly from source, or by the Mycenaeans and Greeks, who acquired them through the Mediterranean trading networks. The materials worked in the workshops of the late second-millennium settlement of Frattesina in northern Italy included ostrich eggshell.

Chalk

Chalk, the waste product of flint mining, was carved by miners into cups for use as oil lamps. It was also used in the Neolithic period to make pendants and a number of possibly ritual objects including phalli, figurines, miniature axes, and balls. The most mysterious objects of chalk are the "Folkton drums," three decorated cylinders found in a barrow at Folkton in northern England. In the Iron Age chalk was used for pendants, loomweights and spindle whorls, and figurines.

READING

General

Champion et al. 1984: general; Hodges 1988, 1971: technology; Jochim 2002c, Mithen 1994: Mesolithic; Whittle 1994, 1996, Sherratt 1994a, Milisauskas 2002b, Milisauskas and Kruk 2002a, 2002b: Neolithic; Harding 1994, 2000, 2002, Demakopoulou et al., eds.

1999: Bronze Age; Cunliffe 1994c, 1997, Sievers et al. 1991, Wells 1995a, 1995b, 2002, James 1993, Collis 1984a: Iron Age; Spindler 1995: Iceman; Darvill 1987, Adkins and Adkins 1982: Britain; O'Kelly 1989: Ireland; Cunliffe 2001a: Atlantic; Perles 2001: Neolithic Greece; Bailey 2000: Balkans.

Wood

Piggott 1995, Leakey 1954: general; Midgeley 1992: Christiansholm; Hingley 1998: Ballachulish; Coles 1984: waterlogged finds; Coles 1987, Coles and Coles 1986: Somerset Levels; McGrail 1995, 1998: boats; O'Kelly 1989: Ireland; Manning 1995, Stead 1981: wheels; Jensen 1999a: Danish coffins; Harrison 1988: Spain.

Textiles, Leather, Basketry, Nets, and Mats

Barber 1991: textiles; Forbes 1954a: dyes; Zohary and Hopf 2000: plant fibers and dyes; Harding 2000, Perles 2001, Crowfoot 1954, Grant 1954: basketry and mats; Gilbert 1954: ropes; Wallace and O'Floinn 2002: Twyford; Sheridan 1999: bark coffin cover; Denison 2000a: Palaeolithic.

Leather and Furs

Harding 2000, Waterer 1956, Spindler 1995: general; Ritchie 1995: Orkney; Coles 1973: experiments; Barth 1991: clothing; Leitner 1999, Whittle 1996, Spindler 1995: Iceman; Noe-Nygaard and Richter 2003: Agernaes; O'Kelly 1989: shields.

Bone, Horn, Antler, and Ivory

Wells 2002, Guilaine 1994, Champion, S. 1995: general; Cole 1954: antler and bone; Craddock 1995: bone and antler mining tools; Hodges 1988, Cunliffe 2001a, Wells 2002: ivory; Sheridan 1999: Scotland; Ritchie 1995: Orkney; Scarre 1998: Hochdorf.

Stone

Sherratt 1997, Shepherd 1980, 1994, Bromehead 1954: mining; Shepherd 1980: Spiennes; Bromehead 1954: Obourg; Whittle 1996: Krzemionki Opatowskie; Kaelas 1994a: Thisted; Mercer 1981, Darvill 1996, Topping 2003: Grimes Graves; Darvill 1996: Great Langdale, Mynydd Prescelly; Ritchie 1995: Orkney; Turner 1998: Shetland; Leakey 1954, Oakley 1975, O'Kelly 1989: stone working; Cunliffe 1993: Iron Age.

Salt

De Roche 1997, Adkins and Adkins 1982: evaporating seawater; Barth 1991, Kristiansen 1998, Bromehead 1954, Weller 2002: salt mining; Harding 1978, Cunliffe 1997, Moosleitner 1991: Dürrnberg.

Metallurgy

Craddock 1995, Tylecote 1987: general; Shepherd 1980, Bromehead 1954: mining; Forbes 1954b, Maryon and Plenderleith 1954: metallurgy; Budd 2000, Timberlake 2001, Pare 2000, Sperber 1999, Dayton 1993, Dungworth 1997, Denison 2000b, Ixer and Pattrick 2004: ores; Harrison 1988: tools; Rothenberg and Blanco-Freijero 1981, Harrison 1988: Río Tinto/Chinflon; Darvill 1996, Denison 2001b: Great Orme's Head; Denison 2001a: lead at Cymystwyth; Bailey 2000: Varna; Wallace and O'Floinn 2002: Ireland; Marazov 1998: Thrace; Northover 1995, Manning 1995: Iron Age metallurgy; Biel 1986, Wallace and O'Floinn 2002, Northover 1995, Sheridan 1999: torcs; Taylor 1999: Wessex; Berresford Ellis 1988, Cunliffe 1997, Darvill 1987, Grierson 1956, Adkins and Adkins 1982: coin production.

Ceramics

Gibson and Woods 1997: general; Scott 1954: pottery production, Eilean an Tighe; Childe 1954: potter's wheel; Midgeley 1992: TRB; De Roche 1997,

Gibson 1995: Iron Age; Harrison 1988: Spain; Cunliffe and De Jersey 1997, Gibson 1986, 2002: Britain.

Vitreous Materials

Renfrew and Bahn 2004, Freestone 1997, Harden 1956: technology; Dayton 1993: glass; Maryon 1956: enamelling; Harding 1994, Angelini et al. 2003: Frattesina; Berresford Ellis 1988: Iron Age; Sheridan 1999, 2003, Shortland 2003: faience; Taylour 1983: Mycenaeans.

Other Materials

Wells 2002, Guilaine 1994, Champion, S. 1995: general; Sheridan 1999: Scotland; Darvill 1996, Cunliffe 2001a: Hengistbury; Collis 1984a: sapropelite; Ritchie 1995: Orkney; Beck and Bouzek, eds. 1993, Wallace and O'Floinn 2002: amber; Cunliffe 2001a, Guilaine 1994: callaïs; Turner 1998, Wickham-Jones 2001: steatite; Sheridan 1999, O'Kelly 1989, Wallace and O'Floinn 2002: jet.

7

RELIGION

The religious monuments of prehistoric Europe are the most impressive and enduring remains of their makers. While in many periods and areas the houses of the living are hard to trace, the people's presence is clearly manifest in the stone monuments they created. Many of these were tombs, while others, such as the Maltese temples and the British stone circles, were sacred places. In general, however, the latter are also elusive, since natural features rather than built shrines were often the main focus of European worship. Not all burials were in impressive stone or earthen structures, but many cemeteries have also been uncovered, a major source of information about life in prehistoric Europe. On the other hand, in some areas and periods the rites for disposing of the dead have also left little trace.

The prominence of the monuments contrasts with the paucity of knowledge about the belief systems that they reflect. Conjectures on the basis of the iconography and the practices that can be reconstructed combine with classical references and later Celtic, Germanic, and Nordic beliefs and practices to shed some light on Iron Age religion and inform speculation on that of earlier times, but there is much that can never be known.

Many objects are interpreted, on the basis of their iconography or context and associations, as having ritual or religious significance, and this is true also of many structures and practices that can be reconstructed. The compartmentalization of religion and other aspects of life, however, is a modern construct. In antiquity it is likely that every aspect of life was imbued with some ritual or religious significance, and it is therefore difficult to consider religion separately from the daily lives of prehistoric Europeans.

RELIGIOUS BELIEF AND PRACTICE

Reconstructing Religion

CLASSICAL SOURCES

Classical observers of the religion of barbarian Europe found much to fascinate and repel them, particularly the practice of human sacrifice, though they themselves had only recently abandoned this. While they seized upon certain attributes of Celtic deities by which they might identify them with their own gods, notably Jupiter, Mars, and Mercury, there was superficially little common ground between Roman and Celtic religion, and much of what they wrote is tainted by incomprehension and sensationalism. Nevertheless, it is to Roman authors that we are indebted for much of what is known of Celtic and Germanic religion and particularly for knowledge of Druidism.

LATER RELIGION

The Romans suppressed Druidism, which they regarded as the source of abominable practices but, perhaps more important, also as a focus of political opposition. Under Roman rule, however, many aspects of Celtic religion continued to flourish. In Ireland and other areas outside the empire traditional religious practices and beliefs endured. Knowledge of later religion in Europe, therefore, can shed considerable light on Iron Age beliefs and practices. Religions nevertheless evolve and so later beliefs and practices cannot be assumed to be a faithful reflection of those of the Iron Age.

ARCHAEOLOGY

Many of the religious symbols and artifacts familiar from later religion and classical sources are known from Iron Age art and from the objects themselves, and some of these, such as the wheel of the sun, can be traced back into the Bronze Age. Similarly, many archaeological sites have yielded evidence of practices that are described in classical and later literature, such as human sacrifice and the veneration of watery places; some, like the latter, seem to have been present from Mesolithic times. Where artifacts and sites show continuity back into deeper prehistory in this way, it may be suggested that the beliefs and practices to which they related also originated earlier.

There is much that is known only from archaeology. For example, classical sources refer to sacred groves, lakes, and rivers, but it is archaeology that reveals the similar importance of placing offerings in the ground. For the greater part of prehistory archaeological findings are the only source of information on religion: Little can be deduced about the beliefs held through this long time span, and only certain of the practices can be reconstructed. Even the artifacts and locations pertaining to religion cannot always be identified with certainty, though many, such as stone circles, relate more plausibly to religion than to other aspects of life. Ethnographic observation, however, makes it clear that the attempt to divorce religion from other aspects of daily experience is misguided; in most societies they are inextricably entwined.

Beliefs

What is known of the religion of the Celts, and of their Germanic neighbors, shows that divine power was perceived to lie within the natural world, embodied in locations such as lakes, rivers and springs, hills, woods, and the sky, in animals and birds, in the Sun and the thunder, in creation and destruction within nature. Some man-made objects could also be invested with power, the hammer, for example. Some divinities were benevolent, but in general they were unpredictable and potentially dangerous. It was necessary to make offerings and sacrifices and perform prescribed rituals in order to obtain their goodwill, avert their wrath, and reward their beneficence. Their will could be determined through divination.

Priests

Classical writers provide some information on the priests of Iron Age communities; their observations mainly concerned the Druids, the chief religious authorities and keepers of knowledge, but they also mention several classes of lesser priests. The *Vates, Ouateis,* or *Manteis* were diviners who interpreted natural phenomena and the results of sacrifices; their training lasted 12 years, and they were skilled in poetry. Bards, who trained for seven years, were masters of poetry through which they were believed to be able to bring misfortune, injury, and even death, as well as good fortune. Other kinds of priests, such as *gutuatri* and *antistes*, were mentioned though little was said of their roles. There were also

priestesses, though no female Druids; priestesses shared the Druids' defense of Mona, unnerving the Roman soldiers sent against them.

Little can be said of priests in the prehistoric period, though the evidence of religious practices implies their existence. It is probable that, like the Druids, they conducted sacrifices, studied and interpreted natural phenomena, and might exercise some temporal authority. The occasional discovery of evidence of hallucinogenic substances, such as henbane, and of other substances that induced altered states of consciousness, such as cannabis and alcohol, suggests that these may have been used by priests or shamans in the performance of rites; the geometric patterns of megalithic art are said to match the visions experienced under the influence of hallucinogens. Paraphernalia used by religious practitioners, such as conical headdresses of sheet gold, have sometimes been identified. Some unusual burials may be those of shamans or priests: For example, in the Mesolithic cemetery of Oleneostrovski Mogalnik four individuals were buried in an upright position, accompanied by a considerable quantity of grave goods.

DRUIDS

According to the classical sources, the Druids were the religious leaders of the Celtic tribes of Britain and Gaul, an order that may have originated in Britain. Druidical training took 20 years and involved the oral transmission of knowledge of the heavens, natural phenomena, medicine, law, and other branches of learning; classical authors reported a prohibition on committing any of this information to writing. The Druids conducted sacrifices, interpreted the omens revealed by these and by the heavens, as well as interceding with the gods. The Druids were said to meet annually in the territory of the Carnutes, where they elected a leader. Among their reported rites was the gathering of mistletoe from an oak tree, cut with a golden sickle and collected in a white cloak on the sixth day of the moon, accompanied by the sacrifice of two white bulls.

Druids were probably of elite birth and might be political as well as religious leaders; rival factions in the Aedui, a tribe allied with Caesar, were led by the chief magistrate and a Druid who was his brother. It was more their hostility to the Romans than the stated reason of their abhorrent sacrificial practices that made the Druids the target of Roman campaigns aimed at their eradication. Despite the destruction of their base on Anglesey, the Druids continued to practice within and outside the Roman Empire and were on occasion consulted as soothsayers by the Romans themselves.

Deities

CELTIC DEITIES

Many Celtic deities are named in inscriptions or in classical writings. Often, on the basis of some of their attributes, these were identified with Roman gods and goddesses, and the worship of the two might be combined in a Roman shrine. Celtic deities continued to be venerated in Roman times in Celtic regions, and some became popular farther afield: For example, altars to Epona are known in North Africa.

Those deities that are known about in any detail were generally associated with particular features of the natural world, such as lakes or rocks, with such phenomena as thunder, and with animals; they were also often linked to aspects of the human world, such as warfare. Frequently, they were credited with the power to change shape, assuming animal forms particularly. They were often worshipped as the numen (divine essence or spirit) of a natural phenomenon and represented by symbols, such as the wheel of the sun; it was not until the period when the Celts were in regular contact with the classical world that the deities began to be personified. Earlier the Celtic leader Brennus is said to have viewed with contempt the stone and wooden Greek gods in human form set up by the Greeks in the temples at Delphi that were attacked by the Celtic army in 279 B.C.

The Celts did not have a universally accepted pantheon. Some known deities were local to a particular location or tribe, while others were more widely worshipped; across Europe, however, among Celtic, Germanic, and neighboring communities similar deities were worshipped who were associated with natural phenomena and could be readily equated with one another. For example, the famous Gundestrup cauldron, found in Denmark north of the Celtic realms and probably made in Thrace to the east, is decorated with symbols, deities, and ritual scenes that are at home within the Celtic tradition, but which also have links as far afield as India. (Although it was not made by the Celts, it is the most frequently reproduced exemplar of Celtic religious iconography.)

Some deities appeared in pairs; more common, however, were the gods thought of as triads since three was a sacred number. These might be a single deity with three heads, such as Cernunnos, or a set of three deities making up three aspects of a single power, such as the triple mother goddesses.

Camulos   A war god known from a number of locations in Britain and Gaul and equated by the Romans with Mars. Camulodunon, the Fort of Camulos, the Catuvellaunian capital, took its name from a shrine to Camulos at the heart of the oppidum.

Cernunnos   God of fertility and living things, whose name meant "horned one." He is generally depicted with antlers and wearing a torc around his neck and his horns, and sometimes also has three heads. He is shown, for example, in Val Camonica and on the Gundestrup cauldron seated cross-legged surrounded by animals such as a stag, a symbol of fertility, and a snake with ram's horns, a symbol of regeneration. He also often holds a cornucopia or bowl overflowing with grain.

Coventina   A goddess of water and healing, particularly associated with Britain but known also from Gaul and northwest Iberia. A spring and associated shrine dedicated to Coventina was located on Hadrian's Wall in northern England, where it received many offerings from Roman soldiers of Celtic or Germanic extraction.

Epona   Goddess of fertility, generally depicted with horses, particularly mares and foals, or as a horsewoman; her name comes from the Celtic word for horse. She was worshipped widely, from Britain to the Balkans, but particularly in the Rhineland and Gaul, where the Aedui and Lingones were famous horse breeders, and was adopted by the Romans, who incorporated a festival to her in their sacred calendar. Epona seems to have been associated with healing and with death as well as fertility: the passage into, through, and out of life.

Esus A title meaning Good Master, applied to a deity associated with woods. He was mentioned by the Roman author Lucan as one of the gods encountered by Caesar in Gaul, whose cult involved human sacrifice. Victims were apparently suspended from trees and wounded, the pattern of their blood flow being used in divination.

Hammer God A popular nature deity in Gaul, sometimes named as Sucellus. He was generally depicted in Roman times holding a hammer and a pot; he was also associated with wine, represented by a barrel, and sometimes with the Sun. The hammer god's associations seem to have been with natural bounty and regeneration, as were those of his consort.

Hunter God A frequently represented deity was related to both the pursuit and the protection of wild animals and was particularly associated with the hunting dog and with the hunted stag and boar. As well as reflecting the close relationship between the Celts and the natural world, the hunter god and the divine hunt may have been connected to the passage between life, death, and rebirth.

Lug (Lugh) A god of light (Irish *lugh:* "shining light") and perhaps of the Sun, whose symbols included the raven, Lug was widely worshipped in western Europe. He was identified with Mercury by the Romans.

Mother Goddess A mother goddess figure was widespread in the Celtic world and beyond, and may have been present in European religions from Neolithic times. A goddess concerned with human procreation and fertility is common to many religions, but whether it is legitimate to identify female figurines from prehistory as mother goddesses is debatable. The Celtic mother goddess was depicted holding a baby or with symbols of fertility such as bread and fruit. She was often represented as a triad, either of three young goddesses or of two matrons

and a younger woman. In inscriptions of the Roman period they were often referred to as *Deae Matres* or *Matronae.*

Nantosuelta A goddess known in Gaul and Britain whose symbols of a dish or pot and a house on a pole suggest a concern with domestic life and well-being. She was also associated with the raven, a creature linked with the battlefield and symbolizing war, and was the protector of souls in the Otherworld. She was the consort of the hammer god Sucellus.

Nehalennia A goddess associated with the North Sea and venerated in two shrines on the Dutch coast, Domburg and Colijnsplaat. Her name may mean "Steerswoman," and she was worshipped by seafarers, including traders and sea captains who dedicated altars to her in the Roman period. These often depict the goddess with part of a ship or other sea motifs, and usually with a dog.

Nerthus A Germanic earth goddess who rode around in a wagon, probably bringing fertility to the land. She may be the goddess represented on a seventh-century bronze model cart from Strettweg in Austria; here a goddess holds a bowl above her head while around her are smaller figures of armed men, with a stag with huge antlers at each end.

Sequana A goddess of healing and the numen of the Seine River. A shrine to Sequana at the source of the river contained a statue of the goddess and numerous votive models of body parts and wood and stone images of pilgrims, generally depicted as peasants wearing the characteristic Celtic hooded cloak.

Sky God Equated with the Roman sky god Jupiter in later times, the Celtic sky god was symbolically represented by the wheel of the sun and the thunderbolt or as a figure holding these. He was also shown as a horseman using a thunderbolt to fight a serpentine monster, which represented evil. He was master of all the celestial elements and their effects, including the Sun, rain, thunder, storms, lightning, drought, and floods; he also represented day, life and light, battling with the evils of night, death, and darkness.

Sucellus A name given to the hammer god, meaning the "good striker." He seems to have been associated with fertility, and the purpose of his hammer may have been to ward off disease or famine. In many cases he was shown as half of a divine couple with Nantosuelta.

Sulis An important British goddess of water and healing, known also in continental Europe. She was associated particularly with the mineral springs at Bath, which became a major spa in Roman times but which must have been a place of pilgrimage in Celtic times also. Sulis also had a connection with the Sun. The Romans identified Sulis with Minerva, a goddess who also included healing among her attributes; votive body parts were among the offerings thrown into the waters of the springs in Roman times, in gratitude for successful cures.

Sun God The Sun was worshipped as a life-giving deity, symbolically represented by a sun disc or wheel. A Bronze Age model chariot in gilded bronze bearing a sun disc from Trundholm in Denmark shows that the cult went back at least to the 13th century B.C., and the sun disc or wheel was frequently depicted in Scandinavian rock art. The sun god was also associated with fertility and healing. Another sun symbol was the swastika, widely used as a symbol of good fortune.

Taranis The Thunderer, the numen of thunder, whose cult was said by the writer Lucan to have been exceptionally cruel, involving human sacrifice by burning. Taranis was widely worshipped but was not a major deity. His cult may have been linked to war. The Romans equated him with Jupiter, who was also linked with thunder.

Teutates (Toutatis) Teutates seems to have been a title given to the deity who protected a tribe and was probably given to different gods in different regions. The Teutates encountered by Caesar in Gaul seems to have been a god of war and was later identified with the Roman god Mars. He was described by Lucan as a god to whom people were sacrificed by drowning; a figure on the Gundestrup cauldron may show this god drowning a victim in a bucket.

7.1 A bronze figurine of a deity wearing a horned helmet and a torc, from Grevensvaenge, Zealand, Denmark. The right arm, now missing, held an ax or hammer, suggesting that the figure represented the god of thunder. (Worsaae, J. J. A. The Industrial Arts of Denmark. London: Chapman and Hall, 1882)

War God Figures of warriors, sometimes nude but always bearing weapons, were widespread both in Celtic Europe and in earlier times. Given the importance of warfare in Bronze and Iron Age Europe, it is assumed that at least some of these figures represented war deities, probably protectors of their individual tribes. Some of these figures were shown riding a horse, the perquisite of the elite, and carrying a severed head, the symbol par excellence of the successful warrior.

Cult Objects and Iconography

A variety of cult objects and sacred symbols are known from Celtic contexts, and some of these are attested to in earlier times: mainly from the Bronze Age but occasionally as far back as the Mesolithic. These included animals and birds, trees and other natural phenomena, as well as manufactured objects such as wheels and axes. In some cases their significance is known from classical and later writings; in others it is more speculatively derived from the contexts in which they are known.

Some of these objects and symbols are shown in art as the attributes of various deities, but in many cases they were also used in other ways: in the performance of rituals, as votive offerings, as ritually significant elements in funerary contexts, and as items of ritual dress.

SYMBOLS AND CULT OBJECTS

Musical Instruments The carnyx, a trumpet blown on the battlefield to instill fear in the hearts of the enemy, was a long pipe with a trumpet end in the form of a boar's head, a powerful symbol of ferocity. Warriors blowing carnyxes are depicted among the ritual scenes on the Gundestrup cauldron, and a fine example is known from Deskford in Scotland. The lur, an enormous horn in the form of a curved pipe with a disc-shaped end, was probably used in religious ceremonies; figures blowing lurer appear regularly in Bronze Age Scandinavian rock art and in votive deposits in bogs. Other instruments possibly used in religious rites included rattles.

Cauldron Sheet bronze cauldrons were manufactured from the Bronze Age onward as vessels for preparing and serving food and drink at feasts. By the Urnfield period they were also used as receptacles for cremations and votive deposits. They appear in art and sculpture as cult vessels. In later mythology they were associated with the Otherworld, feasting, abundance, and regeneration: For example, in Welsh literature dead warriors were reborn from a magical cauldron.

Gundestrup Cauldron Discovered in a Danish bog at Gundestrup, this magnificent silver-gilt cauldron was probably made in Thrace. Among the cult scenes shown on its decorated panels were a procession of warriors, some blowing boar's-headed carnyxes; a deity (possibly Teutates) apparently pushing a man headfirst into a bucket or pit; a horned deity surrounded by animals, probably Cernunnos; and a deity with a wheel, probably the sky god.

Wheel and Circle By the mid-second millennium, the spoked wheel was a common iconographic element, probably representing the Sun. Examples of wooden wheels and model wheels in bronze are known from votive deposits in bogs, rivers, shrines, and other ritual contexts, and from burials. Miniature wheels were worn as amulets. Circles or solid discs also represented the Sun.

Nebra Sky-Disc (Germany) A hoard deposited around 1600 B.C. within a hilltop enclosure at Nebra near Mittelberg in central Germany allegedly included not only two swords, two axes, a chisel, and arm rings but also an extraordinary bronze disc, 1 foot (30 centimeters) wide, inlaid with gold in the shape of the Sun, the crescent Moon, and 32 dots presumably representing stars, some of which have been tentatively identified as the Pleiades. Two strips of gold lie along either side of the disc, and a thin gold crescent along the bottom resembles the boats shown in Bronze Age rock art, with notches suggesting oars. A series of holes around its rim suggest that the disc was originally nailed up somewhere, perhaps in a shrine. Not all scholars accept the authenticity of the disc: The hoard was found by illegal metal detectorists who attempted (unsuccessfully) to sell it on the black market. Nevertheless,

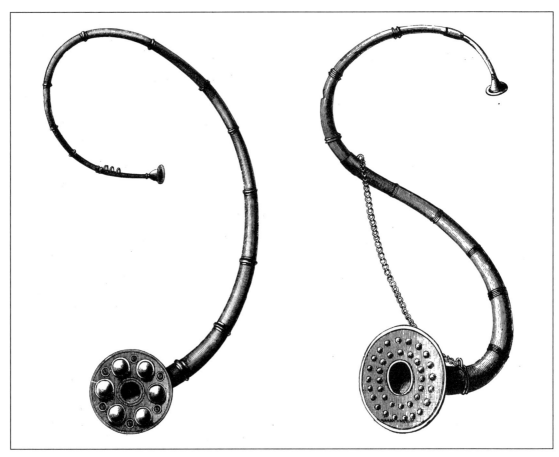

7.2 *Two of the huge horns known as lurer, which are believed to have been used in religious ceremonies* (Worsaae, J. J. A. *The Industrial Arts of Denmark*. London: Chapman and Hall, 1882)

chemical tests on its degree of corrosion do support the date suggested by the other artifacts in the hoard, and other analyses have shown that the disc was made of copper from Mitterberg and Carpathian gold, both consistent with the metal in circulation at that date.

Neck and Chest Ornaments Beautifully decorated lunulae, sheet-gold flat oval pectoral ornaments, were among the finest products of Bronze Age craftsmanship. They are known mainly from votive hoards in the ground or in water, in Ireland, Iberia, and Brittany. Other types of gold pectorals

and collars were made in other parts of Atlantic Europe such as Iberia. They may have been worn, but it is likely that they were also used to decorate the images of gods, which were probably made mainly from wood.

In the Iron Age the torc (neck ring) was similarly used as a symbol of elite, royal, or divine status. Torcs of bronze and gold were major vehicles of Bronze and Iron Age decorative craftsmanship. Many are known from elite burials, including that of the Vix "princess" and from votive contexts. Representations of both warriors and gods frequently show them with a torc around the neck, and some deities also wear them in other places, such as on Cernunnos's horns, or hold one in their hand. Some known examples were too heavy for wear and were probably regalia, to be borne for a limited time on ceremonial occasions.

Ax A symbol that is known from the Neolithic period when fine polished stone axes were deposited as ritual hoards. Axes were prominent symbols in the art engraved on megalithic monuments, including Stonehenge. Model axes of pottery or bronze were among the grave goods in Urnfields and later burials and were common as votive offerings. They were probably also worn as good luck charms.

Mask Hollow metal masks known from a few Celtic ritual sites were perhaps worn by priests performing certain ceremonies or fastened to cult statues. The use of masks goes back to the Mesolithic period, when deer antlers still attached to part of the skull were worn by the people of eighth-millennium Star Carr and other Mesolithic sites, perhaps for use in ritual dances.

Clay masks deposited in some cenotaphs in the Varna cemetery in Bulgaria may have served a different purpose, perhaps symbolizing a person whose body could not be placed in a grave.

Cones Four tall cones of sheet gold have been found on Bronze Age sites in Germany (Etzelsdorf, Schifferstadt) and France (Avanton). They were decorated with bands of repoussé designs, particularly circles, but also stars, eyes, triangles, and wheels. Residues inside the Schifferstadt example indicate that aromatic resins were placed inside, and the design and the presence of a brim in some examples suggest that they were worn as hats, with some form of padding, by individuals who stood in an elevated position (where the designs inside the brim would be visible). Some individuals depicted in rock art appear to be wearing headdresses of this type.

Other Symbols Other motifs and symbols that also frequently appeared on Celtic and earlier objects included an equal-armed cross, often associated with the wheel; the swastika, symbolic of good luck over an area extending as far as India and associated with the Sun in Celtic contexts; double spi-

rals, often called S-symbols, associated particularly with the Sky god and perhaps representing his thunderbolt; and the rosette, a symbol of death and the otherworld, also associated with the Sun god.

RITUAL VEHICLES

A number of bronze models of vehicles with religious scenes or symbols are known. Most appeared on carts or chariots: For example, the Trundholm sun cart, the Late Bronze Age cart from Orastie in Romania bearing a cauldron and a number of birds, and the seventh-century Strettweg cart, which bears a hunt scene and a goddess possibly to be identified as Nerthus, whose cult involved being drawn in procession in a wagon. There were also a few on boats, notably the boat from Roos Carr in England, a wooden model on which stood five large warrior figures, presumably gods. Model boats without passengers are also known from votive deposits such as those at Broighter in Ireland, which yielded an exquisite detailed model in sheet gold, and at Nors

7.3 Two pieces from a cauldron found in a bog at Rynkeby in Fünen, Denmark. Like the more famous Gundestrup cauldron, this bears religious symbols, including here a god wearing a torc, bulls, a wild boar, a wolf, and a triskele. (Worsaae, J. J. A. The Industrial Arts of Denmark. London: Chapman and Hall, 1882)

Thy in Denmark, where 100 tiny vessels of leaf gold were found.

Boats and chariots also figured prominently in rock art, which is thought to have had a ritual context. European mythology links the boat as a symbol with the Sun's movements during the night.

Trundholm Sun Cart (Zealand, Denmark) A bronze model cart drawn by a single horse dated around 1400–1300 B.C. It bears a disc decorated with concentric circles of geometric patterns, including many circles. The disc is gilded on one side, thought to represent the Sun by day, while the other side is ungilded bronze, interpreted as the Sun by night.

BIRDS AND ANIMALS

Celtic and later deities were often attributed the power of shape-shifting, generally assuming an animal form. A number of deities also had animal features, such as hooves, goats' and rams' horns, or antlers; a number of images of horned deities seem to have been associated with war. Animals associated with the gods might also have elements of other animals, as, for example, with the ram-headed snake of Cernunnos. Animals themselves played an important role in Celtic mythology and religious practice. Birds were important in Celtic and earlier iconography, representing the liberated souls of the dead, and other supernatural roles. Some creatures were considered taboo by the Celts: For example, Caesar reported that certain British tribes would not eat geese, hares, or chickens.

Ducks Figures of ducks and duck motifs in art are common from the Bronze Age, for example, as plastic decoration on cauldrons, jugs, and flesh hooks and alternating with wheels or discs in the hammered decoration on sheet metalwork. The association of ducks and other waterbirds with both the air and the water, two sacred realms, gave it particular significance. The statue of the water goddess Sequana at Sources-de-la-Seine shows her in a duck-shaped boat.

Eagle The religious association of eagles dates back into Neolithic times, when eight sea-eagles were placed in a megalithic tomb at Isbister in Orkney. Later, the eagle was an attribute of the Sky god, although this may be a late borrowing from classical mythology in which the eagle is associated with Jupiter.

Ravens and Crows Celtic deities, including Lug and Nantosuelta, were frequently depicted with crows and ravens, which were sometimes regarded as prophetic birds. Their presence on the battlefield gave them an association with war and death and hence with the Otherworld.

Swan In a Mesolithic burial at Vedbaek a stillborn baby was laid on a swan's wing in the grave beside his mother. Swans were frequently represented on Bronze Age and Hallstatt bronzes, and they often appeared in later mythology as people who had been enchanted to change shape.

Cattle The formidable native European wild cattle (aurochs, *Bos primigenius*) must always have been regarded as the epitome of ferocity and strength and the bulls of virility, qualities they symbolized in Celtic religion, where they were associated with Cernunnos. Representations of bulls on vessels such as the Gundestrup cauldron and as figurines are well known in the Iron Age, and cattle are well represented among sacrificial victims in Celtic shrines. That at Gournay-sur-Aronde contained the burials of old cattle that may have died naturally. Cattle and particularly bulls were part of ritual practices from the Neolithic onward; shrines associated with cattle are known in the seventh millennium B.C. at Çatal Hüyük in Anatolia and in the Bronze Age Aegean, and some cattle were buried by the TRB culture.

Horse From the time of their introduction horses were generally associated with the elite and particularly with warriors. As well as the prestige attached to them horses were seen as embodying virility, masculinity, fertility, speed, beauty, and aggression. Horses therefore played an important role in religion, with particular rites associated with them. Some gods and goddesses were regularly shown with horses or as horse riders, notably Epona, the Sky god, and war deities. Horses were important sacrificial victims within some sacred places, for example, at Gournay-sur-Aronde. In a number of Iron Age hillforts horse skulls or jawbones were placed in storage pits. Horses were often used as a symbol on Celtic coinage. The magnificent hill figure at Uffington in England depicts a horse.

Dog   Many Celtic deities were accompanied by a dog; gods associated with hunting had dogs to aid them in the chase, but dogs also seem to have been associated with healing, as, for example, in the shrine of Nodens at Lydney in Britain in the Romano-British period and in the shrine of Sequana. Dogs were also commonly buried in ritual pits and shrines.

Snake   Snakes were represented with a number of Celtic deities and seem to have symbolized regeneration, fertility, and healing. Cernunnos was often accompanied by a snake with rams' horns.

Stag   Deer and particularly stags may have had some ritual significance as early as Mesolithic times. Bronze Age rock art frequently shows stags, and they are also common in Iron Age art, such as the stags with enormous antlers on the bronze cart model from Strettweg. They probably symbolized fertility, while antlers were a symbol of regeneration.

Boar   The ferocious and dangerous wild boar was a frequent symbol in Celtic art, associated particularly with war; the trumpet end of carnyxes (war trumpets) were usually in the form of a boar's head, and Tacitus commented that boar-shaped amulets were worn by Germanic warriors. Classical and vernacular literature refers to wild boar as the food regularly served at feasts in the world of the dead, and many pig bones have been found in Iron Age shrines and ritual pits.

Other Creatures   Many other animals were also associated with Celtic deities or venerated in local cults. These included bears, rams, and dolphins, cocks, cranes, doves, and geese. A dolphin is shown on the Gundestrup cauldron, and they were associated with several water deities. The bones of hares, lambs, pigs, and birds, as well as those of cattle, deer, and dogs, were deposited in ritual pits and within sacred enclosures. Geese were placed as grave goods in a number of Iron Age burials, and a large sculpture of one was placed on the lintel of the skull por-

tico at Roquepertuse in France. Artistic representations of rams as decoration on objects such as drinking horns and flagons may have had some ritual significance.

Monster   As well as real animals, fantastical and hybrid beasts feature in Celtic iconography. These are generally predators and are often shown devouring people or holding human heads. The *Tarasque* of Noves (Provence, France), a third-century stone statue of one such monster, resembles a lion or wolf and has an arm in his jaws and his clawed forepaws upon two severed heads. The Linsdorf monster, from Alsace in France, is similar.

VEGETATION

Plant motifs were common in Celtic art, including sacred objects such as pillars.

Trees   Classical references to the Druids and to Celtic religion emphasize the importance of trees, particularly the oak tree, though others, including yew, ash, hazel, beech, and elm, were also venerated in various places. A model tree from Manching with ivy leaves and fruit made out of wood, sheet bronze, and gold is presumed to have had a ritual purpose. Groves in the forest were among the sacred places of the Celts, where Druids met and sacrificial victims were hanged in trees. The Galatians, Celtic settlers in Anatolia, had a sacred oak grove known as Drunemeton.

The use of trees as sacred objects and for creating places of worship probably dates back to the Mesolithic period, when a series of four massive tree trunks were erected at Stonehenge, and it is underscored by the Neolithic monument known as Seahenge, an enormous tree erected upside down within a ring of posts. Tree trunks were also erected in some Iron Age sacred sites.

Mistletoe   According to Pliny, the Druids cut mistletoe from a sacred oak tree, using a golden sickle. Mistletoe was thought to give fertility, and a drink prepared from mistletoe was given to animals to treat barrenness. Pollen from mistletoe was present in the last meal consumed by the man sacrificed at Lindow Moss.

SEVERED HEADS AND SKULLS

Common among the images of Celtic art is the severed head. These were often represented on carved pillars, and skulls have been found in many shrines. Classical literature describes the Celtic practice of decapitating fallen enemies and nailing up the heads on their houses as trophies, with particularly prestigious heads being embalmed in oil. Severed heads were also impaled on the poles at the gateways of hillforts and oppida in Britain and Spain. The entrance to the shrines at Roquepertuse and Entremont in France had niches holding skulls, and classical sources record the offering of enemy heads in Celtic shrines. A carving at Entremont shows a mounted warrior with a trophy head hanging from his horse's neck, another practice described by classical authors. One broken sculpture at Entremont seems originally to have depicted a seated warrior or deity holding a heap of six severed heads. As the seat of the soul the heads of enemies may have been regarded as a means of controlling their spirits. The cult probably had very ancient roots: A nest of skulls dating to the seventh millennium B.C. was found in a rock shelter at Ofnet (Germany); at the opposite end of Europe collections of skulls were found in some cemeteries of the fifth-millennium Dnepr-Donets culture in the Ukraine; and skulls were often placed in the ditches of Neolithic causewayed enclosures.

MEGALITHIC ART AND SYMBOLS

A number of fifth-millennium Breton standing stones, often broken up and reused in later megalithic tombs, were decorated with symbols, such as plows, axes, and cattle. The crook, a line bent into a tight L-shape, was very common. Some passage graves in Brittany and developed passage graves in Britain were decorated with motifs on the stones of their passage, chamber, or facade or on associated objects, including recumbent or free-standing stones. Many of these designs were geometric, particularly spirals, concentric arcs, zigzags, boxed rectangles, cup marks, and lozenges. There were also daggers and axes. The crook motif was echoed in fourth-millennium southwest Iberia in the schist crosiers, L-shaped objects that were covered with zigzag geometric decorations mirroring those on the associated schist plaques. These bore zones of geometric patterns, but two holes near the top and the layout of the design gave them an anthropomorphic appearance; some also had breasts.

ROCK ART

Engravings and paintings on rocks, in caves and rock shelters, and in open-air sites are known from many parts of Europe from Palaeolithic times onward. Mesolithic rock art comes particularly from the Spanish Levante and Galicia, the Alps, Norway, and Sweden, areas where later rock art is also abundant, but rock art is also known in other regions such as Bulgaria and Britain. In many cases the engravings are geometric symbols such as cup marks, but in some places, notably Val Camonica in Italy and Bohuslän in Sweden, the engravings include numerous depictions of people, animals, and artifacts. Ships also feature in Scandinavian rock art. Much of the art is located in situations far from human habitation, and it has been suggested that these were places of sanctity and pilgrimage; some art was closely associated with settlements, such as cup marks in Scandinavia. Although the rock images probably had many purposes and meanings, it is likely that religion and ritual were among them.

Figurines and Statues

Figurines were made in stone, pottery, metal, and wood, though few of the latter have survived, and there were also larger figures in stone and wood. Although some represented animals, most were in the form of humans who were often schematically depicted. The making of images in human form goes back to the Upper Palaeolithic period, when the famous Venus figurines and other human and part-human figures were made of ivory, wood, stone, and fired earth. The contexts in which later figurines and statues have been found, including watery places and shrines, burials and megaliths, suggest that they generally had a ritual significance.

POTTERY FIGURINES

Many human figurines and model cattle, sheep and goats, houses, tools, and furniture were made in

Greece and the Balkans in the Neolithic period. Many of the figurines were female and very schematic, with faces, exaggerated hips and buttocks, and sometimes small arms and breasts; some scholars interpret these as evidence of a Mother Goddess cult. These figurines were frequently placed together in buildings that were probably shrines. For example, a large building at Nea Nikomedeia contained several pottery sheep and goat figurines, and three stone carvings of frogs, and a number of pottery figurines of stylized women. Some figurines were worn as pendants. Others were found in ordinary houses and may have been used in domestic rituals. Some hollow figurines of the Tripolye culture were filled with grain, suggesting their use in rituals relating to agricultural productivity. Later Neolithic cultures in Southeast Europe also made pottery vessels with human faces, and others are known from Iron Age eastern Europe. Pots in the form of ovens, wagons, and other objects were also made, though in the Balkans figurines ceased after around 4000 B.C., reappearing around the 14th century B.C.

WOODEN FIGURES

Wooden statues of deities were probably common in Celtic shrines, though they survive only in water-logged contexts. One from Broddenbjerg in Jutland was a naturally forked piece of wood, slightly modified to create a figure with two legs tapering up to a head carved with a face, and an enormous phallus. Such figures were also erected beside trackways; a number of figures with a head and a schematic body were found beside the turf and wood path at Ipfweger Moor in Germany. Some were also known from earlier times.

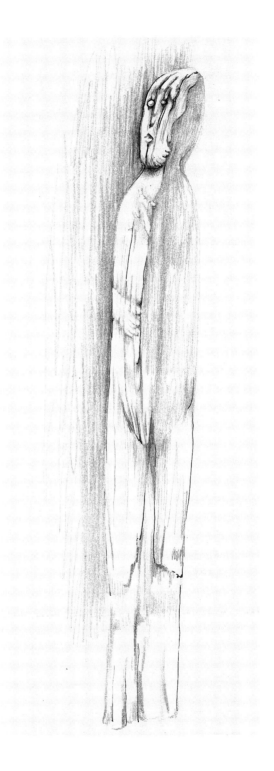

7.4 The near-lifesize figure of a goddess, made of oak with eyes of quartz, found in the 19th century under layers of peat at Ballachulish Moss in Scotland and now badly distorted by drying out. Made around 600 B.C., the figure originally stood in a wicker structure, probably a small shrine, which was deliberately dismantled and buried with the figure beneath it. (Drawing by Audrey McIntosh, from material in the National Museums of Scotland, Edinburgh)

In the Iron Age figures the emphasis was on the head, usually shown with eyes and nose and often with a mouth. Some figures had legs or sexual features and sometimes arms. Others, however, such as the figures from the Late Iron Age shrine at Sources-de-la-Seine, were shown with clothing. Around 200 figures of oak wood were found here, generally depicting people clad in thick hooded cloaks.

BRONZES

A number of bronze figurines of animals from ritual contexts included a Hallstatt-period bull from the cave of Byci Skála in Moravia made of bronze with inlays of iron on its shoulders and forehead and inlaid eyes, now missing but probably originally of glass. Later figures of boars are known from sites across Europe; these were usually shown with a raised crest along their backs. Small examples may have been worn on helmets, but at least one, from Neuvy-en-Sullias in France, was nearly life size. Other Celtic bronze figures included birds, stags, and bulls. Bronze was also used in the second and first millennia to model scenes such as the cult vehicle from Strettweg, which included human and animal figures. The people of Bronze Age Sardinia made distinctive human figures of bronze, some in the form of warriors armed with bows, swords, daggers, and shields, and wearing tunics, bossed belts, and helmets; these were often placed as votive offerings in sanctuaries and sacred springs.

STONE FIGURES

Divine Images?   Stone figures that may represent gods are known in the Mesolithic period, when river boulders were set up in the houses at Lepenski Vir in Serbia. These were carved with goggle eyes, drooping fishy mouths, and patterns like scales, and it is thought that they represented fishy deities.

Human Figures   Many stone figures were found in the Maltese temples and hypogea, including vast obese figures with enormous legs and tiny feet who are generally referred to as goddesses, although in many cases their gender is unclear. Figurines of white marble were produced in the Cyclades in the Early Bronze Age. Elsewhere standing stones and stelae were carved with human features, often extremely schematic or stylized, by many Neolithic and later communities; some were probably divine figures, while others may have been gravestones.

Stone statues were more widespread in the Iron Age. A broken head with a torc around its neck found in the ritual enclosure at Mšecké Žehrovice in the Czech Republic may have come from the statue of a god. A complete naked male figure carved of sandstone, wearing a conical cap, a torc, and a belt with a dagger, and with his arms across his chest, was associated with the sixth-century princely barrow burial at Hirschlanden in Germany. It was four feet, 11 inches (1.5 meters) high and had originally stood on the summit of the barrow. In northwest Iberia life-size statues of warriors (*guerreros galaicos*) were erected at the entrance to *castros* (fortified villages); they were clad in shirts and kilts and carried a circular shield and a dagger.

Landscape Statues   During the Iron Age in parts of western Iberia *verracos*, granite models of bulls and boars, creatures with great religious significance for the Celts, were erected as markers of pastureland, while in the northwest statues of animal heads were similarly placed.

HILL FIGURES

A number of hillsides in England were carved with figures that must have had some ritual significance, though they were probably also territorial markers. These were made by cutting away the turf to expose the chalk beneath, or by digging trenches that were then filled with chalk, creating a figure whose contrasting white color stood out well from the green of the surrounding grass or soil. Although these figures have been constantly renewed down the ages, stylistic features indicate that some were created in the Iron Age.

Uffington White Horse   (Oxfordshire, England) The powerful figure of a horse shown in motion, depicted in a series of elegant curving lines. It measures 360 feet (111 meters) from head to tail. Investigations of this figure using a recently developed technique, optical simulated luminescence dating (OSL), have demonstrated that the figure was created sometime between 1400 and 600 B.C.

Shrines and Sacred Places

In Southeast Europe from the Neolithic period onward, villages often included a building that was probably a shrine, and houses may also have contained domestic shrines. Sacred buildings also appeared in other parts of Europe at various times, but in general the ritual emphasis was on natural features, such as trees, rivers, and caves, or on areas of the landscape enclosed or defined by man-made features, ranging from small ditched enclosures to the famous circular structure at Stonehenge. Landscape features were also venerated in parts of Southeast Europe, such as the peak sanctuaries and sacred caves of the Minoans. Watery places such as bogs, lakes, and rivers attracted many offerings from Mesolithic times onward, some of them very lavish. Many other votive deposits were placed in pits in the ground, probably reflecting the worship of chthonic deities. It has been suggested that souterrains, underground tunnels and chambers used in Iron Age Brittany and western Britain for storage, may also have had a religious dimension: the entrusting of stored food to the realm of the earth deities for safekeeping and particularly the placing of the seed corn here in order to ensure its fertility by divine intervention.

Sacred Places

CLASSICAL EVIDENCE

A number of classical authors describe the veneration of natural places throughout barbarian Europe, from Iberia to the Galatian realm in Anatolia. These included capes and promontories, lakes, rivers, and islands, all locations for which there is also archaeological evidence of veneration. Of particular interest are these writers' horrified descriptions of sacred groves: ghastly places where the trees dripped with blood and even the Druids were afraid to visit after dark. Hanging from many of the trees were human victims subjected to ritual wounding for the purpose of divination.

The classical world itself, though generally worshipping in built shrines, also had sacred places in natural locations, such as the cave on Crete where Zeus was born, Mount Olympus, home of the Greek gods, and Lake Avernus in Italy, reputedly the entrance to the Underworld. After the Roman conquest many native sacred places continued to be venerated, and in some cases Roman shrines were built there. Inscribed offerings from the Roman period, such as altars, provide information about the names of deities associated with these locations and their significance. From this it is known, for example, that many rivers were regarded as female deities: These included the Marne (the goddess Matrona meaning Mother), the Severn (the goddess Sabrina), and the Seine (the goddess Sequana).

Sources-de-la-Seine (Burgundy, France) The Fontes Sequanae at the source of the river Seine was a Celtic sacred place dating back to the first century B.C. where many pilgrims, male and female, offered votive wooden figures of themselves. In the Roman period two temples and a colonnaded precinct were added, along with a bronze statue of the goddess Sequana, the spirit of the river, and votive figures of stone, shown carrying gifts of fruit or animals, were offered to the deity. Other offerings in the shrine included a pot filled with models of human body parts in silver and bronze, reflecting Sequana's role in healing, and numerous others in oak were thrown into the spring pool here.

Drunemeton (Anatolia) Strabo refers to a sacred grove known as Drunemeton ("oak sanctuary"), where 300 men elected by the three tribes of the Galatians met in council. (The Galatians were Celts who had migrated in the third century and settled in Anatolia.)

Mona (Anglesey, Wales) The island of Anglesey was said to be a major center of Druidism. As such it was targeted by the Romans when they attempted to suppress the Druids. The Roman governor of Britain, Suetonius Paulinus, led an assault on the island in A.D. 60. According to Tacitus, the Druids and "black-robed women with disheveled hair like Furies" paralyzed the superstitious Roman soldiers with their appearance and screamed curses, though the Roman officers shamed their men into attacking and defeating the defenders, and razing the sacred groves.

Loire (France) Strabo, quoting Poseidonius, describes an island off the mouth of the Loire, where dwelt a community of priestesses dedicated to a fertility cult, whose rites included human sacrifice and cannibalism.

VIERECKSCHANZEN (SACRED ENCLOSURES)

Many Iron Age shrines took the form of a square or rectangular space enclosed by a bank and a ditch in which offerings were placed, and often by a palisade. Offerings were also buried inside the enclosed space; these might include the bones and flesh of people and animals, wooden figurines, and artifacts. Sometimes these were arranged in zones. In some cases the enclosure contained a built structure, but in many the focus of worship was a single large post or tree trunk or a deep shaft, sometimes with a post set in it. Alternatively, the shrine might contain a number of posts or a series of pits; in the enclosure at Bliesbruck in Germany there were 100 pits in which offerings and tree trunks or living trees were placed. Classical authors reported that a Celtic open-air shrine was called a *nemeton;* this may have referred to such ritual enclosures as well as to groves and other natural features. Shrines were often placed in liminal situations, such as the boggy areas between land and water or at the boundary between territories as was the case of the Gallic shrine at Gournay.

Libenice (Bohemia, Czech Republic) This enclosure with sides 300 feet (90 meters) long contained a sunken area at one end. Within this were a standing stone and two wooden posts, possibly carved in human form wearing the two bronze torcs found beside them. Offerings had been placed in pits in the floor, which had then been filled in. Human and animal bones from the shrine were probably the remains of sacrifices, while the burial of a woman in a coffin with many items of jewelry may have been that of a priestess.

Gournay-sur-Aronde (France) This banked and ditched enclosure, founded in the fourth century

B.C., was situated on the border of three Celtic tribes and close to that of another. Initially a pit was dug in which the corpses of elderly cattle were exposed; these may have been sacrificed or reverently placed here after their death. After exposure for some months the bones were removed and buried in the ditches. Elsewhere in the ditches were buried the bodies of dead horses and the bones of sacrificed lambs, calves, and pigs, each in a separate zone. Dismembered human bodies were also buried in the ditches; these may have been sacrifices or individuals who had died heroically in battle. In the late third century a structure of posts and a roof was built over the pit. Numerous ritual pits were dug in the interior. More than 2,000 deliberately broken iron weapons were placed as offerings in the ditches. The shrine was burnt down in the first century B.C., but a Romano-Celtic temple was constructed on the site some centuries later, showing that its sanctity had continued.

Lowbury (Oxfordshire, England) In this shrine, enclosed by a bank and ditch, a number of trees were planted in the first century A.D. The enclosure also contained offerings of spears and coins and the burial of a woman with a mutilated face.

Roquepertuse (Bouches-du-Rhône, France) This enclosure in the hills near Entremont had an entrance portico formed of three uprights spanned by lintels and originally painted with bands of color, geometric patterns, and horses. Niches in the uprights held skulls (probably placed there as severed heads). Other architectural remains from the sanctuary included a stone engraved with horses' heads and a stone carving of two heads placed back to back; these had originally been painted, the faces red and the hair black.

WELLS AND SHAFTS

Deep shafts were the focus of worship in some ritual enclosures, but there were also others without an enclosure ditch or palisade. Some may have begun life as wells, others were probably dug primarily as ritual features, but, given the sanctity of watery places in prehistoric Europe, the distinction between functional wells and ritual shafts may in any case have been blurred. Such deep shafts are known from the Late Bronze Age onward, but it is worth noting that wells in which offerings were deposited were dug around 8000 B.C. by the earliest inhabitants of the island of Cyprus, part of the Near Eastern world but also within the Mediterranean. The ritual shafts, which were often more than 100 feet (30 meters) deep, contained many offerings, particularly of animals. Human body parts were also included, as were a range of artifacts.

Wilsford (Wiltshire, England) This Middle Bronze Age shaft, 108 feet (33 meters) deep, was dug into solid chalk. Offerings deposited in it included many wooden objects, pottery, beads, and other jewelry, as well as animal bones.

Holzhausen (Bavaria, Germany) This ritual site began life as a palisaded enclosure in which a shaft was dug; a second pit was added, and the site further enclosed by a ditch and bank. A timber building was erected in one corner, and then a third shaft was dug. Excavations in one of these shafts revealed that it had held a post around the base of which traces of flesh and blood were detected.

Fellbach Schmiden (Germany) A timber-lined well with a ladder made of projecting pegs was excavated inside an enclosure: it has been dated to 123 B.C. by dendrochronology. Offerings within it included pottery, a wooden sword, two wooden figurines of goats, and one of a stag.

ROUTES AND TRACKWAYS

Although trackways were generally laid to give access from one place to another across wet or marshy ground, they probably also had a ritual dimension, perhaps because of their association with the wetland environment. The massive corduroy timber track at Ipfweger Moor in Germany had wooden posts and wooden figures set along it, and offerings were placed along others, such as the Sweet Track in the Somerset Levels, England.

Flag Fen (East Anglia, England) An artificial island constructed in the second millennium in the East Anglian Fens near Whittlesea was connected to the fen edge by alignments of oak posts with a brush-wood causeway between them. Over more than a millennium, from around 1600 to 200 B.C., people visiting the island, which may itself have been a ritual site, threw more than 300 objects among the piles or along the southern side of the barrier; these included many pieces of metalwork, from small humble domestic objects to swords and other prestige objects such as a pair of shears in a purpose-made wooden box. A tin workshop at the landward end of the causeway may have specialized in making objects for deposition. While these offerings were confined to the south side, several dogs, a complete human skeleton, and parts of several other people were laid in the water on the north side of the barrier.

CAVES AND ROCK FISSURES

In many parts of Europe votive offerings were placed in caves or rock fissures, places that may have been seen as a way into the sacred realms of the earth and the mountains, or a link with the Other-world of the dead. Offerings of food and drink were frequent, as were those of artifacts, which might be placed as hoards. In some cases human sacrifices took place in caves, while in others these places were used as tombs for those who had died naturally.

Byci Skála (Moravia, Czech Republic) During the Hallstatt period and into the later Iron Age some 40 people, mainly women, were sacrificed in this limestone cave, and their heads and sometimes hands or feet were cut off. One skull was placed in a cauldron, and another had been modified to form a drinking vessel. Two horses were cut into quarters and deposited here along with many pots, objects of bronze including a bronze bull figurine, and a wagon sheathed in bronze. The cave also contained a number of funeral pyres.

CLIFF CASTLES

Cliff castles, which were headlands and promontories cut off from the mainland by banks and ditches, may have served a religious purpose as well as being used for defense. Classical authors writing of Iberia mentioned that such places were sacred to the gods, and in many parts of the Atlantic region evidence suggests that capes and headlands had some special, probably religious, significance back into the Neolithic period; this may have been bound up with their importance as landmarks for seafarers but related also to their liminal situation, between land and sea.

Votive Deposits and Sacrifices

The deposition of votive offerings was practiced throughout European prehistory, from Mesolithic times onward. These offerings were placed in the ground, in caves, and in a variety of watery places, as well as in shrines and other sacred locations. Classical

7.5 A small hoard of bronzes found in a bog at Sma'Glen, Corrymuckloch, in Perthshire, Scotland, comprising a sword blade, deliberately snapped in two; three socketed axes; and a unique ladle. This collection of objects was probably buried as a votive offering around 800 B.C. (Drawing by Audrey McIntosh, from material in the National Museums of Scotland, Edinburgh)

literature also refers to offerings in places that have left no archaeological trace, such as groves in forests. Offerings included fine stone tools in the Mesolithic and Neolithic periods and a great variety of metalwork in later times, as well as pottery, animals, and wooden vehicles. Objects were often dismantled or deliberately damaged before deposition; swords might be bent or broken into pieces, for example. Human bones might also be deposited, and in the Iron Age in particular human sacrifices were made in these locations. Food was likely to have been common among the offerings made to the gods, though this is harder to demonstrate. For example, in Scotland pots or packages of "bog-butter" have been found, probably placed in bogs or lakes in the Bronze or Iron Age. These may have been votive offerings or simply butter placed in water to keep cool in summer months and never retrieved.

The practice of making votive offerings was not continuous either in space or time, but related to factors of which we can have no knowledge. For example, in central Europe it was common around 2000 B.C. to place votive hoards of metalwork in the ground, but the practice was then abandoned for about a millennium. In Ireland and Brittany around the same time gold lunulae and other objects were placed as votive hoards in the ground or in water, whereas in mainland Britain gold objects were placed as grave goods in elite graves. While funerary offerings are generally interpreted in social terms, they would also have had a religious significance and should perhaps be considered equivalent in some ways to votive offerings made in other contexts. These also had a social dimension, since the sacrifice of expensive objects will have conferred considerable prestige on their donors.

DEPOSITS IN WATERY LOCATIONS

The European practice of depositing votive offerings in water dates back as far as the later Mesolithic period, when the Ertebølle people placed polished stone axes, pots, and probably antlers in bogs. Their TRB successors also made ritual deposits in bogs, their offerings including polished stone axes, amber jewelry, and pottery vessels that may have held food. A number of objects placed beside the fourth-millennium Sweet Track in the Somerset Levels,

England, may also have been votive offerings rather than objects lost by people walking across the trackway; these included pots of hazelnuts and a very fine jadeite ax imported from Switzerland.

From the Bronze Age onward the practice was widespread in temperate Europe, with fine metalwork, particularly jewelry and weapons, being thrown into many rivers, lakes, and bogs. The date range of material found in some locations indicates that some spots were venerated for long periods, during which many offerings were made there. The practice continued through the Roman period and into post-Roman times. Rivers, lakes, springs, bogs, and other watery places seem to have attracted particularly lavish offerings, which included many fine pieces of parade armor, bronze cauldrons, wooden vehicles, and in one case a boat containing many weapons. The latter shows that very substantial numbers of objects might be deposited as a single offering, something that seems to have occurred in a number of sites.

Llyn Cerrig Bach (Anglesey, Wales) The island of Anglesey, known to the Romans as a Druid stronghold, was an important religious center in the later Iron Age. A high cliff overlooking the lake of Llyn Cerrig Bach was used as a prominent place from which offerings could be thrown into its sacred waters. These numbered around 150 pieces and included two cauldrons, slave chains, horse trappings, swords, spears, shields, and other valuable prestige goods that seem to have come from sources over a wide area, including Ireland. Although these were probably thrown into the lake on a succession of occasions over the course of three centuries, it is possible that these were the offerings accumulated over that period in a shrine and that all of them were consigned to the lake when the Romans attacked Anglesey in A.D. 60.

Duchcov (Czech Republic) "Giant's Springs," a natural spring where in the third or second century B.C. a huge bronze cauldron was deposited containing around 2,000 pieces of bronze jewelry including bracelets, fibulae, and rings.

Thames (England) A number of votive objects have been recovered from the River Thames. These include the Battersea shield, a fine piece of parade armor, a horned helmet from Waterloo Bridge in London, and hundreds of skulls of young men.

La Tène (Lake Neuchâtel, Switzerland) A wooden bridge or pier was used as a platform from which many offerings were thrown into the lake. These included more than 165 iron swords, 295 spears, shields, razors, pottery, bronze jewelry, particularly 385 fibulae, coins, tools, iron ingots, cauldrons, and wooden objects, including a wheel, yokes, and parts of vehicles, as well as numerous skulls and some other human bones. Dendrochronology dates the structure to 251 B.C. and the wooden objects between then and 38 B.C.

Huelva (Huelva, Portugal) Some 400 10th-century bronze objects, including 78 swords, 88 spearheads, a helmet, 22 daggers, and many brooches, were found in the estuary of the Odiel River near the Tartessian town of Huelva. This may have been the cargo of a wrecked ship, but the composition of the collection, weapons and jewelry, mirrors that of many votive hoards, suggesting that this may have been a votive offering of exceptional munificence.

Broighter (Co. Derry, Ireland) A small hoard of goldwork deposited close to the shores of Lough Foyle in the first century B.C. included an elaborate and massive torc, two lighter torcs made of twisted gold bars, a model boat of sheet gold, a model cauldron, and two neck chains of gold wire. Lough Foyle was connected in Irish mythology with the sea god Manannan Mac Lir, the protector of Ireland, and the presence of a model seagoing boat in the hoard emphasizes the possibility that the gold work was an offering to this deity.

Boats Occasionally whole boats were sacrificed as votive deposits; the earliest of these was at Hjortspring in Denmark in the fourth century B.C., but there are a number from Roman and later times. The Hjortspring boat was packed with more than 300 weapons, including spears, swords, shields, and chain mail, and several sacrificed animals and was then dragged out into a bog and sunk, using stones to weigh it down. It has been surmised that this was a thank offering by those who had defeated the warband that had owned the weapons.

BURIED AND HIDDEN OFFERINGS

From the Mesolithic period onward, and particularly in the Bronze Age, votive offerings were placed in holes in the ground or hidden under stones, in rock crevices and caves, or other places that transferred them to the keeping of the gods. From the later Bronze Age they were also deposited in deep shafts. Offerings were also placed in ditches, from the Neolithic causewayed enclosures to the ditched sacred enclosures of the Iron Age. The foundations of buildings sometimes included offerings of artifacts, animals or joints of meat, and sometimes people. Offerings were probably also deposited in the open air in places of sanctity, including in trees but also on the ground; rarely have circumstances allowed the discovery of these, but the famous Gundestrup cauldron was dismantled and the pieces placed among the grass on dry land (this ground became part of a bog that formed later, where the cauldron was found).

The stone, metal, and salt mines of prehistoric Europe have revealed a number of votive deposits, often placed in shafts that proved unexpectedly unproductive or in which the roof had collapsed, presumably to placate the spirit of the place and obtain future safety and prosperity. For example, in the flint mine at Grimes Graves in England two antler picks, a polished greenstone ax, and the skull of a phalarope, a bird rarely found in Britain, had been arranged in one gallery.

A study of Danish Bronze Age hoards shows that many small offerings, containing domestic items such as knives, axes, and jewelry, were deposited near settlements and were probably offerings made by individuals or small communities, whereas larger hoards were found in places well away from settlements, these probably representing regional sacred places. In addition to objects, these sacred sites sometimes had evidence of large-scale feasting, such as the hundreds of cooking pits at Rønninge Søgard.

In the later Neolithic period hoards of beautiful polished stone axes were placed in the ground in parts of western Europe. These were generally completely pristine, suggesting that they were created as offerings. Axes, now made of bronze, were also common votive offerings in Bronze Age hoards, as were various kinds of weapon, particularly swords. In Únětice central Europe, *ösenringe* were frequent offerings; some hoards contained 500 or more. Hoards of gold lunulae were deposited in contemporary Ireland and Brittany. In the Late Bronze Age hoards became very numerous; while earlier hoards had generally been composed of fine objects, many of these were made up of broken tools. These may have been collections of scrap metal intended for recycling, but other hoards, particularly those containing weapons, probably continued the practice of votive deposition. In the Iron Age ritual shafts and pits within settlements and sacred enclosures often had offerings placed within them, and in the latter the offerings might also be laid on the ground surface. Bronze and gold jewelry and weaponry were common offerings, as were animals, and human bones were also often included.

Hajdúsámson (Hungary) In a Carpathian Bronze Age hoard carefully arranged in the ground, a sword with a solid hilt was placed with its blade pointing due north and across it were laid 12 shafthole battle-axes with their blades to the west. Each of these had been separately made and was unique, unlike the mass-produced axes characteristic of the period.

Snettisham (East Anglia, England) In this area of around 3 acres (1.2 hectares) at least a dozen small pits were dug, probably in the mid-first century B.C., and were tightly packed with valuables. The majority of these were torcs of gold, silver, or electrum, though bronze torcs, other pieces of jewelry, and coins were also deposited. In some cases the objects were placed in two layers, separated by a layer of soil. The area of the hoards lay within a 20-acre (8-hectare) ditched enclosure; finds from the ditch gave a date in the first century A.D., and an illicitly excavated hoard of silver and gold coins and ingots in a silver bowl, dated to the early first century A.D., is reputed to have been found near the ditch. Opinions on these hoards are divided; were they votive offerings or a tribal treasury, buried for safekeeping? Perhaps they were both: wealth entrusted to the protection of the gods.

HUMAN SACRIFICES

Classical authors were both fascinated and appalled by the Celtic and Germanic practice of human sacrifice, and their more extravagant claims may be exaggerated. For example, Strabo reported that the Druids sacrificed large numbers of people by burning them alive in a huge model of a man made of wicker. The classical authors linked death by drowning to the worship of Teutates. They described groves in which human victims were suspended from trees and wounded, and referred to a Druidic practice of divination by observing the struggles of stabbed individuals. The Druids were also said to have divined the future by cutting the throats of victims and studying their blood; it is probably significant that a number of the bog bodies had had their throats cut. In the case of Lindow Man, the cut would have drawn blood but not killed him.

It is impossible to distinguish between sacrifices and the ritual disposal of human remains after death and particularly death by violence (such as murder, execution, and death in battle). Many Iron Age ritual enclosures and pits contained human skeletal remains from people who were either sacrificed or buried there after death. Similarly, it is usually impossible to ascertain whether graves that contain more than one burial represent the sacrifice of individuals such as slaves, followers, or wives to accompany an important person into death; such sacrifices are attested to in Thracian, Scythian, and other steppe burials but may not have been practiced elsewhere. The fortuitous preservation of Iron Age bodies in bogs, however, confirms the classical references to human sacrifice. Such bog bodies were rare in other periods but not entirely absent: For example, the bodies of two fourth-millennium individuals who had suffered an unnatural death were found in a bog at Stoney Island in Ireland, and a few others are known from Denmark. Since the deposition of votive offerings goes back to Mesolithic times, it is possible that some of the early collections of human remains, such as the Ofnet skull nest and the Talheim massacre, may also be evidence of human sacrifice.

BOG BODIES

Many hundreds of sacrificed people have been discovered in the bogs of northern Europe (mainly Denmark but also Germany, the Netherlands, and Britain), mostly dating to the late centuries B.C. and early centuries A.D. They are often intact, depending on the conditions of preservation and discovery, though in very acid bogs the bones are destroyed, leaving the hair, nails, and tanned skin. Textiles have also preserved well, but most of the bog bodies were naked, so these are generally restricted to small items such as caps, belts, and blindfolds. They also include the ropes used to garotte the victim.

In many cases the bog people were killed using several methods in conjunction, presumably for ritual reasons. These methods did not usually include decapitation, a striking contrast to the Iron Age treatment of enemies; the few decapitated bog individuals may have been deposited for other reasons. Examination of the victims' hands has generally revealed that they had been exempted from manual labor, suggesting that they were marked for sacrifice and treated in special ways in advance of their deaths. Comments by Caesar indicate that at least some sacrificial victims were criminals, condemned but not executed until a sacrifice was required, perhaps years after their crime. The stomach contents of some of the bog bodies have been examined, revealing details of their last meal. This was often a gruel or porridge made with a variety of plants; these indicate that the victims were often slain in the winter, suggesting their sacrifice may have related to rites for the return of spring.

Not all bodies found in bogs were those of sacrificial victims. Others may have been people who accidentally drowned or who were murder victims. A woman found at Juthe Fen in Denmark and a man from Datgen in Germany had both been pinned down in the bog with pieces of wood, and the Datgen man decapitated; these unusual arrangements suggest that these were not normal sacrificial victims but perhaps individuals feared in life, held down to prevent their spirits returning to haunt the living. The Roman writer Tacitus reported that unnaturally wicked individuals were drowned in bogs under a wooden hurdle.

Borremose (Denmark) Three bog bodies were found in the large raised bog at Borremose: a man who was garotted and hit on the head, and two women. One of the women was covered by a woolen skirt, while a drape and a shawl were placed over the naked body of the other. The famous Gundestrup cauldron was found 2 miles (3 kilometers) away in what is now an adjacent bog, Raevemose, which was dry land at the time of its deposition.

Grauballe (Denmark) The man found at Grauballe had been hit on the head and his throat had been cut. His last meal had been a gruel containing a small amount of meat and many seeds.

Lindow Moss (Cheshire, England) A man, dubbed "Pete Marsh," was found during mechanical peat cutting in Lindow Moss in 1984. He had been stunned by two blows to the head and garotted with a knotted cord, and his throat had been cut before he was placed facedown in a pool. He was dressed only in a fox-fur band around his forearm, and traces of copper on his skin suggest that his body was painted. Among the remains of his last meal, of bread made with a variety of different grains, was mistletoe pollen, probably included for ritual reasons. Parts of at least one other body have been recovered from the same peat deposit: a man who had been decapitated and his head deposited separately.

Rappendam (Denmark) A peat bog containing a number of offerings including a man, parts of a number of animals, and many wooden wheels.

Tollund (Denmark) Discovered in 1950, Tollund Man was the first bog body to be scientifically studied. He was clad only in a leather cap and belt and had been killed by garotting before being placed in the bog around 200 B.C.

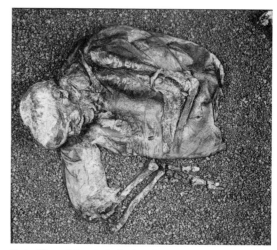

7.6 *"Pete Marsh," the bog body discovered in Lindow Moss in England, a man in his mid 20s who was sacrificed in the Late Iron Age or possibly in the Early Roman period* (TopFoto.co.uk, © The British Museum/HIP, Photographer: Unknown)

Shrines

Buildings within which ritual activities occurred were less common than other kinds of sacred place, except in Southeast Europe from early times and later in parts of the Mediterranean. These ranged from the house shrines of the Neolithic Balkans to the monumental temples of Malta.

HOUSE SHRINES

From the time of the first farmers onward in Greece and the Balkans, buildings within the settlement were the focus of religious practices. In some villages one building was set apart, containing no domestic material but a large number of other objects such as human and animal figurines. Domestic houses might also contain such figurines as well as model houses that are thought to have been shrines. In some houses one area was set aside for religious observances: For example, at Slatina a small strip at the back of the building was partitioned off and contained a box on feet, which could have been one such house model. Tools and food were also stored here. The association between stored produce and ritual paraphernalia was not uncommon; since the family and community depended on stored food to get through the time between harvests, a ritual connection between food and the gods was one way to attempt to ensure its safety during the course of the year. Later villages in Southeast Europe often had a separate shrine among the buildings of the settlement, containing figurines, animal heads, and pottery vessels with human faces. A model from Căscioarele on the lower Danube suggests that there were two-story temples in the Gumelnitsa period.

Nea Nikomedeia (Greece) A large building in the center of this Early Neolithic village contained a number of human figures and three model frogs of polished stone.

Ovcharovo (Bulgaria) A house shrine here contained a cult scene made up of three figurines seated on model chairs, a number of other chairs, a standing figurine, and three model tables bearing miniature pots, as well as screens and three cylinders that may have represented drums.

Platia Magoula Zarkou (Greece) A model house recovered from a pit beneath a house at Platia Magoula Zarkou contained eight human figures of various sizes, including a man with four legs, as well as an oven and a raised platform.

OTHER SHRINES

Although the greater number of Iron Age shrines were enclosures without structures, in some cases wooden buildings have been identified, in some cases inspired by Greek, Etruscan, or Roman architecture. However, the discovery of the Bronze Age structure at Bargeroosveld shows that religious buildings also existed in earlier times, although nothing is known of the rites associated with this structure. The survival of evidence of this building in a remote waterlogged setting illustrates the very limited chances of discovering such shrines.

Bargeroosterveld (Drenthe, Netherlands) In this Bronze Age shrine, constructed on boggy ground, a ring of stones surrounded a construction of two sleeper beams each holding two pairs of stout posts, surmounted by four beams with their ends carved into horns. In each pair of posts one had a round section, the other square. The structure was later dismantled.

Závist (Bohemia, Czech Republic) The highest part of this sixth-century hillfort was enclosed by a palisade, within which a succession of ritual structures were constructed of timber and stone. These seem to have included a wooden temple, a ritual pit, stone platforms, and a triangular stone altar. A stone wall and rock-cut ditch were also constructed around the sanctuary. Along the road leading up to the enclosure's entrance were workshops in which objects were manufactured for visitors to offer in the shrine.

Entremont (France) A large public building with a pillared portico occupied a prominent position in the town of Entremont, between two towers of the town's inner wall. Its first-floor hall was decorated inside with stone laid in geometric patterns and contained slabs decorated with severed heads and skulls. Severed heads were nailed to the front of the building.

MALTESE TEMPLES

From around 3600 to 2500 B.C. monumental stone temples were constructed in Malta, with walls of earth and rubble faced with huge dressed limestone blocks, some of which were decorated with spiral motifs. Stone balls found in the temples were probably used in the transport of the stones from quarries that were often several miles away. The structures resembled a clover leaf in plan, with a central passage surrounded by three to six semicircular apses, which may have been partially roofed with timber beams and clay. Crushed limestone plaster or stone slabs were used to make the floor. A monumental entrance doorway was surmounted by a huge stone lintel; sometimes the facade was two stories high. Inside these temples were a number of altars and cult statues, including enormous obese figures wearing ribbed and fringed skirts. The temples were often built in pairs or groups, and in two cases were associated with hypogea.

Tarxien (Malta) Three or four adjoining temples were built here, the largest group on Malta. The stones used to construct the eastern temple were carefully dressed so that they fitted precisely together. An altar at the back of the southern shrine was decorated with a procession of animals. A pair of connected holes in the floor before the altar may have been used for tethering sacrificial animals; animal bone was found in various parts of the temple complex. The central shrine, unusually, has six lobes in its plan, and was the latest to be built, squashed between the southern and eastern temples and accessible only through the southern temple. A stair may have led from here to the roof. A basin in the central temple had held a fire.

Ggantija (Gozo) Of two adjoining temples on the island of Gozo, known as Ggantija or Giant's House, the first was built around 3700 B.C., and the second added some four centuries later. The interior walls were made smooth with a wash of lime plaster, painted red.

OTHER

Galician saunas (Galicia, Spain) The first-millennium B.C. *castros* of northwest Spain included among their buildings structures that seem to have been used as saunas, it is presumed for ritual purposes. These were sunken rectangular buildings with a stone entranceway decorated with designs that, it is thought, represented fire, water, and wind. The Roman author Strabo may have been referring to these when he described vapor baths that used cold water and heated stones.

Monuments

A great variety of religious monuments were constructed in prehistoric Europe. These included a variety of enclosures defined by ditches and banks, mounds, megaliths, stone orthostats, and wooden posts. In some cases the ritual significance of the act of construction was of as much importance as the subsequent existence of the finished monument. Many in the Neolithic period were linked with funerary practices, including long barrows, megalithic tombs, and mortuary enclosures. While funerary monuments, mostly in the form of round barrows and stelae, continued to be erected down the ages, from the late fourth millennium onward, new types of monument reflected religious preoccupations apparently involving observation of the heavens and particularly the movements of the Sun and Moon.

CAUSEWAYED ENCLOSURES

During the Neolithic period in parts of northern, western, and central Europe, sites enclosed by interrupted ditches and banks or palisades were constructed, apparently for a variety of purposes. Some were defended settlements, but in many cases they seem likely to have served some ritual purpose, perhaps defining a sacred space separate from the normal world. Groups from a wide area may have met at the causewayed enclosure periodically to celebrate a festival or a ceremonial occasion by feasting. This is suggested by the presence in many of the ditches of animal bones, broken pottery, and smashed stone tools; often these were prestige objects, obtained from distant sources. The ritual aspect is emphasized by the presence in many of some human bones, such as skulls set upright on the bottom of the ditch, or sometimes complete inhumations. In the waterlogged ditch of the causewayed enclosure at Etton in eastern England, a pot set on a reed mat and heaps of particular bones and other material were arranged within the ditch. The ditches seem often to have been backfilled after the deposits were placed in them, and some were repeatedly recut or cleaned out and refilled.

Windmill Hill (Wiltshire, England) Three concentric rings of interrupted ditches enclosed an area of around 24 acres (9.6 hectares). Numerous pits had been dug in the interior, stone blocks had been placed within them, and the pits backfilled. The crouched inhumation of a man lay under the outer bank. The pottery and stone tools deposited in the ditches derived from a wide area, including Cornwall, Wales, and Cumbria.

CURSUSES

A *cursus* was an exceptionally long monument, a type probably confined to Britain, comprising a strip of ground defined by two parallel ditches and internal banks or lines of pits that, at least in some cases, once held timbers. The Dorset *cursus*, the longest known, was 6 miles (10 kilometers) long, with ditches 300 feet (90 meters) apart. Generally, they seem to have been constructed in stages. *Cursuses* often enclosed earlier long barrows within their length.

BANK BARROWS

Bank barrows, also known as long mounds, were narrow earthen mounds more than 330 feet (100 meters) long. Some were constructed partially over earlier causewayed enclosures. They seem generally to have been constructed in stages. An example at Crickley was found to have had offerings of animal bone under flat stones placed at intervals along its length.

Cleaven Dyke (Perthshire, Scotland) This monument began as an oval burial mound over which a long barrow was constructed. The mound and parallel ditches of the long barrow were then extended around 3300 B.C. in a series of 34 stages, creating a structure around 1.25 miles (2 kilometers) long, a cross between a bank barrow and a *cursus*.

OTHER

Mesolithic Stonehenge   (Wessex, England) The earliest known wooden monument, three postholes that had held massive pine tree trunks arranged in a line and another nearby, dated to the eighth millennium and was therefore erected by Mesolithic people. This alignment was discovered at the famous and extensively investigated site of Stonehenge when an area was stripped to build a car park; there are probably many other Mesolithic monuments lying undiscovered in less well studied areas of the European landscape.

Silbury Hill   (Wessex, England) An enormous mound 131 feet (40 meters) high and covering 5.5 acres (2.2 hectares) was constructed at Silbury Hill near Avebury during the third millennium B.C. A round mound of turf and gravel was covered with chalk rubble and earth and an outer layer of chalk rubble, quarried from the huge surrounding ditch. Despite numerous exploratory excavations of the mound, no funerary or ritual remains have been found associated with this artificial hill, the largest man-made mound in Europe, whose purpose is still totally unknown. It is calculated that it would have taken nearly 2 million man-days to build.

HENGES

Henges, which began to appear in Britain in the late fourth millennium, consisted of a circular ditched enclosure with an external bank interrupted by one, two, or four entrances. The arrangement of bank and ditch, the opposite of that used for practical defense, has provoked considerable speculation as to its function, with a popular suggestion that the ditch delimited a sacred area in which rites were performed that could be observed by spectators seated on the bank. Another view is that the bank effectively hid from profane view the activities taking place in the interior. A number of henges contained one or several concentric circles of standing stones or wooden posts, either freestanding or roofed. Henges were often associated with elaborately decorated Grooved Ware pottery that may have been used for preparing drugs used in rituals. Henges could be 150–650 feet (50–200 meters) in diameter, though there were also small henges (hengiform monuments). A number of henges were reused in later times as enclosures for cremation burials.

Stonehenge   (Wessex, England) Although it is the site from which henge monuments take their name, Stonehenge is atypical in having its bank inside rather than outside the ditch. The monument underwent several stages of construction and re-modeling during its long history. Around 3100 B.C. a ditch and internal bank were created, and a circle of 56 wooden posts was erected just inside the bank. Around 2500 B.C. 82 bluestones were brought the 130 miles (210 kilometers) from the Prescelly Mountains of South Wales, probably by raft across the sea and up the River Avon. From there they were dragged to Stonehenge, where they were erected in two arcs. The work was abandoned before it was completed, but around 2300 B.C. the bluestones were shifted to their current layout along with 30 sandstone sarsen stones hauled to Stonehenge from the Marlborough Downs 20 miles (32 kilometers) away. The sarsens were huge, each up to 30 feet (9 meters) long and 45 short tons (40 tonnes) in weight. The stones were linked by lintel stones, fastened by mortise-and-tenon joints between the lintels and the stone uprights and tongue-and-groove joints between the lintel stones. The raising of the orthostats and in particular the placing of the lintels must have required great technical ingenuity as well as considerable manpower; it is probable that ramps of sand, rollers, and ropes pulled by a large number of people were used. The Avenue, a path defined by two parallel banks with internal ditches, ran from the entrance to Stonehenge northeast for two miles (3 kilometers). Within it, just outside the enclosure, stands the Heelstone, a sarsen, and nearby is a large hole that had, it seems, originally held a similar stone. These were placed so that at midsummer sunrise the Sun would shine exactly between them into the center of the monument.

Woodhenge (Wessex, England) At the opposite end of the Avenue from Stonehenge is Woodhenge, a small henge that originally held a timber building consisting of six concentric rings of wooden posts, probably with a wooden roof. A pit in the floor at the center of the henge contained the body of a three-year-old child, apparently sacrificed.

Avebury (Wessex, England) The largest henge monument, its enclosure has an internal diameter of 1,140 feet (347 meters) and an area of 28.5 acres (11.5 hectares). The enormous ditch was as much as 33 feet (10 meters) deep and the bank originally 55 feet (16.7 meters) high. A great circle of 98 huge stones was erected around the inside of the ditch, and within the enclosure two smaller circles, the northern one containing a setting of three massive orthostats (known as the Cove) and the one in the south a single huge stone (the Obelisk), 21 feet (6.4 meters) high. The West Kennet Avenue, a route marked by 100 pairs of standing stones, led from Avebury's south entrance two miles (3 kilometers) to the Sanctuary, a circular monument built of concentric rings of timber posts and one of standing stones, enclosed within a stone circle. The stones of the Avebury circles and avenue were of two forms, one tall and rectilinear, the other shorter, wider, and diamond-shaped; these are often referred to as male and female stones, although the original significance is unknown. A number of human skulls and longbones were buried within the ditch, and in the terminal end a complete female dwarf, possibly sacrificed.

CIRCLES

Rings of wooden posts or standing stones were erected as religious monuments in parts of Britain and Brittany in the third and second millennia B.C., stone often replacing earlier timber circles. After they had ceased to be used for their original purpose, many were reused as cemetery enclosures, indicating their continued sanctity. Circles of wooden posts were also a common feature of Bronze Age burials, erected around the grave before the mound was heaped up.

Wooden Circles Single or concentric rings of posts are known from a number of sites; these included the interior of henges and monuments where the wooden posts were later supplemented or replaced by standing stones. For example, Stonehenge had a ring of wooden posts set inside the bank in its first stage of construction; a number of stone circles on Machrie Moor on Arran, Scotland, replaced earlier timber circles. Rings of posts also created enclosures within which one or a number of burials were placed.

Stone Circles Circles of standing stones were erected in various parts of Britain, particularly Scotland and eastern England. Circles of closely spaced stones generally had a wider space between two stones, forming an entrance, and in some these stones were taller than the rest. Some circles were placed within preexisting henges, while others were built in new locations. A few contained a horseshoe setting of stones (a "cove"). Stone circles were often associated with avenues and alignments.

Recumbent Stone Circles Contemporary with the henges in other parts of Britain, recumbent stone circles were being built in northeast Scotland. A large stone was laid horizontal on the ground in the south or southwest arc of a circle of standing stones, usually flanked by a pair of taller stones. The stones were arranged so that the midsummer moon rose between the uprights over the recumbent stone, shedding light into the interior of the circle.

Seahenge (East Anglia, England) Discovered on the Norfolk seashore at Holme-next-the-Sea in 1998, this surprising structure was immediately dubbed "Seahenge," although it lacks the characteristic ditch and external bank of henge monuments. It consists of a massive oak tree, removed from the ground in 2050 or 2049 B.C. and erected upside down, with its roots sticking into the air. A circle of 55 wooden posts was constructed around it. Subsequently, a second, larger, post circle was also found nearby. Ax marks in the timbers of Seahenge show that at least 51 different axes were used, indicating the minimum number of individuals involved in the construction.

MENHIRS AND ALIGNMENTS

In Brittany the megalithic tradition began in the fifth millennium with the erection of a number of massive orthostats, some of which were carved, associated with long chambered mounds. The largest of these is the Grand Menhir Brisé. After a few hundred years, however, these standing stones were taken down. Some of them were broken up and the pieces incorporated into passage graves. One example was broken into three pieces, of which two were used as capstones in the passage graves of La Table des Marchand and Gavrinis, while the third was perhaps built into the chamber of a long mound at Er-Grah.

The practice of erecting standing stones in Brittany was revived later, probably in the third millennium, when numerous alignments of many menhirs were created in the Carnac region. The menhirs were arranged in parallel rows or in lines that fanned out, often associated with rectangles or circles of standing stones. At least six such fields of menhirs were raised, probably over a long period, each containing from several hundred to more than 1,000 stones.

Standing stones also formed part of a number of late fourth- and third-millennium ritual monuments in Britain. They were arranged in pairs, or as single or multiple rows; some formed avenues (double rows of stones attached to henges or stone circles), while others were part of the same landscape as circles or tombs but were not directly associated with them. Alignments were erected in northern Scotland, western Wales, and Ireland, and isolated examples are known in a few other parts of Britain;

7.7 *A view of the alignments at Carnac, Brittany, France. This group consisted of 11 parallel rows of menhirs, running for 3,300 feet (1,015 meters).* (Figuier, Louis. *Primitive Man.* London: Chatto and Windus, 1876)

avenues were found mainly in southern and north-western England. The Avenue attached to Stonehenge was flanked by a pair of standing stones and the West Kennet Avenue at Avebury was lined by 100 pairs of orthostats. Other single or grouped orthostats occur elsewhere in both monuments.

Grand Menhir Brisé (Carnac, Brittany, France) This huge stone, now broken into four pieces, would have stood 66 feet (20 meters) high. The stone was quarried and roughly shaped 7.5 miles (12 kilometers) to the northwest of its current location, to which it was dragged. It would have formed the largest of a row of 18 standing stones, erected around 4500 B.C. A design carved on it may represent an ax or a plow; a similar sign was carved on the former standing stone that was broken into three pieces, two of which were reused as capstones in the Gavrinis and La Table des Marchand passage graves.

Kerlescan (Carnac, Brittany, France) This is one of the fields of stone rows at Carnac running east-west. Eight rows of standing stones start close together in the east but steadily diverge and increase in number to end as 13 rows, fanned out along one long side of a U-shaped arrangement of closely placed standing stones, 260 by 300 feet (80 by 90 meters), that forms a courtyard in front of a long mound. There are 514 extant stones in these alignments.

Callanish (Hebrides, Scotland) At Callanish on the island of Lewis in the Outer Hebrides a circle of tall stones was erected with a cruciform arrangement of stone rows running away from it in the cardinal directions, an alignment on the south, east, and west sides and on the north an avenue. The avenue seems to have been arranged to define the midsummer setting of both the Moon and the Sun.

Stanton Drew (Somerset, England) Located in the Severn region, an area where megalithic and nonmegalithic traditions overlapped, Stanton Drew survives as three massive stone circles, up to 370 feet (113 meters) in diameter. Avenues were attached to two of the circles.

STELAE AND ANTHROPOMORPHIC STONES

Stones carved with a few human features were erected in various parts of prehistoric Europe. In many cases these probably represented deities, erected in open-air sanctuaries, while others may have been grave markers or stelae commemorating the dead. Some fourth-millennium barrow graves in Southeast Europe had stelae erected on their summits decorated with people holding or wearing hafted axes. Funerary stelae might also take the form of stones bearing scenes or images of artifacts and people. Standing stones were used as boundary markers, and many had a ritual significance.

Statue Menhirs Standing stones engraved or carved in relief to represent schematic human figures are known from the fourth to third millennia and sometimes later, in parts of Italy, Sardinia, Corsica, Iberia, southern France, and the Channel Islands. Known as statue menhirs, they depict heavily armed men and women wearing jewelry. Some wear lunulae or neck rings (*gargantillas*) of types familiar from Ireland and Iberia. If these figures represent deities, it may be that lunulae, which have been recovered from a number of votive hoards, were made to be worn by divine images carved in wood. In the Alpine fringes of northern Italy and Switzerland the statue menhirs bore stylized representations of people wearing clearly depicted necklaces and equipment such as bows, daggers, axes, and belts with pouches. In Corsica anthropomorphic menhirs wore a neck ring and a sword or dagger in a sheath, and plain menhirs arranged in rows were also erected.

Cabeço da Mina (Vila Flor, Portugal) This sanctuary took the form of a hill that was probably entirely surrounded by stelae of granite and schist in the fourth or third millennium B.C. Among the 50 surviving stones are 21 carved to represent schematic people with faces, necklaces, and belts; the rest are undecorated.

Saint-Martin-de-Corléans (Aosta, Italy) This sacred place had several phases of different activity. In the

Neolithic period postholes were dug and ox and ram skulls placed in some. A row of ritual pits were later dug to contain offerings of millstones and grain. An area of ground was plowed and sown with human teeth. Later, two stone platforms were constructed and 40 anthropomorphic stelae erected in three rows. In the Beaker period the stelae were taken down and used in the construction of megalithic tombs. Cists were later erected there, again reusing stelae, and the site continued in use into the Early Bronze Age.

Funerary Stelae   Stone stelae carved with weapons, particularly short swords, hafted axes, and double axes, were erected in southwest Iberia during the second millennium. In the early first millennium these became more widespread, bearing depictions of swords, spears, shields, and sometimes warriors and chariots.

Markers   In Iron Age Brittany stone stelae were erected as territorial markers but also as religious symbols; these were sometimes decorated with geometric designs. Many of these stelae were tall columns, some of them fluted, while others were low and rounded. Ones similar to the latter are also known from Ireland.

Pillars   A number of stone pillars carved with human heads and often decorated with heads and floral motifs have been found in Iron Age sites, probably including Pfalzfeld in Germany; although the top of this pillar had broken off, it had probably originally had a head. Conversely, a broken head found at Heidelberg in Germany may have come from one such pillar. In some cases these pillars were erected in shrines where they may have been a focus of worship analogous to the trees or wooden posts from which human heads might be hung. A stone pillar from the oppidum of Entremont was carved with skulls. One from Euffigneix in France had a rudimentary face and arms and wore a torc around its neck, but also had the figure of a boar carved over its front and a large eye on its left side. Other pillar figures were carved with two heads, back to back, like the Roman god Janus; one such paired head was found at Roquepertuse. An example from Holzgerlingen in Germany was carved down to the waist and

had arms. This and many of the Iron Age heads had a headdress of two large balloonlike leaves or petals.

RITUAL LANDSCAPES

Prehistoric Europeans had an intimate relationship with the landscape, which was imbued with religious significance. From the earliest times natural features were the subject of veneration. This is most clearly seen in the Iron Age, when many votive deposits and human sacrifices were placed in bogs, lakes, rivers, the ground, caves, forest groves, and the sea, but offerings had been made, probably in all these different locations, since the Mesolithic period.

In addition, monuments were built that were closely linked to natural features of the landscape, while others created artificial landscape features. These functioned partly as territorial markers, defining the area belonging to a community, but they also served an important religious function. Different types of monuments were constructed in different periods, but these were often closely integrated, creating a ritual landscape of monuments and natural features whose arrangement would have had religious (and social) significance for the region's inhabitants. These included megalithic tombs, standing stones and wooden posts or tree trunks set in postholes, circles of stone or wood, earthen barrows and stone cairns, and a great variety of enclosures demarcated by ditches, banks, pits, wooden palisades, and stone walls. The sanctity of particular locations survived changes in the forms taken by ritual or funerary structures. Some locations in particular functioned as sacred foci for millennia, accumulating monuments of different periods. The length of time that this might endure is brought home by the discovery at Stonehenge of a Mesolithic monument of four enormous posts dated to the eighth millennium, thousands of years before the erection of the famous stone monument. The Wessex area of Britain and the Carnac area of Brittany have the most spectacular built ritual landscapes; in many other areas monuments were less prominent or were absent altogether, features of the ritual landscape being marked in different ways, including some delineated only in the minds of the worshippers.

Carnac   (Brittany, France) The siting of the monuments in the Carnac area emphasizes the

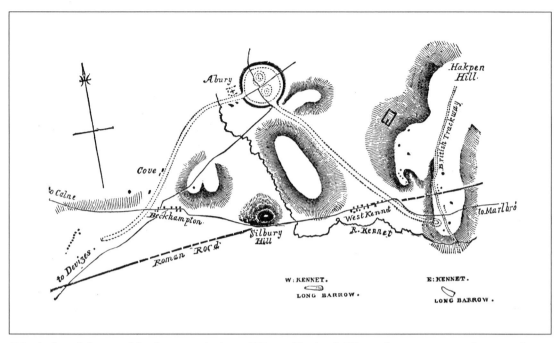

7.8 A plan of the ritual landscape at Avebury, Wessex, England. The earliest monuments here are the Neolithic long barrows of West and East Kennet and the causewayed enclosure of Windmill Hill to the northwest, just outside the area covered by the map. Later in the Neolithic the Sanctuary was erected on Overton Hill, in the southeast of the map, and the great mound of Silbury Hill, followed shortly by the great henge of Avebury with its stone circles. The West Kennet Avenue, lined with orthostats, was built joining Avebury and the Sanctuary; the western (Beckhampton) avenue may be imaginary. Later constructions here included Bronze Age round barrows. Also marked is the Ridgeway ("British Trackway"), an ancient route. (Lubbock, John. Prehistoric Times. New York: D. Appleton and Company, 1890, after Dr. Thurnam's plan in Archaeologia, *Vol. 38)*

importance of the sea to the prehistoric inhabitants of the area around the Bay of Quiberon. The important Mesolithic coastal settlements of Hoëdic and Téviec with their cist burials lie within the adjacent Morbihan region. It was in the Carnac area that the first megalithic tombs, chambers under long mounds, were erected in the fifth millennium, along with a number of menhirs, including the Grand Menhir Brisé. After some centuries the menhirs were taken down, and broken sections from them were incorporated into passage graves such as La Table des Marchand, which appeared in the region in the mid-fourth millennium. At some time, probably later, huge

numbers of menhirs were erected in alignments and other arrangements.

Wessex (England) The Wessex region was a favorable area for agriculture and pastoralism and well placed for trade from the Atlantic west and lands across the North Sea and the English Channel. In the Neolithic period monuments built here included long barrows, other tombs, a small *cursus*, and causewayed enclosures. In the third millennium the area saw the construction of Stonehenge, a number of henges including four of exceptional size (Avebury, Marden, Mount Pleasant, and Durrington Walls), a large *cursus*, several avenues, a large number of Beaker burials, including that of the Amesbury Archer, and the unique mound of Silbury Hill. The area, and particularly the Salisbury Plain, where Stonehenge stands, was a focus for the construction of Bronze Age barrow cemeteries during the second millennium, including a number of wealthy burials belonging to the Wessex culture, and in the Late Bronze Age many cremation cemeteries developed in the area. The Wilsford shaft, a Bronze Age ritual shaft, also lay within the Stonehenge area. Wessex was divided into a number of ritual landscapes, some of them focused on the four exceptional henges.

Stenness (Orkney, Scotland) A narrow strip of land between two lochs on Mainland, Orkney, and the adjacent ground was chosen as the area in which to erect a large number of monuments, including three henges (the Rings of Brodgar, the Stones of Stenness, and the Ring of Bookan), the passage grave of Maes Howe, a number of standing stones, and numerous small barrows.

Astronomy

Knowledge of the annual calendar of the heavens was of major importance to farming communities that needed this information to determine when to perform key activities such as sowing their crops. Although the extent of prehistoric European knowledge of the heavens is still controversial, there is a growing body of evidence to suggest that by the third millennium B.C., if not earlier, the movements of the Sun and Moon were well known.

MEGALITHIC ASTRONOMY

The purpose of Stonehenge and other stone monuments has been much debated, though there has been a considerable consensus that they were religious structures. One view that has gathered momentum since the 1960s is that some at least of the monuments were designed to record key moments in the movements of the heavens. Many scholars, and notably the engineer Alexander Thom, surveyed a number of monuments to determine whether they recorded astronomical phenomena.

While the more extravagant claims have not been supported, the frequent coincidence between a major event, such as sunrise at the summer or winter solstice, and features of a number of stone circles and developed passage graves has led many people to accept that these monuments were designed to record key annual astronomical events. For example, the hole above the lintel over the entrance to the Newgrange passage grave directs the Sun at the midwinter solstice into the central chamber; sunrise on midsummer's day is visible between two of the orthostats at Stonehenge, and the Avenue follows this alignment.

LATER ASTRONOMY

Nebra Sky-Disc The recently discovered Nebra sky-disc, from second-millennium central Germany, may indicate that detailed knowledge of the heavens was widespread in later prehistoric Europe. The disc shows the Moon and the Sun, and between them a number of stars, among which scholars think they have identified the constellation of the Pleiades. The latter was visible in the night sky between March and October, important dates in the agricultural year. In addition, on each side a strip of gold covers 82 degrees of the disc's circumference, this being the distance traveled by the Sun between the solstices in the latitude from which the disc came. Furthermore, the disc was (probably) found within an enclosure orientated so that at the equinoxes the Sun viewed from here would set behind the highest peak of the Harz Mountains. Like the British monuments, the Nebra sky-disc and its enclosure must therefore have been used in recording astronomical movements.

Coligny Calendar The Druids were said by classical authors to have knowledge of the heavens, and this was confirmed by the find at Coligny, Bourg-en-Bresse, France, of a fragmentary sheet bronze calendar with holes for pegs to mark the days. This was written in the Gallic Celtic language, using the Roman script and dated to the first century B.C. or the first century A.D. It recorded five years, composed of 62 lunar months of 29 or 30 lunar nights, with two intercalary months to rectify the difference between the solar and lunar years; the insertion of these extra days was probably staggered over the whole five-year period. Major festivals were marked, and each month was divided into auspicious and inauspicious nights, vital information for organizing important activities.

READING

General

Cunliffe, ed. 1994, Milisauskas, ed. 2002, Champion et al. 1984.

Religious Beliefs and Practices

Whitehouse 1992: development of religion; Bradley 1998: Mesolithic religion; Harding 2000, Demakopoulou et al., eds. 1999: Bronze Age religion; James 1993, Green 1992, Cunliffe 1997: Celtic religion; Green 1992, Bökönyi 1991, MacKillop 1998: deities; Piggott 1970, Green 1992: cult objects and iconography; Durrani 2000, Catling 2005a, 2005b, Anon. 2005: Nebra sky-disc; Maier 1991b: Manching tree; Green 1997, Ross 1995, 1999, Piggott 1975: Druids and other priests; Kruta 2004: Gundestrup cauldron; Eluère 1999a, Wallace and O'Floinn 2002: torcs and lunulae; Menghin 1999, Springer 1999: cones; Bradley 1997, Anati 1999, Capelle 1999, Thrane 1999a, Eluère 1999a, Harding 2002: rock art; Milisauskas 2002b, Marthari 1999, Todorova 1999: figurines; Darvill 1996: hillside figures.

Shrines and Sacred Places

Whittle 1996, Bradley 1998: Neolithic; Harding 2000: Bronze Age; Caesar 1951, Tacitus 1970, 1971, James 1993, Piggott 1970, Cunliffe 1997, Kruta 2004: Iron Age; Woodward 1992: British Iron Age; Darvill 1987, 1996, Parker Pearson 1993: Britain; Hingley 1998, Armit 1997, Barclay 1998, Ashmore 1996: Scotland; Cunliffe 2001a: Atlantic region; Whitehouse 1992: Italy; Thrane 1999a: Scandinavia; Coles 1984: waterlogged remains; Brothwell 1986, Turner and Scaife, eds. 1995, Glob 1969: bog bodies; James 1993, Green 1992, 1997, MacKillop 1998, Webster 1995: Celtic sacred places; Planck 1991: Fellbach-Schmiden; Pryor 1991, 2003: Flag Fen; Motykova et al. 1991: Závist; Scarre 1999: Bargeroosterveld; Hunter 1997: hoards; Kelly 2002, Wallace and O'Floinn 2002: Broighter; Delgado 1997: Hjortspring; Garrison 1997: La Tène; Scarre 1998: Entremont, Borremose; Stead 1998: Snettisham; Trump 1980, 2002, Scarre 1998: Maltese temples; Mercer 1990, Oswald et al. 2001, Darvill and Thomas, eds. 2001, Varndell and Topping eds. 2002: causewayed enclosures; Mercer 1980: Hambledon; Barclay and Harding, eds. 1999: cursuses; Clarke et al. 1985: megalithic monuments; Wainwright 1989: henges; English Heritage 2005, Chippendale 1994, Richards 1991, Scarre 1998: Stonehenge; Malone 1989: Avebury; Pryor 2001, 2003: Seahenge; Burl 1985, 1993, Scarre 1998: Carnac; Burl 1993: standing stones; Jorge 1999b, 1999c, Lenerz-de Wilde 1995, Lo Schiavo 1999, De Marinis 1999, Eluère 1999b: stelae; Ross 1995, Green 1997, Kruta 2004: Coligny calendar.

8

DEATH AND BURIAL

FUNERARY PRACTICES

Funerary Beliefs

Cemeteries may have played some part in reinforcing group identity and integration, and the selection of people and objects for interment may have related to social practices and beliefs, for example, expressing continuity between the living and their ancestors.

Red ochre had been scattered on burials in the Palaeolithic period, and this continued in many Mesolithic graves, as well as later, for instance, in steppe burials. It is widely considered that this reflects a symbolic identification with blood and hence life, perhaps giving the deceased new life in the Otherworld.

A number of Mesolithic cemeteries in the north were located on islands. It is possible that this reflects a desire to separate the spirits of the dead from the world of the living, to prevent them bringing misfortune. The Saami people, who inhabited northern Russia in recent historical times, believed that the spirits of the dead could carry off the living or disturb their fishing and hunting grounds and so also buried their dead on islands.

The Celts believed in the transmigration of souls. The dead passed first to the Otherworld, a happy place similar to the world of the living, in which warriors passed their time in combat and feasting, and there was peace and prosperity. Eventually, the soul was reborn in a new body.

8.1 An imaginative reconstruction of a funeral procession to bury an individual in a tomb resembling the passage grave at Rödinge in Denmark. In some cases people were buried directly within megalithic tombs, but it was more common for bodies to be exposed before their bones were interred. (Figuier, Louis. *Primitive Man.* London: Chatto and Windus, 1876)

Burials

TREATMENT OF THE BODY

Various methods were used for disposing of the dead in ancient Europe. Inhumation of the whole body had the most enduring and widespread popularity, but cremation was also known from Mesolithic times onward and was the predominant rite in the later Bronze Age over much of Europe. During the Neolithic, exposure and the burial of defleshed bones was associated with megalithic tombs, and throughout prehistory there seem also to have been practices in which the dead were not buried at all.

PLACES OF BURIAL

Bodies were often laid in graves; cremations were also buried directly in the ground or placed in urns within graves or pits. Burial containers such as coffins, wooden chambers, stone cists, and monumental tombs were also widely used, and some burials were made in natural features such as caves. It is possible that bodies, bones, or ashes were also disposed of in other places such as trees, rivers, and the sea. In some cases burials were placed within earlier monuments; some Beaker burials, for example, were inserted into earlier megalithic tombs, and the interiors of stone circles and henges were sometimes used as Bronze Age funerary enclosures. Some bodies or bones, however, were disposed of in settlements, beneath house floors or in pits. The bones of the dead were also treated in other ways; the heads of enemies were displayed or carefully preserved by Iron Age warriors, and some groups removed the skulls or other bones of family members for curation in various ways.

GRAVE MARKERS

Many burials were marked by the erection of long barrows, round barrows, cairns, or tumuli over the grave or funerary chamber. In some cases these had additional markers, such as standing stones, wooden posts, or sculptures erected nearby or on the mound. In flat grave cemeteries small mounds may have been raised that have since been eroded or plowed away, while in other cases the graves were originally flush with the ground. Sometimes these graves were delineated by a surrounding ditch, bank, or low wall. Funerary stelae were erected by some cultures, particularly in southern Europe. Other burials were probably also marked in some way since in many densely packed cemeteries the graves do not overlap.

SOCIAL CONTEXT

Two contrasting types of disposal were practiced at various times, single burial and communal disposal, and these are thought to reflect differences in social attitudes and the role of the dead in the society of the living. Single burial was more common, with each body treated as an individual whose place in society was often reflected in the practices involved in his or her disposal, including the arrangement of the body, the choice of inhumation, cremation or other rite, the form of grave or funerary structure, and the accompanying grave goods.

In contrast, communal burial subsumed the individual within the society. After death the body was placed with others in situations where the bones soon became intermingled, by exposure leading to excarnation or insertion within a communal tomb where the earlier skeletons were pushed to one side or sorted into collections of particular bones such as skulls or long bones. Though grave goods were sometimes placed within these tombs, they did not accompany and relate to an individual, but had some significance for the community. This was the characteristic practice in megalithic tombs, but communal burials also characterized parts of the Mediterranean and perhaps go back 300,000 years when the people of Atapuerca in Spain disposed of their dead by dropping them into a natural rock shaft.

GRAVE FURNISHINGS

The majority of burials were furnished with grave goods of some kind, though they were not generally associated with individuals in megalithic tombs. In many cases the grave goods were simply the clothes and personal ornaments in which the deceased was clad. Sometimes the body was wrapped in a shroud or textile. Food and drink might also be placed with the dead. Often small personal objects were also included; these were frequently related to age and gender, adult males having weapons and women jewelry, for example. Objects such as metalworking tools might also reflect the occupation of the deceased. Individuals of a higher status often had both a larger quantity of grave goods and objects that were more valuable, in terms of their material, rarity, or expense, or the craftsmanship of their manufacture, including gold work, swords, horse harness, and sometimes a vehicle, or goods associated with elite activities such as luxury tableware and wine. Horses sometimes accompanied vehicle burials, particularly in the steppe. On occasion dogs or other animals were also buried, either with their owners or in separate graves. Animal bones often represented joints of meat offered as food, but in some cases related to rituals or beliefs. For example, a Mesolithic baby buried at Vedbaek was placed on a swan's wing, and a megalithic tomb at Isbister in northern Scotland contained a number of sea eagles.

ACCOMPANYING RITES

While the remains of the dead in their final resting place provide evidence of the means of disposal and accompanying practices, far less is known of what took place between the death and the final disposal. Animal bones from the forecourts of megalithic tombs suggest funerary feasting and perhaps later commemorative feasts, and these are likely to have been a frequent feature of funerary rites. A rare glimpse of funerary rites comes from a Bronze Age cist burial at Bredadör, Kivik, in Sweden, whose stone walls were carved with a funeral procession. Mourners, some blowing lurer (horns) and beating drums, followed a chariot drawn by two horses. Other slabs bore images of ships, axes, and wheels, symbols with religious meaning.

Barrows

From the Mesolithic period onward, barrows of various sizes were often erected over graves. Small mounds were probably very widespread but have often been removed by cultivation. The larger mounds covering megalithic tombs have survived better, as have the substantial mounds built in the Bronze Age in many parts of Europe. Large mounds

continued to be constructed through the Iron Age and Roman periods into later times. These substantial barrows were often associated with elite burials; in some periods cemeteries of smaller barrows erected over the graves of ordinary people have also survived.

LONG BARROWS

Long barrows were characteristic of the Neolithic period in western, northern, and central Europe when mounds of earth, stones, or both were erected over megalithic tombs and similar mounds covered wooden mortuary structures. These mounds were generally rectangular or trapezoidal in shape, tapering downward toward the narrower end, with the funerary chamber taking up a small area under one part of it, usually one end (the wider end in the case of trapezoidal mounds). Some megalithic tombs had an elaborate entrance court with the mound extended-round it in two pincerlike arms. Generally the barrow was covered with turf and frequently edged with curbstones or revetted with wood and some had a facade of orthostats. The two long sides of the barrow were often edged by ditches; these may have been an important part of the design or may just have been quarry ditches for the soil to build the mound.

ROUND BARROWS

Throughout prehistory and into later times the majority of funerary mounds were hemispherical in form. Small round mounds were raised over some burials in the Mesolithic period. In the Neolithic period round barrows were erected over megalithic burials or mortuary chambers in some areas, and the developed passage graves of the late third millennium were covered by huge round mounds with a stone curb. Barrows were a regular feature of steppe burials. From the later third millennium onward round barrows were raised over inhumation and cremation graves over much of Europe, in some cases creating barrow cemeteries.

In the Bronze Age a few larger mounds were erected over wooden chambers containing the rich burials of important individuals. Different forms of this combination of large barrow and elite burial were found in later times, such as the barrows with wooden chambers of Hallstatt chiefs, the massive barrows covering the lavish burials of the steppe elite, complete with sacrificed horses and people, and the *tholoi* of Southeast Europe. In some periods and regions the graves of less important people were inserted into the mound, or arranged around them in flat graves or under smaller mounds. A mound might also be raised over a cemetery of flat graves as a final ritual act.

Round barrows were generally of earth, but stone cairns also occurred, and stone and earth might be combined. Turf often covered the mound, and in some cases, such as the Neolithic mounds over megaliths and the Hallstatt mounds, a curb of upright stone slabs revetted the mound. An encircling ditch was common, perhaps originally incorporated as a quarry for earth for the mound. Some Bronze Age barrows in the Wessex region of England used various forms of mound, berm, and ditch to create a range of barrow forms such as disc, saucer, and pond barrows. Round barrows might be combined with a variety of other structures, such as wooden mortuary chambers or rings of wooden posts.

North Mains (Tayside, Scotland) Excavation of the 130-feet (40-meter)-wide mound at North Mains has given a detailed picture of its construction. First a small pear-shaped timber enclosure was erected at the center of the site. Panels of wattle fencing were put up radiating out from this, and the bays between them filled with soil taken from a ditch that was dug around the outside. A fenced passage was left open to give access to the central enclosure, in which one or two burials were placed around 2000 B.C. before the remaining areas were filled with earth. A bonfire was lit on the top of the mound, which was then covered with turf and stone. Two further burials and eight cremations, most of several individuals, were placed in cists in the mound's surface.

STEPPE CULTURES AND SOUTHEAST EUROPE

Round barrows were built over the wooden burial chambers or pit burials of steppe cultures, and this form of burial spread through Southeast Europe as far as the Carpathian basin. Often the complete body or cremated remains were placed at the bottom of a pit, sometimes placed on a mat, and scattered with ochre. Wooden beams were placed over the top of the pit and a mound of stones and earth raised over it. Sometimes a stone anthropomorphic stele was erected on top of the mound. Later burials were often dug into the mound or around its base and were themselves covered by a mound.

Plachidol II (Bulgaria) This mound was more than 10 feet (3 meters) high and 136 feet (42 meters) in diameter, with a grave under its center containing an inhumation burial orientated northeast-southwest. Eight other burials, all oriented in the same direction, were added to the mound later, and more soil was heaped over them, expanding the mound to its present extent. These burials, which included men, women, and children, often had red ochre placed on them, and some had a pot or a few small copper objects as grave goods.

CORDED WARE CULTURE

Corded Ware men were buried in a flexed position on their right side, with cord-decorated pots, and sometimes copper objects, battle-axes, arrowheads, and boar's-tooth pendants, while the women were placed on their left side with pots and sometimes ornaments. Although many of the graves were covered by a small barrow, some may have been flat graves.

WESSEX CULTURE

In the second millennium a number of well-furnished graves beneath barrows were constructed in southern England, probably the burials of chiefs or other elite members of society. The Wessex area included a number of "fancy" forms, often constructed largely of turfs. bell barrows, which had a berm (a flat area between ditch and mound); saucer barrows, which had a bank around the outside of the ditch; pond barrows, where a hollow was substituted for the mound; and many others. Cemeteries of these barrows developed over the centuries, with later burials placed around the major burials in flat graves or under small mounds. Many were located in the vicinity of henges and other earlier monuments.

The graves included both inhumations and cremations; those of the early second millennium (Wessex I) included some very rich burials, furnished with objects of gold, copper, faience, and amber.

Bush Barrow (Wessex, England) One of a group of barrows on Normanton Down near Stonehenge, the Bush Barrow covered the burial of an adult man buried with three bronze daggers and several pieces of gold work. These comprised two sheet-gold lozenges that had probably decorated his clothing, a gold belthook cover, and a large number of gold nails that had been set in a pattern in the handle of one of the daggers. A stone mace head whose haft was ornamented with zigzag bone rings is considered to have been a symbol of authority.

TUMULUS CULTURE

During the early to mid-second millennium single burials under round mounds (tumuli) became common from the western Carpathian region to eastern France, an area where flat-grave cemeteries had previously been the norm. Tumulus burials were often placed in a wooden coffin beneath the mound; the majority were contracted inhumations, though cremations are also known.

URNFIELD PERIOD

Although the majority of burials in the Late Bronze Age were simple cremations with few grave goods, in Scandinavia and northern Germany there were a few exceptional burials under massive barrows. The grave goods in these burials, in some cases including a wagon, reflect the deceased's elite status as a warrior.

Håga (Near Uppsala, Uppland, Sweden) A mound known locally as King Björn's Mound was constructed over a cremation burial that had probably been placed in an oak coffin, now decayed away. The middle-aged individual was accompanied by a gold-plated sword with a gold pommel, a gold-plated fibula, bronze buttons, pendants, razors, and tweezers. Over the coffin a layered mound of oak boles, stones, and earth was erected, 26 feet (8 meters) high and 150 feet (45 meters) in diameter, incorporating the bones of three other individuals, two women and

a man, as well as the bones of oxen, pigs, and sheep that are presumed to be the remains of a funeral feast.

Seddin (northeast Germany) Known as the King's Grave, a mound 420 feet (130 meters) in diameter and 36 feet (11 meters) high covered a vaulted stone chamber whose walls had been plastered with designs in red, white, and black. Within this were the remains of two women and an amphora containing the bones of a man, accompanied by a sword, a miniature spear, a decorated knife, metal vessels, razors, tweezers, and unique pottery vessels. Several other urn burials were placed within the mound but outside the chamber. The mound was part of a cemetery also containing a few other rich cist graves and many ordinary urn graves.

Exposure

In many areas and for long periods it seems to have been the usual practice to expose the dead to allow the flesh to rot away or to be removed by carrion-eating birds or animals. Bodies exposed to the elements would rot and eventually be reduced to bones. Those exposed at ground level would be vulnerable to scavenging animals who could carry away any part of the skeleton: Placing the bodies within a securely fenced or walled enclosure or an unroofed wooden chamber or on a platform well above the ground would prevent this, but some small bones might be carried off by carrion birds; bodies placed within closed wooden chambers would be protected from scavenging birds and animals, but excarnation would take longer. Evidence from different sites shows that all these strategies were adopted. In some cases the bones were subsequently buried, while in others they may just have been left for the elements and wild life to destroy completely.

Some of the fifth-millennium burials in Mesolithic cemeteries in northern Europe seem to have been of collected bones from bodies that had probably previously been exposed on wooden structures before the bones were arranged anatomically in the grave. Sometimes bones were not buried but were kept apart in the settlement or were buried in ritual contexts: this was particularly true of skulls.

During the Neolithic period many of the people buried in megalithic tombs were exposed first and their bones then collected and placed within the megalithic chamber. Earthen long barrows, generally found in different areas from megalithic tombs but overlapping with their distribution in Britain, were also communal burial places. The bodies of the dead were apparently exposed on or in a mortuary structure that was eventually covered by a long barrow. Whereas a long barrow erected over a mortuary chamber signaled the end of the use of the mortuary structure, megalithic tombs could be entered on many occasions to place bodies or bones within them, and may have been used in this way for hundreds of years. In many communities only some bones were accorded burial within the chambered tomb or long barrow, and it is possible that other bodies were left permanently in the place of exposure or deposited elsewhere; for instance, some skulls were placed in the ditches of causewayed enclosures.

In the Bronze and Iron Ages many people were interred or cremated, but it is likely that exposure was also practiced; occasional human bones in Iron Age rubbish pits may have derived from exposed bodies. Some excarnated bones may have been given their final resting place in rivers or lakes, the foci of Iron Age religious activities.

MORTUARY ENCLOSURES

Ditched and fenced enclosures similar in plan to long barrows were used as places to expose the dead in the Neolithic period; the bodies were probably placed on platforms erected within them. The evidence from at least one such enclosure at Inchtuthil in Scotland, dated around 3900 B.C., indicates that the enclosure fence was eventually set on fire, the posts pushed over, and the whole enclosure covered with earth. Some causewayed enclosures also served as places to expose the dead.

Hambledon Main Enclosure (Dorset, England) The main causewayed enclosure at Hambledon in England served as a necropolis where the dead were left exposed to the elements and carrion eaters before their defleshed remains were collected and placed either in the two associated long barrows or as single skulls or groups of bones within the surrounding ditch, where they were associated with pottery, stone tools, and animal bone. The bodies must have been exposed on the ground surface, as in one ditch the central part of a body (thigh bones and lower trunk) was found, evidently dragged there by dogs or other scavenging animals before the corpse had fully disintegrated. Pits dug in the interior of the enclosure had been used to hold offerings of exotic pottery and stone axes.

MORTUARY STRUCTURES

Platforms or other raised structures were probably built within Neolithic mortuary enclosures. Some of the unfenced two- and four-post structures in Iron Age settlements were probably also used as platforms for exposing the dead.

Stone pavements, wooden posts, rubble banks, and stone slabs were used to create various forms of mortuary house, often with a facade of wooden posts or of stone. These were used as burial chambers accessible over a period of time before being sealed under a barrow. In many cases the chamber was set on fire before the earth was heaped over the top.

Haddenham (East Anglia, England) A mortuary house constructed of massive oak planks, with a large post at each end and with a wooden vestibule, in which five bodies were buried. Later, the chamber was covered by a long barrow.

Street House Farm (Cleveland, England) This mortuary structure, dated around 3500 B.C., was built of stone and wood and contained burnt human bones and a partially articulated skeleton. To one side of this was a rectangular curbed area with two entrances, within which were two areas of paving that may have been used for exposing the dead. On the other side of the structure was a forecourt defined by a semicircle of large wooden posts with a huge one at the center. Eventually, the mortuary structure was burnt down and a cairn erected over the complex, leaving the forecourt visible.

Balfarg (Fife, Scotland) This was focus of ritual activity for millennia, from the late fifth millennium when ritual pits were dug, in one of which burnt pottery was carefully deposited, to the Bronze Age when cremations were deposited here within an Early Bronze Age ring cairn and stone circle. Two rectangular mortuary enclosures were constructed between 3700 and 3300 B.C.; these had an enclosure wall of wooden posts filled in with wickerwork. Inside them two-post structures supported timber platforms on which the dead were exposed. Around 3100 B.C. one of these enclosures was covered by a low mound of earth; the other may have been similarly treated. Later, a ring cairn was built partially over one, and the other was enclosed within a henge.

Containers and Chambers

While in many areas and periods burials were placed directly in the ground, in others they were placed within a coffin or pottery vessel. These included the urns and other types of pot in which cremations were placed. The grave might be lined with stones, or a stone cist or wooden chamber might be built within it to house the burial. Burials might also be made in caves.

STONE-LINED GRAVES AND CISTS

Burial chambers built out of stones or graves lined with stone slabs were created from the Mesolithic period onward. These included fifth-millennium graves in Brittany and stone-lined graves constructed in the fourth millennium by hunter-gatherer and farming groups in the forest steppe of Southeast Europe. In the same period cist burials surrounded by stone circles were constructed in Corsica and Sardinia, while cist burials without circles were made in Spain. On the limestone plateaus of southern France in the third millennium burials were placed in stone cists covered by round cairns, known locally as *dolmens simples*. In the Bronze Age when single burials, often under small round mounds, came into vogue across much of Europe, some burials were placed in cists beneath the mound. These included richly furnished Armorican burials in Brittany around 2200–1800 and the cist burials beneath mounds that were common in Scotland. In Scandinavia cist burial was the norm, male

burials being accompanied by flint daggers skillfully imitating Únětice bronze daggers. In southwest Iberia some single burials were placed in cists; others were placed in pits that were furnished with stone slabs and a curb of stone uprights. The Iberian burials were accompanied by few grave goods, the most impressive being riveted daggers and small gold ornaments.

Hoëdic and Téviec (Brittany, France) These two Mesolithic cemeteries were within coastal settlements, Téviec dating around 4500 B.C. and Hoëdic around 4600. The dead were placed in cists built of stone slabs, earlier burials being pushed aside when a new one was added. Bone daggers, flint blades, bone cloak pins, and jewelry made of animal teeth and shells were placed with the bodies, which were strewn with red ochre. A few individuals were buried with antlers. Fires were lit above the roof slabs, and hearths beside the graves were probably used to cook meat for a funeral feast. Some graves at Téviec were covered by a small mound.

Kernonen (Brittany, France) The burial was placed on the wooden floor of a stone chamber accompanied by two bronze axes, two bronze daggers, and a short sword, the hilts of all three decorated with gold pins, a bronze dagger with a bone pommel, 12 amber pendants, and 60 flint arrowheads. Some of the grave goods had been placed in three oak boxes within the chamber. A cairn and mound 20 feet (6 meters) high and 160 feet (50 meters) in diameter covered the cist.

COFFINS

Wooden coffins were used by a number of groups, including the widespread Tumulus culture, who buried their dead under round mounds (tumuli). Only a few have survived, due to waterlogging, notably from 14th-century B.C. Scandinavia, where turf mounds covered coffins made of oak tree trunks, split in half lengthwise and hollowed out in the same way that dugout canoes were made. Some mounds contained several coffins. The deceased, presumed to be members of the elite, were buried in their woolen clothing and bronze jewelry and wrapped in an oxhide or a blanket. Along with the corpse some personal possessions and other objects of wood and bark were interred. A few graves contained Mycenaean folding stools with otter-fur seats. In the Late Bronze Age tree-trunk coffins were used to hold cremation burials. A few Bronze Age tree-trunk coffins have also survived in Scotland.

Egtved (Jutland, Denmark) A coffin 8.5 feet (2.5 meters) long made from a tree felled in the summer of 1370 B.C. contained the burial of a girl in her late teens. She wore a skirt and blouse, a belt with a bronze disc, and bracelets on her arms. Her body was wrapped in a coarse woolen blanket and a cowhide. Also placed in the coffin were a container made of birch bark that had held mead, a bronze dagger, and a little cloth bundle containing the cremated remains of a girl aged six to eight years.

POTS

Pottery vessels were often placed in graves as funerary offerings, in many instances containing food or drink. In southeast Spain from around 2200 B.C. single burials were often placed in large pottery storage vessels. More widespread was the use of pottery vessels to house the calcined bones and ashes of individuals who had been cremated. Some cremations were placed in purpose-made cinerary urns, others in domestic pots. In Villanovan Italy the cremated remains were placed within hut urns, models in pottery of houses with pitched roofs, with a removable door or front panel through which the ashes and grave goods were inserted.

WOODEN CHAMBERS

In the Neolithic period long barrows often contained the remains of a wooden mortuary chamber or other wooden structure that had been used for the exposure of the dead. These were communal burial facilities. In contrast, in later times wooden chambers were unusual and generally housed a single principal burial of an elite individual. This became a common practice in the steppe region in the early third millennium and spread from there into other parts of Europe. Rather different wooden chambers under enormous barrows were occasionally built in central Europe in the Early Bronze Age

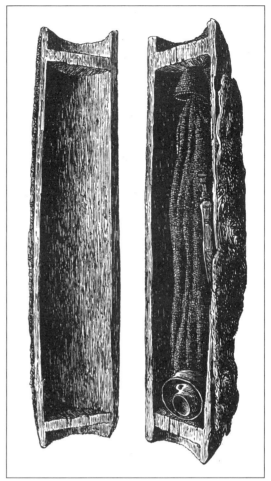

8.2 A Danish tree-trunk coffin containing the burial of an individual with a woolen hat and cloak, several pottery vessels, and a sword (Lubbock, John. *Prehistoric Times.* New York: D. Appleton and Company, 1890)

to house particularly important burials. Exceptional burials in some areas during the Iron Age were also placed in wooden chambers, notably in the Hallstatt period in western and central Europe.

Kurgans Wooden chambers housed burials of the early third-millennium steppe people (Pit Grave Culture), placed in pits under round barrows known as kurgans: some contained sacrificed horses. A few kurgan burials were found as far west as the Carpathian basin. Similar burials continued in the steppe region and through central Asia, becoming more elaborate in the mid-second millennium, when burials were placed in timber chambers resembling houses (Timber grave culture). Some Iron Age examples were lavishly furnished with large numbers of sacrificed horses and people as well as gold work, textiles, and fine objects of wood, many of which were preserved in the frozen tombs of the Altai region of central Asia.

Leubingen (Saxo-Thuringia, Germany) This earthen mound 28 feet (8.5 meters) high and 110 feet (34 meters) wide covered a cairn of stone slabs under which was a large triangular (tent-shaped) wooden chamber, made of timbers felled between 1942 and 1900 B.C. A man was laid on the floor of the chamber, facing its open end, and across his legs was placed the body of a young woman. The grave goods, which included weapons (a halberd, three daggers, and two axes), tools for carpentry and metalworking (three chisels, a serpentine pickax, and a whetstone), and jewelry (two spiral rings, two gold dress pins, a massive arm ring, and a spiral bead) all seem to belong to the man, and it has been suggested that the young woman was sacrificed to accompany him, although there is no evidence of this.

Łęki Małe (Poznań, Poland) In this cemetery of 11 mounds set in a row in a valley, one mound covered a chamber of wood, stones, and clay in which a man and a woman were buried. He was accompanied by jewelry and an array of weapons: a dagger, a flanged ax, and a halberd of bronze, a bronze pin, and a gold spiral. The woman wore two massive bronze anklets. Five pots and a number of wooden objects were also placed in the grave. Elsewhere in the mound another individual was buried with a chisel, a dagger, a flanged ax, three spiral gold rings, two amber beads, two dress pins, and five pots.

Vix (Burgundy, France) This sixth-century B.C. burial was associated with the hillfort of Mont Lassois, probable residence of a chief who benefited from trade with the Greeks. This is reflected in the grave goods, which included the famous Vix krater, probably a diplomatic gift, and other vessels for serving wine: an Etruscan bronze flagon and two Attic Greek cups (*kylixes*). The Vix "princess," aged around 35 and wearing a heavy gold torc, was laid out on a vehicle as a bier; its wheels were removed and stacked against the side of the plank-built wooden burial chamber, whose walls were hung with textiles. A stone cairn covered the chamber. Nearby was a large rectangular enclosure in which some funeral rites may have taken place. Pottery and animal bones in the ditches suggest feasting. A pair of life-size statues flanked the entrance to the enclosure; they represented a man with weapons and a woman wearing a neck ring.

CAVES

Natural caves were widely though infrequently used for burial chambers, though in some regions they were more common: For example, they were used in southern France and parts of Iberia in the fourth millennium and in the third millennium in northern Crete.

Margaux (Belgium) In this cave nine Early Mesolithic individuals were buried, with stones over and around them. Some were accompanied by stone tools.

Cueva de los Murciélagos (Almería, Spain) In this cave located high in the side of a gorge, a number of people were laid to rest around 4000 B.C. The arid environment has preserved the clothes in which they were clad and the artifacts of organic material placed with them: These included hats, tunics, belts, sandals, bags, and coiled baskets of esparto grass. Some baskets were filled with poppy heads, perhaps used as a drug.

Sculptor's Cave (Moray Firth, Scotland) This natural rock cleft was used between 800 B.C. and 700 A.D. as an ossuary, in which the bones of more than 2,000 people, particularly children, were deposited. Some had been decapitated. With them were offerings of bronze objects and exotic items such as imitation Roman coins.

Settlement Burials

In some of the Mesolithic settlements in the Iron Gates Gorge, such as Lepenski Vir, children were interred in the center of the house near the hearth and adults between the houses with their heads pointing downstream.

Human bones found in some Mesolithic shell middens suggest that graves were sometimes dug into these accumulations of domestic rubbish, although more frequently burials were placed in cemeteries. Middens in the Tagus estuary in Portugal covered burials in graves, sometimes lined with stones.

In Southeast Europe in the Neolithic people were often buried beneath the floors of houses, a practice common in the Near East. Burials might also be placed inside the oven or outside the house within or on the outskirts of the settlement. Some burials were cremations, though the majority were inhumations. A few grave goods, such as pottery, ornaments of bone and shell, tools such as bone awls, animal bones, and, later, small copper objects were placed with some of these individuals. Some burial within settlements continued after 4000 B.C., but by then burials were more commonly placed within an external cemetery.

In some Iron Age settlements human bones and on occasion complete corpses were placed in disused storage pits or settlement ditches; these may have been burials or sacrifices.

Inhumation Burials and Cemeteries

Inhumation of complete bodies was the predominant rite for the disposal of the dead in Southeast Europe throughout prehistory, though other rites also occurred, and was practiced in other areas from Mesolithic times onward. LBK burials were placed in small flat-grave cemeteries, some with inhumation, some cremation; the cemeteries were attached to individual hamlets or shared between a number of homesteads. Axes, arrowheads, and shell ornaments accompanied the men, and the women were furnished with grindstones and awls. In various parts of Iberia and Italy individual burials were placed in flat graves in the fourth millennium, but in both the Mediterranean and western Europe communal burial was the more usual method of disposal until the later third millennium, when single-grave burial was gradually adopted. Individual inhumations, with or without a barrow, became the norm throughout the western half of Europe from the late third millennium, although cremation was practiced in some areas. After an interval in the Late Bronze Age when cremation was the predominant rite, inhumation again became a common practice from the early first millennium, although throughout the Iron Age practices were quite varied.

MESOLITHIC CEMETERIES

Cemeteries were widespread in the later Mesolithic period in coastal regions of northern and western Europe, from Russia to Portugal; some were located beside the settlement, though in the north island cemeteries apart from the settlement were also common. The majority of these cemeteries contained inhumations of single individuals, though occasionally two or more people were buried together, and in some cases the graves contained cremations or collected bones. The associated grave goods were generally personal ornaments such as necklaces of perforated shells. Red ochre was widely used, and many graves contained antlers that often framed the body in the grave.

Mesolithic inhumation cemeteries are also known from other parts of Europe. In the Iron Gates Gorge of the Danube, settlements such as Vlasac had an attached cemetery of flat graves. Large cemeteries that began in the Mesolithic period and continued in use for millennia were created by the inhabitants of the Dnestr and Dnepr region of eastern Europe, such as the cemeteries in the Dnepr Rapids region of the Ukraine.

Oleneostrovski Mogilnik (Russia) This island was used by Mesolithic people as a cemetery during the seventh millennium B.C. The dead were buried with their heads toward the east; men with bone points, pins, and harpoons, and knives and daggers of slate; old men just with bone points; and women often with beaver-teeth beads. Pendants of beaver, elk, and bear teeth were also buried with some of the dead, the latter exclusively with young men. Nine individuals were accompanied by effigies of snakes, humans, or elks. In four of the 170 graves the bodies had been placed upright with a large number of grave goods; it has been suggested that these were shamans.

Skateholm (Sweden) This Mesolithic settlement at the head of a lagoon, which was inhabited in the winter, was associated with cemeteries placed on two small nearby islands. The great variety of different funerary rites practiced here suggests that the settlement and cemeteries were used by a number of separate family groups, each with their own practices, which included orientation in different directions, extended and flexed burials, inhumations, cremations, and partial burials, single and double burials, and burials with dogs. Other grave goods included jewelry of animal bone with women and flint blades and axes with men, and there were also separate burials of dogs, complete with their own grave goods.

Vedbaek (Denmark) This lagoon had a scatter of Mesolithic settlements around it. A cemetery at Bøgebakken serving one of these communities around 4800 B.C. had a number of graves neatly arranged in rows. Within these the bodies had been laid on their backs with their arms by their sides. In one grave a young woman was laid with her head on a folded garment, wearing a dress decorated with snail-shell beads and a number of pendants. Beside her, placed on a swan's wing, was her newborn son, accompanied by a flint blade like the other males in the cemetery. Red ochre was scattered over the baby and over his mother's pelvis and face. An adult male in another grave was placed on two antlers, with red ochre under his head and stones around his feet.

Vlasac (Serbia) Burials were concentrated in areas on the borders of the settlement, beyond the houses. More than 100 burials have been uncovered, arranged in several clusters. Some were accompanied by personal ornaments or materials such as ochre and graphite that could have been used in personal decoration. There were also a few cremations.

SOUTHEAST EUROPE

Inhumations within the settlement or on its outskirts was usual in Southeast Europe during the Neolithic period, but by the fifth millennium these were often placed in deserted parts of the settlement. Separate cemeteries began to be created in the late sixth millennium in some areas such as Bulgaria, and by the mid-fifth millennium such cemeteries were widespread in the southeast. The graves were often laid out in rows and did not overlap, showing that they were marked. People were placed in the grave in a crouched position, with their personal possessions, such as pottery, jewelry, and bronze tools and weapons, and sometimes gold work. Some graves contained two or three individuals. Inhumation in large flat-grave cemeteries continued to be the most common method of disposal in the southeast throughout prehistory, although other practices also appeared, such as communal burial in third-millennium Crete, and elite cremation burial in *tholoi* in Iron Age Macedonia.

Cernavoda (Romania) In this fifth-millennium cemetery of around 400 burials, divided into two areas, people were buried with jewelry made of copper, spondylus and dentalium shells, and marble, pottery figurines, animal bones, and stone axes and chisels.

Varna (Bulgaria) This exceptional cemetery on the Black Sea coast dated around 4500–4000 B.C., contained some 300 graves. Around 60 of these contained ornaments and other objects of gold, copper, and spondylus shell, and fine flint blades, but in most cases no associated body. Some of these cenotaphs also held clay masks, perhaps representing deceased individuals whose bodies had not been recovered. A few of the richly furnished graves did contain bodies; some individuals in other graves were buried with no grave goods, some with only a few, and others with more than 10 objects, of which pottery was the most common; shell and copper ornaments and flint tools were also included.

Tiszapolgár-Basatanya (Hungary) In this large cemetery of the late fifth millennium women were buried on their left side, accompanied by stone or shell necklaces, bone awls, pots, and sometimes copper rings and bangles, while men were laid on their right side with copper daggers, axes, pins, and awls. Some graves contained no grave goods, others had many; one man aged around 25 was buried with a dog at his feet, bones and antler from wild animals, a copper bracelet, four flint blades, eight pots, an antler hammer-ax, and a boar's tusk pendant.

BEAKER BURIALS

In the third millennium single burial became quite widespread in temperate Europe and the Mediterranean, often associated with Beakers: Although some Beaker burials occurred within megalithic tombs, most were in flat graves or graves under mounds; in some areas such as Scotland the grave might be lined with stones. Small cemeteries might be enclosed within a ring ditch or stone curb; in some a central burial furnished with numerous grave goods were surrounded by other graves with few or no objects. A mound might eventually be erected over the cemetery. In other cases an individual burial might have its own mound.

Male Beaker inhumations were usually accompanied by a Beaker vessel, and often weapons and archery equipment including barbed and tanged arrowheads and a stone wristguard. Both men and women might be buried with personal ornaments such as V-perforated buttons of jet or schist and copper pins.

Barnack (East Anglia, England) The burial of a man with a fine beaker, a copper dagger, a wristguard, and a bone pendant was surrounded by the graves of 15 other individuals, 12 of them without grave goods. All were placed within a ring ditch, and the cemetery was covered by a large barrow.

Amesbury Archer (Wiltshire, England) The richest Bronze Age burial in Britain was found near Stonehenge in A.D. 2002. The man, aged 35–45 when he died, was crippled by a serious knee injury. He was buried in a grave lined with wood, probably under a barrow, and was accompanied by more than 100 objects. These included three copper knives, five beakers, two archer's wristguards, 16 flint arrowheads, a bone pin, flint- and metalworking tools, and personal ornaments including boar's tusks

and a pair of gold earrings or hair tresses. The date of this burial, around 2400–2200 B.C., coincides with the period during which the bluestones and the sarsens were brought to Stonehenge, prompting speculation that this man may have been the leader responsible for one of these major feats of engineering and organization. Adjacent to his grave was the burial of a younger man, also furnished with a pair of gold earrings and a boar's tusk. A bone abnormality shared by the two indicates that they were related, perhaps father and son. Examination of the older man's tooth enamel shows that he had spent his childhood in a colder environment than Britain, probably in central Europe or the Alps: the "King of Stonehenge" was therefore an immigrant. The younger man, however, had grown up in Britain, spending his childhood in the south and his adolescence farther north.

IRON AGE BURIALS AND CEMETERIES

Inhumation was a common method of disposal in the first millennium, with cemeteries such as that at Hallstatt emerging early in the period. Burials of the elite often contained weapons, fine pottery, and metalwork, and sometimes horse harness. In some elite graves the body or the grave goods were laid on a wagon or chariot.

Hallstatt (Austria) The long-lived cemetery at Hallstatt contained more than 2,500 burials of individuals who had been involved in the salt-extraction industry. Wealthy women were buried with gold jewelry, while the richest male burials contained bronze daggers or swords of bronze or iron, several with gilded hilts. Other parade weaponry, bronze vessels, bronze helmets, and fine jewelry also accompanied elite burials, which were located in a secluded part of the cemetery. At the opposite end of the range were poor individuals buried without any grave goods.

Somme-Bionne (Marne, France) In this late fifth-century burial the man's body was placed on a two-wheeled vehicle, along with weapons including a sword in an engraved bronze scabbard, horse-trappings, and feasting gear, including a Greek Attic cup.

Cremation

Cremation was the custom of some groups in parts of Europe at various times throughout prehistory. For example, some of the graves in the cemetery at Mesolithic Skateholm in Denmark contained cremated remains; cremation as well as inhumation was practiced by Southeast European and LBK farmers; cremation was the custom in Hungary in the Early Bronze Age, when inhumation was the norm in the rest of central Europe; and in Britain, northwest France, and the Netherlands cremation was common throughout the second millennium, the ashes being deposited in urns or large pots, accompanied by few grave goods.

Cremation became the predominant rite across a large part of Europe (Urnfield Culture) in the later second millennium and early first. Thereafter, inhumation again became more common, but cremation was popular in some regions at some times, such as in the later Iron Age. Flat-grave cemeteries of cremation burials were the norm in Thrace in the Iron Age for ordinary people, while the elite were accorded more elaborate burials.

URNFIELDS

Urn burial was the principal method of disposal over most of Europe in the Late Bronze Age. The bodies were cremated, and the ashes and calcined bones were collected into urns of various forms, which were buried in vast urnfields. In the western part of the Urnfield zone some urn burials were surrounded by ditched enclosures; some of these were circular, while others took various forms, including keyhole-shaped. Small barrows were erected over the burial pits in some areas.

The fashion for inurned cremation burial probably originated in the middle Danube region, where cremation had been the usual rite in the earlier Bronze Age. It spread into Italy, through central and eastern Europe, and then western Europe, reaching Iberia by the ninth century. Urnfield burial was not adopted in the Atlantic region or the north, though other forms of cremation burial were common in these regions. Some urnfields also included a number of inhumations, ranging from a few to more than the number of cremations.

The grave goods associated with Urnfield burials were usually confined to a few small ornaments, such as fibulae and pins, and other small personal possessions such as razors, along with pottery. A few elite individuals were placed on a wagon on the funeral pyre, and their grave goods included fine tableware and a sword.

SCANDINAVIA

In Scandinavia tree-trunk coffins had earlier been used for inhumation burials. In the Urnfield period these were still used, but now held the calcined bones and ashes of the deceased, along with unburnt grave goods, usually personal possessions but also miniature swords. Often the graves in which these were placed were surrounded by a low stone setting in the shape of a boat.

IRON AGE

Cremation was practiced in some regions during the Iron Age, including southeast England in the last

8.3 A cinerary urn and lid. In the later Bronze Age cremation was widespread across Europe, and the ashes and calcined bones were collected and placed within an urn, which was deposited in the ground or in a tomb. (Worsaae, J. J. A. The Industrial Arts of Denmark. London: Chapman and Hall, 1882)

century B.C. where a number of rich cremation burials are known.

Welwyn Garden City (Hertfordshire, England) A deep pit contained the cremated remains of a young man surrounded by five wine amphorae, a number of silver, bronze and wooden vessels for serving and drinking the wine and other food, including a bronze strainer, a bronze nail cleaner, a number of other small personal objects, and various pieces of jewelry made of bronze, glass, and amber, 24 glass gaming pieces, and a wooden board.

Other Ways of Disposal

BODY PARTS

Burial was not always complete or final. Body parts, and particularly skulls, were kept back or removed from burials by Mesolithic people and treated in certain ways. On Oronsay in Scotland finger bones were inserted into middens, in some cases placed on seal flippers. The Mesolithic collection of skulls from Ofnet in Germany may be an extreme example of this practice. The Neolithic people of the western half of Europe also moved bones around, placing some in ritually significant places such as the ditches of causewayed enclosures and others in tombs, organized in various ways. Bones might be sorted into different types, which were stacked separately. Finger bones were pushed between the stones of one British tomb. In the Iron Age particular attention was paid to severed enemy heads and skulls, which were nailed up on houses or impaled on gateway posts, or carefully preserved in oil as trophies. Human body parts or bones were placed in a variety of ritual contexts, including shafts and enclosures.

ABSENT RITES

In many periods and places the number of burials that have been found seem far too few to account for all the dead. It is probable that cremation was far more widespread than can be demonstrated, given the difficulties of discovering or identifying unmarked graves containing calcined bone or ash and few grave goods; cremated remains might also be scattered to the wind or deposited in rivers and lakes, leaving no trace. For example, in Southeast Europe in the Neolithic period when the number of bodies found in the settlement is too small to represent the entire population it has been suggested that cremation was also practiced.

In other cases cremation was not the answer. For example, in the Iron Age funerary rites were extremely varied, changing with fashion or beliefs through time and from region to region; for much of the time, burial seems to have been eschewed, perhaps in favor of exposure since human body parts turn up in excavated rubbish pits. Some of the common two- and four-post structures on settlements may have been excarnation platforms. Other possibilities include the consignment of bodies to rivers, the air, and the sea. A cluster of material found in a dried-up channel of the Thames confirms this suggestion: It shows that between 1300 and 200 B.C. human bodies and defleshed bones were placed in the river beside an island, weighed down to prevent them being carried away by the river. Finds of first-millennium skulls in a number of British rivers also support the suggestion.

CANNIBALISM?

A number of instances of butchery marks on human bones show that sometimes the flesh was cut from the skeleton; this might have been part of a ritual that reduced a corpse to bones, since burial of excarnated bones was a practice of many prehistoric European groups. Usually, however, bones treated in this way were defleshed by exposure.

More controversially, butchery marks may be evidence of cannibalism, and this is supported by the discovery of human long bones broken in the way that would allow the marrow to be extracted. Cannibalism has been suggested by finds, for example, in some Mesolithic settlements, including Vedbaek and Dyrholm in Denmark, transitional Mesolithic-Neolithic Fontbrégoua in France, and in Iron Age deposits in rivers in Britain. Cannibalism was generally a ritual rather than a survival practice in recorded ethnographic and historical cultures, and this was probably true also of prehistoric Europe. Often cannibalistic practices revolved around the transfer of the spirit or powers of the deceased to the living, and so relatives and enemies might both be treated in this way by different groups.

MONUMENTAL TOMBS

In the Mesolithic period some burials were placed in stone-lined graves, and during the Neolithic period substantial chambered tombs were constructed, including megaliths in the western part of Europe and hypogea in the Mediterranean. Massive barrows covered wooden chambers in many areas of Europe, a tradition that began in the Neolithic period and continued in different forms into post-Roman times; in contrast, megalithic chambered tombs gradually went out of use during the third and second millennia though massive stone *tholoi* and smaller stone cists were built in some circumstances in later times.

Monumental tombs acted as a very visible statement of ownership, signaling a community's ancestral rights to its territory or a leader's control over it. The size of these monuments reflected the community or ruler's ability to mobilize an appropriate labor force for the task of construction, whether drawn from the community itself and undertaken as a pious communal task, or from neighboring communities induced to contribute labor, for example, in the context of a feast. It is likely that communities competed to make their own monumental tombs more impressive than those of their neighbors.

Megalithic Tombs

From the early fifth century funerary monuments constructed of stone began to appear in Brittany and Iberia; they spread along the Atlantic facade from Iberia through Brittany and western Britain to Scandinavia, and into parts of the interior of western Europe and the Mediterranean, notably southern Spain, the Pyrenees, central France, and the western Mediterranean islands, during the fourth millennium. Although they generally shared some features, such as the use of large stones in their construction and the practice of communal burial rites, the forms that they took were extremely diverse. Not only were the megalithic tombs of different regions distinct from one another, but tombs were frequently added to and changed through time and new forms adopted. Megalith building came to an end in most areas by the late third millennium, although some tombs were constructed even in the second millennium. Some megalithic tombs continued to be used for burial, often sporadically, long after the practice of erecting them had ceased, although many others were put out of commission by having their entrances sealed with stone rubble.

MEGALITHIC ARCHITECTURE

The megalithic tombs of Europe took a bewildering diversity of forms, depending in part on the materials locally available and in part on other considerations of which we have no knowledge. Each region developed its own characteristic forms of these megalithic monuments, variations on the theme of a circular, rectangular, or polygonal burial chamber constructed of massive, largely undressed, stones, often with drystone walling between them.

Some had a separate passage opening into a wider chamber or chambers (passage graves), while others were rectangular, with or without internal divisions (gallery graves). Often the tomb had an elaborate facade and entrance and a forecourt. Many tombs were roofed with stone slabs laid horizontally, but others had corbel vaulting.

The tombs varied considerably in size, from small cists to large passage graves with side chambers. In some cases the megaliths were freestanding, but generally they were covered by a mound often many times the size of the tomb and frequently delimited by a stone curb or wooden revetment and ditches. Most mounds covered a single chambered tomb, but under some there were two or more chambers. In some regions similar long barrows covered wooden mortuary structures. These also might have stone forecourts or facades. Pits, hearths, and human bones in the forecourts of chambered tombs were probably the result of rituals performed there.

MEGALITHIC BURIALS

Many rites were associated with megalithic tombs, including cremation, complete inhumation, and the interment of bones from corpses that had been excarnated, while some contained no funerary remains. In some cases many excarnated bones were burnt on a communal pyre. Within the tomb the bones were often arranged and rearranged in various ways, such as placing skulls in one area and long bones in another. In some cases it is possible that the tombs contained the bones of all the people of the local community, but frequently this was not so, certain individuals or a selection of bones being used as representatives. Although in some megalithic burials individuals were furnished with grave goods, in general the offerings placed in the tombs were not associated with individuals but with the community of the dead in general.

In contrast, some megalithic tombs were reused by later groups who practiced single burial, placing complete bodies and associated grave goods within the tomb, generally near its entrance.

EARLY MEGALITHS

The earliest megaliths were constructed in coastal Brittany and Iberia in the early fifth millennium. In western Brittany these took the form of one or several small chambers, each accessed by a passage, under a stone mound. In the Carnac region long mounds known as *tertres tumulaires* were erected, covering hearths, post settings, and small cists with human bones. Single standing stones or arrangements of menhirs were often associated with these mounds. In the Alentejo and Estremadura region of Iberia the earliest megalithic tombs were passage graves.

PASSAGE GRAVES

Around 3800 B.C. the chambered mounds of coastal Brittany were replaced by passage graves, under round or elongated mounds; some mounds covered more than one tomb. In a number of cases the menhirs that had accompanied the earlier graves were broken into pieces and reused as capstones in the passage graves. These were built until around 3500 B.C. but continued in use for a long time thereafter.

A great variety of forms of passage grave were constructed during the fourth millennium, from Sardinia, southern Spain, and Portugal, through Brittany and western Britain to Scandinavia and northern Germany, where TRB tombs were erected from around 3700 B.C. These tombs all had an entrance passage that led into one or several rectangular or polygonal chambers, constructed of orthostats and roofed with stone slabs or by corbelling. Generally, the tomb was covered by a large mound of stones or earth. The passage gave access to the tomb chamber, allowing burials or bones to be placed inside or reorganized, something not possible with cists or wooden mortuary chambers sealed inside their mound.

Swedish passage graves, generally erected in the period 3600–3300 B.C., had a large oval or rectangular chamber at right angles to the passage, covered by a round mound of stones, burnt flint, and turf with a stone curb. The Danish passage graves, known as *jaettestuer* ("giants' tombs"), had a low passage leading into a high chamber roofed by an enormous capstone, which generally protruded from the top of the round mound that covered the tomb.

In Britain early simple passage graves had a small round or oval mound covering the tomb; later this was often incorporated into a much larger long barrow. In some cases the original tomb was at one end and still accessible; in others it was entirely covered and a new tomb was built at one end. At the same time entirely new passage graves in long barrows were also constructed.

Although megalithic tombs in Britain generally went out of use in the later third millennium, in eastern and northern Ireland, northern Wales, and Orkney a new form developed from around 3300 B.C., known as the developed passage grave. This had a very long entrance passage leading to a circular or polygonal central chamber often with side chambers creating a cruciform plan. The passage was roofed with slabs and the chamber usually corbel-vaulted. These passage graves were contained within a massive round cairn with a curb of stone orthostats and sometimes a stone revetment at the tomb entrance; some mounds covered one tomb, as at Newgrange, while others covered several, for example, Knowth, which had two. In Ireland the burials within these tombs were usually cremations, though excarnated bones were also included; these belonged to many individuals. The funerary remains were often placed in the side chambers or in stone basins within the tomb. The Orkney passage graves

8.4 *A round mound covering two passage graves, from Röddinge in Denmark, and a plan of the same mound.* (Lubbock, John. *Prehistoric Times.* New York: D. Appleton and Company, 1890)

contained communal inhumations; that at Quanterness held the remains of more than 150 men, women, and children. Features of these tombs were connected with megalithic astronomy. These tombs were often decorated with spirals and other megalithic motifs. The tombs often occurred in closely grouped cemeteries of passage graves, often with associated standing stones or stone circles, dolmens, or other megalithic tombs, and Bronze and Iron Age burials in or around the tombs show the continued sanctity of the cemetery area.

In the Almeria region of southern Spain burials were made by the Millaran culture in similarly elaborate passage graves with side chambers and capstones or corbelled roofs, entered through portholes. These were covered by round barrows with stone curbs and

a great semicircular forecourt, surrounded by a circle of one or several rows of stones. Stelae (*baetyls*) were associated with some.

Hunebedden "Giants' beds," the passage graves of the TRB culture in the Netherlands, had a very short passage, generally constructed of a single pair of orthostats, and a long rectangular chamber set at right angles to it, under an oval mound edged with orthostats.

Clava Cairns (Inverness, Scotland) A round cairn covered a central passage grave opening to the southwest, sometimes housing a single inhumation. A stone circle might surround the cairn. The Clava cairns are confined to northeast Scotland and probably date to the late third millennium.

Entrance Graves A variant form of passage grave was found in Ireland, Cornwall, and the Scilly Isles, in which the sides of the passage diverge from the entrance to form a wedge-shaped chamber undifferentiated from the passage, under a round cairn.

Wayland's Smithy (Oxfordshire, England) A stone pavement with a low stone bank and six posts around it was used as the burial place for 14 individuals. Later, this mortuary house was incorporated into the center of a trapezoidal long barrow with a passage grave and a stone facade at the east end.

Boyne Valley (Ireland) The Boyne Valley cemetery area included the tombs of Newgrange, Dowth, and Knowth, and a number of smaller passage graves, some of them earlier, within an area of around 2 by 3 miles (3 by 4 kilometers), in which

8.5 A detail of the entrance to the great passage grave at Newgrange (Boyne Valley, Ireland), showing the massive carved entrance stone and the roofbox through which the sun shines at the midwinter solstice (© 2003 Charles Walker/Topfoto)

DEATH AND BURIAL

there were also standing stones, enclosures, and a ritual pond. Three other similar cemeteries are known in a band across Ireland, at Loughcrew, Carrowkeel, and Carrowmore. The passage graves were always built on hilltops or elevated ground.

Newgrange (Boyne valley, Ireland) A mound around 260/275 feet (80/85 meters) in diameter and 50 feet (15 meters) high was built of earth, stone, clay, and turf, enclosed in a ring of decorated curbstones above which a retaining wall 10 feet (3 meters) high had originally stood. By the entrance to the chamber this wall was constructed of boulders of white quartz and gray granite. A passage grave with an elaborate facade lay under a small part of the mound. A stone "roof-box" above the lintel allowed light to shine down the passage to the back of the chamber at the midwinter solstice, lighting up the tomb's interior for about 15 minutes. Great engineering skill was involved in building the tomb in the correct alignment to create this effect. Many of the stones of the structure, including the boulder lying across the entrance, some of the curbstones, and other stones outside and within the chamber were decorated with spiral and geometric patterns. Several of the stones also bore surveyor's marks used in the original layout of the monument. The tomb contained cremation burials, unburnt bones, antler pins, pottery, and stone pendants, though most traces of these had been removed or destroyed by the stream of visitors since the tomb was opened in 1699; it is likely that both bones and grave goods had originally been placed in the stone basins in the recesses.

Maes Howe (Orkney, Scotland) A stone and clay mound originally 125 feet (38 meters) in diameter and 26 feet (8 meters) high, surrounded by a bank and rock-cut ditch, enclosed a beautifully constructed cruciform passage grave with a vaulted roof. Some of the stones used in its construction were huge, while others were small slabs built up in horizontal layers. A massive triangular stone was used to seal the tomb and was kept in a recess when the tomb was open. A small gap left at the top of the doorway when the slab was in place directed the sun's light at midwinter sunset down the passage into the main chamber. The tomb was cleaned out at

8.6 A gallery grave from Bagneux near Saumur in France (Figuier, Louis. *Primitive Man.* London: Chatto and Windus, 1876)

a later date, so nothing is known of the burials that were originally placed within it.

Gavrinis (Brittany, France) A passage grave erected on what is now the small island of Gavrinis in the Gulf of Morbihan, formerly a promontory. A passage around 40 feet (12 meters) long led to the chamber; these lay under the eastern part of a huge cairn 200 feet (60 meters) in diameter, revetted with drystone walling. The tomb was richly decorated, most of the orthostats being carved with curvilinear geometric designs, axes, and crooks.

Los Millares (Almeria, Spain) A cemetery of passage graves stood outside the bastioned site of Los Millares, some with corbelled roofs. These tombs held collective burials, but the cemetery may have been divided socially, those nearest the monumental wall holding the most important people, accompanied by rich grave goods that included ostrich eggshells, ivory, callaïs beads, and small copper objects such as daggers, as well as larger quantities of more mundane objects such as flint arrowheads.

GALLERY GRAVES

Gallery graves were tombs in which the passage and chamber were not differentiated. The rectangular gallery might be divided into chambers by cross slabs. They were widely distributed, from Iberia and Sardinia through France and Germany to Sweden.

Allées Couvertes   In the later fourth millennium gallery graves, known locally as *allée couverte*, began to be built in Brittany; these consisted of a long rectangular chamber of orthostats, uniform in width and roofed by slabs. These were subsequently built also in other parts of France, such as by the Seine-Oise-Marne (SOM) culture in the Paris Basin. They were used generally for collective burial until around 2200 B.C., except in southern France, where burials continued to be made into the early second millennium. In some cases the gallery graves may have been freestanding, while in other cases they were covered by a mound. Compared with the offerings placed in passage graves, those deposited in gallery graves seem relatively poor. Tombs closely similar to those of SOM were also found in parts of Germany and Sweden.

Sepultures Coudées   Also known as angled gallery graves, these were a type of gallery grave, largely confined to Brittany, in which the gallery turned at the end to form a chamber at right angles to the gallery.

Court Cairns   These were built in northern Ireland and parts of western Britain, probably during the third millennium. The gallery of orthostats was divided by cross slabs into two or three chambers, containing cremated or unburnt remains or both. The gallery was accessed through an unroofed courtyard lined with orthostats, set within a rectangular or trapezoidal cairn, which also covered the gallery grave.

Wedge Tombs   These developed in western Ireland in the later third millennium and were used until 1200 B.C. or later, generally for cremation burials. The tomb was higher and wider at one end, usually the southwest, and completely enclosed in a round cairn with a curb of orthostats. There were two variant forms. In one the chamber was rectangular and built of a double row of orthostats set close together on each side; the chamber was probably completely enclosed by the cairn. The other form was probably open at the front, giving access to the gallery, which was rectangular with a rounded end. The chamber had a second, wider setting of orthostats around the first, hidden by the cairn.

Stalled Cairns   Stalled cairns were common in northern Scotland, including Orkney; in these the gallery was separated into chambers by cross slabs. The stalled cairn at Isbister in Orkney also had several small side cells opening off the main gallery. The tomb, which probably served as the repository of all the dead from a small community, contained many bones arranged into groups by type, skulls in one place, long bones in another, or into heaps of bone from a number of individuals, with a skull placed on top. The bones of eight sea eagles were also placed in the tomb.

DOLMENS

Dolmens were characterized by two to four massive orthostats supporting an enormous capstone. Probably originally enclosed or set within a mound or cairn, many are now freestanding and their contents long gone. They were constructed particularly in northern Europe and western Britain, and were often earlier than passage graves in the same regions.

Dysser   Dolmens, known as *dysser* in Denmark, were among the forms of megalithic tomb built by TRB in Denmark, Germany, and Sweden from around 3700 B.C. They were enclosed within round or long rectangular mounds and were probably inaccessible after the mound was constructed, though it has been suggested that access to the tomb could be gained by removing the capstone.

Portal Dolmens   Found in Ireland, Wales, and southwest England, portal dolmens were often defined by a setting or chamber of low orthostats. Two massive portal stones marked the entrance; a massive capstone was poised on these at the front, sloping down to rest at the back on a third orthostat or the stones of the chamber. Though many have no surviving ancient contents, cremations have been found in a few.

MEGALITHIC CISTS

Cist burials under mounds also occurred in a number of areas in the fourth millennium. The Globular Amphora culture in eastern and central Europe reused earlier TRB megalithic tombs or constructed cists with stone and earth mounds over them. In Britain and Brittany cist burials were earlier than some of the other megalithic tombs.

Rotunda Graves   In the Severn-Cotswolds region of England, round cairns of stone covered a central cist in which one or several inhumations were buried. Some were incorporated into the mounds of later passage graves.

Grands Tumulus   During the earlier fourth millennium B.C. huge mounds, known as Carnac mounds or *grands tumulus*, often more than 300 feet (100 meters) long and up to 30 feet (10 meters) high, were erected in the Carnac region. These were often built over smaller cairns, containing a square stone burial chamber with a massive capstone in which one or several people were buried along with a number of special objects, including stone axes and callaïs beads and pendants.

GIANTS' GRAVES AND NAVETAS

In parts of the western Mediterranean megalithic tombs continued to be built in the second millennium and were used for collective burial. In Sardinia these are known as *tombe di giganti* (giants' graves). These were gallery graves built of enormous dressed (*cyclopean*) slabs with a facade extending into a horned forecourt. In the center of the facade was a large slab with paneled decoration forming the entrance to the tomb.

The Balearic tombs known as *navetas* were also a form of gallery grave of cyclopean masonry, but their ancestry was probably in the local rock-cut tombs. The navetas often had an antechamber between the entrance and the tomb chamber, which had a rounded end and was sometimes oval rather than rectangular. Some navetas were divided into an upper and lower chamber. The name reflects the resemblance of the covering mound to an upturned boat.

Long Barrows

From around 4700 B.C. a tradition began in the northern parts of Europe of building long funerary mounds of earth and stones. These were rectangular or trapezoidal in shape, recalling Danubian longhouses in plan. Some were revetted with timber posts or drystone walling, and they were often flanked by ditches. The tradition may have begun in Kujavia in Poland. These long mounds were constructed by TRB in parts of Jutland and across the North European Plain from the Elbe to the Vistula and by the Neolithic inhabitants of eastern and lowland Britain, as well as in southwest England, where megalithic tombs were also built. Like contemporary megaliths, these mounds often contained the collected bones of a number of individuals; in Britain the mound often covered a mortuary house in which the bodies had been exposed for excarnation. Not all earthen long barrows contained collected bones, however.

Tholoi

In third-millennium southern Crete, communal burials were placed in *tholos* (or *beehive*) tombs, circular tombs built aboveground with a single entrance and probably with a vaulted roof, though these are not preserved. Some had attached antechambers. *Tholoi* seem to have been a Cretan invention, perhaps erected as artificial caves. In the second millennium rather different *tholoi* were constructed by the Mycenaeans, such as the magnificent "Treasury of Atreus" at Mycenae. These consisted of a long stone-lined open passage (*dromos*) leading to a circular corbel-vaulted chamber. The *tholoi* were dug into the hillside or built on the ground and set within a large round mound; mounds might also be built up over tombs cut into the hillside. Early examples were built of small flat stones, but later dressed stones of increasing size were used, and the final examples were constructed of huge blocks. *Tholoi* were used for the burial of royal families and contained few burials except in Messania, where they were family vaults used over many generations.

The use of *tholoi* for burial died out in classical Greece but continued farther north. In Macedonia the magnificent tombs at Vergina housed the remains of the Macedonian royal family; a tomb excavated here in the 1970s may be that of Philip II of Macedon, father of Alexander the Great. The Thracians also buried their royalty in *tholoi*, along with many ornaments, vessels, weapons, and pieces of armor made from gold and silver. One such tomb at Kazanluk in Bulgaria had a funeral banquet painting on its ceiling, while battle scenes were painted on its *dromos*.

Rock-Cut Tombs

Rock-cut tombs were constructed in some parts of Europe, particularly the Mediterranean regions. Some were subterranean and are known as *hypogea*, while others, including some Etruscan tombs, were cut into hillsides. Rock-cut tombs were excavated in the fourth millennium in Malta, Sardinia, Sicily, southern regions of France, parts of Iberia, and much of Italy. Collective burials were placed within them. The tombs generally had an entrance shaft leading into an often hemispherical chamber (from which the Italian examples take the name *tombe a forno*, "oven tombs"), and might be elaborated by the addition of a passage, an antechamber, or side chambers. Rock-cut tombs continued in use in the third millennium and later, but now they were used for single burials, often richly furnished with grave goods such as fine pottery drinking vessels, jewelry, and weapons of copper or stone. Elite burials in Iron Age Thrace were placed in rock-cut tombs, accompanied by rich grave goods of silver and gold vessels and jewelry.

MALTESE HYPOGEA

The best-known and most elaborate hypogea are in Malta, constructed in the fourth millennium.

Hal Saflieni (Malta) Also known as the Hypogeum, this massive labyrinthine underground rock-cut tomb near the temples of Tarxien resembled the Maltese temples in plan and was divided into a number of chambers with rock-cut pillars, lintels, and benches, and red-painted walls with spiral patterns. It held the remains of as many as 7,000 people and probably had a religious as well as a funerary function. It probably went out of use around 2500 B.C.

Brochtorff Circle (Gozo, Malta) In an area of natural caves used for burial, to which rock-cut tombs were added in the late fifth millennium, one excavated tomb contained the remains of 65 people, placed in the tomb over a period of time, the bones from earlier burials being pushed out of the way or removed when each new body was added. Around 3000 B.C. the burial site was transformed; a stone circle was built around it, with an entrance flanked by two large orthostats facing the nearby Ggantija temple. The caves were extended and the rock quarried away to create an underground complex of chambers approached down a flight of steps at the foot of which was a trilithon. Nearby were a large human statue, an area where bodies were displayed, and a pit where the bones of earlier burials were placed along with a quantity of red ochre. There was also an altar with a number of stone figurines, including two seated corpulent women and six schematic people with heads, belts, and tapering tunics.

WITCHES' HOUSES

In Sardinia rock-cut tombs were known as *domus de gianas* or witches' houses; the best known is Anghelu Ruju. These were cut into the hillside and had an antechamber, sometimes imitating a hut, from which one or a number of burial chambers opened. One tomb, at Mandra Antine, had painted walls. Many burials were placed in these tombs over a long period and included a range of Neolithic and Beaker pottery among the grave goods. The latter were mostly pots, but there were also stone tools and occasional copper daggers, axes, or awls.

READING

General

Cunliffe, ed. 1994, Milisauskas, ed. 2002, Champion et al. 1984.

Funerary Practices

Bradley 1998, Mithen 2003: Mesolithic; Whittle 1996: Neolithic; Kristiansen 1998, Harding 2000: Bronze Age; Collis 1984a, Lloyd-Morgan 1995, Jope 1995, James 1993, Ritchie and Ritchie 1995, Green 1992, Cunliffe 1997: Iron Age; Denison 2000c: deposition in water; Bailey 2000: Balkans; Cunliffe 2001a: Atlantic; Thrane 1999b, Jensen 1999a, Christensen 1999, Bogucki 2001: Scandinavia; Clarke et al. 1985, Darvill 1987, 1996, Burgess 1980, Bradley 1984, Parker Pearson 1993, Pryor 2003, Cunliffe 1995: Britain; Barclay 1998: Scotland; Barker and Rasmussen 1998, Trump 1980, Peroni 1996: Mediterranean; Ecsedy and Kovaćs 1996: Tumulus burials; Vandkilde 1999: Leubingen, Leki Małe; Srejović 1969: Lepenski Vir; Venedikov 1976, Renfrew 1980: Varna; Fitzpatrick 2005, Wessex Archaeology 2005: Amesbury archer; Thrane 1999b: Seddin, Håga, Bredadör; Carr and Knüsel 1997: Iron Age excarnation; Denison 2000c, Taylor 2001: cannibalism; Green 1992, 1997: Celtic funerary beliefs.

Monumental Tombs

Mohen 1989, Sherratt 1997, Daniel 1963, Renfrew 1981, Kaelas 1994b, Giot 1994, Bradley 1998: megaliths; Fitton 2002, Taylour 1983, Venedikov 1976, Andronikos 1980: *tholoi*; O'Kelly 1989: Ireland; Clarke et al. 1985, Darvill 1987, 1996, Burgess 1980: Britain; Barclay 1998, Ashmore 1996: Scotland; Ritchie 1995: Orkney; Tilley 1999, Glob 1974: Scandinavia; Bakker 1979, 1992: *hunebedden*; Guilaine 1992, Pericot Garcia 1972, Lanfranchi 1992, Trump 1980, 2002, Leighton 1999: Mediterranean; O'Kelly 1982, Stout 2002, Scarre 1998: Newgrange; Hedges 1984: Isbister; Chapman 1990: Los Millares; Venedikov 1976, Marazov 1998: Thracian tombs; Selkirk, Selkirk, and Selkirk 2004: Brochtorff circle.

9

WARFARE

The fragmentary evidence can support contradictory interpretations of the origins and development of European warfare. Death by violence can be detected only when it left some mark on the skeleton, except in the rare cases of individuals whose soft tissue is preserved (such as bog bodies). Often it is difficult to distinguish whether injuries were inflicted before or after death.

Even when the evidence of death by violence is unequivocal, it is often impossible to determine whether the death was an accident (due to a poorly aimed hunting weapon, for instance), a homicide, a ritual act, a judicial execution, or the result of armed conflict. A collection of skeletons including some with evidence of violent death may seem likely to represent a massacre during an armed attack, but could equally be an accumulation of sacrificial victims, or a community's dead, some of whom had suffered accidental death, laid to rest following tradition.

This evidence is viewed through the lens of opinions on the nature of humanity: Some scholars see people as inherently violent, while others believe people are driven to conflict only by external pressures such as starvation. As a result, reconstructions of Europe's past range from a Utopian vision in which warfare had no place before the time of the "war-mad" Celts to a grim picture of intercommunity violence stretching back deep into the Palaeolithic period. The truth probably lies somewhere between. While many archaeologists argue against warfare in the absence of pressure on land or resources, this is not the only potential casus belli, as historical and ethnographic studies show; others include xenophobia, competition for women, and greed. Social tensions or quarrels may escalate into long-running feuds in the absence of social mechanisms to resolve them. Some societies regard warfare as an extreme sport.

There seems to be general agreement that there is little sign of conflict in Southeast Europe during the Mesolithic and Neolithic periods. In contrast, the incidence of skeletal damage found among Mesolithic burials in northern and western Europe suggests that violence was a regular part of life, particularly in the Later Mesolithic, due perhaps to pressure on resources. Among the LBK farmers of central Europe there seem to have been episodes of extreme violence in which whole communities may have been massacred. In Neolithic western Europe some enclosed settlements were apparently attacked and their inhabitants killed, and some collective tombs included individuals who had suffered violent death.

Violence, therefore, was present in the early periods of European prehistory, but it is difficult to characterize; sporadic flare-ups generally seem more likely than the organized and institutionalized violence of warfare. There seem to have been no objects designed solely for attacking people; domestic tools and hunting weapons were used to inflict the injuries that have been identified. Nor were settlements generally defended against human attack, although the ditches, banks, wooden palisades, and stone walls used to demarcate settlements and keep animals in or out could also offer protection when violence erupted.

From the Chalcolithic period onward, however, the evidence suggests conflict was becoming both expected and managed. Sites in many parts of Europe, from the steppe through the southeast into central Europe and in the western Mediterranean, now had more businesslike defenses. Objects perhaps specifically designed as weapons, such as battle-axes, were now appearing, and the Beaker emphasis on archery equipment suggests that suitable tools were also being promoted as weapons. Individuals, particularly males, were regularly buried with such equipment, showing that being a warrior was now among the social roles marked in funerary ritual.

By the early second millennium warrior status and weaponry were becoming more apparent, and both developed rapidly, daggers giving way to swords of increasing efficiency and body armor appearing. Various clues, such as the emphasis on finely decorated weapons in some burials, depictions of warriors on rock art and stelae, and analogies with the nature of warfare in Mycenaean Greece, give an impression of societies where warfare was small-scale but persistent, where champions engaged in single combat and armed bands raided their neighbors to rustle cattle or women, and where honor depended on bravery in combat. The construction of defended houses and settlements, such as nuraghi and hillforts, offered protection for people and livestock against such raids. By the Late Bronze Age, perhaps as a result of the problems caused by climatic deterioration, warfare was becoming increasingly serious, with many well-fortified sites that suffered armed attacks, large numbers of weapons in circulation, and continuing innovation in military technology. These trends continued throughout the first millennium, and by the time classical authors were observing the peoples of barbarian Europe, warfare was a way of life for many men, large armies could be raised, and warrior bands might travel across Europe or into the lands beyond. Defended settlements were common, and fortifications were becoming increasingly sophisticated.

WEAPONS AND ARMOR

Weapons

Skeletons of people who died by violence during the Mesolithic and Neolithic periods show that everyday objects were used as weapons: Heads were hit with stone axes and antler picks and bodies were pierced by hunting spears and arrows. Maces, known from sometime in the Neolithic period, may have been the first purpose-made weapons or may have served some utilitarian function as well. Daggers were developed as Chalcolithic weapons, being elongated into swords during the Bronze Age. Weapons, particularly swords and spears, were subject to continuous change and improvement.

AXES

Holes and dents in some of the skulls found at late LBK Talheim and Schletz exactly match the blade shape of the axes and adzes used for woodworking and other domestic activities, so there is no doubt that these were employed as offensive weapons. Late Neolithic and Chalcolithic stone battle-axes and ax-

hammers and copper shafthole axes may have been intended primarily as weapons.

BOW AND ARROWS

The bow, used for hunting from the Late Palaeolithic period, was probably turned on people at an early date. Mesolithic rock art from the Spanish Levant shows groups of archers firing at one another. Many Mesolithic and later skeletons have been found with arrowheads or bone points imbedded in them, some undoubtedly killed during an armed attack, like the Neolithic man shot in the back while carrying a child from the Stepleton enclosure (Hambledon, England). Bows and arrows probably reached their peak of popularity in the Chalcolithic period, when many Beaker men were buried with archery equipment, including a wristguard to protect the wrist from the backlash of the bowstring. By the Middle Bronze Age bows and arrows were less important, but they continued in use in later times and were mentioned by Caesar.

Across much of Europe yew was the wood most generally used, since it is very hard but elastic. Some arrows were simple shafts with a sharpened wooden tip or a stone, bone or metal arrowhead; others were fletched with feathers. One of the Iceman's arrows was made in two pieces, joined with birch tar and thread, a feature shared by a number of other prehistoric arrows; this was probably so that they would break off in the wound, making them harder to withdraw.

The Iceman   (Alps, Italy) Among the equipment that the Iceman was carrying were an unfinished yew bow stave, a damaged fur quiver, two arrows with flint arrowheads and fletching, both broken, 12 unfinished arrow shafts, a bowstring, and fragments of antler for making arrow points. He had a stone arrow in his shoulder, having been shot from behind. This did not wound him fatally, but may have weakened him, combining with the effects of a recent illness to make him succumb to the elements on the high Alpine track he was following when he died. The most recent analyses suggest that he may have been fleeing an attack at the time; he had received a number of cuts, and his arrows and clothing bore traces of the blood of four other people.

SLINGS

It is assumed that slings were used throughout prehistory both for hunting and for fighting, though the evidence is slight. The baked clay balls and small stones that are sometimes found may have been used as slingshot. Dumps of large numbers of these in some fortified sites support their defensive use, for example, in the Chalcolithic Portuguese site of Castro de Santiago and by the gateways of a number of Iron Age hillforts. Caesar reported that the Gauls fired slag as slingshot.

SPEARS

Spears were used from the Palaeolithic period for hunting, both handheld and as projectiles, and also served as weapons in early times, though it was not until the Middle Bronze Age when socketed metal spearheads began to be developed that spear superseded arrows as the preferred projectile. Their frequency in Bronze and Iron Age burials shows that they were used by all warriors and particularly by fighters who did not own a sword. Small spears were used as projectiles, and these and large spears were both used as thrusting weapons; some Iron Age examples were as much as 8 feet (2.5 meters) long. The spearhead took many forms, with straight or serrated edges; some third-century examples became extremely long, resembling bayonets.

MACES

Disc-shaped stone objects with a shafthole were made in the Neolithic period and are generally thought to have been mace heads, used as weapons, although there is no clear evidence of this before the Chalcolithic period. Horse-headed scepters, characteristic of the Yamnaya culture of the steppe, may also have been used as maces.

KNIVES, DAGGERS, AND HALBERDS

Stone knives, potentially vicious weapons, would have inflicted damage mainly on soft tissue, so the evidence of their use is slim. Daggers were among the early objects made from copper, and these were imitated in stone; they were probably for display but may also have been functional weapons. By the Early Bronze Age daggers were very widespread and were among the grave goods in many elite burials, especially of men, as well as being frequently represented in art. They could have been used only at close quarters, and would therefore suggest single combat between warriors and surprise assaults by raiders rather than pitched battle. Blades were also mounted at right angles to a wooden staff as halberds in the Early Bronze Age: they were unreliable weapons as they tended to shear at the rivets joining blade to shaft.

RAPIERS AND SWORDS

During the second millennium daggers became longer, evolving into rapiers; long, slender blades with sharp points for thrusting at the opponent. These were difficult to wield efficiently; examples where the rivets between blade and hilt had given way show the strain imposed when warriors attacked with a sweeping action. By the later second millennium narrow rapiers had developed into wider swords with cutting edges, suitable for dealing slashing blows, and Carp's-Tongue swords (a long blade with a long narrow point and slotted hilt) designed both to thrust and to cut. At the same time hilts also evolved, giving a better grip and replacing the weak riveted join between blade and hilt with a flange extending from the blade to which a hilt of other materials was fastened. There were also solid-hilted swords; these were often badly balanced and in general show less use-wear than flange-hilted swords. In the first millennium iron blades gradually replaced those of bronze across Europe. Swords and before them daggers were confined to the elite. This is shown not only by their presence in rich graves, but also by the valuable materials used to decorate their hilts, including gold, bronze, coral, glass, and enamel. Parade weapons might also have decoration on their blades. Scabbards were made of metal, wood, and leather and were also often richly decorated. Winged chapes were developed in the Iron Age so a swordsman could steady his scabbard with his foot, allowing him to draw his sword with one hand.

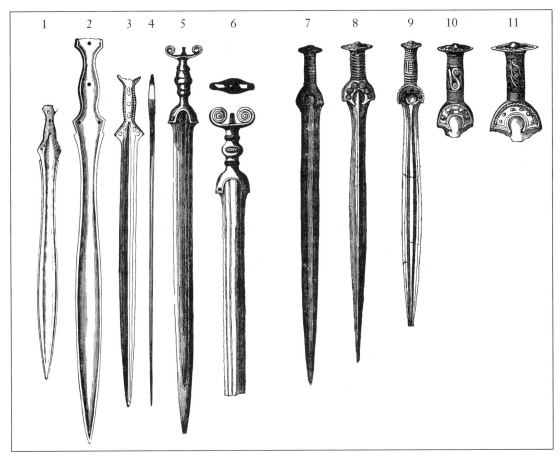

9.1 A selection of Bronze Age swords, including highly decorated solid-hilted thrusting swords typical of central and northern Europe (7–11), flange-hilted cut-and-thrust swords (1–4), and Late Bronze Age antenna-hilted swords (5, 6) (Lubbock, John. *Prehistoric Times*. New York: D. Appleton and Company, 1890)

Armor

Protective equipment is virtually unknown before the third millennium and was only seriously developed in the Bronze Age, when weapons became common and conflict more formalized and predictable. Shields and armor gave good protection in close-range conflict but were less effective against projectiles. As well as practical equipment, fine parade armor, often richly decorated, was made for show.

SHIELDS

The earliest surviving shield comes from a Globular Amphora tumulus at Langeneichstädt in Germany. Bronze Age shields were generally round, with a notch in one side, perhaps to allow a spear to be couched close to the body. Often they were decorated and strengthened with raised rims and bosses. Most surviving examples are of bronze, although several wooden molds used to make leather shields of the same design, two shields of alder wood, and one of leather are known from Ireland. Though rarely preserved, wooden or boiled leather shields were probably always more numerous than those of metal, which were generally far less tough. Identical shields are depicted in Bronze Age art.

Other designs were developed in the Iron Age. That most favored by the Celts was a flat elongated oval shield constructed of a single piece of wood or of two wooden panels held together with a central metal rib and boss. The latter covered the space left in the shield for the warrior's fist holding the horizontal metal hand grip and was also useful for punching an opponent, while the rim of the shield could be used to deal him a powerful blow under the chin.

HELMETS

Leather and bronze helmets were developed in the Bronze Age, the latter often for ceremonial use. An impressive pair of Late Bronze Age helmets were recovered from Viksø in Denmark; they bore long curved horns and a face made up of eyes, eyebrows, and a curling beak. In the Iron Age stronger helmets were made of iron. Some were plain domes, while others had extra features such as a top button, a neck guard, and cheek pieces. There were also tall helmets rising to a spike and helmets with horns or crests. More elaborate arrangements on the top included figures or heads of animals, such as boars and birds, intended to make the wearer appear larger and more menacing; one third-century helmet from Çiumeşti in Romania bore a huge raven with wings that flapped as the wearer charged. Helmets used for display, such as those found at Agris and Amfreville in France, might be covered with gold or bronze plating, decorated with intricate patterns, and embellished with silver, glass, and coral. Some Celtic tribes, however, did not wear helmets but went into battle bareheaded.

BODY ARMOR

Leather breastplates, body armor, and padded clothing of leather or thick wool may have been worn as a protection against arrows; a warrior depicted on a Chalcolithic stele from Petit-Chasseur in Switzerland probably wore such a garment, and Bronze Age figurines from Sardinia appear to be clad in leather tunics and kilts with small bronze bosses for added protection. Iron Age figurines also wear leather cuirasses. Most body armor dates from the Urnfield period or later. Corselets of bronze were often too thin to offer serious protection and were probably used mainly for show. Around 300 B.C. the Celts invented chain mail, a much more effective body protection. This was made of numerous interlocking

9.2 A shirt of chain mail from a Danish bog. This efficient body protection was probably a Celtic invention. (Worsaae, J. J. A. The Industrial Arts of Denmark. London: Chapman and Hall, 1882)

iron rings, individually forged, so they were expensive and time-consuming to make. Mail shirts, therefore, were confined to the elite, who probably handed them down to their descendants. The mail shirt might weigh up to 35 pounds (15 kilograms). Leg armor (greaves) of leather, bronze, or iron might also be worn.

Chariots

Light, extremely maneuverable chariots were developed during the first millennium. Chariot fittings in graves and wooden parts preserved in lakes allow the design of Celtic chariots to be reconstructed. The two wheels were fastened to the axle with linch pins, allowing them to be easily removed for lubrication, repair, or replacement. The chariot pole was attached to the axle, with a yoke at its front end to fasten across the neck, withers, or back of a pair of ponies. A flat platform was fastened to the axle; an arrangement of cotter pins and straps probably provided suspension so that the platform did not suffer the bumps and jolts of the wheels' passage over rough terrain. Arched wooden frames filled with wickerwork or leather or other types of side panel were erected on either side of the platform. The chariot generally held two people; a charioteer who sat at the front of the platform, holding the reins and flourishing a whip, and a warrior who sat or stood behind.

FORTIFICATIONS AND DEFENSES

Although settlements in prehistoric Europe were often open, from the Neolithic period onward many were surrounded by defenses in the form of a ditch, often with a bank, a stone wall, a timber palisade, or a combination of these elements. These protected the settlement against wild animals and kept domestic animals from straying. Substantial defenses were also designed to impress, defining the settlement,

making it visible, and emphasizing the power of its inhabitants. These defenses could also protect the settlement against intruders and attackers, and the growth of intercommunity conflict gave impetus to their development and elaboration. Many defended sites were located on high ground or on promontories, but there were also some low-lying settlements, sturdily fortified. Defended sites often served as a place of refuge for the rural population.

Fortified sites were designed for protection against sudden attacks and many show signs of violent destruction and abandonment. Many hillforts lacked a supply of drinking water or were unfit in other ways to withstand a siege, and siege warfare seems not to have played a part in prehistoric European warfare outside the Mediterranean.

Banks and Ditches

Ditches dug around settlements or houses and banks constructed of the earth taken from them presented a barrier that slowed the advance of intruders and put them at a disadvantage, exposing them to missiles (arrows, spears, and slingshot) fired by the defenders from the elevation of the bank. Earthen ramparts absorbed the attackers' missiles without significant damage and were hard to demolish, though they required constant maintenance to counteract erosion. Banks and ditches were used from the Neolithic period onward. In the east ditches were often combined with stone ramparts, and ditches were also regularly dug in front of timber palisades in later Europe. A number of Iron Age hillforts were defended by a series of bank-and-ditch circuits (multivallation). Sites that took advantage of promontories surrounded by water or steep cliffs were frequently protected by banks and ditches on their landward side.

CAUSEWAYED ENCLOSURES

A few of the causewayed enclosures of Neolithic northern and western Europe, with their interrupted ditch-and-bank defenses, seem to have served as fortified settlements, their banks enhanced by the addition of a stout wooden palisade.

Crickley Hill (Gloucestershire, England) This promontory was completely enclosed by defenses that began as a ditch, low bank, and fence with three to five entrances. It was later reconstructed into an enclosure with a massive ditch broken by two entrances. A palisade surrounded the settlement inside the ditch, with two timber-lined gateways. The settlement was the subject of a massive attack by a party armed with bows and arrows; more than 400 arrows were found at the gateways alone. The settlement was abandoned thereafter.

LATER EARTHEN RAMPARTS

Dump Rampart The dump rampart lacked any internal structure; a defensive line of earth was piled up into a bank and was often topped by a palisade; some examples were built of stones instead of earth. They were particularly effective against arrows, slingshot, and other missiles.

Fécamp Rampart A variation, used in France, in which the rampart was combined with a wide flat-bottomed ditch; it may have been devised specifically as a defense against Roman artillery.

Stone Fortifications

Stone walls around settlements were most common in the Mediterranean and the Atlantic west, including the cyclopean defenses of the Mycenaean world and simpler walls of drystone or roughly shaped stone blocks. Stone was also used to construct defensive houses and towers, designed to withstand lightning raids but not a siege.

STONE RAMPARTS

Carn Brea (Cornwall, England) A Neolithic hilltop enclosure combining a boulder wall and a stretch of ditch with natural granite outcrops, protecting a settlement, Carn Brea fell to an attack in which hundreds of arrows were fired, including more than 800 that landed within the settlement; many of these were calcined, showing that the settlement was burned down.

Murus Duplex A form of rampart was described by Caesar, in which walls of drystone with stone facings were constructed in layers outward, with several facings within the wall. This imparted strength to the wall, making it harder to demolish.

IBERIAN FORTRESSES

The late fourth-millennium fortified settlements of Los Millares, Vila Nova de São Pedro, Zambujal, and others in southeast Spain and southern Portugal were surrounded by massive walls with great bastions and elaborate gateways. Though these are generally

9.3 Reconstruction of an attack on the causewayed enclosure of Furfooz in France, the attackers armed with bows and arrows, the defenders using stone from the walls as weapons. A British enclosure at Carn Brea, similarly incorporating stone walls in its defenses, fell to a massive assault by archers. (Figuier, Louis. Primitive Man. *London: Chatto and Windus, 1876)*

thought to have been designed to impress rather than as functional defenses, some scholars note their effectiveness against attack with arrows and point out possible slits in the walls for returning fire.

DOMESTIC STRONGHOLDS

Tower Houses During the second millennium fortified dwellings were constructed in Sardinia (nuraghi), Corsica (*torre*), and the Balearic Islands (talayots). These had two or three floors reached by stairs and corridors built inside a double wall of stone and served as a place of refuge during intercommunity raids. Stone bastions or houses with stone walls were constructed around the base of some of these towers from the 12th century to accommodate whole communities in safety. Towers (*morras* or *motillas*) were also constructed in southeast Spain; these were surrounded by several stone walls between which were areas partitioned for storage or industrial activity. The houses of the community were located outside these walls. In the late first millennium tower houses (brochs) were built in Scotland; these had massive double walls with a stair between them leading up to storage cells, and an interior space used for accommodation. Stone-walled houses were built around the outside of some Orcadian examples, housing larger communities, with a defensive wall surrounding the whole settlement. There is little evidence from the brochs of actual attacks, suggesting that the existence of such strongholds acted as a deterrent.

Stone-Walled Houses and Settlements A number of different forms of stone-walled house were constructed in Iron Age Scotland, including wheelhouses and aisled roundhouses, accommodating an extended family. More widespread were farming settlements with drystone walls that surrounded or incorporated buildings; these included the Iron Age forts, rounds, raths, and duns of western Britain and Brittany and the polygonal walled pastoral enclosures of Chalcolithic southern France.

Ramparts

Timber palisades and earth and stone ramparts were combined with banks and ditches from the Neolithic period onward. During the Iron Age in particular, many varieties of rampart were developed, making use in different ways of stone, timber, and soil. In central Europe these often took the form of an outer facing of upright timbers or stone on an earthen bank; soil and stone ramparts reinforced with horizontal timbers, very resistant to assault, were more usual in western Europe. Ramparts using timber in the construction might have towers but generally carried the rampart up to the required height. In contrast, stone walls and dump ramparts could be lower and often had timber breastworks and parapets above.

PALISADES

A simple timber palisade was a widespread form of defensive circuit. This was constructed of close-set timber uprights driven into the ground or erected within a foundation trench. Many early hillforts were defended by a timber palisade as was the famous Polish settlement of Biskupin. The defenses might be strengthened by digging a ditch in front of the palisade and banking up the soil behind it.

IRON AGE RAMPARTS

Kastenbau Rampart Many timbers were laid crisscross to create boxes that were filled with soil.

Timber-Laced Ramparts The *murus gallicus* was a form of timber-laced rampart described by Caesar as characteristic of Gaul. The front of the rampart was faced with a skin of stonework through which protruded the ends of a series of massive timber beams. These ran through to the vertical face or a sloping ramp of earth at the rampart's rear and were interlaced with other timbers laid at right angles; iron spikes were driven through the intersections. The core of the rampart was filled with stones and earth. The simpler Ehrang rampart was similar but lacked the iron spikes.

Timber-Reinforced Ramparts Timbers ran through the core of the Preist-Altkànig rampart joining front and rear faces: these had a stone lower portion and timber above. Other ramparts had timbers running from the front face into the core: the Kelheim rampart was faced with vertical posts separating stone panels, while the Abernethy rampart had a rubble and earth core faced with a drystone wall at front and rear. Ramparts of the latter type built using igneous or metamorphic stone are known particularly in Scotland and France, where their destruction by fire caused the stones to fuse, creating "vitrified forts."

Box Rampart The front and rear walls of the rampart were formed of timber uprights infilled with wicker work. Between them was a core of earth. The Hod Hill version had a slighter rear revetment, lower than the front face and not anchored into the ground.

Other Defenses

CHEVAUX-DE-FRISE

A number of Iron Age sites, particularly in Iberia but also in parts of Britain, had a *chevaux-de-frise*, an additional defense designed to slow the advance of attackers and prevent the approach of mounted men. This was composed of a large number of sharp stones placed facing outward in offset rows so that people approaching had to weave their way in and out. Similar obstacles in timber may have been more widespread.

GLACIS

Hillforts built on a slope were sometimes defended by a glacis, a spread of artificial scree. This made it extremely difficult to walk up the slope to the foot of the defenses, and impossible to run or to approach silently. A glacis could very effectively be laid on a bank that ran continuously from the base of the ditch to the base of a timber or stone breastwork.

WATER

Some settlements were located to make use of bodies of water in their defenses. Iron Age crannogs (artificial islands) were situated in lakes, with access either by boat or across a narrow causeway, which might include a drawbridge, although their location was probably more for prestige than for defense. Other island settlements were more substantially

defended: For example, the Late Bronze Age settlement of Wasserburg in southern Germany was surrounded by a palisade set on piles. This incorporated towers and watergates and was linked to the island settlement by bridges.

Promontories jutting out into lakes or surrounded on most sides by a river were also chosen for defense. For example, the Polish town of Biskupin was built on a promontory, with its landward end protected by a swamp. A long, narrow bridge from firm ground skirted the town's stockade, allowing the inhabitants to overlook, and if necessary bombard, those approaching the gate.

Gateways and Entrances

The entrance to a site was generally the most vulnerable place in the defensive circuit and other features of the defenses, such as a glacis, might channel attackers toward it. Entrances were therefore often heavily defended, incorporating features such as massive gates, towers, bastions, guard chambers, entrance passages, and outworks.

GATEWAYS AND ENTRANCE PASSAGES

The gap in a rampart was often lined with timber to form an entrance passage into which a single gate or a pair of gates were set. In some cases the ends of the rampart were turned inward, creating a more substantial passage. Many had timber or stone guard chambers immediately behind the gate.

A number of Iron Age Scottish dwellings, including duns and brochs, were entered via a passage that ran through the thickness of the stone wall. A heavy door partway down closed the passage, with drawbars that could be shot behind it. In some cases a guard chamber was let into the thickness of the wall so that attackers who managed to force the door could be dealt with before they left the confinement of the passage.

TOWERS AND BASTIONS

Towers might be erected flanking the gateway in a palisade, but they were not common in temperate

9.4 Depictions of Bronze Age warriors in Scandinavian rock art. The pair in the boat (left) wear horned helmets, carry round shields, and are perhaps armed with axes, as is the warrior on the right. (Worsaae, J. J. A. *The Industrial Arts of Denmark.* London: Chapman and Hall, 1882)

Europe. In some hillforts a bridge was constructed above the gate, linking the two sides of the rampart, and in others, for example, at Biskupin, a tower was erected over the gateway. These constructions allowed the defenders to fire or drop missiles on attackers as they attempted to force an entry. Bastions projecting from the line of the wall or rampart allowed the defenders to cover the approach to long stretches of the defenses with missile fire. Rare examples of bastions are known in the Chalcolithic fortified sites of southern Iberia such as Los Millares. They were also present at the Heuneberg in Germany as part of the unusual mud brick wall erected here at the time of Greek trading contact in the sixth century B.C.

OUTWORKS

Various arrangements might be made to slow the approach to the gateway and expose the enemy to attack from the ramparts. One simple method was to construct a freestanding bank-and-ditch outwork immediately in front of the entrance, forcing the attackers to pass round it to right or left, exposing

their unprotected flanks. Another employed a bank and ditch extending like a horn from one end of the rampart, forming a corridor down which the attackers had to pass. More elaborate versions multiplied these arrangements, leading attackers down a tortuous network of passages flanked by earthworks from which the defenders could rain down missiles.

WARRIORS

Although Mesolithic and Neolithic conflict could result in extreme violence, it was not until the Chalcolithic period that burial evidence and artistic representations indicate that men (or at least the elite) were regarding themselves as warriors, equipped with bows, battle-axes, and daggers. The increasing importance of warrior status in the second millennium was reflected in votive hoards and warrior burials, which frequently included weapons and parade armor. While bows and throwing spears enabled people to be killed at a distance, the development of daggers, halberds, and rapiers implies fighting at close quarters; it seems likely that the matching of champions and the concept of honor in overcoming an opponent in personal combat, strongly developed in Mycenaean and later Celtic society, had their beginnings at this time. By around 1300 slashing swords were the elite weapon, while ordinary soldiers were equipped with spears. Considerable edge damage to swords shows that they were used in combat, not just for show. While raiding and single combat seem likely to have been the main forms of Bronze Age warfare, pitched battles may also have occurred. Warfare was a major preoccupation during the Iron Age, and this was reflected in the continued deposition of weapons and parade armor in graves and votive hoards. By Roman times the Celts, Germani, and other European peoples were engaged in endemic warfare, conducting raids against their neighbors and raising armies that crisscrossed Europe. Some warrior bands sought employment as mercenaries; in other cases whole communities, men, women, and children, would move together, fighting to gain booty or land on which they could settle.

Warrior Burials

Grave goods frequently reflect the status and social personae of the deceased. From the Chalcolithic period onward, men, and particularly the elite, were buried with weapons, implying that society viewed them as warriors. Many male Beaker burials were furnished with archery equipment. In Southeast Europe copper daggers accompanied some fourth-millennium male burials and these became more widespread in the third millennium, while in the north they were imitated in flint. Elite burials in the Early Bronze Age were furnished with rapiers, spears, and wooden or leather shields, while the graves of less important individuals often contained spears, frequently deposited in pairs. By the 13th century elite burials had a sword and bronze body armor. Well-furnished male graves in the Iron Age contained a range of weapons and armor, with carts or chariots and horse harness in some.

Warriors in Art

Artistic representations of conflict and warriors are known from the Mesolithic period onward.

ROCK ART

Rock paintings in the Spanish Levant show warriors armed with bows and arrows, sometimes alone but often lined up as opposing war bands in scenes full of movement. Some of these date to the Mesolithic period, while others, on the evidence of arrow form, may be later. Some warriors are wearing headdresses, perhaps of feathers, and occasionally body ornaments, probably also of feathers.

Bronze Age rock engravings from Scandinavia show (often ithyphallic) men brandishing swords and axes on long shafts, singly or opposing each other in pairs, sometimes on the deck of boats. The rock engravings of Val Camonica also feature warriors brandishing swords and holding up shields.

SCULPTURE, FIGURINES, AND RELIEFS

Many of the Chalcolithic and Bronze Age statue menhirs of the Atlantic and Mediterranean regions represent warriors, often wearing a neck ornament and a belt and perhaps a leather chest protection. Some were equipped with a bow and a dagger, others with a battle-axe and a dagger or later a sword. Many of the bronze figurines of Late Bronze Age Sardinia depicted warriors, clad in tunics with metal bosses, helmets, greaves, and bossed belts, carrying bows, swords, daggers, and shields.

Funerary slabs in southwest Iberia in the second millennium were carved with short swords and axes. By the first millennium they depicted a round shield with a notch, a sword and spear, and personal equipment such as a mirror; sometimes they also showed a stick figure and his chariot or war cart. The warrior statues erected in Iron Age northern Spain held a small round shield against their abdomen and a dagger in their right hand. These are shown also in Greek-inspired sculptures in eastern Spain, where the warrior wears a circular breastplate. An Etruscan funerary stele from Bologna depicts a fight between a mounted Etruscan warrior and a naked Celt armed with a short sword and a shield that protects him from chin to thigh. In the Hallstatt chief's burial at Hochdorf a bronze couch was decorated with a frieze of warriors fighting in pairs with sword and shield, framed by a wagon at each end. Warriors were also depicted on some Iron Age bronze vessels, including the Gundestrup cauldron, where a file of foot soldiers marches, carrying long rectangular shields with metal bosses, followed by others blowing carnyxes.

Celtic Warriors

Classical authors such as Strabo regarded the Celts as war-mad, welcoming every opportunity to engage in warfare. For the elite, armed raids and single combat were probably major activities in their normal lives, whereas the farmers and other ordinary people became involved in warfare only when they were threatened. Individual chiefs and nobles, armed with swords and owning horses and chariots, were supported by parties of followers armed with spears; farmers and other occasional combatants probably mainly fought with bows and arrows and slings.

Feasts, where drunkenness was a normal part of the enjoyment, were often the scene of contests between warriors; these were undertaken as a sport but could nevertheless end in serious injury or death. Feasts were also an occasion for an ambitious and adventurous warrior to recruit a war band of volunteers who would go off to seek their fortune. These might join with bands from other tribes to form large forces of confederate warriors such as the Gaesatae. Some bands found employment as mercenaries for the Macedonians, Egyptians, Carthaginians, Romans, and various Anatolian states; others grew rich on the spoils of armed expeditions like that in 387 B.C. during which Rome was sacked, a humiliation the Romans never forgot.

Although battles could involve thousands, barbarian Europeans fought more as individuals than as cooperating armies. Disciplined Roman troops were often able to overcome much larger parties of Celts or Germani, who would throw away tactical advantage in pursuit of personal glory. A warrior marked his success by cutting off the heads of defeated opponents, tying them to his horse's neck

or impaling them on his spear, and on his return home nailing them up as trophies on his house walls. Some Celtic warriors such as the Gaesatae, who faced the Romans at Telamon, enhanced their prestige by fighting naked (a practice that, while exposing them to greater likelihood of injury, ironically greatly reduced the risk of their wounds becoming infected).

CHARIOTS

From the fifth century two-wheeled chariots developed as an important arm of Celtic combat, to be superseded by cavalry by the second century. Only in Britain did the chariot remain important, surviving in Ireland into post-Roman times.

The cost of commissioning a chariot and maintaining a chariot team meant that only the elite owned them. Celtic warrior nobles would begin a battle by driving around hurling spears at their opponents. Chariot forces were often deployed on the flanks. After the charge, however, chariot fighters would dismount to engage in hand-to-hand fighting on foot while the charioteer drew up the chariot on the sidelines, ready to drive his warrior swiftly away from the battlefield. The Celts became exceptionally skillful in maneuvering their chariots at speed and could perform feats such as running along the chariot pole while the chariot was in motion. Irish literature asserted that a skilled charioteer could make the chariot leap ditches and could stop or change direction suddenly.

IRON AGE HORSEMEN

Horse riding was developed and perfected in the steppe and from there spread into Europe. However, the difficulty of controlling horses with the harness available (reins and bar bits) made it impractical to fight on horseback until the Late Iron Age, when the four-pommelled saddle was introduced, probably from the steppe region. The saddle, which had two pommels behind the rider and two in front curving back over the rider's thighs, provided a firm seat, allowing the rider to maneuver and use weapons. Germanic warriors, however, were said to find the use of the saddle shameful, preferring to depend upon their own skill to keep their seat. Elite cavalry became widespread in the later first millennium. The Celts gained a reputation in the classical world as skilled horsemen and mounted warriors, and Gallic and Iberian cavalry were employed as mercenaries by the Carthaginians. Mounted warriors were generally heavily armed. In battle, hurling javelins, they would attack the infantry with ferocious charges designed to break the foot soldiers' nerve. Some groups fought on horseback, using lances and swords, and art shows horsemen with spears. In general, however, once fighting began in earnest they would dismount and engage in hand-to-hand fighting on foot.

Female Warriors

The Greeks had stories of the Amazons, female warriors of the steppe. A number of steppe burials from the fifth century onward were of warrior women, buried with military equipment including arrows, swords, spears, shields, and armor. Celtic women were renowned for their courage and ferocity; they did not usually go into battle, according to classical sources, but were often stationed on the sidelines, giving vocal encouragement to their own forces and abusing the enemy. At times, however, they were moved to take part: For example, when the Roman general Marius fought the Ambrones, the women, armed with swords and axes, set upon both their fleeing menfolk and the pursuing Romans. Queen Boudicca of the Iceni was actively involved as one of the leaders of the British uprising against the Romans in A.D. 60, and in the same year the Roman troops had been disturbed by being opposed by belligerent women when they attacked the island of Anglesey, stronghold of the Druids.

CONFLICTS, BATTLES, AND WARS

The victims present the most graphic evidence of conflict. Many Mesolithic burials, for example, at Schela Cladovei in Romania, Téviec in France, and Vedbaek in Denmark, are of individuals with fractured skulls or arrows still imbedded in their skeletons. Some LBK communities seem to have suffered wholesale massacres. Skeletons and arrowheads at some causewayed enclosures in Britain underline the occurrence of armed attacks in the Neolithic period, at least in the western half of the continent. A small proportion of individuals in Neolithic and Chalcolithic burials and communal tombs in France and Iberia exhibited clear evidence of violence, particularly blows to the head and arrow wounds, the latter increasing in frequency after 3500 B.C. Some individuals had healed injuries. A few bones bore marks of knife attacks; these were probably more common since knife wounds inflicted on soft tissue could have caused death without leaving any skeletal trace.

Burials in later times continued to include individuals who had suffered injury or violent death, and occasionally there are remains that suggest mass murder. Many hillforts or fortified settlements were abandoned after armed attack. Combat seems to have become more formalized and fighting a male activity; there is less evidence of the wanton killing of women and children. In the Late Iron Age classical sources provide written accounts of battles.

Victims of Violence

Dnepr Rapids (Ukraine) In an Early Mesolithic cemetery at Voloshkii three of the 19 burials were of individuals who had died from arrow wounds. Similar evidence comes from two cemeteries at Vasilyevka, dated around 9000 B.C., where nine out of 70 skeletons had projectile injuries and a further two had suffered heavy blows.

Ofnet (Bavaria, Germany) Two pits ("skull nests") were discovered here, containing between them the carefully arranged skulls and jaws of 34 (or 38) Mesolithic individuals, mainly women and children. All four adult men, half the children, and a quarter of the women had suffered blows to the head. The victims had all been decapitated, though it was not clear whether they were killed in this way or if their heads were cut off immediately after death. Mollusk shells and perforated deer teeth indicate that most were wearing a decorated cap or jewelry. The heads may not all have been buried at the same time.

Talheim (Neckar valley, Germany) At Talheim a large pit containing the jumbled remains of at least 34 late LBK men, women, and children with multiple injuries was found. Most were killed by blows to the head with a stone ax, and some had been struck so hard that the ax made an ax-shaped hole in the skull. Others had been shot with arrows. All appeared to have sustained their injuries from behind, indicating that they were fleeing rather than fighting. Several were struck repeatedly after they had fallen; evidently the aggressors were intent on ensuring that their victims were dead. The bodies were tidied into a pit without any attempt at funerary treatment, presumably the disrespectful action of the victors. Analysis of the victims' DNA indicates that all were related, suggesting the mass murder of an entire extended family, ranging from children to one individual over 60; only the infants (if there were any) were spared.

San Juan Ante Portam Latinam (Alava, Spain) A rock shelter was used between 3800 and 2800 B.C. as a communal burial place in which some 300 individuals were interred. Among them were nine men with arrows lodged in their skeletons. Most had been shot from behind by crouching archers, implying surprise attacks rather than combat. The presence of 55 arrowheads in the rock shelter suggests that other individuals had died from arrows penetrating their soft tissue. Some people had suffered injury to their head or to forearms raised to protect their head from blows. The incidents in which the injuries were sustained occurred throughout the period in which the tomb was used, but most bodies showed no trace of violence.

Wassenaar (Netherlands) A mass grave dated around 1700 B.C. contained the remains of seven men, three women, and two children, perhaps a family killed in a raid. One young man had a flint arrow lodged between his ribs, three other men had suffered blows to the head, and one of the children was buried with his head separated from his body.

The group was carefully arranged in two rows, one facing east, the other west, with their legs overlapping, the men in the center flanked by the women, with the children at the edges.

Velim (Czech Republic) At Velim a series of Middle Bronze Age pits formed interrupted ditches that contained the bones of several hundred people, probably the victims of violent death. Some were whole individuals, others were incomplete skeletons, and some bore cut marks suggesting dismemberment or even cannibalism. Men, women, and children were represented. Most appeared to have been tipped in rather than carefully buried, and there was little in the way of accompanying material.

Maiden Castle (Dorset, England) This 43-acre (17-hectare) hillfort was defended by three to four massive ditches with banks surmounted by a high stone and wooden wall, their layout dictating a tortuous and exposed approach to the summit. A group of 14 graves at the eastern entrance was identified by Sir Mortimer Wheeler as a war cemetery for the hillfort's final defenders during the Roman conquest of Britain. At least one individual here had indeed been killed by the Romans, since he had a Roman spearhead in his spine. Others had sustained sword cuts or spear wounds to the head, and four also had partially healed injuries. It now appears, however, that the hillfort was largely deserted by the time of the Roman conquest. The "war cemetery" formed part of a much larger cemetery used for more than a century, in which three-quarters of the burials were of uninjured individuals. The bodies may have been brought here for burial from the surrounding area.

Battles

Classical sources record that the Celts were ferocious and brave but undisciplined fighters. Armies were drawn up in contingents by tribe, each with its own battle standards. In the lead-up to a battle the Celtic forces would engage in activities intended to intimidate their opponents and awaken their own battle frenzy: flaunting themselves and their military equipment, demonstrating their skills in maneuvering

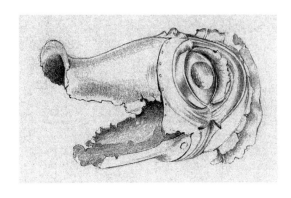

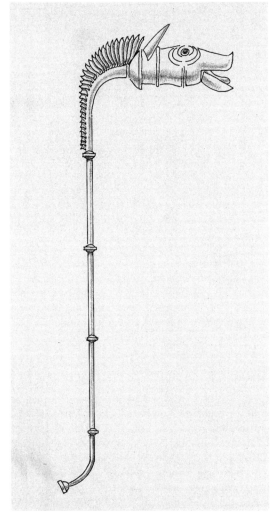

chariots and managing horses, blowing the raucous war trumpets (carnyxes), yelling battle cries, shouting boasts, singing battle songs, and hurling insults. They would often sit watching while their champions engaged in single combat.

After these initial exchanges battle would be joined. The elite would charge down in chariots or on horseback, raining javelins upon their enemy. Behind them came the foot soldiers, also at the charge. The elite would dismount and join them, and hand-to-hand fighting would begin. The battle lines would quickly break up into individual contests. Classical authors reported that the Celts were ferocious and utterly fearless fighters in the initial part of the battle, but easily gave up if they did not quickly succeed in disheartening or routing the enemy. Battles between Celtic forces seldom lasted more than an hour or two. Individual warriors or groups of fighters might decide the day was going badly and retreat, particularly when faced by classical armies who stood fast and cooperated as a single body. The Romans' weapons were also superior to those of the Celts for formation fighting. The Germani resembled the Celts in their fighting techniques and approaches to battle.

Telamon   (Italy) A force of around 70,000, made up of Gaesatae from beyond the Alps and north Italian Celts, including 20,000 cavalry (chariots and horse), launched a freebooting expedition into Etruria in 225 B.C. Returning north laden with booty, they were intercepted at Telamon by two Roman armies. The Gaesatae, a close-knit force of young men at the peak of fighting fitness, chose to fight naked save for their gold torcs and other ornaments, displaying their magnificent physiques to awe their opponents. The Celts seized control of a hill where they installed their booty, drawing up their forces around it facing

9.5 The trumpet-head of a carnyx (war trumpet) in the form of a boar's head from Deskford, Banffshire, Scotland, and a reconstruction of the complete carnyx, which was made in the mid-first century A.D. (Drawing by Audrey McIntosh, from material in the National Museums of Scotland, Edinburgh)

the Romans, with their cavalry and chariots on the flanks. At first they were successful, terrifying the Romans with their ferocity, braying trumpets, and savage war cries, and killing and decapitating one of the Roman generals. The Romans, however, hurled flights of javelins, killing many of the Celts, and their cavalry took the hill. The majority of the Celts stood firm, and around 40,000 were killed. The Celtic cavalry fled, but 10,000 Celts were taken prisoner, including one of the kings; another Celtic king committed suicide to avoid capture.

Delphi A large Celtic force invaded Greece in 279 B.C., aiming to plunder the famously rich shrine at Delphi. Despite Greek resistance, they reached Delphi in the middle of winter. Sources are divided on whether they succeeded in sacking the treasuries here. An earthquake and thunderbolts shook the Celtic forces during the night and rock slides followed the next morning, natural disturbances that apparently unnerved the superstitious Celts. The Greeks attacked at dawn, surprising the Celtic army with a combined assault from front and rear, and inflicting heavy casualties, including injuries to the Celtic leader, Brennus. The Celts were seized with panic and fled, killing their wounded as they retreated to prevent their capture; in all some 26,000 Celts are said to have died.

CELEBRATING VICTORY

Hjortspring (Island of Als, Denmark) The votive offering of a boat containing a large collection of arms around 350 B.C. in a bog at Hjortspring is generally interpreted as a thank-offering, presumably deposited by the island's residents after a victory over armed attackers. The weapons suggest that a war band of around 80 men arrived in four war canoes; each held a crew of up to 18 oarsmen, with a steersman, a coxswain, and two other senior crew members. The military equipment included 10 mail shirts, 11 swords, eight lances, and 11 or 12 narrow shields, presumably the equipment of the leaders, and infantry equipment for about 65 men, each comprising a spear, a javelin, and a shield. About half also had an additional javelin with a bone or antler head. Details of the equipment indicate that the war band may have come from the Hamburg region.

Ribemont-sur-Ancre (France) After a battle in the third century B.C. between two Celtic armies, of local Belgae and Lexovii from Armorica, the victors erected a unique war memorial. Within a large ditched enclosure they built at least six cubic structures from daub and the longbones of around 300 people, presumably the losers, mixed with those of some horses. Within these structures they placed the calcined bones of their own dead. Outside the enclosure they set up the bodies of many more of the dead, around 140 individuals, having first hacked off their heads as trophies. All the bones on the site were from men aged between 15 and 40. Broken and discarded weapons, such as arrowheads and spearheads, were also found in considerable numbers, and seem originally to have been displayed on a platform. This monument was a place of reverence for several centuries, where offerings of weapons and food were made, and eventually it was replaced by a Romano-Gallic shrine.

Campaigns, Migrations, and Wars

Although warfare was endemic in Iron Age society, much of it was on the level of raids to acquire booty, cattle, and women, as well as slaves to supply the insatiable requirements of the Mediterranean world. Successful raids required mobility; chariots, horses, or boats were essential to make the attack swift and unexpected and to evade pursuit. Raiders were therefore generally a select band of nobles and their personal followers.

Warfare was also for glory and honor. A losing leader often deliberately died in battle or committed suicide rather than concede defeat. The demonstration of personal prowess was important in battle and often interfered with the efficient actions of the fighting force as a whole. Successful warriors collected the weapons and the severed heads of enemies as trophies. Later Irish literature suggests that wars ended with the defeated community becoming the client of the victor, giving hostages for their good faith.

There were also armed expeditions by war bands made up of young men with a taste for adventure, which often traveled considerable distances and swelled in size with success. Occasionally, whole communities migrated, fighting their way and accumulating booty, until they found a place where they chose to settle. A large number of Helvetii, for example, left Switzerland in 58 B.C. in search of new land in southern France, but were turned back by Caesar, with the loss of 250,000 Helvetic lives. The progress of migrating groups was inevitably slowed down by the baggage train: women, children, household possessions, and booty.

GALATIANS

The huge band of migrating Celts who invaded Macedonia in 279 B.C. quarreled and divided, with one group continuing east to Anatolia, where they took service as mercenaries. Here they founded a small state and gained a comfortable living raiding their neighbors. Several times defeated and checked by Anatolian kingdoms, they were finally suppressed by the Romans in 25 B.C.

ROMAN CONQUEST OF GAUL

Southern Gaul, an area long exposed to classical influences, had by 100 B.C. been absorbed by the Romans. In 58 B.C. several local military crises gave Caesar, the region's governor, an excuse to keep an army in the field, and he set about conquering the rest of Gaul, making use of intertribal hostilities to gain alliances with some tribes against others. Some tribes quite quickly admitted defeat, allowing Caesar to move on. Others, including the Nervii, the Veneti in Brittany, and the Belgae and Eburones in Belgium, put up strong and determined resistance. Caesar mercilessly punished them, massacring thousands or cutting off their hands and selling thousands of others into slavery. A coalition of tribes, led by Vercingetorix of the Arverni, rose against Caesar in 53, and, forgetting their internecine feuding in the face of the common enemy, almost all the remaining Gallic tribes joined them. Initially, the Gauls enjoyed some success and their scorched earth policy made life extremely difficult for the Romans. After a defeat, however, Vercingetorix made the mistake of falling back on the oppidum of Alesia. The experienced Romans built military camps, ramparts, towers, pits with stakes, and other traps around the oppidum. A large Gaulish force attempted to relieve the siege but was defeated, and the starving defenders were forced to surrender. Resistance ended the following year.

READING

General

Carman and Harding 1999, Guilaine and Zammit 2005: warfare; Vencl 1999, Whittle 1996: Neolithic; Harding, 2000, Osgood and Monks 2000: Bronze Age; Ritchie and Ritchie 1995, James 1993, Connolly 1998: Iron Age.

Weapons and Armor

Harding 1999b, 1999c, Kristiansen 1999: Bronze Age; Rapin 1991: Iron Age; Chapman 1999: weapons; Mithen 1994, Mercer 1999: bows and arrows; Spindler 1995, Renfrew and Bahn 2004: Iceman; O'Kelly 1989: Ireland; Furger-Gunti 1991: chariots.

Fortifications and Defenses

Ralston 1995, Cunliffe 1974, Collis 1984a: Iron Age defenses; Lenerz-de Wilde 1995: Iberia; Ritchie 1988: brochs; Mercer 1990, 1999: enclosures; Scarre 1988, Kristiansen 1998: Wasserburg; Armit 1997, Morrison 1997: crannogs; Scarre 1998: Biskupin.

Warriors

Dolukhanov 1999b: Neolithic warriors; Harding 1999c, Jensen 1999b, Kristiansen 1999: Bronze Age warriors; Parker Pearson 1999, Ehrenberg 1989: female warriors; Anati 1999, Capelle 1999, Scarre 1998, Frey 1995: warriors in art.

Conflicts, Battles, and Wars

Jochim 2002c, Cunliffe 2001a, Vencl 1999, Dolukhanov 1999b, Whittle 1996, Mithen 2003: Mesolithic; Chapman 1999, Dolukhanov 1999b: Neolithic; Lloyd-Morgan 1995, Frey 1995, Randsborg 1999, Twist 2001, Rapin 1995: Iron Age; Bahn, ed. 2001b: Talheim; Parker Pearson 1999, Clason 1999: Wassenaar; Gill and Kaner 1996, Sharples 1991: Maiden Castle; Polybius 1979: Telamon; Randsborg 1999: Hjortspring; Caesar 1951, Ralston 1995: Caesar in Gaul; Furger-Gunti 1991: chariotry; Centre Archaeologie Departemental de Ribemont-sur-Ancre 2005, Bahn 2003: Ribemont.

10

LANGUAGE, LITERATURE, AND THE ARTS

Few cultures in prehistoric Europe were literate; knowledge of the continent's languages and literature, therefore, depend largely on oral traditions and reconstruction on the basis of what was recorded by literate classical cultures or survived into later times.

Abundant evidence of the visual arts survives from prehistory, going right back into Palaeolithic times; in contrast, very little can be said about prehistoric European music, dance, or other performing arts.

EUROPEAN LANGUAGES

The vast majority of languages spoken in modern Europe belong to the Indo-European language family. Of those that do not, some are post-Roman arrivals: these include both the languages spoken by recent immigrants from Asia and elsewhere, and ones such as Hungarian and Turkic that were brought in earlier by invaders, particularly from the steppe region. There are also a few languages that probably descend from those spoken by the original inhabitants of Europe: a group of Finno-Ugric (Uralic) languages in the far north, and in the Pyrenean region Basque, a language isolate. Other languages were recorded in prehistoric and early historic times. The key question in reconstructing the linguistic prehistory of Europe is when the Indo-European languages were introduced, a matter of continuing controversy. Was proto-Indo-European the language of the first farming immigrants into Europe, a view espoused by Colin Renfrew (1987) but not widely accepted, or was it brought in later by immigrants from the steppe? The latter is linguistically acceptable but hard to demonstrate archaeologically or explain.

Indo-European Languages

ORIGINS AND SPREAD

Although the original homeland of Proto-Indo-European (PIE) is still a subject of debate and con-troversy, many scholars, on linguistic and archaeological grounds, favor the region between the Black Sea and the Caspian and argue that the language began to spread from this region into other areas in the fourth to third millennium. By the late first millennium B.C. Indo-European languages were certainly spoken over a vast area from Europe through Anatolia and Iran into South Asia and in central Asia as far as Chinese Turkestan.

GREEK

The existence of the Linear B script, used to write an early form of Greek, demonstrates that by 1450 B.C. an Indo-European language was being spoken by the Mycenaeans on the southern Greek mainland. Archaeological and linguistic evidence suggest the arrival of early Greek speakers here late in the third millennium B.C., though some scholars would place this intrusion earlier or later and others consider that it did not occur at all. Mycenaean Greek may have been related to Indo-European languages in Anatolia, such as Luwian. Greek in the first millennium was spoken not only in Greece and the Greek islands but also in Cyprus, Asia Minor, and the Greek colonies, and was spread farther afield by the conquests of Alexander the Great.

SOUTHEAST EUROPE

The first-millennium inhabitants of the Balkans, the Illyrians, Dacians, Getae, and Thracians, spoke Indo-European languages. Shared names suggest possible links with some of the language groups in Anatolia. Archaeological evidence may support the arrival of Indo-European speakers in the Balkans in the later fourth millennium. Modern Albanian is probably descended from Illyrian; Thracian and Dacian (possibly related dialects rather than separate languages) died out.

ITALIC

Indo-European languages probably reached Italy via Southeast Europe during the second or possibly third millennium B.C. The best known is Latin, spread by the Roman conquest into many parts of Europe, where it evolved into the modern Romance languages (Italian, French, Spanish, Portuguese,

Romanian, and others). In the earlier first millennium B.C. Latin was confined to the region of Rome, and other languages were spoken elsewhere: Siculan in Sicily, Umbrian and Oscan in the center and southwest, Messapic in the southeast (possibly related to Illyrian), and Picene (East Italic) to its north, all known from inscriptions. Venetic at the head of the Adriatic may have been related to the Italic languages or have belonged to a separate subgroup of Indo-European.

EASTERN EUROPE

Speakers of Slavic languages occupied the region between the upper Vistula and the Dnepr perhaps as early as the second millennium B.C. They were recorded as raiders in Southeast Europe in the first millennium A.D., the period when they also spread into areas to the north formerly occupied by Baltic speakers. Slavic languages are spoken today over much of the Balkans as well as in eastern Europe from the Czech Republic and Poland to Russia.

Baltic languages were spoken in classical times in an area east of the Baltic Sea and as far south as the northern Dnepr basin; much of this area was later overrun by Germanic and Slavic speakers, and Lithuanian and Latvian are the only modern survivors of the Baltic languages.

GERMANIC

In late prehistory Roman authors noted the presence of Germanic tribes east of the Rhine and west of the Oder, in northern Germany and southern Scandinavia. Migrations during the first millennium A.D. took Germanic speakers, such as the Goths, into much of Europe, though in many areas they were assimilated and lost their languages. Germanic languages are spoken today in Britain, northern Europe, the Low Countries, and Germany.

CELTIC

In the early first millennium B.C., and probably considerably earlier, Celtic languages were spoken in the area from eastern France to Bohemia. Before 500 B.C. speakers of Celtiberian (Hispano-Celtic) spread into Iberia, establishing themselves over most of the country, with the exception of the south and east. Celtiberian was related to Gaulish, spoken in France and adjacent areas to the east, and Lepontic, spoken in the Alpine regions and the far north of Italy. The eastern area was home to speakers of another block of Celtic languages, Eastern Celtic. At some time, probably during the first millennium, Celtic languages also spread to Britain, where they developed into the only Celtic languages that have survived into the modern world: Welsh, Scots and Irish Gaelic, and Breton, the latter thought to descend from the language of British immigrants into Brittany in the fifth century A.D. Celtic migrations took members of Gaulish-speaking tribes such as the Boii, Insubres, and Senones into northern Italy, probably in the sixth century, and other Celtic speakers in the third century B.C. into Anatolia (Galatia), where their language survived into the fifth century A.D.

Inscriptions from the last three centuries B.C. show that the cultural division made by the Romans between Celts and Germani did not coincide exactly with the distribution of speakers of Celtic and Germanic languages: though there was broad coincidence, there were also overlaps and considerable mixing between these languages at their interface.

PICTISH

Pictish, a language spoken in Scotland in classical and early historical times, is known from inscriptions that provide only a limited vocabulary and therefore only limited scope for comparing Pictish with other languages. Although some scholars consider it to have been a non-Indo-European language, the currently favored view is that Pictish was probably a form of Celtic.

THE SPREAD OF INDO-EUROPEAN IN EUROPE

When and how the precursors of the Celtic, Germanic, Baltic, and Slavic languages spread into northern and central Europe is controversial. Attempts to identify their arrival archaeologically have often focused on the third-millennium Corded Ware Culture, widely distributed and having some elements strongly reminiscent of steppe culture, though other elements show local antecedents. The mechanism by which the Indo-European language might have become established here is obscure. An alternative identification with the sixth-millennium LBK culture, though perhaps archaeologically seductive, is linguistically untenable.

Surviving Non-Indo-European Languages

URALIC

The Uralic language family comprises two groups: Samoyedic, spoken by reindeer herders and hunters across northern Siberia, and Finno-Ugric. The latter has two branches. Ugric is spoken mainly on and east of the Ob River, but also includes Magyar (Hungarian), introduced to Hungary by settlers in the ninth century A.D. Finnic, including Finnish, Lapp, and Estonian, is now spoken east of the Baltic and west of the Urals. It has been suggested that the speakers of the early Uralic languages be identified with the Mesolithic inhabitants of the boreal region, who in the fourth millennium made pottery with comb and pit-marked decoration. Mutual linguistic influences show that Proto-Uralic and Proto-Indo-European were spoken by people who occupied adjacent areas during the third millennium B.C.

BASQUE

Basque is spoken today in a small area of northeast Spain and southwest France, but originally covered a much wider region, including the area in France and much of northern Spain known to the Romans as Aquitania. It is not related to any known language.

Dead European Languages

IBERIA

The pre-Celtic languages of Iberia are known from a number of inscriptions. Iberian was spoken along the east coast, and inscriptions in Iberian are concentrated particularly around the Ebro. Tartessian was the language of the southern quarter of the peninsula. It is likely that both were more widely spoken before the arrival of Celtiberian speakers. The indications are that neither language was related to Basque.

ITALY

A large number of mainly short texts survive in Etruscan, spoken in central Italy in the first millennium and probably the language of the indigenous people of the region from earlier times. The Romans were familiar with Etruscan, but it died out by the fourth century A.D. The only language that was clearly related to Etruscan was Lemnian, the language of a handful of inscriptions from the north Aegean island of Lemnos, said by the Greeks to be inhabited by Tyrrhenians, a loose term that included Etruscans and pirates, both of which descriptions may have applied to the inhabitants of Lemnos. Place names suggest the existence of other indigenous languages, in Sardinia, the western Alps, northwest Italy (Ligurian), and the northeast (Raetic). It is likely that these formed part of a group of non-Indo-European substrate languages stretching across the Mediterranean.

GREECE

The Linear B script, used to write an early form of Greek, was developed from Linear A, the script used by the Minoans, and studies have demonstrated that the sound values assigned to the signs in the two scripts often coincide. From this it is clear that Linear A rendered an unknown language (Eteo-cretan), which most scholars believe was not a form of Greek. It may have been a Semitic language, though this is not widely favored, or related to a language spoken in western Anatolia, such as the Indo-European languages Lycian and Luwian.

On mainland Greece many names of individuals, divinities, and places and words for many plants, animals, objects, and materials used by the Mycenaeans were non-Indo-European, demonstrating that other languages were spoken in the region into the Bronze Age. These may have been related to non-Indo-European Anatolian languages such as Hattic, and may also have been spoken in the Balkans.

HISTORICAL INTRUDERS

Phoenicians from the Levant who spoke a Semitic language established colonies in the western Mediterranean during the first millennium B.C.

WRITING

The scripts that developed in Mesopotamia (cuneiform) and Egypt (hieroglyphic) during the late fourth and third millennia made use of logographic and syllabic elements. A number of other scripts developed from these, including the hieroglyph-inspired alphabetic script of the Phoenicians: this was ancestral to most scripts used in Europe.

Pre-alphabetic Scripts

CRETAN SCRIPTS

From around the beginning of the second millennium B.C. the Minoans made use of seals bearing symbols that are known as Cretan hieroglyphs. Around 1750 B.C. another script, Linear A, also came into use on Crete, used primarily for accounts written on clay tablets. Both seem to have been Cretan inventions, inspired by the scripts used in contemporary western Asia but not directly based on any of them. Both scripts were syllabic; neither has been deciphered, though comparisons with Linear B have enabled many of the sounds of the Linear A signs to be determined.

LINEAR B

Developed by the Mycenaeans from Linear A and Cretan hieroglyphic, Linear B was a syllabic script with around 90 signs, used to write an early form of the Greek language. Most of the documents in Linear B are clay accounting tablets and sealings. The script died out around 1100 B.C.

Alphabetic Scripts

The alphabetic script of the Levant was written from right to left and had 22 letters representing conso-

nants only, since the Semitic languages use consonantal roots, allowing the vowel sounds to be deduced from the context. This script was adopted by the Greeks before 800 B.C. and adapted to include vowels and a few additional consonants. By the sixth century Greek was being written from left to right. Greek eventually gave rise to most other European scripts.

IBERO-TARTESSIAN

The Phoenicians introduced writing into Iberia. By the seventh century the Tartessians had developed a script based on that of the Phoenicians, and this was later adopted by the Iberian speakers of the east. This script had 28 alphabetic letters but also employed some syllabic signs. It was used to write short inscriptions such as legends on coins.

ITALIAN SCRIPTS

Around 700 B.C. the Etruscans adopted the Greek alphabet from Greek colonists settled in Italy, making some modifications, including the addition of letters to represent *f* and *u*. The direction of writing was from right to left. More than 10,000 Etruscan inscriptions and other texts are known, most of them short. Although the script can easily be transliterated, the language in which it is written is still very poorly understood.

The speakers of the Messapic language in southeastern Italy also adopted the Greek alphabet. Other regional scripts, including Faliscan, Oscan, Umbrian, and Latin, were developed from the Etruscan script. Latin inscriptions are known from the sixth century onward, using 21 letters. Later, two more letters not needed by the Latin language, *y* and *z*, were adopted from Greek to write Greek loanwords. The spread of Roman power in Italy led to the Latin script eventually replacing other Italian scripts.

TRANSALPINE EUROPE

The Celts in north Italy and the Alps adopted the Etruscan script, and it was used here from the sixth century until the first, when it was finally superseded by the Latin script. The Greek alphabet, introduced by the Greek colony at Massalia, was used in southern France, and was also known in central Europe. Caesar, writing in the first century B.C., noted that the Gauls regularly used the Greek alphabet for business and private matters.

The extension of Roman influence and later of the Roman Empire into other parts of Europe spread the Latin script widely. By the mid-first century the Boii in central Europe were using it on their coins. It was employed in Gaul from the same period and a little later in Britain to write Celtic inscriptions. Some included modifications of the Roman alphabet to render sounds not used in Latin, such as *ch* as in *loch*.

The Latin script survived the collapse of the empire to become the basis of western European literacy. The Greek script was used in the longer-lasting Eastern Roman Empire and was ancestral to the scripts of eastern Europe and Russia.

OGHAM

Ogham, a script inspired by alphabetic writing but derived from the use of tally sticks, evolved in Britain in the early centuries A.D. It was inscribed on stones and probably wooden wands, using the side of the object as a center line. The consonantal signs consisted of one to five lines arranged perpendicular or at an oblique angle to the center line, on one or other or both sides, and one to five short lines or dots placed on the line represented the vowels.

Other

Symbols such as spirals and crosses found on pottery and other objects from the later Neolithic Balkans, including three tablets from the Vinča settlement of Tartaria, are thought by some scholars to represent an early script. The symbols are likely to have had some significance, perhaps indicating ownership, but, like symbols in many other places and periods, do not have the features of a fully fledged writing system.

LITERATURE

Texts

Pre-classical texts from Europe are mainly very short inscriptions, the majority on stone or metal, including epitaphs and legends on coins. The most extensive texts are a 200-word Celtiberian inscription from Botoritta near Saragossa in Spain, probably a land contract, another inscription from this site, and the five-year calendar from Coligny in France. Finds from settlements in central Europe show that Celtic people also wrote on bone tablets covered with wax, using bone or metal styli, and the use of papyrus in British coin molds suggests that papyrus was also imported into transalpine Europe as a writing medium. Around and after the Roman conquest texts also included dedications on altars and other votive offerings, and tablets and strips of lead bearing curses, prayers, and other magico-religious texts.

Oral Traditions

The oral literature of the post-Roman Celtic, Germani, and Nordic societies have many similar stories of gods and heroes, suggesting the existence in prehistory of shared traditions. These include common themes such as shape-shifting, particularly the assumption by deities and magicians of bird and animal forms; heroic quests; feuds, raids, and armed conflicts between rival warrior bands, champions, or kingdoms; and struggles between mortals and supernatural beings. Nonhuman races, such as dwarfs, fairies, and elves, and monsters that assumed fair animal or human form, such as the demonic kelpie of Scottish legend, are also common participants in these myths and legends. Although these traditions do not allow detailed reconstructions of European prehistoric oral literature, they give some impression of the tales likely to have been told or sung by prehistoric bards and storytellers.

The vernacular literature of Ireland gives a glimpse of the Celtic world in the early centuries A.D. Made up of songs, tales, and poems transmitted orally, they were written down by Christian monks from the fifth century A.D. onward. Now known as the Ulster Cycle, they centered on the prose epic *Táin Bó Cúailnge* (*The Cattle Raid of Cooley*). This recounts the warrior deeds of the hero Cú Chulainn, fostered at the court of his uncle Conchobar, legendary king of Ulster. The *Mabinogion*, a Welsh collection of prose tales, although mainly medieval, also draws on earlier Celtic tradition.

Druidic Education

Classical authors such as Caesar described the role of Druids in Celtic education in Britain and Gaul. Young noblemen came in large numbers to study with the Druids, who themselves underwent a 20-year training during which they acquired knowledge of astronomy and calendrics, natural science, medicine, law, tribal history and traditions, philosophy, and literature, as well as religious lore and ritual. Although educated Celts used writing in their everyday life, it was thought improper to commit Druidic knowledge to writing, so all Druidic teaching was conducted orally. Students were expected to commit to memory great quantities of information in the form of poetry. The first-century A.D. author Pomponius Mela recorded that the Druids taught in secluded and remote locations, perhaps in response to Roman persecution; in contrast, Tacitus referred to a Celtic school within the oppidum of Bibracte, which was superseded in 122 B.C. by a Roman school in the nearby new town of Autun.

VISUAL ARTS

Prehistoric art was executed in many media. The magnificent art of the Upper Palaeolithic period included figurines, particularly of women, powerful cave paintings and rock engravings of bulls, horses, and other animals, and exquisite carvings on bone, ivory, and antler artifacts such as spearthrowers. Later paintings are rare. Decorated ceramic, stone, bone, and antler objects, and metalwork comprise most of the extant art of prehistoric Europe; few textiles and objects of leather and wood survive. A considerable proportion of prehistoric European art is abstract, often using geometric patterns. Many designs incorporate symbols, ranging from abstract elements such as spirals, through symbols such as circles and wheels representing the sun disc, to naturalistic elements such as ducks and plants. Figurative art is much less common; sometimes the human form is minimally represented by features such as eyes, breasts, and significant dress and equipment; often there is a concentration on the head at the expense of the rest of the

10.1 *An intricately carved stone ball from Towie, Aberdeenshire, Scotland, dated around 2500 B.C. These enigmatic objects were confined to northeast mainland Scotland and Orkney.* (Drawing by Audrey McIntosh, from material in the National Museums of Scotland, Edinburgh)

body; and complete figures are rare except in rock art and occasional statues in bronze or stone. The most common medium using the human form is the pottery figurine, but here also a few features were often represented rather than the whole. Animals are common in rock art and occasionally appear as sculptures and figurines. Unlike the classical world, where pottery was often decorated with naturalistic scenes, the ceramics of prehistoric Europe rarely had figurative decoration. One exception, Iron Age vessels from Sopron in Hungary, shows people spinning, weaving, riding, and playing music, but even here the figures are shown as triangles with limbs, woven into panels of geometric decoration.

Mesolithic Art

The early postglacial inhabitants of Europe produced a number of fine carvings, including wooden elk's heads from Oleneostrovski Mogilnik, amber figurines from Scandinavian sites in the north, and fish-faced stone sculptures from Lepenski Vir in the south. Rock paintings were executed in eastern Iberia. Many Mesolithic objects bore geometric designs, such as the elaborately decorated antler from Sjöholmen in Sweden, which had two fish woven into an intricate geometric pattern, and the paddles from Tybrind Vig in Denmark, on which fine carved patterns were inlaid with a brown substance. A number of pebbles painted with lines and dots were found at Mas d'Azil in France and other sites in western Europe; these undoubtedly had some more than decorative significance, perhaps being used in calendrics.

Sculpture and Figurines

Sculptures and figurines of stone, bronze, pottery, and occasionally other materials, were made in various parts of Europe; in the southeast they were common in most periods, but in other areas they appeared only in certain cultures. Sculptures

10.2 A pottery bowl from a Danish megalithic tomb. Pottery gave almost infinite scope for variations in design, representing many techniques. (Worsaae, J. J. A. *The Industrial Arts of Denmark.* London: Chapman and Hall, 1882)

included the huge obese statues of people (perhaps women) in ribbed skirts placed in the Maltese temples; the bronze model cult vehicles from Bronze Age transalpine Europe; and Iron Age stone statues such as the male figures erected on the summit of Hallstatt period barrows, the well-equipped warriors guarding the entrance to settlements in Galicia, and the landscape figures of bulls, boars, and animal heads in western Iberia. Also from Iron Age Iberia come a number of limestone sculptures of men and women with detailed depiction of clothing and equipment; these show Phoenician and Greek influences. Naturalistic sculptures became common elsewhere in Celtic Europe in the last centuries B.C., similarly reflecting classical influences.

POTTERY FIGURINES

Pottery figurines of people and less frequently animals were made in Southeast and eastern Europe from the Neolithic period onward. Often these were schematic, having a head, generally with eyes and often with a nose, and a sticklike body on which a few features were modeled such as jewelry, a phallus, or breasts and a pubic triangle, although many were sexless. Others showed more detail, including limbs, for example, and sometimes lines suggesting clothing. A series of later Bronze Age figurines from the Iron Gates region of the Danube took the form of a rounded upper body incorporating rudimentary arms, a neck, and sometimes a head, and a bell-shaped skirt, covered in geometric designs arranged to give some impression of patterned clothing, jewelry, hair, and facial features. More naturalistic were the fine seated figurines of the Hamangia culture of fifth millennium Romania, and the Aegean region also made more naturalistic figures, including the lovely Cycladic marble sculptures of the Early Bronze Age. At the other extreme pots with painted or modeled human features, generally faces, are known from the Balkans.

SARDINIAN BRONZES

A number of bronze figurines are known from Late Bronze Age Sardinia. These mainly depicted well-armed warriors clad in tunics, but also other male figures and occasionally women. Made by cire perdue casting, the figures are long and thin but otherwise naturalistic, with carefully modeled details such as faces, decoration on clothing, and features of weapons and equipment.

Reliefs and Engravings

Objects with relief decoration, such as stelae, were created in many parts of Europe from the fourth millennium onward. These included the schist plaques associated with Iberian megaliths, which bear geometric designs suggesting human features, and Chalcolithic statue menhirs in the Mediterranean and Atlantic Europe, which were often carved with necklaces, belts, weapons, and human faces, schematically representing people. From the second millennium funerary stelae were produced in Iberia, engraved with weapons, and by the Iron Age also a shield, jewelry, a mirror, a chariot, and a warrior shown as a stick figure.

MEGALITHIC ART

Engravings on many megalithic monuments featured geometric motifs such as spirals, concentric arcs and rectangles, zigzags, lozenges, and cup marks. Carvings on these monuments also included a small but widespread repertoire of symbols, primarily axes and daggers.

SITULA ART

Iron Age beaten bronze buckets (*situlae*) from northern Italy and the area around the head of the Adriatic provide a rare example of a figurative art style. This was strongly influenced by oriental styles transmitted via the Etruscans. The punched and incised decoration was arranged in friezes; early examples, from the seventh century, showed grazing animals; later ones scenes from life such as fighting, sport, processions, sexual activity, and feasting, as well as mythical beasts. This decoration was also applied to other objects such as lids, belt plates, and plaques. A fourth-century scabbard from Hallstatt bears a design of two figures holding a wheel; by this time, however, the style was in decline.

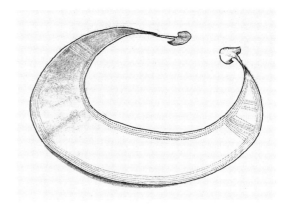

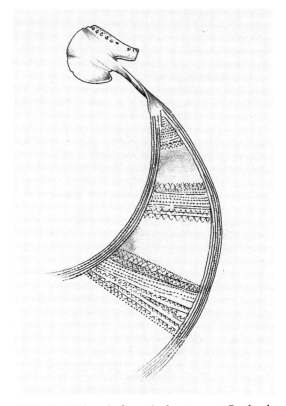

10.3 *A gold lunula from Auchentaggart, Scotland, and a detail of its finely incised geometric decoration. Such objects are often shown on depictions of people or gods, such as statue menhirs.* (Drawing by Audrey McIntosh, from material in the National Museums of Scotland, Edinburgh)

Rock Paintings and Engravings

Rock paintings and engravings are a European tradition going back into Palaeolithic times. In the postglacial period the majority of rock art was located in Galicia and the Levante region of Spain, Val Camonica and Mount Bego in the Alps, northern Scandinavia, particularly the Bohuslän region of Sweden, and Britain. In addition, rock art is scattered across many other regions, including the Mediterranean, and Southeast and central Europe. Many of the eastern Spanish rock paintings date from the Mesolithic and Neolithic periods; some of the Scandinavian engravings belong to later Mesolithic and Neolithic times, but the majority are from the Bronze Age; engravings in the Alps range from Mesolithic to medieval times. The engraved designs were mainly executed by grinding and pecking.

Much of the rock art of eastern Spain, the Alps, and Scandinavia is figurative. The eastern Spanish paintings, executed in red, black, and brown, show both individuals engaging in activities such as collecting honey, and large groups fighting, hunting, or dancing.

Symbols such as the sun disc were common in Bronze Age art, and animals were frequently shown in all periods. The main themes of Bronze Age Scandinavian rock art were people, especially warriors, boats, vehicles, weapons, plowing scenes, and trees. In the same tradition are scenes and motifs engraved on slabs in a few Scandinavian burial mounds. Earlier art in Scandinavia included hunting scenes and perhaps processions and dances.

Many of the Alpine engravings show scenes from daily life, such as hunting, plowing, weaving and other domestic chores, houses and settlements, as well as weapons, vehicles, and many animals. There were also many symbols and geometric patterns. Rock art in Galicia, western Ireland, Scotland, and northeast England, probably dating from the Bronze Age, was mainly abstract, including many enigmatic cup marks, rounded holes pecked into the surface of rock outcrops and boulders, often surrounded by one or several rings. These were also common in Scandinavia. As well as such abstract designs, Galician art included animals, particularly stags, and weapons.

10.4 A bucket (situla) of beaten sheet bronze, elaborately decorated with repoussé designs, principally featuring the sun disc and ducks' heads, typical Late Bronze Age motifs (Worsaae, J. J. A. *The Industrial Arts of Denmark*. London: Chapman and Hall, 1882)

Celtic Art

The La Tène period saw the flowering of what is known as Celtic art, expressed in many media and particularly in metalwork, including vessels such as jugs and cauldrons, jewelry, horse-harness and chariot fittings, scabbards, and parade armor such as helmets and shields. This art had its roots in the skilled craftsmanship and exuberant decorative techniques of the Bronze Age and earlier Iron Age, which combined geometric and abstract designs with the use of symbols such as ducks and the sun disc. In the sixth century imported pottery and bronze vessels introduced transalpine Europe to the repertoire of Greek and Etruscan decorative motifs, such as lotus flowers rically arranged floral patterns (Early Style). These were applied to luxury objects such as jewelry, sword scabbards, and metal and ceramic tableware. Metalwork was decorated with inlays of glass and coral. Intricate patterns were laid out precisely using compasses, and included openwork metal sheets used to embellish objects in other materials, such as the wooden bowl overlaid by openwork gold decoration from Schwarzenbach in Germany.

From the late fourth century the designs became more curvilinear, with complex interwoven patterns of plant elements such as tendrils and leaves, and barely recognizable animal elements, particularly human, bird, and animal heads, sometimes leading into sinuous bodies (Waldalgesheim Style). Many motifs were stylized to the point of geometric abstraction. These included fibulae with bows in the form of animals (mask brooches), made in southern Germany and western Austria. In some cases designs on pottery were built up of motifs applied from pre-cut stamps.

In the third century curvilinear geometric designs were engraved on many iron scabbards, still using plant motifs and abstract patterns (Sword Style). Often these created an asymmetric decorative panel. Many pieces of jewelry, such as armlets, and bronze vessels were embellished with substantial three-dimensional elements such as knobs, bosses, and highly stylized and often grotesque heads of birds, animals, and humans (Plastic Style).

Insular artistic designs developed in Britain. Mirrors and other objects were engraved with elaborate geometric compass-drawn designs of swirling curves and circles filled with cross-hatching (Mirror Style). Later Celts carried both technical expertise and design intricacy to even greater heights in the pagan and Christian art of the post-Roman period.

10.5 *A bronze flagon from Basse-Yutz, Lorraine, France, one of a matching pair from a rich late-fifth-century grave. While the form was inspired by Etruscan examples, the elaborate decoration, including coral and red glass inlay, human heads, and three-dimensional figures (a pack of hounds chasing a duck) is purely Celtic.* (TopFoto.co.uk © The British Museum/HIP. Photographer: Unknown)

and palmettes and human faces, as well as designs of sinuously distorted and sometimes imaginary animals derived ultimately from the steppe and the Near East, such as griffins and sphinxes. Celtic artists in the fifth and fourth centuries adapted these, weaving them into their own traditional designs. Natural elements were fantastically transformed, producing grotesque human heads with popping eyes, animal heads, and elaborate, geomet-

PERFORMING ARTS

Very little evidence survives of the music and dance that were undoubtedly part of life in prehistoric Europe. Rock art depicts people dancing and playing instruments, and there are a few other representations.

Some classical sources commented on the practices of the Celts and other cultures, and very occasionally instruments themselves have been found. Like the barbarian inhabitants of later Europe, the people of the Iron Age and probably earlier were entertained and educated with songs and tales from their own traditions, performed by bards and storytellers to the accompaniment of music.

Music

Mammoth bones from the Palaeolithic site of Mezin in Russia may have been used as drums, rattles, and even perhaps like a xylophone. A number of Gravettian bird-bone pipes with finger holes were found in a cave at Isturitz in France and part of an earlier Mousterian object, which might have been a pipe in Yugoslavia, made on a bear femur. Bone flutes were also found in the Neolithic settlement of Anza in the Balkans. The classical author

Diodorus wrote that the Celts had bards who sang their poetry to the accompaniment of instruments resembling lyres; some depictions of these are known, for example, on an Iron Age pot from Sopron in Hungary. One of the marble figurines from the third-millennium Cyclades is also playing a lyre while another plays a pipe.

Lurer and carnyxes are shown in rock art. The lur, a long curved tube with a disc end, was probably used in religious ceremonies. Small jingles were hung from the back of the disc and beside the mouthpiece, which resembled that of a modern trombone. Lurer were probably played in pairs, since many have been found in pairs that were tuned together. In Ireland smaller horns of bronze seem likely to have been modeled on those of the aurochs (wild cattle); they were probably not blown but sung into. The carnyx was the Celtic war trumpet, made of bronze, wood, or horn, with a long straight tube and a bell end in the form of an animal's head, especially that of a wild boar; it made a loud and penetrating noise.

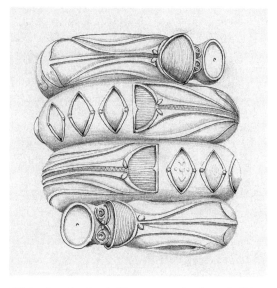

10.6 A snake-headed bronze armlet from Culbin Sands, Scotland, dated to the early centuries A.D. The use of animal motifs was typical of Celtic art. (Drawing by Audrey McIntosh, from material in the National Museums of Scotland, Edinburgh)

READING

European Languages

Dalby 1998, Crystal 1987: general; Mallory 1989, Renfrew 1987: Indo-European languages; Mallory 1989, Robinson 2002: non-Indo-European languages; Fitton 2002, Chadwick 1987, Gordon 2000: Aegean languages; Lenerz-de Wilde 1995: Iberia; Frey 1995, Barker and Rasmussen 1998, Bonfante 1990: Italy; Wells 2002, Cunliffe 2001a, Collis 2003: Celtic languages; Carver 1999, Foster 1996: Pictish.

Writing

Coulmas 1996, Robinson 1995, 2002: general; Chadwick 1987, Fitton 2002: Aegean scripts; Healey 1990: alphabet; Frey 1995, Barker and Rasmussen 1998, Bonfante 1990: Italy; Lenerz-de Wilde 1995: Iberia; Kruta 1991, Piggott 1975: Celtic writing.

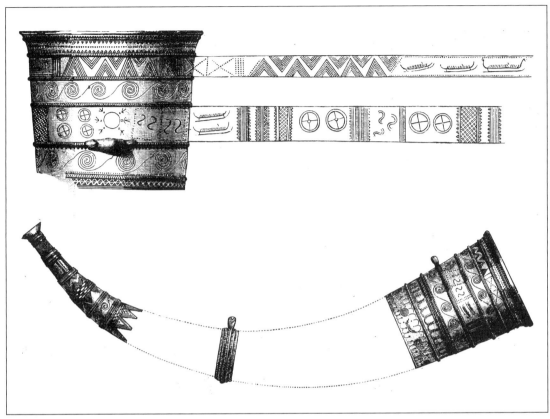

10.7 An elaborately decorated bronze horn found in a bog at Wismar, Mecklenburg (Worsaae, J. J. A. *The Industrial Arts of Denmark*. London: Chapman and Hall, 1882)

Literature

Cunliffe 1997, Kruta 2004: texts; James 1993, Mac Cana 1995, Davies 1995: vernacular literature; Green 1997, Piggott 1975: role of Druids in education.

Visual Arts

Sandars 1985, Milisauskas, ed. 2002, Cunliffe, ed. 1994: general; Mithen 1994, 2003, Bradley 1998: Mesolithic art; Bradley 1997, Harding 2000, Guilaine and Zammit 2005, Anati 1999, Capelle 1999, Scarre 1998: rock art; Anati 1965: Val Camonica; Cunliffe 2001a, Shee Twohig 1981: megalithic art; Whittle 1996, Bailey 2000, Perles 2001, Todorova 1999, Marthari 1999, Gimbutas 1956, 1991: figurines; Lenerz-de Wilde 1995, Jorge 1999b, De Marinis 1999, Kristiansen 1998: reliefs and stelae; Jacobsthal 1944, Megaw and Megaw 1989, 1995, Filip 1976, James 1993, Wells 2002: Celtic art; Collis 1984a: *situla* art.

Performing Arts

McIntosh and Scarre 1998, Green 1997, Milisauskas ed. 2002, Fagan, ed. 2004: music.

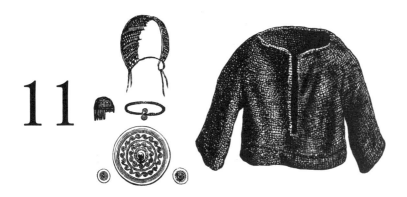

11

SOCIETY AND LIFE

SOCIAL AND POLITICAL ORGANIZATION

Various sources are used to gain an idea of social organization in prehistoric Europe, including status differentials manifest in burial practices, grave goods, and other artifacts; the existence of monuments whose construction implies the organization of communal endeavor; trading patterns; and settlement size. In most prehistoric European settlements, however, there is little evidence of social differentiation being manifest in the size or complexity of individual houses. Classical texts and later vernacular literature shed some light on later Iron Age society, and modern ethnography also offers some insights into social organization.

The Evolution of Social Hierarchy

The evidence suggests that earlier Mesolithic communities were largely egalitarian, with some division of responsibilities and role differences probably being made on the basis of age and gender. At Vedbaek, for instance, men were generally buried with stone blades and bone daggers and women with ornaments. Other status differentials, however, seem to have been developing within many Late Mesolithic communities in northern and western Europe. Individual burials in cemeteries were furnished with differing quantities of goods such as beads, other jewelry, figurines, and tools; some individuals had none, others many, with some well-endowed burials being those of children, for example at Zvejnieki in Latvia. In many cases, however, the best furnished graves were those of young men in their prime (for example, at Oleneostrovski Mogalnik in Russia), suggesting that physical might conferred status. In addition, some individuals seem to have been honored for other reasons. For example, at Oleneostrovski Mogalnik four individuals were buried in an upright position, with many grave goods: they may have been shamans. Cemeteries with differing practices and the distribution of certain styles of artifact suggest that these Mesolithic communities were also divided into clans.

Europe's early farmers seem to have been small egalitarian groups. In the eastern part of the continent cemeteries contained burials with similar grave goods or ones differentiated by age and gender. In the west megalithic tombs reflect a society in which membership of the community was emphasized and individual identity suppressed in death. The erection of monuments such as the megalithic tombs implies the ability of these communities to bring together large work parties, but ethnographic analogies suggest that these were assembled by calling in

11.1 One of the rich graves in the Chalcolithic cemetery at Varna in Bulgaria (Courtesy of Ancient Art & Architecture Collection. ©2004 AAAC /TopFoto.co.uk)

help from kin and favors from neighbors on a reciprocal basis, with a feast rewarding the participants on completion of the construction work.

Widespread changes took place in the fourth and third millennia, beginning in the southeast. Growing differentials appeared in grave goods, with some individuals being buried with none while a few had a large number, often made from imported prestige materials. In the west communal burial practices gave way to single graves in which the deceased was for the first time treated as an individual. In part social inequality may have been related to the growing importance of land differentials, control over better land giving some members of the community more power or economic prosperity. Competition among communities may also have been a catalyst to the development of social hierarchy, with those leaders able to organize the manpower and cooperative effort to construct ever more impressive monuments (such as Stonehenge and other henges and stone circles, or the Maltese temples) growing in authority and enabling their community to outshine their neighbors. Leaders could also enhance their own and their community's prestige by controlling the extraction of minerals or successfully manipulating trade to obtain prestige materials such as fine flint, metal, and amber. The accumulation of large herds of cattle, often by raiding, also increased the status of leading individuals. Other leaders in this period may have been bullies capable of organizing and using force to coerce other members of society.

By the second millennium it is thought that ranked societies had emerged in many parts of Europe, reflected particularly in burials but also in the ostentatious deposition of hoards of valuable objects. Social hierarchy was not generally marked by differentials in housing; for instance, in the settlement of Biskupin, in the early first millennium, there were 120 houses of similar size. The settlement, however, had some occupational divisions. A fishermen's quarter lay near the center of the settlement, with fishing gear stored in their outer rooms.

By the mid-first millennium there was also evidence of some settlement hierarchy, with the rural population in hamlets and farmsteads being tributary to and dependent upon hillforts and other larger settlements that housed the local leader and his entourage. Hierarchical societies were found in

11.2 Two Danish flint axes of exceptional size and quality, one chipped, the other polished. Fine stone axes like these were status symbols in the Neolithic period. (Worsaae, J. J. A. *The Industrial Arts of Denmark.* London: Chapman and Hall, 1882)

many regions of Europe, status differences still being most clearly visible in burials. For instance, Thracian kings were buried in *tholoi* with sacrificed wives or servants and magnificent gold and silver vessels, jewelry, and armor; the pastoral warrior nobility had rock-cut tombs or burials under barrows and were accompanied by smaller quantities of fine objects; and the common people, who were farmers and artisans, were cremated and their ashes buried in flat cemeteries. Although by this period rank was dependent on birth, status within one's social station was dependent upon personal achievement.

Celtic Social Organization

CHIEFDOMS

Traditional Celtic and Germanic societies were ruled by chiefs who maintained an entourage of nobles and other supporters, including artisans and bards, furnishing them with meat and drink and rewarding them for particular services or military prowess with gifts such as jewelry, dogs and horses, and booty from raids. Nobles owned horses and a full panoply of weapons, including a sword. Chiefs and war leaders were drawn from their ranks, gaining power from the size of the following they were able to attract and maintain. Their entourage would be drawn from their kin in the first instance but also included client nobles from other lineages. The chief's wealth came from a variety of sources, including land revenues, livestock, warfare and raiding, trade, and clientage. Spiritual power was wielded by the religious authorities: in Gaul and Britain the Druids. These were recruited from the nobility and might also exercise temporal power: For example, Diviciacus, the leader of the Gallic tribe of the Aedui at the time of Caesar, was a Druid.

Below the nobles in status were the artisans and other specialists, many of whom were part of the chief's entourage. Farmers, the backbone of society, were answerable either to nobles or directly to their chief, providing goods and produce in return for protection and patronage. In later Irish society clients of nobles and chiefs undertook a contract whereby they were given cattle in return for service in war and peace and a return on the cattle at a rate that could be as high as one-third of the number in the original grant, over a three-year period. A similar system seems to have operated in pre-Roman times.

People of different ranks each had their "honor-price," the amount that they were entitled to receive in the event of injury or death at the hands of another. This specified their status in many aspects of life: For example, in the case of litigation an individual's honor-price determined the value placed upon his testimony.

Chiefs controlled small tribes or tribal groups. Many of these were united into larger tribes under a tribal leader or king, and, in southern Gaul at least, these tribes often became clients of a major tribe; in the time of Caesar the Sequani and the Aedui held this dominant position, competing with each other to attract the allegiance of lesser tribes, the Sequani with German military support, the Aedui backed by the Romans. Greek descriptions of the society of the Galatians, Celtic immigrants into Asia Minor, show that the Galatian state was ruled by a council drawn from all the smaller chiefdoms within the state, who met in a grove (Drunemeton) to make decisions of state.

MAGISTRATES

Early classical writings refer to the chiefs and kings of a number of tribes, and this form of organization was still in place in many areas, including Britain and Germany, in later times. By the first century B.C., however, some regions adjacent to the Roman provinces had developed an oligarchic system of government. Among the Helvetii, magistrates were chosen annually from among the leading noblemen. Orgetorix, the wealthiest of these, attempted in 60 B.C. to subvert the system and was accused of conspiring to become king, a capital offense. The size of his personal following, however, some 10,000 people, enabled him to resist arrest, but he died mysteriously soon after. The Aedui elected a magistrate, the Vergobret, who for a year held the power of life and death within the tribe but operated within certain restrictions, including a prohibition on leaving the tribal territory during his magistracy. All members of the magistrate's family were debarred from the council of nobles who worked with him. An assembly of all free tribesmen met on occasion to decide the most serious issues such as declaring war. In Caesar's day two individuals rose to prominence among the Aedui. Dumnorix, magistrate for the year 60 B.C., used his popularity and power to monopolize the contract for collecting taxes and river dues, which was annually auctioned, thus gaining control of enormous funds. His brother Diviciacus led the rival faction and gained the upper hand by allying himself with the Romans; Dumnorix was eventually captured and executed by the Romans.

CRIME AND PUNISHMENT

Theft probably occurred only rarely in small communities where everyone knew one another. The development of oppida in the last centuries B.C. marks a change, the development of communities that were not only large enough to contain people who were unknown to one another but also cosmopolitan, housing unrelated people from a variety of different sources. Security now became an issue: numerous keys (something not previously known) were found in the oppidum of Manching, implying both wealth and suspicion of the neighbors, a reflection of the change from kin-based social relationships to the anonymity and independence of individuals in urban situations.

Traditional societies probably had their share of other crimes, however, including offenses against the social norms such as incest and adultery, infringements of religious strictures, and antisocial behavior such as murder, as well as imagined crimes such as witchcraft when ill fortune struck individuals or communities. The Roman author Strabo noted that obesity was punished among the Gauls. Although there is limited information on crime and punishment in prehistoric Europe, the discovery of people who had been killed prompts speculation. For example, the woman found pinned down in a bog at Juthe Fen in Denmark may have been a criminal who was executed, a witch placed under restraint after her death to prevent her harming the community, or one of the numerous sacrificial victims deposited in bogs. Classical sources state that some at least of the Iron Age sacrificial victims were condemned criminals who were saved up, often for years, until required for a sacrifice.

A grave in the Iron Age cemetery of Garton Slack in Yorkshire, England, contained the bodies of a young man and a woman around age 30, apparently executed together, perhaps for adultery. They were placed with their arms pinned together by a stake and were probably buried alive. A fetus was found below the woman's pelvis. Tacitus, however, describing Germanic practices, wrote that adulterous women were punished by having their hair cut, being stripped naked and beaten publicly, but not executed.

THE ORGANIZATION OF INDUSTRY

In the Mesolithic period and for most of the Neolithic period, artifacts were produced by members of the community, but specialization began to develop alongside the growth of status differentials in the Late Neolithic and Chalcolithic periods and became well developed in the later Iron Age, when many products became quite standardized. Some crafts were practiced in the home, with every household probably meeting their own requirements; these included spinning and weaving, making baskets and simple pottery, carving wooden tools, knapping flints, and working leather, bone, and antler. Some crafts were technologically within the scope of everyone but required collective input: building houses, for example.

An interesting insight into the organization of early industry comes from the Lengyel settlement of Brześć Kujawski in Poland. Here the manufacture of antler axes was undertaken in a single house and apparently away from prying eyes. Since such axes were a typical product of the earlier Mesolithic inhabitants of the region and their TRB descendants, it has been suggested that this was the household of an "outsider" TRB craftsman.

More elaborate products and ones that required particular skills or equipment were manufactured by specialists, particularly in later periods: For example, fine wares such as the wheel-turned ceramics of the later Iron Age were created by master potters. Objects required by the elite were made in the centers where the leaders lived, by artisans who were probably part of their entourage. For example, craftsmen based in the Bronze Age regional centers of the Carpathian basin, such as Malé Kosihy, carved the decorated bone cheekpieces for the horses owned by the elite; others produced large quantities of fine textiles that were probably prestige goods. Another example is the goldsmith who worked for the Wessex chieftains, whose handiwork has been identified in a number of Wessex elite burials. The later Iron Age saw the concentration of many craft specialists in the emerging oppida and towns, where they may have produced goods for sale as well as for their aristocratic patrons.

Small-scale mining and metal production was often undertaken by small groups who saw the work through from mining to metal. Early metal mining was an occasional rather than continuous activity in many areas. This is shown by the large numbers of discarded hammerstones found at many mines; for example, at Cwmystwyth in Wales, where the hammerstones came from around 20 miles (30 kilometres away), the numbers show that these were brought by the miners on each visit and abandoned here when the mining trip was complete. Many of the larger mines and associated centers of production, however, such as those of the Mitterberg, probably engaged hundreds of people working full-time on different tasks, such as winning the ore, hauling it to the surface, felling timber and making charcoal, and smelting. Smiths who used the metal to create artifacts probably worked mainly in settlements from which their products were traded, but some were itinerant workers. Rich burials containing metalworking tools imply that, in the Early Bronze Age at least, smiths enjoyed considerable social status, and Irish literature indicates that they still did so in early historical times.

Stone working similarly could involve a network of people who quarried the stone or flint; roughed out the tools from the raw material; traded or exchanged the roughouts; and finished the tools. Many flint mining sites were visited periodically, probably seasonally by groups who lived elsewhere for most of the year. Although obtaining the stone must have been a specialism or seasonal activity of certain communities or individuals, the technology for shaping and finishing stone tools was probably common to most (men), so this industry was not fully specialized. Specialization probably also

increased through time, as communities became larger and social organization more complex, though this was no means a linear progression.

GENDER

Gender distinctions are often shown in burial rites, both in the layout of the body in the grave and in the grave goods placed with the body. For example, women in Lengyel and Tiszapolgár cemeteries were placed on their left side and men on their right. Men were often buried with hunting tools or weapons, such as arrows, daggers, and knives, while jewelry was often placed with women, though these associations were by no means universal.

The Division of Labor

PROVIDING FOOD

In hunter-gatherer societies some division of labor is usual, with men hunting larger animals, sea fishing and catching sea mammals, and other activities requiring strength, prolonged absence from home, or danger, while women, accompanied and assisted by children, gather plants, catch small game, collect shellfish, and obtain other foods within walking distance of the settlement. Men also gather these foods, and men, women, and children eat as they gather; women differ from men in also bringing home gathered food to feed the rest of the community such as the elderly and disabled. The relevant contribution of men and women to the food supply depends to some extent on latitude—meat caught by men being a major part of the diet in cold regions, whereas in the Tropics the foodstuffs collected by women provide the bulk of the diet. During the cold periods of the Palaeolithic and in the extreme north, when it was occupied, it is likely that men were significant providers, but during warmer episodes and in the postglacial period Europe's hunter-gatherers are likely to have foraged much of their food for themselves, supplemented on a daily basis by the food obtained by women and less regularly by game and fish provided by men. Ethnography also suggests that men would butcher the game they caught but that other food preparation would be the responsibility of women.

Although there is no way of determining the division of labor in early European farming communities, ethnographic and historical studies indicate that most of the work was done by women, including some ground preparation, sowing, hoeing, weeding, and harvesting, with tasks requiring greater strength, such as forest clearance, being the province of men. The introduction of the plow shifted much of the responsibility for cultivation to men. While women continued to be involved with many agricultural activities, it is likely that the beginning of plow agriculture and the use of animal transport and traction introduced a division in labor, men working the fields and managing draft animals and women tending vegetable plots and farmyard animals, with the whole family playing a part in major tasks such as harvesting. Pastoralism, on ethnographic analogy, also gave men a greater role in food production.

DOMESTIC WORK

Traditionally, work within the home has been the responsibility of women. This included food preparation, cooking, and cleaning. While mothers probably generally kept their babies with them while they worked, the care of small children probably devolved mainly on grandmothers and other women no longer able to undertake demanding physical work.

The production of tools and equipment was shared between men and women. Domestic pottery was generally made by women, and stone tools and weapons and wooden objects probably generally by men. Women spun thread, wove cloth, and prepared skins. A number of Bronze Age female graves at Singen contained awls used for working leather. Rare representations of people at work in prehistoric European art show women spinning and weaving. The ubiquity of surviving spindle whorls demonstrates how widespread was the practice of spinning, which must have occupied many hours of most women's time, often performed while doing other things such as minding sheep or children.

House construction was a joint activity, men undertaking the heavy work involved in erecting the framework of wood or stone and women performing many of the other tasks such as cutting straw, mixing and applying daub, and preparing other materials.

The development of metallurgy may have seen a shift in gender relations: men would have obtained metal ores and smelted and worked metals, and from this developed other more specialized industrial activities such as the manufacture of jewelry and weapons, the production of glass, and so on.

Power

Celtic women enjoyed greater freedom and power than their classical counterparts. The existence of two British Celtic queens who ruled in their own right, Boudicca and Cartimandua, demonstrates that authority was not confined to men. Vernacular literature shows this to have been an established tradition in Celtic society also in later times, at least in Britain.

Everyday Life

Family Life

MARRIAGE AND SEXUAL MORES

Most traditional societies have rules or customs that determine the range of acceptable marriage partners. Acceptance of incest is rare, though many societies permit or encourage marriage between certain more distant relations such as cousins or uncles and nieces. Most have some pattern of exogamy, taking marriage partners from neighboring or more distant communities rather than from their own, a survival mechanism presumably developed in the remote past. Exogamy became less essential as communities grew in size and the pool of available partners increased. Marriage was generally still within a kin group, which was often also an occupational group. In hierarchical societies groups drew marriage partners from among those of their own rank. Classical literature refers to dynastic marriages within the nobility of Celtic society, political ties between the leading men of Celtic and other tribes being forged and cemented by intermarriage. For example, around 60 B.C., when the kingdom of Noricum was threatened by an alliance between the Celtic Boii and its neighbors, the Helvetii, the Norican king married his sister to Ariovistus, chief of the Suebi, a powerful Germanic tribe. Ariovistus was also allied to the Sequani, enemies of the Aedui, two leading Gallic tribes that were at that time engaged in a power struggle; a leading member of the Helvetian nobility, Orgetorix, forged an alliance with the Aedui by marrying his daughter to one of their chiefs, Dumnorix.

Marriage patterns may be one way to shed light on prehistoric kinship organization. The work is still in its infancy, but DNA studies and other physical or chemical analyses of bones have the potential to track the movement of individuals from birthplace or childhood home to later residence or place of death. Stable isotope analysis of bones from the Mesolithic cemeteries of Hoëdic and Téviec shows that women came from areas inland to marry the men of these coastal communities.

Intermarriage may have been one of the mechanisms involved in the transition from hunting and gathering to farming, marriage partners being exchanged, for example, between LBK and Ertebølle communities. Often attempts have been made to trace marriage patterns by looking for nonlocal items of material culture, such as tools or pieces of jewelry, that might have been brought into the community by a person from another community at the time of their marriage. Where these have been identified, the vast majority are artifacts associated with women, indicating that in general in prehistoric Europe it was girls who moved into the households of their husbands rather than men into those of their wives. A number of Bronze Age women's burials in northern Europe contained complete sets of ornaments characteristic of other areas, a north German set in a grave on the Danish island of Zealand, for example, and a number of north German graves with Scandinavian ornament sets: It is suggested these women were buried in the jewelry that they brought with them when they moved to their final home as brides.

Vernacular literature refers to three grades of wife in Irish law. According to Caesar, in Gallic law the bride's family contributed a dowry, which was matched by a bride-price from the groom's family. The combined sum was inherited by one partner on the death of the other. The Romans were shocked by the freedom enjoyed by Celtic women, although Caesar commented that husbands had the power of life or death over both their wives and their children. Classical accounts perhaps misinterpreted Celtic sexual practices, which, they said, included wives being shared among the 10 or 12 men of an extended family, and girls inviting intercourse, taking offense if their offer was refused. Vernacular literature indicates that the rules of society permitted sexual activity outside marriage for friendship or profit.

CHILDREN

Irish vernacular literature describes the practice of sending children to foster parents, preferably of a higher status to their own parents, from age seven to 14 (marriageable age) in the case of girls and 17 (military age) in the case of boys. This may also have been a Celtic practice since Caesar states that it was considered unacceptable for a boy to approach his father in public before he reached military age. Boys did not become full members of adult society until they inherited land; before this they were landless members of the war band.

SLAVERY

The economies of the Mediterranean civilizations came to depend on slave labor, and barbarian Europe became a valued supplier: It is probable that slaves were among the commodities sought by Greek traders in the sixth century. How much earlier slave trading occurred is unknown, but by the late centuries B.C. large numbers of individuals were being captured in Celtic and Germanic wars and sold to the Greeks and Romans. Within Iron Age barbarian Europe, however, it seems slaves were of much less importance, though in later Irish society they had an important economic role.

Entertainment and Sport

A few musical instruments are known from prehistoric Europe, undoubtedly only a tiny fraction of those once used. Mesolithic and later rock art depicts individuals and groups of people dancing and taking part in processions. These may have been ritual in nature, but such events would also have added interest to the lives of their participants.

Communal activities such as house construction probably culminated in a feast. Pits full of animal bones in the floor of the wheelhouse at Sollas on North Uist (Scotland), for example, are thought to be the remains of such a feast. Feasting was a major source of entertainment, often within the context of events such as births, marriages, and deaths, as well as of religious festivals but probably not exclusively so. Certainly by the later Iron Age feasting was a regular and important activity among the elite, and involved the consumption of large (and excessive) quantities of alcohol and food. Elite graves often contained fine tableware for serving and consuming meat and alcohol, both native beer and mead and imported wine. The drunken fights that inevitably followed were also part of the entertainment for both the participants and the appreciative spectators, though they frequently resulted in serious injury or even death. Alcohol was not necessarily always consumed in excess; it may originally have played an important role in ritual practices.

Board games and games with dice were also in vogue by the Iron Age; dice made of bone or antler and glass gaming pieces have been recovered from a number of elite burials, for example, at Welwyn Garden City in southern England, which contained 24 glass gaming pieces and a wooden board. Vernacular sources show that gambling on the outcome of dice games and other games of chance was rife and the stakes could be extremely high; this was likely also to have been the case in earlier times.

Most entertainments have left no archaeological trace; these probably included physical contests between young men to demonstrate excellence in strength, stamina, and endurance, and the recital of tales and songs enshrining community history and tribal lore.

Domestic Arrangements

FAMILY ACCOMMODATION

The layout of houses suggests a variety of domestic arrangements and family groupings in different areas. In Neolithic Southeast Europe the houses, which were built close together in settlements, seem designed to accommodate nuclear families: a couple and their preadult children. Later Neolithic houses in the Balkans often had two rooms and some had four. Houses in the Swiss lake villages and in many other areas also probably accommodated nuclear families.

The LBK first farmers in central Europe lived in longhouses, often laid out so that each had its own surrounding space, often with gardens and outbuildings. These longhouses probably accommodated extended families: a couple, their children, and their grandchildren. This arrangement continued in much of western, northern, and central Europe throughout prehistory and well into historical times.

In other parts of western Europe different forms of houses were also probably home to extended families; these included the large roundhouses of wood or stone in British Iron Age settlements, holding the whole extended family. Modular units of smaller houses grouped together, also familiar from British Bronze and Iron Age settlements, may have housed the nuclear units of an extended family; similarly, the Neolithic settlement at Skara Brae was made up of a series of interconnecting rooms, each with a hearth and beds, which probably housed a nuclear family, linked by a passage and grouped together within a single complex with a turf and stone outer wall.

Domestic animals might be corralled in the open in the areas adjacent to the houses, stalled in separate byres, or accommodated in the house along with the family. Many longhouses of all periods included partitions for animal stalls at one end; substantial Scottish Bronze and Iron Age stone houses may have accommodated the animals on the ground floor and people on an upper floor, while in single-story roundhouses the animals were kept in one section of the interior.

FITTINGS AND FURNITURE

The majority of European houses had a hearth used for cooking, heating in the winter, and light; the household would sit round it together while eating, working, talking, and entertaining themselves and visitors. Houses in the Balkans also had ovens for cooking. In some houses a hole in the

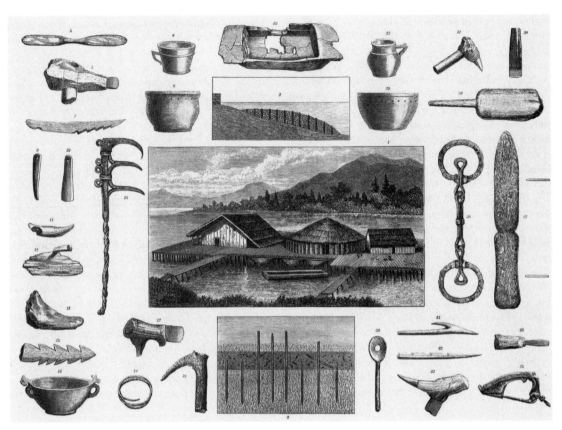

11.3 An illustration of a lake settlement discovered at Meilen on Lake Zurich in 1853–54 and the material recovered in its investigation by Ferdinand Keller. Waterlogged settlements like these provide some of the richest sources of information on daily life in prehistoric Europe. (Courtesy of Ann Ronan Picture Library / HIP / TopFoto. ©2004 Ann Ronan Picture Library)

roof above the hearth drew out the smoke from the fire. In thatched houses, however, the smoke generally found its own way out through the material of the roof; the interior of the house must often have been smoky and dark. Storage was essential in agricultural settlements where the annually harvested grain and other storable foods such as fruit and pulses had to be kept for use throughout the year. Hunter-gatherers also stored food such as nuts and fruit. Other produce such as skins and wool also needed to be stored. Pottery jars, stone or clay storage bins, wooden buckets and barrels, bags, and sacks were used inside the house; central

and western European Neolithic longhouses had a loft for storage. Water was also necessary but was probably fetched daily from a nearby river or lake or drawn from a well and kept in small containers. Many Scottish houses from the Neolithic period onward had watertight stone tanks, perhaps for storing fish or fishing bait. External storage facilities included pits and small wooden granaries, sheds, and barns.

Some houses had a platform built out from the house wall to serve as a bed at night and a place to sit and work during the day. In others such as Slatina in the Neolithic Balkans the beds were constructed of wood. Box beds of stone slabs were built along the walls of the rooms at Skara Brae. Miniature furniture from some Balkan settlements suggests that chairs and tables were used, but logs or boughs of wood were probably more usual seats. According to classical authors the Celts ate sitting on the ground or on wolf or dog skins, with the food placed on a low table before them. Other furniture might include a wooden chest for storing clothing and coverings, and some houses had shelves; those at Skara Brae in Neolithic Orkney were built out of stone slabs, forming freestanding "dressers," while the brochs of Iron Age Scotland often had recesses built into the walls to serve as cupboards. More elaborate pieces of furniture have occasionally been found, such as the elaborately decorated wooden object, possibly a chest of drawers, from fourth-century B.C. Cancho Roano in Spain. Some exotic furniture was imported, probably as prestige items, such as the Mycenaean folding wooden stool with an otterskin seat from a Danish tree-trunk coffin at Guldhøj.

Burnt mounds, large heaps of charred stones often arranged in a horseshoe shape around a small wooden or stone tank, may be the remains of Bronze Age and Early Iron Age saunas. The stones were heated and dropped into the water to raise its temperature and produce steam.

DOMESTIC ACTIVITIES

The house was the scene of much domestic activity. In addition to food preparation, the women would have spent much of their time cleaning and treating skins, spinning and weaving wool or linen thread, and sewing clothing. An upright loom was a fixture in many European houses, generally set near the door to take advantage of daylight. There were many other tasks that were constantly being performed, such as mending broken tools, making fishing nets, or shaping pottery. It is unlikely that anyone sat idle: there were always tasks to engage the hands, though the brain might be focused on conversation or storytelling.

Many activities took place outside the house; these included tasks that produced a lot of debris such as flint knapping and whittling wood and might also have included tasks that involved bad-smelling

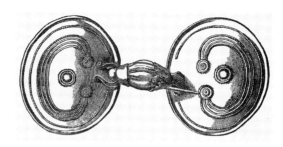

11.4 A large fibula, richly decorated and highly valued, that had broken across the bow connecting the two plates. This was mended by casting-on: The break was coated in wax, the whole fibula encased in clay, and the wax melted out, forming a mold into which metal was poured. The result is a little rough but serviceable; it may have been a domestic job or the work of an itinerant metalsmith. (Lubbock, John. *Prehistoric Times.* New York: D. Appleton and Company, 1890)

or otherwise offensive materials, such as tanning leather. For example, at the Mesolithic site of Vaenget Nord in Denmark bone tools were made and repaired inside the hut, while cooking, stone working, and hide scraping and preparation took place in the area around the hut.

PERSONAL APPEARANCE

Since the dawn of consciousness people have been using their appearance to make statements about themselves, giving information about their cultural, ethnic, political, and religious affiliations, their occupation, and their status, the latter both in terms of age, marital state, and gender, and in terms of social hierarchy. Identity can be shown by varying aspects of clothing, personal ornaments, and hairstyles, and by altering the body, all means that were employed in prehistoric Europe.

Bodies

The Scythians and other steppe peoples decorated their bodies with tattoos. Several of the frozen bodies recovered from the steppe mounds at Pazyryk bore elaborate designs, including animals, and the steppe dwellers on the European margins were similarly elaborately tattooed; the practice is mentioned by Herodotus. Faint blue patterns on parts of the Iceman's body, including his spine, ankles, right knee, and left calf, indicate that he had been tattooed. His skin was punctured with a very sharp instrument and a paste, probably made from charcoal mixed with water, was rubbed in. Though this may have been decorative, it was more probably intended as a medical treatment for joint pain.

Classical authors stated that the Britons painted their bodies, particularly before fighting naked. Although the term used for this paint is usually translated as woad, studies of the blue designs on the body of the bog man from Lindow Moss show that they were executed with a mineral pigment, including copper and iron, and the Latin term has been reexamined: it now seems it may refer to this pigment.

Hair

Occasionally the hair of prehistoric individuals has survived, including that of several bog women. This shows that European hairstyles could be elaborate. Women generally had long hair, but this was often braided, pinned into a bun or twisted up onto the head. Long hair was also often caught up into a hairnet or tight-fitting cap. Men also wore their hair long, often under a cap, and the Celts often braided their hair to keep it out of the way. Some bog men and women had elaborate arrangements constructed from several braids, interwoven or knotted. Classical sources reported that the Gauls used a limewash on their hair, making it stiff and spiky. The Celtic elite favored long mustaches, and facial hair was kept neat using razors, which are known from the Middle Bronze Age onward. Combs, used by the Mesolithic period, were made of antler, bone, horn, wood, or metal, and might have both coarse and fine teeth, the latter for removing nits.

Clothing

Bone needles for sewing garments were used from the Gravettian period around 25,000 years ago. Clothing was stitched from leather or cloth made from various fibers, including flax, wool, grass, and hemp, and leather might also be laced together with sinews. There were also untailored draped garments fastened with belts, brooches, and pins. Cloth was generally woven, but plaiting, felting, netting, twining, and other techniques were also used. Few actual garments have been found; most come from the bog bodies and tree-trunk coffins of the north and the lake villages of the Alpine regions. The Iceman has provided an exceptionally full picture of one individual's clothing. Evidence also comes from representations of people in various media and from the arrangement of ornaments used to fasten or decorate clothing.

MATERIALS

The cloth from which garments were made might be colored. A range of natural shades were available; linen naturally had a golden color that could be bleached in sunlight to cream; the natural colors of wool were a spectrum from white and fawn to dark brown and black. Wool could be dyed as could some plant fibers, but linen did not take dyes easily. The colors produced by dyeing with plant, animal, and mineral pigments included greens, blues, reds, browns, and yellows. The *pintaderas* (pottery stamps) common in Southeast European Neolithic sites may have been used to stamp colored designs onto cloth, and stamp-decorated cloth is known from the Swiss lake village of Ledro. Leather was also dyed, sometimes in patterns, and designs could be embossed on it.

Patterns could be woven into cloth; some woven designs depended on the use of different-colored threads, such as the checked designs (resembling modern tartans) apparently favored by the Celts; others used a single color, but varied the arrangement of the threads, producing twills and other textured cloth. In a few cases the warp and weft were of different fibers, usually wool and linen. Woven cloth could also include borders and panels of contrasting weave, and fringes and tassels were added to some.

Cloth and clothing was also embroidered with thread (including silk in a few instances) or decorated with sewn-on beads and other small elements such as tiny shells. Quantities of tiny beads on the heads and bodies of Palaeolithic people buried at Arene Candide in Italy and Sungir in Russia show the shape of headgear and clothing to which they were sewn as decoration.

GARMENTS

An extraordinary garment was recovered from a girl's log coffin at Egtved in Bronze Age Denmark. It consisted of a woven waistband, from which hung down a series of threads twisted together in fours to form heavy cords. These were fastened together at the bottom by a twined cord, beneath which the loop ends of the cords protruded decoratively. This see-through garment, which was quite short, offered neither warmth nor decency, and its significance is unknown. It was wrapped twice around the girl's waist, presumably to make it as warm as was possible in the circumstances.

In general, women wore long skirts and blouses, fastened with brooches, ties, or fibulae. Some women wore a jacket. A belt might hold the skirt in place. Women's clothes from the Scandinavian log coffins were often worn with a bronze disc at the waist. Shawls and cloaks might be worn over the top. Men also wore cloaks or capes; the Iceman had an outer cape of grass and beneath it a short-sleeved deerskin coat. In the Late Iron Age the Celts produced waterproof hooded capes of coarse wool, the *sagum* and the *byrrus.*

The main male garments were tunics, kilts, and shirts, often belted at the waist. The Iceman had a leather pouch attached to his belt, probably a common accouterment. The Celts, and probably earlier inhabitants of transalpine Europe, also wore trousers (*bracae*). The Iceman wore fur leggings, perhaps the precursor of these trousers. The Gundestrup cauldron depicts a file of warriors with long-sleeved shirts and tight knee-length trousers. Occasionally, undergarments have also been found: the Iceman wore a loin cloth as did some men from the log coffins. A gold penis sheath was among the objects worn by a man in one of the rich Chalcolithic graves at Varna in Bulgaria; this may have been a luxury translation of a garment more usually made in leather. It had small holes at the wider end, probably to enable it to be attached to clothing.

Caps and hoods of various materials, including plaited or twined fibers, fur, and leather, and even leather lined with fur, were frequently worn; the Iceman had a cap with a chin strap of fur. Shoes were also common, some with a leather sole and a cloth upper, others made entirely of leather. Often they were made of a single piece of leather drawn up around the foot and laced or fastened by a strap right around the foot, passing under the instep, though some were shaped and stitched. The Iceman and some of the Scandinavian bodies had their shoes stuffed with grass, an excellent insulator, to cushion their feet and keep them warm.

Ornaments

DECORATED HEADGEAR

The Mesolithic Ofnet skulls wore caps decorated with shells and perforated deer teeth. A Bronze Age woman buried at Grundfeld in Germany had a band decorated with rings around her head and a band joining it over the top of her head, decorated with beads. Bronze Age pottery figurines from the Carpathian basin are shown with an ornament hanging down their back, fastened to a plait, and similar ornaments were found in hoards. These consisted of a central metal plaque in a geometric shape from which dangled chains and metal rings or other shapes. Later head ornaments included gold tress rings.

Earrings of bronze and gold were popular in some periods. Among the fine jewelry in Beaker and later graves were gold earrings in the form of tiny baskets or boats.

NECK AND CHEST ORNAMENTS

The Iron Age elite wore torcs around their necks; the finest were of gold, but there were also examples in bronze. Massive collars of beaten gold (gorgets) were also worn in Ireland. In the Bronze Age divine statues and elite individuals wore collars; these included the *gargantillas* of Iberia and the magnificent gold lunulae of Ireland, decorated with fine designs, as well as a unique "cape" (pectoral) of beaten gold found at Mold in Wales, dating to the early second millennium, and elaborately decorated with embossed geometric designs. Necklaces and pendants were more widely distributed and common. These included collars made of rows of beads

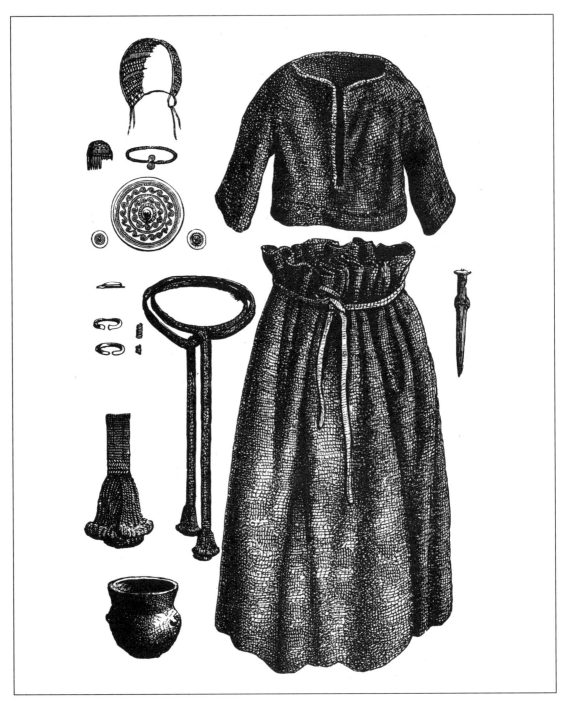

11.5 The woolen garments worn by a woman found in a Danish Bronze Age tree-trunk coffin at Borum Eshøj, including a hairnet (top left), a woven and stitched jacket, and a long woven skirt with a tasselled girdle. Buried with her were a pottery vessel, several ornaments including a decorated disc apparently worn at the waist, a dagger, and a decorated horn comb (left, second from top). She was buried wrapped in a deerskin cloak (not illustrated). (Worsaae, J. J. A. *The Industrial Arts of Denmark.* London: Chapman and Hall, 1882)

joined by spacer beads, made of amber, jet, and other prized materials.

PINS AND BROOCHES

Clothing was fastened or decorated with a variety of brooches and pins, often with decorated heads. Particularly distinctive are the fibulae (safety-pin brooches), which were invented in north Italy or the eastern Alps in the 15th century B.C. These offered three areas for decorative elaboration—the bow, the spring, and the catchplate—all of which were exuberantly explored in Iron Age Europe. The spring could be a simple double turn in the center of the pin, but was developed in some instances into a large series of coils protruding on either side of the essential spring. The catchplate, at its simplest a piece of metal curved over to hold the point of the pin, was in many cases elongated and formed into a variety of elaborate shapes. The bow, forming the curve from spring to catchplate, was often embellished with luxury materials such as glass or gemstone, or had a bronze figure molded onto it.

OTHER ORNAMENTS

Finger rings, bracelets, leg ornaments, and anklets were known in many prehistoric European societies, made from shell, stone, metal, or glass. Shale, jet, and related materials were popular for bracelets. Some Iron Age bronze arm rings were massive, with

11.6 Two fibulae, one of bronze from a Bronze Age tree-trunk coffin, the other of iron from Lake Neuchâtel (Worsaae, J. J. A. *The Industrial Arts of Denmark*. London: Chapman and Hall, 1882; Figuier, Louis. *Primitive Man*. London: Chatto and Windus, 1876)

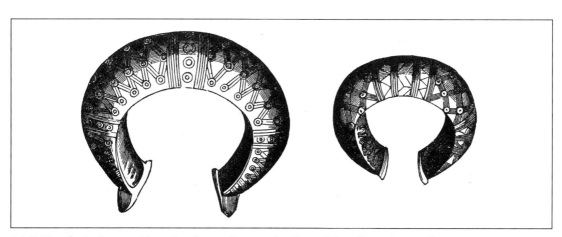

11.7 Two finely decorated bracelets from a Bronze Age Swiss lake village. Personal ornaments were worn by men and women from the Palaeolithic period onward. (Lubbock, John. *Prehistoric Times*. New York: D. Appleton and Company, 1890)

grotesque plastic decoration. In the Bronze Age and early Iron Age many ornaments incorporated a "spectacle" design, in which a bronze wire was tightly coiled into a pair of spirals.

BEADS

Many ornaments, such as necklaces and bracelets, were made of beads. Some were perforated natural objects, such as small shells, fish vertebrae, or animal teeth; others were made from decorative stones, amber, jet, bone, antler, shell, metal, glass, or other attractive materials. Beads were also sewn as decoration onto clothing, bags, and other objects.

Toilet Equipment

Various implements were used from early times to improve personal appearance, including combs.

Bronze tweezers, nail parers, and razors were in regular use from the second millennium. Mirrors of polished metal became popular accessories in the Iron Age; these were placed in women's graves but were perhaps also used by men if the objects shown among warrior equipment on Iberian grave slabs have been correctly identified.

FOOD

Food and Cooking

The diet of Mesolithic and later hunter-gatherer groups was probably quite varied but was influenced by location: coastal communities ate a high proportion of marine foods, particularly in the north,

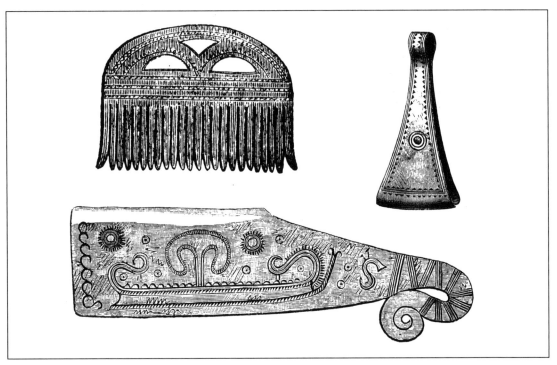

11.8 A selection of personal equipment from Danish sites: a horn comb from the tree-trunk coffin at Treen-hoj, a bronze razor decorated with a ship, and a pair of tweezers (Lubbock, John. *Prehistoric Times.* New York: D. Appleton and Company, 1890; Worsaae, J. J. A. *The Industrial Arts of Denmark.* London: Chapman and Hall, 1882)

whereas farther south plant foods and meat were also significant; on inland sites meat was the principal food, but in riverine locations such as Lepenski Vir fish predominated. Apart from the far north where suitable plants were restricted in their availability, plant foods were important in the Mesolithic diet.

In contrast, grain was the staple of purely agricultural communities, supplemented by pulses, some vegetables and fruits, milk, cheese, and meat. Many farming communities, however, also made some use of wild foods, particularly coastal and lake or riverside communities that caught fish. Calculations of meat consumption at a number of sites show that meat often contributed significantly to the diet, although such figures are at best a very rough approximation. Some groups such as the TRB inhabitants of Bronocice consumed as much or more meat than the modern people of some European countries. Meat could be eaten fresh or preserved, for instance, as hams or sausages. Meat fat, particularly pork lard, was an important dietary element, as was oil from plant seeds; these were also used in medicines and for lighting.

GRAIN

Grain was cooked with liquid as the basis for gruel or soup or made into bread (this was one of the last foods eaten by the Iceman). North Italian Bronze Age sites suggest it was also made into gnocchi (boiled balls made from flour paste). Flour for bread could also be made of pulses, acorns, and nuts. Small loaves made of unleavened wheat flour was found in the Neolithic settlement of Twann in Switzerland, and this site also yielded evidence of porridge. Oval or rectangular saddle querns and rubbers of hard stone were used to grind grain for most of prehistory in Europe. By the fourth century B.C. rotary querns were in use; these had a fixed lower millstone on which an upper stone was rotated. A central hole in the upper stone was used as a funnel down which the grain was slowly poured as the grinding took place, and a section cut out of the lower stone acted as a spout through which the flour came out. A small slot in the upper stone held a handle for turning it.

MILK PRODUCTS

Perhaps from the Early Neolithic period and certainly by the mid-fourth millennium milk from cat-

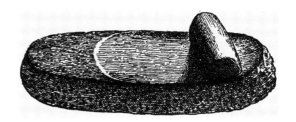

11.9 A saddle quern used for grinding grain, a daily task (Figuier, Louis. *Primitive Man.* London: Chatto and Windus, 1876)

tle, sheep, and goats was being consumed, particularly in transalpine Europe. Most humans cannot digest lactose, present in raw milk, after they cease to produce the enzyme lactase in early childhood. Lactose tolerance is an adaptation that has developed in cattle-keeping populations around the world; many Europeans, central Asians, and South Asians have this adaptation, as do the pastoral peoples of Africa, while most other groups, such as the Chinese, most Africans, and others, including many in the Mediterranean, do not, and experience severe discomfort if they consume raw milk. It is not known how early this adaptation took place in Europe; even in the Iron Age milk was probably mainly made into cheese.

When milk is processed by heating or fermentation to make yogurt, butter, and cheese, the lactose is broken down, avoiding the problem. Vessels for collecting and processing milk, known by the fourth millennium, included pottery strainers, ceramic and wooden bowls, wooden whisks, pottery churns, and hollowed log churns. Cheese-making equipment included baskets and Apennine milk-boiling vessels that had a perforated lid sitting on a ledge partway down the vessel.

COOKING

Most food was either roasted directly over the fire on sticks or metal spits or cooked with water in vessels. These included pottery cooking pots placed directly on the hearth, supported by stones, and metal cauldrons suspended over the fire. Food could also be cooked in stone tanks or skins filled with liquid into which heated stones were dropped to bring the liquid to the boil and maintain it at a simmer.

The Roman writer Poseidonius, describing southern Gaul in the early first century B.C., referred to meals of bread and large amounts of meat, cooked by boiling, roasting, or charcoal grilling, and fish baked with cumin, salt, and vinegar.

Drink

The main drink consumed by everyone in prehistory was water, drawn from wells, rivers, lakes, or ponds. The earliest well known in Europe, dated to 5089 B.C., was found in the LBK settlement of Erkelenz-Kückhoven. Wooden buckets for drawing water have been found in a number of sites. Farming communities, and especially those specializing in animal husbandry, may have drunk milk and the related substances, buttermilk and thin yogurt.

The techniques used to produce alcohol may have been introduced from the Near East, where wine and beer were being brewed by the early third millennium. In temperate Europe the techniques were applied to produce alcohol (mead) from honey. This, however, was not easily obtained or abundant, so mead must have been a prestigious commodity. It is known from residues in vessels that mead was being drunk in temperate Europe by the third millennium. Wine drinking in Greece and probably Iberia began around the same time. The handled cups and jugs that appeared in Southeast Europe and farther north from the fourth millennium were probably for consuming alcohol. Drinking vessels, including Globular Amphora and Corded Ware beakers, became more widespread in the later fourth millennium and reached western Europe with the appearance of the Beaker complex. Lime, heather, and plantain honey were used in the mead drunk from a beaker at Ashgrove Farm, Scotland; this was flavored with meadowsweet. Mead found in birch-bark pots in the Bronze Age log coffin at Egtved in Denmark was brewed from wheat and honey flavored with cranberries, other fruit, and leaves. Mead residues were also found in the massive bronze cauldron in the sixth-century chieftain's grave at Hochdorf.

Beer, which could be brewed from barley, wheat, oats, or millet, was probably produced from emmer wheat by the Beaker period, if not earlier, and beer became common from Urnfield times with the intro-duction of two-row barley. The Roman author Poseidonius describes a beer known as *corma*, brewed from wheat, which he said was the drink of the common people, sometimes mixed with honey.

Drinks made with drugs may also have been consumed: A residue of black henbane in a Grooved Ware vessel from Balfarg in Chalcolithic Scotland may have been the remains of a hallucinogenic drink. Opium was used in temperate Europe by LBK times, perhaps infused in a drink. Other narcotics included birch bark, which was chewed like gum. Cannabis was used in the steppe region by the third millennium and probably in other parts of Europe; it was burned and its smoke inhaled, although it may also have been eaten. Small braziers or lamps ("altars") from the fifth-millennium Balkans may perhaps have been used for heating poppy heads or cannabis. Probable braziers have also been found in other parts of Europe such as Neolithic Brittany.

By the second millennium wine was widely made and drunk in the Mediterranean and was introduced into barbarian Europe by the sixth century. The elite rapidly developed a taste for wine, which they drank neat, to the disgust of classical writers (who watered their wine), becoming roaring and violently drunk. The Celts also drank beer, described by Dionysius of Halicarnassus as "a foul-smelling liquor made from barley rotted in water" (*Roman Antiquities* XIII, 10, quoted in Sherratt 1997: 394).

Feasting

The Celts' love of feasting was described by classical authors. Meat was roasted on spits or stewed in large cauldrons suspended on chains from a tripod or the roof beams. Fleshhooks were used by feasters to fish out tasty morsels to eat. Residues in cauldrons found in the Iron Age British hillfort of Danebury show they were used for stewing pork. Wealthy later Iron Age graves often contained a pair of firedogs, vertical iron stands decorated with an animal head at each end, which were used to support spits for roasting large joints of meat. The choicest joint of meat, known as the champion's portion, was presented by later Irish chiefs to warriors who had showed particular prowess, and it is likely that a similar practice existed in the Iron Age.

Serving Food

At all periods it is likely that food was eaten from bowls or dishes of wood, though they have survived only in rare waterlogged sites such as Iron Age Glastonbury. Pottery vessels might also have been used. Wooden and pottery bowls were also used for drinking in the earlier Neolithic, but later a range of different drinking vessels began to appear, including beakers. Animal horns were made into drinking vessels; a set of such drinking horns, decorated with gold and bronze bands, was found in the sixth-century chieftain's grave at Hochdorf in Germany. Metal vessels were made for the elite in Bronze Age Europe from copper or gold; these often had handles. During the Iron Age Mediterranean fine tableware, including bronze flagons and fine pottery drinking cups, was imported by European chieftains for serving wine.

HEALTH AND MEDICINE

Examination of skeletons from prehistoric Europe has furnished some insights into health, injuries, treatment, and life expectancy, while occasional completely preserved bodies have provided more detailed evidence, including conditions that affected only soft tissue.

Health and Diet

The mixed and varied diet enjoyed by many Mesolithic groups promoted their health. In contrast, there is evidence of some malnutrition in agricultural communities; LBK children, for example, suffered from scurvy (vitamin-C deficiency), and by the Bronze Age scurvy was more prevalent. Rickets, a condition caused by vitamin-D deficiency, was also common. Markings on bones known as Harris lines, which indicate periods of malnutrition, are frequently seen: For example, they were present on the bones of the Iron Age girl sacrificed at Windeby. Hunter-gatherers who depended to a significant extent on fish, such as Iron Gates communities and the inhabitants of Vedbaek in Denmark, often suffered from fish tapeworms and other intestinal parasites ingested with the fish; these caused malnutrition and unpleasant symptoms such as bloating and diarrhea. Material recovered from the guts of bog bodies and the Iceman and from other sources show that prehistoric communities often suffered debilitating infestations of parasites such as intestinal worms, some of which caused damage to the kidneys or lungs. Skeletons in LBK and later cemeteries, including Bronze Age ones in Spain, Italy, Moravia, and Germany, show that many children suffered from *Cribra orbitalia*, an anemic condition that produces spongy bone above the eye sockets. Various explanations for this include malnutrition, malaria, or infestation with intestinal parasites due to eating untreated beef and dairy products or living in close proximity to domestic animals.

Dental caries, a condition linked to the consumption of foods rich in carbohydrates, was associated with a diet in which plant foods predominated; it was rare in Mesolithic Scandinavia but more common in southerly latitudes, in areas such as Brittany, Portugal, and Italy. Mediterranean communities, which had a significant plant component in their diet, suffered severe caries. Farmers experienced many problems with their teeth, their grain-based diet encouraging dental caries, while the minute pieces of grit that resulted from the grinding of the grain caused the teeth to become worn and chipped. Abscesses and tooth loss are also known. Tooth wear was also common among hunter-gatherers; this resulted not only from erosion by grit or bone mixed in with food but also from the use of the teeth as tools, for instance for softening hides by chewing them. Women suffered more from tooth problems than men, probably due to calcium deficiency when bearing and nursing children.

Hygiene was an important factor in health. Sedentary settlements where food waste, dung, and feces accumulated promoted diseases among farming and settled hunter-gatherer communities, which were avoided by mobile hunter-gatherers and pastoralists.

Ill Health

Evidence of a number of diseases and medical conditions have been found; these included malaria, spina bifida, osteomyelitis, kidney stones, polio, eye problems, ear infections, arthritis, rheumatism, slipped discs, various skeletal deformities, and tumors. The Iceman, who was probably around 45 years old when he died, was beginning to suffer from arthritis. Injuries were also common, some from falls or accidents, others deliberately inflicted in domestic disputes or armed combat. Death from infected wounds was probably as common as death from injuries themselves. Many individuals were permanently crippled by badly healed injuries. People buried in the later Neolithic cemetery of Tizsapolgár-Basatanya had sustained injuries to their heads and spines, and suffered from paralyzed limbs, deformed skulls, brain tumors, osteoporosis, rheumatism, arthritis, and other conditions. The "Amesbury Archer," the man recently discovered in a rich burial near Stonehenge, was age 35 to 45 when he died. He had a permanent limp from a serious knee injury that discharged continuously and also suffered from an abscess, both of which caused him constant pain.

Medical Treatment

Illness and injury were treated with herbal remedies and magical practices. A Bronze Age man at Hvidegård in Denmark wore a leather purse containing various objects that were probably charms, perhaps intended magically to ensure health: dried roots and bark, a squirrel's jaw, a grass snake's tail, and a falcon's claw. The Iceman carried two pieces of birch fungus on a thong; this may have been a prophylactic charm against disease or a portable supply of a material thought to be medicinal. Alcohol and narcotics were presumably used as anesthetics and medical drugs.

Cures might also be sought by appealing to the gods. The shrine of the goddess Sequana at Sources-de-la-Seine (Fontes Sequanae) in France received many votive offerings in the form not only of small figurines of patients but also models of various parts of the body, deposited either in supplication for a cure or in thanks for having obtained one. Eye problems and chest diseases were the most common afflictions.

Medical instruments have been found in a number of Iron Age graves; these included saws, rasps, and spatulas. That of the "warrior-surgeon" at München-Obermenzing in Germany, dating from the third or second century B.C., included a trepanning saw and medical probes, while the first-century A.D. collection from Stanway in England comprised needles, hooks, a saw, forceps, and scalpels. The skill of prehistoric surgeons is clear from the evidence of trepanning, which goes back to the seventh millennium B.C. This operation, in which a disc of bone was removed from the skull, was potentially fatal since it required working with sharp instruments near the brain. Many of those who underwent this operation did indeed die, but as many as two-thirds survived, and in some cases were successfully trepanned several times. The operation may have been performed to relieve pressure from skull injuries or brain tumors or to treat mental disorders, or may have had some magical function. The circle of bone could be removed by cutting around it with a special saw, drilling out a circle with a hollow cylindrical drill (trepan) or with a more advanced drill with a central anchoring pin to prevent the drill slipping (trephine), or by scraping the bone away.

Life Expectancy

The limited evidence available on the age structure and mortality pattern of ancient European communities shows that infant mortality was high, perhaps as high as one in two; many children died in childhood or adolescence and many more people in young adulthood. Mesolithic life expectancy was around 30 to 34 years. Burials at the Neolithic Greek settlement of Nea Nikomedeia included many infants and children, while the adults averaged around 30 years old when they died. Examination of seven women showed that they had borne an average of five children each. In the Corded Ware cemetery of Żerniki Górne, the average age of the adult males was 43 and women 36, and many individuals had died in childhood. People buried in the Late Tripolye cemetery of Vikhvatinski had had around a one-in-six chance of reaching the age of 50; this compares favorably with an earlier cemetery where people only had a one-in-eight chance of reaching this age, and with Bronze Age Britain where the chance was less than one in twenty. Few individuals survived beyond 35 in the Bronze Age and very few beyond 45. By the Iron Age life expectancy had risen a little; a high proportion of the population still died in infancy, childhood, or young adulthood, but those who survived the hazards of these years might live to 60, 70 or even more. Women were more at risk than men of dying young, due to the dangers of childbearing.

Population

There has been a general trend toward population increase throughout prehistory and history. In mobile communities where infants had to be carried during the frequent changes of location, births tended to be spaced at intervals of three or four years. In sedentary communities, however, there were no such constraints, so young women might bear a child every year.

The population of Europe around 5000 B.C. has been estimated at between 2 and 5 million; this is comparable with the population of some modern cities. Settlements were generally small, many occupied by a single family, numbering perhaps 20 people, while larger settlements probably had no more than 200 inhabitants. By the Late Iron Age Europe's population had risen to between 15 and 30 million, with Italy and Greece being the most densely settled regions. The majority of settlements in the rest of Europe still housed fewer than 50 people. Earlier Iron Age hillforts and other more substantial settlements may have had populations, in some cases, of as many as 1,000 people, and some of the oppida that emerged in the last centuries B.C. may have accommodated as many as 10,000 people, though others were smaller.

READING

General

Milisauskas, ed. 2002, Cunliffe, ed. 1994, Champion et al. 1984, Cunliffe 2001a: general; Whittle 1996: Neolithic; Harding 2000: Bronze Age; Cunliffe 1997, James 1993, Collis 1994a: Iron Age.

Social and Political Organization

Mithen 2003, Bradley 1998, Jochim 2002c: Mesolithic; Renfrew 1973, Scarre 1998, Bradley 1998: the social context of monument construction; Bailey 2000, Sherratt 1997: Neolithic; Audouze and Büchsenschütz 1992: Bronze Age; Moosleitner 1991, Maier 1991a, Motykova et al. 1991, Champion, T. 1995: Iron Age; Caesar 1951: Celtic political history; Frey 1995: magistrates; Taylor 1994, Venedikov 1976, Marazov 1998: Thracians; Parker Pearson 1999, Carman and Harding, eds. 1999: status in burials.

Crime and Punishment

Maier 1991b: keys; Brothwell 1986: bog bodies; Green 1992: Garton Slack; Lloyd-Morgan 1995: Iron Age.

The Organization of Industry

Jope 1995, Wells 1995a: Iron Age industry; Midgeley 1992: Brześć Kujawski.

Gender

Ehrenburg 1989, Lloyd-Morgan 1995, Finlayson 1998: women's roles.

Personal Appearance

Schumacher-Matthaus 1999, Glob 1974: Bronze Age; Barber 1991: Egtved skirt; Lloyd-Morgan 1995, Hingley 1998, Pyatt et al. 1995: body painting; Spindler 1995: Iceman; Kruta 2004: Celts;

Lloyd-Morgan 1995, Hingley 1998, Bahn, ed. 2003: hair; Bahn, ed. 2003, Spindler 1995: tattoos; Hingley 1998: clothing; Champion, S. 1995: jewelry.

Everyday Life

Scarre 1998: Skara Brae; Lloyd-Morgan 1995, Champion, T. 1995, Ritchie 1988, Hingley 1998: Iron Age; Champion, T. 1995, Ehrenburg 1989: women.

Food

Barker 1985, Garrison 1997: types of food; Cunliffe 1995, Coles 1973, 1987, Barker 1985: cooking equipment; Bökönyi 1991, Sherratt 1997: milk products; Barclay 1998, Sherratt 1997: henbane drink; Sherratt 1997, Bogucki 2001: alcohol.

Health and Medicine

Fitzpatrick 2005, Wessex Archaeology 2005: Amesbury archer; Green 1992: Fontes Sequanae; Kunzl 1991, Fagan 2004: surgical equipment; Trump 1980, Kunzl 1991, Guilaine and Zammit 2005, Schultz 1999, Walker 1998: trepannng; Mithen 2003: parasites; Bahn, ed. 2001b, 2003, Parker Pearson 1999, Hingley 1998, Mithen 2003, Schultz 1999: illness; Bahn, ed. 2003, Hingley 1998, Lloyd-Morgan 1995, Ashmore 1996: life expectancy.

CHRONOLOGICAL CHART

7 million years ago

Divergence of hominid and chimpanzee lineages

2.5 million years ago

Emergence of first members of genus *Homo* and first stone tools

1.9 million years ago

Emergence of *Homo ergaster* in Africa and rapid spread of *Homo* across Asia

800,000 years ago

First secure evidence of humans (*H. antecessor*) in Europe

500,000–300/250,000 years ago

H. heidelbergensis present in Europe. Earliest known European camp sites and wooden tools.

300,000/250,000–45/40,000 years ago

Neanderthals in Europe, possible development of burial and simple art

Evolution in Africa culminating in emergence and spread of *H. sapiens*

45/40,000–28,000 years ago

Neanderthals and *H. sapiens* both occupying Europe

Probable emergence of spoken language; beginning of many cultural and aesthetic advances

26,000–12,700 B.C. (28,000–14,650 years ago)

Neanderthals extinct

Upper Palaeolithic cultures flourishing in Ice Age environment

Glacial maximum c. 18,000–16,000 B.C. (20,000–18,000 years ago)

12,700–9600

Global warming to 10,800; dramatic return of glacial conditions

9600–7000

Beginning of Holocene

Mesolithic cultures adapting to new opportunities offered by postglacial environment

Yoldia Sea 8300–7800

7000–5500

Britain separated from the continent and Doggerland drowned by c. 6000

Ancylus lake 7800–5500

Spread of farming

Greece—Pre/Proto-Sesklo, Early Elateia, PPN Argissa to 6000; Sesklo from 6000

Balkans—Karanovo I and II, Starčevo, Criş from c. 6500/6000

Hungary—Körös from c. 6500/6000

Ukraine and Moldavia—Bug-Dnestr from c. 6200/6000

South and Central Italy—Impressed and Red-Painted Ware cultures from 6800/6000

Po plain—Castelnovian (Padan variety)

Rest of Mediterranean—Impressed Ware cultures from 6500/6000 including Danilo-Smilčič in the eastern Adriatic

Southern France—Castelnovian, Sauveterrian, Cardial Impressed Ware

Temperate Europe—Mesolithic cultures

Scandinavia—Kongemose

Western Europe (Belgium, N. France)—Limburgian, Tardenoisian

Northwest Switzerland—Birsmattian

5500–5000

Black Sea coasts flooded c. 5500

Further spread of farming and infilling

First cold-hammered copper artifacts

Litorina sea by 5500

Greece—Sesklo

Balkans—Karanovo III, Vădastra, Early Vinča (Vinča-Tordos), Dudeşti

Ukraine and Moldavia—Bug-Dnestr, Eastern LBK

Eastern Slovakia—c. 5300–5000 Bükk

Mediterranean—continuing spread of Impressed Ware cultures

South and central Italy—Impressed and Red-Painted Ware cultures

Po plain—Castelnovian

S. France—Epicardial

Iberia—Late Cardial

Central Europe—LBK

Rhine-Neckar valley—La Hoguette

Temperate Europe and Atlantic—Mesolithic

Denmark—Ertebølle from 5400

5000–4000

Beginning of metallurgy in Balkans and later in Iberia

Farming adopted in most of Europe

Megalithic tombs began to be constructed

Greece—Late Neolithic: Tsangli to 4500 then Dimini

Balkans—Karanovo IV–VI, Vinča (Vinča-Tordos then Vinča-Pločnik), Boian to c. 4700 then Gumelnitsa, Hamangia to c. 4500 then Varna

Ukraine and Moldavia—Cucuteni-Tripolye, Dnepr-Donets including Mariupol complex; LBK Notenkopf

Hungary—Tisza to c. 4600; Tiszapolgár

Southern Italy—Trichrome to 4500, Serra d'Alto

Northern Italy—Impressed Ware, Bocca Quadrata; Fiorano, Vhò (both acculturated Mesolithic); Castelnovian

France—Chasseen from 4500

Iberia—Almerían, Alentejan

Eastern Switzerland—Egolzwil then Cortaillod, Pfyn from 4500

Atlantic facade—Mesolithic, early Megalith-building cultures

Britain—Mesolithic and Early Neolithic

Northwest France—Cardial Atlantique 5000–4500; Castellic-Chambon-Sardun 4500–4000

Paris Basin—Mesolithic; LBK 5000–4500; Cerny 4500–4000, Rössen 4200–4000

North France/Rhine—Limburg

Central and eastern Europe—Danubian II: Bischeim, Hinkelstein/Grossgartach, Rössen, Stichbandkeramik (SBK), Lengyel; Aichbühl

Low Countries and North European Plain—Mesolithic including Swifterbant, Ellerbek, Wistka

Scandinavia—Ertebølle

Northeast Europe—Narva, Neman, Combed Ware

Northern Poland and Neman Basin—Comb and Pit wares from 4800

4000–3500

Farming becoming main way of life

Growing focus on burials and monuments

Metallurgy becoming more widespread

Greece—Sitagroi

Balkans—Karanovo VI, Bodrogkeresztúr, Cernavoda, Salcutsa, Bubanj Hum

Ukraine and Moldavia—Cucuteni-Tripolye, Sredny Stog

Steppe—Lower Mikhailovka-Kemi Oba culture

Switzerland—north: Michelsberg; east: Pfyn, Cortaillod

Southern and central Italy—Diana

Northern Italy—Bocca Quadrata, Lagozza

Iberia—Almerian, Alentejan, Sepulcros de Fosa

Northwest France—Carn-Cous-Bougon

France—Chasseen

Central Europe—TRB

Low Countries / Rhine—Michelsberg, Swifterbant/Hazendonk 4000–3800; TRB from 3800

Poland—Sarnowo and Comb and Pitted Wares 4200–3700; from 3700 TRB

Denmark—Ertebølle to 3900; TRB

Northern Europe (North European Plain, Polish uplands, German uplands, southern Sweden)—TRB

Northeast Europe—Comb and Pit Wares, Neman, Pit-comb Ware

Atlantic—Developed Megalith-building cultures

Britain—Grimston-Lyles Hill

3500–3200

Farming almost universal

Spread of innovations ("secondary products revolution")

Metallurgy spreading

Increasing trade especially in flint and stone

Greece—Final Neolithic, Rakhmani, Sitagroi

Balkans—Ezero, Coţofeni, Pit-grave, Bubanj Hum, Cernavoda

Ukraine and Moldavia—Tripolye, Usatovo (hybrid culture), Yamnaya

Southern Central Europe—Baden

Eastern Switzerland—Horgen

Southern and central Italy—Diana

Northern Italy—Lagozza

France—Chasseen

Iberia—Almerian, Alentejan, Sepulcros de Fosa

Northern Central Europe—Globular Amphora

Scandinavia—TRB

Northeast Europe—Pit-comb Ware

Britain—Windmill Hill, Lyles Hill

3200–2200

Animal husbandry becoming increasingly important

Emerging social hierarchy in some areas

Single burial replacing communal rites

Copper and gold metallurgy in most regions

Greece—EBA prepalatial period 3200–1950: Early Minoan 1, Early Cycladic 1, Early Helladic 1; from c. 2800 Early Minoan 2, Early Cycladic 2, Early Helladic 2

Balkans—Final Ezero, Coțofeni, Glina, Schneckenberg, Karanovo VII

Hungary—Vučedol

Ukraine, southern Russia—Pit-Graves

Italy—Gaudo, Rinaldone, and Remedello from c. 3100; Beakers

Northern France—SOM then Beaker

Belgium—SOM, Wartburg-Stein-Vlaardingen

Low Countries—Wartburg-Stein-Vlaardingen, Corded Ware (PFB); Bell Beaker from 2500

Northern Europe—Corded Ware, Pitted Ware

Poland—Globular Amphora then Corded Ware

Northeast Europe—Boat Axe culture, Pit-comb Ware culture, Corded Ware from c. 2700

Scandinavia—TRB to 2800 then Single Grave Culture = Corded Ware

Central Europe including eastern Switzerland—Corded Ware to c. 2600; Bell Beaker

Northwest France—Kerogou 3200, Conguel 2800

Western Europe—Beakers from 2800

Southern France—Ferrières and Fontbouisse

Iberia—Millaran, VNSP to c. 2700; Bell Beaker, Chalcolithic

Britain—Peterborough Ware, Grooved Ware, Bell Beaker

2200–1800

Bronze metallurgy

Developing international trade

Increasing social hierarchy

Greece—EBA protopalaces from c. 2300 Early Minoan 3, Early Cycladic 3, Early Helladic 3; from c. 2000 Middle Minoan (early palaces), Middle Cycladic, Middle Helladic

Ukraine, South Russia—Pit-Graves to c. 2000, Catacomb Graves

Southeast Europe—A1 Final Glina, Nagyrév; then Hatvan, Monteoru

Central Europe—Bronze A1 2200–1800/1950 Singen, Nitra, Únětice

Scandinavia—Late Neolithic / Dagger period

Iberia—Later Beakers, Palmela complex, Ciempozuelas; EBA (Bronce Antiguo), Argaric Bronze Age, *motillas*

Britain—Late Beaker; Food Vessel; Wessex I 2000–1700; Migdale

Atlantic and Western Europe—later Beaker

Southern France—Fontbouisse, Bell Beaker

France—Late Beaker; EBA

Italy—Laterzo, Rinaldone, Proto-Apennine (center and south), Polada (north)

1800–1500

Burial under tumuli adopted in many regions

Bronze metallurgy becoming widespread

Greece—Middle Minoan, Middle Cycladic, Middle Helladic to c. 1600; Late Minoan (Late Palaces), Shaft Graves Late Helladic

Southeast Europe—A1 Kisapostag, Hatvan, Monteoru, Otomani; A2 Tumulus

Ukraine—Middle Dnepr, Catacomb Graves

Central Europe—Bronze A2—Únětice and related cultures; Bronze B Tumulus

Scandinavia—Bronze Age 1 Tumulus

France—EBA (Bronze ancien) to c. 1700, MBA (Bronze moyen—Tréboul); Breton tumuli

Italy—Polada then Fiavé (north), Proto-Apennine EBA

Mediterranean islands—Nuraghic (Sardinia), Castelluccio (Sicily), Capo Graziano (Aeolian Islands)

Britain—Collared Urns, Food Vessels, Late Beakers; Wessex I to 1700; Wessex II c. 1700–1400; Acton Park

Iberia—Bronce Medio, Argaric Bronze Age

1500–1200

Growing evidence of conflict

International trade flourishing

Greece—Late Minoan, Late Helladic Mycenaean

Ukraine—Timber grave culture

Southeast Europe—A2 Tumulus

Central and Western Europe—Bronze B-C Tumulus culture to 1300; Lausitz; Bronze D Urnfields from c. 1400

Scandinavia—Bronze Age 2 Tumulus, tree-trunk coffins

Britain—Deverel-Rimbury, Acton Park then Taunton Ornament Horizon

France—MBA (Bronze moyen—Tréboul); Breton tumuli

Iberia—Cogotasl, Bronce Medio to c. 1350; Bronce Tardio, Cogotas

Italy—*Terramare* (north), Apennine Bronze Age

Mediterranean islands—Nuraghic (Sardinia), Thapsos (Sicily), Milazzese (Aeolian Islands)

1300/1200–1000

Agricultural intensification

Cremation and urn burial widely practiced

Fortified settlements widespread

Bronze in common use

Greece—Late Helladic IIIC, Dark Age destructions, SubMycenaean then ProtoGeometric

Steppe—Timber grave culture

Southeast Europe—EBA including Urnfields

Central Europe—Urnfields—Hallstatt A (1250–1050), Hallstatt B1 (1100–1000); Lausitz (southern Poland and eastern Germany)

Scandinavia—Bronze Age 3

Italy—Peschiera (north), Sub-Apennine; Proto-golasecca (north), Protovillanovan

Mediterranean islands—Nuraghic (Sardinia), Pantalica (Sicily), Ausonian (Aeolian Islands)

Britain—Deverel-Rimbury, Penard, Wilburton

France—EBA (Rosnoen), Urnfields

Iberia—Bronce Final, Urnfields

1000–800

Environmental deterioration

Iron gradually coming into use

Urnfields widespread

Phoenicians active in central and western Mediterranean

Greece—Early Geometric

Steppe—Timber Grave culture, Cimmerians

Southeast Europe—EBA including Urnfields

Central Europe—Hallstatt B2/3 (1050–800/750)—Urnfields

Scandinavia—Bronze Age 4–5

Britain—Ewart park, Dowris to c. 750

France   Bronze final IIIa, St-Brieuc-des-Iffs to c. 850; IIIb Carp's Tongue

Iberia—Bronce Final, Urnfields; Phoenicians (coast)

Mediterranean islands—Nuraghic (Sardinia), Pantalica (Sicily), Ausonian (Aeolian Islands)

Italy—Este, Bologna, Golasecca (north), Terni, Villanovan (center and south)

800–700

Greek colonies established in the central and western Mediterranean

Elite wagon burials

Greece—Middle Geometric, Late Geometric

Steppe—Cimmerians

Southeast Europe—Early Iron Age

Central and Western Europe—Hallstatt C

Italy—Este, Bologna, Golasecca (north); Villanovan, Greeks

Iberia—Hierro (Iron Age), Castros (northwest), Tartessians (southwest), Phoenicians (coast)

Britain—Llyn Fawr to 750

Scandinavia—Bronze Age 5

700–600

Salt mining at its peak

Ironworking widespread

Greece—Orientalizing, Archaic

Steppe—Scythians

Southeast Europe—Early Iron Age

Central and Western Europe—Hallstatt C

Italy—Este, Bologna, Golasecca (north), Etruscans, Greeks

Iberia—Iberians, Castros, Celtiberians, Tartessians; Phoenicians (coast)

Scandinavia—Bronze Age 6

Britain—Early Iron Age

Atlantic—Atlantic Iron Age

600–500

Greek traders penetrating central Europe via the Rhône

Chieftains' burials with Mediterranean luxuries

Greece—Archaic

Steppe—Scythians

Southeast Europe—Thracians

Central and western Europe—Hallstatt D

Italy—Este, Bologna, Golasecca, Celts (north); Etruscans, Latins, Greeks

Iberia—Iberians, Castros, Celtiberians, Tartessians; Carthaginians, Greeks (coast),

Scandinavia—Early Iron Age

Atlantic—Atlantic Iron Age

500–400

Celts and Etruscans trading across the Alps

Iron used across Europe

Greece—Classical from 480

Steppe—Scythians

Southeast Europe—Thracians

Central and western Europe—Hallstatt D to 450; La Tène A 500–400, Celts

Italy—Celts (north), Etruscans, Latins, Greeks

Iberia—Iberians, Castros, Celtiberians; Carthaginians, Greeks (coast)

Atlantic—Atlantic Iron Age

400–300

Celtic migrations

Greece—Classical; Macedonian from 338

Steppe—Scythians

Southeast Europe—Thracians

Iberia—Castros, Celtiberians, Iberians; Carthaginians (coast)

Central and western Europe—La Tène B

Italy—Gauls (north), Etruscans, Rome, Samnites, Greeks

Carpathian basin—Galatians

Atlantic—Atlantic Iron Age

300–200

Celtic culture widespread

Greece—Hellenistic

Steppe—Sarmatians

Southeast Europe—Thracians

France to Balkans —La Tène B to 275; La Tène C

Eastern Europe—Germani

Eastern Alps—Noricum

Iberia—Castros, Celtiberians, Iberians; Carthaginians (south)

Italy—Gauls (north), Etruscans, Romans (center), Greeks; Romans from 218

Atlantic—Atlantic Iron Age

200–100

Oppida emerging in western and central Europe

Progressive Roman expansion in Mediterranean

Greece—Hellenistic; Romans from 146

Steppe—Sarmatians

Southeast Europe—Thracians

France to Balkans—La Tène C to 150; La Tène D

Eastern Europe and Scandinavia—Germani

Italy—Romans

Iberia—*Castros*, Lusitanians, Celtiberians; Romans (south and east)

France—Romans from 120 (south), Gauls

Atlantic—Atlantic Iron Age

100–0

Oppida widespread

Roman conquest of western Europe

Steppe—Sarmatians

Southeast Europe—Thracians, Dacians

Central and western Europe—La Tène D

Eastern Alps—Noricum

Europe east of the Rhine and Scandinavia—Germani

Mediterranean, western Balkans—Romans

France—Gauls; Romans from 51

Atlantic—Atlantic Iron Age

Sources: Whittle 1996, Milisauskas, ed. 2002, Cunliffe, ed. 1994, Cunliffe 2001a, Harris, ed. 1996, Champion et al. 1984, Harding 1994, Bailey 2000, Scarre 1988, Twist 2001.

LIST OF MUSEUMS WITH IMPORTANT EUROPEAN MATERIAL AND OPEN-AIR MUSEUMS

ALBANIA

Tirana: Archaeological museum

AUSTRIA

Vienna: Naturhistorisches Museum
Graz: Steiermarkisches Landesmuseum Johanneum
Hallein: Keltenmuseum
Salzburg: Museum Carolino Augusteum
Hallstatt: Hallstatt Museum
Asparn an der Zaya: Museum für Urgeschichte

BOSNIA

Sarajevo: National Museum of Bosnia and Herzegovina

BULGARIA

Sofia: National History Museum; Archaeological Institute and Museum
Varna: Archaeological Museum
Plovdiv: Archaeological Museum
Lovech: Museum of History

CROATIA

Zagreb: Archaeological Museum

CZECH REPUBLIC

Prague: Národní Muzeum

Brno: Moravské Zemské Muzeum
Roztoky: Středočeské Muzeum

DENMARK

Copenhagen: Nationalmuseet
Lejre: Lejre Experimental Centre
Moesgaard: Forhistorisk Museum
Silkeborg: Silkeborg Museum

ESTONIA

Viljandi: Museum of Viljandi

FINLAND

Helsinki: National Museum
Turku: Aboa Vetus
Espoo: Glims Farmstead Museum

FRANCE

Saint-Germain-en-Laye: Musée des Antiquités Nationales
Aix-en-Provence: Musée Granet
Lyon: Musée de la Civilisation Gallo-Romaine
Dijon: Musée Archéologique
Marseilles: Musée d'Archéologie Méditerranéene
Châtillon-sur-Seine: Musée Archéologique
Vannes: Musée de Prehistoire
Rennes: Musée de Bretagne
Châlons-en-Champagne: Musée Municipal

GERMANY

Berlin: Staatliche Museen; Museum für Vor- und Frühgeschichte; Antikenmuseum
Bonn: Rheinisches Landesmuseum
Stuttgart: Württembergisches Landesmuseum
Schleswig: Schleswig-Holsteinische Landesmuseum
Eberdingen-Hochdorf: Keltenmuseum Hochdorf
Munich: Prahistorische Staatssammlung
Nuremberg: Germanisches Nationalmuseum
Saarbrücken: Landesmuseum

GREECE

Athens: National Archaeological Museum
Thessaloniki: Archaeological Museum

HUNGARY

Budapest: Magyar Nemzeti Múzeum
Sopron: Soproni Múzeum
Debreccen: Déri Múzeum

IRELAND

Dublin: National Museum of Ireland
Boyne Valley: Brú na Bóinne Visitor Centre

ITALY

Bolzano: South Tyrol Museum of Archaeology (including the Iceman)
Brescia: Museo Civico
Capodiponte: Parco Nazionale delle incisioni rupestri
Bologna: Museo Civico
Rome: National Museum of Prehistory and Ethnography; Antiquarium Communale
Milan: Archaeological Museum
Verona: Natural History Museum
Este: Museo Nazionale Atestino
Ancona: Museo Archeologico Nazionale delle Marche

LATVIA

Riga: History Museum of Latvia

LITHUANIA

Vilnius: National Museum of Lithuania

LOW COUNTRIES

Liège: Museum of Prehistoric Archaeology
Leiden: Rijksmuseum van Oudheden
Brussels: Musées Royaux d'Art et d'Histoire
Luxembourg: Musée National d'Histoire et d'Art
Libramont: Musée des Celtes

MALTA

Valletta: National Museum of Archaeology

MACEDONIA

Skopje: Archaeological Museum

NORWAY

Trondheim: Vitenskapsmuseet
Oslo: University Museum of National Antiquities
Bergen: Museum of History
Stavanger: Arkeologisk Museum

POLAND

Warsaw: Panstwowe Muzeum Archeologiczne
Biskupin: Biskupin Museum
Poznan: Muzeum Archeologiczne

PORTUGAL

Lisbon: Museu Nacional de Arqueologia

ROMANIA

Bucharest: Muzeul National de Istorie a Romaniei
Cluj-Napoca: History Museum of Transylvania
Iassy: Moldova National Museum

RUSSIA

St. Petersburg: State Hermitage Museum

SERBIA

Belgrade: National Museum

SLOVAKIA

Bratislava: Slovenské národné múzeum
Nitra: Archeologický ústav SAV

SLOVENIA

Ljubljana: Narodni Muzej Slovenije

SPAIN

Madrid: Museo Arqueológico Nacional
Cordoba: Archaeological Museum
Palma de Mallorca: Museu de Mallorca
Barcelona: Museo Arqueológico

SWEDEN

Stockholm: Statens Historiska Museet
Tanum: Hällristningsmuseet

SWITZERLAND

Bern: Bernisches Historisches Museum
Geneva: Musée d'Art et d'Histoire
Zürich: Schweizerisches Landesmuseum
Biel: Musée Schwab
Neuchâtel: Musée Cantonale d'Archéologie

UNITED KINGDOM

London: British Museum; Museum of London
Edinburgh: Museum of Scotland
Oxford: Ashmolean Museum
Cambridge: Museum of Archaeology and Ethnography
Cardiff: National Museum of Wales
Salisbury: Salisbury Museum
Lerwick: Shetland Museum
Andover: Museum of the Iron Age
Dorchester: Dorset County Museum
Devizes: Devizes Museum
Chalton: Butser Ancient Farm
Peterborough: Flag Fen Visitor Centre
Kirkwall: Tankerness House Museum
St. Fagans: Museum of Welsh Life
Belfast: Ulster Museum

UKRAINE

Kiev: Ukraine National Historic Museum
Odessa: State Archaeological Museum
Pereiaslav-Khmel'nyts'kyi: State Historical Archaeological Preserve

BIBLIOGRAPHY

Adkins, Lesley, and Roy A. Adkins. *A Thesaurus of British Archaeology*. London: David and Charles, 1982.

Ammerman, A. J. *Acconia Survey: Neolithic Settlement and the Obsidian Trade. Occasional Publication 10.* London: Institute of Archaeology, 1985.

Anati, Emmanuel. *Camonica Valley. A Depiction of Village Life in the Alps from Neolithic Times to the Birth of Christ as Revealed by Thousands of Newly Found Rock Carvings.* Translated by Linda Asher. London: Jonathan Cape, 1965.

———. "The rock sanctuaries of Europe." In Demakopoulou et al., eds. 1999.

Andronikos, Manolis. *The Royal Graves at Vergina.* Athens: Archaeological Reipts Fund, 1980.

Araújo, Ana Cristina, Cláudia Umbelino, Eugénia Cunha, Carla Hipólito, João Peixoto Cabral, and Maria do Carmo Freitas. "Long-term change in Portuguese early Holocene settlement and subsistence." In Larsson et al., 2003.

Arca, Andrea. "Fields and settlements in topographic engravings of the Copper Age in Valcamonica and Mt. Bego rock art." In Della Casa, ed. 1999.

Armit, Ian. *Celtic Scotland.* London: Batsford / Historic Scotland, 1997.

Ashmore, P. J. *Neolithic and Bronze Age Scotland.* London: Batsford / Historic Scotland, 1996.

Audouze, Françoise, and Olivier Büchsenschütz. *Towns, Villages and Countryside of Celtic Europe.* Translated by Henry Cleere. London: Batsford, 1992.

Bahn, Paul. "A war monument in Gaul." In Bahn, ed. 2003.

Bahn, Paul, ed. *Tombs, Graves and Mummies.* London: Weidenfeld and Nicolson, 1996.

———. *The Penguin Archaeology Guide.* London: Penguin, 2001a.

———. *The Archaeology Detectives.* Lewes: The Ivy Press, 2001b.

———. *Written in Bones. How Human Remains Unlock the Secrets of the Dead.* New York: Firefly, 2003.

Bailey, Douglass W. *Balkan Prehistory. Exclusion, Incorporation and Identity.* London/New York: Routledge, 2000.

Bakker, Jan Albert. *The TRB West Group. Studies in the Chronology and Geography of the Makers of Hunebeds and Tiefstich Pottery.* Amsterdam: Albert Egges van Giffen Instituut voor Prae- en Protohistorie, 1979.

———. *The Dutch Hunebedden. Megalithic Tombs of the Funnel Beaker Culture. International Monographs in Prehistory. Archaeological Series 2.* Ann Arbor, Mich.: International Monographs on Prehistory, 1992.

Barber, Elizabeth J. W. *Prehistoric Textiles.* Princeton, N.J.: Princeton University Press, 1991.

Barclay, Alistair, and Jan Harding, eds. *Pathways and Ceremonies. The Cursus Monuments of Britain and Ireland. Neolithic Studies Group Seminar Papers 4.* Oxford: Oxbow Books, 1999.

Barclay, Gordon. *Farmers, Temples and Tombs. Scotland in the Neolithic and Early Bronze Age.* Edinburgh: Canongate Books / Historic Scotland, 1998.

Barker, Graeme. *Prehistoric Farming in Europe.* Cambridge: Cambridge University Press, 1985.

———. "Bronze Age landscapes in southern Europe." In Harding, ed. 1999.

Barker, Graeme, and Tom Rasmussen. *The Etruscans.* Oxford: Blackwell, 1998.

Barnett, William K. "Cardial Pottery and the agricultural transition." In Price, ed. 2000.

Barth, Fritz Eckart. "The Hallstatt salt mines." In Moscati et al., eds. 1991.

Barton, Nicholas. *Stone Age Britain.* London: Batsford / English Heritage, 1997.

Beck, Curt W., and Jan Bouzek, eds. *Amber in Archaeology. Proceedings of the Second International Conference on Amber in Archaeology. Liblice 1990.* Prague: Institute of Archaeology, 1993.

Becker, Marshall Joseph. "Cultural uniformity during the Italian Iron Age: Sardinian nuraghi as regional markers." In Tykot and Andrews, eds. 1992.

Berresford Ellis, Peter. *The Ancient World of the Celts.* London: Constable, 1988.

Bevan, Bill. "Bounding the landscape: Place and identity during the Yorkshire Wolds Iron Age." In Gwilt and Haselgrove, eds. 1997.

Bewley, Robert. *Prehistoric Settlements.* Stroud, U.K.: Tempus, 2003.

Biel, Jorg. "Treasure from a Celtic tomb." *National Geographic,* 157, 1986.

Binder, Didier. "Mesolithic and Neolithic interaction in southern France and northern Italy: New data and current hypotheses." In Price, ed. 2000.

Black, Jeremy, ed. *DK Atlas of World History.* London: Dorling Kindersley, 1999.

Boardman, John. *The Greeks Overseas. Their Early Colonies and Trade.* 4th edition. London: Thames and Hudson, 1999.

Bocquet, Aimé, Jacques L. Brochier, Aline Emery-Barbier, Karen Lundstrom-Buadais, Christian Orcel, and Françoise Vin. "A submerged Neolithic village: Charavines 'Les Baigneurs' in Lake Paladru, France." In Coles and Lawson, eds. 1987.

Bogucki, Peter. "How agriculture came to north-central Europe." In Price, ed. 2000.

———. "Egtved. A Bronze Age discovery." In Bahn, ed. 2001b.

Bökönyi, S. "Agriculture: Animal husbandry." In Moscati et al., eds. 1991.

Bonfante, Larissa. *Reading the Past. Etruscan.* London: British Museum Press, 1990.

Bonzani, René M. "Territorial boundaries, buffer zones and sociopolitical complexity: A case study of the Nuraghi of Sardinia." In Tykot and Andrews, eds. 1992.

Bowen, H. C. *Ancient Fields.* London: British Association for the Advancement of Science, 1961.

Bradley, Richard. *The Social Foundations of Prehistoric Britain.* London: Longman, 1984.

———. *Rock Art and the Prehistory of Atlantic Europe. Signing the Land.* London: Routledge 1997.

———. *The Significance of Monuments. On the shaping of human experience in Neolithic and Bronze Age Europe.* London: Routledge, 1998.

Braudel, Fernand. *The Mediterranean in the Ancient World.* Translated by Sian Reynolds. London: Allen Lane the Penguin Press, 2001.

Briggs, Daphne Nash. "Coinage." In Green, ed. 1995.

Bromehead, C. N. "Mining and Quarrying." In Singer et al., eds. 1954.

Brothwell, Don. *The Bog Man and the Archaeology of People.* London: British Museum Publications, 1986.

Bruck, Joanna, ed. *Bronze Age Landscapes. Tradition and Transformation.* Oxford: Oxbow Books, 2001.

Burgess, Colin. *The Age of Stonehenge.* London: J.M. Dent, 1980.

Burl, Aubrey. *Megalithic Brittany.* London: Thames and Hudson, 1985.

———. *From Carnac to Callanish. The Prehistoric Stone Rows and Avenues of Britain, Ireland and Brittany.* New Haven, Conn./London: Yale University Press, 1993.

Butzer, K. *Environment and Archaeology.* London: Methuen, 1972.

Caesar, G. Julius. *The Conquest of Gaul.* Translated by S. A. Handford. Harmondsworth, U.K.: Penguin, 1951.

Capelle, Torsten. "The rock art of the north." In Demakopoulou et al., eds. 1999.

Carman, John and Anthony Harding, eds. *Ancient Warfare. Archaeological Perspectives.* Stroud, U.K.: Sutton Publishing, 1999.

Carr, Gillian and Christopher Knüsel. "The ritual framework of excarnation by exposure as the mortuary practice of the early and middle Iron Ages of central southern Britain." In Gwilt and Haselgrove, eds. 1997.

Carver, Martin. *Surviving in Symbols. A Visit to the Pictish Nation.* Edinburgh: Canongate / Historic Scotland, 1999.

Catling, Christopher. "More on the Nebra astronomical disk." *SALON* 107, 10 January 2005.

———. "More on the Nebra disk." *SALON* 108, 24 January 2005.

Chadwick, John. *The Mycenaean World.* Cambridge: Cambridge University Press, 1976.

———. *Reading the Past. Linear B and Related Scripts.* London: British Museum Press, 1987.

Champion, Sara. "Jewellery and adornment." In Green, ed. 1995.

Champion, Sara and Tim Champion. "Biskupin." In *The Atlas of Archaeology*, edited by Keith Branigan. London: Macdonald, 1982.

Champion, Timothy. "Power, politics and status." In Green, ed. 1995.

Champion, Timothy, Clive Gamble, Stephen Shennan, and Alasdair Whittle. *Prehistoric Europe.* London: Academic Press, 1984.

Chapman, John. "The origins of warfare in the prehistory of central and eastern Europe." In Carman and Harding, eds. 1999.

Chapman, Robert. *Emerging Complexity. The Later Prehistory of South-East Spain, Iberia and the West Mediterranean.* Cambridge: Cambridge University Press, 1990.

Childe, Vere Gordon. "Rotary motion." In Singer et al., eds. 1954.

Chippendale, Christopher. *Stonehenge Complete.* Revised edition. London: Thames and Hudson, 1994.

Christensen, Kjeld. "Tree-ring dating of Bronze Age oak coffins from Denmark." In Demakopoulou et al., eds. 1999.

Cizmarova, Jana, Vladimir Ondrus, Jaroslav Tejral, and Milan Salas. *Moravia in Prehistoric Times.* Brno: Moravian Museum, 1996.

Clarke, David L. "Mesolithic Europe: The economic basis." In *Problems in Economic and Social Archaeology*, edited by G. Sieveking, I. H. Longworth, and K. E. Wilkinson. London: Duckworth, 1976.

———. "A provisional model of an Iron Age society and its settlement system." In *Models in Archaeology*, edited by David L. Clarke. London: Methuen, 1982.

Clarke, D. V., T. G. Cowie, and A. Foxon. *Symbols of Power at the Time of Stonehenge.* Edinburgh: National Museum of Antiquities of Scotland, 1985.

Clason, A. T. "What's new in the Bronze Age? The livestock and gamebag of the Bronze Age farmers in the western and central Netherlands." In Sarfatij et al., eds. 1999.

Cole, Sonia M. "Differentiation of non-metallic tools." In Singer et al., eds. 1954.

Coles, Bryony. "Tracks across the Wetlands: Multidisciplinary studies in the Somerset Levels of England." In Coles and Lawson, eds. 1987.

———. "Somerset and the Sweet conundrum." In Harding, ed. 1999.

Coles, Bryony, and John M. Coles. *Sweet Track to Glastonbury. The Somerset Levels in Prehistory.* London: Thames and Hudson, 1986.

Coles, John M. *Archaeology by Experiment.* London: Hutchinson, 1973.

———. *The Archaeology of Wetlands.* Edinburgh: Edinburgh University Press, 1984.

Coles, John M., and Anthony F. Harding. *The Bronze Age in Europe.* London: Methuen, 1979.

Coles, John M., and Andrew J. Lawson. *European Wetlands in Prehistory.* Oxford: Oxford University Press, 1987.

Collis, John. *The European Iron Age.* London: Batsford, 1984a.

———. *Oppida: Earliest Towns North of the Alps.* Sheffield, U.K.: University of Sheffield, 1984b.

———. "The first towns." In Green, ed. 1995.

———. *The Celts. Origins, Myths and Inventions.* Stroud, U.K.: Tempus, 2003.

Connolly, Peter. *Greece and Rome at War.* Philadelphia: Stackpole Books, 1998.

Cornell, Tim, and John Matthews. *Atlas of the Roman World.* New York/Oxford: Facts On File, 1982.

Coulmas, Florian. *The Blackwell Encyclopedia of Writing Systems.* Oxford: Blackwell, 1996.

Craddock, Paul T. *Early Metal Mining and Production.* Edinburgh: Edinburgh University Press, 1995.

Crowfoot, Grace M. "Textiles, basketry and mats." In Singer et al., eds. 1954.

Crystal, David. *The Cambridge Encyclopedia of Language.* Cambridge: Cambridge University Press, 1987.

Cunliffe, Barry. *Iron Age Communities in Britain. An Account of England, Scotland and Wales from the Seventh Century BC until the Roman Conquest.* London: Routledge and Kegan Paul, 1974.

———. *Danebury.* London: Batsford / English Heritage, 1993.

———. "Introduction." In Cunliffe, ed. 1994a.

———. "Iron Age societies in Western Europe and beyond, 800–140 BC." In Cunliffe, ed. 1994b.

———. "The impact of Rome on barbarian society, 140 BC–AD 300." In Cunliffe, ed. 1994c.

———. *Iron Age Britain.* London: Batsford / English Heritage, 1995.

———. *The Ancient Celts.* Oxford: Oxford University Press, 1997.

———. *Facing the Ocean. The Atlantic and Its People. 8000 BC–AD 1500.* Oxford: Oxford University Press, 2001a.

———. *The Extraordinary Voyage of Pytheas the Greek. The Man Who Discovered Britain.* London: Allen Lane, Penguin Press, 2001b.

———. *Danebury Hillfort.* Stroud, U.K.: Tempus, 2003.

Cunliffe, Barry, ed. *The Oxford Illustrated Prehistory of Europe.* Oxford: Oxford University Press, 1994.

Cunliffe, Barry, and Philip de Jersey. *Armorica and Britain. Cross-Channel Relationships in the Late First Millennium BC. Studies in Celtic Coinage 3. Oxford University Committee for Archaeology Monograph 45.* Oxford: Oxbow Books, 1997.

Dalby, Andrew. *Dictionary of Languages. The Definitive Reference to More Than 400 Languages.* London: Bloomsbury, 1998.

Dani, A. H., and Jean-Pierre Mohen, eds. *History of Humanity. Volume II. From the Third Millennium to the Seventh Century BC.* Paris / London: UNESCO / Routledge, 1996.

Daniel, Glyn. *The Megalith Builders of Western Europe.* Harmondsworth, U.K.: Penguin, 1963.

Darvill, Timothy. *Prehistoric Britain.* London: Batsford, 1987.

———. *Prehistoric Britain from the Air. A Study of Space, Time and Society.* Cambridge: Cambridge University Press, 1996.

———. *The Concise Oxford Dictionary of Archaeology.* Oxford: Oxford University Press, 2002.

Darvill, Timothy, and Julian Thomas, eds. *Neolithic Enclosures in Atlantic Northwestern Europe. Neolithic Studies Group Seminar Papers 6.* Oxford: Oxbow Books, 2001.

Davies, Sioned. "Mythology and the oral tradition: Wales." In Green, 1995.

Dayton, John. *Minerals, Metals, Glazing and Man.* London: Harrap, 1978.

———. *The Discovery of Glass. Experiments in the Smelting of Rich, Dry Silver Ores, and the Reproduction of Bronze Age-type Cobalt Blue Glass as a Slag. American School of Prehistoric Research Bulletin 41, 1993.* Cambridge, Mass.: Harvard University Press, 1993.

De Laet, S. J., ed. *History of Humanity. Volume I. Prehistory and the Beginnings of Civilization.* Paris / London: UNESCO / Routledge, 1994.

Delgado, James P. "Hjortspring." In Delgado, ed. 1997.

Delgado, James P., ed. *British Museum Encyclopaedia of Underwater and Maritime Archaeology.* London: British Museum Press, 1997.

Della Casa, Philippe, ed. *Prehistoric Alpine Environment, Society, and Economy. Papers of the International Colloquium PAESE 97 in Zurich.* Bonn: In Kommission bei Dr. Rudolf Habelt GmbH, 1999.

Demakopoulou, Katie, Christiane Eluère, Jørgen Jensen, Albrecht Jockenhövel, and Jean-Pierre Mohen. *Gods and Heroes of the European Bronze Age.* London: Thames and Hudson, 1999.

De Marinis, Raffaele C. "Chalcolithic stele-statues of the Alpine region." In Demakopoulou et al., eds. 1999.

Dennell, Robin. *European Economic Prehistory.* New York: Academic Press, 1983.

De Roche, C. D. "Studying Iron Age production." In Gwilt and Haselgrove, eds. 1997.

Dixon, Philip. *Barbarian Europe.* London: Phaidon, 1976.

Dolukhanov, Paul. "Timber-Grave culture." In Shaw and Jameson, eds. 1999a.

———. "War and peace in prehistoric Eastern Europe." In Carman and Harding, eds. 1999b.

Doumas, Christos. "The Aegean during the Neolithic." In De Laet, ed. 1994.

Dungworth, David. "Copper metallurgy in Iron Age Britain: Some recent research." In Gwilt and Haselgrove, eds. 1997.

Durrani, Nadia. "The Nebra Sun-Disc." *Current World Archaeology* 5. May / June 2004.

Ecsedy, Istvan, and Tibor Kovacs. "Central Europe." In Dani and Mohen, eds. 1996.

Egloff, Michel. "130 years of archaeological research in Lake Neuchâtel, Switzerland." In Coles and Lawson, eds. 1987.

Ehrenberg, Margaret. *Women in Prehistory.* London: British Museum Press, 1989.

Eluère, Christiane. "The golden treasures of the European Bronze Age." In Demakopoulou et al., eds. 1999a.

———. "The world of the gods in the Bronze Age." In Demakopoulou et al., eds. 1999b.

Fagan, Brian, ed. *The Seventy Great Inventions of the Ancient World.* London: Thames and Hudson, 2004.

Fenwick, Valerie, and Alison Gale. *Historic Shipwrecks. Discovered, Protected and Investigated.* Stroud, U.K.: Tempus, 1998.

Filip, Jan. *Celtic Civilization and Its Heritage.* Prague: Academia, 1976.

Finlayson, Bill. *Wild Harvesters. The First People in Scotland.* Edinburgh: Canongate Books / Historic Scotland, 1998.

Fischer, Anders. "Seasonal movement, exchange and Neolithisation." In Larsson et al., 2003.

Fischer, Anders, and Kristian Kristiansen. *The Neolithisation of Denmark. 150 Years of Debate.* Sheffield: J. R. Collis Publications, 2002.

Fitton, J. Lesley. *Peoples of the Past. Minoans.* London: British Museum Press, 2002.

Fokkens, Harry. *Drowned Landscape. The Occupation of the Western Part of the Frisian-Drentian Plateau, 4400 BC–AD 500.* Assen, Netherlands: Van Gorcum, 1998.

Fontana, Federica, and Antonio Guerreschi. "Highland occupation in the southern Alps." In Larsson et al., 2003.

Forbes, R. J. "Chemical, culinary, and cosmetic arts." In Singer et al., eds. 1954a.

———. "Extracting, smelting, and alloying." In Singer et al., eds. 1954b.

Foster, Sally M. *Picts, Gaels and Scots.* London: Batsford / Historic Scotland, 1996.

Freestone, Ian C. "Vitreous materials. Typology and Technology." In Eric M. Meyers, ed. *The Oxford Encyclopedia of Archaeology in the Near East.* 5. Oxford: Oxford University Press, 1997.

Frey, Otto-Herman. "The Celts in Italy." In Green, ed. 1995.

Furger-Gunti, Andres. "The Celtic war chariot. The experimental reconstruction in the Schweizerisches Landesmuseum." In Moscati et al., eds. 1991.

Gamble, Clive. "The peopling of Europe, 700,000–40,000 years before the present." In Cunliffe, ed. 1994.

Garasanin, Milutin. "The Balkan peninsula and south-east Europe during the Neolithic." In De Laet, ed. 1994.

Garrison, Ervan. "Lake Neuchâtel." In Delgado, 1997.

Giardino, Claudio. "Nuraghic Sardinia and the Mediterranean: Metallurgy and maritime traffic." In Tykot and Andrews, eds. 1992.

Gibson, Alex M. *Neolithic and Early Bronze Age Pottery.* Princes Risborough, U.K.: Shire Publications, 1986.

———. "The art of the potter." In Green, ed. 1995.

———. *British Prehistoric Pottery.* Stroud, U.K.: Tempus, 2002.

Gibson, Alex M., and Ann J. Woods. *Prehistoric Pottery for the Archaeologist.* Leicester, U.K.: Leicester University Press, 1997.

Gilbert, K. R. "Rope-making." In Singer et al., eds. 1954.

Gill, David, and Simon Kaner. "Battle cemeteries." In Bahn, ed. 1996.

Gilman, A., and J. B. Thornes. *Landuse and Prehistory in South-East Spain. The London Research Series in Geography 8.* London: George Allen and Unwin, 1985.

Gimbutas, M. *The Prehistory of Eastern Europe.* Cambridge, Mass.: Peabody, 1956.

———. *The Civilization of the Goddess: The World of Old Europe.* San Francisco: Harper, 1991.

Giot, Pierre-Roland. "Atlantic Europe during the Neolithic." In De Laet, ed. 1994.

Glob, P. V. *The Bog People.* London: Faber and Faber, 1969.

———. *The Mound People.* London: Faber and Faber, 1974.

Gordon, Cyrus H. "Recovering Canaan and ancient Israel." In Jack M. Sasson, ed. *Civilizations of the Ancient Near East.* 4 volumes. Peabody, Mass.: Hendrickson Publishers, 2000. (Reprint of 1995 edition. New York: Scribner).

Graham-Campbell, James, ed. *Cultural Atlas of the Viking World.* Oxford: Andromeda, 1994.

Grant, Julius. "A note on the materials of ancient textiles and baskets." In Singer et al., eds. 1954.

Green, Miranda. *Dictionary of Celtic Myth and Legend.* London: Thames and Hudson, 1992.

———. *Exploring the World of the Druids.* London: Thames and Hudson, 1997.

Green, Miranda J., ed. *The Celtic World.* London: Routledge, 1995.

Grierson, Philip. "A note on stamping of coins and other objects." In Singer et al., eds. 1956.

Grimal, Pierre. *In Search of Ancient Italy.* Translated by P. D. Cummins. London: Evans Brothers Limited, 1964.

Guilaine, Jean. "The megalithic in Sardinia, southern France and Catalonia." In Tykot and Andrews, eds. 1992.

———. "Western Mediterranean cultures during the Neolithic." In De Laet, ed. 1994.

Guilaine, Jean, and Jean Zammit. *The Origins of War. Violence in Prehistory.* Translated by Melanie Hersey. Oxford: Blackwell Publishing, 2005.

Gwilt, Adam, and Colin Haselgrove, eds. *Reconstructing Iron Age Societies. Oxbow Monograph 71.* Oxford: Oxbow Books, 1997.

Halstead, Paul. "The development of agriculture and pastoralism in Greece: When, how, who and what?" In Harris, ed. 1996.

Harden, D. B. "Glass and glazes." In Singer et al., eds. 1956.

Harding, Anthony F. "Reformation in barbarian Europe, 1300–600 BC." In Cunliffe, ed. 1994.

———. "North-south exchanges of raw materials." In Demakopoulou et al., eds. 1999a.

———. "Swords, shields and scholars: Bronze Age warfare. Past and present." In Harding, ed. 1999b.

———. "Warfare: A defining characteristic of Bronze Age Europe?" In Carman and Harding, eds. 1999c.

———. *European Societies in the Bronze Age.* Cambridge: Cambridge University Press, 2000.

———. "The Bronze Age." In Milisauskas, ed. 2002.

Harding, Anthony F., ed. *Experiment and Design. Archaeological Studies in Honour of John Coles.* Oxford: Oxbow Books, 1999.

Harding, Dennis. *The Making of the Past. Prehistoric Europe.* London: Elsevier Phaidon, 1978.

Harmatta, J. "The emergence of the Indo-Iranians: The Indo-Iranian languages." In A. H. Dani and V. M. Masson, eds. *History of Civilizations of Central Asia. Volume I. The Dawn of Civilization: Earliest Times to 700 BC.* Paris: UNESCO, 1992.

Harris, David R., ed. *The Origins and Spread of Agriculture and Pastoralism in Eurasia.* Washington, D.C.: Smithsonian Institution Press, 1996.

Harrison, Richard J. *Spain at the Dawn of History. Iberians, Phoenicians and Greeks.* London: Thames and Hudson, 1988.

———. "Arboriculture in southwest Europe: *Dehesas* as managed woodlands." In Harris, ed. 1996.

Haselgrove, Colin, and Martin Millett. "Verlamion reconsidered." In Gwilt and Haselgrove, eds. 1997.

Healey, John F. *Reading the Past. The Early Alphabet.* London: British Museum Press, 1990.

Hedges, John. *The Tomb of the Eagles.* London: John Murray, 1984.

Hernek, Robert "A Mesolithic winter site with a sunken dwelling from the Swedish west coast." In Larsson et al., 2003.

Hingley, Richard. *Settlement and Sacrifice. The Later Prehistoric People of Scotland.* Edinburgh: Canongate Books / Historic Scotland, 1998.

Hodges, Henry. *Technology in the Ancient World.* Harmondsworth, U.K.: Penguin, 1971.

———. *Artifacts. An Introduction to Early Materials and Technology.* Kingston, Canada: Ronald P. Frye, 1988.

Hoffman, George W., ed. *A Geography of Europe. Problems and Perspectives.* 5th edition. New York: John Wiley and Sons, 1983.

Hunter, Fraser. "Iron Age hoarding in Scotland and northern England." In Gwilt and Haselgrove, eds. 1997.

Hunter, John, and Ian Ralson, eds. *The Archaeology of Britain. An Introduction from the Upper Palaeolithic to the Industrial Revolution.* London: Routledge, 1999.

Jacobsthal, Paul. *Early Celtic Art.* Oxford: Clarendon Press, 1944.

James, Simon. *Exploring the World of the Celts.* London: Thames and Hudson, 1993.

Jensen, Jørgen. "Oak coffin-graves of the northern European Bronze Age." In Demakopoulou et al., eds. 1999a.

———. "The heroes: Life and death." In Demakopoulou et al., eds. 1999b.

Jochim, Michael A. "The Lower and Middle Palaeolithic." In Milisauskas, ed. 2002a.

———. "The Upper Palaeolithic." In Milisauskas, ed. 2002b.

———. "The Mesolithic." In Milisauskas, ed. 2002c.

Jockenhövel, Albrecht. "Bronze Age fortresses in Europe: Territorial security." In Demakopoulou et al., eds. 1999.

Jope, Martyn. "The social implications of Celtic art: 600 BC to AD 600." In Green, ed. 1995.

Jorge, Susana Oliveira. "Bronze Age settlements and territories on the Iberian peninsula: New considerations." In Demakopoulou et al., eds. 1999a.

———. "Bronze Age stelai and menhirs of the Iberian peninsula: Discourses of power." In Demakopoulou et al., eds. 1999b.

———. "Cabeço da Mina (Vila Flor, Portugal): A late prehistoric sanctuary with 'stelai' of the Iberian peninsula." In Demakopoulou et al., eds. 1999c.

Kaelas, Lili. "The northern European lowlands. Neolithic acculturation." In De Laet, ed. 1994a.

———. "Megalithic monuments of Europe." In De Laet, ed. 1994b.

Kellner, Hans-Jorg. "Coinage." In Moscati et al., 1991.

Kelly, Eamonn P. "The Iron Age." In Wallace and O'Floinn, eds. 2002.

Kiple, Kenneth F., and Kriemhild Conee Ornelas. *The Cambridge World History of Food*. Cambridge: Cambridge University Press, 2000.

Klassen, Lutz. "The Ertebolle cultures and Neolithic continental Europe: Traces of contact and interaction." In Fischer and Kristiansen, eds. 2002.

Kovács, Tibor. "Tell settlement in the Danube region." In Demakopoulou et al., eds. 1999.

Kristiansen, Kristian. *Europe before History*. Cambridge: Cambridge University Press, 1998.

———. "The emergence of warrior aristocracies in later European prehistory and their long-term history." In Carman and Harding, eds. 1999.

Kruta, Venceslas. "Celtic writing." In Moscati et al., ed. 1991.

———. *Celts*. London: Hachette Illustrated UK, 2004.

Kunzl, Ernst. "The tomb of the warrior and surgeon of Munchen-Obermenzing and other archaeological evidence of Celtic medicine." In Moscati et al., eds. 1991.

Kuster, Hansirg. "The history of vegetation." In Moscati et al., eds. 1991.

Lanfranchi, François de. "The megalithic monuments of Corsica and Sardinia: A comparative study." In Tykot and Andrews, eds. 1992.

Larsson, Lars, Hans Kindgren, Kjel Knutsson, David Leoffler, and Agneta Åkerlund, eds. *Mesolithic on the Move: Papers Presented at the Sixth International Conference on the Mesolithic in Europe, Stockholm 2000*. Oxford: Oxbow Books, 2003.

Leakey, Louis S. B. "Working stone, bone and wood." In Singer et al., eds. 1954.

Leighton, Robert. *Sicily before History. An Archaeological Survey from the Palaeolithic to the Iron Age*. London: Duckworth, 1999.

Leitner, Walter. "Ötzi—the man in the ice." In Demakopoulou et al., eds. 1999.

Lenerz-de Wilde, Majolie. "The Celts in Spain." In Green, ed. 1995.

Lillie, Malcolm. "Late Mesolithic to Early Neolithic communities in the Dniepr rapids region of Ukraine: Chronology and socioeconomic continuity." In Larsson et al., 2003.

Liversidge, Joan. *Everyday Life in the Roman Empire*. London: Batsford, 1976.

Lloyd-Morgan, Glenys. "Appearance, life and leisure." In Green, ed. 1995.

Lo Schiavo, Fulvia. "The Nuragic bronze statuettes." In Demakopoulou et al., eds. 1999.

Louwe Kooijmans, Leendert P. "Hardinxveld, two late Mesolithic/Early Swifterbant sites in the Rhine delta wetlands and the persistence of the foraging tradition in the lower Rhine basin." In Larsson et al., 2003.

Lumley, Henry de. "A Paleolithic camp at Nice." *Scientific American* 220 (1969): 42–50.

Luning, Jens. "Central Europe during the Neolithic." In De Laet, ed. 1994.

Mac Cana, Proinsias. "Mythology and the oral tradition: Ireland." In Green, ed. 1995.

MacKillop, James. *Dictionary of Celtic Mythology*. Oxford: Oxford University Press, 1998.

Maier, Ferdinand. "The *oppida* of the second and first centuries B.C." In Moscati et al., eds. 1991a.

———. "The *oppidum* of Manching." In Moscati et al., eds. 1991b.

Mallory, J. P. *In Search of the Indo-Europeans. Language, Archaeology and Myth*. London: Thames and Hudson, 1989.

Malone, Caroline. *Avebury*. London: Batsford / English Heritage, 1989.

Manning, W. H. "Ironworking in the Celtic world." In Green, ed. 1995.

Marazov, Ivan, ed. *Ancient Gold: The Wealth of the Thracians. Treasures from the Republic of Bulgaria*. New York: Harry N. Abrams, 1998.

Marthari, Marina. "Cycladic marble idols: The silent witnesses of an island society in the Early Bronze Age Aegean." In Demakopoulou et al., eds. 1999.

Martinez, Alfredo Jimeno. "Numantia." In Moscati et al., eds. 1991.

Maryon, Herbert. "Fine metal-work." In Singer et al., eds. 1956.

Maryon, Herbert, and H. J. Plenderleith. "Fine metal-work." In Singer et al., ed. 1954.

McGrail, Sean. *Ancient Boats*. Princes Risborough, U.K.: Shire Publications Ltd., 1983.

———. "Celtic seafaring and transport." In Green, ed. 1995.

———. *Ancient Boats in North-West Europe. The Archaeology of Water Transport to AD 1500*. 2d edition. London / New York: Addison Wesley Longman, 1998.

McIntosh, Jane, and Chris Scarre, eds. *Atlas of the Ancient World*. CD-ROM. Maris Multimedia, 1998.

Megaw, J. V. S., and M. R. Megaw. *Celtic Art from Its Beginnings to the Book of Kells*. London: Thames and Hudson, 1989.

Megaw, Ruth, and Vincent Megaw. "The nature and function of Celtic art." In Green, ed. 1995.

Melchert, H. Craig. "Indo-European languages of Anatolia." In Jack M. Sasson, ed. *Civilizations of the Ancient Near East*. 4 volumes. Peabody: Hendrickson Publishers, 2000 (Reprint of 1995 edition. New York: Scribner).

Mellars, Paul. "The Upper Palaeolithic revolution." In Cunliffe, ed. 1994.

Mellars, Paul, and Petra Dark. *Star Carr in Context*. Cambridge: Macdonald Institute of Scientific Research, 1998.

Melton, N. D., and R. A. Nicholson. "The Mesolithic in the Northern Isles: The preliminary evaluation of an oyster midden at West Voe, Sumburgh, Shetland, U.K." *Antiquity* 78, no. 299 (March 2004).

Menghin, Wilfried. "The Berlin gold hat: A ceremonial head-dress of the Late Bronze Age." In Demakopoulou et al., eds. 1999.

Mercer, Roger. *Hambledon Hill: A Neolithic Landscape*. Edinburgh: Edinburgh University Press, 1980.

———. *Grimes Graves, Norfolk. Excavations 1971–2*. 2 volumes. London: Dept. of the Environment, 1981.

———. *Causewayed Enclosures*. Princes Risborough, U.K.: Shire Publications Ltd., 1990.

———. "The origins of warfare in the British Isles." In Carman and Harding, eds. 1999.

Mercer, Roger, ed. *Farming Practice in British Prehistory*. Edinburgh: Edinburgh University Press, 1984.

Merpert, Nikolai J. "The European part of the former USSR during the Neolithic and the Chalcolithic." In De Laet, ed. 1994.

Midgeley, Magdalena S. *TRB Culture. The First Farmers of the North European Plain*. Edinburgh: Edinburgh University Press, 1992.

Milisauskas, Sarunas. "The present environment, a geographic summary." In Milisauskas, ed. 2002a.

———. "Early Neolithic, the first farmers in Europe, 7000–5500/5000 BC." In Milisauskas, ed. 2002b.

Milisauskas, Sarunas, ed. *European Prehistory. A Survey*. New York: Kluwer Academic / Plenum Publishers, 2002.

Milisauskas, Sarunas, and Janusz Kruk. "Middle Neolithic, continuity, diversity, innovations, and greater complexity, 5500/5000–3500/300 BC." In Milisauskas, ed. 2002a.

———. "Late Neolithic, crises, collapse, new ideologies, and economies, 3500/3000–2200/2000 BC." In Milisauskas, 2002b.

Millett, Martin. *The Romanization of Britain. An Essay in Archaeological Interpretation*. Cambridge: Cambridge University Press, 1990.

———. *Roman Britain*. London: Batsford 1995.

Mithen, Steven. "The Mesolithic Age." In Cunliffe, 1994.

———. *The Prehistory of the Mind. A Search for the Origins of Art, Religion and Science*. London: Thames and Hudson, 1996.

———. *After the Ice. A Global Human History 20,000–5000 BC*. London: Weidenfeld and Nicolson, 2003.

————. *The Singing Neanderthals. The Origins of Music, Language, Mind and Body.* London: Weidenfeld and Nicolson, 2005.

Mohen, Jean-Pierre. *The World of the Megaliths.* London: Cassell, 1989.

————. "Introduction." In Dani and Mohen, eds. 1996.

Moosleitner, Fritz. "The Dürrnberg near Hallein: A centre of Celtic art and culture." In Moscati et al., eds. 1991.

Morrison, Ian. "Crannogs." In Delgado, ed. 1997.

Moscati, Sabatino, Otto Herman Frey, Venceslas Kruta, Barry Raftery, and Miklos Szabo, eds. *The Celts.* New York: Rizzoli, 1991.

Motykova, Karla, Petr Drda, and Alena Rybova. "The *oppidum* of Zavist." In Moscati et al., 1991.

Nash, Daphne. *Coinage in the Celtic World.* London: B. A. Seaby Ltd., 1987.

Noe-Nygaard, Nanna, and Jane Richter. "A late Mesolithic hunting station at Agernaes, Fyn, Denmark. Differentiation and specialisation in the late Ertebolle culture—heralding introducton of agriculture?" In Larsson et al., 2003.

Northover, Peter. "The technology of metalwork: Bronze and gold." In Green, ed. 1995.

Oakley, Kenneth P. *Man the Toolmaker.* London: British Museum, 1975.

O'Brien, Jacqueline, and Peter Harbison. *Ancient Ireland. From Prehistory to the Middle Ages.* New York: Oxford University Press, 1996.

O'Brien, Patrick K., ed. *Philip's Atlas of World History.* London: Georg Philip Ltd., 1999.

O'Kelly, Michael J. *Newgrange: Archaeology, Art and Legend.* London: Thames and Hudson, 1982.

————. *Early Ireland. An Introduction to Irish Prehistory.* Cambridge: Cambridge University Press, 1989.

Osgood, Richard, and Sarah Monks, with Judith Toms. *Bronze Age Warfare.* Stroud, U.K.: Sutton, 2000.

Oswald, Alastair, Carolyn Dyer, and Martyn Barber. *The Creation of Monuments. Neolithic Causewayed Enclosures in the British Isles.* Swindon: English Heritage, 2001.

Pare, Christopher F. E. "Wagon-graves of the Late Bronze Age." In Demakopoulou et al., eds. 1999.

————. "Bronze and the Bronze Age." In Pare, ed. 2000.

Pare, Christopher F. E., ed. *Metals Make the World Go Round. The Supply and Circulation of Metals in Bronze Age Europe.* Oxford: Oxbow Books, 2000.

Parker Pearson, Mike. *Bronze Age Britain.* London: Batsford / English Heritage, 1993.

————. *The Archaeology of Death and Burial.* Stroud, U.K.: Sutton, 1999.

Pearce, Mark, and Armando De Guio. "Between the mountains and the plain: An integrated metals production and circulation system in later Bronze Age north-eastern Italy." In Della Casa, ed. 1999.

Pericot Garcia, L. *The Balearic Islands.* London: Thames and Hudson, 1972.

Perles, Catherine. *The Early Neolithic in Greece.* Cambridge: Cambridge University Press, 2001.

Peroni, Renato. "Southern Europe." In Dani and Mohen, eds. 1996.

Perring, Dominic. *Town and Country in England. Frameworks for Archaeological Research. CBA Research Reports 134.* York: CBA, 2002.

Petersen, Erik Brinch "Mesolithic cremations at Vedbaek." In Larsson et al., 2003.

Philip, George. *Philip's Atlas of the World.* London: George Philip, 1991.

Piggott, Stuart. *Early Celtic Art.* Edinburgh: Edinburgh University Press, 1970.

————. *The Druids.* London: Thames and Hudson, 1975.

————. "Wood and the wheelwright." In Green, ed. 1995.

Planck, D. "The Fellbach-Schmiden sanctuary." In Moscati et al., eds. 1991.

Polybius. *The Rise of the Roman Empire.* Translated by I. Scott-Kilvert. Harmondsworth, U.K.: Penguin, 1979.

Price, T. Douglas. "The introduction of farming in northern Europe." In Price, ed. 2000.

Price, T. Douglas, ed. *Europe's First Farmers.* Cambridge: Cambridge University Press, 2000.

Pryor, Francis. *Flag Fen.* London: Batsford / English Heritage, 1991.

————. *Seahenge: New Discoveries in Prehistoric Britain.* London: HarperCollins, 2001.

————. *Britain BC. Life in England and Ireland before the Romans.* London: HarperCollins, 2003.

Pyatt, F. B., E. H. Beaumont, P. C. Buckland, D. Lacy, J. R. Magitton and D. M. Storey. "Mobilisation of elements from the bog bodies Lindow II and III and some observations of body painting." In Turner and Scaife, eds. 1995.

Raftery, Barry. "Paths, tracks and roads in early Ireland: Viewing the people rather than the trees." In Harding, 1999.

Rahtz, Philip. *Glastonbury*. London: Batsford, 1993.

Ralston, Ian. "Fortifications and defences." In Green, ed. 1995.

Randsborg, Klavs. *The First Millennium AD in Europe and the Mediterranean. An Archaeological Essay.* Cambridge: Cambridge University Press, 1991.

———. "Into the Iron Age: A discourse on war and society." In Carman and Harding, eds. 1999.

Rapin, André. "Weaponry." In Moscati et al., eds. 1991.

Reed, Michael. *The Landscape of Britain. From the Beginnings to 1914.* London: Routledge, 1990.

Renfrew, Colin. *Before Civilization.* London: Jonathan Cape, 1973.

———. "Ancient Bulgaria's golden treasures." *National Geographic* 158, no. 1 (1980).

———. *Archaeology and Language. The Puzzle of Indo-European Origins.* London: Jonathan Cape, 1987.

Renfrew, Colin, ed. *The Megalithic Monuments of Western Europe.* London: Thames and Hudson, 1981.

Renfrew, Colin, and Paul Bahn. *Archaeology: Theories Methods and Practice.* 4th ed. London: Thames and Hudson, 2004

Reynolds, Peter J. *Ancient Farming.* Princes Risborough, U.K.: Shire Publications, 1987.

———. "Rural life and farming." In Green, ed. 1995.

Ritchards, Julian. *Stonehenge.* London: Batsford/ English Heritage, 1991.

Ritchie, Anna. *Prehistoric Orkney.* London: Batsford / Historic Scotland, 1995.

Ritchie, J. N. Graham. *Brochs of Scotland.* Princes Risborough, U.K.: Shire Publications, 1988.

Ritchie, J. N. G., and W. F. Ritchie. "The army, weapons and fighting." In Green, ed. 1995.

Robinson, Andrew. *The Story of Writing. Alphabets, Hieroglyph and Pictograms.* London: Thames and Hudson, 1995.

———. *Lost Languages. The Enigma of the World's Undeciphered Scripts.* Maidenhead, U.K.: McGraw-Hill Education, 2002.

Ross, Anne. "Ritual and the Druids." In Green, ed. 1995.

———. *Druids.* Stroud, U.K.: Tempus, 1999.

Rothenberg, Beno, and Antonia Blanco-Freijero. *Studies in Ancient Mining and Metallurgy in South-West Spain. Explorations and Excavations in the Province of Huelva.* London: Institute of Archaeology, 1981.

Rowley-Conwy, Peter. "The laziness of the short-distance hunter: The origins of agriculture in western Denmark." In Fischer and Kristiansen, eds. 2002a.

Sacks, David. *Encyclopedia of the Ancient Greek World.* London: Constable, 1995.

Sandars, Nancy K. *Prehistoric Art in Europe.* 2d edition. Harmondsworth, U.K.: Penguin, 1985.

Sarfatij, H., W. J. H. Verwers, P. J. Woltering, eds. *In Discussion with the Past. Archaeological Studies presented to W.A. van Es.* Amsterdam: Foundation for Promoting Archaeology (SPA), 1999.

Scarre, Chris. *Exploring Prehistoric Europe.* Oxford / New York: Oxford University Press, 1998.

———. "From the megaron to Stonehenge." In Demakopoulou et al., eds. 1999.

Scarre, Chris, ed. *Ancient France. 6000–2000 BC.* Edinburgh: Edinburgh University Press, 1987.

———. *Past Worlds. The Times Atlas of Archaeology.* New York: Times Books, 1988.

Schulting, Rick J. "The marrying kind: Evidence for an exogamous marriage pattern in the Breton Mesolithic, and its implications for the process of Neolithisation." In Larsson et al., 2003.

Schultz, Michael. "Bronze Age man." In Demakopoulou et al., eds. 1999.

Schumacher-Matthäus, Gisela. "Clothing and jewellery." In Demakopoulou et al., eds. 1999.

Scott, Lindsay. "Pottery." In Singer et al., eds. 1954.

Selkirk, Andrew, Wendy Selkirk, and Rob Selkirk. "The Brochtorff Stone Circle." *Current World Archaeology* 7 (September/October 2004).

Sharples, Niall M. *Maiden Castle.* London: Batsford, 1991.

Shaw, Ian, and Robert Jameson, eds. *A Dictionary of Archaeology.* Oxford: Blackwell, 1999.

Shee Twohig, E. *The Megalithic Art of Western Europe.* Oxford: Oxford University Press, 1981.

Shepherd, Robert. *Prehistoric Mining and Allied Industries.* London/New York: Academic Press, 1980.

———. "Mining in Europe during the Neolithic and the Chalcolithic." In De Laet, ed. 1994.

Sheridan, Alison. "Drinking, driving, death and display: Scottish Bronze Age artefact studies since Coles." In Harding, ed. 1999.

Sherratt, Andrew. "The transformation of early agrarian Europe: The Later Neolithic and Copper Ages, 4500–2500 BC." In Cunliffe, ed. 1994a.

———. "The emergence of elites: Earlier Bronze Age Europe, 2500–1300 BC." In Cunliffe, ed. 1994b.

———. *Economy and Society in Prehistoric Europe. Changing Perspectives.* Princeton, N.J.: Princeton University Press, 1997.

Sievers, Susanne, Radomir Pleiner, Natalie Venclova, and Udo Geilenbrugge. "Handicrafts." In Moscati et al., eds. 1991.

Singer, Charles, E. J. Holmyard, A. R. Hall and Trevor I. Williams. eds. *A History of Technology. Volume I. From Early Times to Fall of Ancient Empires.* Oxford: Oxford University Press, 1954.

———. *A History of Technology. Volume II. The Mediterranean Civilizations and the Middle Ages.* Oxford: Oxford University Press, 1956.

Skeates, Robin. "The Neolithic enclosures of the Tavoliere, south-east Italy." In Varndell and Topping, eds. 2002.

Smrz, Zdenek. "The early La Tène court residence at Drouzkovice." In Moscati et al., eds. 1991.

Sperber, Lothar. "Crises in Western European metal supply during the Late Bronze Age: From bronze to iron." In Demakopoulou et al., eds. 1999.

Spindler, Konrad. *The Man in the Ice.* London: Orion, 1995.

Spivey, Nigel, and Simon Stoddart. *Etruscan Italy. An Archaeological History.* London: Batsford, 1990.

Springer, Tobias. "The gold cone of Ezelsdorf-Buch: A masterpiece of the goldsmith's art from the Bronze Age." In Demakopoulou et al., eds. 1999.

Srejović, Dragoslav. *Lepenski Vir.* London: Thames and Hudson, 1969.

Stead, Ian. *The Gauls. Celtic Antiquities from France.* London: British Museum Press, 1981.

———. *The Salisbury Hoard.* Stroud, U.K.: Tempus, 1998.

Stout, Geraldine. *Newgrange and the Bend of the Boyne.* Cork: Cork University Press, 2002.

Straus Lawrence G., and Manuel R. Gonzalez Morales. "The Mesolithic in the cantabrian interior: Facts or fiction?" In Larsson et al., 2003.

Stringer, Chris, and Peter Andrews. *The Complete World of Human Evolution.* London: Thames and Hudson, 2005.

Tacitus, Publius Cornelius. *Agricola.* Translated by M. Hutton. Revised by R. M. Ogilvie. *Germania.* Translated by M. Hutton. Revised by H. Warmington. *Dialogus.* Translated by W. Peterson. Revised by M. Winterbottom. Loeb Classical Library. Cambridge, Mass.: Harvard University Press, 1970.

———. *The Annals of Imperial Rome.* Translated by Michael Grant. Revised edition. Harmondsworth, U.K.: Penguin, 1971.

Taylor, Joan J. "Gold reflections." In Harding, ed. 1999.

Taylor, Timothy. "Thracians, Scythians, and Dacians, 800 BC–AD 300." In Cunliffe, ed. 1994.

Taylour, Lord William. *The Mycenaeans.* Revised edition. London: Thames and Hudson, 1983.

Thomas, Julian. "The cultural context of the first use of domesticates in continental central and northwest Europe." In Harris, ed. 1996.

Thorpe, I. J. *The Origins of Agriculture in Europe.* London/ New York: Routledge, 1996.

Thrane, Henrik. "Bronze Age settlement in south Scandinavia—territoriality and organisation." In Harding, ed. 1999a.

———. "Princely graves of the Late Bronze Age in the north." In Demakopoulou et al., eds. 1999b.

Tilley, Christopher. *The Dolmens and Passage Graves of Sweden. An Introduction and Guide.* London: Institute of Archaeology, University College, London, 1999.

Timberlake, Simon. "Mining and prospection for metals in Early Bronze Age Britain—making claims within the archaeological landscape." In Bruck, ed. 2001.

Todd, Malcolm. *The Barbarians. Goths, Franks and Vandals.* London: Batsford, 1972.

———. "Barbarian Europe, AD 300–700." In Cunliffe, ed. 1994.

Todorova, Henrietta. "The Late Bronze Age idols of the Danube." In Demakopoulou et al., eds. 1999.

Trump, David H. *The Prehistory of the Mediterranean.* London: Allen Lane, Penguin Press, 1980.

———. *Malta. Prehistory and Temples.* Malta: Midsea Books, 2002.

Turner, R. C., and R. G. Scaife, eds. *Bog Bodies. New Discoveries and New Perspectives.* London: British Museum Press, 1995.

Turner, Val. *Ancient Shetland.* London: Batsford / Historic Scotland, 1998.

Twist, Clint. *Philip's Atlas of the Celts.* London: George Philip Ltd., 2001.

Tykot, Robert H., and Tamsey K. Andrews, eds. *Sardinia in the Mediterranean: A Footprint in the Sea. Studies in Sardinian Archaeology Presented to Miriam S. Balmuth.* Sheffield, U.K.: Sheffield Academic Press, 1992.

Tylecote, R. F. *The Early History of Metallurgy in Europe.* London/New York: Longman, 1987.

Van Andel, Tjeerd H., and William Davies, eds. *Neanderthals and Modern Humans in the European Landscape during the Last Glaciation: Archaeological Results of the Stage 3 Project.* Cambridge, U.K.: MacDonald Institute, 2004.

Van Andel, Tjeerd H., and Curtis Runnels. *Beyond the Acropolis. A Rural Greek Past.* Palo Alto, Calif.: Stanford University Press, 1987.

Vandkilde, Helle. "The princely burials of the Únětice culture." In Demakopoulou et al., ed. 1999.

Varndell, Gillian, and Peter Topping, eds. *Enclosures in Neolithic Europe.* Oxford: Oxbow Books, 2002.

Vencl, Slavomil. "Stone Age warfare." In Carman and Harding, eds. 1999.

Venedikov, I. *Thracian Treasures from Bulgaria.* London: British Museum, 1976.

Verhart, Leo. "Mesolithic economic and social changes in the southern Netherlands." In Larsson et al., 2003.

Verjux, Christian. "The function of the Mesolithic sites in the Parisian Basin (France): New data." In Larsson et al., 2003.

Waddington, Clive, Geoff Bailey, Ian Boomer, Nicky Milner, Kristian Pederson, Robert Shiel, and Tony Stevenson. "A Mesolithic settlement at Howick, Northumberland." *Antiquity* 77, no. 295 (March 2003).

Wainwright, Geoffrey. *The Henge Monuments. Ceremony and Society in Prehistoric Britain.* London: Thames and Hudson, 1989.

Wallace, Patrick F., and Raghnall O'Floinn, eds. *Treasures of the National Museum of Ireland. Irish Antiquities.* Dublin: Gill and Macmillan, 2002.

Waterer, John W. "Leather." In Singer et al., eds. 1956.

Webster, Jane. "Sanctuaries and sacred places." In Green, ed. 1995.

Weller, Olivier. "The earliest rock salt exploitation in Europe: A salt mountain in the Spanish Neolithic." *Antiquity* 76, no. 292 (June 2002): 317–318.

Wells, Peter S. *Culture Contact and Culture Change.* Cambridge: Cambridge University Press, 1980.

———. "Resources and industry." In Green, ed. 1995a.

———. "Trade and exchange." In Green, ed. 1995b.

———. "The Iron Age." In Milisauskas, ed. 2002.

Whitehouse, Ruth D. *Underground Religion. Cult and Culture in Prehistoric Italy. Specialist Studies on Italy 1. Accordia Research Centre.* London: University of London, 1992.

Whittle, Alasdair. "The first farmers." In Cunliffe, ed. 1994.

———. *Europe in the Neolithic. The Creation of New Worlds.* Cambridge: Cambridge University Press, 1996.

Wickham-Jones, Caroline. *The Landscape of Scotland. A Hidden History.* Stroud, U.K.: Tempus, 2001.

Winghart, Stefan. "Mining, processing and distribution of bronze: Reflections on the organisation of metal supply between the north Alps and the Danube region." In Pare, ed. 2000.

Woodward, Ann. *Shrines and Sacrifice.* London: Batsford / English Heritage, 1992.

Zeuner, F. E. "Cultivation of plants." In Singer et al., eds. 1954.

Zilhão, João. "From the Mesolithic to the Neolithic in the Iberian peninsula." In Price, ed. 2000.

Zohary, Daniel, and Maria Hopf. *Domestication of Plants in the Old World.* 3d edition. Oxford: Oxford University Press, 2000.

Zvelebil, Marek. "Wetland settlements of Eastern Europe." In Coles and Lawson, eds. 1987.

———. "The agricultural frontier and the transition to farming in the circum-Baltic region." In Harris, ed. 1996.

ELECTRONIC RESOURCES _____

Angelini, I., G. Artioli, P. Bellintani, V. Diella, and A. Polla. "Protohistoric vitreous materials of Italy: From early faience to final Bronze Age glasses." Available online. URL: http://www.historyofglass.org.uk/AIHV2003/Bronze%20Age.htm. Updated September 27, 2003.

Arizona University. "The Blytt-Sernander Sequence." Available online. URL: http://www.geo.arizona.edu/palynology/geos462/02holocene.html. Cited June 8, 2005.

Budd, Paul. "Meet the metal makers." *British Archaeology*. 56 (December 2000). Available online. URL: http://www.britarch.ac.uk/ba/a56/ba56feat.html#budd. Posted February 2001.

Centre Archéologique Départemental de Ribemont-sur-Ancre. Homepage of Ribemont excavations. Available online. URL: http://www.ribemontsurancre.cg80.fr/. Cited March 22, 2005.

Cunliffe, Barry. "People of the sea." *British Archaeology* 63 (February 2002). Available online. URL: http://www.britarch.ac.uk/ba/ba63/feat2.shtml. Posted April 2002.

Denison, Simon. "Woven clothing dates back 27,000 years." *British Archaeology* 52 (April 2000a). Available online. URL: http://www.britarch.ac.uk/ba/ba52/ba52news.html#woven. Posted June 2000.

———. "Welsh gold." *British Archaeology* 53 (June 2000b). Available online. URL: http://www.britarch.ac.uk/ba/ba53/ba53news.html#inbrief. Posted August 2000.

———. "Burial in water 'normal rite' for 1,000 years: Skeletons, animal skulls and other Iron Age offerings found in Thames." *British Archaeology* 53 (June 2000c). Available online. URL: http://www.britarch.ac.uk/ba/ba53/ba53news.html#burial. Posted August 2000.

———. "Earliest evidence of lead mining at Cwmystwyth." *British Archaeology* 58 (April 2001a). Available online. URL: http://www.britarch.ac.uk/ba/ba58/news.shtml#item1. Posted June 2001.

———. "Great Orme." *British Archaeology* 58 (April 2001b). Available online. URL: http://www.britarch.ac.uk/ba/ba58/news.shtml#inbrief. Posted June 2001.

———. "Neolithic farmhouse found in Scotland." *British Archaeology* 62 (December 2001c). Available online. URL: http://www.britarch.ac.uk/ba/ba62/news.shtml#item2. Posted February 2002.

———. "Log boat from Tay estuary dated to the later Bronze Age." *British Archaeology* 63 (February 2002). Available online. URL: http://www.britarch.ac.uk/ba/ba63/news.shtml#item3. Posted April 2002.

———. "Tale of the Bronze Age barge sunk in Trent." *British Archaeology* 69 (March 2003a). Available online. URL: http://www.britarch.ac.uk/ba/ba69/news.shtml. Posted May 2003.

———. "Shipping news." *British Archaeology* 73 (November 2003b). Available online. URL: http://www.britarch.ac.uk/ba/ba73/news.shtml#item4. Posted January 2004.

———. "Mesolithic houses in both Scotland and the North East." *British Archaeology* 69 (March 2003c). Available online. URL: http://www.britarch.ac.uk/ba/ba69/news.shtml#item4. Posted May 2003.

Dolukhanov, Pavel. "Geographical environment and ecology of the Black Sea: Past and present." Available online. URL: http://www.biaa.ac.uk/babsi/abstracts.rtf. Posted March 2003.

English Heritage. "Stonehenge. Forever a mystery." Available online. URL: http://www.english-heritage.org.uk/server/show/ConWebDoc.1914. Cited June 8, 2005.

Fitzpatrick, Andrew. "The Amesbury archer: The king of Stonehenge?" Available online. URL: http://www.bbc.co.uk/history/archaeology/king_stonehenge_01.shtml. Cited February 3, 2005.

Ixer, R. A., and R. A. D. Pattrick. "Copper-arsenic ores and Bronze Age mining and metallurgy with special reference to the British Isles." Available online. URL: http://www.rosiehardman.com/fahlerz.htm. Posted 2004.

Kurz, Siegfried. "Heuneberg. Latest Research." Available online. URL: http://www.dhm.de/museen/heuneburg/en/neuforsch1.html. Cited February 3, 2005.

Mellars, Paul "Revising the Mesolithic at Star Carr." *British Archaeology* 48 (October 1999). Available online. URL: http://www.britarch.ac.uk/ba/ba48/ba48feat.html#mellars. Posted December 1999.

Metindex. "Historical weather events." Available online. URL: http://homepage.ntlworld.com/booty.weather/climate/wxevents.htm. Updated March 27, 2005.

Mitchell, Jacqueline S. "The truth behind Noah's Flood." Available online. URL: http://www.pbs.org/saf/1207/features/noah.htm. Cited April 5, 2004.

"Nebra Skydisk." Available online. URL: http://en.wikipedia.org/wiki/Nebra_skydisk. Updated May 3, 2005.

Noble, Gordon. "Islands and the Neolithic farming tradition." *British Archaeology* 71 (July 2003). Available online URL: http://www.britarch.ac.uk/ba/ba71/feat3.shtml. Posted September 2003.

Rowley-Conwy, Peter. "Great Sites: Balbridie." *British Archaeology* 64 (April 2002b). Available online. URL: http://www.britarch.ac.uk/ba/ba64/feat3.shtml. Posted June 2002)

Shepherd, Alexandra. "Great sites: Skara Brae." *British Archaeology* 55 (October 2000). Available online. URL: http://www.britarch.ac.uk/ba/ba55/ba55feat.html#shepherd. Posted December 2000.

Sheridan, Alison. "Supernatural power dressing." *British Archaeology* 70 (May 2003). Available online. URL: http://www.britarch.ac.uk/ba/ba70/feat3.shtml. Posted July 2003.

Shortland, Andrew. "Making a talisman." *British Archaeology* 70 (May 2003). Available online. URL: http://www.britarch.ac.uk/ba/ba70/feat3.shtml. Posted July 2003.

Shwartz, Mark. "Electronic tags reveal transatlantic migrations and breeding grounds of Atlantic bluefin tuna." Available online. URL: http://www.stanford.edu/dept/news/pr/01/tunastudy822.html. Posted August 21, 2001.

Smithsonian Institute. "Hall of Human Ancestors." Available online. URL: http://www.mnh.si.edu/anthro/humanorigins/ha/ances_start.html. Updated June 2004.

Taylor, Timothy. "The edible dead." *British Archaeology* 59 (June 2001). Available online. URL: http://www.britarch.ac.uk/ba/ba59/feat1.shtml. Posted August 2001.

Topping, Peter. "Great sites: Grimes Graves." *British Archaeology* 70 (September 2003). Available online. URL: http://www.britarch.ac.uk/ba/ba72/feat2.shtml. Posted November 2003.

Uscinowicz, S. "Late Glacial and Holocene of the southern Baltic shoreline displacement." Available online. URL: http://www.lgt.lt/geoin/files/Szymon_Uscinowicz.doc. Posted September 2000.

Walker, Amélie A. "Mesolithic surgery." Available online. URL: http://archaeology.about.com/gi/dynamic/offsite.htm?site=http://www.he.net%7Earchaeol/onlin e/news/trepanation.html. Posted April 9, 1998.

Wessex Archaeology Ltd. "The Amesbury archer." Available online. URL: http://www.wessexarch.co.uk/projects/amesbury/archer.html. Updated December 10, 2004.

Wickham-Jones, Caroline. "The tale of the limpet." *British Archaeology* 71 (July 2003). Available online. URL: http://www.britarch.ac.uk/ba/ba71/feat4.shtml. Posted September 2003.

INDEX

Page numbers in **boldface** indicate major treatment of the subject. Page numbers in *italic* refer to illustrations. Page numbers with the suffix *m* refer to maps. Page numbers with the suffix *c* refer to the chronology.

animals
 and aesthetic/symbolic
  behavior 22
 in agriculture **124–125**
 burials 274
 Celtic art 325, 326
 as commodity **174–175**
 Corded Ware culture 59
 as cult objects/symbols
  248–249
 environmental change 12
 Holocene 26
 Late Glacial Period 23–24
 Mesolithic art 322
 Palaeolithic period 22
 sheep 32, 34, 48, 55, 58, 59,
  110, 345
 travel by **181**
 visual arts 321
 as wild resources **114–116**
animals, domestic **107–112.** *See also*
 cattle; horses
 the Balkans 32
 Britain 44
 cats **112**
 dogs 23, 27, 38, *112,* **112, 249,**
  274
 Eastern Europe 33, 41
 environmental change 12
 family accommodation 337
 Greece 32
 hunter-gathers/farmers 43
 Late Glacial Period 23
 Later Eneolithic 49
 LBK culture 35, 37
 Mediterranean 34, 42
 Neolithic consolidation 41–44
 Neolithic period 29, 32–34
 pigs 29, 32, 34, 55, 59, **108,**
  119
anthropomorphic carvings and
 stones 54, **266–267**
antlers 18, 43, **204–205**
A1 Final Glina 354*c*
A1 Kisapostag 354*c*
Apennine Bronze Age 106, 355*c*
appearance, personal **339–344**
appliqué (on ceramics) **229**
aquatic resources **116–117**
arboriculture 106
archaeology xi–xii, 16, **240–241,**
 296, 317–318
archery 296, 297. *See also* arrows;
 bows
architecture. *See also* houses
 circular houses **137–138**
 ephemeral housing **132–133**
 housing construction 128

longhouses 44–45, 109,
 136–137, 146, 337, 338
mansions **139–140**
Mesolithic houses **133–134**
monumental 16, 353*c*
oppida 94, 95
square and rectangular houses
 134–136
storage facilities **140**
strongholds **138, 139**
Arctic Circle 10
ard 46, 49, 52, **119–120,** 161
Arevaci 156
Argaric Bronze Age 124, 354*c,* 355*c*
Argaric culture 106, 124
Ariovistus (chief of the Suebi) 95, 336
armlet *326*
armor 77, **299–301**
arrows 23, 27, 38, 43, 116, **297,** 309.
 See also bows
art. *See also* Celtic art; rock art;
 specific headings, e.g.: sculpture
 aesthetic/symbolic behavior
  22–23
 Bronze Age 73
 Greece 83
 Iberia 87
 Iron Age 83, 87
 Late Glacial Period 23
 megalithic **250, 323**
 Mesolithic period 29
 Minoan Crete 73
 Neanderthals 19
 Palaeolithic period 22–23
 performing **325–326**
 Roman Empire 98
 settlement/movement/society
  29
 visual 316, *321,* **321–325**
 warriors in **306–307**
artifacts
 the Balkans 32
 coal/shale **233–234**
 Danubian II 44
 Greece 32
 marriage and sexual mores 336
 religious **240–241**
 visual arts 321
 wood **192–193**
Asia 20
astronomy **269–270**
Athens, Greece 83
Atlantic Ocean 2, 8, 9
Atlantic region (zone) 352*c*–354*c,*
 356*c,* 357*c*
 Bronze Age 63, **69–71, 75–76,**
  80
 domestic architecture 132

Early Postglacial Europe
 37–39
fortifications 149
geography of **8–9**
Holocene 24
Iron Age **87–88**
megaliths/funerary monuments
 45
Mesolithic society **42–43**
Neolithic consolidation **42–45**
Neolithic period 46, **52–54**
roundhouses 144
settlement 141
stone fortifications 302
trade routes **178**
Urnfield burial 284
Atrebates people 96
Aurignacian periods 20
aurochs 248
Ausonian 355*c*
Austria 175, 216–217, 358
Avaricum 157
Avebury **264**
Avenue (Stonehenge) 263
Avernus, Lake **253**
axes **297**
 the Atlantic region 43, 54
 ax-hammer, stone *210*
 the Balkans 32
 battle-axes **59,** 60, 62, 67, *210*
 Britain 55
 bronze *215*
 Bronze Age *68*
 domestic wood equipment 194
 Greece 32
 humans, early 18
 industry, organization of 333
 LBK culture 35
 Mediterranean 49, 50
 Neolithic consolidation 39
 Neolithic period 32, 49–52, 54,
  55
 northern Europe 43
 as offerings 258
 Southern Central Europe 52
 stone *36, 170, 210,* **247**
 TRB culture 50, 51
 wood felling/preparation 192
azurite **213**

B
Baden culture 52, **109,** 134, 353*c*
Balbridie, Scotland 54, 137
Balearic Islands 150, 303
Balfarg **277**
the Balkans 352*c*–354*c,* 357*c*
 callaïs 235
 Chalcolithic period **58–59**

England *(continued)*
    coal and shale sources 232
    Danebury 155
    domestic wood equipment 194
    Dover Boat 186
    Ferriby boat 186–187
    flax preparation 196
    Great Langdale quarry 210
    Grimes Graves flint mine 207
    Hasholme logboat 185
    Hengistbury Head shale
      production 233–234
    Langdon Bay shipwreck 188
    metal mining 213
    Moor Sands shipwreck
      187–188
    Neolithic period 48
    northern European trade routes
      179
    oppida 95
    pottery 175
    roads 182
    rounds 151
    Seahenge 264
    Somerset Levels 183
    Star Carr 182
    trackways 182
    trade patterns 166
    water travel 188
    Wessex barrow burial area 222
English Channel 9, 10, 24
engravings *323*, **323, 324**
entertainment **336–337**
entrance graves 289
entrance passages **304, 305**
Entremont 92, **156, 261,** 267
environment xii, **10–12, 26**
environmental change **10–12,** 16,
  23, 39, 82, 351*c*, 355*c*
ephemeral housing **132–133**
Epicardial 352*c*
epitaphs 320
Epona **242–243**
equipment, domestic **194, 195,** *198*
Ertebølle 352*c*, 353*c*
    the Atlantic region 42, 43
    Bronze Age 66
    domestic wood equipment 194
    furs 202
    Neolithic consolidation 42, 43
    Neolithic period 51
    Northern Europe 42, 43
    trade patterns 166
    TRB culture 51
Erzgebirge. *See* Bohemian Ore
  Mountains
esparto grass (in textiles) **197,** 201
Este 355*c*, 356*c*

Estonia 358
Esus **243**
Etruscan language 318, 319
Etruscans 84, **84,** 85, 89, 356*c*, 357*c*
Etton, England 262
Euboea 84
Europe
    development of 16–98
    far Northern **9–10**
    grain crops 116
    political map of *3m*
    temperate **5–8**
    topography of *6m*
European language **316–319**
Europeans **18**
everyday life 18, 75, 324, **335–339,**
  338
Ewart park 355*c*
excarnation 285, 287
exogamy 335
exposure (as funerary practice) 273,
  276–278, 285
Eyni, Estonia 134
Ezero 353*c*, 354*c*
Ezinge **148**

F
fahlerz **213**
faience beads **173, 230–231**
fairies 320
family accommodation **337**
family life **335–336**
farmers 40, 44, 86, 97, 330, 332, 347
farming. *See* agriculture and farming
farms **144, 145, 150–152**
fastenings (wood) **193**
fauna
    environmental change 12
    Far North 10
    Holocene 26
    humans, early 18
    Late Glacial Period 23
    Mediterranean 4
    Mesolithic period 26–27
    Palaeolithic period 17
    temperate Europe **7–8**
feasting 82, 262, 307, 337, **346**
Fécamp rampart **302**
Feddersen Wierde **148**
Fellbach Schmiden **255**
Ferriby, North **186–187**
Ferrières 354*c*
Fiavé 355*c*
fiber crops **107**
fibers (textiles) **196–198.** *See also*
  specific headings, e.g.: silk
fibulae 84, 284, *339*, 341, 343, *343*
fields 66, 77, **118–119,** 123

fights 337
figs 105–106
figurative art 321, 324
figurines **250–252,** *251,* 260,
  306–307, 322–323
    Bronze Age 80
    god of thunder *244*
    Later Sesklo-Vadastra-Vinča-
      Karanovo III-Dudeşti 37
    Mediterranean 80
    pottery **250–251,** 321, **322**
    religious **250–252,** *251,*
      306–307
    Sardianian bronzes **322–323**
    visual arts 321
Finland 7, 9, 10, 181, 197, 358
Finnish language 318
Fiorano 352*c*
fire 17–18, 21, 22, 28
firing (clay pottery) **227–228**
First Palace period 67
fish 7, 9, 26, 28, 33, 37
fishing **116, 117**
    the Atlantic region 38, 42–43
    economy 26, 28
    fishhooks, bronze *117*
    Mediterranean 42
    Mesolithic period 26, 28, 38
    Neolithic consolidation 42–43
    Neolithic period 46, 50
    northern Europe 38, 42–43
    sea trade routes 177
    temperate Europe 7
    TRB culture 50
fish traps 116–117
fish weirs 116–117
Flag Fen **255**
flagons 89
flagstone 130
flask, collared *228*
flax **105, 107, 196**
flint 353*c*
    axes *331*
    blades 41
    climate/flora/fauna 8
    as commodity **169–170**
    Mediterranean 42, 49
    microliths 114
    Neolithic consolidation 42
    Neolithic period 49–51
    sickle *121*
    temperate Europe 8
    tool making **206, 209**
    TRB culture 50, 51
    wood felling/preparation 192
flint mining 48, 51, **206–209,** *208,*
  334
Flood stories 26